This Kind of War

THE CLASSIC KOREAN WAR HISTORY

T. R. Fehrenbach

BRASSEY'S
WASHINGTON • LONDON

For Lillian

Fehrenbach, T. R.
This kind of war: the classic Korean War history/T. R.
 Fehrenbach.—1st Brassey's ed.
 p. cm.
Originally published: This kind of war: a study in unpreparedness. New York: Macmillan, 1963.
 Includes index.
 ISBN 0-02-881113-5
 1. Korean War, 1950–1953. I. Title
DS918.F37 1994
 951.904'2—dc20   94-10908
                                   CIP

10 9 8 7 6 5 4 3 2 1

Printed in the United States of America

CONTENTS

Contents

PART III: BLUNDERING

ACKNOWLEDGMENTS

T HIS BOOK IS compiled from many sources, official records, operations, journals, histories, memoirs, and newspapers; the greater portion, however, is culled from the personal narratives of men who served in Korea. In this sense, portions of the book may be more hearsay than history—and a sense of personal outlook must color each narrative.

There may be errors in these narratives, for memory is often a fragile thing. Wherever possible, all statements have been checked against official sources, to verify dates, unit designations, and names of personnel or commanders.

To a very great extent not high commanders but the men who stood around them were sought out. It is often painful for generals and commanders to talk, and besides, they tend to write their own memoirs. This is very much a platoon leaders' book based on the actions of men who led small units across the bloody face of Korea from June 1950 until July 1953. The majority of the men in these pages were professional soldiers, and therefore the outlook is not warlike, but military. Men who did not lead troops in combat in Korea may disagree with them—but are in no valid position to contradict.

In many cases the names of the men through whose eyes the action was seen are not reported, for various reasons. In any case the names are not important. What happened is.

Grateful acknowledgment is made to the hundreds of individuals, in service or out, who contributed to this book, and to George C. Lambkin, Fort Sam Houston, Texas, who knows what a Public Information Officer should be. Without each of these, there might have been no book.

An AUSA Book

The Association of the United States Army, or AUSA, was founded in 1950 as a not-for-profit organization dedicated to education concerning the role of the U.S. Army, to providing material for military professional development, and to the promotion of proper recognition and appreciation of the profession of arms. Its constituencies include those who serve in the Army today, including Army National Guard, Army Reserve, and Army civilians, and the retirees and veterans who have served in the past, and all their families. A large number of public-minded citizens and business leaders are also an important constituency. The Association seeks to educate the public, elected and appointed officials, and leaders of the defense industry on crucial issues involving the adequacy of our national defense, particularly those issues affecting land warfare.

In 1988 the AUSA established within its existing organization a new entity known as the Institute of Land Warfare. Its purpose is to extend the educational work of the AUSA by sponsoring scholarly publications, to include books, monographs, and essays on key defense issues, as well as workshops and symposia. Among the volumes chosen for designation as "An AUSA Institute of Land Warfare Book" are both new texts and reprints of titles of enduring value that are no longer in print. Topics include history, policy issues, strategy, and tactics. Publication as an AUSA Book does not indicate that the Association of the United States Army and the publisher agree with everything in the book, but does suggest that the AUSA and the publisher believe this book will stimulate the thinking of AUSA members and others concerned about important issues.

FOREWORD

Regard your soldiers as your children, and they will follow you into the deepest valleys; look on them as your own beloved sons, and they will stand by you even into death.

If, however, you are indulgent, but unable to make your authority felt, kindhearted but unable to enforce your commands; and incapable, moreover, of quelling disorder, then your soldiers must be likened to spoiled children; they are useless for any practical purpose.

—From the Chinese of Sun Tzu, THE ART OF WAR

TEN YEARS AFTER the guns fell into uneasy silence along the 38th parallel, it is still impossible to write a definitive history of the Korean War. For that war did not write the end to an era, but merely marked a fork on a road the world is still traveling. It was a minor collision, a skirmish—but the fact that such a skirmish between the earth's two power blocs cost more than two million human lives showed clearly the extent of the chasm beside which men walked.

More than anything else, the Korean War was not a test of power—because neither antagonist used full powers—but of wills. The war showed that the West had misjudged the ambition and intent of the Communist leadership, and clearly revealed that leadership's intense hostility to the West; it also proved that Communism erred badly in assessing the response its aggression would call forth.

The men who sent their divisions crashing across the 38th parallel on 25 June 1950 hardly dreamed that the world would rally against them, or that the United States—which had repeatedly professed its reluctance to do so—would commit ground forces onto the mainland of Asia.

From the fighting, however inconclusive the end, each side could take home valuable lessons. The Communists would understand that the free world—in particular the United States—had the will to react quickly and practically and without panic in a new situation. The American public, and that of Europe, learned that the postwar world was not the pleasant place they hoped it would be, that it could not be neatly policed by bombers and carrier aircraft and nuclear warheads, and that the Communist menace could be disregarded only at extreme peril.

The war, on either side, brought no one satisfaction. It did, hopefully, teach a general lesson of caution.

The great test placed upon the United States was not whether it had the power to devastate the Soviet Union—this it had—but whether the American leadership had the will to continue to fight for an orderly world rather than to succumb to hysteric violence. Twice in the century uncontrolled violence had swept the world, and after untold bloodshed and destruction nothing was accomplished. Americans had come to hate war, but in 1950 were no nearer to abolishing it than they had been a century before.

But two great bloodlettings, and the advent of the Atomic Age with its capability of fantastic destruction, taught Americans that their traditional attitudes toward war—to regard war as an unholy thing, but once involved, however reluctantly, to strike those who unleashed it with holy wrath—must be altered. In the Korean War, Americans adopted a course not new to the world, but new to them. They accepted limitations on warfare, and accepted controlled violence as the means to an end. Their policy—for the first time in the century—succeeded. The Korean War was not followed by the tragic disillusionment of World War I, or the unbelieving bitterness of 1946 toward the fact that nothing had been settled. But because Americans for the first time lived in a world in which they could not truly win, whatever the effort, and from which they could not withdraw, without disaster, for millions the result was trauma.

During the Korean War, the United States found that it could not enforce international morality and that its people had to live and continue to fight in a basically amoral world. They could oppose that which they regarded as evil, but they could not destroy it without risking their own destruction.

Because the American people have traditionally taken a warlike, but not military, attitude to battle, and because they have always coupled a certain belligerence—no American likes being pushed around—with a complete unwillingness to prepare for combat, the Korean War was difficult, perhaps the most difficult in their history.

In Korea, Americans had to fight, not a popular, righteous war, but to send men to die on a bloody checkerboard, with hard heads and without exalted motivations, in the hope of preserving the kind of world order Americans desired.

Tragically, they were not ready, either in body or in spirit.

They had not really realized the kind of world they lived in, or the tests of wills they might face, or the disciplines that would be required to win them.

Yet when America committed its ground troops into Korea, the American people committed their entire prestige, and put the failure or success of their foreign policy on the line.

The purpose of this book is to detail the events of that action, and what led to it, and not to explore controversy. It does not seek to exalt the military nor to deride the traditionally liberal American view toward life. There is no desire to add fuel to the increasingly bitter dialogue between traditionalists, military officers, and "liberals" that has resulted from those events—a dialogue brought about more by the fact that the liberals would feel safer if the military would feel emotionally more at home in a society that was a bit more spartan, than by a clear assessment of the needs of the country.

The civilian liberal and the soldier, unfortunately, are eyeing different things: the civilian sociologists are concerned with men living together in peace and amiability and justice; the soldier's task is to teach them to suffer and fight, kill and die. Ironically, even in the twentieth century American society demands both of its citizenry.

Perhaps the values that comprise a decent civilization and those needed to defend it abroad will always be at odds. A complete triumph for either faction would probably result in disaster.

Perhaps, also, at the beginning a word must be said concerning discipline. "Discipline," like the terms "work" and "fatherland"—among the greatest of human values—has been given an almost repugnant connotation from its use by Fascist ideologies. But the term "discipline" as used in these pages does not refer to the mindless, robotlike obedience and self-abasement of a Prussian grenadier. Both American sociologists and soldiers agree that it means, basically, self-restraint—the self-restraint required not to break the sensible laws whether they be imposed against speeding or against removing an uncomfortably heavy steel helmet, the fear not to spend more money than one earns, not to drink from a canteen in combat before it is absolutely necessary, and to obey both parent and teacher and officer in certain situations, even when the orders are acutely unpleasant.

Only those who have never learned self-restraint fear reasonable discipline.

Americans fully understand the requirements of the football field or the baseball diamond. They discipline themselves and suffer by the thousands to prepare for these rigors. A coach or manager who is too permissive soon seeks a new job; his teams fail against those who are tougher and harder. Yet undoubtedly any American officer, in peacetime, who worked his men as hard, or ruled them as severely as a college football coach does, would be removed.

But the shocks of the battlefield are a hundred times those of the playing field, and the outcome infinitely more important to the nation.

The problem is to understand the battlefield as well as the game of football. The problem is to see not what is desirable, or nice, or politically feasible, but what is necessary.

T.R.F.
JULY 4, 1962
SAN ANTONIO, TEXAS

PART I

Beginning

1

Seoul Saturday Night

Who desires peace, should prepare for war . . . no one dare offend or insult a power of recognized superiority in action.

—From the Latin of Vegetius, MILITARY INSTITUTIONS OF THE ROMANS

ON 8 JUNE 1950, newspapers of the city of P'yongyang, capital of *Chosun Minjujui Inmun Kongwhakuk,* the North Korean People's Republic, printed a manifesto of the Central Committee of the United Democratic Patriotic Front. The manifesto announced as a goal for the Central Committee, elections to be held throughout both North and South Korea, and the parliament so elected to sit in Seoul no later than 15 August, fifth anniversary of the liberation from Japan.

No mention was made of the *Taehan Minkuk,* the Republic of Korea, which south of the 38th parallel was United Nations–sponsored and American-backed, and of which Dr. Syngman Rhee was president.

The manifesto was picked up by *Tass,* Russian news service, and reprinted in *Izvestia,* 10 June 1950. By devious routes a copy of *Izvestia* came to the Library of Congress, untranslated from the Russian.

This manifesto made interesting reading. It was a storm signal. It seems a pity no one in the West bothered to read it.

But then, if it had been read, it would have been ignored. Storm signals had been flying for more than four years. In Asia, Nationalist China had fallen. There was Communist-directed war in Indo-China. World Communism, from its power base in Soviet Russia, undeterred by the nuclear bomb, continued its aggressive course, causing misgivings in the West, making its nations sign defensive alliances.

But the West did not prepare for trouble. It did not make ready, because its peoples, in their heart of hearts, did not want to be prepared.

It would not have mattered if anyone had read the P'yongyang Manifesto.

* * *

Senior Colonel Lee Hak Ku, thirty years old, was Operations Officer, II Corps, of the *Inmun Gun*, the North Korean People's Army, and all week he had been working very hard. Since 15 June 1950, every regular division of the Inmun Gun had moved from their normal billets and had been deployed along planned lines of departure just north of the 38th parallel. It had meant staff work, and lots of it.

Only now, as darkness fell on Saturday, 24 June, could Lee Hak Ku allow the hard lines of his square young face to relax, and to permit himself leisurely to enjoy a cigarette. In a people's republic Saturday night meant nothing, but every unit of the Inmun Gun had been in position since midnight 23 June, and for a few hours there was really nothing more to do.

And that was good staff work.

Standing relaxed in his somewhat shoddy Russian-style blue uniform with its flaring breeches and polished high boots, Senior Colonel Lee could review the turmoil and ferment of the last few days. Eighty thousand men had been moved, some divisions coming down from the high and distant Yalu, and it had all been done smoothly. Beyond doubt, the running dogs of the American imperialists, the South Koreans, suspected nothing.

The commander of the Inmun Gun, Chai Ung Jun, and his staff of veterans from the Manchurian wars, could take deep pride in their work. Since the meeting of high Soviet and Chinese Communist officials in Peiping in January to plan the invasion of the United Nations and American-backed Republic of Korea, the Inmun Gun had achieved prodigies for so small and so new an army.

There had been the dumps and depots to build near the parallel, to hold the mountains of arms and equipment shipped in by freighter from the Soviet Union. There had been the crews of the 105th Armored Brigade to train in the use of the Russian T-34, the main battle tank that had stopped panzer leader Guderian in front of Moscow, and young fliers to be accustomed to the intricacies of YAK fighters. And there had been the thousands of Korean-extraction veterans of the Chinese Communist Forces to reintegrate into the Inmun Gun. With Chiang Kai-shek defeated and his Nationalist remnants exiled to Taiwan, Red China could release her Korean-speaking soldiers; by June 1950, they made up 30 percent of the Inmun Gun.

On Friday, 23 June, shortly before midnight, 90,000 men stood ready in the misting rain. In addition to their 150 medium tanks and 200 aircraft, they had small arms and mortars in profusion, backed up by plentiful 122mm howitzers and 76mm self-propelled guns. They were seven infantry divisions, one armored brigade, a separate infantry regiment, a motorcycle regiment, and a brigade of the fanatical Bo An Dae, the Border Constabulary.

Beginning 18 June, Senior Colonel Lee Hak Ku and his brother officers had seen to it that their orders went out.

First, Reconnaissance Order 1, in the Russian language, had come down from Intelligence, directing that information concerning South Korean defensive positions along each division's projected route of attack be obtained and verified no later than 24 June.

The Inmun Gun had hundreds of spies across the parallel, many of them working directly for the American advisers to the South Korean Army. The mysterious officers in Intelligence, who wrote in Russian script, received what they asked for.

By 22 June the divisions issued their operations orders, in Korean. The 1st, 3rd, and 4th divisions attacked down the Uijongbu Corridor toward Seoul, armored elements leading. Other divisions attacked in the east. Common soldiers were to be told they were on maneuvers. Officers were to know it was war.

Red-eyed, smoking too much, young Senior Colonel Lee waited now in his Operations Post, listening to the torrential showers of the beginning monsoon slash down into the green paddies outside, smelling the pungent odors of earth and fertilizer the rains released. He was tired, but he was also spring-tight with a disciplined excitement, waiting for the hours to pass. He looked at his cheap watch. He did not have long to wait.

The orders had gone out, and he knew they would be obeyed. Aside from its fanatical core of Russian- and Chinese-trained veterans, there were many conscripts, rice Communists, in the ranks of the Inmun Gun. But even these men would obey.

Hesitancy, in the Inmun Gun, was cured neatly, efficiently, and permanently by the application of a pistol to the back of the head.

* * *

As Saturday waned, Major General Chae Byong Duk, Deputy Commander—under Syngman Rhee—of the Republic of Korea Armed Forces, was not content. For "Fat" Chae, five foot five, two hundred and fifty pounds, darling of the Seoul cocktail set, was not completely a fool.

For years the Communists north of the parallel had been making trouble in the South. They made rice raids across the border; they fomented disorder and subversion in the cities. They incited and supplied the rebel guerrillas in the southern mountains, doing everything in their power to destroy the Republic of Korea. They kept a third of Fat Chae's Army tied down on constabulary work.

March, particularly, had been a bad month. But then, unaccountably, all activity had ceased. Fat Chae was worried.

Chae had talked to the Americans about it, but the Korean Military Advisory Group was not concerned. One officer told Chae that the Communists were becoming more sophisticated, settling down at last. The Americans seemed to feel that when Communists left you alone, it was all to the good. But Chae worried. He might be handier with a whiskey and soda than with command of the Army, but he was not completely a fool.

Chae had read *Time,* which three weeks before had printed a splendid article on the Korean Military Advisory Group and its work with the Korean Armed Forces. Like most people outside the United States, Chae Byong Duk knew that what *Time* printed was not only true, but official.

Time had said the Republic of Korea Army was the best outside the States. That was one thing that comforted him, as more and more reports reached

Seoul from refugees from the northern regime, informers, and his own officers stationed along the parallel. Because General Chae Byong Duk had no
great trust in Communists, despite the Americans.

But now the bright lights were coming on in Seoul, and, shrugging, Chae
Byong Duk prepared for the evening's battle. As he got into his well-tailored
American-style uniform, he knew that many of his officers from the border
would be down this night, and before they departed their posts they would
sign passes for many of their men, who also liked to get away now and then.
The American advisers had been very persuasive with their discussions of
troop morale.

It grew dark. General Chae prepared to go out. He could accomplish nothing by brooding, and he might accomplish a great deal drinking with the
Americans.

As evening fell, among the teeming, raucous hordes of white-clad people
thronging the streets and alleyways from North Gate to the massive railway
station to the odorous reaches of Yongdungp'o, the talk was of rice and of
rain. As always before the monsoon, the price of grain had skyrocketed; the
green seedlings, already transplanted, were parching. Only the monsoon rains,
with promise of a good crop, would bring ease to the people's mind.

Even now a great black cloud was forming over North Mountain, and toil-
ers, shopkeepers, even *yangban*—those who did not work—watched it hopefully. There was prayer that a storm, indeed, was brewing.

Never far from the smell of the brown soil, or starvation, the desperately
poor masses of Koreans talked of rain and rice.

But as the dark clouds soaked up the last of the fading daylight, the current
of Seoul's social life quickened. It had been a hot and muggy day, with showers in the morning. At the Sobingo Gun Club on the banks of the Han, the
KMAG officers and civilian members had worked up a fine sweat over the
traps. With the last clay target shattered, they had eased their bodies with a
short dip in the KMAG pool, followed by a long cool one at poolside.

Slowly, the American colony came to life. The largest American mission in
the world was based in Seoul, two thousand strong, and they had had a busy
week.

Foster Dulles had been in town. He'd got the usual tour, in VIP fashion: up
to Uijongbu on the parallel, to be snapped staring across no man's land, surrounded by grinning ROK officials. The usual press release had to be handled
smoothly: something about continuing American interest in South Korea, and
the pride in its progress toward democracy and a vitalized economy. After
that, Dulles got back on his plane at Kimpo, to his own and the American
Mission's relief.

But from the roof gardens of the Naija to the lounge of the Traymore, in
the carefully cordoned embassy bars where men and women gathered, there
was no talk of crops. Over tax-free liquor, the colony laughed over Foster's
visit, and over the official who had been caught keeping North Korea's Number One female spy. This man had even bought the woman a short-wave
radio, and it was said the ROK's would shoot her.

In spite of American influence, the ROK's were still extremely brutal to leftist elements in their midst. Of course, they could not shoot the American official.

There had been a child, towheaded yet, the American wives in Seoul told each other. Some American couple would, of course, adopt it.

Now the embassy taxi service began to hum, ferrying couples from the Traymore to the Banto, and from the Banto to the Chisan. Two topflight cocktail parties were scheduled, and there was the regular Saturday-night dance at that palatial symbol of midcentury Occidental culture, the KMAG Officers' Open Mess.

None of the Americans knew that Captain Vyvyan Holt of the British Legation had advised His Majesty's subjects to get out of town. Like Chae Byong Duk, Captain Vyvyan was uneasy. He had heard things.

American Intelligence, Seoul-bound, heard things, too. They reported them. But each report crashed headlong into a wall of belief that despite the recent takeover in Czechoslovakia, the unpleasantness in Berlin, and the military conquest of China, Red designs for the world were not too inimical to those of the West. And since Topside failed to worry, Intelligence relaxed.

So behind its walls and screens, carefully cordoned from the distasteful Orient about them, the American colony went about its Saturday-night business. It was no different from any other American colony, from the Straits of Gibraltar to Hong Kong, no better, and no worse. It was certainly no wiser.

As the bars filled in Seoul, Brigadier General William L. Roberts, lately commanding KMAG, the Korean Military Advisory Group, was on a States-bound ship. His time was in; he was going home. And his tour had been capped by an interview by *Time*.

Time had quoted him correctly: "The South Koreans have the best damn army outside the United States!"

The ROK's had eight divisions. Except those fighting guerrillas in the South, they were armed with American M-1 rifles. The guerrilla fighters had to make do with old Jap Model 99's. The ROK's had machine guns, of course, and some mortars, mostly small. They had five battalions of field artillery to back up the infantry divisions, all with the old, short-range Model M-3 105mm howitzer, which the United States had junked.

The best damn army outside the United States had no tanks, no medium artillery, no 4.2-inch mortars, no recoilless rifles. They had no spare parts for their transport. They had not even one combat aircraft.

They didn't have any of those things because the American Embassy didn't want them to have them. KMAG was not under the United States Army, or even responsible to the aloof and powerful satrap in Tokyo, MacArthur. Because the United States was determined to show the world that its intentions in Korea were nonaggressive, KMAG was under the State Department.

Most KMAG officers recognized this policy was nonaggressive. But as they told their Korean colleagues, who asked plaintively about guns and jets, "You can't fight city hall."

Ambassador John J. Muccio had been instructed to take no chances of the South Koreans attacking the Communists to the north. An attack would certainly convince the Soviets that America was not really bent on co-existence.

Ambassador Muccio had taken none, though his First Secretary, Harold Noble, had announced, "The ROK's can not only stop an attack but move north and capture the Communist capital in two weeks."

Whether they could or not, such reassurance was good for ROK morale.

Lynn Roberts had told *Time* that while the troops were excellent, the Korean officers' corps was not so hot. After all, in only eleven months staffs and commanders could not be made and trained, starting from scratch. Lynn Roberts, a professional soldier, also knew that soldiers are only as good as their officers make them. But that kind of attitude sounded un-American and was not popular in Washington, and there was no point in playing it up.

Not knowing the kind of tough, doctrinaire, disciplined armies that were being built in Asia by the Communists from Vietnam to Manchuria, KMAG and Ambassador Muccio really did not expect the ROK's to have to fight.

Now, sailing home on Saturday night, 24 June 1950, Lynn Roberts' sense of timing, at least, was perfect.

* * *

As the music started up in Seoul, in Kokura, Japan, Major General William Frishe Dean was guest of honor at a 24th Division Headquarters costume party. Which was one way for infantrymen to try to forget Secretary of Defense Louis Johnson and his fat-cutting, the supercarrier, the Strategic Air Command, and the nagging feeling that in the Atomic Age footsloggers might be obsolete.

Bill Dean came as a Korean *yangban,* one of the aristocratic class who did no work, with a black stovepipe hat perched on his close-cropped head, and a long, flapping robe covered his two-hundred-pound, six-foot frame. The 24th Division Staff thought he was hilarious.

Bill Dean remarked to his wife, who also came dressed as a Korean—they had both been in the Occupation Forces—that he felt a bit ridiculous. Besides, as the evening wore on, the hard hat hurt.

* * *

It was Sunday morning in Seoul now, and the embassy bars were closing. Only a few dreaming—or drunken—young people still lingered in the KMAG Officers' Open Mess. It was almost dawn, and even the private parties were dying.

Any young officer who had not made out by now never would.

And the storm that had hovered over the high peaks of Bukhan Mountain north of the city broke. The rain sheeted down, true monsoon, and it was good to sleep by. People woke, smiled in the dawn's freshness, and returned to sleep. Workers, passing out of the city through Namdai Mun, the South Gate, laughed and sang as they crossed the bridge over the Han. Below them the gray shapes of massive junks and the thin shadows of motor launches lay quietly on the rain-speckled dark water.

White-clad farmers smiled as they scooped up chamber pots outside the surrounding villages' doors, and filled their reeking honey buckets. Life was hard, but again the people would be able to buy rice.

The million and a half people of Seoul did not expect the future to be good. The expected to survive.

And miles to the north, beyond where the roads the Americans had named Long Russia and Short Russia ended, beyond the religious missions on the parallel at Kaesong, where the Methodist missionaries, reassured by Ambassador Muccio, still slept, far to the east of Seoul in a town called Hwach'on, Senior Colonel Lee Hak Ku looked once again at his watch.

He looked up, met the eyes of the booted and blue-breeched officers standing about him in the Operations Post. They were all young, and hard, and most of their adult lives had been spent at war, with the Chinese, with the Soviets. They had fought Japanese; they had fought Nationalists. Now they would fight the running dogs of the American Imperialists, or whoever else got in their way.

All around, men in mustard-colored cotton uniforms were moving in the wet, predawn murkiness. Covers were coming off stubby howitzer muzzles; diesel tank engines shuddered into raucous life. The monsoon was turning into drizzle now along the dark hills that framed the demarcation zone.

The varihued green paddies glistened with water, but the roads were hard and firm. The big long-gunned tanks began to move.

Back along the valley, where two divisions awaited the order to slash southward, officers raised their right arms. Section chiefs filled their lungs for shouting. The heavy guns had been trained and loaded long before.

Then men shouted, and dark cannon spat flame into the lowering sky. From the cold Eastern Sea to the foggy sandbanks of the Yellow Sea to the west, along every corridor that led to the South, night ended in a continuous flare of light and noise.

The low-slung, sleek tanks attached to the 7th Division spurted forward, throwing mud from their tracks. Designed for the bogs of Russia, they rolled easily over the hard-packed earth. Behind them poured hordes of shrieking small men in yellow-brown shirts.

"Manzai!" Senior Colonel Lee Hak Ku said, and, eyes gleaming, his staff repeated it.

It was 4:00 A.M., Sunday, 25 June 1950. The world, whether it would ever admit it or not, was at war.

2

The Crime of Marquis Ito

The twentieth century knows no greater crime. . . .

—Under Secretary of State Summer Wells, speaking of the Japanese occupation of Korea, 1905–1945.

THERE HAVE BEEN three Korean Wars in modern times. Each time, foreign powers have fought in Chosun, and each time the Korean people have been the losers. It is already an old pattern, and it seems one likely to continue, so long as the empires of man collide.

Korea, or Chosun, is a peninsula, 575 miles in length, averaging 150 miles across. It resembles in outline the state of Florida, though bigger. Along its eastern coast a giant chain of mountains thrusts violently upward; the west coast is flat and muddy, marked by estuaries and indentations. Inland the country is a series of hills, broad valleys, lowlands, and terraced rice paddies. Its rivers run south and west, and they are broad and deep.

It is a country of hills and valleys, and few roads. Most of Korea is, and always has been, remote from the world.

Chosun is a poor country, exporting only a little rice. But its population density is exceeded in Asia only by parts of India. For four thousand years the Koreans have tilled their misty valleys, forming a separate culture, with distinct language, literature, and ethos, within the broader frame of Sinic Civilization. Koreans are neither Chinese, Manchu, nor Japanese. They took their basic civilization from ancient China, passed it on to the then barbarous islands of Japan, but always, shrouded by their hills and bordering seas, the people of the Hermit Kingdom wished to be left in peace.

The wish is hopeless, for Korea is a buffer state.

It juts southeastward for Chinese Manchuria, and touches the maritime eastern province of Russia. One hundred and twenty miles from its southern tip lie the islands of Japan. To Japanese eyes, looking upward, Chosun is a dagger, aimed eternally at her heart.

Neither China, nor Russia, nor whatever power is dominant in the Islands of the Rising Sun, dares ignore Korea. It is, has been, and will always be either a bridge to the Asian continent, or a stepping-stone to the islands, depending on where power is ascendant.

Throughout history the great powers surrounding Chosun have proclaimed and guaranteed its continued freedom and independence. But none of them have truly accepted such guarantees. They dare not, because they do not trust each other.

So Korea has suffered, without profit to herself. So she is suffering still. The crimes against her have been continuous, for Korea is a breeding ground for war.

* * *

From the time of the Manchus China controlled Korea, but with a lax and distant hand. But by the nineteenth century Manchu power had decayed, and the stars of Russia and Japan were rising in the East. Collision was inevitable.

The cause of collision was not the poor land of Chosun with its teeming millions, but vast and wealthy Manchuria, looming high beyond the Yalu. Manchuria is the richest area in all East Asia, with iron ores, coal, water power, food, and timber, and whoever owns Manchuria, to be secure, must also own Chosun.

The newly awakened Empire of Japan began to put fingers of economic penetration through Chosun, inching toward Manchuria. In 1894 Japan and the Empire of China went to war, in Korea.

Near P'yongyang, the Japanese met the Chinese hordes, and defeated them. By the Treaty of Shimonoseki, signed 17 April 1895, the Manchu Empire renounced all influence in Chosun, and ceded to Japan the Island of Taiwan. The weakness of China was revealed, and the Western powers, unconcerned with the Rising Sun, gathered for what loot could be had. Russia gained forts and bases in Manchuria, and pressed down across the Yalu, seeking to control North Korea.

All powers agreed to the continuing freedom of Chosun.

Russian troops, however, garrisoned the north, while Japanese corporations began to swallow up the south. It was an uneasy situation that could not last.

In 1904 Japan and czarist Russia went to war. Japanese troops debarked at Inch'on, Korea, and marched north. They attacked across the Yalu River, and defeated Russia in a brilliant campaign. Meanwhile, the Japanese signed a treaty with Chosun, guaranteeing the Hermit Kingdom's independence, in return for the use of its territory as a base of operations.

It is the nature of peoples to see the ancient foes, and to ignore those newly arising. Japan defeated Russia with the moral and material aid of Great Britain and America, who had watched the Russian advance to the Pacific with unconcealed dread. Japan, with far greater ambitions than the rotting Empire of the Bear had ever entertained, now was the dominant power in East Asia, and America and Britain applauded.

They did not sense that, in time, Japan would overthrow the old order completely.

At the Treaty of Portsmouth, signed in New Hampshire under the good offices of President Theodore Roosevelt, Russian influence in Manchuria was checked. All powers again guaranteed the freedom of Chosun, but the treaty recognized Japan's "paramount political, military, and economic interests in Korea."

The Empire of Japan was free to move.

In the crisp, smoky early fall of 1905, the Marquis Ito was called to Tokyo. The Marquis Ito—Japan had now adopted French-style titles for its aristocracy—was not only a member of the high nobility but also one of the most capable men under the Rising Sun.

In Tokyo, the Foreign Office briefed Ito on recent events. The *Tenno,* the Son of Heaven, he was told, had sent a personal message to the king of Chosun, asking the king to bring his small realm into the friendly arms and great prosperity of the Rising Sun. But the king and cabinet of Chosun were most shortsighted. They did not understand that Japan must control Manchuria, or see that to exploit that province, Japan must hold a land bridge to its wealth.

In short, both king and cabinet wanted no part of the Rising Sun. This, in itself, was sacrilege—but worse, the king had dispatched a note to the President of the United States, begging help against Japanese pressure.

The Marquis Ito, a small and dapper brown-skinned man, winced. He knew a great deal about the American President, who sometimes spoke softly, but always maintained an uncomfortably large navy.

"When will the message arrive?" he asked.

The Foreign Office, whose spies reached even into the royal gardens at Seoul, had learned the name of the ship on which the note had sailed. They could calculate the days, and there was very little time. If the White House received the note, the Chrysanthemum stood to lose much face, and worse, its immediate hopes of dominating Chosun.

The Marquis Ito was ordered to go to Seoul at once, and to do whatever must be done to retrieve the situation. If agreement with the Government of Korea, the Taehan Minkuk, could be reached prior to the delivery of the note, Roosevelt could do nothing.

The victorious Japanese Army had not yet left Korean soil, and its commander, General Hasekawa, was placed at the disposal of the Marquis Ito.

Ito went at once to Seoul. There he conferred with General Hasekawa, while awaiting audience with the Hermit King. Hasekawa suggested that he had sufficient troops in the Seoul area to settle the matter handily, if the Marquis Ito so desired. Gently, Ito explained to the bluff and honest samurai the facts of international diplomacy, and why it would not do to blow down the palace walls. But he suggested that Hasekawa march his men about for exercise and that the horse artillery indulge in target practice.

The cold winds had just begun to blow out of the north, and the brown paddies were freezing by night. Across them Hasekawa's soldiers marched singing and shouting, carrying the banner of the Rising Sun, and the artillery, horses stamping and leaving smoking droppings on the dark earth, wheeled shining field guns into place near the city's walls.

The cannon barked into the wind, sending up great gouts of black smoke. The noise crashed across the peaceful gardens and still pools of the palace grounds, shaking the leaves of the ancient gingko biloba and other venerable trees in the groves beneath Royal Mountain. It rebounded from Namdai Mun, the great South Gate of the city, to Taihan Mun, the Red Gate built in the Middle Ages.

And on the walls of ancient Seoul, seven miles long, twenty-five feet high and ten feet thick, the cabinet of Chosun gathered and watched. They were scholars of the mandarin caste, not soldiers, but even they knew that no walls of dressed stone would stand against the modern power of *Dai Nippon.*

But the king had written to the great Roosevelt, and they pressed him to deny the Marquis Ito's audience. The king did so. He sent word to the Japanese that he was not well, and could not leave the royal apartments.

The acting prime minister of Chosun, Han Kyu Sul, a man more brave than wise, ordered the cabinet to resist the Japanese demands for a protectorate to the death, if necessary. Han Kyu Sul was loyal to his king, but he also knew that ten years earlier a party of drunken Japanese officers under the Viscount Miura had murdered the queen, and with her, his sovereign's courage.

But the Marquis Ito understood the people of Chosun. He knew they were a peaceful race, puritan in habit, whose highest caste were not samurai, as in Europe or Japan, but scholars. He knew that Chosun had no army, and he knew, moreover, that the Koreans were the Irish of the Orient, changeable, mercurial. And he knew that a mercurial race, with its moods of alternate elation and despondency, may often be manipulated. Marquis Ito waited, while Hasekawa's men marched and Hasekawa's cannon thundered.

Finally, on 17 November 1905, he demanded that the cabinet meet with him, the king in attendance, to discuss the matter of a Japanese protectorate. He gave abrupt orders to Hasekawa, who bowed. The Koreans had been frightened enough; it was time to act.

Quietly, as dark fell on 17 November 1905, a battalion of Japanese regulars entered the city. They marched through Namdai Mun and Taihan Mun, and they entered the palace grounds. They girdled the ancient courtyards and took up positions at the gates. They lighted flaming torches, and they fixed long, glittering bayonets.

Now, boldly, the Marquis Ito, the bandy-legged, taciturn Hasekawa at his side, trailing a long samurai sword, marched into the Hall of Bright Rule, the vast audience chamber. Here, the nervous cabinet awaited him, but the king was not in sight.

Ito demanded audience with the king. Messengers were sent, but the king refused to appear.

Smiling coldly, Ito brushed the retainers aside and went into the king's private apartments. He did not stop until he had burst in and was face to face with the paling monarch. Then he bowed. He begged audience. Matters, he said, were pressing.

The king had no stomach to face the smiling Japanese. "Please go away," he stammered. "My throat is very sore. Discuss your matter with my ministers."

Ito smiled, bowed, and withdrew. He marched back to the audience hall and told the cabinet ministers, "Your king has commanded you to settle this matter with me now."

Han Kyu Sul leaped angrily to his feet. "I will go myself to see the king!" he shouted.

Ito, without expression, watched the prime minister leave. He knew that Han Kyu Sul alone was holding the cabinet together and that Han was braver than his king. He had anticipated this, and imperturbably, he allowed Han to pass through the door.

Outside, the secretary of the Japanese Legation pressed a revolver barrel in Han Kyu Sul's side. "Be quiet, or I shall kill you!"

Han was forced into a small side chamber, and onto his knees.

Now the Marquis Ito appeared. He told Han Kyu Sul that the prime minister could be very useful to the Chrysanthemum and that it was time to recognize the march of history, time to bend and so profit by it rather than to fight it and die.

Han spat at him.

"Would you not yield, if your king commanded you?" Ito asked, at last.

"No. Not even then," Han said bitterly.

Ito met his stubborn black eyes, sighing almost regretfully. Han, of course, could be broken, but a broken tool is of no use. Leaving Han kneeling on the floor, he went again to the king's apartments.

"Han Kyu Sul is a traitor to you," he told the king abruptly. "He defies your order to treat with me; he will obey none of your commands."

Trembling, the king agreed that Han Kyu Sul should be removed. Ito's cold eye saw that the House of Lee was much decayed. He had also heard that the heir apparent was mentally retarded from birth. He made a mental note, that if all went well this night, the king would not live long.

Now the Marquis Ito went arrogantly from the king's presence, and spoke to the soldiers outside the Hall of Bright Rule. Then he went inside, seeing the worried faces of the Koreans turn toward him. Han Kyu Sul had been gone an hour, and courage was oozing minute by minute from these venerable, scholarly graybeards.

Ito squared his shoulders and threw back his head. He no longer smiled. He shook himself, and suddenly shrieked at them: "Han is dead! The Chinese are gone; the Russians are defeated. America is too far away to help you, in spite of your Treaty of 1882. You are all alone. Agree with us now and be rich—oppose us, and die!"

The cabinet grew frightened. They talked among themselves in low voices.

Now Hasekawa came in. Beating on the table with his sword, he raved that he would turn his soldiery loose upon the city, unless the cabinet signed a treaty of protection with Japan. Screaming and roaring at the shocked *yangban,* the Japanese threw off all restraint. Relentlessly, they hammered at the Koreans. None was allowed to leave; soldiers with bayoneted rifles guarded every exit.

Long past midnight, tears streaming down his face, the foreign minister used a newly installed device of the foreign devils, the telephone, to call for the Seal of State, so that a treaty might be signed.

The Keeper of the Seal, who knew what was afoot, refused to deliver it. Japanese soldiers found him and tore the Seal from him by force. The Seal was taken triumphantly to the Hall of Bright Rule by a grinning subaltern.

In this manner, the Marquis Ito negotiated a treaty of protection between Chosun and the Empire of the Rising Sun. He would become Governor-General of Chosun, because if he had not served his *Tenno* nobly, he had at least served him well.

* * *

Fourteen years after Chosun became a part of the Japanese Empire, the Reverend Edward W. Twing, of Boston, visited Korea as Oriental Secretary of the International Reform Bureau.

The Reverend Mr. Twing saw at once that a flush of enthusiasm for democracy and self-determination was sweeping Korea, just as in 1919 it was sweeping all the earth.

But in Chosun the movement was getting nowhere at all. The Japanese authorities, as a matter of policy, were extremely bitter about the whole thing, even about peaceful protests and demonstrations. The mere idea that the people of Chosun might desire separation from the Japanese East Asia Co-Prosperity Sphere was more loss of face than they could bear.

One day Mr. Twing saw a group of Korean girls of school age shout *"Manzai!"*—which means merely "Hoorah!"—at passing Japanese soldiers. The Japanese immediately opened fire on them. Another group of schoolgirls walking down the road, not even shouting, were set upon by the angry troops. The Japanese beat them with rifle butts, knocked them down, tore away their clothing. Then, as Mr. Twing related back in Boston, "the soldiers treated them in a most shameful fashion."

The Koreans had to be taught that they were inseparably citizens of the empire, whatever the class rating of their citizenship might be. They were taught so well that, during three months of 1919, more than fifty thousand of them were killed or at least hospitalized by the lesson.

Above all, Mr. Twing reported back, the Japanese were out to teach Korean Christian converts that contact with the philosophies of the West was dangerous. And it was. Christian men and women were dragged into Shinto temples, tied to crosses, and beaten savagely. Young girls of Christian families were stripped, fastened to telegraph poles by their hair, flogged, and left exposed to public view.

Mr. Twing let no one mistake that he found this highly distressing. Years later, survivors of Nanking, Malaya, and the Bataan Death March—not the travelers who stopped at the Imperial Hotel and were charmed by gentle smiles and ritual deference—would have understood what Mr. Twing was talking about. In 1919 nobody much cared. After all, the Koreans were Asiatics, and someone had to keep them in hand.

Mr. Twing told also about the great reforms the Japanese had instituted in Korea, and of which they eternally boasted. But Mr. Twing's version differed slightly from the official one.

The Japanese had reformed the ancient tongue of Chosun, Mr. Twing said, by abolishing it. Korean archives and treasures of literature were purified by burning, since there was no place in the bright new twentieth century for a separate Korean culture. Not only was Japanese the language of Korean courts; it was the only one allowed in the schools.

Beyond literacy, Koreans were to receive no education. No Koreans were allowed abroad to study, except a few trusted ones who were permitted to enter Japan. Even here they might not study religion, history, economics, politics, or law. Koreans were to be hewers of wood and haulers of water; Japan had already more scholars and subversives than the samurai could stomach.

Reform of the primitive economy was accomplished by placing almost all of it into the hands of pure-born Japanese, hundreds of thousands of whom were encouraged to emigrate.

Judicial reforms included mandatory flogging for minor offenses for which Japanese drew a monetary fine. Justice was also refined by the reintroduction of an ancient tool, the rack. Japanese police took over law enforcement, slowly training a corps of loyal Koreans to handle the minor details, such as traffic duty and beating of prisoners.

The legal reform of the country brought on social reforms. Very soon, patriotic Koreans found it expedient to lie, cheat, steal, and malinger on the job. And they became brutalized with brutal treatment. Some of the habits would be hard to break.

All told, more than a million and a half Koreans fled the country. Some went to China, many to Russia, a few even to the United States. One refugee in the States, a Dr. Syngman Rhee, embarrassed the government. He had entered on an old Korean passport at the time of the takeover, and now in 1919 he requested a visa to visit the League of Nations, to make a protest over the treatment of his countrymen. Washington emphatically told him no, since he had no valid Japanese passport, and Washington did not want to offend its late ally, Japan. Generously, however, since Dr. Rhee had influential friends, he was allowed to remain in the United States.

In 1919, and later, the Japanese rulers of Chosun never quite dared expel the Western missionaries, probably not realizing in how little repute these emissaries were held in the Western capitals. For years the only contact the Korean people had with outside was through these missionaries. In Chosun, no anti-Western bias ever developed.

Koreans had learned the hard way that imperialism comes in many forms, and it can be black or brown or yellow, as well as white. Koreans would never afterward feel any sentimental racial cohesiveness with the rest of Asia. The Japanese occupation and policy of extirpation took care of that.

In 1919, and afterward, the Reverend Mr. Twing and many others came back from Chosun and tried to make the world know what was happening there.

But the world was not interested. In Washington, Mr. Twing was told that Korea, after all, was an internal problem of the Japanese. It could be of no more concern to the United States than how Mississippi planters paid their field hands could be of interest to Japan.

It was not until long afterward, after a rather hot time one Sunday morning at a place called Pearl Harbor, that anyone in government would listen.

3

To Make a War . . .

The water downstream will not be clear if the water upstream is muddied.
—Korean Proverb.

O N A STEAMING AUGUST night of 1945, if anyone along the Potomac had gone in to see what the boys in the back room would have, they'd have found them sweating over a brand-new problem: Korea. The men of Swink—the State-War-Navy Coordinating Committee, or SWNCC—had been told to come up with something on Korea and to do it fast.

For after three years of working on it, two days after the Bomb went off over Hiroshima, the United States had finally finagled Soviet Russia into the war against Japan. And even before they declared war, the Russians had sent their armies crashing into Manchuria, and across the Korean border.

Colonel General Ivan Chistyakov crossed the Yalu with 120,000 men, and pushed south. On orders from Tokyo the Japanese were falling back.

The men of Swink knew that the Cairo Declaration of December 1943 had promised a free and independent Korea in due time, and they knew that at Yalta, and later at Potsdam, the big powers had agreed on some form of international trusteeship for Chosun. Russia had accepted the Potsdam agreements. On the surface, then, it did not seem to matter that Russia was now overrunning the Japanese Empire on the continent of Asia.

But there were hard-bitten, unidealistic types on Swink—men who doubtless had never truly accepted the Russkies as comrades-in-arms—who thought the United States had better get some troops up that way pretty quick. Ivan could manage the surrender of Japanese troops alone, of course—but that was not the point.

The Government of the United States agreed with them. It was decided to ship troops to Korea as soon as possible.

But it was also apparent that an untidy situation could arise from having armed Americans, armed Russians, and gun-toting Japanese all milling about in one small peninsula. Swink was given the problem of hacking out zones of

18

operations for the two Allied powers, within which each would accept the Japanese surrender.

"We'll have to draw a line of demarcation; they handle the Japs on one side, we handle them on the other," it was suggested.

Everyone on the committee bought that. Agreement those days in the Pentagon was somewhat easier, since there was as yet no independent Air Force to protest the role of strategic bombing in the surrender.

But where to draw the line?

Some of the men of the unidealistic group asked, "Why not the Yalu?"

But it was too late for that; the Russians had already crossed the Yalu. And a man from State wanted it understood that if the military were going to view the Russians with suspicion, it would thoroughly louse up the bright new world everyone had fought for. As a mater of courtesy, the Soviets could not be asked to retreat from territory they had already captured.

"Let's look at the map," Army suggested.

Navy agreed, though Navy couldn't be of too much help there. The strategic wall map didn't show fathoms.

A line or zone had to be found that was far enough north not to jeopardize the future role of the United States, but also far enough south so that the Russian Army could not have already crossed it.

It was noted that the 38th parallel of latitude cut the peninsula almost in half. "How about that?"

State liked it, for the line put the political capital of Chosun in the American sector.

Navy liked it, because it gave the United States two larger ports. "This Fusan"—Navy was looking at a Japanese map—"down here in the south is the biggest port in the country—"

"Anybody got a better idea?"

Nobody had.

"Let's take it upstairs, then."

And upstairs they bought it—the 38th parallel to serve as a temporary line of demarcation dividing Russo-American responsibility for the Japanese surrender. The line was incorporated into General Order Number 1, the protocol for the surrender of Japan, and it was flashed to London and Moscow for confirmation.

Good show, London agreed. The Russians said *Da,* for once.

And the 38th parallel it was.

The men of Swink could not anticipate that the world was not going back to what it had been in 1939, only with the bad boys removed, and that there was now a distressing bipolarity of power in the world, split between two essentially hostile philosophies. Anyway, it wasn't their job.

Nor was it their job to worry over what the Russians might do, or to fear that the temporary lines of expediency being drawn now across the earth might become hard political frontiers.

The Army and the Navy had been directed to win a war, and they had done just that. And the State Department, to quote Mr. W. Walton Butterworth,

Assistant Secretary for Far Eastern Affairs under Marshall, "should have no opinions about anything," especially on career-officer levels.

To anticipate what might happen politically was the responsibility of the highest circles of civilian government, the men surrounding the President, who should have been planning beyond 1948, 1952, or even 1964.

Now, in late summer 1945, pending a final solution to the problems of the world and of the war, American troops entered Korea.

* * *

Lieutenant Colonel William P. Jones, Jr., of Morrisonville, Illinois, was redeployed with his 1108th Engineer Combat Group Headquarters from Leghorn, Italy, to the Pacific during the summer of 1945. Sailing through the Panama Canal, the 1108th reached the Philippines in September. The war was over, and the troops were clamoring to go home.

The XXIV Corps, under Lieutenant General John R. Hodge, had gone to Korea, to take the Jap surrender and serve as occupation troops, and General Hodge needed engineers. But he wasn't going to get them from the 1108th, as Colonel Jones soon discovered.

A new discharge and rotation list had been published after VJ-Day, and almost all officers of the group, including the surgeon and dentist, and all but fifteen of the eighty enlisted men of Group Headquarters were eligible to go home. Only two officers of the Corps of Engineers branch would remain, with the exception of Jones himself, who was Regular Army, and not going anywhere.

Bill Jones, a stocky, square-jawed man with a moustache and thinning hair, protested the removal of his troops. How the hell was he going to get anything done, if all the trained men were sent home?

Up at Headquarters he was told that nothing, absolutely nothing—not the occupation, the surrender, or anything else—could take precedence over sending the boys home. The Regular Army, which was about two hundred thousand men, would have to carry on by itself. Congress had decided that the most urgent matter had come before it for four years was the question of whether some of the brass were nefariously plotting to keep a lot of men in uniform beyond their time.

Congress, and the American people clamoring behind them, needn't have worried. Most of the brass just sighed, and gave up.

The boys went home.

Colonel Jones received replacements, of course. He got officers from the Quartermaster Corps and the Infantry, and plenty of basic riflemen from the eighteen-year-olds just drafted, who didn't have Skill One, even for basic riflemen. Engineers he didn't get. Engineers, like most professional men, serve in the military only when the draft moves them.

With a Group HQ that didn't know a crowbar from a wrecking iron, and who thought a balk was part of baseball, Colonel Jones, as part of "Blacklist Forty" (code name for Korea), reported to General Hodge in Korea. Hodge sent him to Pusan, to take control of some three thousand engineer troops in the area. The engineers' mission was to construct housing for the United

States occupation troops and otherwise furnish engineer support, after, of course, all the boys had been sent home.

These were days and weeks to break a career officer's heart. The United States Army, which had been the most powerful in the world, did not melt away in an orderly fashion. It disintegrated into a disorganized mob, clamoring to go home. Men who had come into the service three months before, now that the war was over, figured they should go home too. No one gave much thought to the work that had to be done.

Fortunately for Jones, the Jap soldiers in Korea waiting to be sent home were willing workers. Both Koreans, drunk with new liberation, and Americans, already mentally wearing civilian clothes, grew sullen at the idea of labor. The Japs, now that the Greater East Asia Co-Prosperity Sphere was gone, were affable, smiling, professional, and entirely helpful. Jones put them to work. Somebody had to get the job done.

Eventually, though, all the Japs had to be repatriated. They took with them, when they left, every military officer, every professional man, every engineer, bank teller, and executive in the Pusan area. They left behind a hell of a mess.

Like most Americans, Colonel Jones was not prepared to take Chosun. The appalling poverty, the dust, dirt, filth, and eternal clamor of Pusan repelled any man accustomed to the West. Orphan children, with running sores, lay in the streets. Society, with the iron Japanese hand gone, was in dissolution. Money was worthless, since the Japanese had printed billions of yen prior to the surrender and passed it out to all who wanted it. Almost all responsible Koreans, particularly the educated were—rightly—tarred with the collaborationist brush.

Yangban, in conical hats, white robes, graybearded and wise with years, got roaring drunk and staggered through the streets. Women and children fell beside the roads, and died, ignored by both authorities and passersby. Jones saw one old woman try to cross a street of Pusan against the orders of the traffic policeman on duty. The cop pushed her back and knocked her down. Nobody bothered to help her up.

Forty years of slavery and brutality could not be brushed aside in a month, or in a year. Military Government had a hell of a situation on its hands, Jones realized.

He never got used to the stink. Inside the city, the odors were of decaying fish, woodsmoke, garbage, and unwashed humanity. Outside, the fresh air was worse. Koreans, like most Orientals, use human fertilizer. Their fields and paddies, their whole country smells somewhat like the bathroom of a fraternity house on Sunday morning.

Clothing washed in their rivers turns a sickly brown.

But slowly, holding their noses, the officers of the Occupation and Military Government tried to get things organized. None of them had had any experience with the job, or with Orientals. In Germany, or even Japan, the problem was much easier. There were, after all, skilled people to call upon, once the formality of Denazification was over.

In Korea, there were no trained administrators for either government or business, regardless of their politics.

Colonel Jones became acquainted with the complexities of Korean politics only indirectly. As an engineer, he became responsible for fire fighting in Pusan, and he noticed a great number of fires were breaking out. He asked a Korean fireman about this.

"Oh, it is the different factions, setting each other's houses afire," the Korean answered cheerfully. With most of Pusan constructed of wattle with tile roofing, Colonel Jones soon had his hands full.

Once he attended a fire personally. He saw the Korean firemen, with high courage, battling the flames with their old Jap equipment. Then, close by, he heard screams.

He turned, and saw several firemen and a policeman torturing a Korean. He ran over. An American major touched his sleeve. "Don't interfere with them, Colonel. They're trying to solve who set the fire!"

Later, one of his trucks ran down a Korean child. The officer he sent to investigate reported that the family was unconcerned. Life was hard and bitter and apt to be short, and now there was one less mouth to feed.

He soon learned to use Korean guards for U.S. military stores. The Koreans were desperately poor, and would steal anything, even if nailed down—nails had commercial value—but American sentries would not willingly shoot down women and boys carrying off gas cans and water buckets. Not after they had killed two or three, anyway—they lost all heart for it. But Korean guards would shoot or beat hell out of the thieves, if they caught them. By using Korean guards, the U.S. saved money.

Because he was a sincere, conscientious man, Colonel Jones of Illinois did the best he could. But he never learned to understand the people of Chosun, and he felt, reluctantly, that any hope for real democracy on the American pattern in that land was wishful thinking.

But he didn't know what to do about it, and he was glad when his time came in early 1946, and he, like the boys a year before, went home.

* * *

Captain Edward H. Landers, Infantry, arrived at Inch'on, Korea, in 1946. He went to XXIV Corps at ASCOM City, between Seoul and Inch'on, as Troop Information Officer. Tall, slow-talking, he was an Army brat, born in old Fort Dupont, in Delaware.

ASCOM City had been built by the Occupation Forces, and was the center of the Army Service Forces in Korea. From the first, Captain Landers didn't like it. But that was nothing startling—nobody in his right mind liked being in Korea.

The summers were hot and dusty, or hot and rainy, with hundred-degree temperatures. The winters were Siberian. The country literally stank, except for the few months during which the ground stayed frozen.

Nor did Captain Landers like his job. Nobody cared much for Troop Information. You had to watch what you said, or somebody wrote to Congress. Landers, a sincere man, felt about as useful as the proverbial appendages on a male pig.

Troop morale was lousy. All the men wanted to go home; some of them could get pretty nasty about it. In the meantime, they made out as best they could. Korean girls ran up and down the barracks at night, and everybody made black-market deals. There was no discipline among the troops.

When Landers spoke to any of the junior officers, they shrugged. "What can you do? The war's over."

A deadly thing had been done to the Army, which even the Army had not yet fully understood. The Doolittle Board had been convened in 1945 to iron out the inequities of the so-called "caste system" of the Army. The board interviewed a total of forty-two witnesses, and read approximately one thousand letters. Most of the letter writers were unhappy. In all fairness, many of them had a right to be. In making an Army of eight million men, the United States had commissioned many thousands of men who should never have risen above PFC. Some lousy things happened, particularly in the Service Forces. Officers and noncommissioned officers, in some cases, did abuse their powers.

Basically, there were two ways to reduce abuses of power in the service. One was to overhaul the officer procurement system, make damned certain that no merely average man could ever be commissioned, and have fewer officers, but better ones. The other way was to reduce the power to abuse anybody.

The Doolittle Board, probably thinking of a long period of pleasant peacetime coming up, in early 1946 chose to recommend the second.

It was a good idea, but it wouldn't work. The company commanders in Korea watched the girls run in and out of the barracks, had men talk back to them, and didn't know what to do about it. In fact, they weren't sure but what the American thing to do was to ignore it, and get a girl of their own.

Which many did.

What the hell, the war was over. Anybody who said a new one was brewing was definitely a goddam Fascist, or something.

Besides, contracting a venereal disease was no longer a court-martial offense. That kind of thinking had gone out with the horse, with saluting except on duty, with the idea that you should respect a sergeant.

Captain Landers made some contacts with the natives. After all, the American Army was in Korea for their benefit—or that was what he kept telling the troops. He met newspapermen from Seoul, and a Dr. Ahn of Inch'on. He learned to take off his shoes, even in winter, and sit politely in a Korean house. But the conversation with these intelligent Koreans sometimes threw him.

"What is democracy?" asked Dr. Ahn.

"Why is your democracy good for Korea?" the newsmen asked.

"Why do Americans refuse to have anything to do with the people of Chosun?" Dr. Ahn asked. "Why do you try to re-create your own way of life in our country?"

"Why do MP's throw Koreans out of the American compartments on the trains? Why do your allies the Russians keep Korea divided at the parallel?

Why do you not go home and let us rule our own country?" Koreans were very inquisitive.

"But what *really* is democracy?" Dr. Ahn still asked, after Landers had spent half an hour telling him.

"Let me ask you one," Captain Landers said. "Yesterday, I saw a Korean girl fall alongside the road near the Education Center. I called the Special Korean Police. They wouldn't come. Only after I had called three times did they show up to take the girl away."

"Ah," said Dr. Ahn. "They did not want to accept responsibility."

"Don't your people have compassion?"

"Of course. But it is always wise to shun the unfortunate," Dr. Ahn said, wisely. "Now, tell me what democracy is, and why it is best—"

Captain Edward H. Landers, Infantry, walked back to his quarters, thinking. He passed a group of drunken colored soldiers coming back from town. They pretended they didn't see him, so they wouldn't have to salute.

At ASCOM City, plenty of girls were hanging around, waiting for the lights to go out. Captain Landers remembered the Korean word for young girl was *seikse*. Like the Chinese, the Koreans optimistically refer to their young women as virgins.

Many a young Korean woman of the better class, approached by an American soldier, said, "Oh, no—oh, no! I am *seikse!*"

This sometimes confused the issue beyond repair. The girls were often beyond repair, too, but that was life.

Captain Landers was old Army. He could not understand Korea or the Koreans, and he could no longer understand the Army itself.

He requested separation.

First Lieutenant Charles R. Fletcher came to Korea in July 1946. Things were better now; the first complete chaos of the early months had gone. But the squalor, the smells, and the hopelessness of a conquered, brutalized people produced the same sense of shock in him as it produced in most of his countrymen. Lieutenant Fletcher had been born and raised on a farm near Wichita, Kansas, but this was no preparation for Chosun.

A hundred years before, Americans might have gone to Korea and taken it in stride, but no longer. America had changed, both materially and subtly over the decades, and now in the Orient American soldiers could not live without insulating themselves from the life around them.

It was not that Americans came with arrogance or with a feeling of insurmountable superiority. They simply would not—could not—accept the way the people of Chosun lived.

No matter how cultured or ancient the civilization, no average American is going to condone the absence of flush toilets. Not now, not ever. The United States Government and international planners may as well face that simple fact.

Because Fletcher, a good-looking, quiet, pipe-smoking young man, planned to stay in the service, he made the best of what he considered a bad deal. His wife, who came over later, reminded him that some people were occupying Germany or Austria, but there was nothing he could do about that.

He was assigned to Major Herbert Van Zandt, who ran the huge New Korea Company. American occupation officers still had control of all important parts of the Korean economy; South Korea had not been able to develop the necessary capable executives since the Japanese surrender.

Neither Americans nor Koreans were enthusiastic about the arrangement.

The New Korea Company was actually the old Oriental Development Company, that Japanese octopus of industry that had dominated the Far East before the war. It had owned mines, mills, shipyards, factories, smelters, and farmland. Now, for the most part, only farmlands remained.

Van Zandt installed Fletcher, an infantry officer, as Director of Mining Industry and Engineering, an imposing title for a farm boy from Kansas. However, Fletcher soon found that most of the mines were in the North, where he might as well forget them, and that engineering was defunct.

By this time, most American Military Government officers realized that they might never be able to restore the Korean economy. Certain things had come to light since 1945: two-thirds of Korea's people lived and farmed south of the 38th parallel, but almost the entire industry and mineral wealth of the country lay in the north.

By themselves, the two halves might possibly build a viable economy by the year 2000, certainly not sooner.

And Fletcher soon found that the occupying Russians to the north intended that the country be joined on their terms, or not at all. Their terms included formation of a "democratic"—Communist—government for the entire peninsula. They allowed neither Koreans nor Americans to enter their zone.

Korea had always been a homogeneous nation. There was no difference between the North and South, no cultural line such as divides the United States along the Ohio Valley, no separate ethos, no distinct dialect. The split made absolutely no sense—except to two mutually hostile occupying powers, each with its own irons in the fire.

The Russians would not cooperate with American attempts to rebuild the South. Worse, they meddled. They fomented economic disorder and political protest. They demanded conferences, and requested joint commissions. If a commission met, they made demands. If the demands were met, they made further demands. If something was asked of them, they yelled, "Unfair!" picked up their marbles and went north. In short, they acted as Russians had acted around the world since the war.

Finally, Military Government in Korea quit trying to do business with them. General Hodge was criticized for this inflexible attitude; the world had not yet learned that it is completely impossible to do business with Russians except from either a position of power or upon Russian terms.

Soon enough, the Director of Mining Industry and Engineering found that his job was not all gravy. The Koreans working for him tended to be temperamental and sullen. Some of them thought they knew as much about mining industry and engineering as he did. None of them could distinguish between right now, tomorrow, or next year, when asked to do something.

Nor was the living exactly high, even on directorate level. Winter came, and Charles Fletcher had to wear overcoat and gloves at his desk. Once, as an experiment, he put a glass of water on his space heater. The water turned to ice. Two weeks later, checking, he found it was still ice.

His wife had servants, but she had to cook on a wood range. The range was used for heating the house, too. Often, Charles Fletcher found it expedient to stay late at the office, even in gloves and overcoat.

The Army did what it could, but in 1946 Korea was logistically at the end of the line. Most Army equipment had been diverted to surplus sales, to ease the screaming civilian demand for goods, and short of war, there was likely to be no new appropriation.

At his desk one day, Fletcher heard that there was trouble in Samch'ok, on the east coast. He left his office in Seoul to investigate. At a company iron-ore mine, he found agitators were encouraging idle workers to carry away company property. He had the Korean Special Police arrest the agitators, and beat hell out of them.

Back at Seoul, there was some criticism—but nobody had a better idea.

The policy now became one of giving Korean nationals control of the company. The new executives learned some things quickly. They became adept at losing company property, mostly into their own pockets.

Meanwhile, a crisis developed with the Russians just across the border from Seoul Province. The waters that irrigated company rice paddies flowed down from the north, and suddenly the Russians dammed them off. The company agricultural adviser, PFC Peavey, was sent up north to investigate.

The Russians were not offended by negotiating with a PFC. They had political officers masquerading in low ranks in their own forces; they understood perfectly *Gospodin* Peavey's desire not to appear conspicuous. They sat down with Peavey and informed him they wanted a portion of the company's rice harvest in return for the water.

Peavey argued awhile. Finally, getting nowhere, he figured, what the hell? He was due to rotate out any day and become a civilian. He agreed to everything. He returned to Seoul, and soon the water flowed south.

When asked how he had outwitted the Ivans, Peavey would only smile gently. A few weeks later, he sailed for the States.

When fall came, the Russians asked for their rice. Military Government, of course, with some confusion, explained why they couldn't have it.

Next summer, the New Korea Company had a hell of a time getting water.

* * *

Meanwhile, political organizations and parties were springing up all across the South. Most, like the Full Moon Mating Society, had small success, unless that faction had something to do with the exploding population.

Through a hassle for power, a group of conservatives led by Dr. Syngman Rhee were gradually consolidating their hold on the country. General Hodge himself personally disliked Rhee, who could be both cantankerous and autocratic, but Rhee had a big lobby in Washington. A Christian, he had the missionary group behind him.

And the choice was not between Rhee and middle-of-the-roaders. Outside the Anglo-Saxon countries, there are few middle-of-the-roaders. It was, to Fletcher, a choice between right and left.

Charles Fletcher's daughter was born in Korea, and shortly afterward he was sent home. He did not feel that he had done a good job, although he had tried to do his best. But the country was just too damn poor, too primitive, too temperamental, too stinking, for Americans to like or understand. Charles Fletcher had become aware that few Americans, forced to live for an extended period in a land without safe drinking water or plumbing, can keep both equilibrium and an open mind.

By 1947 the Government of the United States, as well as the men still stationed in Chosun, was sick of the Korean problem. A great deal of effort had been made; a great deal of money had been thrown at it; but the problem wouldn't go away.

As long as Military Government remained, South Korea would remain in chaos; no lasting solution to the country's ills could be made. And the forty-five thousand men tied down there were desperately needed elsewhere by the shrunken American ground forces.

And the Korean problem could not be solved of itself; it was part of a larger problem: that freezing of boundaries and attitudes men were beginning to call the "cold war." It had become obvious to many men in Washington that the world was split between two hostile groups, that the danger of a collision was increasing, and that something must be done, either to ease the tension or to strengthen the largely disarmed West.

But the deadly weakness of the Truman Administration was that Truman's domestic supporters, in the main, were indifferent to foreign policy. And domestic leaders of the Democratic Party were totally unfit by training and inclination for playing roles in foreign affairs. In general, Republicans, even of the liberal sort, left Washington at the end of the war, and businessmen would have nothing to do with the Administration. To execute his foreign policy Truman was forced to fall back on the great foundation bankers, who were largely isolated from the mainstream of American liberal tradition, soldiers, and career diplomats. On the whole these men, the Marshalls, the Clays, the McCloys, Forrestals, and Kennans, were professional, patrician, and conservative, much in the way the proconsuls of the early Roman Empire must have been: they disliked the violent enthusiasms sweeping the postwar world; they desired above all else order; and they were instinctively and instantly hostile to world Communism.

Their thinking, on the whole, was concise and clear, but it was unfortunately thinking isolated and often opposed to the thinking of the bulk of the American people. During the war, some members of the government had made an incalculable mistake: they had propagandized the Russians as heroic brothers-in-arms, indicated to the public that Stalin and associates were democrats at heart, and led the people to believe that Russia had fought the war from motives as pure as America's own.

All of which, even as early as December 1945, had been proved nonsense— but many people still believed it. Fortunately, there was government by consent of the governed in America—but just as unfortunately, such governments dearly hate to admit a mistake. The image of the Russians was not corrected.

The problem was that America had fought the war—as she had most of her wars—as a crusade, while Russia had fought first for survival, then for power. Crusades are usually inconclusive; it was no accident that Russia won the peace.

And it was no accident, in the late forties, that the makers of American policy, unwilling to backtrack with the public, began to try to isolate foreign-policy decisions *from public and Congressional control.* The great decisions—the Marshall Plan, the Truman Doctrine—that gave the earth a hope of eventual order were not instantly popular with the American people. There was no great attempt to sell them—it was significant that every historic decision of the Truman Cabinet was debated by Congress only after it had been made irreversible. The makers of foreign policy, not by accident, universally held Lockean notions of federal executive power; and, not by accident, they escaped the popular will.

They began, knowingly and cunningly, to contain the spread of Communism through whatever policy, short of war, might be required. This containment was vital to American interests, but it must always be remembered that the mere mention of such a policy would have sent millions of patriotic, well-meaning American liberals into convulsions. Liberal thought, which had scented Hitler early, seemingly remained tragically blind to Communist tyranny.

Before any attack on the morality of the men who formulated the policy of Communist containment may be made, several things should be recalled: these men had no designs on the world. They had no nationalist or imperialist policies to foist on anyone; they wanted to keep order and, so far as possible, the status quo, in an era when the Soviet Government clearly desired the opposite. The Soviets were doing their utmost to create chaos, so that they might then impose their own tyrannical system over an ever-widening circle.

If the popular will of the earth desired the Communists to be given a free hand, if it did not have either the physical or moral hardness to offer opposition—then the popular will, for its own sake, needed circumvention.

Thus in the Truman Administration there existed a basic dichotomy, between the politicians and liberals, the Hannegans, McGraths, McGrannerys, on the one hand, and the soldiers and bankers on the other. Each operated almost in a vacuum where the other was concerned.

The one rare exception to the pattern, Louis Johnson, was the most tragic figure of all. Johnson was a businessman liberal, a "go-getter," the sort of man who would later look for a "bigger bang for a buck." When Louis Johnson began to cut the armed forces, it must be remembered he was giving the bulk of the American public, liberal and business-conservative alike, precisely what it wanted.

Truman's own tragedy remained that the people on whom he depended for domestic support would simply not support his foreign policy. For the policy that evolved in the 1940's was new to American thought. It was not underprivileged Democratic, nor was it business Republican. It was orderly, world-seeing, pragmatic, and conservative—but conservative in the British or ancient Roman sense, not in the American sense.

Denied popular support, Truman functioned without it. Possibly history will accord him that as his greatest feat. History must also condemn him, with his Cabinet, for his inability to communicate. Wherever there is rule by consent of the ruled, the rulers must always be salesmen, however difficult the task.

For the first time in history, or at least for the first time since before the War Between the States, America had embarked upon a foreign policy that was not at least partially a crusade. The policy was the restoration of order in the world, and the orderly containment of Communism—not its hysteric extirpation, as with Hitler and "Kaiser Bill," by means of cataclysmic war that could, at best, solve nothing.

Since Wilson's time, some Americans had learned much.

In Europe, beginning with 1947, the policy succeeded brilliantly. It succeeded without the *sine qua non* of international politics, armed force, for both sides understood the stakes in Europe were too vital to risk less than all-out effort, if force were used.

The policy in Asia succeeded less well, because American planners were slow to see the importance of the East, and did not early recognize the Soviet shift to that area in 1949. Because of a certain indecisiveness on Asian policy, apparent to the Soviets, there would be war.

But even then it would be war different from all wars in American experience, except the Indian campaigns on the Plains. It would not be a crusade, because neither Harry Truman nor the men who handled his foreign policy were crusaders across the water. Because it was different, it would have far-reaching results. It would be the first war to bring down a government, to oust a party in power, not because of the actions that party had taken, but because the policy makers were never able adequately to explain those actions to a troubled and increasingly hostile public.

Like the Indian Wars, it would leave a troubled feeling, a trauma, in its wake. Crusades, even when failures, are emotionally satisfying. Wars of containment, wars of policy, are not. They are hard to justify unless it is admitted that power, not idealism, is the dominant factor in the world, and that idealism must be backed by power.

It was hard for a nation and a people who had never accepted the idea of power, not as something immoral in itself, but as a tool to whatever ends they sought, to fight and die for limited goals. In short, it was hard to grow up.

The Korean problem came again in Swink in 1947. Now the men of the State-War-Navy Coordinating Committee understood three things:

1. The Russians had different ideas as to what should be the solution to the Korean problem, and they would not cooperate, not now, not ever.

2. Without massive American support and economic aid, Korea would never achieve a viable economy.

3. And in event of large-scale war, Korea was a liability; the men based there would be lost to the services.

Swink wanted a way out of Korea, if there was a graceful one to be found. They requested the views of the Joint Chiefs of Staff. A complete decision was not, of course, the responsibility of the Joint Chiefs, who should have had no influence on what was, essentially, a political rather than a military matter. But in 1947, the civilian branches of government were letting Asian policy fall to the military by default—someone, qualified or not, had to make decisions, however painful such decisions might be to make.

Later, this power of decision would be taken away from the military, just as it should never have been given them. But it must be remembered that all through the 1940's civilian policy makers tended to shun Asian questions, letting the military have a disproportinate voice. Only when it came to cutting back military strength and expenditures did civilian planners advance with firm and happy tread.

At the end of World War II, American military policy, digesting the Japanese lessons in China, was to control air and sea lanes throughout the East but never to engage in ground hostilities on the Asian mainland. As one spokesman put it, "There was no point to mucking about through Manchuria."

The only war that military planners could envision was a big one between the United States and the Soviet Union. They assumed that in the future, as historically, America would never fight for limited goals; in the event of actual war, an all-out effort would be made to break or destroy the Soviet homeland. This was neither faulty thinking nor planning. The military men were following what had been American experience in the twentieth century. Many of the military planners themselves were not aware of the change to conservative, pragmatic thinking in certain quarters of Washington—thinking that was never explained to the public or to the military. The military continued to plan for the only kind of war they had been told to plan for: worldwide, atomic holocaust.

On 26 September 1947 the JCS sent Secretary of Defense Forrestal their reply:

> *From the standpoint of military security, the United States has little strategic interest in maintaining the present troops and bases in Korea.*

Thinking of the then-American atomic monopoly, the JCS wrote:

> *. . . Enemy interference from Korea could be neutralized by air action, which would be more feasible and less costly than large-scale ground operations.*

But the JCS made one other point very clear:

> *A precipitate withdrawal of our forces . . . would lower the military prestige of the United States, quite possibly to the extent of adversely affecting cooperation in other areas more vital to the security of the United States.*

The JCS, then, clearly understood that the problem was in essence not military but political. They were nervous and uncomfortable at having to make recommendations on it. They knew that military considerations, as they foresaw them, required the removal of troops from the Korean periphery, but also that the "rat leaving the sinking ship syndrome" was very prevalent in Asia. Korea was not militarily vital to American security. But American withdrawal from Korea might discourage Japan, which clearly was. American refusal to interfere with the fall of Nationalist China was already hurting American prestige in the Far East.

There were American planners who saw that a million ground troops, and a billion in aid, could hold the problem in check. But these planners knew that such things were not in the cards. The pragmatists in the high echelons of foreign policy could accomplish many things by fiat or executive agreement, but they could not raise troops or money against the popular will. This was a basic weakness to the policy of containment inherent in any parliamentary democracy, and as it proved in Asia, an insurmountable one, that would recur again and again, in China, in Korea, and finally in Vietnam.

Listening to the Joint Chiefs, the Government saw an out—one that got the United States off the hook militarily, and yet seemed to promise stability for Korea. They offered the question to the United Nations, which immediately, at American urging, accepted responsibility, voting Korea a U.N. ward and establishing a U.N. mandate over the divided nation.

On the surface, it look like a good solution, in keeping with the United States' professed aims in the world. Yet under the surface it was and remained an American withdrawal. There were only two centers of power in the world, and the United Nations was neither of them.

Stalin, who had asked how many divisions the Pope had, knew exactly how many divisions the U.N. maintained: none. When UNCOK, the United Nations Commission on Korea, tried to cross the dividing parallel, the Russians weren't even polite. UNCOK, after much debate, was able to accomplish nothing toward the reunification of Korea.

Despairing, the United Nations proposed free elections in South Korea to set up a rump state. After much political turmoil, these elections were held 10 May 1948.

The elections were reasonably honest, but Koreans were a disorganized and submissive people, almost without political education. It is not always easy to get an honest count in Chicago or Jersey City; what happened in Pusan or Seoul cannot be considered too harshly. The conservative parties behind Syngman Rhee came legally to power, and by 15 August the Taehan Minkuk, the Realm or Republic of Korea, had been established.

Russia protested each proceeding. Then, in September 1948, Russia established the Chosun Minjujui Inmun Kongwhakuk, the Korean Democratic People's Republic, in the North. This "republic" was in all respects what has since become known as a "tank democracy"; however, from the million Korean refugees that had fled Japanese tyranny Russia was able to cull many able, dedicated Communists to organize its government. Kim Il Sung, a Soviet citizen and officer, became Premier. Kim Il Sung could and did call upon the thirty thousand Korean veterans of the Chinese Communist and Soviet armies to return to form the nucleus of his Inmun Gun, or People's Army.

From its start, the North Korean State had a cohesion that the South lacked. It also had a purpose expressly denied Syngman Rhee, however much he might threaten it: the unification of the country.

The Russians had eyed the United States withdrawal, and misinterpreted it. But if the Soviets misunderstood American policy, it was perhaps because Americans did not clearly understand it, either. All the riddles within riddles wrapped in enigmas were not in the Kremlin.

To make a war, it is sometimes necessary that the eventual antagonists not know, or understand, what the other is doing. Russian policy had shifted to limited war, to subversion and terror and military operations on the periphery. American policy had drawn a line in Europe, but had not yet firmed in Asia. Russians had already moved in China, and in Indo-China, and set the future pattern. The United States had given no indication that it would oppose the Soviet game, provided its vital interests, such as Japan, were not involved.

The Russians, who had kicked up the dust, saw Americans waiting for the dust to settle. They could draw their own conclusions.

Americans, blissfully unaware of their weaknesses in conventional military strength, assumed that their government would, by blowing up any troubles, solve them, so that the Soviets would never dare to act.

To make a war, sometimes it is necessary that everyone guess wrong.

In the South of Korea, the economically impossible, democratically imperfect regime of Syngman Rhee struggled with massive problems. In the North, the Chosun Minjujui Inmun Kongwhakuk struggled only to overthrow Rhee. It used border raids, sabotage, guerrilla action, and propaganda, plus economic pressure.

One irrefutable measure of the success of cantankerous, autocratic, and Christian old Syngman Rhee was that the North failed. In spite of massive infiltration, treason, and chaotic political turmoil in South Korea, the majority of the people south of the parallel wanted no united nation that would be a tool of the Soviets.

On 1 January 1949 the United States recognized the new Republic of Korea. Special Representative to Korea John J. Muccio became the United States' first ambassador; the last American occupation forces were quickly withdrawn, though the United States by treaty agreed to help train ROK security forces. And economic aid continued; the Republic of Korea could not exist without it.

On 12 January 1950 Secretary of State Acheson spoke to the National Press Club in Washington. During the speech it came to public light that neither Korea nor Taiwan were within the United States' security cordon in the Far East. This was nothing new. The Korean decision had been made prior to 17 September 1947, when the United States had informed Russia of its intention to place the Korean problem before the United Nations. And the United States was still cautiously waiting for the "dust to settle" on the Chinese question.

Mr. Acheson neither blundered nor gave away state secrets. In global war—which was the only kind American policy makers contemplated or for which any service was preparing—neither Taiwan nor Korea was of much use. But neither Mr. Acheson nor his colleagues, who understood the European situation very well, quite knew or understood what was happening in Asia.

Europe could no longer be lost without a big war, but Asia had begun to teeter on the brink. There were plenty of farsighted men who were uneasy at the prospect, but in each case the dichotomy of the Truman Administration kept them hamstrung. Pragmatists and conservatives might be willing to put ground troops in Asia to fight "agrarian reformers and starving peasants"— but American liberal opinion was not.

The bulk of the people, indifferent as they were, might have been convinced, but the intellectuals, never. And the Democratic Administration did not feel it could completely circumvent its liberal spokesmen at home.

Dean Acheson drew his soon famous line, but he told the Russians nothing. By their process of reasoning, the United States had abandoned any real interest and power position in Korea when it had sent the question to the United Nations. Even as Mr. Acheson spoke, Russian and Chinese and North Korean leaders conferred in Peiping, agreeing that if the waters were muddied further in Korea the United States would stand aside, as it had during the fall of Nationalist China. They agreed that there would be no resort to atomic war if Korean attacked Korean; and observing American armed strength in the Orient, they correctly assumed that the United States had no other capability.

The United States could not be bought, or even intimidated, but it had a long history of looking the other way if not immediately threatened.

A war is made when a nation or group of nations is frustrated in political aims or when ends can be achieved in no other way. Communism was receding from its high-water mark in Europe, and the Atlantic Treaty Organization promised new stability there. It was succeeding in Asia, but the United Nations–sponsored Taehan Minkuk stood in its way. The Republic of Korea was not vulnerable to subversion, but it was vulnerable to armed force. And if it fell, the Russians saw, as the Americans did only imperfectly, that Communist control of the peninsula would soon become disastrous to the American presence and prestige in Japan.

Clausewitz, whom the majority of Americans read only to try to refute, had written: *War is not pastime, no mere passion for daring and winning, no work of a free enthusiasm; it is a serious means to a serious end. War always arises from a political condition and is called forth by a political motive.* Beside this passage, Lenin had drawn a marginal line.

A war is made when a government believes that only through war, and at no serious risk to itself, it may gain its ends.

Even before Dean Acheson spoke and told the Russians what they already knew, the Communist leaders were agreed. Soon, Senior Colonel Lee Hak Ku and his brother staff officers would receive orders, in Cyrillic script, to be translated into the Korean Hangul.

It was to be a bold stroke, with every chance of success.

It would almost succeed.

4

The Plan of General Chae

Surprise may decisively shift the balance of combat power in favor of the commander who achieves it. It consists of striking the enemy when, where, or in a manner for which he is unprepared.

—Field Service Regulations, Operations, United States Army.

THE ONLY AMERICAN soldier on the 38th parallel on Sunday morning, 25 June 1950, awoke at daylight to the sound of cannon. Captain Joseph R. Darrigo, Assistant Adviser to the 12th Regiment, 1st ROK Division, had quarters in a house just northeast of Kaesong. Half awake, he lay in bed, listening; it had been raining, and the sound he heard could have been thunder. Then he heard the whine of shell fragments through the air and the slap of small-arms fire against the house.

Captain Darrigo came awake. He found his trousers, and with his shoes in one hand and his uniform shirt in the other, he rushed from his bedroom. He ran into his frightened Korean houseboy on the stairs.

Darrigo's jeep was parked just outside the house, and the two of them made a dash for it. Outside they saw no one, but the sound of firing was continuous, reverberating from the bare hillsides and amplified by the low clouds. Darrigo started up the jeep and spurted southward toward Kaesong.

Arriving at the traffic circle in the center of the city, he stopped and looked around. He saw the railroad station, less than half a mile away, and noticed that a dozen railway cars had just pulled into it. As he watched, what seemed a full regiment of men in mustard-colored brown uniforms began leaping from the train.

Darrigo knew that the rail line, which had been torn up across the demarcation zone just north of Kaesong when the bamboo curtain crashed down, must have been relaid during the night by the Inmun Gun. Then they had loaded a train with troops, and while their artillery and frontal assault crashed against the thinly held position along the parallel, this train had puffed calmly into Kaesong to take the ROK's in the rear.

Men began advancing toward the traffic circle, and rifle fire slashed near Darrigo's quarter-ton. Captain Darrigo saw that there was nothing he could do in Kaesong; he could not even rejoin the 12th Regiment beyond the town. He put the jeep in gear and roared south, speeding across the Imjin River to Munsan-ni.

* * *

The assault of the North Korean People's Army—the NKPA, in United States Army terminology—while completely coordinated did not fall everywhere at once. Rather, it came in a series of blows, beginning at exactly 0400 in the west and continuing eastward for more than an hour.

Since the South had been heavily infiltrated with line crossers and Communist agents, the NKPA without exception knew the location of every South Korean defense unit, and sent superior forces against it. And almost without exception, the assault took the ROK units by complete surprise.

Many officers, most American advisers, and a large number of enlisted men were absent on pass to Seoul or other towns. And while the ROK's had deployed four divisions along the border, only one of the three regiments of each division was actually occupying its preplanned defensive position. The remaining regiments generally were in reserve areas from ten to forty miles south of the parallel.

The armored fist of the NKPA, then, struck not only against an utterly surprised ROK army, but a ROK army not deployed for battle. This factor, even more than lack of equipment or status of training, was to be decisive.

At approximately 0600, KMAG HQ in Seoul received a radio message from the advisers of the ROK 17th Regiment on the Ongjin Peninsula west of Seoul. They reported: "Regiment under heavy attack, about to be overrun." They requested instructions. No orders had been issued to KMAG to cover the situation developing on Sunday morning. Were the American officers to fight alongside the ROK's, or merely to continue their advisory duties, or to withdraw, since this was a war of Korean against Korean?

Ambassador Muccio's feeling was that KMAG should stand aside, following the precedent set earlier in China's civil war. Two volunteer aviators from KMAG HQ flew the five Americans on the Ongjin Peninsula back to Seoul in light L-5 liaison planes.

The Ongjin Peninsula west of Seoul had been considered defensible, but within hours the remnants of Colonel Paik In Yup's 17th Regiment were evacuated by LST's to Inch'on.

Farther east, the assault that had awakened Captain Darrigo rolled up the defenses north of Kaesong. Only two companies of the ROK 12th Regiment were able to flee south across the Imjin River; the others were killed or captured. The remaining regiments of the ROK 1st Division, the 13th and 11th, were at Korangp'o-ri, fifteen miles east of Kaesong, and in reserve just north of Seoul. They were commanded by Colonel Paik Sun Yup, a very young but able officer.

At the time Captain Darrigo was watching the NKPA detrain in Kaesong, Colonel Paik and several of his staff were in Seoul, beating on the door of the

KMAG compound where Darrigo's boss, Lieutenant Colonel Lloyd Rockwell, was sleeping. As soon as they had got Rockwell awake, the Koreans told him of the NKPA assault. Colonel Paik then got in touch with his 11th Regiment by phone and ordered it to move north to Munsan-ni, south of the Imjin River, and to take up already prepared defensive positions alongside its sister regiment at Korangp'o-ri.

In earlier discussions, both Rockwell and Paik had agreed that the 1st Division could hold against an attack from the north only on the south side of the Imjin. Now they and the staff proceeded immediately up to that river and ordered the bridges blown. But the NKPA was so close upon the rear of the retreating 12th Regiment that the order could not be executed.

The 11th and 13th regiments, by midmorning, were heavily engaged with the NKPA 1st Division and the 105th Armored Brigade. Korean soldiers were as brave as any, but they soon found they had no weapons to halt the Russian-built T-34 tanks. The 2.36-inch rocket launchers furnished them by the U.S. Army could not be counted on to penetrate the Russian armor, and they were very weak in artillery. But the 1st Division held at Korangp'o-ri.

ROK soldiers, seeing all else fail, seized packets of high explosive and threw themselves under tank treads, trying to disable the steel monsters. Others ran at the advancing tanks with satchel charges, or charges fixed to long poles. Still others leaped upon tank decks, and desperately attempted to pry open the turret hatches with iron bars and hooks, so that they might drop hand grenades inside. In open terrain, and against tanks deployed in number, such tactics were suicide. A tank or two slued aside or blew up, but the ROK soldiers died.

They died chopped down by the tank machine guns, or shot by the supporting NKPA infantry. They died shrieking under the tank treads. When almost a hundred had been killed in this manner, the desire to fight tanks barehanded began to leave the survivors.

Still the 1st Division held its ground. It was still holding, desperately, when disaster to the east forced it to withdraw.

* * *

The main attack of the NKPA burst down the Ch'orwon Valley toward the Uijongbu Corridor, the main gateway from the north to Seoul. On the left the 4th Division, NKPA, attacked southward along the Yonch'on-Tongduch'on-ni road into Uijongbu; on the right the 3rd Division moved along the P'och'on-Kumwha road. In front of each division roared and clanked a regiment of forty tanks.

A single ROK division, the 7th, with its 1st Regiment scattered along the parallel, its 9th Regiment at P'och'on, and its 3rd Regiment at Tongduch'on-ni, took the full force of the assault.

At 0830 a staff officer of the 7th Division radioed the ROK Minister of Defense in Seoul: "We are under general attack and heavy artillery fire near the parallel. The enemy has already seized his initial objectives. We require immediate reinforcements. Our reserve is engaged."

There were no reinforcements available, and there was no way to stop the onrushing tanks—no rivers, no ridges to bar the way. Fighting, the 7th Division fell back toward Uijongbu. By evening of 25 June, worried civilians there could hear the sound of guns, coming closer.

If Uijongbu fell, Seoul was defenseless.

Farther east, south of Hwach'on and the great Hwach'on Reservoir, near which NKPA II Corps had its headquarters, lay the ancient and lovely town of Ch'unch'on, atop whose Peacock Mountain was the most famous shrine in Korea, a building with bright-lacquered pillars and dull red roof tiles, which the South Koreans had turned into a library. Against Ch'unch'on II Corps threw its 2nd Division, without tank support.

The 2nd Division was to take Ch'unch'on no later than Sunday afternoon, while II Corps' 7th Division, which had tanks, was to attack toward Hongch'on, which lay southeast of the Shrine City.

The attack of the 7th Division south from Inje was immediately successful. What happened at Ch'unch'on, however, is significant.

The ROK 6th Division's 7th Regiment stood in dug-in concrete pillboxes and bunkers on the high, pine-covered ridges north of Ch'unch'on. The positions on Sunday morning were fully manned by grousing ROK soldiers; Colonel Kim Chong O, the division commander, had permitted no weekend passes. The American adviser, Lieutenant Colonel McPhail, was at Wonju with Division HQ. The 6th Division artillery was well trained.

The attack of the NKPA stalled in the mountains north of Ch'unch'on. Well-placed artillery fire shattered the NKPA 6th Regiment. There was no panic, no confusion among the defenders, who had been ready.

At midmorning, Colonel McPhail rushed up from Wonju to be on hand during the battle, and by late afternoon the reserve regiment of the 6th Division entered the town. Despite desperate attacks and bitter fighting, the NKPA 2nd Division could not force its way into Ch'unch'on.

With the fall of dark, there was annoyance in the Operations Post of II Corps at Hwach'on. Senior Colonel Lee was ordered to divert the 7th Division from its push toward Hongch'on and bring it back to join in the drive on Ch'unch'on. The 2nd Division, in only one day's fighting, had been badly mauled. It had suffered almost 40 percent casualties.

Fighting unsurprised, fully manned, and against troops without armor, the ROK Army was more than holding its own. For three days the ROK 6th Division would hold Ch'unch'on, retreating only when disaster to its east and west made its strongly held positions untenable.

* * *

Far across the peninsula, on the other side of the rugged and almost impassable Taebaek Range, the ROK 8th Division, which was stationed in coastal cities along the Sea of Japan, had been fighting Communist guerrillas. Several of its battalions were detached for service in the mountains on Sunday, 25 June; the others were stretched out from the parallel down to Samch'ok.

At first light on Sunday morning Korean staff officers burst in on Major George Kessler, adviser of the 10th Regiment. They told him, "We are under heavy attack across the parallel!"

Before any moves could be made, reports by telephone said that enemy soldiers were landing on the coast both north and south of Samch'ok. Whatever might be happening along the parallel, this last was serious. Kessler jumped into his jeep, and with the commanding officer of 10th Regiment, drove east to the sea north of Samch'ok.

Kessler stopped the jeep on a high hill overlooking the sea. Offshore, he and the regimental C.O. saw a vast flotilla of sampans and junks. Below them, on the beach, they saw a battalion-sized group of Inmun Gun coming ashore and spreading out. Kessler backed around and got out of there.

Driving south of Samch'ok, they saw approximately the same scene. ROK gunfire opened up and sank two boats offshore, but at least a thousand armed men came ashore. These men, mostly guerrilla cadres, did not engage the ROK forces, but slipped into the Taebaek Mountains and linked up with the guerrilla forces already fighting there.

And north, along the parallel, the NKPA 5th Division, supported by the 766th Independent Unit, crashed against the spread-out ROK 8th, driving it southward down the coast. The division commander informed the ROK chief of staff before withdrawing, in good order. No matter what happened, the campaign would not be won or lost in the remote east.

By midmorning on Sunday, General Chae Byong Duk and his principal advisers knew that the assault in progress was no rice raid.

In ROK Headquarters at Seoul there was confusion, but as yet no panic among the rank and file. After all, plans had been laid for just such an eventuality as this attack of the Inmun Gun.

In Seoul the officers knew that the key to the capital lay in the Uijongbu Corridor; any serious threat against Seoul must come that way, and if the enemy should get past Uijongbu, there was no feature, manmade or natural, that could hinder him short of the Han, on Seoul's south side. Obviously, and according to well-thought-out plan, the major ROK effort would be made in the Uijongbu Corridor, where now General Yu Hai Hyung's 7th Division was falling back under heavy pressure.

General Chae Byong Duk, Chief of Staff, began nervously to issue orders. All reserves of the ROK Army were to move north toward Seoul, and through the city into the Uijongbu Corridor.

The ROK 2nd Division was at Taejon, ninety miles south. The 5th was near Kwangfu far to the southwest, and the 3rd was across the peninsula at Taegu.

The ROK 2nd was the first to receive its orders, and to move. Its lead elements, accompanied by their American advisers, departed north by rail at 1430. By nightfall on 25 June parts of the 5th were on the road, and some units of the 3rd were also in motion.

The ROK divisions were not mechanized or mobile. Most of their transport was on deadline for lack of spare parts, and they were not organized for rapid movement. But they did the best they could, beginning to move north in piecemeal fashion.

As his orders went out, "Fat" Chae grew more nervous. Accompanied by his American staff adviser, Captain Hausman, he made two trips up to the

Uijongbu area, trying to hammer out a plan of action. Chae was certain that something had to be done very quickly, or it would be too late.

In that surmise he was correct—but what he would do was wrong. It would lose the war.

* * *

In Seoul there was no more talk of rain and rice. As word of the Communist attack spread, the people rose in a spasm of patriotic fury. There was relief in their fervor, too—all Koreans had considered the division of their country unbearable; from cranky old Syngman Rhee in the government palace to the landless peasant in the south ran strong agreement on that issue.

Now the puppet state to the north had attacked, and it would soon be over. North Korea would be overrun by the victorious troops of the Taehan Minkuk. It would be united again. The people, fed on statements by their government and the broadcasts of the Voice of America, believed implicitly in their army. They believed implicitly in the mountains of military aid the Americans had promised, and in final victory.

At 0900 Kimpo Airport reported that it was under air attack, and at mid-morning Russian-built YAK fighters screamed over Seoul's main avenue, strafing—but no one understood the significance of this. The only people in Seoul who were shaken by the appearance of the enemy aircraft were some members of the American colony—who knew the true status of the ROK forces where equipment was concerned.

By midday, ROK Army units were streaming north through Seoul. They came through in long columns of trucks, rail cars, jeeps, bicycles—and oxcarts. To the people of Seoul the oxcarts did not seem odd. Nor did they seem to notice that their army had no combat vehicles, such as tanks.

The soldiers sang as they poured through Seoul, and vast crowds of civilians gathered at every street corner, cheering them. From Taihan Mun to the solid stone of the railway station, Seoul went wild with emotion.

Peasants in traditional white, elderly *yangban* graybearded in black hats, and neat businessmen in Western suits screamed their encouragement. The sight of the khaki-clad ROK troops moving north suddenly united all the segments of Seoul in one vast frenzy.

Manzai! Victory! *Manzai!* Unification! *Manzai! Manzai!*

All day Sunday, the khaki columns rode, pedaled, or limped by, moving north.

But among the American colony of Seoul, which had its women and children far from home, men were growing nervous. A fish merchant named John Caldwell, who had once been attached to the embassy staff, called a high embassy official, asking for news, just after the YAK fighters had been reported over Seoul.

The embassy man was very angry. He said: "John, this thing is serious. They strafed an American plane at Kimpo. That's destruction of American property!"

At four o'clock on Sunday afternoon Ambassador John J. Muccio went on the air over the embassy radio station, WVTP, to reassure the American colony. He stated that there was no reason for anyone to be afraid and that the ROK army had already contained the Communist offensive. There was to be no evacuation.

But KMAG officers, who were getting frantic reports by telephone from the length of the 38th parallel, were hardly so sanguine. They began to argue with the ambassador, who was still in command. At least the women and children should be flown out, many of them said.

All afternoon and far into the night, an argument raged. Ambassador Muccio cannot be blamed for his attitude. A diplomat, he was suddenly in command during a military disaster, with no instructions from home, no clear-cut policy, no idea of the course the United States should follow. Muccio felt he must continue to show confidence, and at the same time he sincerely believed the United States would not become involved, at least not directly.

At midnight, Muccio suddenly yielded to the pleading for evacuation. But he would not listen to a plan for removal of the American civilians by air; Communist planes were in the air, and if one of them should shoot down a plane loaded with refugees it would become an international incident.

There was a small Norwegian ship at Inch'on, and all 682 women and children would have to sail for Japan aboard this. The Norwegian ship carried a full load of fertilizer, and it had accommodations for only twelve passengers.

On this point Ambassador Muccio, a tall, dark, bespectacled man, given to wearing bow ties, was adamant. Generally, too, he was set against any evacuation, since he felt that even if the Inmun Gun should by some miracle capture Seoul, the Americans there would be granted diplomatic immunity by the Communists. The British, who had recognized Red China, also planned to keep their diplomatic staff in Seoul.

The British, some of whom would not live to see England again, also did not fully understand the nature of the Communist foe.

Radio Station WVTP ordered all dependent American women and children to assemble at certain designated locations to be picked up by embassy busses for the trip to Inch'on. From there the tiny freighter *Reinholt* would take them to Kokura, Japan.

Three days later, when the *Reinholt* docked, fifty of its passengers had to be removed to hospitals by stretcher. Exposure, lack of food, crowding, and the horrible odor of commercial fertilizer had prostrated the majority. But at that the women and children were lucky.

* * *

On late Sunday, with the sound of the guns coming ominously closer to the vital center of Uijongbu, General Chae held a hurried conference with his major subordinate commanders. Chae had formed his plan of battle.

Yu Jai Hyung's 7th Division, which was holding both approaches to Uijongbu, was to swing to the west, onto the Tongduch'on-ni road, up which it would attack at dawn.

The arriving 2nd Division, under Brigadier General Lee Hyung Koon, would take over the entire P'och'on sector, and attack up the right-hand road in a coordinated effort with that of 7th Division.

Counterattacked, the advancing Inmun Gun would be halted short of Uijongbu, and, with luck, destroyed.

Brigadier General Yu accepted his orders, and began to move his units westward at midnight.

Lee Hyung Koon did not buy the plan at all. He explained that his division was still on the road and that only his Division HQ and two infantry battalions had closed in on Uijongbu. He said he could not possibly deploy the entire division north of Uijongbu by morning—it would not even have arrived.

Chae told him, "You will attack with whatever troops you have available."

"But I shall have to attack piecemeal, throwing in small units one at a time. And my men cannot march all night and fight at dawn. We must defer the counterattack until all my division, or at least most of it, is in position!"

Chae said, "No. You are overruled. The attack will proceed as I have planned."

Lee looked at Captain Hausman, the American KMAG officer. Hausman agreed with Lee, and said so. Lee's 2nd Division would be in no position to make a major effort; in fact, such a commitment risked its destruction.

But Hausman had no command here. He was an adviser lent by a friendly government, and at the moment even his status was not clear. Even had he been a major general, he could not overrule, and would not have felt justified in an attempt to overrule, the ROK chief of staff.

Chae, his huge bulk sweating, would listen to no more argument. Furious, General Lee departed for his command post at Uijongbu.

The hours of remaining darkness passed swiftly. General Yu, with his weary, half-demoralized troops strung out along the Tongduch'on-ni road after many of them had made a night march, gave orders for a counterattack to be launched at daylight, and when the orders had gone out, paced up and down inside his CP, watching the intermittent flashes of gunfire to the north. At dawn, he would see to it that his 7th Division attacked.

But on his right flank, at Uijongbu, General Lee Hyung Koon, surrounded by his Division HQ, with two tired battalions dozing along the road, did nothing.

He had made up his mind, and he had no intention of doing anything.

5

Disaster

Do something, even if it's wrong. . . .
—Unofficial doctrine of the United States Army Infantry School.

ECAUSE OF THE International Date Line, there is a day's difference in
time between Korea and the United States; it was still Saturday, 24
June, in Washington when word of the North Korean attack arrived.

Early Sunday morning, Korea time, both the military attaché and Ambassador Muccio had cabled the Assistant Chief of Staff for Intelligence and the State Department, respectively. Muccio said, in part:

"It would appear from the nature of the attack and the manner in which it was launched that it constitutes an all-out offensive against the Republic of Korea."

Meanwhile, newsmen from the various wire services sent their own messages from Seoul.

The word, from varying sources, first reached Washington at about eight Saturday night; Muccio's cable came in at nine-thirty. On Saturday night in Washington, particularly in summer, things were slow. It was not until the next day, Sunday morning, that even a good panic could get organized.

At nearly the same time, members of the United Nations Commission that was still in Korea reported to U.N. Headquarters in New York. Secretary General Trygve Lie was at his Long Island estate; receiving the news by telephone, the rotund Norwegian blurted, "This is war against the United Nations!"

Lie, furious, called an emergency meeting of the Security Council to convene at 2:00 P.M. Sunday.

Official Washington, meanwhile, had been taken completely by surprise. As General Lyman Lemnitzer reported to an angry Secretary of Defense a few days later, while United States Intelligence knew that North Korea had had the capability to attack the South, similar capabilities had existed all along the Soviet periphery, and not one intelligence agency had singled out Korea as an imminent danger point.

When the Soviet pressure had relaxed in Europe in 1949, with the ending of the Berlin blockade and the formation of the North Atlantic Treaty Organization, Washington had tended to relax also. Owing to American commitments and atomic superiority, no war seemed imminent in Europe—and Asian policy had not been completely firmed.

The shift of Soviet strategy away from Europe, which after all remained the major prize, to the periphery of Asia had not been understood in the West. And the West tended to think only in terms of an all-out Soviet attack, of which there was no evidence. Almost no one had considered the possibility of limited military operations, for which the Western powers were completely unprepared.

Now, on 25 June and later, Washington could never be sure that Korea was not merely a smokescreen, to divert American attention and troops while an assault against Europe was being prepared. For this reason, even after it had committed itself to the defense of Korea, the United States Government was reluctant to throw any major portion of its strength into the peninsula.

Only gradually did American planners realize that the Soviets might attempt to achieve their ends by bits and pieces rather than in the traditional American way, with one fell swoop. Soviet strategy, like Soviet thinking, has always been devious where American has been direct.

On Sunday, 25 June, the government was stunned by the Communist action. In the climate of opinion prevailing in Washington, such an overt military operation was unthinkable.

The surprise pointed up a continuing of American Intelligence. The various intelligence agencies poured a vast amount of information into Washington; they knew the numbers of divisions, guns, tanks, and naval craft of potential enemies. But this intelligence could not be evaluated because Washington had not even one pipeline into official circles of enemy capitals; they could not even estimate what the potential aggressor was thinking or might do.

This was no change from the past. In December 1941, American Intelligence knew that strong carrier task forces of the Imperial Japanese Navy had left port. But not understanding official Japanese thinking, the fact had meant nothing to Washington.

The situation in 1950 was no change from the past, and there would be little change in the future.

Now, Sunday morning 25 June, there were observers in Washington who recalled a similar shock on another Sunday eight and one half years before.

President Truman was in Independence for the weekend. He immediately prepared to fly back to the capital and called a conference of high Defense and State officials at Blair House that evening.

But the shock in Washington was more of anger and annoyance than of alarm. No one yet could know the real extent of the military disaster that had already overtaken the Taehan Minkuk.

As the shock wave set off by the overt Communist aggression against the Republic of Korea reverberated through the West, Seoul began its second day of war, and by now the city was relatively calm.

Confidently, their initial hysteria drained away, Seoul's million and a half inhabitants waited for word of their army's victories in the North. Troops still streamed through Seoul toward Uijongbu and other points north, and soothing statements came over the national radio.

The day passed quietly; then in the afternoon of 26 June, Seoul broadcast the news that the 7th Division had counterattacked north of Uijongbu.

Fifteen hundred enemy soldiers had been killed, fifty-eight tanks destroyed, and a mountain of other matériel had been captured. Listening, the people shouted with enthusiasm.

But as evening fell, an ominous tide of frightened, fleeing refugees began to pour into the suburbs from the north, and, by listening closely, men could hear the distant mutter of cannon on the wind. The sound seemed to be coming closer.

* * *

On the morning of 26 June both the 3rd and 4th Divisions of the Inmun Gun were poised above Uijongbu, spearheaded by powerful armored elements. After pausing briefly for reorganization during the night, both divisions attacked on a converging axis toward the Uijongbu Corridor, the 3rd along the P'och'on road, and the 4th down the road from Tongduch'on-ni.

Immediately the 4th Division ran into trouble. The ROK 7th Division struck them with a violent counterattack, and during the morning a bitter fight developed in the west. Genera Yu Jai Hyung's division was not making anything like the progress the Seoul radio later claimed, but it was at least containing the attack.

But to the east, on the 7th's right flank along the P'och'on road, American advisers entering Brigadier General Lee Hyung Koon's 2nd Division command post found the general sitting among his staff officers. He had placed his two infantry battalions along the road approximately two miles north of Uijongbu, told them to dig in, and now Lee Hyung Koon did nothing.

Believing an attack by his feeble battalions futile, he never ordered it. And at 0800, his men saw the NKPA columns advancing south on the road. They opened fire with artillery and mortars.

A column of forty tanks led the NKPA attack, and when the artillery first crashed among them, the tanks halted momentarily. Then, spotting the ROK infantry along the road, the tanks clanked forward, firing.

The light fieldpieces of the ROK's scored some direct hits, but even these could not halt the thickly armored T-34's. The tanks rumbled through the ROK lines and crashed into Uijongbu.

Behind them, bayonets fixed, charged the North Korean infantry. As the tanks overran their positions, the soldiers of the ROK 2nd Division began to leave their holes. Within minutes, the survivors had melted into the encircling hills.

Brigadier Genera Lee and his staff fled south.

Fighting stubbornly along the Tongduch'on-ni road, Yu Jai Hyung heard that the enemy was in Uijongbu. Flanked, about to be cut off, Yu ordered his attack broken off. Raggedly, the 7th Division fell back south of Uijongbu.

The 2nd Division had virtually disappeared; it was fighting now with disorganized small units. And during the unexpected retreat, 7th Division also began to come apart. Only the best trained and best led troops can execute an orderly withdrawal under heavy pressure. Outnumbered, outgunned and with no way to counteract the freezing terror—which the Germans call panzer fever—caused by the unstoppable Russian tanks, the 7th took frightful losses.

The NKPA 3rd and 4th divisions joined in Uijongbu, and again the tanks of the 105th Armored Brigade rolled south.

But now, as darkness fell on 26 June, there no longer remained any effective ROK force above Seoul that could affect the situation.

General Lee had disobeyed orders—but the complete shattering of his forces, even in defensive positions, revealed that even had he obeyed Chae and attacked, he would have failed. The ROK plan of maneuver had been hasty, ill advised, and impossible. A competent, adequately trained basic rifleman could be made in eleven months. Competent, well-schooled commanders and staffs could not.

There was nothing wrong with either the stamina or courage of the ROK soldier. Too many thousands of them died above Seoul proving otherwise.

On Sunday, 25 June, Colonel Wright, KMAG Chief of Staff and senior officer of that group now that Brigadier General Lynn Roberts had left, was in Japan. On Saturday night his wife had sailed from Yokohama for home, and Colonel Wright expected to follow her in a matter of days. But as he attended church services on Sunday morning, a messenger sought him out, bent over and whispered, "Colonel, you'd better get back to Korea right away!"

Wright left church and telephoned Seoul. What Seoul told him caused him to hop a plane, and he flew into Kimpo Airport just before dawn on Monday 26 June.

Before leaving Japan he set in motion a plan to evacuate American dependents from Korea. American ships were diverted to Korea, and Air Force cover was ordered for such ships. Planes were to screen the Norwegian fertilizer ship *Reinholt* as it left Inch'on early on Monday morning.

Now, in Seoul, Wright conferred with his boss, Ambassador Muccio, and they agreed to evacuate all of KMAG, too, with the exception of thirty-three officers Wright wanted to keep in ROK Army HQ. The word was passed, and KMAG officers began to leave the front. Most of them were flown to Japan from Suwon Airfield early the next morning.

All during the 26th of June, KMAG HQ in Seoul was getting confused but accurate reports from its officers in the field. The reports were not good.

And during the hours of darkness on 26 June, the Government of the Taehan Minkuk was getting accurate reports, too, despite what the people were told. And the Government of the Taehan Minkuk began to grow increasingly nervous. During the night it planned to move from Seoul to Taejon, ninety miles to the south. The members of the National Assembly engaged in acrid and shouting debate in the early morning; the National Assembly voted to remain in Seoul no matter what the ministers did.

Just after midnight on the morning of the 27th, Ambassador Muccio received orders from the Department of State to leave Seoul. He planned to take his staff south of the Han to Suwon, while Colonel Wright and his selected KMAG officers crossed to Sihung-ni, a town some five miles south of Yongdungp'o, to which ROK Army HQ had already gone, without notifying the Americans.

Now the American evacuation, which had been held in abeyance for two days, began in a sort of panic. Ambassador Muccio and his staff went to Suwon at 0900 Tuesday, 27 June. Under American fighter cover from Japan, the civilian and KMAG staff began to fly from Suwon Airfield. Behind them, the American evacuation of Seoul was both hasty and chaotic, and in some respects, tragic.

The fifteen hundred vehicles belonging to Americans, both government and private, were abandoned; no effort was made to turn them over to the ROK Army, which desperately needed them. More than twenty thousand gallons of gasoline were abandoned in the embassy motor pool. A tremendous amount of food, valued at $100,000, and the entire July quota of liquor—$40,000 worth, tax free—were left for the Inmun Gun.

But these losses, aid to the enemy aside, were replaceable. The ghastly mistake made during the early hours of 27 June was that the personnel records of more than five thousand Korean employees of the embassy were left in their files. While the confidential records of the American Mission were burned, no one thought of the dossiers of its loyal Korean workers—or more likely, no one on the embassy staff really understood the nature of the Communist foe they faced.

These files would fall into the hands of the Inmun Gun, and none of the employees who remained at their homes in Seoul would survive the Communist occupation.

But the 2,202 American citizens were evacuated from Korea, without loss of life.

Colonel Wright, as Chief of KMAG, drove to Sihung-ni to hunt up General Chae and the ROK Army HQ, who had taken off from Seoul without informing him.

On the way, Wright received a radio message from General MacArthur in Tokyo. MacArthur stated that the Joint Chiefs of Staff had directed him to take command of all United States military personnel in Korea, including KMAG. He was sending an advance command and liaison group—called ADCOM—into Korea at once. KMAG was home again.

Arriving at Sihung-ni, Wright received a fresh message from MacArthur: "Personal MacArthur to Wright: Repair to your former locations. Momentous decisions are in the offing. Be of good cheer."

Colonel Wright had no idea what was up, but at least he recognized MacArthur's hand in the message. With both messages as authority, he began arguing with General Chae to return the ROK HQ to Seoul. It was not an easy task, but by evening of the 27th the HQ had returned to the capital.

But inside Seoul itself panic was erupting. The people had not been told of the failure of the counterattack at Uijongbu, but civilian refugees and wounded soldiers were streaming down into the city, and slowly a feeling of panic spread. North Korean planes flew over the city, dropping surrender leaflets. Fear grew. Then Marshal Choe Yong Gun, field commander of the Inmun Gun, beamed a broadcast into Seoul: "Surrender!"

By nightfall 27 June the city was in turmoil, and thousands of civilians began to flee southward over the Han bridges.

The military authorities in Seoul had devised a roadblock and demolition plan that was supposed to blow all bridges north of Seoul, and, on order, destroy the great modern spans leading south across the Han. But by dark on 27 June the civilian terror had spread to the soldiers, too. Men falling back from the north told of the terrible tanks that could not be stopped. It must be recalled that Korean soldiers had not even been told much about tanks, let alone given them, and the tanks assumed the proportions of invincible monsters as the tales spread. And the ROK Army had not even one antitank mine.

The roadblocks were not defended; the bridges to the north were not blown. Thousands of defeated ROK troops began to pour into Seoul, and as they did so, the rearguard detachments left to delay the enemy melted away.

And now a new menace appeared. Thousands upon thousands of Communists and Communist sympathizers had infiltrated Seoul during the years, and as the Inmun Gun approached, these men came out into the open. Suddenly no one could be trusted; even on the ROK Army Staff men began to shout "Communist!" and "Traitor!" at each other.

By midnight the ROK Army Staff was close to a state of funk.

The leading units of the Inmun Gun had already entered Seoul at 1930, but desperate fire from the defenders forced them back temporarily. At 2300 a single T-34 and a platoon of soldiers reached the gardens of the Chang-Duk Palace in the north of the city. Somehow, amazingly, the Seoul Police Department was able to destroy the tank and disperse the accompanying infantrymen.

On the ground, the situation in Seoul was far from hopeless. There were thousands of heavily armed ROK troops within the walls, and the city itself was an immense obstacle. Fighting street by street, using delaying tactics, the ROK's Army could delay the Inmun Gun for days, while more of their reserves moved north.

The bulk of the ROK Army was still north of the Han River.

But the ROK Army was at this moment almost devoid of leadership.

At approximately midnight, an American lieutenant colonel named Scott was on the G-3 (Operations) desk at ROK Army HQ. The phones were beginning to report breakthroughs all along the northern edge of the city. As the reports came in, Scott saw ROK officers of the G-3 Section start to take down and fold their maps.

Going to General Chae Byong Duk, Chief of Staff, Scott asked "Have you ordered this headquarters to leave?"

"No," Chae said.

At about this time, Colonel Wright issued orders that most of his principal KMAG officers try to get a little sleep. The majority of KMAG, including Colonel Wright, had been on their feet since Sunday morning, and were nearing exhaustion. The KMAG quarters were a little distance from ROK HQ, connected by phone.

Colonel Wright, and his Chief of Staff, Lieutenant Colonel Greenwood, turned in. Almost immediately Colonel Greenwood's phone rang. It was Major Sedberry, G-3 Adviser to the ROK Army, who now had the desk over at ROK HQ.

"My God, Colonel, the ROK's are going to blow the Han bridges," Sedberry said. "I'm trying to get the Deputy Chief of Staff, General Kim, to hold off until all the troops and supplies in Seoul can be removed to the south side—"

The KMAG officers on duty in ROK HQ now tried to reach Colonel Wright, but the officer who took his calls refused to disturb his chief. The solicitude was understandable, but it would almost cause Wright to lose his life.

There had been a firm agreement between KMAG and General Chae that the Han bridges south of Seoul would not be blown until enemy tanks reached ROK HQ itself. But when Colonel Greenwood rushed to ROK HQ, he could not find Chae.

There were three ROK divisions still holding Seoul, with all their arms and military transport. It did not appear that the enemy could reach the center of the city before noon the following day, and there was plenty of time to blow the bridges later.

But Chae Byong Duk was gone—he had been hustled out of the HQ, apparently against his will, and put on a southbound truck. General Kim Paik Il was now in charge.

Kim Paik Il told Greenwood that the Korean Vice-Minister of Defense had ordered that the bridges be blown at 0130 and that he had no authority to countermand the order.

A few minutes later General Lee Hyung Koon, commander of the 2nd Division, which had now finally arrived in Seoul, entered the HQ and was told that the bridges were to be blown. Lee rushed to Kim and began to plead with him.

"At least let me evacuate my troops, with their equipment, to the south side of the river! This order does not make sense!"

Shaken by Lee's arguments, Kim at last turned to the ROK Army G-3, Major General Chang Chang Kuk.

"Drive to the river and tell the chief engineer to stop the demolitions!"

As soon as he had ordered this, Kim directed the HQ to pack up and depart.

The KMAG officers were still not able to reach Colonel Wright.

General Chang, who well understood the situation, ran outside and started his jeep. He headed for the great highway bridge, but by now the streets were so clogged with refugees and frightened civilians, men, women, children, and animals, that he could make no progress. Cursing and blowing his horn, he pushed his way through. He had to reach a police telephone box on the north end of the bridge, which was the only point from which the ROK engineers on the south side could be contacted.

At 0214 he had arrived at a point only 150 yards from the northern end of the highway bridge. The highway and the bridge itself were jammed with masses of vehicles and pedestrians—fleeing refugees, army trucks, soldiers, and civilians filling all eight lanes of the road and the three lanes of the bridge. Chang could see that there were many thousands of civilians and soldiers actually crossing the bridge itself. Sweating, he angrily bulled the jeep foot by foot across the stream of traffic.

He knew he had very little time.

Two of Wright's KMAG officers, Colonel Hazlett and Captain Hausman, had been sent south at midnight to Suwon, there to establish communications with Tokyo. They had just jeeped across the highway bridge when Hausman looked at his watch: 0215.

At that moment the bridge blew. A sheet of orange fire burst across the dark night, and the ground shook. With an ear-shattering roar, two long spans on the south side of the river dropped into the swirling dark water.

No one will ever know how many soldiers and civilians died in the explosion or were hurled screaming into the Han to drown. The best estimates indicate the number was near one thousand.

There had been no warning of any kind to the traffic thronging the bridge. Later, the ROK chief of engineers would be tried by court-martial and summarily shot for his part in the demolitions. But no one in the Rhee Government ever brought up the matter of the Vice-Minister of Defense, who had given the order that ensured the destruction of the ROK Army.

Trapped by the premature blowing of the Han bridges, 44,000 men of the divisions north of the river would die or disappear. Their vital artillery and equipment would be lost with them.

A few got out. Brigadier Yu Jai Hyung, whose 7th Division had charged the buzzsaw, reached the south side of the river with 1,200 men and four machine guns. Colonel Paik, whose 1st Division soldiers had fought tanks with iron bars, brought 5,000 men across the Han near Kimpo, but had to leave his artillery behind.

At Ch'unch'on to the east, the gallant 6th Division heard the news, and prepared to abandon its pillboxes and bunkers north of Peacock Mountain. At Samch'ok, on the Sea of Japan, the 8th began its own retreat. These two divisions were the only ones of the ROK Army still intact, and they were isolated.

General Lee got out, and lived to explain to Colonel Wright why he had not obeyed Fat Chae's orders. But the majority of the Korean officers died with their men.

On the 28th of June, only a rabble held the south shores of the Han. The ROK Army Command could account for only 22,000 men of the 98,000 its rolls had carried out on the 25th.

The Army of the Taehan Minkuk, which had been called "the best damn army outside the United States," had not merely been defeated.

It had been destroyed.

6

The U.N. Cloak

We see, therefore, that war is not merely a political act, but a real political instrument, a continuation of political intercourse, a carrying out of the same by other means. . . .
—From the German of Karl von Clausewitz, ON WAR.

A T THE UNITED NATIONS, Secretary-General Tryve Lie had already established a tradition that was to last and that perhaps would eventually allow the world body to survive. As the first man to hold the office of Secretary-General, the Norwegian Lie considered that he was no mere lackey of the member powers, great or small, nor even an executive agent at the Council's beck and call. He considered himself an executive, much as the President of the United States is an executive, and as such, he might place questions in consideration before his legislature, composed of the Security Council and the General Assembly. Like the President, his power must stem from those legislatures' consent—but like the President, also, he could propose, direct, and ask for support.

From the moment he was informed of the Communist assault upon the Republic of Korea, Trygve Lie saw the immediate crisis and inherent danger to the future of the U.N. A body like the U.N. had been formed to keep the peace of the world—perhaps a hopelessly ambitious gesture—and each breach of peace inevitably carried it to the edge of the abyss. If the U.N. succeeded, it merely bought a little more time. But if it failed completely, then it was dead in the hearts of men, and its formal death, like that of the League of Nations, was only a matter of time.

A native of a small and powerless nation that in his lifetime had been brutally treated by a more powerful neighbor, Trygve Lie believed deeply in the purposes and necessity of the United Nations. If the U.N. proved it could not offer at least some protection to the weak, then it was useless, and would disappear.

And Lie, who as Secretary-General had helped set up the U.N. Commission on Korea, which had brought the Taehan Minkuk into vigorous life, also took the bald Communist assault as a personal affront.

50

Moving swiftly, and with the complete backing of the United States—whose own feelings were affronted—Lie convened an emergency meeting of the Security Council at 2:00 P.M. 25 June, New York time. With unprecedented swiftness—for there was only one "neutral" on the Council in 1950—that body proposed, debated, revised, and adopted a resolution on the Korean crisis.

But for all his determination and swiftness of action, only one fact allowed Lie to succeed: the Soviet Union, which with the other four great powers enjoyed the veto, was not in attendance. On 10 January 1950, the Soviet delegate had not only pulled one of the now famous Soviet walkouts but had also continued to boycott the Council meetings over the issue of seating Red China.

If Andrei Gromyko or his ilk had been in New York on Sunday afternoon, the U.N. would not have taken action on the Korean question. And the U.N. might not have enjoyed another dozen years of life.

Taking advantage of the Soviets' tactical mistake, Lie and the Western powers passed a strong resolution stating that the armed assault upon the Republic of Korea constituted a breach of the peace. The resolution called for:

1. an immediate cessation of hostilities, and

2. the authorities of North Korea to withdraw their forces back to the 38th parallel, and

3. all members to render every assistance to the United Nations in the execution of this resolution and to refrain from giving assistance to the North Korean authorities.

Voting for the resolution were Nationalist China, Cuba, Ecuador, Egypt, France, India, Norway, the United Kingdom, and the United States. At the time both Cuba and Egypt, untroubled by revolution, were in the Western bloc. Only Communist Yugoslavia, which hated Americans because they were capitalists and Russians because they were Russians abstained.

Shortly after 6:00 P.M. the resolution was released.

A few hours afterward, in Blair House across from the White House—which was undergoing repairs—President Truman met with the "guts" of his Administration, the important members of Defense and State.

Here, by 10:30 P.M. American policy in the Far East had solidified. The real, if uneulogized, foreign policy of the Truman Administration was the containment of Communism, and there was general agreement that the United States had better begin containing.

While the immediate security of the United States was not threatened, its political order in the world was. China had disappeared into the hostile camp, provoking great unease not only among Americans but also among many of the Cabinet who had not dared act, for with its loss the balance of power in Asia had shifted. Now, if Korea were lost, Japan would hang by a thread—and if Japan went, America would be back where it was after Pearl Harbor.

The interests of the United States demanded action, and now two things had occurred that would permit the Administration to act: the United Nations had taken a hand, which gave the United States an international sanction it could not have had otherwise in protecting its own interests—and the Communists had this time used overt, brutal armed force against a peaceful people, provoking immediate disapproval among the American public, among liberals, leftists, conservatives, and mugwumps alike.

Truman, who liked to say, pointing to his desk, "The buck stops here," was not a man to shirk a decision. He had acted—not intemperately or rashly, no matter how intemperate or rash he might be on other things—on the decision to drop the nuclear bomb. He had bought the Marshall Plan, and proclaimed the Truman Doctrine in Greece and Turkey. Harry Truman, however confused his ideas on domestic matters might become, never passed the buck or dropped the ball.

The Government of the United States, realizing completely the importance of halting Communist encroachment not only in Europe but everywhere in the world, resolved to assist the Republic of Korea. For whatever the truth might be, the world regarded Korea as an American protégé, and American prestige in Asia hung in the balance.

But at 10:30 P.M. on 25 June 1950, Washington time, no one knew how hard it was going to be to help the Taehan Minkuk.

* * *

By teletype, the Joint Chiefs of Staff authorized General MacArthur, Commanding General, FECOM, to send ammunition and military equipment to Korea to prevent the loss of the Seoul-Kimpo area, and to provide requisite air and naval cover to assure its arrival, to provide ships and aircraft to evacuate American civilians from the peninsula, and finally to dispatch a survey party to see the situation at firsthand and to decide what aid the Republic of Korea might require.

At the same time orders were received by the Seventh Fleet to sail from its bases in the Philippines and Okinawa to Sasebo, Japan, there to come under the operational control of Commander United States Naval Forces, Far East.

MacArthur immediately sent his radiogram to Colonel Wright, KMAG Chief, at the time on the road from Seoul to Sihung, telling him to be of "good cheer."

A few hours later three Russian-built YAK fighters, sighting American Air Force planes over Inch'on, opened fire on them. The Americans were over Korea only to provide air cover against attack on the evacuating civilians and dependents—but with the bullet holes in their wings, the American pilots declared open season. They shot down all three YAK's.

A few hours later, four more YAK's were shot out of the skies over Seoul. That day the 68th and 339th All-Weather Fighter Squadrons, and the 35th Fighter-Bomber Squadron, Fifth Air Force, flew 163 sorties from Japan. The ancient YAK fighters of the Inmun Gun proved no match for the F-80 and F-82 jets.

Americans, unknown to the public at home, were already engaged.

* * *

In Seoul, in the early hours of 28 June, even while "Momentous decisions were in the offing," Colonel William H. S. Wright, KMAG Chief of Staff, was having his difficulties.

Since 0100, when the ROK's decided to blow the Han bridges, officers on duty at ROK HQ had tried to reach him. They wanted to tell him that the ROK HQ was leaving Seoul, and wanted to know if KMAG should also leave.

But the officer taking Wright's calls determined to let the Old Man sleep, and it was not until a KMAG officer, Lieutenant Colonel Lewis Vieman, went personally to Wright's quarters and routed out Wright's houseboy that the message got through.

Once Wright was awake, Vieman briefed him on the chaotic situation at ROK Army HQ. He had just finished when the Han bridges blew. After the great flash of orange and thunderclap of sound from the south, Wright, exhausted as he was, was fully alert.

He immediately got all the American officers together, found trucks, and started them in convoy for a bridge on the east side of Seoul. They were almost there when ROK troops informed them that this bridge, too, was gone. The convoy turned back to a KMAG housing compound in the Sobingo area near the river to wait for daylight.

Parts of Seoul were aflame; firing was heard continually as the retreating ROK's battled the NKPA within the city, and the city was in confusion. In the dark, disorganized ROK soldiers were falling back to the river, firing at anything that moved.

At dawn, KMAG sent out a small recon party, which soon reported back that the ferries just east of the blown highway bridge were still in operation. This party also made contact with Lieutenant Colonel Lee Chi Yep, an officer who greatly liked Americans. This was a fortunate break, for Lee said he understood their plight and would help them to get across the river.

Along the banks of the Han this Wednesday morning, Colonel Wright and his group found complete chaos. ROK soldiers and civilians were milling about the ferry, fighting each other, shooting at the boatmen who were trying to retain possession of their craft. Colonel Lee Chi Yep ordered a ferryman to carry the KMAG party across. When the Korean refused to bring his boat alongside the milling crowd on the riverbank, Lee shot a hole in the man's shirt.

In this way, Lee got attention, and a few at a time, taking two hours, the KMAG party finally crossed the broad Han. Colonel Wright crossed last, insisting the command radio truck be ferried across with him. The radio was KMAG's only link with Japan. When Wright finally got truck and radio into a ferryboat, artillery fire was bursting along the riverside, and he could hear the sharp *whack* of tank guns close by.

On the south bank, Colonel Wright went ahead with a small advance group to Suwon. The others walked fifteen miles to Anyang-ni, where at 1500 trucks sent by Colonel Wright picked them up and brought them to Suwon.

The KMAG party had come through without the loss of a man.

* * *

At approximately 1900 hours, 27 June, MacArthur's survey party from Tokyo landed at Suwon Airfield, where it was met by Ambassador Muccio. This party consisted of thirteen officers and two enlisted men from MacArthur's GHQ, under command of Brigadier General John H. Church. After the survey party had left Japan, MacArthur received authority from the Joint Chiefs to assume command of all military personnel in Korea, and he immediately redesignated the survey party GHQ Advance Command and Liaison Group in Korea (ADCOM), giving it the added mission of assuming control of KMAG and assisting the ROK Army.

In Suwon, General Church, a slender, hatchet-faced officer in neat khakis, telephoned Colonel Wright, who was still in Seoul. Wright advised him not to try to enter Seoul that night, and ADCOM took over the Experimental Agriculture Building in Suwon to await further developments.

At 0400 the next morning, Colonel Hazlett and Captain Hausman, who had missed being blown up with the Han highway bridge by a matter of five minutes, drove their jeep into Suwon. They reported immediately to General Church.

They told him that the Seoul bridges were blown, that there were already NKPA tanks inside the city, and that the ROK Army was falling apart. They were very much afraid that the KMAG officers still in Seoul were trapped.

General Church realized he had walked into a hell of a situation, one that no one in Tokyo had understood at all. Now he ordered Hazlett to locate the ROK chief of staff, General Chae.

When Fat Chae finally came into ADCOM HQ, Church informed him that General MacArthur had taken charge of U.S. operations in Korea. He suggested that Chae move his own HQ into the same building with ADCOM. A subtle but very real change had come into American-Korean relations, for Church, listening to the complaints of KMAG officers, realized that someone had to take charge.

He strongly urged Chae to order the ROK troops still in Seoul to continue fighting, to establish straggler points south of the Han, and to put together enough troops to defend the Han Line at all costs.

Chae was able to collect about a thousand officers and eight thousand men to deploy along the river in provisional units.

Then Church, feeling as gloomy as he looked, radioed MacArthur that the United States was going to have to commit ground troops if it wanted to restore the original border of Korea. In the early evening he received a return radiogram stating that a high-ranking officer would fly into Suwon the next morning, and asking if Suwon Airfield was still operational. Church replied affirmatively.

* * *

Shortly after 0800 on 29 June, Major General Earle E. Partridge, acting commander of the Far Eastern Air Force, received a radio message from his chief, General Stratemeyer, who was already aloft in MacArthur's personal C-54, the *Bataan*.

The message said, succinctly:

"Stratemeyer to Partridge: Take out North Korean Airfields immediately. No Publicity. MacArthur approves."

The Far Eastern Air Force was the largest body of American air power outside the continental United States. Lieutenant General Stratemeyer had nine groups of combat planes, or a total of about 350 operational combat aircraft. Only four groups were initially in position to support the fighting in Korea, but immediate orders went out to the more distant units to close in on Japan.

And immediately, FEAF began to wreak havoc on the North Korean Air Force. The propeller-driven YAK's, and their pilots, were no match in the air for the American jets. And while Communist air was being shattered, FEAF flew hundreds of missions against the advancing ground troops of the NKPA.

In the first few hours they did more harm than good. Without ground-control parties, and with the situation on the ground so confused, FEAF pilots could not tell friend from foe.

Young Colonel Paik Sun Yup, trying to bring the remaining half of his 1st Division back across the Han, was struck by American air.

The U.S. planes rocketed and strafed his columns, killing or wounding dozens, sending Paik and his staff scrambling into the ditches.

When the jets, their ammunition exhausted, sighed high and away, Paik got his shaken staff together. "You see," he told them, "you did not believe the Americans would come to help us. Now you know better!"

The staff had to agree that the Americans, indeed, were in the war.

But while FEAF could quickly wipe out the small NKPA air forces, it immediately became obvious that American air power alone could not seriously affect the outcome on the ground. The NKPA took their losses and came on.

Meanwhile, an American ground force unit had already entered Korea. Designated only as Detachment X, 33 officers and men of the 507th Antiaircraft Artillery Battalion had flown into Suwon and emplaced their four M-55 machine guns about the airfield. A few minutes after the *Bataan* flew out, this unit engaged four YAK fighters, shooting down one.

MacArthur, Stratemeyer, and a party of high-ranking officers were on the way to Suwon Airfield, which was being strafed at the moment by Russian-built YAK's.

As the *Bataan* landed on the Suwon strip, a wrecked United States C-54 was flaming on the runway.

On the ground, MacArthur, wearing his gold-braided cap, a leather jacket over his khaki uniform shirt, and his long corncob in his left hand, was met by President Syngman Rhee of Korea, Ambassador Muccio, and General Church. They all entered an ancient sedan and were driven to Church's ADCOM HQ.

Church told MacArthur that by nightfall he expected to be able to account for about 25,000 ROK troops south of the Han. MacArthur insisted upon going personally up to the river to see the situation at firsthand. On the trip, he saw enough to tighten his lean face.

Thousands upon thousands of white-clad Korean refugees were fleeing south. Among them, completely disorganized, were thousands of ROK soldiers—also moving south.

MacArthur quietly told Church that in his opinion the situation called for the immediate commitment of American ground troops. He stated he would request the JCS for such action as soon as he returned to Tokyo.

At 1800 the *Bataan* was airborne for Japan.

* * *

In New York, the Security Council of the United Nations convened again on the night of 27 June. By this time it had become obvious that the U.N. resolution calling for an end to hostilities was going to be ignored by the Communist nations, and also by this time the United States had become determined to halt the aggression in Korea.

The Russian delegate was still not in attendance.

In 1950 United States influence in the U.N. was still preponderant; the NATO allies and the Latin-American nations voted consistently with the Americans, and these votes could be counted on for a majority both on the Council and in the Assembly.

Now the Security Council passed a resolution commenting on its fruitless efforts to halt the war, and ending, at American urging, as folows:

> . . . *Recommends that the members of the United Nations furnish such assistance to the Republic of Korea as may be necessary to repel the armed attack and to restore international peace and security in the area.*

Bespectacled, white-haired Warren Austin, the U.S. delegate, had in essence what he wanted. The United States, which had already decided to go to the aid of Korea, now had woven a U.N. cloak under which to carry out its national policy.

In the future, this "cloak" would become both a help and a hindrance.

The Soviet Government, receiving information of this resolution, decided its own representative had better get back to minding the store. But it was already too late for effective Russian obstruction.

In Washington, as reports on the debacle of the ROK Army filtered in, tension increased. Before noon on the 29th, Secretary of Defense Louis Johnson telephoned President Truman.

Of all the Cabinet, Johnson was probably the most shocked at the developments. Honestly believing that the United States would never again fight a ground war, Johnson had made it almost impossible for the U.S. Army to do so. But even Johnson did not fully understand the extent of American weakness to handle a situation of this kind—for in cutting the "fat" from the ground forces, Johnson had—along with public opinion generally—not only cut deeply into their strength but also into their morale and effectiveness.

He and other leaders met with the President during the afternoon, and at this time a new directive was issued to the Far East commander:

1. MacArthur was authorized to use Army service forces in Korea to maintain communications and supply services for the ROK's;

2. to employ Army combat troops to ensure the retention of an air and naval base in the Pusan-Chinhae area;

3. to use both naval and air forces against military targets in North Korea—but to stay well away from the Chinese and Russian frontiers;

4. to defend Taiwan from Chinese Communist invasion, but also to prevent any attack on the mainland by Chiang Kai-shek; and finally,

5. to send whatever supplies and munitions the ROK's might need to the Korean Government.

This directive also ended with a clear statement that there was no decision to engage in war with the Soviet Union, even if Soviet forces should intervene in Korea. Already, a firm determination to limit this engagement—if possible—had appeared in Washington.

Officials were still apprehensive of the role of the Soviet Union. No one could be sure that general war would not begin at any moment. Never before having accepted the idea of limited goals in war, Washington still found it difficult to follow Soviet reasoning. But as President Truman stated later, the United States Government saw absolutely no chance of forcing its will—as it had on Germany and Japan—upon the vast land masses of Russia and China, even by means of general war. They felt that such a war against these powers would solve nothing for the United States, and should as far as humanly possible be avoided. If the Communist powers held back from total war, the United States would follow suit.

But the Communists had made a strong move on the politico-military chessboard, and there was immediate determination that the Soviet gambit must not be allowed to proceed unchecked.

This directive had been out only hours when MacArthur's report of his personal reconnaissance to Korea hit Washington like a bomb. From the above directive it is obvious that the government felt that American troops would not become engaged on the peninsula except in the air or at sea, where the United States was well prepared to engage and where casualties could be expected to be light.

MacArthur's cable read:

"The only assurance for the holding of the present line, and the ability to regain later the lost ground, is through the introduction of U.S. ground combat forces into the Korean battle area. To continue to utilize the forces of our Air and Navy without an effective ground element cannot be decisive."

MacArthur further asked for permission to move a regimental combat team into Korea, to be built up later into a two-division force as needed.

The message was too hot for General J. Lawton Collins, Army Chief of Staff, to handle. He called the Secretary of the Army, Frank Pace, and ordered a hot teletype connection set up with Tokyo.

Over the teletype, MacArthur reiterated that the authority he already had, to put troops into the Pusan area, would not fulfill the mission. He also asked Collins to make up his mind. "Time is of the essence, and a clear-cut decision without delay is essential!"

Collins replied he would kick it upstairs, and would reply within thirty minutes. Then he got Pace on the wire and repeated the teletype conversation. As soon as Collins had hung up, Pace called Blair House.

It was 0457, on 30 June, Washington time, but Harry Truman was already up. He listened to Pace's report.

The United States, in effect, was already committed. Its air forces were shooting down North Korean planes and bombing North Korean airfields. But no one in Washington, either civilian or military, had understood the real extent of the Communist action, or the countermoves that would be required.

Already, the Korean incident was escalating into real war for the United States, step by step. But Truman still could not anticipate at this time the true measure of the difficulty the United States faced in stemming the North Korean invasion. He could only continue to anticipate that an American breakdown now, or a failure to carry through, might tip the balance of the world fatally by the loss of all Asia.

When Frank Pace had given him the substance of the MacArthur-Collins conversation, Truman without hesitation told Pace to go ahead with the regimental combat team. He would let Pace know within two hours on the matter of the two divisions.

The word flashed to MacArthur immediately.

Then, at midmorning 30 June, Truman met with important members of State and Defense. At this time, Truman agreed to two recommended moves: two Army infantry divisions should be sent into Korea from Japan, and North Korea should be blockaded by the Navy.

Now that the Communists had moved overtly and dramatically, and the U.N.—which ironically held the emotional support of the very elements who opposed containment of Communism on moral grounds—had provided a legal and moral cloak under which the U.S. might act, the tougher members of State and Defense felt that their hands were free. Many of them had long writhed under the mistaken attack of conservatives who did not understand the government's dilemma vis-à-vis its own intellectual elements and the American public. They were ready to fight.

In using whatever means necessary to stem the attack against South Korea, the government of Harry Truman unquestionably acted in the best interests of the United States and of the world.

But characteristically, that government took action in a manner that could only make later trouble. As with every major policy decision that Administration had made, it was announced to the public only after the decision was irrevocable. With the orders already speeding to Tokyo, Truman called in the balance of the Cabinet, the Vice-President, congressional leaders of both parties, and told them what he had done.

In effect, Truman had engaged the nation in war by executive action.

Some of the leaders were understandably shaken.

In the afternoon, President Truman issued a terse statement to the press, terming the Korean venture a "police action."

At about the same time, Warren Austin addressed the Security Council in New York, and told the world that the action taken by the United States in Korea was strictly in conformity with the resolutions passed on 25 and 27 June.

Something new had happened. The United States had gone to war, not under enemy attack, nor to protect the lives or property of American citizens. Nor was the action taken in crusading spirit, as in World Wars I and II, to save the world. The American people had entered a war, not by the roaring demand of Congress—which alone could constitutionally declare a state of war—or the public, but by executive action, at the urging of an American proconsul across the sea, to maintain the balance of power across the sea.

Many Americans, who had never adjusted to their country's changed position in the world, would never understand.

Harry Truman had ordered troops into action on the far frontier. This was the kind of order Disraeli might have given, sending Her Majesty's regiments against the disturbers of Her Majesty's peace. Or the emperor in Rome might have given such a command to the legions when his governor in Britain sent word the Picts were over the border.

This was the kind of war that had bleached the bones of countless legionnaires on the marches of the empire, and had dug the graves of numberless Britons, wherever the sun shone.

In 1950 there was only one power and one people in the world who could prevent chaos and a new, barbarian tyranny from sweeping the earth. The United States had become a vast world power, like it or not. And liking it or not, Americans would find that if a nation desires to remain a great and moral power there is a game it must play, and some of its people must pay the price.

Truman, sending the divisions into Korea, was trying to emulate the Roman legions and Her Majesty's regiments—for whether the American people have accepted it or not, there have always been tigers in the world, which can be contained only by force.

But Truman and the American Republic had no legions.

The President and the American people had ten Army divisions, the European Constabulary, and nine separate regimental combat teams, all of which, except the one in Europe, were at 70 percent strength. Each regiment had, instead of its normal three battalions, only two, and each artillery battalion had not its proper three firing batteries, but two.

No division had its proper wartime quota of weapons and equipment, and each had only light M-24 tanks. What equipment each division had was World War II worn, and old.

But the greatest weakness of the American Army was not in its numbers or its weapons, pitiful as they were.

The United States Army, since 1945, had, at the demand of the public, been civilianized. The men in the ranks were enlistees, but these were the new breed of American regular, who, when they took up the soldier, had not even tried to put aside the citizen.

They were normal American youth, no better, no worse than the norm, who though they wore the uniform were mentally, morally, and physically unfit for combat, for orders to go out and die.

They wore the uniform, but they were still civilians at heart.

* * *

The ancient legions, and the proud old British regiments, had been filled with taverns' scum, starvelings, and poor farm boys seeking change. They had been inducted, knocked about, ruled with a rod of iron, made into men of iron, with iron discipline. They were officered by men wholly professional, to whom dying was only a part of their way of life. To these men the service was home, and war—any war—their profession.

These legions of old, like the sword itself, were neither moral nor immoral. Morality depended upon the use to which their government put them. But when put to use, they did not question, did not fail. They marched.

In 1950 America, imperfectly understanding her position in this new world, had no legions. She had even no men in "dirty-shirt blue," such as had policed the Indian frontier. She had an army of sorts of citizens, who were as conscious of their rights and privileges as of their duties. And she had only a reserve of more citizens to fall back upon.

Citizens fly to defend the homeland, or to crusade. But a frontier cannot be held by citizens, because citizens, in a republic, have better things to do.

In 1950, as later, President Truman and his Cabinet might have sounded the clarion call, aroused the nation to frenzy, ushered in World War III. But they saw no profit in holocaust, nor was there any.

The balance of power can be maintained short of holocaust, but only if the trumpet is not sounded. The world of 1914 learned that lesson much too well.

The foreign policy of the Administration had never been that of destroying Communism, which could not be done without Armageddon, but to contain it until the natural balance of world power was restored and there was no void imperialist Communism could fill.

By attacking the Republic of Korea, the Communist world was not proclaiming jihad; it had not sounded its own trumpet of war to the death. It was probing. It was playing the game of limited war and power politics as the kings and tyrannies of old had played them.

The American Government would have preferred not to play. But the game was thrust upon them. There was no alternative to playing, other than surrender or holocaust.

The single greatest weakness of a free people is always their moral doubts. Fortunately for the world, in 1950 the men in the United States Government overcame theirs.

Harry Truman, President, ordered the legions to the frontier. He prepared to back them up with the civilian might of the nation. He sent them not to destroy the unholy, but merely to hold the line.

But Harry Truman, President, had not true legions. He had a citizen army, backed by civilians who neither understood nor approved the dangerous game. Few of them preferred surrender; but most thought of war only in terms of holocaust. They were not prepared.

Citizens, unless they hear the clarion call, or the angel's trumpet, are apt to be a rabble in arms.

PART II

Battle

7

Task Force Smith

No commander likes to commit troops piecemeal, and I'm no exception.
—Major General William Frishe Dean, CG, 24th Infantry Division.

AT A LITTLE PAST eight on the morning of 1 July 1950, Lieutenant Colonel Charles B. Smith, commanding 1st Battalion, 21st Infantry, reported to his division commander, General Dean, at Itazuke Air Base. Standing behind Brad Smith in the slanting monsoon rain were just over four hundred officers and men, the first troops designated to go into Korea by air. They stood in fatigue uniforms and steel helmets, holding rifles and a conglomeration of old and worn supporting weapons. Each man carried 120 rounds of ammunition and two days' C rations.

Most of them were not yet twenty, and hardly one in six had heard a shot fired in anger.

Major General Dean, tall and close-cropped, his face serious under his sandy short hair, shook hands with Smith.

"When you get to Pusan, head for Taejon. We want to stop the North Koreans as far from Pusan as we can. Block the main road as far north as possible. Make contact with General Church. If you can't find him, go to Taejon and beyond if you can. Sorry I can't give you more information—that's all I've got. Good luck, and God bless you and your men!"

Smith, a good-looking young man of thirty-four, West Point class of 1939, saluted and ordered his men into the waiting C-54 transports.

They were Task Force Smith, which MacArthur termed an arrogant display of strength, sent ahead into Korea to give the Communists pause. General Dean had been ordered to move his entire 24th Division to the peninsula, but it was scattered the length and breadth of Japan, near six separate ports, and there were no ships immediately available. It would have to go in bits and pieces, of which Task Force Smith was the first.

Five days later, Task Force Smith was dug in along the main highway between Suwon and Osan, which lay a few miles south. Two understrength infantry companies, with headquarters and communication personnel, it had, in addition to its rifles, two 75mm recoilless rifles, two 4.2-inch mortars, six 2.36-inch rocket launchers, and four 60mm mortars. A battery of six light howitzers from the 52nd Field had joined them, and these went into place two thousand yards behind the infantry.

They dug in on low rolling hills, on a ridge that ran at right angles to the road, commanding it. The weather was rainy, and cold, but from the highest point of the ridge, some three hundred feet above the highway, Smith could see almost into Suwon.

Brigadier General Church, of ADCOM, had told him: "We have a little action up here. All we need is some men up there who won't run when they see tanks. We're going to move you up to support the ROK's and give them moral support."

Now, waiting confidently at dawn on 5 July, Task Force Smith covered approximately one mile of front. As soon as the light was good, the riflemen test fired each of their weapons, and the artillery registered on the surrounding hills. Then everyone went to breakfast, which consisted of cold C rations.

One of the artillerymen was worried. He knew the battery had only six rounds of antitank ammunition—one-third of all that could be found in Japan—and he asked, "What will happen to the guns if the North Korean tanks get through the infantry up there?"

One of the infantry officers told him smiling, "Don't worry; they'll never get that far."

It was generally agreed that the North Koreans, when they found out who they were fighting, would turn around and go back. The young soldiers of Task Force Smith were quite confident; at this point none of them felt fear. At Pusan, when they had boarded the train, the Koreans had unfurled gay banners and bands had played in the station yard.

They had been told that this was a police action, and that they'd soon be home in Japan. It was a happy thought—life in Japan was very good. Almost every man had his own shoeshine boy and his own *musame;* in a country where an American lieutenant made as much as a cabinet minister, even a PFC could make out. And the training wasn't bad. There were no real training areas in crowded Nippon, so there wasn't much even General Walker of Eighth Army could do about that, though he made noises.

The young men of Task Force Smith carried Regular Army serial numbers, but they were the new breed of American regular, who, not liking the service, had insisted, with public support, that the Army be made as much like civilian life and home as possible. Discipline had galled them, and their congressmen had seen to it that it did not become too onerous. They had grown fat.

They were probably as contented a group of American soldiery as had ever existed. They were like American youth everywhere. They believed the things their society had taught them to believe. They were cool, and confident, and figured that the world was no sweat.

It was not their fault that no one had told them that the real function of an army is to fight and that a soldier's destiny—which few escape—is to suffer, and if need be, to die.

At about 0700, through the sweeping rain, Colonel Smith saw movement on the road in the direction of Suwon. By 0730, he could clearly see a tank column, eight in all, grinding toward his ridge.

At 0800, or thereabouts, the forward observer with the infantry along the road picked up his field phone and called, "Fire Mission!"

The rounds went into the stubby 105's; breechblocks clicked home. Gunners set their sights, leveled the bubble, and section chiefs' arms went up. At 0816, Number 2 howitzer spat flame into the murky sky, one round, two. All guns joined in the barking chorus.

The tanks were now about two thousand yards in front of the infantry holes, and still coming. Bursting HE shells walked into the tank column, spattering the advancing armor with flame and steel and mud.

"Jesus Christ, they're still coming!" an infantryman shouted.

Colonel Smith knew that the 75mm recoilless rifles he had placed covering the highway had very little ammunition; he now ordered them to hold their fire until the tanks got within 700 yards.

The NKPA tanks, dark and wicked and low-slung on the road, advanced arrogantly, seeming unconcerned by the exploding HE shells about them.

Antitank mines placed in the road would have stopped them. But there was not a single antitank mine in Korea. Air support might have stopped them, but because of the rain the planes could not fly.

Now the troops dug in along the ridge could count more than thirty tanks strung out on the road.

At 700 yards, both recoilless rifles slammed at the tanks. Round after round burst against the T-34 turrets, with no apparent effect. But with this opposition, the tanks stopped and turned their 85mm cannon on the ridge. They fired, and their 7.62mm coaxial machine guns clawed the hillsides. Suddenly, American soldiers pulled their heads down.

Lieutenant Ollie Connor, watching, grabbed a bazooka and ran down to the ditch alongside the road. Steadying the 2.36-inch rocket launcher on the nearest tank, only fifteen yards away, Connor let fly. The small shaped charge burned out against the thick Russian armor without penetrating. Angrily, Connor fired again, this time at the rear of the tank where the armor protection was supposed to be thinnest.

He fired twenty-two rockets, none of which did any damage. Some of the rounds were so old they did not explode properly. The tankers, thinking they were up against only a small roadblock, made no real attempt to engage Task Force Smith, but continued down the road.

The enlisted men of Task Force Smith stuck their heads out of their holes and watched them disappear around the bend, heading for the artillery positions.

There was nothing mysterious about the Russian T-34, as some newspapers later claimed. Of obsolescent design, it had been used against the German panzers in front of Moscow in the early forties; perhaps it was the best all-around tank developed in World War II, with very high mobility, a good low silhouette, and very heavy armor plating. It could be stopped—but not with the ancient equipment in the hands of the ROK's—or Task Force Smith.

The American Army had developed improved 3.5-inch rocket launchers, which would penetrate the T-34. But happy with having designed them, it hadn't thought to place them in the hands of the troops, or of its allies. There just hadn't been enough money for long-range bombers, nuclear bombs, aircraft carriers, and bazookas too. Now, painfully, at the cost of blood, the United States found that while long-range bombers and aircraft carriers are absolutely vital to its security, it had not understood in 1945 the shape of future warfare.

To remain a great power, the United States had to provide the best in nuclear delivery systems. But to properly exercise that power with any effect in the world—short of blowing it up—the United States had also to provide the bread-and-butter weapons that would permit her ground troops to live in battle.

If it did not want to do so, it had no moral right to send its troops into battle.

The two lead tanks rumbling down on the howitzer positions were struck head on by HEAT rounds, damaging them. They pulled off the road, so the others could get around them. One of the damaged tanks burst into flames. Two of its crew leaped from the turret with their hands up; the third came out holding a burp gun.

This soldier, seeing an American machine-gun crew dug in beside the road, fired at it, killing an assistant gunner. The Americans immediately shot down all three tankers. But the first American had been killed in Korea.

Very soon the dead American would have company.

The other tanks still did not stop, but continued on down the road. The howitzer gunners relaid their pieces directly on the tanks, and fired. At ranges from 300 to 150 yards, the 105's just bounced off.

But the tankers had buttoned up, and could not locate the artillery's firing position. Answering the fire only haphazardly, they continued down the road, past the artillery site and beyond. One more tank was hit in the track and immobilized. But the antitank ammunition was now gone, and a badly shaken group of American gunners watched the Communist armor rumble on.

After the main body of the tanks had disappeared, Colonel Perry, commanding the 52nd Field, who had come up to fight with his single engaged battery, organized a squad of men to destroy the halted tank. He called for its crew to surrender, and was shot through the right leg for his efforts.

The howitzers slammed at the tank until its crew deserted it. The two men who got out were killed in a brief fire fight with some of Perry's men.

Now it was found that the tanks had cut all the wires leading up to the infantry positions farther north. The radios were wet and old and wouldn't work, and the gunners had no idea of what was happening up ahead. They knew only that a hell of a lot of tanks had come through, and that wasn't supposed to happen to them.

Ten minutes later, another long string of tanks poured down the road toward the guns emplaced alongside it. They came singly, in twos, and threes, apparently without any organization, and, like the first, not accompanied by enemy infantry.

To any troops with solid training, armed with the weapons standard to any advanced nation at the middle of the century, they would have been duck soup. But Task Force Smith had neither arms nor training.

As the new wave of tanks burst into view, the artillery battery started to come apart. Officers ordered fire on the tanks, but the crew members began to take off. Some men scuttled off; others simply walked away from the guns. The officers and senior sergeants suddenly found themselves alone.

Cursing, commissioned officers of the battery grabbed ammunition and stuffed it into the tubes. The noncoms laid the guns and pulled the lanyards.

Again, the tanks did not pause to slug it out with the battery but passed through the gap to the south.

Colonel Perry, hobbling on one leg, leaning against a tree, together with First Lieutenant Dwain Scott, talked the men into coming back on the guns. Many of the second echelon of tanks did not fire on the battery at all, and the guns were able to knock out one more by disabling its track.

But one howitzer had been struck by an 85mm shell, and destroyed, and a great many of the battery vehicles, which had been parked off the road, were smashed and burning. Other than Colonel Perry, only one other artilleryman had been hit.

Farther north, Colonel Smith's infantry had lost some twenty dead or wounded to tank fire.

After the last tank had passed, the roadside grew quiet again. The gunners sat down around their guns, resting, while the riflemen began to dig their holes deeper. The steady rain continued to come down.

Then, after an hour had passed, Smith through his glasses saw a long column of trucks and walking infantry moving south from Suwon. At first sight he estimated the column to be at least six miles in length. Leading this new column were three more tanks, followed by trucks and miles of marching men.

This column was the 16th and 18th regiments of the NKPA 4th Division, the conquerors of Seoul.

For about an hour, the column closed upon Task Force Smith's position. The men were no longer cocky or happy. They were scared.

Smith held his fire until the leading tanks and trucks were only a thousand yards away. Then he said, "Throw the book at them!"

The North Korean column was congested on the narrow road; it was not prepared to fight. Apparently it was not even in communication with the tank columns of the 105th Armored Brigade that had preceded it down the road, and it did not anticipate trouble.

While tough and battle-hardened, with a core of veterans, and psychologically prepared for battle, the NKPA was by no means a scientific military instrument by twentieth century standards. With no body of technical skills to fall back upon, the handling of communications and mechanized equipment, or even of artillery larger than mortars, by its peasant soldiery was inept. When its core of veterans had been exhausted in battle, the newer forced-inductees would be less reliable, and the NKPA would falter.

But in the early months of the war, the NKPA was a better army, more ready for war, than those it faced.

Colonel Smith gave the order to fire. Behind the ridge, mortars coughed, throwing their shells in a high arc over the ridges, sending them crashing down on the truck column. Trucks exploded and burst into flame. Shouting Koreans ran for the ditches. Machine guns ripped at them as they ran.

Some died on the road. Others reached the ditches, and were blown apart by the 4.2 shells that fell among them. The column of North Koreans stopped and began to pile up in confusion.

But now again Colonel Smith had nothing with which to stop the three tanks. The armored vehicles moved up close to his ridges, only 200 yards from the holes, and began to shower them with machine-gun slugs and to belt them with cannon fire. Americans began to die along the ridge.

Now, behind the smoke of the burning trucks, Smith could see a thousand North Koreans in mustard-colored uniforms start to deploy out into the rice paddies beside the road. A wave of them started for his ridge; it was broken up by rifle and machine-gun fire.

Surprisingly, although they brought some machine guns around, the enemy made no real effort to flank the ridge.

Enemy artillery began to burst along his position now—but Smith had no communication with his own supporting battery. Either artillery or air could have wreaked havoc on the North Koreans congested on the road in front of him, but he had neither. Smith believed the artillery had been destroyed by the tank column, though actually only one howitzer had been knocked out.

While the infantry fought along the ridge, the artillery sat it out. Twice Perry ordered wire parties to try to get the lines back in, but twice the men came back, complaining that they had been fired on.

Wet and old, none of the radios would work.

Smith, a courageous and competent officer, held his ridge as long as he dared. He held fast until the early afternoon, blocking the enemy, but he was running low on ammunition, and he realized that he was going to have to extricate his force, and soon, if he was going to save any of it from destruction.

Not only did he have a great number of enemy in front of him, but now men with automatic weapons were flowing across his flanks.

A withdrawal under fire is one of the most difficult of all military maneuvers. With seasoned troops it is dangerous, but with green men, undisciplined, badly shocked by the new and terrifying experience of battle, it can be fatal.

Smith ordered his two companies to leapfrog backward down a finger ridge on his right, toward Osan. While one platoon was to withdraw, others would cover it by fire.

C Company started back first, followed by the medics and battalion HQ.

But one platoon of B Company never received the withdrawal order. Fighting, Lieutenant Bernard, its commander, suddenly realized he was all alone on the position. He gave orders for his men to pull out after the others had already gone.

The withdrawal immediately became ragged and chaotic. Nobody wanted to be last in a game where all advantage obviously lay with being first. The men got out of their holes, leaving their crew-served weapons. They left their machine guns, recoilless rifles, and mortars for the enemy.

Getting up from its holes to withdraw, Task Force Smith now came under heavy machine-gun fire from the flanks, and here it took its heavy losses. At close range, automatic weapons chewed the retreating Americans, breaking them up into small, disorganized units.

They left their dead where they lay, and abandoned the thirty or so wounded who were too hurt to walk. One medical sergeant, whose name has been lost, refused to leave the wounded. He was not heard from again.

With his last company leaving the hill, Colonel Smith struck off toward Perry's position, to tell the artillery that the infantry was pulling out. Finding Perry, Smith was amazed to find five guns operable and only one man other than Perry wounded. But it was too late now for the artillery to take a hand.

The artillerymen were quite ready to go. Quickly, they lifted sights and breech locks from their howitzers, and took them to their vehicles. Smith, the hobbling Perry, and many of the gunners then walked back to Osan, three miles away, where the artillery had left many of their trucks, which they found undamaged.

But Osan was occupied by enemy tanks. The little convoy struck out on a dirt road to the east, trying to reach Ansong. Soon they overran straggling groups of infantry struggling over the hills and sloshing through the rice paddies. Covered with slime, running, these men had tossed aside their steel helmets. Some had dropped their shoes, and many had lost shirts. None of them had weapons other than a few rifles, and two or three clips of ammunition per man.

They shouted at the trucks as they passed. The artillerymen stopped and picked up about one hundred men of this group. Then they continued eastward, away from the enemy.

The NKPA, apparently satisfied with taking the ridge, did not pursue. Besides, the Americans had left many good things behind to occupy the victors.

Early the next morning, 6 July, Colonel Smith could account for only 185 men. Later, the C Company commander came in with 65 more. The artillery was missing 5 officers and 26 men.

Survivors straggled into several Korean towns for a number of days. Some men walked all the way to the east coast; some reached the Yellow Sea on the west. One man finally came into Pusan by sampan.

Task Force Smith, designed to be an arrogant display of strength to bluff the enemy into halting his advance, had delayed the Inmun Gun exactly seven hours.

8

The Late Company A

Tragically . . . when the fighting was over the militiamen who had scampered remained to be war-battered heroes. Campaigners for public office told them how gallant they had been; expounded on the glories of New Orleans and the Thames and Lundy's Lane and ignored Hull's surrender, Wilkinson's failures, the scuttle at Blandensburg. . . . the lessons and problems were forgotten by people and government.

—James E. Edmonds, FIGHTING FOOLS, concerning the War of 1812.

A T THE TIME Task Force Smith saw its first tanks north of Osan, the 24th Division's 34th Regiment was in P'yongt'aek, a dirty little town of wattle huts and muddy streets fifteen miles south. Bit by bit and piece by piece, the 24th Division was arriving in Korea, coming into Pusan by LST or transport, then by rail northwestward to Taejon and points north.

And rapidly now, the burden of the war was falling on its back.

The heart of the ROK Army, with the loss of its best men north of the Han, had broken. It had little equipment remaining from the Seoul debacle, and the troops who had been in the south were poorly armed, with old Jap matériel. The staff had fallen into controversy, with more than one high officer shouting "Communists!" at his colleagues. Fat Chae was gone. Lee Bum Suk, who had graduated from the United States Army Infantry School, became temporary chief of staff.

It was the Communist tanks, the ever-present, ever-leading T-34's, which could not be stopped and could not be destroyed, that wrecked every plan and every hope of the ROK commanders. Lee Bum Suk had sound notions for fighting tanks—but now he could no longer find any ROK soldiers with the heart to try them. The rash and the brave die early in a war.

Lee's successor, Chung Il Kwon, dropped the whole problem in the Americans' laps. They were here now; their advisers had talked endlessly about the insignificance and vulnerability of Soviet tanks—now let the men from *Mikuk,* the Beautiful Land, fight the Communist tanks.

At the first the men from *Mikuk* were not worried. They were pretty well convinced that they were better than any gooks, North or South.

On 5 July, as the 1st and 3rd battalions of the understrength 34th Infantry closed in on P'yongt'aek, General Dean realized that he must make a strong defense of the P'yongt'aek-Ansong line. Here an arm of the Yellow Sea protected his left flank, and to the right there were mountains and poor roads. The main communications to the south came through P'yongt'aek and Ansong. South of them, the peninsula broadened out in all directions, particularly in the west, making defense much more complicated there than along this line.

Dean, who had flown in Korea 3 July, ordered 1st Battalion, 34th Infantry, north of P'yongt'aek to block the main road. The 3rd he sent to Ansong, a few miles to the east.

The young men of 1st Battalion resembled those of Task Force Smith. Already they had seen all of this stinking country they wanted to. They were ready to head back to their nice billets in Japan where their Japanese girl friends were probably already growing restless.

All of them were convinced they would be only a few days in Korea, at most. They had been told very little, for their officers themselves didn't know much. But as everyone said, "Just wait till the gooks see an American uniform—they'll turn around and run like hell!"

Coming north on the train from Taejon, 1st Battalion had picked up a new C.O., Lieutenant Colonel Ayres, who had had a fine record in Italy. Ayres confidently told his company commanders:

"There are supposed to be North Korean soldiers north of us. These men are poorly trained. Only about half of them have weapons, and we'll have no difficulty stopping them."

It was never disclosed who had briefed Colonel Ayres.

The company officers went back to their men and told them that this whole affair was only a police action and that, before long, everybody'd be back in good old Sasebo, Japan.

It is not certain that the young Americans knew what a police action was—but it is certain that none of them associated the term with combat.

The battalion marched north of P'yongt'aek in the same cold rain that soaked Task Force Smith. It halted in the green, grassy hills two miles north of town. Here both the highway and railbed ran through a cut with a low hill on each side, a good spot to defend. Colonel Ayres put B Company to the east of the road, and ordered C into reserve.

Captain Leroy Osburn's Able Company he placed on a hill to the left, with its line running down the hill through a rice paddy to the highway and railroad cuts.

A Company dug in. The reddish-brown earth was coarse, and turned easily, but in the pelting rain the foxholes began to fill with cold, dirty water. And because the front was wide for a weak company, the holes were far apart. The men of Lieutenant Driskell's 1st Platoon, down by the road, could not see the company CP up on the green hill.

The 2nd and 3rd platoons dug in along the hill; Weapons Platoon went in generally behind them. A Company's roster carried only 140 names, less than two-thirds its authorized wartime strength. For in America it was still peace-time, and had been for five years.

Each soldier carried either an M-1 rifle or a carbine, with less than 100 rounds of ammunition. The company had three light machine guns, with four boxes of ammunition for each gun. Each platoon had only one Browning Automatic rifle, with a total of 200 rounds per weapon.

The Weapons Platoon dug in only three 60mm mortars. It also had 75mm recoilless rifles, but these it could have left behind, for the powers that be had issued no ammunition for them.

Nor were there any hand grenades.

When their holes were dug, the young men of A Company sat outside them in the rain, occasionally shouting back and forth to one another. During the day nothing happened.

A small reconnaissance force went north on the road and reported back that there were tanks south of Osan. Then, after dark, four tired and somewhat incoherent survivors from Task Force Smith stumbled into Colonel Ayres' CP. They told a rather wild story, which Colonel Ayres didn't exactly buy.

Brigadier General Barth, who was acting division artillery commander of the 24th while awaiting the arrival in Korea of his own 25th Division, stopped by the CP. Barth had talked with Colonel Perry of Task Force Smith after his escape from Osan. Now Barth—who was not in communication with Dean and who did not know Dean's plan of maneuver—put an oar in proceedings at P'yongt'aek. Somewhat shaken by the disaster that had overtaken the delaying force north of Osan, Barth ordered Ayres to hold only as long as he could, and to take no chance of being flanked or surrounded.

"Don't end up like Brad Smith," he told Ayres.

Then Barth went on to the 34th Regiment's CP, and suggested to its com-mander, Colonel Lovless, that the regiment should consolidate its battalions to the south at the town of Ch'onan. Lovless did not know exactly where Barth stood in the chain of command or general scheme of things but Barth was a brigadier general, and Lovless now made a tremendous error. He sent word to his 3rd Battalion to pull back from Ansong, although the battalion had not yet made contact with the enemy. The right flank was left exposed.

Lovless had inherited the 34th only a short time before from an officer who had been relieved for incompetency.

The rain continued to fall on the waiting 1st Battalion all night. A few of the men, hearing rumors, grew nervous. They were told emphatically by an officer, "This is a police action, nothing more!"

Captain Osburn of A Company figured an attack was possible, but not like-ly. He had received word to be on the lookout for stragglers from Smith's bat-talion, but somehow these instructions did not get down to the platoons.

Daylight came 6 July, and now all the foxholes were filled with water. One man, PFC James Hite, told his platoon sergeant, "I'd sure hate to have to get into that hole."

A newly joined platoon sergeant, SFC Collins, who had been in combat before, walked up and down his line of holes. He told his men that they'd better eat while they had the chance, and to break out the C's. Then he took out a can of cold beans and sat down to eat it.

The morning was misty and foggy, but Collins, half through his beans, thought he heard the sound of engines to the north. He took up his field glasses and made out the faint outlines of several tanks on the road. Behind the tanks, he saw a great number of brown-uniformed infantrymen spreading out in the varicolored green rice paddies.

He called to his platoon leader, Lieutenant Ridley, "Sir, I think we got company!"

Ridley answered that what he saw must be part of Task Force Smith withdrawing down the road.

"These people got tanks. The 21st Infantry hasn't any," Collins yelled back.

Meanwhile, Colonel Ayres walked up to Captain Osburn's command post. From there both officers could see the infantry spreading through the rice fields, but visibility was too poor for them to identify the troops.

Osburn and the colonel agreed these must be some of Smith's boys, and continued to watch them for several minutes. Only when they had counted more than a battalion of soldiers deploying, with more beyond, did they come awake.

Immediately, Ayres called for the mortars to open fire. The first rounds burst in the fields, and the oncoming infantry spread out a little farther. It did not stop advancing.

Sergeant Collins, up on the hill, saw the turret hatches of the lead tank slam down. The long, wicked tube of the tank's 85 swung toward him.

"Here it comes!" Collins bellowed to his men. "Get down!"

The shell screamed into the hill, burst, and showered mud over the cowering riflemen. The men began jumping into their holes, sounding like frogs diving into a pond.

"Commence firing! Commence firing!" Collins shouted. Two other men, who were veterans of World War II, took up the shout.

The Americans on the hill could see the advancing Koreans plainly now, but almost no one fired. Collins turned to the two riflemen in his own hole.

"Come on! You got an M-1—get firing! Come on!" He jabbed one of them sharply.

But most of the men stood slack-jawed, staring at the advancing Koreans, as if unwilling to believe that these men were really trying to kill them. For many minutes, only the squad and platoon leaders did any shooting, and more than half of the men never got off a round.

Back in the Weapons Platoon, PFC Hite was still sitting beside his hole. He saw explosions on the hill near Captain Osburn's CP. "Must be short rounds—"

"Hell! That isn't short—that's an enemy shell!" his platoon sergeant told him. With a great splash, Hite turned and dived into his watery hole. The platoon sergeant joined him.

Colonel Ayres, standing at Osburn's CP, watched the attack for a few minutes. Then, shaking his head, he told Osburn to withdraw his company. Ayres then left the hill, walked back to his own CP, and ordered it to move back.

NKPA soldiers were coming across the fields in numbers frightening to the Americans on the hill. B Company, on the right, was also under attack. More than a dozen tanks converged bumper to bumper on the road, a beautiful target, and on the hill SFC Collins cursed because he had no ammo for the 75's.

He called for fire from the battalion's 4.2—mortars-but a tank cannon shell burst near the single mortar observer, not harming him, but shocking him into speechlessness. No one else knew how to direct the mortars, and in the confusion the tubes stood idle.

Now the advancing and firing North Koreans were only a few hundred yards away, so close Collins could see them stop to load fresh cartridges into their long rifles. B Company began to move down off its hill on the east, withdrawing to the south.

Captain Osburn shouted down to his men, "Prepare to withdraw—but stay to cover B Company first!"

A Company was still putting out only a ragged volume of fire. The men just watched, seemingly dazed. The Weapons Platoon, hearing Osburn's shout, immediately got up and moved to the rear.

Then the two rifle platoons on the hill, not worrying about B Company, began to get out of their holes. The men left their field packs behind, and most of them forgot their spare ammunition. A few even left rifles in the rush. They started down to the south side of the hill, where a small village of straw houses stood in the mist. Here Captain Osburn and his officers started to organize A Company for withdrawal.

As the last two squads came off the hill, an automatic weapon snarled at them. The two squads panicked. Men started running.

The running men tore past Osburn, and some of the men with him began to run away, too. The panic was contagious.

Osburn and the other officers screamed at their men to halt. A few did stop, but the majority kept going. Running about, Osburn got together as many men as he could.

The 1st Platoon, dug in the flat ground toward the road, was more exposed to fire than the two on the hill. Hearing orders to withdraw, four men jumped up and ran back across the soggy green fields. Rifle fire hit one of these men in the back. The rest of the platoon now were too afraid to desert their holes, and refused to move.

Seventeen men under Lieutenant Driskell had been dug in along the railroad embankment and could not see the rest of A Company from their position. Now they did not even get the withdrawal order.

Suddenly they saw NKPA soldiers standing on the hill to their left. Understandably, Driskell became nervous. He asked his sergeant, a combat veteran, "What do you think we should do now?"

"Get the hell out of here," the sergeant replied.

Driskell ordered his men to move back along the railway embankment. A large number of them, however, confused and frightened, refused to move. Driskell, after moving to the rear, missed these men, and went back to get them. A few minutes later, while searching the Korean mud houses for possible wounded, a squad of North Koreans surrounded him and the four men with him. Driskell tried to surrender.

One of the NKPA shot him dead, and then the enemy fired on the other four, killing three. The fourth ran away.

The men who refused to leave their holes were not seen again.

A couple of miles to the rear in P'yongt'aek, Captain Osburn began to get his company back under control. The long run took most of the steam out of the men, and they recovered from their panic. They stood waiting in the rain until Osburn came to break them down into some semblance of order for a further retreat.

Sergeant Collins, disgusted that so many of his men hadn't fired on the enemy, went among his survivors, asking them why they hadn't fired. A dozen of them said their rifles wouldn't work. Checking, Collins found the rifles were jammed with dirt, or incorrectly assembled after cleaning.

Many of the men did not know how to put a rifle together. It wasn't Collins' fault, since he had joined the company only one day before.

Once assembled, A Company began the move south. This time, the men obeyed their sergeants' orders—just as long as they were moving south.

One-fourth of the company was missing.

The wounded who had made it could walk, but the shell-shocked mortar observer wandered around aimlessly if not helped. Men took turns helping him along.

The rain stopped, and the day became steamy, humid, and miserable. The men sweated. They had thrown away their canteens, and now they were forced to drink like animals from the muddy ditches and stinking rice paddies, fertilized with human feces.

All along the road south, they saw a litter of American equipment thrown aside by the other elements of 1st Battalion who had preceded them: helmets, rain gear, cartridge belts, even rifles. By late afternoon, men began to falter, and the company column spread out over two miles.

Captain Osburn passed the word that any man who fell out would be left behind. No one said very much. They all kept going.

The mortar observer kept moaning to himself, over and over, "Rain, rain, rain."

"Why the hell don't you shut up?" one of the men helping him asked bitterly.

At dark, a ragged, disheartened, stumbling mob of men straggled into Ch'onan. Here they found the rest of 1st Battalion, who had got there first, snoring in the muddy streets, tired, uncaring.

Captain Osburn located some trucks of the ROK Army and loaded his men in them. Battalion ordered him to take his company two miles south of Ch'onan and prepare a defensive position.

A Company moved into their designated area after dark. The men now had no entrenching tools. A few men scraped out shallow foxholes with their hands or mess utensils. Most of them fell down on the soggy earth and went to sleep.

* * *

General Dean, at Taejon, after hearing the full story of Task Force Smith, did not feel too badly about the situation. Smith had done the best he could, and he had allowed the 34th Infantry precious hours to prepare the P'yongt'aek-Ansong defense line.

Bill Dean knew very well that the holding of the P'yongt'aek-Ansong line was vital to his plan of defense. Where he made his mistake was believing that the understrength, untrained, undisciplined, and unprepared regiment to which he gave the orders was capable of carrying out such a mission against a foe as tough and numerous as the Inmun Gun.

At about 1600 on 6 July, Dean learned that not only had the 1st Battalion fallen back all the way below Ch'onan; more than fifteen miles below the natural defense terrain, but that the 3rd Battalion, which he had left at Ansong, had retreated back twenty miles to Ch'onan without even making contact with the enemy.

Dean turned his jeep toward Ch'onan. There, in the CP of Colonel Lovless, the commander of the 34th Infantry, he blew his top.

The withdrawal from P'yongt'aek had exposed his entire left flank. There were some ROK's on the left, called the Anti-Communist Youth Group, but in these Bill Dean rightly placed no confidence.

Lovless told him about Barth's instructions to bring the troops back from Ansong. Dean, who had been out of communication with Barth—few of the available radios would work in the rain—had to accept that.

Dropping Ansong, Dean demanded to know who had authorized the retreat from P'yongt'aek.

There was a long silence in the CP. Lovless looked at Colonel Ayres, who finally said, "I'll accept the responsibility for that."

Dean almost told them to turn around and get their tails going north. But as he opened his mouth, he realized that it was already dark, and there could be danger of a night ambuscade on the march. He figured that there had been enough confusion already.

He made a painful decision to let the error stand.

But just as soon as he had returned to his own command post, he thought better of it. He sent word to Lovless to advance his regiment north until contact was made, and then to fight a delaying action.

Dean took responsibility for the precipitate drawback on himself, since he considered he had not made his intentions clear to all hands.

But wherever the fault lay, the result was tragic.

* * *

Late in the afternoon of 7 July, Major John J. Dunn, Operations Officer of the 34th Infantry, was with the 3rd Battalion of that regiment moving north from Ch'onan pursuant to Dean's orders. The battalion was able to advance only a few miles out of town before its lead elements were fired upon. The advance halted.

The 3rd Battalion deployed out into an area along the road that had excellent fields of fire, and prepared to delay the enemy.

While Major Dunn talked with the battalion commander, the Intelligence and Reconnaissance Platoon leader, who had driven ahead of the battalion in a jeep, reported to the CP. The I&R Platoon leader showed a couple of bullet holes in his jacket, and one through his canteen. His platoon had been ambushed by a party of some forty enemy up ahead in a tiny village, but all except three of his men got out.

The leading rifle company of the battalion immediately started forward to rescue these men; Dunn went with it. On the way, they met Major Seegars, the Battalion S-3, who said that he had already found the missing men. Hearing this, Dunn told the rifle company to hold off its attack, and to take up a blocking position on the road.

As the company moved back, it drew a small amount of rifle fire. Immediately, some American soldiers began firing wildly and indiscriminately; Dunn was able to halt this only with difficulty. Suddenly, friendly mortar shells began dropping on the company's position.

Dunn angrily went to the rear to get somebody straightened out.

When he arrived at the 3rd Battalion's holding positions, he was surprised to find the battalion falling back along the road. He was not able to locate either the battalion commander or the exec at the CP.

Dunn then drove back to the regimental command post and reported the 3rd Battalion's action. A brand-new colonel, Robert R. Martin, was with Lovless. Martin had been hurriedly flown in from Japan, and he was wearing low quarter-shoes and an overseas cap. He had been sent to Korea at the express request of General Dean, who had known him in World War II, and at 1800 Dean had given him command of the 34th.

After listening to Dunn, Martin asked if Dunn thought the regiment would take orders from him.

"Yes, sir," Dunn said.

"Then put them back in that position!"

Dunn roared back up the road, stopped the retreating battalion, and headed it back. As soon as it was turned around, Dunn picked up Major Seegars and two of the battalion's company commanders in his own jeep, and followed by a second jeep with a few enlisted men, pulled out ahead of the battalion.

A few hundred yards short of the abandoned good position, small-arms fire blazed at the two jeeps from close range. A group Dunn estimated to be about forty men had ambushed them.

Both Dunn and Seegars were hit immediately, Seegars very badly. Several other men were wounded. The jeeps slued to a stop under the hail of bullets, and the men in them tumbled to the road.

Dunn was wounded severely in the head; an artery was pulsing bright red blood on the road. With great effort Dunn crawled off the road into a clump of bushes, and here he was able to stanch his bleeding. One of the enlisted men dragged Major Seegars to cover.

One of the officers with the party, unhit, said he would bring help, and took off to the south.

Keeping low, surrounded by enemy scouts, Dunn crawled up onto a small knoll. Down the road he could see the leading rifle company of the 3rd Battalion, which had been just behind the advance party. When the shooting began, these men had hit the dirt and commenced firing.

They were close enough for Dunn, too hurt to move, to recognize some of the men. But they did not advance, even though their officers knew that wounded men lay directly to their front, and they constituted a superior force to the scattered scouts before them.

Then Dunn heard an officer shout nervously, "Fall back! Fall back!"

The rifle company, under no pressure from the enemy, fell back.

Unbelieving, sickened, Major Dunn, who would spend three years in a North Korean prisoner-of-war camp, watched his men fall back with no attempt to rescue their own.

Two hours later a large force of North Koreans advanced down the road and took Dunn and the other men prisoner. During the evening, Major Boone Seegars died beside the road.

All day on 7 July, Company A of the 1st Battalion waited on the road south of Ch'onan, improving its positions with shovels borrowed from Korean farmers—most of whom were now abandoning their fields, and fleeing south. The monsoon rain continued to fall during the day, and the men sat around in it, talking.

Somehow, a new rumor made the rounds, one that pleased everyone. A Company was going back to Japan. Other than rumors, nothing much of importance passed during the day. The only food the company could get was from the Koreans, and many of the men went hungry.

There was fighting north of them during the night in the town of Ch'onan, but it was too far off for them to get the wind up.

* * *

Colonel Bob Martin, now in command of the 34th Infantry, had inherited a debacle. With a disintegrating command, it was not enough to issue orders; orders had a way of being ignored on company and platoon level. Martin did the only thing he could do, which was to try to set a personal example.

His 3rd Battalion retreated through Ch'onan in disorder; in the early evening of 7 July Martin joined the battalion and ordered its C.O. to return and defend the town. Then, with a small group of soldiers, Martin went inside Ch'onan.

Confused fighting developed to the west of the town during the night, where elements of the 3rd Battalion were defending. After midnight 8 July, word arrived at the regimental command post south of Ch'onan that Colonel Martin and eighty men were cut off inside the town and that North Korean tanks were in the city.

General Dean, hearing this report, was too upset to sleep during the night. He had Martin shipped to Korea at his personal request.

But Martin came out, and reported that the supply lines into the city were clear and that the defenders needed ammunition. Then, just before daybreak on 8 July, he returned into the beleaguered town.

Now a half-dozen tanks were in the streets of Ch'onan, firing on the rail station, the church, and any Americans or vehicles in sight. The battle for Ch'onan devolved into disorganized street fighting. North Korean infantry marched inside at 0600, and the two rifle companies still defending were cut off.

In the early morning, Bob Martin was hunting through the streets of Ch'onan with a 2.36-inch bazooka. It was no job for a regimental C.O.—but somebody had to do it. Leading the attack, gathering a small group of men about him, Martin engaged the enemy tanks.

With his regimental S-3 sergeant, Jerry Christenson, he stood in a hut east of the main street of Ch'onan, facing a T-34. Martin, acting as gunner, aimed the rocket launcher, and fired. The small, obsolete rocket charge fizzled out against the tank's steel hull.

At the same time, the tank fired. At a range of less than twenty-five feet, the 85mm shell blew Bob Martin into two pieces.

The concussion burst one of Christenson's eyes from its socket, but in great pain he managed to pop it back in. He was taken captive by the North Koreans.

With Martin's death, the defense of Ch'onan came apart. There was a great deal of bugging out. The troops that did not bug were chopped up by a superior and better-armed enemy.

* * *

While the last fighting was going on in Ch'onan, Company A was getting breakfast, their first good meal in two days. After eating, the company could see American troops pulling out of Ch'onan, but it was not until several hours later that artillery shells began to fall in their own area.

When the first shell burst, Captain Osburn gave the order to pull back south. The entire 1st Battalion was moving out again.

All afternoon and half the night the company marched south, keeping a fast pace. Then, after daylight, the company was shuttled by truck into new positions along the Kum River. Here the men dug new holes, and this time, deep ones. They received their first resupply of ammunition.

The rumor about going to Japan began to die a natural death.

* * *

On the morning of 8 July, Lieutenant General Walton Walker flew into Dean's HQ in Taejon. He informed Dean that help was on the way—the entire Eighth Army, all four divisions under Walker himself, were coming to Korea.

MacArthur had already requested from the Joint Chiefs the following troops and equipment from the continental United States and elsewhere.

The 2nd Infantry Division, then at Fort Lewis, Washington; a regimental combat team from the 82nd Airborne, a regimental combat team from the Fleet Marine Forces, with heavy Marine air and beach parties, Army engineers, and three tank battalions—of which there had been none in the Far East.

MacArthur had already envisioned his plan of maneuver for ending the war—the end run to the west coast and the Inch'on landings. But neither he nor any one else had realized yet how hard it was going to be to stop the North Korean advance long enough to put the Inch'on show on the road. As the days went by, MacArthur would continually increase the list of his requirements.

On 8 July General Dean sent him the following message: "I am convinced that the North Korean Army and the North Korean soldier, and his status of training and equipment have been underestimated."

MacArthur directed Lieutenant General Stratemeyer to use his bomber forces against North Korean ground troops—an inefficient employment of heavy bombers, but there were simply not enough ground-support groups available. The Air Force had never anticipated having to support a large-scale ground war.

Air power was not able to halt the North Korean advance. But without the air cover and timely air support and supply FEAF gave them, the American ground units would have been in far worse condition.

MacArthur then cabled the JCS:

"The situation in Korea is critical. . . . This force more and more assumes the aspect of a combination of Soviet leadership and technical guidance with Chinese ground elements. While it serves under the flag of North Korea, it can no longer be considered as an indigenous N.K. military effort.

"The situation has developed into a major operation."

* * *

Ch'onan was a transportation hub, from which good roads ran west and south. When P'yongt'aek was abandoned, General Dean's entire left flank had been exposed, and with the capture of Ch'onan, the North Koreans had entry into most of western and southern Korea. Dean was forced now to try to defend along the Kum, which was the first large river south of the Han. It was a natural defense line, a great watery moat almost encircling the important city of Taejon.

Taejon was the last militarily important center in South Korea, with the exception of Taegu and Pusan behind the Naktong River, far to the southeast. If Taejon fell to the enemy, there was no real defense line short of the Naktong—and on that river the defenders would hold only a tiny corner of Korean earth.

More and more units were coming into Korea, and General Dean was assembling more forces. He could expect the 25th Infantry Division to go into action in a few days, and the 1st Cavalry (actually a TO&E infantry division retaining a famous name) was arriving. But for the next crucial battle, Dean would have to depend on his own 34th, 21st, and 19th Infantry regiments.

Late 8 July, Dean issued a formal operations order, confirming fragmentary verbal instructions put out during the day: "Hold Kum River Line at all costs. Maximum repeat maximum delay will be affected."

He placed his regiments, the 19th, 21st, and the now battered and bedraggled 34th, into a great semicircle along the Kum River. Dean now realized that if this line could not be held, Taejon itself, with its important roads and rail lines, was doomed.

On 9 July A Company was still north of the Kum, in well-prepared positions. During the afternoon it came under heavy shelling, and then enemy infantry struck against its left flank, held by the 1st Platoon.

Most of the 1st Platoon had stayed in their holes at P'yongt'aek, and it contained only about a dozen men. Quickly, the Inmun Gun poured over it, firing at the men in their holes.

Five men got out, running down the hill.

Men in the 2nd Platoon, dug in to the right, looked up on the hill where 1st Platoon had been. "Who the hell put the flag up there?" a sergeant asked.

Then a shout went up. "That's a North Korean flag!"

Shrieking and shooting, a wave of Koreans poured down from the hill toward 2nd Platoon. The platoon had not dug its position for all-around defense. It could not now fire effectively to its left flank.

"Let's get the hell out of here!"

Taking its weapons and some of the wounded, 2nd Platoon took off.

The remainder of A Company held out until dark. Then orders came to pull back out of rifle range. Early the next morning, the company crossed south of the Kum.

Here they had a breathing spell, until the NKPA boiled across the river. At daybreak on 20 July, A Company held the main road into the north side of Taejon; four men from the Weapons Platoon were down on the road with a rocket launcher. As it grew lighter, they saw three long skirmish lines of Korean infantry pass over a hilltop to their right. Looking left, they saw more enemy.

The men ran some five hundred yards back to the battalion CP. There the senior man, a sergeant, reported to the battalion commander.

The C.O. remarked that the sergeant seemed a bit excited. The sergeant asked him to take a look down the road. The colonel went outside the command hut, and at that moment red flares burst against the lightening sky.

All hell broke loose. Artillery, mortar, small-arms, and tank-gun fire pelted the area.

The urge to pull out was once again irresistible.

The battalion moved south, beyond Taejon. At first A Company kept good order, but men from other units became enmeshed with them, and these men wouldn't take orders from A's officers. Soon there was confusion.

Men threw away their shoes, because it was difficult to walk in the mud. They had no canteens, and they had no food. They were tired and dispirited, and some were bitter. The sun burned out of the clouds, and now the full brazen heat of Korean midsummer baked them. Some men grew dizzy and sick.

They told bitter jokes: "If I'm a policemen, where the hell's my badge?" And, "Damn, these crooks over here got big guns!"

None of them had been told why they were in Korea, or why the United States was fighting North Korean Communists. None of them cared. They wanted only to get back to Japan.

Instead, they were heading for the Naktong River Line, there to make a final stand. There they would realize their government had no intention of withdrawing them; if they wanted to live, they would have to fight.

They were learning, in the hardest school there was, that it is a soldier's lot to suffer and that his destiny may be to die. They were learning something they had not been told: that in this world are tigers.

Behind them, platoons and companies from new divisions, fresh from Japan, went into line to take up the fight. These companies and platoons were manned by men like those of A Company, young Americans, no better, no worse, than the society from which they sprang. Some would do better than A Company, some less well. No matter how they did, there would not be enough of them.

No American may sneer at them, or at what they did. What happened to them might have happened to any American in the summer of 1950. For they represented exactly the kind of pampered, undisciplined, egalitarian army their society had long desired and had at last achieved.

They had been raised to believe the world was without tigers, then sent to face those tigers with a stick. On their society must fall the blame.

9

Taejon

I have no intention of alibiing my presence in Taejon. At the time I thought it was the place to be.

—Major General William Frishe Dean.

I N THE FIRST terrible, shattering days of July 1950, casualties among officers of high rank of the United States Army were greater in proportion to those of any fighting since the Civil War. They had to be. There were few operable radios with the regiments in Korea, and almost no communication from command posts down to the front positions.

If commanders wanted to know what was happening, or make their orders known, they had to be on the ground.

And the troops themselves, who had never developed any respect for N.C.O.'s or junior officers, often would ignore their orders—particularly if the order involved something unpleasant or unpopular.

Understandably, the junior leaders soon became defeatist. A great many of them died, recklessly, but it was not enough.

It was not because the colonels and generals had lost their minds that so many of them began to stand with bazooka teams or to direct rifle fire. There was no other way. So it was that men like Bob Martin were blown apart doing a rifleman's job, or battalion commanders like Smith of the 3rd, 34th Infantry, collapsed and had to be evacuated, and men like Major Dunn, marching ahead of a rifle company, were lost.

The high-priced help was expendable, true. They too were paid to die. But it was no way to run a war.

While the 34th Regiment was getting chewed in Ch'onan, the 21st—"Gimlets"—were in delaying position to the east, near Choch'iwon. Here Colonel Stephens—Big Six to his men—found a scene of mass confusion. Supplies for his men and the neighboring ROK troops arrived by rail, mixed together. The Korean trainmen were impossible to control; some trains, still loaded, bolted for the rear. Refugees were everywhere.

Stephens, a tough and rugged officer, was told by Dean to hold for four days. He was given an artillery battery, some engineers, and a company of light tanks. On 10 July his composite battalion, made up of men of the 21st who had not flown in earlier with Brad Smith, held a ridge along a three-quarter-mile front, north of Choch'iwon.

Stephens was up on the ridge with his troops.

In the early morning, mist and fog hung over the green rice paddies to the front. Soon, Korean voices could be heard through the fog. Some of the American soldiers began shooting, wildly.

Dick Stephens roared at them to stop, and they did.

A platoon on a single hill to the left of the position now came under vicious attack. Mortar fire slashed the ridge, and men could hear tank engines in the fog. But preplanned mortar and artillery fires turned back the wave of North Korean infantry that began to dribble forward.

Gradually, the fog lifted. But now Stephens had lost communication both by wire and radio with his supporting mortars. They fell silent.

At 0900, enemy infantry tried to climb to the American positions. Now the artillery battery, firing repeatedly, drove them back again. But four tanks moved out of a small village and began pelting the ridges with automatic fire. Nothing could be done about them.

At 1100, lacking close-in mortar support, the lieutenant holding the single hill on the left was unable to keep the enemy at a distance. This officer, Bixler, radioed to Stephens: "I need reinforcements; have many casualties; request permission to withdraw."

"Hold on—relief is on the way," Stephens told him.

Stephens had recalled for an air strike. Soon, the planes screamed over the hill, rocketed the tanks—without visible effect—and scattered the attacking infantry. But soon the planes expended their ammunition, and sighed off to the south.

And something else had happened during the air strike—enemy fire had cut the wire from the ridge to the artillery position, and the forward observer's radio had conked out.

The North Koreans started upward once again, and now friendly artillery whistled down on the American defenders. The artillery, with the idea that the enemy had overrun Stephens' ridge, had decided on their own to fire upon the ridge.

Stephens, cursing, ran to his own command jeep. He called his regimental HQ to contact the artillery to lay off—but the shells kept whooping in.

Crouching on the ridge under his own shellfire, Stephens took another message from Bixler, that Bixler was surrounded and most of his men were down. Bixler was not heard from again.

During the fire fight, a few men here and there on the right flank of the ridge had been seen moving back. Now a yell went up.

Dick Stephens saw a number of men running to the rear. He shouted: "Get those high-priced soldiers back into position! This is what they're paid for!"

A corporal, a Japanese-American from Hawaii, did his best to stop the panic, but was able to collect only a few men.

Within a few minutes, Stephens saw that the ridge would have to be abandoned. He signaled the small group still with him to fall back, and they crossed the rear slope of the ridge and floundered through the stinking rice paddies. On the way, two American planes dived down and strafed them. No one was hurt, but the men, forced to wallow face down in the odorous night soil, lost any future love of rice.

Coming into the position of his 3rd Battalion, Stephens immediately ordered Lieutenant Colonel Jensen to counterattack the lost ridge. Jensen went forward and after a sharp fight retook the ground—all except Bixler's hill.

And on the retaken ground Jensen found six American soldiers with their hands tied behind their backs, shot in the head.

The 21st Infantry continued fighting, though it was forced back from the ridge toward Choch'iwon. The North Koreans, the veteran 3rd Division, which Kim Il Sung had designated "Seoul," crashed into the 3rd Battalion early on 11 July. It was a beautifully executed assault, following the pattern of most NKPA attacks.

While heavy fire held down the American front, troops and tanks passed through and around them, setting up roadblocks. Again—as continually happened—tanks tore up the wire, and radios fizzled. Colonel Jensen and a very high percentage of his battalion staff were killed or missing in action, while more than 60 percent of the battalion went down the drain.

Overrun, the survivors streamed to the rear. The men who came out had no canteens or ammunition. They lost their shoes in the muck of the rice paddies, and threw away their heavy helmets. Nine out of ten left their weapons behind.

Behind them, Colonel Stephens had organized the remnants of the 1st Battalion—the old Task Force Smith—on new positions. Two enemy divisions—the elite 3rd and 4th—were breathing on his neck.

At 1200, 12 July, he radioed General Dean: "Am surrounded. 1st Bn, left giving way. Situation bad on right. Having nothing left to establish intermediate delaying position with am forced to withdraw to [Kum] river line. I have issued instructions to withdraw."

The retreat was orderly. At 1600, except for a few inevitable stragglers, the 21st had crossed south of the Kum. On the south shore Stephens took up a new blocking position. He could put a total of 325 men on line—the total fighting strength of the 1st and 3rd battalions combined.

For three days Stephens had delayed the best of the North Korean Army. His was the first impressive American performance in Korea; some Gimlets had run, but the majority had fought and died.

The Gimlets had done well, but they had paid.

Falling back, they passed through the lines of the newly arrived 19th Infantry, the "Rock of Chickamauga," which had been rushed forward on Dean's orders.

The Chicks needn't have hurried. They were going to get their turn.

* * *

The Kum River is the first wide, deep, defendable stream south of the Han in southwestern Korea. It flows around the important city of Taejon, 120,000 people in 1950, sixth in South Korea, which lies some ten to fifteen miles below it. Between the river and the city is no terrain suitable for any hopeful defense.

If the Kum River were lost, Taejon must inevitably follow, and the American army could ill afford to lose Taejon, with its road and rail network leading to all South Korea.

General Dean was determined not to lose it.

By 12 July he had ordered all his troops to cross to the south bank of the Kum, and to blow all bridges behind them. Along the great arc, a sort of horseshoe bend that the river made about Taejon, he placed the three regiments at his disposal, the 34th Infantry on the left, the 19th on the right, and what was left of Colonel Stephens' 21st in a reserve blocking position on the southeast.

On arrival in Korea, the regiments had been at 70 percent strength—but worse, their tactical integrity had been destroyed. Each regiment had only two battalions, instead of the normal three, and American doctrine and training supposed three battalions. In any situation now in Korea, the regimental commanders could have only one battalion on line and one in reserve, or two on line and no reserve at all.

No American officer had had any experience with this kind of arrangement. The Army schools, assuming that before being committed to action the Army would get its "fat" restored, had developed no new and startling ways of making do with too little, too late.

Facing now its hardest test, the 24th Division was already in poor shape. The 21st Infantry had lost 1,433 men; 1,100 remained. The 34th had 2,020; the 19th, 2,276. With supporting troops the division numbered 11,400.

Attacking this battered American division were the hardened 3rd and 4th divisions, NKPA, supported by at least fifty tanks. The North Korean units stood at from 60 percent to 80 percent strength at this time; they had not fought all the way from the Ch'orwon Valley unscathed. A full-strength NKPA division numbered 11,000 officers and men—therefore, the North Koreans had not quite two-to-one superiority over the Americans.

No staff and command college in the world teaches that a military force with not quite two-to-one numerical superiority has any assurance of success. An attacking force needs heavy superiority in numbers. But staff and command colleges teach also that men are not ciphers. Fighting against great odds, American fighting men have proved that fact time and again. Again and again they have defeated foes vastly superior in manpower.

But in Korea in July 1950, before Taejon, the American 24th Division was on the brink of disaster, and not because of the enemy's numbers.

* * *

On the left side of the American defense line, 3rd Battalion, 34th Infantry, held the south shore of the river. It had dug in Companies L, I, and K, with the mortars of M—Weapons Company—between them. Two and a half miles to the battalion's rear, the 63rd Field, 105's, stood ready to give fire support.

Still farther back, what was left of the 34th's 1st Battalion rested in assembly areas.

The 3rd Battalion had no communications—none between battalion HQ and the companies, very little between company HQ's and platoons and squads. There was no wire for the few phones—most of it had been lost on former positions—and batteries for the old radios had gone out of style. At least, it was a waste of time requisitioning any.

The Love Company Commander, Lieutenant Stith, looked high and low for just one radio with which he could talk to Battalion. He couldn't find it.

The command situation throughout the regiment had, in military parlance, worsened. After Colonel Martin's death, the regimental exec, Wadlington, had taken over, and Pappy Wadlington was doing a good job. But the 3rd Battalion commander, Smith, had exhausted himself and been evacuated, and both the regimental Operations and Intelligence officers had come down with combat fatigue. All through the regiment, command and staff positions were now occupied, from Pappy Wadlington on down, by officers not exactly prepared for them.

And during the first night along the Kum, K Company—now only forty men—had to be withdrawn and sent to Taejon for medical disposition. The company had reached such a state of deterioration that Wadlington felt they would be more liability than asset.

That left only Item and Love holding the river. Item and Love knew that there was no one west of them and that it was some two miles from their right flank to the 19th Infantry on their right.

All night 13 July, it rained on them, and they approached the dawn with no great enthusiasm. Then, early on the 14th, they heard tanks across the river.

Soon, tank cannon began to crack, flailing them with fire and steel. But the T-34's couldn't swim, and the shellfire did no great damage.

At midmorning, a scout ran back to L Company saying that Korean infantry was crossing the Kum two miles below them. More than five hundred were already across.

A liaison spotter plane from the 63rd Field reported NKPA ferrying across the river in two small boats, carrying thirty men each; the 63rd's Operations officer decided to wait for more lucrative targets. Then YAK fighters drove the spotter plane away.

Meanwhile Stith of L Company decided he'd better round up his supporting machine guns and mortars from the Weapons Company. He couldn't find them. Artillery and mortar fire now began to fall on Love.

Stith decided it was time to make tracks. He ordered L to withdraw from the Kum River heights. As L went back, one of its platoon leaders, Sergeant Wagnebreth, stopped to inform an officer of the 63rd Field Artillery that NKPA was south of the river; but the officer did not seem impressed with the news.

L Company went all the way back to Battalion HQ. When the Battalion C.O. found out what had happened, he relieved its commander on the spot and said he would court-martial him.

Meanwhile, I Company's acting C.O., Joe Hicks, was wondering what had happened to Love. He couldn't reach Battalion, either. Feeling rather lonely, Hicks stayed in place all day, under sporadic shelling. About dark, he received orders to rejoin the rest of the 34th back at Nonsan, and he pulled out.

The NKPA regiment that had crossed the Kum hadn't wanted Joe Hicks and Company—their scouts had filtered to the American rear and located a far richer target, the 63rd Field. The artillery battalion, consisting of only two firing batteries—artillery fat, as well as infantry, had been well sliced—Headquarters, and Service Battery, was positioned along a secondary road in the scrub- and pine-dotted low hills.

The 63rd Field was in fashion this Bastille Day, too. Its C.O. had taken sick and been evacuated to Taejon; Major William Dressler was in command. It had no communications with the infantry supposedly holding the Kum River line, and none with its own observers. It could talk only with the 34th HQ, which was to be no help.

In early afternoon, one of its outposts reported that enemy troops were in the hills. Battalion HQ told the outpost what it saw were friendly troops, and not to fire. Shortly thereafter, the outpost was captured, and its machine gun turned to fire on HQ Battery.

In this way, the 63rd Field learned it was under attack.

Mortar shells crashed into HQ Battery area, bursting with clouds of greasy smoke. A shell struck the battalion switchboard, destroying wire communication with the other batteries. Other shells burst on the CP, the medical section, and the radio truck, destroying all remaining communication left to the battalion.

An ammunition truck began to smoke, and when it went up, HQ Battery disintegrated into chaos, with men running in all directions. Machine guns flayed them. Bullets chopped holes in the doors of the Fire Direction Center hut.

Major Dressler jumped into a foxhole with a corporal, trying to fight back. Both men died there.

A few men of the battery escaped up a ravine leading to the south.

A Battery, only 250 yards away, drew fire at the same time. A company of approximately a hundred North Koreans ran into the battery, screaming and yelping, while mortar fire burst among the guns themselves.

Some of A's men fought back courageously with small arms. The battery commander was killed. Finally, some of them made it to the south, almost all without weapons of any kind.

Next, it was B Battery's turn. Four hundred enemy infantry surrounded the battery area, and for several minutes something akin to Custer's last stand was repeated. Then, while a group of ROK horse cavalry, who had ridden out of nowhere to attack the enemy, slashed into the North Koreans on the west, the artillerymen went march order.

They left their guns, after removing locks and sights.

The 63rd Field had now lost all ten guns and eighty vehicles. The five howitzers of A had been abandoned intact. Many men were missing.

Service Battery, overlooked in the first NKPA rush, was alerted by survivors from A. Service Battery marched fifteen miles south to Nonsan.

A straggler reached the 34th Infantry's CP at Ponggong-ni. When Lieutenant Colonel Pappy Wadlington understood what had occurred, he ordered Colonel Ayres' 1st Battalion to rescue the men and equipment that had been lost.

Late in the afternoon 1st Battalion marched north along the road, in attack column. Just as they came in sight of the 63rd's old position, they drew machine-gun and carbine fire.

The small-arms fire halted the battalion.

Ayres had been ordered to pull back if he could not accomplish the rescue by dark; it was now dusk. The 1st Battalion marched back to its old position. It did not remain there. It loaded into trucks and departed south for Nonsan.

That night, General Dean ordered an air strike on the abandoned matériel. The practice was becoming standard operating procedure.

It had been a bloody and tragic afternoon.

* * *

In the fading hours of 14 July, Bill Dean was still optimistic, although everything he knew of the art of war told him his hold on Taejon was precarious. But it was a forlorn optimism—again and again he ordered that the enemy be delayed; again and again his troops fell back, precipitating crisis. He knew that morale was crumbling, and he sent a message to his units:

"Hold everything we have until we find where we stand—might not be too bad—may be able to hold—make reconnaissance—may be able to knock these people out and reconsolidate. Am on my way out now."

His line was breached, and the 19th Infantry's flank exposed.

He was in trouble, but he was not yet beaten.

* * *

The 19th Infantry, the Rock of Chickamauga, on 14 July held the principal crossing places over the Kum, centered on Taep'yong-ni. The 34th Infantry was on its left flank, and ROK Army units held to its right. As the one remaining intact regiment of the 24th Division, the 19th was given the most critical frontage of the river line.

The total front, counting the bends and twists of the Kum, extended for thirty miles. Having only two rifle battalions, the 19th was forced to leave wide gaps between units, and in some places hope for the best. The Kum itself was 200 to 300 yards in width, with four- to eight-foot embankments, and the water varied from six to fifteen feet in depth. It was a formidable barrier to enemy penetration.

But it was also crisscrossed with sandbars, and in some places wadable.

The Chicks were well commanded on 14 July by Colonel Guy S. Meloy, Jr., a combat veteran of the big war. Stan Meloy, a competent and courageous officer, made both his presence and his confidence felt. He placed his 1st Battalion, under Lieutenant Colonel Otho Winstead, to the front, with his 2nd generally to its rear in reserve. He had six batteries of artillery in direct support. He put his regimental CP at the village of Palsan, back from the river on the main road.

During the day, some probing attacks came across the river. All failed.

Then, in late afternoon, Meloy learned of the collapse on his left flank. He had no choice but to move his 2nd Battalion, under Lieutenant Colonel Thomas McGrail, over to the left to prevent his thinly spread line from being taken in the flank and rear. Now he had only one company, F, in regimental reserve.

And he had lost the battle of the Kum River before it began.

He could expect no help from the 21st. Virtually unfit for combat after the battering it had taken, the weak Gimlets had been moved by General Dean east of Taejon to give the ROK's moral support, if nothing else.

As dark fell on 15 July, Stan Meloy alerted all his units to expect a night crossing. For two days an enemy buildup had been observed across the river. Air strikes had slammed into the enemy columns repeatedly, doing damage, but not halting them. The NKPA was growing wise to the ways of the now dominant American air power; it was staying off the roads by day, camouflaging its tanks and vehicles in wattle huts and orchards.

On both sides of the river the mud and straw villages were burning, set afire by air and artillery. As it grew dark, a hot, reddish glow overspread the muddy waters.

Then, small groups of NKPA waded into the river, trying to swim or wade across. The machine guns and recoilless rifles of the 19th butchered the majority of them, but a few sneaked onto the south shore.

As night deepened, there was sporadic firing. Smoke and the smell of cordite lay heavy over the uneasy lines facing the Kum. No one got any sleep.

Then, exactly at 0300 on 16 July, a single North Korean aircraft flew along the river. A flare popped behind it, and at the signal the north bank of the Kum blazed with fire.

Artillery, tank cannon, mortars, and small arms punished the south shore. The volume of fire was as great as anything Stan Meloy had seen in Europe—and under its cover North Koreans streamed down to the river. They jumped on boats and rafts; they waded; they swam, pouring into the river like a swarm of rats fleeing a forest fire.

Stan Meloy met them with everything he had. And at this critical moment one of the inevitable mishaps of war dealt him a damaging blow.

One 155mm howitzer of the 11th Field was firing flares on call. The flares gave 1st Battalion visibility over the river, and light to shoot by, but they were slightly off the main concentration of enemy. Colonel Winstead requested a slight shift in flare area. The shift should have taken at most a minute or two—but the gunners misunderstood the request, and completely moved the gun around.

For many long, crucial minutes the river stayed dark, and enemy infantry poured across.

Once on the south bank, they poured through the gap between Charley and Easy companies and took the 1st Platoon of C under attack. Hearing the violent firing, C's commander called Lieutenant Maher of the 1st Platoon by telephone.

Cheerfully, young Maher said, "We're doing fine."

He put down the phone and took a bullet in the head. Almost immediately, his platoon was overrun. The platoon sergeant was able to rejoin the company with only a dozen men.

Now, under cover of dark, with dawn only an hour away, the NKPA began to filter through the 1st Battalion and to fire on its mortar and CP positions.

To the left of the 19th's front, another crossing was taking place. At first light, men in B Company saw almost a battalion of North Koreans on the high ground to their left and rear. More were coming across every minute.

Then, suddenly, it seemed that the NKPA was everywhere. Colonel Winstead reported to Meloy that his CP and mortars were under attack and that the middle part of his line was falling back. Parts of both Able and Baker companies were overrun. The enemy was coming through the center of the regimental position.

This attack had to be contained. Meloy and Winstead began to organize a counterattack force. With no organized reserve, they called upon all cooks, drivers, mechanics, and clerks in the regiment, and every staff officer present.

This conglomerate force went into action, and by 0900 had driven the attack off. A few North Koreans even fled back to the river and recrossed it. Leading the counterattack, both the 1st Battalion S-3, Major Cook, and the adjutant, Captain Hackett, were killed.

Breathing a sigh of relief, Meloy called Dean and reported he had the situation under control.

But Stan Meloy, this confused morning, did not know the whole picture. Almost immediately, Colonel Winstead reported that enemy units were raising hell in his rear areas, and he had nothing with which to fight them. The artillery batteries were under fire, and screaming for assistance.

Something had happened to the air support, which was supposed to be on call at dawn.

Then, a roadblock was reported three miles behind the regiment on the main supply road. Ammunition trucks could not get up to the units.

Enemy infiltrators struck against F Company, the single reserve force, and pinned it down by fire.

Colonel Meloy and his S-3, Major Logan, went back to check on the roadblock in their rear, which was being rapidly reinforced by the enemy infiltrators streaming through the hills. Many of the enemy wore white robes, disguised as farmers.

At the roadblock, Meloy found a sad situation. The American troops in the area, mostly service troops, were not trying to reduce the block, which was a narrow pass between a stream and a forty-foot embankment covered by fire. These troops were lying around, completely disorganized, firing in the general direction of the block, doing no damage at all.

Meloy immediately jumped in and tried to get some order. As he tried to get a group of men to attack the high ground above the pass, he was hit and severely wounded.

He told Logan to pass the command to Colonel Winstead, of the 1st Battalion. Logan, after notifying Winstead, finally reached through to General

Dean's HQ in Taejon. He told Dean that the situation was poor, Meloy down, and Winstead now in command. Dean, worried, replied that he would send men to force the roadblock, and for the 19th to withdraw at once—but to try to bring its equipment out with it. As soon as these messages had been sent, an enemy shell struck the regimental radio truck, and all contact with Division was cut off.

Winstead then ordered Logan to do something about the roadblock, while he went back to his battalion and tried to bring it back from the river. It was now past noon.

Now, in middle summer, the monsoon rains had finally ended, and the Korean sun was beginning to sear with all its fury. By early afternoon the thermometer reached 100 degrees, and the hillsides became humid furnaces. The soldiers of the 19th were in no better physical shape than the other Japanese occupation troops; they were unused to heat and unused to the steep Korean slopes. This was their first action, but they had had no real rest or sleep for three nights. The long midsummer day, with sixteen hours of daylight, following a night of battle, began to be too much for them.

The lightly armed Koreans continued to pour through the hills and take up positions on the high ground in the regiment's rear. The NKPA ran through the valleys stolidly, and bounded up the ridges like rabbits; they had been doing it all their lives.

If Colonel Meloy had had an adequate reserve, he would not have had to lead men personally against the damaging roadblock. The enemy parties in his rear could have done no real damage, and he could have reduced them one by one, since the main line was able to hold until ordered to withdraw.

But every available fighting man was on line up against the Kum, and there was nothing to wipe up the rampaging infiltrators in the rear. By noon, too, demoralization had begun to set in among the men. The long night and the burning sun had reduced them to panting exhaustion. Ordered to climb the high ground to knock the enemy off the blocking positions, the majority of them lay down and looked the other way.

Under fire, the line companies along the river began to withdraw on Winstead's order. Coming out of line, they found they still had a long way to go. From hills and bushes in their rear, enemy machine guns chattered at them.

Again and again, officers were simply not able to organize attacks against the enfilading hills to clear the way. It wasn't that the men were afraid—they were simply unable to walk up the hills to engage the North Koreans.

Trying to organize his men, Winstead was killed.

F Company, the supposed reserve force, was ordered to attack the major roadblock to the south. It was under fire and could not leave its reserve position.

To the south, General Dean was making every attempt to organize a force to rescue the 19th's 1st Battalion. The 19th 2nd Battalion, under McGrail, was ordered to come up from its position on the east flank and break the roadblock.

Colonel McGrail, coming up the road from the south, ran into heavy North Korean fire. His vehicles were set afire, and he was pinned down in a ditch while many men around him were killed or wounded. His G Company, trying to attack the ridges over the roadblock, took casualties and was forced to dig in. The 2nd Battalion men could not climb the hills, either.

At dusk, the effort to break the roadblock ended.

Meanwhile, all afternoon, the troops on the north had waited for the block to clear. Some men did not wait, but began to head south through the hills. Staff officers decided to place Colonel Meloy in the one light tank available and to try to get him to safety. The tank got through, leading about twenty vehicles. Just south of the roadblock, the tank engine failed.

None of the vehicles it had escorted through stopped to pick up its crew or the wounded Meloy. Meloy, badly hurt but conscious, ordered the tank commander to drop a thermite grenade down the hatch while he lay in the ditch and watched.

Later in the night, an officer finally returned with a truck and rescued Meloy and several other wounded men who had gathered with him.

An hour after Meloy was sent out, the officer commanding north of the roadblock, Captain Fenstermacher, told the 500 men remaining to prepare for movement out cross-country. He passed orders to set the 100 waiting vehicles afire with gasoline, and as he did so, fell shot through the throat. At dusk, the men scattered into the hills.

Some of them made it. Some did not. Some of the wounded they brought out, others they left behind. One chaplain, Herman Felhoelter, refused to leave the wounded when the unhurt men would no longer carry them. A sergeant, watching from another hill through his field glasses, saw Felhoelter killed by the NKPA along with his charges as he knelt over them, praying.

All night, and all the next day, the remnants of the 19th Regiment streamed into Taejon and the surrounding villages. Only two companies, E and G of the 2nd Battalion, were intact. Less than half of the 1st Battalion came back. The regimental HQ had taken unusual losses in both officers and enlisted men. The supporting artillery had lost heavily, too.

On 17 July, General Dean relieved the 19th with B Company of the 34th. The Rock of Chickamauga then moved twenty-five miles southeast of Taejon to reorganize and reequip.

* * *

The battle for Taejon was lost. General Dean knew that he now had only the remnants of three defeated regiments, each one little better than a battalion in size. The 21st had come apart at Osan and Choch'iwon; the 34th had been shattered successively at P'yongt'aek, and Ch'onan; the 19th had bought it at the Kum River. Not only were the regiments weak in men and equipment; they were exhausted and their morale was poor.

Dean himself was worn down. For fourteen days he had lived from crisis to crisis without a breathing spell. He did not plan to make a last ditch stand in Taejon, though he did plan to delay there.

But on 18 July General Walton Walker, commanding Eighth Army, flew into Taejon. Walker had been assembling a great deal of data on the Korean situation, and was becoming nervous to know when and where the enemy was going to be stopped. Back home, the Pentagon was still putting out sweetness and light over the intervention and "police action," but Johnny Walker's own pants were beginning to burn, however confident the Pentagon remained.

On 11 July, an official communiqué reported "65 enemy tanks damaged or destroyed." On the same date Tokyo claimed that the "morale of North Korean troops was reported cracking under the steady hammering from the air."

On 13 July 1950 the *New York Times,* reporting the request of the Army for 20,000 draftees, said, *Draftee duty set—none will go to Korea soon,* "and not many at all," *Army says.*

On 14 July the *Times* also carried the following dispatch, datelined 13 July, Tokyo:

> *Front dispatches have greatly exaggerated American losses in one of the most skillful and heroic holding and rearguard actions in history although out-numbered at times more than 20 to 1, and the casualties inflicted on the enemy have been immeasurably greater than they have sustained.*

On admitting the loss of the Kum River Line, the *Times* quoted the Pentagon as saying: *Enemy said to use 150,000 men in the onslaught, led by Russian tanks, some weighing 60 tons*—though the attack had been mounted by less than 20,000 NKPA, and the largest tank sighted in Korea had been the 34-ton T-34. Bad news was always offset by the mention of insuperable odds.

The *Times,* widely quoted by other newspapers across the land, reported 16 July 1950 that "General Collins (J. Lawton Collins, Chief of Staff) spoke well of American troops and their equipment. 'In spite of their greenness,' the Army Chief said, 'the troops had done an exceptionally fine job.' "

The same day Tokyo commented that "morale and combat efficiency remained excellent despite the necessity of withdrawals and holding actions."

There was constant talk of air power and air attacks and the damage air was doing to the enemy. Gradually, the reports became almost plaintive, as air power remained unable to stem the North Korean advance.

Side by side with the official Pentagon and Tokyo communiqués, however, there were stories by men such as Richard J. S. Johnston and Hanson Baldwin, of the *New York Times.* Johnston reported troops as saying, "I never saw such a useless damn war in my life," and wrote: *In the last few bloody days of fighting the bravado and self-assurance have given way—*

One of the problems, in 1950, was to recognize the problem.

Walker had decided that he could hold along the Naktong River in south-eastern Korea with the divisions and troops now on the way. Already, his boss, MacArthur, had developed plans for taking the enemy in the rear by amphibious assault—but such a plan was worthless unless the enemy advance could be stopped short of the Naktong.

Talking with Bill Dean at the 34th Infantry CP, Walker told Dean he needed two more days' delay in Taejon, so that the 1st Cavalry and 25th divisions could deploy to the city's east. Then he flew back to his own HQ at Taegu, above Pusan.

His chief of staff asked Walker how much rope he had given Dean, and Walker replied, "I told him that I had every confidence in him, and that if it became necessary for him to abandon Taejon earlier, to make his own decision, and I'd sustain him. Dean is a fighter. He won't give an inch if he can help it."

Johnny Walker was right.

General Dean was to be much criticized for remaining inside the city as it fell. The majority of the men complaining did not comprehend the situation on the ground in Korea. They could not understand that a senior commander, issuing orders for a last-ditch defense from a safe position in the rear, was apt to be trampled in the rush.

The United States Army, understandably, has been reluctant to discuss the problem, even among its own. Once it had returned to the bosom of a permissive society, and tried to adopt that society's ways, its own hands were tied. Once it had gone on the defensive to its critics, it would never regain the initiative. When the answer to a problem is not immediately at hand, the better part of valor is to ignore it.

Dean had almost no communications. If he wanted to know what was happening to the front-line troops, he had to be on the front lines. He had found, sadly, that it was much easier to get a message to the rear than it was to get one carried forward.

In the chaotic situation along his front, with units continually breaking contact and moving south, Dean could never be sure of the real situation. This was one reason he would stay so long in Taejon.

He had three basic reasons for remaining inside the beleaguered city; one, to keep up the crumbling morale of the 34th Infantry and the other defenders by the sight of their commander moving shoulder to shoulder with them; two, to set an example for the ROK officers and staffs fighting alongside the Americans, who by now had all virtually climbed on the Pusan Express; and three, Bill Dean wanted to see close up just what kind of fighting cat the North Korean was.

As he would write later, he was too close to the forest to see the trees.

The North Korean assault on Taejon was like all other North Korean attacks—they crashed into the defenders head on pinning them down, forcing them back, while at the same time they flanked or infiltrated to the rear and blocked the defenders' retreat. At any given moment, it was impossible for Dean or any other commander to know what the situation was to his rear; this was a kind of tactic that the Europe-trained American officers, who liked to keep tidy lines, could not grasp until too late.

As it developed, Dean kept what he wanted of the 34th in the city, and sent other elements of the division, including his own HQ, to the east. As he would say much later, what he did afterward could have been done by any competent sergeant—but in saying this, Dean was thinking of the old Army, not the forces of 1950.

There is no point to detailing the day-by-day and street-by-street actions during the next three days. They were repetitions of what befell the Americans earlier. The NKPA attacked. The defenders fought, then fell back. The enemy got into their rear, and cut them off. The Americans disintegrated and saved what they could.

On the morning of 20 July Dean awoke to heavy gunfire as the ragged line drawn around Taejon continued to shrink. The city was now afire in many places, the stench of smoking thatch competing with that of gunpowder and the underlying filth of the Orient. And by the morning of the 20th, Dean realized that his hope that help might arrive if he held two days was fading. The dispirited defenders were beginning to straggle back into town, and the ring of gunfire was drawing tighter.

Then, just after dawn, Dean heard that North Korean tanks were in the town. Dean was at the CP of the 34th Infantry. The 34th had now no further contact with its two battalions—as usual; it did not know where the flanks were, or even where the war was. For the first time in days Bill Dean had no command decisions to make.

He decided to go tank hunting. He did not know it, but Colonel Beauchamp, to whom he had just given command of the 34th, was doing the same. Like Colonel Martin, Beauchamp had found everyone deathly sick of the T-34's, but now things were just a bit better, for a few of the new 3.5-inch bazookas, designed to stop any known armor, had been flown in from the States.

With Beauchamp guiding and directing a team, the 3.5's knocked out one tank west of Taejon.

Inside the city, Dean, with his aide, Lieutenant Clarke, and his ROK interpreter, Kim, found a soldier with one of the new rocket launchers and went tank hunting.

The little party found two on a street, just behind a burning American ammunition carrier. The tanks opened fire with machine guns, forcing the hunters into buildings along the street. But the smoke lay so heavily over the city now that Dean and his men were able to creep up closer, and to the rear of the tanks.

The tanks turned around, and started to come back toward them. The bazooka man took aim, but he was shaking too badly to hold true. When he fired, he blew up the street a few yards in front of him.

He had only one round of ammunition.

Arrogantly, like all the tanks of the Inmun Gun, the T-34 waddled on past Bill Dean and party. Dean lost his temper. Pulling out his .45 automatic, he emptied the magazine at the monster as it clanked past.

Then Dean and party got the hell out of there.

Meanwhile, hundreds of North Korean soldiers, disguised in the white robes of farmers, were infiltrating into the city. Once inside, they threw off the misleading civilian attire and opened fire on American troops. Soon snipers were everywhere.

Using HQ and service personnel, American officers were having very poor success in rooting them out. Most American boys no longer knew how to play cowboys and Indians, particularly with live ammunition.

By afternoon, Dean had located another bazooka man, this time with an ammo bearer.

Dodging sniper fire, shooting a few snipers on the way, his party hunted up another tank. But this target was covered by North Korean infantry, and rifle fire kept them from getting close. Dean and the bazooka men sneaked back through a Korean courtyard, and climbed up to the second story of a house facing the street.

Here, cautiously looking out the street window, Dean saw the muzzle of the tank's 85mm gun pointed at him, not more than a dozen feet away.

The bazooka man aimed where Dean pointed, and fired. The blowback from the rocket shook the whole room. The shaped charge burned into the tank at the juncture of turret and body.

From the tank came a shrill, horrible ululation.

"Hit 'em again!" Dean said.

After the third round, the screaming ended abruptly, and the T-34 began to smoke.

Somehow, the long day drew to an end. Dean knew now that it was time to pull out of the city, and at the 34th's CP he also found that there was a road-block across the escape route east. While he was preparing to shoot his way out of Taejon, several light tanks from the 1st Cavalry fought their way into town to assist Dean's withdrawal.

Dean sent the HQ of the 34th out with them, and soon heard them firing from the edge of town.

It was now dark. Colonel Pappy Wadlington, who had remained with Dean, suggested it was time for Dean to get out himself. He wanted to send a message asking for more tanks to assist the general's retreat.

Dean didn't buy it. It smacked too much of asking for help personally. He did send a message for armor to reduce the roadblock east of Taejon, and then he and the remaining men around him got into their vehicles and started down the street the tanks had gone.

Soon, they reached the earlier convoy. It had been ambushed, and burning trucks filled the streets. The buildings on both sides of the streets were afire, and American infantry was engaged along the side in a vicious battle with enemy troops.

Dean's jeep hurtled through, screeching around the stalled and flaming trucks, while the heat seared him and the men with him. The driver poured it on, and a block farther on, roared through an intersection. Lieutenant Clarke, Dean's aide, shouted, "We missed our turn!"

But sniper fire was smacking the pavement all around; it was impossible to turn the jeep about. Dean ordered the driver to keep straight ahead; they would take the long way around to safety.

It was the long way around indeed. Because he took the wrong turn, Bill Dean would not rejoin the American Army until September, 1953. Thirty-five days later, after wandering lost in the hills, after making heroic attempts to reach his own lines, Bill Dean was betrayed to the Inmun Gun by Koreans. When they jumped him, he tried to make them kill him, but they put ropes around his wrists and dragged him to a police station. There they threw him in a cage, the sort reserved for the town drunk.

Only much later did the Inmun Gun realize that the old-looking, filthy, 130-pound emaciated soldier they had captured was an American general.

General Dean once said that he wouldn't award himself a wooden star for what he did as a commander. His country saw more clearly.

It gave him the Medal of Honor.

10

Retreating

There is no one but yourself to keep your back door open.

—Lieutenant General Walton H. Walker, Commanding Eighth Army, to
Major General Hobart R. Gay, CG 1st Calvary Division, July 1950.

A T NOON 22 JULY, the units of the 24th Division holding at Yongdong
east of Taejon turned over the front to the 1st Calvary Division. At
the same time General Walker ordered Major General John H.
Church to assume command in the absence of General Dean.

In seventeen days of combat, the 24th Division had been driven back one
hundred miles. It had lost enough matériel to equip a full-strength infantry
division. Its losses in personnel had amounted to more than 30 percent, of
which an unusually high portion had been senior officers. More than twenty-
four hundred men were missing in action.

But had it not been committed, the balance of the United States Forces
could never have established themselves in Korea. Without the extra days
General Dean gave Walker at Taejon, the final defense of Pusan probably
would have failed.

There had been hundreds of acts of heroism in the 24th, as well as acts that
reflected no credit on the service. But most of the heroic actions had been
those of individuals, of single officer or men who fought bravely and well.
Because without tight discipline their bravery could not be coordinated into a
team effort, many of these men died in vain.

Every American fighting man, seeing the decimated, dirty, exhausted, and
weaponless 24th Infantry Division pushed back beyond Taejon, could only say
to himself, "There but for the grace of God go I."

For the 24th Division was certainly no weaker than the Army as a whole.
The other divisions from Japan, the 25th, the 1st Cavalry, the 7th Infantry, displayed the identical weaknesses of the 24th as each was committed to action.

None of them were equipped, trained, or mentally prepared for combat. For
the first time in recent history, American ground units had been committed

during the initial days of a war; there had been no allies to hold the line while America prepared. For the first time, many Americans could understand what had happened to Britain at Dunkirk.

Almost subconsciously, Americans had come to believe there would always be someone else to hold the line at first.

Once aroused, a democracy can match a totalitarian state in every facet of strength-it can be stronger, for totalitarianism has built-in bureaucratic weaknesses. A Hitler can command, and men march—but a Hitler can go mad—and there is no one to say him nay.

But the abiding weakness of free peoples is that their governments can not or will not make them prepare or sacrifice before they are aroused.

The majority of the young men of the other divisions thrown into Korea now in late July were no more interested in being soldiers than the men of the 24th had been. They had enlisted for every reason known to man except to fight. They had no real antagonism for the enemy system, nor any desire to oppose it. They had no understanding of their nation's position in the world, or of the course their government must take. And their government was slow to waken to what its supposed legions had become.

Lacking professionalism, the men and junior officers did not have even the dash and pride of standard and outfit that men like De Vigny had been able to restore to the defeated French Army. With this pride of unit and profession, and with iron discipline, they would have fought differently.

The government, slow to understand, did nothing to remedy the situation. It did not seriously explain the world situation to the troops, or the United States' stake in it. Unquestionably, the government had hoped in the early days and weeks that the Korean conflict could be quickly contained, a hope the pitiful condition of its ground forces rendered forlorn from the start.

Soldiers fight from discipline and training, citizens from motivation and ideals. Lacking both, it is amazing that the American troops did even as well as they did. For as Colonel Dick Stephens of the 21st Infantry said, "The men and officers had no interest in a fight which was not even dignified by being called a war. It was a bitter fight in which many lives were lost, and we could see no profit in it. . . ."

And once they were committed, the Pentagon seemed to be living in its own dream world of optimism. It should have been clear from the start that America was entering a very real, if limited, war, and in war the outcome is usually in doubt. Day after day, the official briefings gave neither the public and the troops at home a real picture of the actual situation.

Though a number of armchair strategists and second-year ROTC students with a map could figure it out, and did.

Among those sickened by the official releases, which sometimes approached the dream world of the Imperial Japanese Government while being hammered to pieces by American might in World War II, was the *New York Times* military writer, Major Hanson Baldwin, who wrote, ". . . the Pentagon . . . has too often disseminated a soothing syrup of cheer and sweetness and light since the fighting began."

Nor were all the newsmen, particularly those writing from Korea, clear as to the real facts. Rarely has any conflict been so badly reported. Again and again in late July, dispatches referred to "wave after wave of screaming North Koreans" crashing against American lines. Newspaper after newspaper printed the fact that "we are still outnumbered at least four to one." Some papers put the figure at ten to one. The *New York Times* carried one story in which a junior officer claimed, "We were doing good against odds of better than 15 to 1 until we ran out of ammunition." In this, the Army aided and abetted them, and did nothing to disillusion them. The Army commanders had their own problems without trying to help newsmen understand the war.

In actuality, the NKPA held a slight superiority in men on 20 July. By 22 July, U.N. and North Korean forces were on a par, and by the end of July United Nations forces actually outnumbered the Inmun Gun, an advantage they never again lost.

But men are not ciphers, nor do the battles always go to the big battalions.

The correspondents saw, and were often quick to report, the command failures—which were many. Stories did spread of ranking officers removed from command, or put on planes for Japan in states of nervousness and collapse. Since the occupation divisions had been at full peacetime stance, a certain number of officers with no aptitude for leading men in combat had been assigned to them, as is inevitable in any peacetime army.

But few correspondents saw that officers, giving crucial commands, could never be sure if their orders would be obeyed. A colonel who sends men to hold a vital hill, and who sees them again and again "take a vote on it with their feet" by marching to the rear, is soon apt to be a straitjacket case.

One highly decorated colonel, known to his men as "Cash Pays the Rent" Corley, wrote HQ: "I want double the TO of officers with each unit—one to lead and the other to drive."

Or if they saw, their stories were not printed. A free press is equally free to print the truth or ignore it, as it chooses.

* * *

On 22 July, the 1st Cavalry Division (Infantry) went into action at Yongdong, east of Taejon. The 25th Infantry Division moved into line in the Sangju area, to the southeast.

Yongdong was lost. The 25th moved south.

The fighting was confused, hellish, and bloody. In the main, it repeated the actions earlier in the month. The new divisions repeated the same weaknesses of the 24th, and did no better.

The front continued to move south.

Many men and units, unprepared for combat, fought creditably and more than creditably when unexpectedly thrown into battle. But even these could not stem the tide. From Okinawa, two battalions of the 29th Infantry Regiment were diverted to Korea. Unready for combat, the 29th was promised six weeks of training in Japan in the middle of July. But the front kept moving south, and the promise could not be kept. On 25 July, the two battalions found themselves on the front line at Chinju. In their ranks were four hundred brand-new recruits. Their newly issued rifles were not zeroed; their mortars were yet untest-fired; their new machine guns still oozed cosmoline.

Lieutenant Colonel Harold W. Mott, commanding 3rd Battalion, 29th Infantry, received orders to move forward to seize the town of Hadong.

In Chinju was a ROK major general—Chae Byong Duk. Chae talked to the Americans about the deteriorating situation, and although he had only a few soldiers of his own, begged permission to join the Americans. They agreed to let him come along, but with the understanding that the ROK general was to serve only as interpreter and guide to Colonel Mott. The former chief of staff of the Republic of Korea agreed.

At Hadong Pass the next day, Chae and the American command group saw a group of soldiers approaching their newly prepared defensive positions. Many of these men seemed to be in American uniforms, though some wore the Communist mustard-brown. When the motley group was only one hundred yards away, Chae stepped forward and called to them.

"What unit?"

The group rushed into the ditches. The Americans along the pass opened fire with machine guns. And enemy fire blazed into the pass from the men in the ditches and some who had walked onto high ground to the north.

Chae Byong Duk, struck in the head, fell dead in a great pool of arterial blood. Two of his aides, loyal to the last, picked up his body under fire and took it to a truck. Chae Byong Duk, whatever his failings and whatever his mistakes, died a soldier.

In the same burst of fire Colonel Mott and several of his staff officers were wounded. Immediately, the battalion was under heavy fire, and heavy attack from two sides.

It fought well until enveloped by the enemy. Ordered to withdraw, the battalion experienced the same weakness of many American units; weakened by casualties, particularly among officers, it came apart.

Leaving more than three hundred dead behind it, a hundred prisoners, and most of its officers, the remnants of the battalion reached Chinju. Many men had retained only their boots and shorts by the time they reached safety.

Shortly afterward, the battalion was reorganized, and its companies sent to fill the gaps in the 19th Infantry, 24th Division.

The front continued to move south and east.

Lieutenant General Walton H. Walker, with HQ at Taegu, was aware that Eighth Army was approaching crisis. He was unhappy with the performance of General Kean's 25th Division at Sangju, and he let Kean know about it.

He saw the 1st Cavalry Division falling back on the Taejon-Taegu axis with alacrity. He made known his disappointment to General Hobart Gay, the division commander.

Gay, who had been Patton's chief of staff in Europe, admitted he did not know how to conduct a retreat—thus far in this military experience he had never been involved in one.

In addition to the problems of understrength units and missing batteries and battalions, lack of communications, and poor equipment, shaky morale and weak discipline, Eighth Army faced another problem, one that grew as summer lengthened.

July and August of 1950 were abnormally dry for Korea; the monsoon ended early, in blazing heat and droughts. The temperature soared to unusual heights, reaching 120 degrees at times.

The hillsides of South Korea are steep; often slopes of 60 degrees are found on low ridges. Under the sullen sun, the ridges shimmered like furnaces, and there was almost no shade in the scrubby brush that covered them.

And there is very little drinking water, outside the brownish stuff in the fecal paddies.

The land viewed from afar is beautiful, rolling terraces and rice paddies, each a subtly different shade of green. But each paddy is a humid, stinking oven, and the bare hills are like broiler plates.

When they left their trucks and moved up onto the hills and ridges, American soldiers, as one officer put it, "dropped like flies." Their legs, unused to hard pulls, gave out. The heat and exertion gave them throbbing headaches. During these weeks exhaustion and heat knocked out more men than NKPA bullets.

Short of water, lacking water discipline, they drank from ditches and paddies, developed searing dysentery.

They sweated until their shirts and belts rotted, and their bellies turned shark-white. Salt tablets became such an item of priority that they had to be air-dropped on units, along with vital ammunition.

Korea is a land cut by multiple hills and valleys, lacking roads. It is no terrain for a mechanized army. The principal—and sometimes only—means of getting from one place to another through the hills is shank's mare.

But American troops, physically unhardened for foot marches, were road-bound. They defended on roads, attacked on roads, retreated on roads. If their vehicles couldn't go, they did not go either.

FEAF soon made the roads unpopular with the Inmun Gun. On the roads, tactical air strafed them, rocketed them, burned them. The Inmun Gun left the roads and went over the ridges, and it seemed to bother them not at all. They went stolidly up the slopes with the patient, sideways, Korean peasant tread, and they carried their machine guns, mortars, and mountains of ammunition with them.

They set their guns up on the high ground behind the Americans, interdicting their supply roads. Americans had trouble attacking up the hills to knock them off. And when their roads were blocked, Americans could hardly drag themselves over the hills to safety, let alone their heavy equipment. Second to the Soviets, the American Army became the principal supplier to the Inmun Gun of guns and ammunition.

The great problem was that in 1950, an infantryman in Korea was called on to do almost the same things Caesar's legions had done, and to suffer the same hardships. In twenty centuries, infantry warfare has changed but little in the burdens it puts on the men in the mud. But in 1950, while ground warfare had changed little, the American society and the American soldier had.

In American society the best weapon against a convertible may be another convertible, but in Korea it is apt to be a good pair of legs.

Johnny Walker, a tenacious little bulldog of a Texan, seeing the poor performance of his men, began to feel a certain warmth in his own britches area. He requested MacArthur to come to Korea, and they conferred, with only General Almond present. MacArthur said there was going to be no Korean evacuation, no repetition of Dunkirk. Walker agreed.

Walker moved among his divisions afterward and began to lay down the law. On 26 July he had issued a warning order for a planned withdrawal to defensive position behind the Naktong River, but now he put out an order that was promptly tagged by the press as "stand or die."

Walker knew Eighth Army would have to fall back more—he did not intend the order to be one to stand or die. But he was doing everything he could to slow the southward rush. A determination to stand—somewhere— had to be instilled in all ranks.

Walker's presence up and down the line was felt to good effect, though his order of 29 July had little effect other than in the press.

The front moved south. On 1 August, Walker commanded an orderly withdrawal across the Naktong, the last natural defense barrier to the port of Pusan. Once across, the bridges were to be blown, and all hands were to dig in for a final stand.

Behind the Naktong, Eighth Army would be only fifty miles from the sea.

The American and ROK divisions streamed back across the Naktong for several days, sometimes breaking contact with the NKPA, against Walker's instructions. By the evening of 3 August, all were across except a battalion of the 8th Cavalry, acting as rear guard. This battalion was on the west side of the river at Waegwan, preparing to come across so that the bridge could be dynamited.

But this rear guard had a problem.

Thousands upon thousands of Korean civilian refugees were pressing upon these men, clamoring to be let across the bridge. Hundreds of thousands of South Koreans, frightened of the Inmun Gun, were fleeing south ahead of, with, and behind the fighting forces, complicating their job enormously.

As the rear guard came across the bridge to the east side, throngs of Koreans followed them, filling the bridge with jostling bodies. General Hobart Gay, who had ordered the bridge to be sent up only at his express command, instructed them to go back to the far side, and clear the bridge.

This they did, as dusk approached. Then, with the refugees pushed back onto the west shore, the rear guard turned and pelted across to the friendly bank—but the second they turned, the Koreans dashed madly for the bridge and soon filled it, even before the cavalrymen were across.

Three times, at Gay's order, they repeated the maneuver, without success. Short of shooting them there was no way to keep the Koreans from using the bridge. Even telling them it would be blown did no good.

Now it was growing dark, and the Inmun Gun was closing. As the rear guard recrossed to the east side for the third time, with the mass of Koreans close behind them, Hobart Gay, his face pale, said, "Blow it." He had no other choice.

Several hundred Koreans went into the river with the bridge.

11

Perimeter

There will be no more retreating, withdrawal, or readjustment of the lines, or anything else you want to call it.

—Lieutenant General Walton H. (Johnny) Walker, to the staff of the 25th Division.

B Y 4 AUGUST the entire United Nations force—the U.N. had now given the command of its effort over to the United States, and the Republic of Korea, though not a member, had placed its Armed Forces under U.N. command—had reeled into the Pusan Perimeter. So far only the ROK's and three occupation divisions from Japan had been engaged, and they had been blooded, knocked about, and pushed back. They had lost mountains of equipment and thousands of men. Staggering back into the small remaining toehold at the corner of the peninsula, the fighting men were exhausted, dispirited, and bitter.

Walton Walker reported to MacArthur that the 24th Division needed complete rehabilitation and that he had grave doubts as to the offensive capabilities of the 25th.

Behind the Naktong River the U.N. held only a rectangular box of terrain ranging one hundred miles from north to south and fifty miles across. On the west was the barrier Naktong. Across the north rose high and rugged mountains, difficult for an attacker to penetrate. On all other sides was the sea.

But at the bottom of the rectangle lay the major port of Pusan, now pumping renewed American strength into the peninsula. Working around the clock, transportation and technical-service people poured in ton after ton of supplies to replenish those the divisions lost. More important, men began to arrive in a continual stream. In Japan, Operation Flushout had separated thousands of American troops from their desks and other jobs, and thrown them into the fighting. Replacements were beginning to arrive from the States. All over the world, the Army had turned the vacuum cleaner on, and at its apex was Pusan.

Help was on the way.

And here, behind the Naktong, the tenor of the war began to change.

Within the box, from north to south, Walton Walker had eight divisions: the ROK 3rd, Capital, 8th, 6th, and 1st, plus ROK manpower to assimilate within the weakened American units; the 1st Cavalry, the 24th, and 25th infantry divisions, and 5th Regimental Combat Team from Hawaii.

Now, behind barriers, with a definite piece of ground to defend, Walker could form for the first time a continuous battle line. Eighth Army was spread margarine-thin across the land—but at last it had anchored flanks, refused to the enemy. There were great gaps in the line, but at least it was a line.

And slowly, painfully, reaching eagerly for every man, Walker was putting together a reserve. Each morning he demanded of his chief of staff, "How many reserves have you got me?"

For the first time, American commanders could plan for combat as they had been trained for it—with known friendly forces on either flank, and with help in the form of a reserve to their rear.

A great and continuing weakness of the United States Army fighting in Asia was its tactical and psychological dependence on continuous battle lines, such as had been known in Europe. In Asia, terrain and Communist tactics made such lines rare—Communist armies tended to flow like the sea, washing around strong points, breaking through places where the dams were weak. The "human sea" analogy picked up and headlined by the press was very real—except that the press always gave a misleading indication of the numbers of enemy involved.

Relatively small numbers of enemy flowed around the high ground held by American troops, went behind them, and interdicted their supply roads. Roadbound, the American commanders became understandably nervous. Invariably, both men and leaders began to think of retreat, falling back to form a new line. This was in many respects a frame of mind. The North Korean forces in the American rear were small, ill supplied, and in effect often cut off from contact with their own bases.

Able to live on three rice balls a day, capable of carrying guns and ammunition over the steepest slopes on foot, this isolation bothered the Communists not at all.

It drove the Americans, hating isolated action, dependent upon wheels, to desperation. Ironically, the Indian-fighting army of seventy-five years earlier would have understood the new form of warfare perfectly. On the plains and mountains of the American West, the United States Army had once learned everything there was to learn about hit-and-run tactics and guerrilla warfare. It had learned to ride hard and march hard, live light, and to operate in isolated columns, giving the enemy no rest.

But even hard lessons can be soon forgotten.

In August, however, within a tight little box, the United States Army could at last fight the way it had been trained, and it could finally bring its inherently superior firepower to bear. And its mechanization, a handicap when scattered over long supply lines vulnerable to interdiction, became an asset, since troops could be rushed within the interior lines from one spot to another as needed, faster than the foot-bound enemy could exploit a breakthrough.

Within the perimeter, the American soldier began to put up a better fight, a fight he could hardly have been expected to wage when committed a battalion or a regiment at a time, with no friends to right or left, and his rear vulnerable.

And in August 1950, other factors took effect. After a month and more of battle, the first sense of incredible shock had worn off the green United States troops. They had now learned what to do the hard way.

They had also learned that they would not be withdrawn. Walton Walker told them, "A retreat to Pusan would be one of the greatest butcheries in history." If they did not hold along the Naktong, they stood to be slaughtered. There was, to say the least, an incentive to hold.

And finally, while most Americans can be pushed around a great deal, there comes a time when they will be pushed no more.

They had not been told why they were in Korea or why they must fight and die, but in many men a certain pride took hold. The "gooks" had pushed them around long enough.

Undisciplined, untrained, unhating, they had come to battle. They had been clobbered, as American citizen-soldiers had usually been clobbered in their first battles, from Bull Run to Kasserine. Only gradually did men understand the nature of the job they had to do.

Once they did, they would begin to do it.

*   *   *

It was the boast of the great Frederick that when he went to war neither the peasants of the fields nor the tradesmen of his towns should know or care. Because Frederick involved his small state of Prussia in wars too big for even his iron grenadiers, he was not quite able to live up to his boast—but it is an accurate statement of the conditions of warfare in the Age of Reason.

In the eighteenth century, men and rulers were sick to death of unlimited war. For almost two centuries jihad had been preached; armies had crossed Europe like ravening locusts; millions had died; and at the end of the savagery nothing had been accomplished. The survivors still insisted on being Calvinists, Catholics, or Lutherans, short of extermination.

In Frederick's time men were still men, and they must compete—but they no longer trusted the angel's trumpet, or would have heeded had it blown. Wars there still were, but they developed in a new, a limited, fashion: to snatch a province here, to defend one there, to place a friendly head upon some throne, or to remove an unfriendly one from it.

The statesmen of Europe, even though they fought, wanted a certain order to the world. They called it the balance of power. It was a desperately fragile system, but it was the best they could design.

After two hundred years, and after a new resort to savagery in the period of the "nations in arms," men had still evolved nothing with any more promise. There was a new hope of an eventual world order through the uniting of all nations in peace, but the hope was still only that, and no more. Power remained the fulcrum of world action. And unless some sort of balance could be maintained, the world would once again erupt in perhaps the last of all "holy" wars.

When the Soviet bloc pushed at the balance of world order in 1950, the men in the United States Government reacted the best way they knew how. So far as they would be able, they would reject resort to cataclysmic war. They felt, in their hearts, that a final test of strength between Communist and non-Communist would in the end decide nothing, except who remained alive in a shattered world. They would accept such a test only as a last resort.

They accepted, tacitly, to play the Communist game of limited war, for limited ends. It must never be forgotten that the game was pushed upon them—they did not precipitate it. Their cruel choice was that of cataclysm, humiliation, or surrender.

On 16 July 1950 the *New York Times* in a superbly worded editorial said: *Our emotions as we watch our outnumbered, out-weaponed soldiers in Korea must be a mingling of pity, sorrow, and admiration. This is the sacrifice we asked of them, justified only by the hope that what they are now doing will help to keep this war a small war, and that the death of a small number will prevent the slaughter of millions. The choice has been a terrible one. We cannot be cheerful about it, or even serene. But we need not be hysterical. We need not accept as inevitable a greater war and the collapse of civilization.*

The millions who still mutter that they should have chosen cataclysm forget that while civilizations live, they may still aspire, and hope—as long as their legions can hold the far frontier.

And no free-born American can or could advocate surrender.

The Truman Administration accepted the limitation of the war to Korea, and its decision was never altered. But that Administration must have wished for Frederick's legions, his forty thousand iron grenadiers—for there was never any hope that the men of the fields and the merchants of America could continue undisturbed.

In addition to restraint of objective, the second necessary ingredient of limited war is a professional army large enough to handle any task.

In 1950, even to fight an underdeveloped nation in Asia, America had to fall back upon her citizens. And in this, above all else, lies the resulting trauma of the Korean War.

The far frontier is not defended with citizens, for citizens have better things to do than to die on some forsaken hill, in some forsaken country, for what seems to be the sake of that country.

By July of 1950, the President was forced to authorize the calling of Reserve Forces. MacArthur understood the meaning of American control of sky and sea and was planning that truly American conception of warfare, amphibious assault against the enemy's flank. MacArthur wanted Marines.

The entire Marine Corps stood at less than ninety thousand men, scattered to the seven seas. Asked for a division by the Joint Chiefs, the Corps, with the President's agreement, called its organized reserves.

The Army, Air Force, and Navy quickly saw that all their forces in the Far East, and more, would be involved. There would be nothing left for fresh emergencies. They asked for, and received, permission to induct their own reserves.

The President called four National Guard divisions, hundreds of lesser units, and thousands of individual reservists, at the Pentagon's request. Conscription was immediately necessary to keep the ranks filled.

There was no hope that the men of the fields and of the towns could remain untouched. A modern democracy was not semifeudal Prussia, or Bourbon France, or Whig England, where soldiers could be swept from taverns, pressed from the ranks of the unskilled and unemployed, the disadvantaged put under the rod of iron, to be broken into grenadiers, to voyage and die for the realm, while the stable and fortunate citizenry said good riddance.

The war would touch every metropolis, every town, almost every field. It would touch many hearts, for sons and fathers would suffer mutilation and death. And many, not hearing the angel's trumpet that they had come to associate with the grandeur and horror of war, would never understand.

But suddenly, in late summer, an awareness of war came on the public. There was scare buying. Tires, coffee, sugar were hoarded; there was disruption of economic life.

To this the government could apply restraint. It had no intention of mobilization for a limited war; mobilization was not indeed. It refused to call the war a war, and slowly, gradually, panic faded.

America was rich, and money and munitions were no problem. There had been recession, and this disappeared in the smoke from retooling factories. As in World War II, America, unique in history, could afford both guns and butter. No Congress would refuse a defense budget, and money could be borrowed. There need be no special war appropriation; the fighting could be—and was—financed out of "Miscellaneous." The guns and trucks and combat boots could be—and were—made in idle manufacturing capacity.

The price of labor, food, and fibers rose, and America enjoyed a new flush of wartime prosperity. At home, things were suddenly better than they had been before. The people might have been content. The slack economy hummed, and all seemed well.

But even in the middle of the twentieth century, men were still required for war. Guns, boots, and butter might be bought, but not men. Except for men, who had to suffer and die, all might have been well.

Men listened for the trumpet, but heard only an uncertain sound. The trumpet had to be sounded, a little, but the government wanted no hysteria, no war enthusiasm that might not be restrained. Men did not understand, and grew confused.

The government could handle the problems of butter and bayonets, but it could never solve the problem of men.

After the commitment of United States troops, American newspapers never again devoted much attention to the exploits or condition of the ROK Army. Consequently, few Americans have understood the ROK contribution to the Korean War, and most have tended to deprecate it.

In the first week of fighting, because it had exceedingly poor weaponry and bad training at staff levels, the original ROK Army in the west was largely destroyed. Most of its men and officers died fighting.

In the east, however, the ROK divisions had remained intact, and fought delaying actions down the peninsula.

Beginning in the early part of July, American officers tried to reorganize the ROK's, a difficult job since losses among officers had been ghastly, and because even American equipment was painfully short. By 24 July, however, two ROK corps of five divisions had been organized and outfitted. Their equipment was not equal to and never would equal that of United States divisions throughout the war.

ROK's would remain weak in artillery and without organic tanks for the balance of the conflict. But they would fight.

All during July 1950, ROK units continued in action. Many fought exceedingly well. A comparison of casualties tells the story: in the first six weeks, American losses amounted to 6,000 men; the ROK's lost 70,000 killed, wounded, or missing.

While the Republic of Korea would have been utterly defeated without American help, South Koreans for three years continued to bear the manpower brunt of the war.

And in the summer of 1950, the ROK losses point up a fact that was decisive—by heavily engaging the victorious Inmun Gun again and again, the ROK Army inflicted deadly losses upon it, losses that at the time were not credited to them by American officers. In some cases ROK units, in dying, destroyed North Korean regiments and even divisions; although until NKPA records were captured later the fact was unknown.

When the United Nations reeled behind the Pusan Perimeter, American officers estimated the NKPA had suffered some 30,000 casualties. The actual figure was nearer 60,000, most of which had been inflicted by the ROK's. On 5 August, many of the Inmun Gun divisions facing the Naktong were at half-strength; the total combat strength of its eleven divisions could not have been more than 70,000.

It had no more than forty tanks by 4 August.

Behind the Perimeter on 4 August 1950, the U.N. had a troop strength of 141,808, of which some 82,000 were ROK's. American combat ground strength was 47,000. By the end of August, when the crucial Perimeter battles began, American strength alone would exceed that of the Inmun Gun. By 19 August there would be 500 American tanks within the perimeter, outnumbering the enemy armor by more than five to one.

The United States Far Eastern Air Force had complete supremacy of the air, and could range over the North Korean supply lines at will. It could concentrate tremendous tactical air power against the ground in front of American troops.

For six weeks, the U.N. forces had been trading space for time. Their space was running out—but time was also running out for the Inmun Gun. In a protracted contest with the potential power of the United States, the North Korean State had no real hope of success.

By August the NKPA was bled white; replacements were fed in, some from the population of South Korea. These new men were hardly soldiers, but they were led by sergeants, officers, and generals who were fanatical veterans of the Chinese Communist Forces. Men who did not obey were shot. This system, with Koreans, had some success. It continued to be a matter of some frustration for American officers serving in Korea that Communist methods often turned out fighting men more quickly than the system employed with the ROK's.

By 4 August 1950, the Inmun Gun had actually lost every advantage but two: it still held the initiative; though it was running out of men, supplies, and time, its attack spirit was still strong; and of its seventy thousand men, almost every man was available for the line. Given ammunition, the North Korean soldier could fight on three rice balls a day.

For more than thirty days this tired, decimated, ill-fed army would push American and ROK forces to the very wall. For thirty days the outcome would hang by a slender thread.

Men are not ciphers, and hearts, even Communist hearts, are not potatoes, and Americans would do well to remember it.

* * *

Without complete control of the air and seas during the dark days of midsummer 1950, the United Nations presence on the Korean Peninsula would have ended. The Far Eastern Air Force, aided strongly by Marine and Navy units, had quickly dominated the skies over both North and South Korea and the waters around them. The relative weak and unmodern air strength of the NKPA was soon brushed aside and by August was no longer a factor in the war. Unprepared for tactical ground-support missions, FEAF at first did almost as much harm as good, shooting up American positions and dealing grievous harm to friendly ROK units on the roads, but these mistakes were quickly corrected.

After gaining air control, FEAF began to interdict the ever-lengthening supply lines of the NKPA, throttling a great deal of its resupply to the front. But air over a country like Korea could never be in itself decisive. The country was too broken, and the NKPA was never completely roadbound. Its units and its supplies, often on foot, went through the valleys and over the ridges, and too much of them arrived at the front. The NKPA did not amass the great, vulnerable mountains of matériel common to Western armies, because in the main it did not have them.

Tactical air burned and destroyed much supply on the ground, but more reached the front. This ability to resupply itself over the broken terrain of Korea without transport and in the teeth of airpower was one of the minor miracles achieved by the Inmun Gun.

Because there was a certain lack of good targets in North Korea, but mainly due to the near desperate condition of the defending ground forces, FEAF early in the war devoted itself to supporting the front lines. It is expensive to use aircraft in place of artillery—but in 1950 the United States had more aircraft, relatively, than cannon in the Far East. Without the constant air cover over the Perimeter, without the strafing and rocketing and napalming that greatly hampered the NKPA attacks, it is probable that the Perimeter would have been breached fatally.

All through the Korean War, whenever the enemy came out into the open, he was subject to immediate, effective air attack. Another minor miracle was his ability to learn to live with this handicap. The NKPA became very good at camouflage and at night movement.

The early months of the war were fought under weird circumstances by the American fighter and bomber pilots. Based in Japan, which never changed from peacetime ways, many of them had wives and family stationed at their fields. Many a pilot flew out in the predawn darkness to strafe and rocket enemy troops all day across the burning hills of Korea, then returned to play cards with his wife at night.

This was harder on both pilots and family than if the dependents had been an ocean away.

While the United States Navy never engaged in heavy combat during the Korean conflict, it was as essential as the Air Force to the American continuance on the peninsula. It ferried troops and supplies in endless quantity. Without this ability to reinforce Korea immediately by sea, all would have been lost. Without control of the adjacent waters, the United Nations effort would have been constantly imperiled.

Without both air and sea power no nation can hope to guard the far frontier beyond its shores. While neither air nor sea forces were fully permitted to fulfill their primary mission—the carrying of the war to the enemy—it is more than probable that their very presence enabled the United States to contain the war. In the air, and on sea, America was by no means so weak as she had been on the ground, and she was immeasurably stronger than the immediate enemies, North Korea and Red China.

The enemy never seriously attempted to strike at American bases or lifelines beyond Korea, vulnerable as the bases continued to be. An air or sea strike—and both planes and submarines were available in quantity within the Communist bloc—might have wreaked havoc with American reinforcement of Korea, but it would also have exposed the enemy to even more serious retaliation. During the fighting, both air and sea forces continued to operate from their own "privileged sanctuaries" on both sides.

The fact that the United States was not seriously challenged in the air, or at sea, where it was strong, indicates that had the nation been equally prepared on the ground, the war would not have occurred, or having begun, could have been quickly contained.

But while air power and sea power were absolutely vital to American hope of success, this was to be a ground war, by the enemy's choice. A French minister of state, in the days when Bourbon France was the land power par excellence of the world, once respectfully pointed out to his government that if France seriously intended to challenge Britain, a sea power, she must first have a navy. Two hundred years later the United States was in the same position. If it seriously desired to check the Communist advance on the ground, the United States would have to take to the mud, too.

Korea was an infantry war, essentially no different from any infantry war of the twentieth century. This was one of the factors, along with the political, that made the fighting so distasteful to a people who had subconsciously come to regard infantry warfare as obsolete.

Air Force and Navy fought, and spent long hours on dangerous and arduous duty. Airmen and sailors died—but it was an infantry war. Two typical days' casualties figures for American forces tell the story: Army—615 (20 KIA, 126 WIA, 417 MIA); Navy—0; Air Force—1 (MIA); and Army—328 (20 KIA, 181 WIA, 127 MIA); Navy—0; Air Force—3 (1 WIA, 2 MIA).

It was in the misty valleys and on the cruel mountains and hills that the fighting took place, and it was in these narrow valleys and barren hills that the story of Korea was told.

The North Korean Army came across the 38th parallel as conquerors, and as conquerors it prepared to remain. The Communists, to a greater degree than had been realized, had infiltrated the South, and as the Inmun Gun captured city after city, Communist cadres were ready to assume control.

Hundreds of thousands of South Koreans fled ahead of the armies, but the entire population of twenty million had nowhere to flee. As with most populations, the bulk of the people remained in place, particularly the peasants of the land.

The North Koreans were prepared to assume civilian control, and while the bulk of the Korean population was anti-Communist, the Reds quickly assumed such control. There was a pattern to the conquest following that of all Communist conquest in Asia.

The North Korean rulers had absolutely no interest in the merchants of the towns, or the middle classes, except eventually to get rid of them. Generally, these people were left alone or arrested, for later attention. But other groups received immediate attention. Former officials of the Republic, down to clerks, were jailed or killed. People such as moneylenders and prominent landowners were executed at once for political capital. Few, in any land, love the rich. The North Korean State acted on the assumption that men and women who could not be easily controlled or assimilated into a Communist state must be killed.

What happened in Seoul and Taejon was typical. In Seoul, every man or woman who had worked for the Americans in any capacity was executed if found, and the American Embassy had conveniently left their personnel files behind. All former government employees were killed or jailed. Steps were taken immediately to induct many of the youth of the city into the NKPA, and others in labor forces.

Outside Taejon, after the city had been scoured for possible enemies to a Communist regime, shivering hordes of unfortunates, in groups of one hundred or more, were led to mass graves, hands bound, wired to each other. Then the shooting began. When the United States Army came back through in September, a burial trench containing more than 7,000 bodies, including those of 40 American soldiers, was uncovered.

There were mass graves outside Amui, Mokp'o, Kongju, and Hamyang, wherever the Inmun Gun had marched.

The killing was not sheer savagery. The regime was ridding itself of people it could never trust, for the best of political reasons.

Revolution and terror are synonymous; only with the passage of time does any revolution become respectable. After the military triumph of the American Revolution the hard-core adherents of the Crown—more than a quarter-million out of a population of three million—were stripped of their property and forced into exile in Canada and elsewhere. Much of the success of the United States in early days was due to the lack of organized dissent within the Republic.

After the French Revolution, thousands of aristocrats and others who fought the revolution were permitted to return to France, where their descendants have not accepted the principles of the revolution to this day, causing perpetual instability.

In a hideously practical way the Communists knew what they were doing.

The Korean terror exceeded that of now respectable Western social upheavals only in degree, and in brutal Communist efficiency.

But while it was shooting the officials and anti-Communists, the regime made every effort to cater to the poorer masses. Asian Communists have always realized that in nations largely peasant, the peasantry alone is of any real political value. Land was redistributed. It would be taken back later, when the regime was consolidated—but first, it was a necessary step, as in China, to secure the backing of the millions of the poor.

The middle classes, so vital to Western democracy, do not exist in most of Asia. Where they do exist, they are more of a political liability with the mass of people than an asset, for they are regarded with envy and hatred by men who break their backs on the soil. The peasant feels he can live without them.

While the proscribed classes were being wiped out, the Inmun Gun showed every courtesy to the workers of the soil. When the Inmun Gun required food or lodging of the poor, these were paid for—in worthless currency, but paid for none the less. In Seoul, the Inmun Gun had captured the South Korean Government mints, and the printing presses ran off all the currency the Inmun Gun could ever use.

In a country where 90 percent of the people are peasants, the Communist regime had every expectation of success—because peasants they understood. From the first, the peasantry saw little to lose through Communist rule, and perhaps much to gain. Only much later, when the land is collectivized and the iron hand shows through the paternal glove, and when it is too late, does the peasant who has been Communized realize his loss. Communized, he ceases to be an individual man, losing an identity that even the most abject poverty could not take from his before.

Communism had really nothing to offer the peasant but propaganda—the Communist has no more use for the peasant in his scheme of things than does a purveyor of Rolls-Royces—but Asian Communism has always realized that the good will of the peasant was necessary above all else for its eventual success. Americans, in turn, have been slow to understand the peasant, let alone mix with him.

Americans, who cannot understand or even communicate with peasantry, are growing lonelier in a world where the great majority of men are peasants.

Shooting the members of the *ancien régime,* destroying the merchant and landowning groups, and making certain it respectfully paid cash for every peach its soldiers took from the trees of the farmers, the North Korean State came to stay in the South. Among the people of a nation inured to grinding poverty and accustomed to bloody repression, who had been beaten more than once into sullen submission, its actions aroused no such outcry as might have been expected in the West.

Communism came to stay below the parallel, and had it not been thrown back by force it would be there yet.

12

Fire Brigade

The situation is critical and Miryang may be lost. The enemy has driven a division-sized salient across the Naktong. More will cross the river tonight. If Miryang is lost . . . we will be faced with a withdrawal from Korea. I am heartened that the Marine Brigade will move against the Naktong Salient tomorrow. They are faced with impossible odds, and I have no valid reason to substantiate it, but I have the feeling they will halt the enemy.

. . . . These Marines have the swagger, confidence, and hardness that must have been in Stonewall Jacksons's Army of the Shenandoah. They remind me of the Coldstreams at Dunkirk. Upon this thin line of reasoning, I cling to the hope of victory.

—From a wire dispatched 16 August 1950 by a British military observer at Miryang.

IN FRONT OF almost three-quarters of the Pusan Perimeter of August 1950 wound the Naktong River. Flowing south, the Naktong is Korea's second river; it bends and folds its way between rice paddies and the hills running down to the water's edge. The Naktong averages more than one-quarter mile in width, and more than six feet in depth. At low water, as during the hot, dry summer of 1950, large sandy beaches and bars appear in the river, but it is at all times a formidable obstacle.

Behind the river to the east, the hills rise to twenty-five hundred feet, and on its north, across the top of the Perimeter, they reach three thousand or more. It was here, on the highest hills, that the United Nations Forces, the United States and ROK armies, organized their defense.

There was no hope of organizing a strongly held line; there were still not enough troops for that. Troops dug in on hills that overlooked the Naktong and the major avenues of approach leading east from it. By day these strongpoints served as observation posts, and by night they buttoned up into small tight defense perimeters, acting as listening posts. Between these outposts along the river ran jeep and other mechanized patrols to screen the terrain.

Some miles back from the Naktong the reserve troops were held in readiness to attack against any successful crossing by the enemy. Supporting weapons, artillery and mortars, were also emplaced back in the hills, and registered on all likely crossing sights, and prepared to mass fire against any threatened point.

The object of the defense was to hold the commanding ground east of the river, and the vital road net. There could be no practical hope of holding each inch of ground, as in the position defense, but now the mobility of the American defenders could be brought in play. If the enemy broke across the river at any point, men and firepower could be quickly assembled against him from other parts of the Perimeter.

There were four natural attack routes into the Perimeter. One was on the south through that port of Masan; another through the so-called Naktong Bulge to the important rail and road network at Miryang. A possible corridor of advance ran through the roads and rails to Taegu. Finally, on the far northeast, a valley ran down the seacoast through Kyongju.

As the enemy plan of maneuver developed, it became obvious that the NKPA would attempt all four corridors, almost simultaneously. The NKPA plan assumed that by making a multiple attack against the entire thinly manned line, a breakthrough could be made in at least one area. Because of this plan, the men defending east of the Naktong would be stretched to the breaking point, and the pressure would be felt everywhere.

There was fighting—hard, bitter fighting, along almost all the Perimeter in August. The most dangerous threat developed against the Naktong Bulge, however, and here the action was typical of the whole bitter, desperate month.

After July 1950, it becomes impossible to detail the actions of each division or regiment. Every unit in Korea had its moments of desperation, and many their moments of glory. But by detailing to some extent the experiences of certain units, to a great extent the flavor of the whole action is revealed. For what happened in one stinking paddy valley was very much like what happened in the next, from here to the end of the war.

* * *

A few miles north of the confluence of the Naktong and the Nam, the Naktong forms a wide bow to the west, enclosing a loop of land measuring four miles by five, with the town of Yongsan at its eastern base. The territory within the river bend was called by its American defenders the Naktong Bulge.

The terrain enclosed on three sides by the Naktong is at first hilly, then flattening out to the east, with three large lakes in front of Yongsan. The town of Yongsan itself is a road intersection, with good dirt roads leading east, west, north, and south.

The first serious penetration of the Pusan Perimeter was into the Naktong Bulge.

On 4 August Major General Lee Kwon Mu, Inmun Gun, surveyed the east side of the river from his command post at Hyopch'on. By August, Lee Kwon

Mu was already among the greatest heroes of the North Korean People's Army. He had been made a Hero of the Chosun Minjujui Inmun Kong-whakuk, and awarded the Order of the National Flag, First Class.

His 4th Division, NKPA, had, with the 3rd, spearheaded the drive south, taking Seoul and shattering the American 24th Division at Taejon. The 4th had been given the honorary title "Seoul" Division by Premier Kim Il Sung.

Lee Kwon Mu, as all the senior commanders of the Inmun Gun, had been fighting most of his life. Born in Manchuria of Korean refugee stock, he had joined the Chinese Communist 8th Route Army, fighting both Japanese and Nationalists. He had attended an officers' school in Russia. Now, at the age of forty, Lee stood at the apex of his military career.

His veteran 4th Division still contained 7,000 men, and to it came orders to attack. With almost no preparation, Lee sent his battalions boiling across the Naktong.

At midnight, 5 August, on the signal of a red and a yellow flare, the 16th Regiment, 4th Division, plunged into the broad river at the Ohang ferry, where the water ran only shoulder deep to an adult Korean. Some of the soldiers crossed on makeshift rafts, but most stripped naked, and with both clothing and rifles held high over their heads, waded into the river.

They caught General Church, 24th Division CG, by surprise. Church had felt the blow would fall farther north in his zone.

The 16th Regiment reached the east bank safely, dressed, and marched down a draw between the American defensive strongpoints. They struck into American units, while behind them more North Koreans swarmed across the Naktong. By 7 August, against a 24th Division that was at less than 40 percent efficiency because of losses of men and equipment, with attendant low morale, the NKPA had seized both Cloverleaf Hill and Obong-ni Ridge, dominating the road into Yongsan, five miles to the east. They could see far down the road to Miryang, an important center.

If Miryang fell, the Perimeter would be in deep trouble.

Now the NKPA built underwater bridges across the Naktong at the ferry site, employing an old Russian trick. These bridges were invisible and therefore invulnerable to air attack. Heavy equipment of the 4th Division poured across; their artillery began to fire by battery.

The town of Yongsan came under the North Korean shellfire.

General Church ordered counterattacks. Fresh troops from the 2nd Infantry Division were coming onto line; the 9th Infantry of that Division had arrived from the States.

Along the critical Cloverleaf Hill–Obong-ni Ridge Line vicious combat now raged for ten days. Hills changed daily from hand to hand, and along this line the Perimeter would be held or lost.

First Lieutenant Frank E. Muñoz, of Tucson, Arizona, was the executive officer of H Company (Heavy Weapons), 9th Infantry, the first week of July 1950, when the orders came to pack for Korea. The regiment—the Manchu Raiders—had been at Fort Lewis, Washington, since April 1946, and, as Frank Muñoz put it, the Raiders were at Parade Rest.

Since most of the enlisted men of the regiment had come in at one time
three years before, two months before Korea many enlistments expired, and
most of the men left for civilian life. On 25 June, the parent 2nd Division was
at 50 percent strength, and conducting training. Some of the training was pretty basic, and all of it was peacetime.

When Muñoz heard the news of the North Korean attack, he felt the same
excitement he had known after Pearl Harbor. Then he had been on active service with the Arizona National Guard. After the war he had decided to make
a career of it. A middle-sized, tough, wiry black-eyed man of twenty-eight, he
was what the Army called a "career reservist"—he would stick around as long
as they let him. He felt a deep pride in the uniform, and a deeper pride that
he had become an officer.

The army gave the 2nd Division one week to load on shipboard at Tacoma,
and the same week to fill up to full strength. As Muñoz said: "We turned the
vacuum cleaner on. It sucked up men from everywhere—behind desks, out of
hospitals, from depots. We filled up fast."

Unfortunately, some of the men arriving were not infantrymen, and more
than some were not interested in becoming riflemen.

The 9th Infantry was the first to embark for Korea, preceding the balance
of the division. It landed at Pusan on 31 July 1950, but some of its vital equipment didn't land with it—the regiment had come across on more than one
ship. It took a few days at Pusan to get everything straightened out.

H Company got no formal briefing on the war aboard ship, or before. The
men heard newscasts, and they saw maps in the papers. Other than that, no
one could tell them much. H Company's C.O., young, serious First Lieutenant
Edward Schmitt, talked to the men once during the crossing.

He told them very solemnly: "Men, we're going into war. This will be a
time when mistakes will cost lives." Schmitt had seen combat in World War II,
and he had served in the Occupation of Korea. He talked to them about the
importance of maintaining weapons and equipment, and he tried to tell them
something about the lay of the land in Korea.

But at Pusan, no one would know there was a war on. The waterfront was
raucous and noisy; equipment was piled high in the open; and while there was
a lot of frantic activity, there was nothing to indicate things were desperate in
the west.

The regiment took the train to Miryang, and above Miryang they en-
camped on the high ground. They made liaison and reconnaissance with units
of the 24th and 1st Cavalry divisions, who held the front lines in front of them
along the Naktong.

Here they got plenty of war stories. The heard about the atrocities—dozens
of American soldiers found with hands tied behind their backs, shot in the
head. They were briefed on the guerrilla-like tactics of the NKPA, the night
operations, the probing for weak points, and the use of soldiers disguised as
civilians.

To the Manchu Raiders, fresh from Fort Lewis, the 24th Division looked
beat up, shoddy, and pretty nervous.

Then, five days after the NKPA crossed the Naktong into the Bulge, Schmitt, Muñoz, and company were ordered up to plug a hole that had been sprung in the 24th Division's wall. They marched over hot, dusty roads beside smelly rice paddies, and went up into a series of hills along the Naktong, called the Cloverleaf.

The heat was ghastly, especially to men fresh from the cool Northwest, and it reduced their efficiency. Many of them dropped out.

Lieutenant Colonel Harrison, the six-foot, gray-haired 2nd Battalion commander, like Frank Muñoz a career reservist, spread the Heavy Weapons Company and its automatic weapons and mortars among the three rifle companies, E, F, and G. The battalion occupied its assigned hills just back of the 24th, and for two days nothing happened.

There was heavy fighting all around, but H Company did not become closely engaged. It rained on 14 August, momentarily breaking the heat, but also breaking up supporting air attacks. And on 14 August both 1st and 2nd battalions of the 9th Infantry were ordered to move against the NKPA positions within the Cloverleaf complex.

After heavy fighting, and after heavy loss, both battalions failed to take the high crests of the hill mass. Exhausted after a day of battle in the broiling heat, 2nd Battalion dug in along the ridges, but the fighting did not cease with darkness.

With night, the North Koreans attacked.

Frank Muñoz's first contact with the enemy came when Schmitt called him at his position with the 75mm recoilless rifles in the rear. "Get our boys, the part of the Machine Gun Platoon attached to Fox Company, out of position. Fox has been overrun!"

Muñoz jumped into his jeep and told the PFC driving to make for Fox Company's hill. Coming up behind it, he saw it was under heavy fire from SP 76's the enemy had sneaked across the Naktong. At the rear slope of the hill he left the jeep and went through the dark on foot. In the valley behind the hill, Sergeant Bozarth's Mortar Platoon was firing its 81's steadily, and Muñoz located a number of three-quarter-ton weapon carriers standing by.

But F Company, dug in along the front slope of the hill, had been infiltrated in the dark, and had come apart. Many of the men had pulled back, breaking contact. The company commander was dead. Most of the officers were down. F was no longer an effective military unit.

Somehow, under fire, in the dark, Frank Muñoz got a number of the men together and moved them off the hill. Just to the right rose another hill, this one clear of enemy. Muñoz ordered the men he had collected to move to it, picking up any stragglers, and try to organize this hill for defense.

As they did so, they came across other casualties streaming around the hills through the rice paddies. These men told Muñoz that wounded men were still lying in the fields in front of his new hill. Easy Company had been hard hit, along with Fox, and it had also come apart in the night.

Once he had his scattered remnants together and dug in, Frank called Schmitt by radio. He told the company commander about Easy Company.

"See if you can help 'em," Schmitt ordered.

After a bit, Frank was able to raise E Company by radio. A master sergeant was in command. Lieutenant Schultz of Easy had been hit in the head, and badly wounded. Over the radio, Frank and Sergeant Jordan of Easy established each other's location; most of Easy's men were still down in the paddies in front of the hill.

"I'll send you help to bring in your wounded," Muñoz told Jordan. "Start moving back to me—we'll cover you by fire."

He sent five men to assist Easy, and soon fifteen enlisted men—all that could be found—joined him on the hill. He ordered the wounded out. They went down the rear slope of the hill and disappeared to the east.

He contacted Battalion HQ by radio. He learned that Colonel Harrison had been hit, and the exec had taken command. The exec ordered him to hold where he was, and said he would send him another officer, a Lieutenant Chu Mon Lee.

Lee arrived, and for the balance of the night there was only sporadic shooting around the hill. But occasionally a mortar shell dropped in, and by dawn Frank Muñoz had two more wounded men on his hands. One, hit in the leg but still able to walk, he sent down the hill.

As this man limped to the defilade area behind the hill, he bumped into the ominous, hazy shape of a T-34 tank. Staring, unable to believe his eyes, the soldier saw a tank hatch open, and a North Korean blazed away at him with a submachine gun. But the poor light saved the wounded man; he hit the ground and crawled back to Muñoz on the hill.

Hearing about the tank in his rear, Muñoz said a few unprintable words. Then he got a crew of men together, and with a 3.5-inch rocket launcher they sneaked down the rear slope. It was still dark enough to permit them to crawl within a few yards of the deadly vehicle, and with the first round from the bazooka they put it out of action.

But the crew remained inside—at least, Muñoz saw no one come out.

Warily, they watched the silent steel monster, as light grew in the east and spread across the brown and green paddies. They had no more rocket ammunition.

As it grew light, Lieutenant Schmitt came up behind the hill. For a night Muñoz had held the actual command of two companies, but now, with the arrival of his boss, he reverted to exec of H.

Pointing to the tank, Schmitt wanted to know, "What's with that?"

"The crew is still inside—won't give up," Frank said.

"Hell," Schmitt said. He stood out in the open and began to yell at the tank in the Korean he had picked up during the Occupation. "*Ede wha!*" Come out!

The tank stayed quiet, even when Schmitt went up beside it and banged on the turret with his hand. Then Schmitt climbed up on the sponson and tried to pull open a hatch. Suddenly, then, there was movement inside. A crewman partly opened the hatch, thrust a pistol through, and fired point-blank at the Weapons Company commander.

Unhurt, Schmitt jumped down. "You son of a bitch, we'll fix you!" he said. "Somebody give me a white phosphorous grenade—"

Pulling the pin, Schmitt dropped the incendiary grenade on the tank's back deck, over the air intake.

The North Koreans never did come out, though they made a number of unpleasant noises as they stayed inside and burned.

As exec, Frank returned to his old post at the Company CP to the rear. When he arrived, the battalion operations officer, Major Woodard, was on the phone.

"Listen, Frank," Woodard said. "George Company is in bad shape. Captain Van Oosten has been evacuated with heat stroke. G's got only one officer left, and he's demoralized. How about taking over G?"

"Well, if you tell me to take it, I'll take it," Frank said. "But I won't volunteer." G was a rifle company, like E and F, and commanding a rifle company was somewhat different than acting as exec of a Weapons Company. For one thing, it could be a hell of a lot more dangerous.

"I'm telling you," Woodard said.

So Frank Muñoz assumed command of George Company. Joining the company on the hill, he found that George had taken several frontal assaults during the recent fighting. Many men had been shot at close range with small arms; others had been hit by mortar fragments. Out of a TO strength of 213, Frank had exactly fifty people left.

He found the remaining officer, Lieutenant Hank Merritt, and told him he was the new C.O.

Merritt seemed happy to get out from under. "Glad to have you, Frank," he mumbled.

Quickly, Frank Muñoz understood that G Company was in a state of shock. The men had not been ready for the vicious combat into which they had plunged. The original men, who had been at Fort Lewis, had been on the peacetime training schedule, with frequent half-day training, heavy on athletics and sports. The newer men, the fillers they received in July, had largely come from even softer occupation duty overseas.

It had been a pleasant half-decade since the war ended, but the time had come to pay the price. The price, Muñoz thought, was a hell of a lot of dead people.

Muñoz realized he had not only the problem of too few men to do the job; he had also a morale problem. Almost all of the riflemen, dug in along the rear slope of the hill, had jumped in their holes and pulled the zipper. They didn't want to come out even to shoot.

He knew many of the men by name, and he walked along the foxholes strung out over the ridge, talking to each man. He told them they were fighting for their country, and other things. It was a hard sell.

"Hell," one man told him, "you can't tell me we're fightin' for the U.S.A. ten thousand miles from home!"

Some of the men told him they didn't mind fighting a big war. Americans, he found, tend to take pride in doing things in a big way. But they had no interest in fighting a half-ass war like this one.

But he went from hole to hole, talking to every man, doing the best he could.

Muñoz was an officer, and a good one. He had no personal enthusiasm for this war, either; but he had taken the government's bread and the government's commission, and even for Truman's shilling he would give all he had in return.

He had just finished, and was walking back to his position in the middle of the line, when the NKPA pulled the plug.

Mortar shells hissed down on the ridge, bursting with sharp cracks, spewing gouts of greasy smoke, sending whining metal through the roiling dust. Caught in the open, Muñoz jumped into a foxhole. He had only a .45 automatic pistol. Realizing something was going to happen, he drew the pistol and threw a round in the chamber.

For two minutes the mortar rounds burst along the ridge; then, suddenly, the shelling ceased.

The instant he understood the mortar fire had finished, Frank Muñoz jumped from his hole and ran up to the top of the ridge, where he could see across the rice paddies to the front. Quick as he was, he was too late.

At the top of the ridge, he made eyeball to eyeball contact with a North Korean soldier. Muñoz moved first. His .45 slug killed the Korean at a range of inches. As he shot, he could see two waves of enemy infantry, bayonets fixed, charging up the slope, firing from the hip.

He went into the nearest hole, which was already occupied by a man with a BAR. "Fire to your right front!" he snapped at the BAR man.

The enemy boiled up over the hill and ran at George's thin line of holes. George Company met them with a blast of fire, stopping them only yards away. The first wave fell apart a few feet in front of Frank's own position.

As it did so, he got up and ran back to his regular post in the center of the line, joining Merritt. He had seen two of his own men leave their holes to run, and had seen both shot in the back and killed by rifle fire from the enemy. And he knew that George Company was close to the thin edge.

"Hank, call for final defensive fires!"

Then the second wave of charging Koreans swarmed over the crest. In a wild melee, some of the Inmun Gun jumped into foxholes with Muñoz's men, bayonets flashing.

Muñoz yelled at his Artillery forward observer to bring fire down on the hill. The FO, Lieutenant Hartman, yelled back, "No! I don't want to do it!"

But Frank grabbed a field phone and reached Battalion. He got the Artillery liaison officer there, and he got action—two salvos of 105's, to be put down on his own position.

Seconds later, the shells screamed down, bursting with ear-shattering noise. They caught most of the attacking Inmun Gun still swarming down the ridge.

Dug in, Muñoz's boys suffered no harm. The enemy, in the open, died. And, as suddenly as they had been attacked, George's men were all alone on the hill.

Muñoz reported to Battalion by phone. For the balance of the day there was only desultory firing about the hill. Only a few 82's dropped in.

That night, the higher-ups took George Company off the hill for two days' rest.

* * *

Trying to counterattack, the United States forces had employed all the men and matériel at their command—and had been able to do no more than hold their own in front of Cloverleaf and Obong-ni. Colonel Hill, commanding the 9th Regiment and all other combat forces within the Bulge, had no reserve left, and no hope of maneuver.

Both he and General Church, 24th Division CG, agreed that at the moment all that could be accomplished was a continued defense in place. By 15 August they were having their hands full just to contain the Bulge, without thought of erasing it. Earlier, on the 13th, Church had tried to tell General Walker that the entire NKPA 4th Division was across the Naktong—but this Walker steadfastly refused to believe until after the bloody stalemate along the ridge had become apparent.

Walker at this time was edgy, impatient, and abrupt—but Johnny Walker had his problems. There was trouble everywhere on Eighth Army's front, and everybody was squalling for help.

On 12 August the first United Nations counterattack, Task Force Kean, had run into serious trouble at the valley called Bloody Gulch. The front to the extreme south was in a bad way. And at the same time the Bulge was getting fatter in the west, the NKPA had also forced the Naktong in front of Taegu, and were converging on that vital center. And on the far northeast, the ROK divisions on the coast were being steadily driven southward.

There was, from the second week of August, combat everywhere, and Walton Walker lived in crisis. His command decisions had to be never-ending series of robbing Peter to pay Paul. Faced with danger everywhere along his line, he had to guess where the greatest peril lay, and guess correctly, for in war there is no prize for being almost right.

Walker's military reputation will be secure, for he made the right decisions.

On 15 August, considering the Yongsan-Miryang area the most dangerous enemy axis of attack—a feeling shared by the NKPA—he told Church abruptly: "I am going to give you the Marine Brigade. I want this situation cleaned up, and quick!"

The Marine Brigade, under General Craig, USMC, had newly arrived from the States. MacArthur had wanted to hold it back for future amphibious operations, but the situation along the Naktong had been too critical; the Marines were needed for a fire brigade. At this time, the 5,000-man Marine force was Walker's principal reserve.

While 9th Infantry was being bled and battered on the hill, the Marines were ordered to attack 17 August to erase the enemy bulge east of the Naktong.

* * *

While the U.N. situation within the Pusan Perimeter looked black indeed during these critical days, it can be truly evaluated only in the light of what was occurring with the enemy. On the other side of the hill from American forces, Major General Lee Kwon Mu's 4th "Seoul" Division faced enormous difficulties.

Attacking with three rifle regiments of approximately 1,500 men each, the 4th Division had suffered frightful casualties against the stubborn American defense in front of Cloverleaf and Obong-ni. The division received replacements—often men dragged from the villages of South Korea—but many of these arrived at the front without weapons, let alone military training. As many as 40 percent of these men deserted at the earliest opportunity. The remainder, unfit for the assault elements, were used as general labor troops, digging holes, carrying ammunition, foraging, and the like.

And east of the Naktong, Lee Kwon Mu was experiencing tremendously logistical difficulties. Food was scarce. Ammunition was increasingly difficult to get to the engaged units across the water barrier—not only had the original supply brought out of the North been exhausted, but American air interdiction was beginning to strangle his overextended lines.

Chang Ky Dok's 18th Regiment, holding critical Obong-ni Ridge, was able to procure no resupply of ammunition after 14 August.

Men of the division who were only slightly wounded were returned to duty, without medical attention. There was no way to aid those hurt more severely, and without care these men were dying in high numbers.

But the morale of the North Korean squad and platoon leaders, the men who had fought in China and Manchuria, was still firm. As long as Lee Kwon Mu and Colonel Chang Ky Dok could count on their junior officers and NCO's, they could count on the performance of their units.

Courage and fighting ability come in many creeds and colors. Whatever Americans might feel toward Lee and Chang's cruel and tyrannical system, they could not deny that the Communists' courage remained high.

Lee Kwon Mu, Hero of the People's Republic of Korea, Order of the National Flag, First Class, had no intention of withdrawing.

* * *

When the Korean War broke, somewhat less than 10 percent of the small United States Marine Corps had seen combat. But fortunately for the Corps, the percentage was highly concentrated within officer and key NCO grades; most of the Marine troop leaders knew what war was like.

And the Marines, who had always been largely a volunteer organization, had escaped the damaging reforms instituted within the United States Army at the end of World War II. The public clamor rose against the Army, during the war twenty times the small, parochial Corps' size, and ignored the Marines.

In 1950 a Marine Corps officer was still an officer, and a sergeant behaved the way good sergeants had behaved since the time of Caesar, expecting no nonsense, allowing none. And Marine leaders had never lost sight of their primary—their only—mission, which was to fight.

The Marine Corps was not made pleasant for men who served in it. It remained the same hard, dirty, brutal way of life it had always been.

The Marines may take little credit, either for courage or foresight, in remaining the way they were. The public pressure simply never developed against them in the years after the war, pushing their commanders into acquiescence with the ideals of society. Not long after the end of the Korean conflict, after an unfortunate incident one night at a place called Ribbon Creek, the commandant of the Corps showed no more ability to stand up for his rights in front of a congressional committee than had the generals of the Army.

It is admittedly terrible to force men to suffer during training, or even sometimes, through accident, to kill them. But there is no other way to prepare them for the immensely greater horror of combat.

In 1950 the Marines, both active and reserve, were better prepared to die on the field of battle than the Army.

Asked immediately for a full division by the Joint Chiefs, the Corps could at first put together only a brigade out of the 1st Marine Division, Fleet Marine Force. Ships and shore were scoured for men; all ground reserves were called to the colors. While the Corps made every effort not to send unprepared men into combat, it was still forced to consider the needs of the service first; a certain number of new recruits with less than desired training sailed for the Orient, both in the summer of 1950 and later. And a large number of reservists, just getting started in civilian life, found the callup just as painful as the reserves of other services.

Bitter feelings remain in the Corps, as in other arms, but they have not been so well publicized.

But bitter or not, believing in the reasons for the war or not, the Marines went, and they obeyed orders.

* * *

The 5th Marines, Lieutenant Colonel Raymond L. Murray, moved from dusty Masan in the south to Miryang. Here Murray and General Craig discussed their attack plans, while the tired and sweaty Marines bathed in the brownish waters of Miryang's river, received new clothing and equipment to replace that which had rotted in the slime of rice paddies, and speculated on their mission.

These men had seen only limited combat in the south, but they had already sweated off their shipboard fat, and were beginning to lick the heat. At first they had been no better prepared for the violent sun than had the Army, but, like the Army, they were adjusting.

And these men walked with a certain confidence and swagger. They were only young men like those about them in Korea, but they were conscious of a standard to live up to, because they had had good training, and it had been impressed upon them that they were United States Marines.

Except in holy wars, or in defense of their native soil, men fight well only because of pride and training—pride in themselves and their service, enough training to absorb the rough blows of war and to know what to do. Few men, of any breed, really prefer to kill or be killed. These Marines had pride in their service, which had been carefully instilled in them, and they had pride in themselves, because each man had made the grade in a hard occupation. They would not lightly let their comrades down. And they had discipline, which in essence is the ability not to question orders but to carry them out as intelligently as possible.

Marine human material was not one whit better than that of the human society from which it came. But it had been hammered into form in a different forge, hardened with a different fire. The Marines were the closest thing to legions the nation had. They would follow their colors from the shores of home to the seacoast of Bohemia, and fight well either place.

General Church, to whose 24th Division the Provisional Marine Brigade was attached, considered both Cloverleaf, where the 9th Infantry was engaged, and Obong-ni Ridge parts of the same enemy hill mass; however, Colonel Murray asked for permission for the Marines to reduce Obong-ni before a general assault was made upon the Bulge. Murray felt the Ridge could be quickly and easily reduced, and, secured, it could be used as a line of departure for a general attack. In this he was wrong, but General Church agreed to the proposal.

The Marine order of attack was organized. Lieutenant Colonel Harold S. Roise's 2nd Battalion would lead, followed by 1/5 and 3/5 in that order. A little after midnight 17 August, 2/5 moved into an assembly area in front of Obong-ni Ridge.

D and E companies of 2nd Battalion had been selected to lead the assault. They moved forward in the freshness of early morning, and by 0700 were in position to see their objective, a long, unprepossessing ridge, covered by shale and scrub pine, with six riblike spurs running down from it into the sodden rice paddies. Between the spurs and the low hills behind which the Marines gathered lay a long expanse of open rice fields.

The maps issued to the Marine Brigade, as all the maps used by the United Nations in 1950, were based on old Japanese surveys, and inaccurate. The Marines did not know exactly where they were. Conferring with Captain Sweeney of Easy Company, Captain Zimmer of Dog called the ridge "Red Slash Hill." From the Marine attack position a fresh, gaping landslide scar could be plainly seen in the reddish earth near the center of the ridge.

Andy Zimmer told Sweeney, "I'll take the area right of that red slash." Sweeney agreed. Each company would attack with two platoons forward at 0800, after the air and artillery preparation.

There were only 120 riflemen available to send forward in the first assault wave.

Now, far out in the Sea of Japan, the Navy carriers *Badoeng Strait* and *Sicily* turned into the wind and launched a total of two squadrons of eighteen Marine Corsairs. The gull-winged planes, clumsy under heavy bomb loads, could carry no napalm because of a shortage of fuel tanks.

For ten minutes, artillery of the 24th Division burst on the rear approaches to Obong-ni Ridge, and along the reverse slopes of the ridge itself. Then, when the artillery pounding ceased, the Marine air swarmed over the hill, blasting Obong-ni's spine. Dirt, dust, and flame spurted up in great gouts all along the ridge. To General Church, watching, it seemed as if the ridge were floating away in smoke.

Then, their bomb load exhausted, the Corsairs roared away. At 0800, the four thin platoons of Marines went forward, across the valley and toward the ridge, one thousand yards beyond.

Several war correspondents, watching from the attack positions, asked officers the name of the objective. None seemed to know, and one correspondent wrote "No Name Ridge" on his release.

The Marines splashed across three rice paddies and skirted a cotton field, and they drew fire, not from the ridge, but from automatic weapons on their flanks. The fire grew heavier, and now gaps opened between the attacking platoons.

In spite of the fire, the platoons reached the slopes of Obong-ni. Here mortar shells crashed down on them. And here the ground steepened sharply, forcing the Marines to climb slowly and painfully toward the crest.

Only one platoon, 2nd Lieutenant Michael J. Shinka's 3rd of Dog Company, made the top. Just to the right of the big red slash Shinka found a small rain gulley leading upward, and through this his men crawled, bent over, panting, to the crest. Shinka reached the top of Obong-ni with only two-thirds of his original thirty men—while the other platoons, faced with steep ground and heavy fire, stalled halfway up the slope.

The twenty men atop Obong-ni had no protection to either flank. They found a line of empty foxholes dug by the NKPA, and poured into them, just as a hail of machine-gun fire whipped at them from enemy positions to their right. And then hand grenades soared through the air from enemy holes down on the reverse slope.

The Marines could handle the resistance below them on the slope, but they couldn't stop the enfilading machine-gun fire from their right. Any man who came out of a hole was hit. Within minutes, Mike Shinka had five men down. There were no Marines supporting him, either to left or right. He realized the ridge was too hot. He shouted to his platoon sergeant, Reese, to get the wounded down, and ordered 3rd Platoon back down the hill.

Pulling the wounded men on ponchos, the Marines slithered back down the gulley to a position halfway down the hill, where they had reasonable cover. Shinka raised his company CP by radio.

"We can reach the top and hold it," he told Zimmer, "if you can get that flanking fire off our backs." Shinka, counting, saw he had fifteen men left out of thirty. "Give me an air strike and more men, and we can make it."

"I can't give you any more men," Andy Zimmer said. "But the air strike is on the way."

All of the platoons of Dog and Easy had been stopped along the ridge, and Dog's reserve had had to be committed to assist the platoon on Shinka's flank. Waiting for the Marine Corsairs to return and plaster the hill, Shinka and the other platoon officers did their best to coordinate a fresh attack.

The Marine aircraft buzzed over Obong-ni once again, blasting the snaky spine with high explosives until the ground trembled underfoot. When they finished, American tanks moved out into the open valley east of the ridge line and hurled shells into the sides and crest of Obong-ni.

The decimated Marine platoons went up the hill again. Again the enemy fire blazed up, much of it coming from the Cloverleaf hill complex on the north. North Koreans rushed back into their holes along the top of the ridge, which they had abandoned under the air strike, and rolled hand grenades down the front slope.

Again Mike Shinka and platoon were the only Marines to make the crest. Shinka arrived this time with nine able-bodied men. They saw moving men on the ridge to their left. The platoon sergeant, still on his feet, called, "Easy Company?"

A blast of automatic fire answered him.

"Son of a bitch!" Sergeant Reese yelled, and returned the fire with a BAR.

Again Shinka's platoon was in an untenable position, enemy fire chopping at it from left and right, and from the reverse slope of Obong-ni. Reese fell shot through the leg; another man took a bullet in the stomach.

On the crest a bullet shattered Mike Shinka's jaw. Choking on his own blood, he bent over and hawked to clear his throat. He was unable to use his radio. He motioned his men to get back down the ridge slope.

As he checked the ridge to make sure no wounded Marine had been left behind, a new bullet took Shinka in the arm. The impact knocked him rolling down the slope.

As Shinka and his bloody survivors crawled back to their covered gulley, a storm of fire shattered the entire Marine attack against Obong-ni. By 1500, of the entire 240 men who had been committed against the enemy, 23 were dead and 119 wounded in action.

They hadn't taken Obong-ni Ridge—but a lot of them had died trying.

At 1600, Colonel Newton's 1st Battalion relieved the battered remnants of 2/5 in front of the ridge.

* * *

In command of the 18th Regiment, NKPA, holding Obong-ni Ridge, Colonel Chang Ky Dok knew his situation was increasingly desperate. During the day he had suffered six hundred casualties, forcing the 16th Regiment, which defended Cloverleaf, to reinforce him with a battalion. His ammunition supply was dwindling at a frightening rate. He had no medical supplies, and his wounded were dying from lack of attention.

He knew he could not withstand another day of American air and artillery pounding and a fresh Marine assault up the ridge. Because he had a captured American SCR-300 radio, tuned in on Marine frequencies, he knew that the 1st Battalion had relieved 2/5 along the front of Obong-ni, and he knew approximately where the companies of 1/5 were located, for the Marines talked a great deal over the air.

At last Colonel Murray had realized that Cloverleaf had to be taken before his Marines could assault Obong-ni, and late in the afternoon the 2nd Battalion, 9th Infantry, had pushed the 16th Regiment from that supporting position. The American 19th and 34th regiments were pushing attacks north of Cloverleaf against the right flank of the NKPA salient with some success.

About to be flanked, Chang Ky Dok requested permission to withdraw west of the Naktong. The request was denied.

Colonel Chang, as all senior commanders of the Inmun Gun, was a veteran of Soviet schooling and the North China wars. He knew his only hope was to shatter the American attack before it started on the 18th. He was short of men, short of food, and, worst of all, low on ammunition. But he could still place superior combat power against the thin Marine lines in front of him at places of his choosing.

As dark fell 17 August, he chose to attack.

* * *

A and B Companies, 1/5 Marines, had relieved the decimated 2/5 during the late afternoon of 17 August and continued the attack. They had taken two of the knobs of the Obong-ni ridge line, and with dark, they buttoned up for the night. They adjusted artillery on likely enemy avenues of approach, and in front of their own lines they strung wires to trip flares. They expected a strong enemy reaction by night—but they did not realize that the enemy, monitoring their radio, knew exactly how they were positioned.

At 0230 a green flare rose high over the dark and blasted mass of Obong-ni, and the night exploded into a continuous flare of light and noise. Enemy squads rushed down upon the Marines, hurling grenades and firing automatic weapons furiously. As each squad dashed forward a little way, then hit the ground, fresh squads repeated the attack.

Screaming and firing, the North Koreans pushed into A Company, passed through, and slammed against B Company's perimeter. One platoon of Able was isolated, but the separate platoon positions held together. Finally, Able was forced to retreat off its knob, moving back down the slope into a saddle.

Against Baker's perimeter the North Korean attack broke. For three-quarters of an hour it was touch and go, violent, close-in fighting raging over the ridge knob. Then, gradually, the North Korean assault faltered.

Within two hours, it was growing light, and the assault ended completely as the sky brightened to the east. In the early, shadowy daylight the Marines counted almost two hundred North Korean corpses sprawled in front of the two companies' positions. The number of wounded who had crawled or been carried away could only be estimated—but the 18th Regiment was shattered beyond repair.

But the cost had not been light. Half of the Marines who had watched the evening sun go down were no longer on their feet.

With daylight, those who were took up the attack once more, following the path of the enemy's withdrawal. Soon, a machine gun held up Able's advance.

Captain John Stevens of A called for an air strike on the gun's position. But the gun was only one hundred yards in front of his men, and Battalion HQ refused to allow the Corsairs to strike so close to its own troops. Stevens argued. He said he couldn't go forward against the dug-in fire, and he would lose men trying to withdraw. He said his own men were in holes. Finally, Battalion agreed.

The Corsairs, piloted by men who were also ground officers, took no chances. One plane marked the target with a dummy run; another whistled in with a 500-pound bomb. The hillside surrounding the NKPA machine gun blew up with a tremendous wave of sound.

Stevens' Marines pushed into the smoke and falling rock and earth. They found the gun destroyed, and gunners dead of concussion. One of their own men had been killed, too—but a few minutes later they had the hill.

While 1/5 mopped up on part of the ridge line, Colonel Murray sent 3/5 into action on its north. The 3rd Battalion moved in rapidly, almost without opposition.

Behind Obong-ni, hundreds of defeated and demoralized North Koreans were streaming westward toward the Naktong. Now the artillery forward observers and the tactical aircraft overhead began to have a field day. Forced into the open by advancing Marines, dozens of enemy troops were brought under fire and killed.

By afternoon, 18 August, it was obvious to all that the NKPA 4th Division was in full flight. Marines and soldiers pushed westward, converging on the river, while artillery fell continuously on the Naktong crossings. Early on the 19th, Marines and troops from the 34th Infantry made contact on the riverbank; by that evening patrols could find no enemy east of the Naktong. The first battle of the Naktong Bulge had ended in complete American victory.

Less than 3,000 men of the NKPA 4th Division went back across the river. Its regiments had only from 300 to 400 effectives each. Behind them, they had left more than 1,200 corpses for the Americans to bury. Almost equally important, the 4th Division had left its guns: 34 artillery pieces, hundreds of automatic weapons, thousands of rifles. For all practical purposes, the "Seoul" Division had been destroyed.

The fire brigade had arrived. It had been burned in the flames, but the fire was out.

It was a bitter moment for Major General Lee Kwon Mu, Hero of the North Korean State, when, on 19 August 1950, he received from Kim Il Sung the order, published several days before, that designated the 4th a Guards Division for its heroic accomplishments at Taejon.

13

Death on the Naktong

If the enemy gets into Taegu you will find me resisting him in the streets and I'll have some of my trusted people with me and you had better be prepared to do likewise. Now get back to your division and fight it!

I don't want to see you back from the front again unless it's in your coffin.

—Remarks made by Lieutenant General Walton Walker, commanding Eighth United States Army, during the September crisis, 1950.

A T THE SAME TIME the Naktong Bulge was threatening the existence of the Pusan Perimeter, serious trouble for the Eighth Army continued to develop elsewhere. The 1st Cavalry Division holding the Taegu front was in heavy combat; the line sprang leaks in the far south. And on the east, where the ROK divisions were fighting, in the Kigye and P'ohang-dong areas, the entire front seemed ready to collapse.

Because the east was mountainous, and because he did not have troops and artillery enough to defend everywhere, Walker gambled in the east. It was assumed that the North Korean 12th Division marching down the coast would not be able to cross the mountains in sufficient strength to budge the ROK's.

But the NKPA came across the rugged terrain, surrounded the ROK 3rd Division, and threatened Yonil Air Base. By 11 August, fighter planes flying out of Yonil in support of ground action were beginning their strafing runs almost before their wheels had retracted.

On 13 August, Far East Air Force decided to abandon the field, even though it was surrounded by United States infantry and tank units. The Fifth Air Force withdrew, although there was no fire on the airstrip, and actually it was never brought under effective enemy fire. The planes were vitally needed during the seesaw battle the ROK's and the NKPA waged about the area, and when MacArthur heard the news via United Press, both he and his chief of staff, Ned Almond, were much upset. MacArthur immediately notified FEAF that he intended to hold Yonil and did not want the planes returned to Japan.

Nevertheless, the two squadrons of F-51's flew back to base at Tsuiki on Kyushu.

The embattled ROK 3rd Division fought its way to the seacoast, where on 16–17 August it was evacuated under cover of American air and the U.S. Navy. It was landed farther south to continue the battle.

P'ohang-dong fell to the enemy.

But the ROK's were able to fight the NKPA advance to a standstill. General Walker's estimate that the enemy 12th Division could not cross the mountain barrier had not been wholly wrong. South of the mountains, the 12th Division men were exhausted by the arduous passage; they had left their artillery behind, and their supply difficulties became crucial. For five days after 12 August the division received no food supply and was forced to forage off the countryside. Stretched too far, the North Koreans at last had to retreat north under heavy ROK pressure.

During each of the critical days, Walton Walker spent his time with front-line units, leaving the staff work to his chief of staff, Colonel Landrum. Walker felt, rightly, that he could influence the action more by keeping his finger on the pulse of the engaged units than by monitoring reports at his Taegu HQ.

Defending a front of tremendous width, with its artillery batteries often firing in different directions, 1st Cavalry Division repulsed crossings over the Naktong again and again. Counterattacking on Hill 303 near Waegwan, the 5th Cavalry Regiment came across a group of American soldiers, twenty-six mortarmen of the Heavy Weapons Company, who had been captured earlier by the NKPA. These men lay packed shoulder to shoulder, their feet, bare and covered by dried blood, thrust out stiffly. They had been shot in the back by Russian-made submachine guns.

Each man's hands were bound tightly behind his back with cord or telephone wire.

And along the Perimeter front, as the battle increased in intensity and bitterness, worse atrocities were discovered. American soldiers were found who had been burned and castrated before they were shot; others had their tongues torn out. Some were bound with barbed wire, even around the head and mouth.

As the evidence of battlefield atrocities continued to mount, General MacArthur sent warning messages to the North Korean High Command, threatening them with criminal accountability for these acts. There is no evidence that such acts of barbarism against U.N. soldiers were ever countenanced by NKPA commanders—in fact, orders were issued by the Advanced General HQ of the North Korean Army to prevent the unnecessary slaughter of prisoners of war. But the fruits of the long, brutal Japanese occupation could not be undone in a day; the Korean population, used to cruelty, lacking Western standards of conduct, could hardly be expected to behave other than according to its own lights in desperate situations.

When the tide of combat turned against them or when small units were isolated and in danger of losing their POW's, the vindictiveness of the North Korean soldier could not be restrained. Men accustomed to torture and summary execution all their lives, both from Japanese and Communist rulers, could not be expected to behave with nicety toward foreign captives. Nor did they.

As the pressure on Taegu increased, and its population rose by more than 400,000 refugees, the ROK Government fled south to Pusan.

General MacArthur requested General Stratemeyer of FEAF to divert his heavy bombers to "carpet bombing" of enemy ground troops. Ninety-eight huge B-29's lumbered over the battlefront, unloading almost a thousand tons of general-purpose bombs on 16 August. It was a desperate measure, opposed by the Air Force, for bombing tactical troop dispositions from 10,000 feet had to be a hit-or-miss affair. There was never any evidence that the bombing was effective, and it was not repeated.

In the Sangju-Taegu Corridor—the "Bowling Alley"—the 25th Division's 27th Infantry Regiment, attached to the 24th Division, fought desperately night after night to stem enemy advances. Colonel Michaelis' Wolfhounds were able to stop the NKPA because the ROK 1st Division held the hills surrounding the Bowling Alley, channeling the enemy attack into American guns.

And the destruction wrought against both troop units and supply lines of the NKPA by tactical air was continuous and ruinous. During this period FEAF unquestionably influenced the decision on the ground to a greater extent than at any other time during the Korean War. During July 1950, air strikes had been uncoordinated and haphazard, often damaging friend as much as foe; later, the enemy plan of maneuver was such that air could not be decisive.

But during August, 1950, when enemy supply lines were completely extended, and the NKPA was forced to mass to penetrate the Perimeter, planes flying out of Itazuke and Ashiya air bases in Japan supported each ground division with an average of forty sorties, while at the same time bombardment groups destroyed rail facilities and military matériel all over the peninsula.

While the aerial destruction was tremendous, it will not support claims made at the time. In some cases the discrepancy was thirty to one between pilot claims and actual damage. But there is no question that without this air support, the Army would have been driven from Korea.

During all the desperate days, the United Nations buildup was increasing. More ships, more planes, and, more important, fresh men poured into the Far East. During August, 11, 115 United States replacements arrived at Pusan. In late August the first help from outside the United States and South Korea entered the war—the British 27th Brigade arrived from Hong Kong. The ROK Army itself was improved increasingly by reorganization; and spare ROK manpower was diverted into American divisions, a system that was born of desperation and that was later abandoned as unworkable.

And the buildup succeeded. By the end of August, the United Nations Forces had a large superiority of manpower, nearly 180,000 against less than 100,000 enemy. They held the air uncontested, and the sea as well. Eighth Army had absolute and overwhelming superiority in artillery and mortar fire, and could face the one hundred remaining tanks of the Inmun Gun with some 600 American main battle tanks.

By 31 August the enemy had only one thing in his favor. He still held the initiative.

* * *

During the early days of the war, the North Korean People's Army never varied its tactics. It never had any need to do so. Its general maneuver was to press the ROK or American forces closely, engage with them by means of a frontal holding attack, while at the same time turning the enemy flank and infiltrating troops to the enemy rear. Against both ROK's and United States troops, who were never able to establish a firm battle line, this tactic was ruinous.

But during August 1950, the NKPA tried the same tactics against the Pusan Perimeter, and failed. The U.N. flanks now rested firmly against the Sea of Japan, and the U.N. line, while thin, had no significant gaps.

As August waned, the North Koreans began to realize that the only way they could now hope to gain a decision was by frontal attack against the Perimeter—to break through the wall, then to exploit in the enemy's rear before his reserve could eject them.

In short, they now had to play the game the way most American soldiers had learned it. And frontal assault against American troops, from Breed's Hill to New Orleans to the Pacific Islands of World War II, has always proved both bitter and bloody.

In pushing the Americans into a corner, the NKPA probably made its greatest tactical error, for, more lightly armed than the Americans, it had poor odds of smashing the American forces with direct hammer blows.

For by late August the Inmun Gun was bleeding to death. Its combat efficiency was lower than at any previous time. It had lost irreplaceable tanks, guns, and trained veterans of the China wars. At least one-third of its strength now was composed of inductees from South Korea, many of whom had no weapons, training, or inclination to fight for unification, Communist style. But the morale of its fanatic squad, platoon, and company leaders, as well as its generals, was still firm. And these battle-hardened men still held iron control over the wavering men of the ranks.

One of the Inmun Gun's astonishing feats was the fact that it got any supply at all. Rail transport, while hurt, continued to reach the front in the teeth of American air. Ammunition and motor fuel, while curtailed in quantity, still arrived on the Naktong. While artillery was scarce, there was still steady resupply of tanks, mortars, and small-arms ammunition, in spite of the fact the NKPA's trucks were almost gone.

But much of the vital military stores arrived at the expense of other supplies. The Inmun Gun received no new supply of clothing. Men whose uniforms rotted off in the slimy paddies had to wear captured GI fatigues. And rations grew scarcer. At the best, there was only enough food for one or two meals per day, and every NKPA division was forced to live to some extent off the land about it. By early September, many Communist troops were suffering acutely from hunger.

Fed information by Soviet Intelligence, the high commanders of the Inmun Gun knew of the American buildup across the Naktong during the stalemated August fighting. They understood clearly that time was running out. Either they must penetrate the Perimeter quickly, or they would never penetrate it at all.

Marshal Choe Yong Gun, from Front HQ in Kumch'on, directed North Korean operations. Under him, commanding NKPA I Corps, from Waegwan south to the Korea Strait, was Lieutenant General Kim Ung, the hardest and ablest of Communist field generals, and commanding II Corps, from Taegu eastward, was Lieutenant General Kim Mu Chong, a graduate of the Chinese Whampoa Military Academy. All these top commanders were veterans of the Chinese Communist 8th Route Army of the 1930's and 1940's.

With these men Choe Yong Gun and General Kim Chaek of Front HQ planned a massive blow against the Perimeter on 1 September. They gathered all their effective forces, 13 infantry divisions, 1 armored division, and 2 armored brigades, with security troops, together for a coordinated last offensive. The strength of these divisions ranged from 5,000 to 9,000 men; that of the armored division, 1,000, and the two armored brigades only 500 each. Approximately 100 new T-34's had arrived from P'yongyang. Altogether, Marshal Choe could muster about 98,000 men.

By 20 August, both I and II Corps, NKPA, had issued their attack orders as follows:

a. 6th and 7th divisions to penetrate the U.S. 25th Division in the south.

b. 9th, 2nd, 10th, and 4th divisions to destroy the U.S. 2nd Division before Miryang, and to break through to the Pusan-Taegu Road by way of Yongsan.

c. 3rd, 1st, and 13th divisions to break through the U.S. 1st Cavalry and 1st ROK divisions at Taegu.

d. 8th and 5th divisions to smash ROK 8th and 6th divisions east of Taegu.

e. 5th and 12th divisions to penetrate through the ROK 3rd and Capital divisions to P'ohang-dong, Yonil, and Kyongju Corridor on the east coast.

While the greatest effort was to fall on the Naktong Front, in the already corpse-strewn Bulge area, Choe's plan was to put pressure on the straining U.N. wall everywhere. His hope was that somewhere, surely, it must break.

When First Lieutenant Frank Muñoz's G Company, 9th Infantry, 2nd Division, went back on line on the commanding terrain west of the town of Yongsan, the company had only seventy effectives. Muñoz relieved 3rd Battalion, 19th Infantry, on a front that extended 7,000 meters, which spread him as thin as hot butter. Where the 19th had placed a company, Muñoz was forced to dig in a squad.

But within a few days, while the front remained fairly quiet, George gradually built up to three hundred men. Most of the replacements were men who had been wounded slightly and returned to duty, or who had collapsed from illness or heat in the first days; all had had at least a brush with combat.

George Company was able to police up a lot of abandoned American equipment, too. Now they had two light machine guns in their light-machine-gun squads, plus some Quad .50's and two twin 40mms to sweep the ground, and Regiment attached a platoon of tanks to them.

They were eating one hot meal a day, and for a little while things weren't too bad. George was beginning to pull together. Good leadership could do a great deal, given time.

But on 31 August, Frank Muñoz was smelling something stronger than the usual fecal odor of the rice paddies. George Company, like all American units, had picked up a number of native Korean laborers and servants, and these men demanded their pay on the last day of August. Muñoz explained to them that tomorrow, 1 September, was pay day for the U.S. Army and attached personnel—but the Koreans said they couldn't wait that long. At nightfall the indigenous personnel bugged out, to the last man.

Muñoz smelled a rat. He talked to Lieutenant Pete Sudduth, Battalion Intelligence Officer. Sudduth, who had his own pipelines, acknowledged that something big was in the wind. He said, "Expect something hot tonight, Frank."

"Should I continue those patrols you requested forward of my own lines?"

"Yes," Sudduth said.

Muñoz instructed Sergeant Flowers, the young, slim kid who was to take a standing patrol of four men out to the Naktong bank, to keep his eyes and ears open. Just after dusk, with the night warm and clear and moonless, Flowers and his men moved out.

The patrol had no more than reached its position beside the river when they discovered the night was full of softly moving North Koreans—they were crossing the Naktong in small boats, and the scrub and paddies along the Naktong were alive with padding enemy.

Flowers and his men, unseen, hit the deck. There were already enemy riflemen behind them. Flowers had a walkie-talkie radio. He tried to call Muñoz; the damned thing wouldn't work. All he could do now was to hide out and hope the enemy wouldn't stumble over him.

Then, at 2100 hours, 76mm shells began to sweep George's area. It was haphazard artillery preparation, not aimed. Under the shelling, Muñoz ordered his platoon of tanks to move on line with the riflemen, and to fire on targets of opportunity. Lieutenant Hank Merritt had gone to E Company, and Muñoz talked with his new exec, Lieutenant Joe Manto. He told the New Yorker George was going to hold on its present line no matter what happened.

Manto agreed. They held a good high position, except for the 3rd Platoon, which was on a spur of the ridge, and more accessible to enemy attacking from the front. On their left flank F Company was dug in, and they had contact with units of Colonel Freeman's 23rd Infantry across the road on their right.

Then a violent fire fight blazed in the 3rd Platoon area. The orange-violet winkings of rifle and machine-gun fire flashed all over the finger where the 3rd Platoon had dug in, and the 3rd Platoon leader Sergeant Tworak was on the hot loop, reporting to Muñoz, "They hit us!"

"Stay awake!" Muñoz ordered him.

Then, as usual, the wire to 3rd Platoon failed at a moment of crisis. Immediately the blazing fire fight on the spur increased in viciousness. Muñoz tried to raise the Artillery forward observer with the company; he wanted to put artillery down in front of the 3rd.

He couldn't reach the FO, who seemed to be at the other end of the company line. And then the NKPA hit George all along the line. They came through the night in long lines of skirmishers, firing and screaming:

Manzai! Manzai! Manzai!

They overran the 3rd Platoon, but recoiled from the wall of fire and steel that George threw up from the higher portions of the ridge.

Sergeant Long, 2nd Platoon, reported by telephone that 3rd Platoon had ceased firing at the enemy.

"How are you making out?" Muñoz asked Long.

"I can hold."

"Do it," Muñoz said. Now he had Battalion HQ on the wire, talking to the Artillery liaison officer. "Fire the preplanned concentrations," Muñoz requested. "I'll direct—"

By ten o'clock the artillery was crashing down around George's hill, and the NKPA were giving it a wide berth.

But by now, the entire Naktong front was ablaze with gun and shellfire. Muñoz realized that a general enemy assault was in progress and that there was trouble everywhere. By midnight the NKPA had breached a gap between his right flank and the 23rd Regiment, and they were pouring down the road in strength beyond George's power to stop. Then the enemy turned, and Muñoz could hear them hit the 23rd in the rear.

Contact with Fox Company on the left had been lost.

For the balance of the night, all that Muñoz and George Company could do was to stay on their hill and be thankful that they had not been in the path of the Inmun Gun's main efforts.

* * *

With the launching of the great North Korean Naktong offensive, every American division immediately came under heavy pressure. Immediately, the dike sprang leaks everywhere, and everywhere there was bitter, prolonged, and bloody fighting. A chapter could be written of each engagement alone, for in the first two weeks of September occurred both the heaviest fighting and heaviest casualties of the Korean War.

A major breakthrough anywhere on the five points of pressure might have resulted in disaster, but again, as in August, the deadliest threat to the Perimeter and Pusan developed in the Naktong Bulge on the southwest.

While there was a great similarity to the fighting in each locale, it was in the Bulge again that the most crucial battle raged.

As for the other areas not treated here, let it be said that American and ROK troops fought, bled, died—and held, in the main. Had they not, what occurred in the Bulge would be of little importance.

Just before the great crossing on the night of 31 August, General Pak Kyo Sam, 9th Division, NKPA, opposite the United States 9th Infantry's 20,000-yard front along the Naktong, instructed his division officers as to their mission:

> . . . *To flank and destroy the enemy through capture of the Miryang and Samnangjin areas, thereby cutting off Eighth Army's withdrawal route between Taegu and Pusan . . .*

The 9th Division very nearly succeeded, for with a 20,000-yard front, the companies of the 2nd Infantry Division's 9th Regiment were scattered like dust over a few of the higher hills east of the river. On the far south, or left flank, of the 9th Infantry's area, A Company, with two tanks from A Company, 72nd Tank Battalion, and supporting antiaircraft vehicles, held the Agok area.

In the early evening, heavy fog covered the Naktong, which lay silent except for a continuous barking of dogs from the west bank. Suddenly, at eight, shellfire fell onto the American side, followed by heavy mortar fire.

A half-hour later the fog suddenly lifted, and in the clear night Sergeant Ernest Kouma, commanding one of the two tanks in Agok, was startled to see a bridge already completed across two-thirds of the Naktong. Kouma immediately opened fire on this bridge with his tank's 90mm; the second tank and the ack-ack vehicles joined in. The bridge collapsed.

But the enemy had already crossed the river elsewhere. Sudden firing in A Company's perimeter; the infantrymen were being forced back into the hills. As the company withdrew, a soldier shouted to Kouma, "We're pulling out, tankers!"

It was a bad night for Kouma's men and those in the other tank, commanded by SFC Berry. Koreans dressed in American uniforms approached them and spoke in English, then attacked them with hand grenades, wounding Kouma with fragments. Other Koreans slaughtered the more poorly protected crew of the Quad .50 antiaircraft vehicle parked nearby; the twin 40mm M19 crew was wounded but managed to escape.

Kouma and Berry slued their Pershing tanks out of Agok onto open ground, where they had clear fields of fire. Here they killed or drove off repeated waves of North Koreans, until Berry's tank engine began to overheat. He told Kouma by radio he was withdrawing. After proceeding about one mile, Berry's tank caught fire, and Berry and his crew abandoned it.

Sergeant Kouma held his ground, firing at any enemy who threatened his Pershing. After daylight 1 September, he fought his way back to American lines, shooting up enemy troops and positions all the way.

After being initially overrun, A Company reassembled on a ridge in perimeter defense, and passed the night.

North of A, C Company, 9th Infantry, was assaulted near midnight to the accompaniment of green flares, screams, and shrilling whistles. The attack was unusually heavy, and Charlie soon broke under it. About half the company escaped southward into the lines of the 25th Division below the Nam River.

Five full miles north of Able Company, Baker had held a ferry crossing over the Naktong from Hill 209. And here, as the North Korean offensive broke, the 9th Infantry had been planning a show of its own, called "Operation Manchu." While Baker held the crossing site, the regimental reserve, E Company, had been ordered to cross west of the Naktong on an aggressive foray against the enemy 9th Division. Two heavy Weapons companies of the 9th Infantry, Dog and How, were to furnish supporting fires, while a platoon of the 2nd Engineer Combat Battalion ferried Easy across the river.

Operation Manchu misfired before it could even begin.

At dark, Lieutenant Edward Schmitt of H Company, accompanied by Lieutenant Caldwell of Dog, moved his company and weapons up behind Hill 209 to furnish a base of fire for the crossing. E Company at this time was still forming up with the Engineers back near Yongsan.

Around 2100, Schmitt and Caldwell went up Hill 209, showing their NCO's where they wanted each of the weapons emplaced. It was here, on the slopes, that the North Korean's attack took them by surprise, and swamped them. Colonel Hill, the 9th's C.O., who had been with the men of the Heavy Mortar Platoon, barely escaped with his life. His operations officer was less lucky.

When Hill got back and contacted Division HQ, it took Division only a little while to decide to call Operation Manchu off.

The men of Dog and How companies, taken flat-footed, fought their way onto a knob of Hill 209—but they were still half a mile distant from Baker's perimeter higher on the ridge. The survivors had only a jumble of assorted weapons—a radio, three operable machine guns, one BAR, a few rifles, and approximately forty carbines and pistols. On the knob Lieutenant Schmitt took command of some seventy-five men and officers.

They passed the night, and with daylight saw they were completely surrounded. Where B Company had been the night before, they saw only mustard-colored cotton caps. Below them, all along the river, they saw streams of enemy supply parties passing through to the east. And the enemy saw them.

During the night the NKPA had pushed B Company from Hill 209, inflicting heavy casualties upon it. Now they turned to the remnants of D and H on the knob, and a terrible ordeal for the Americans began.

Schmitt had radio contact with his battalion, but all he could get from Battalion HQ were promises. He learned that at 0300 the 9th Infantry had sent its reserve company, Easy, toward the Naktong to take up a blocking position between Obong-ni Ridge and Cloverleaf Hill, to deny this critical terrain to the enemy. Easy was too late; it never reached its assigned position. It came under heavy automatic-weapons fire from the high ground surrounding the road, and its C.O. was killed, along with many of its men. By dawn on 1 September, then,

Cloverleaf and Obong-ni were in North Korean hands; the hills were swarming with enemy, and the United States lines west of Yongsan completely shattered.

But on the knob of 209 Schmitt was determined to hold out. The time when Americans tended to surrender or to try to bug out was fast ending in Korea. Too many U.S. soldiers had been found shot in the back—and all hands knew there was nowhere to go. And, finally, all hands were now aware that they were in a war to the finish, regardless of how they had got into it.

All afternoon and all that night, Schmitt's small party repulsed violent enemy attacks. One master sergeant, Travis Watkins, distinguished himself by conspicuous heroism, killing a dozen of the enemy. Desperately wounded, half-paralyzed, Watkins then refused any of the few rations, saying he deserved nothing since he was now too weak to fight.

Schmitt kept asking for an air drop of supplies, if there was no other way to relieve him. A light plane was able to drop some small-arms ammunition, rations, medical supply, and twenty-one cans of beer. The water cans broke on impact with the ground, and most of the attempted resupply fell into the enemy lines beyond Schmitt's perimeter.

Schmitt was hit, but refused to give up command. His example gave renewed nerve to the tired men on the knob the second day. The enemy sent a captured American up with a message to surrender. Schmitt refused.

From higher ground, enemy machine-gun and mortar fire continued to lash the American position. After dark, the enemy renewed its infantry assaults. Again they were repulsed, but now the list of American dead and dying was growing. Schmitt's men were almost out of ammunition, and food was exhausted. They had no more water. The radio was gone; they were cut off from the world. Dead or wounded men lay in every foxhole, or on the blasted earth around it.

As the sun came up on 3 September, about the only thing left to the pitifully few Americans on the knob was the determination to resist.

*   *   *

At daylight on 1 September the tank platoon leader reported to Frank Muñoz that there was no one alive to be seen within George's 3rd Platoon area except NKPA. But Muñoz, checking the rest of his line, found the remaining rifle platoons in good shape. The enemy had boiled around them during the night, not stopping to finish them off.

Muñoz conferred with his remaining platoon leaders, Lieutenant Mallory and Sergeant Long. Long had been hit, but refused evacuation during the night. Now he asked, "What are we going to do, sir?"

"Stay here until we're told otherwise, Sergeant. I'd hate to have to recapture this terrain."

But with the enemy in the 3rd Platoon area, this ridge was too exposed for last-ditch defense. Muñoz tried to raise Battalion, and failed. In the absence of instructions, he began to look for a better hill, on which George could erect a tight perimeter. Just behind his present ridge rose Hill 211, and on this high ground Muñoz now consolidated his remaining company. And during the morning, stragglers from the 3rd Platoon came in, with Flowers' patrol.

The enemy seemed willing to leave them alone. Muñoz ordered his cooks to prepare a hot meal for noon chow.

At midmorning, more stragglers from Easy Company, which had been shattered between Obong-ni and Cloverleaf, wandered into his lines. Few of these men had any weapons or equipment; Muñoz re-outfitted them from his store of recovered American arms. One of Easy's officers, Lieutenant Day, joined him.

Day told him, "I want to get out of here."

"Hell, no. Let's combine our forces here on 211 and hold till Regiment comes back." Frank Muñoz knew that Regiment would come back. The 9th Infantry had to return, or else.

Morning passed, without action. Then, at 1200, the radio in contact with Battalion HQ squawked. From it came a new order: Move back to Yongsan.

Muñoz argued over the radio. "I can hold here. I want to stay. Look, there are still isolated American troops in this vicinity, wandering over the hills. If I stay, it'll give 'em a place to come to—"

But Frank Muñoz didn't have a Battalion officer on the radio; he was talking to some PFC operator. This operator told him, "Look, Lieutenant—my orders are to tell you to move back to Yongsan. I've done that, and I'm leavin'. Out!"

Muñoz, whose dark eyes were deceptively pleasant in his hawk-nosed face, was furious. He thought, *If I ever catch that SOB, I'll beat his brains out.* Fortunately for his career, he never found that radioman.

There was nothing to do but to move out, however. Right or wrong, he had his orders. He took stock. He had taken some fifteen NKPA prisoners during the night, most of whom were wounded, and he also had a large number of wounded of his own. These men he put in the three deuce-and-a-half trucks parked behind his hill.

At about 1600, George Company moved out. Muñoz formed his men into a long column of twos. At the head of the column he placed two of his supporting tanks, with the remaining two at the rear. He ordered small parties to go ahead to secure the hills on either side of the road to the east.

As he moved out, he could clearly see the North Koreans climbing the hills all around him. They made no move to halt the retreat, nor did they fire on him. They merely stood on the surrounding hills and watched calmly as G Company marched away.

* * *

During the night, the NKPA had passed between the 9th and 23rd regiments, and while the 9th was taking its lumps, C of the 23rd was overrun and destroyed. Only an effort by Headquarters and Service Company personnel halted the enemy advance—the same units that had brushed past the right of Muñoz's hill—close to the 23rd Command Post.

By midmorning, Major General Keiser, CG of the 2nd Division, realized his division was split in two—the 23rd and 38th, which was so far untouched, in the north, out of contact with Division HQ and the reeling 9th Infantry to the south. The enemy 9th Division was locked in heavy combat with the 9th

Regiment, and now Keiser had intelligence that the NKPA 2nd Division had also crossed the Naktong and was on high ground in the 23rd Regiment's sector.

At 0810 he telephoned Eighth Army HQ in Taegu, and reported the crisis.

Within a few hours Eighth Army was aware that a hole more than eight miles deep and six miles across had been sliced into the middle of the 2nd Division front and that the front-line rifle battalions of two of the division's regiments had been hit hard and in some cases were disintegrating. Communication everywhere along the front was spotty or non-existent.

General Walker at 0900 requested Fifth Air Force to make its maximum effort in front of the 2nd Division, and to try at all costs to prevent reinforcement and resupply of the NKPA spearheads across the Naktong. The Far East Command immediately asked the Navy to support this air effort, and at FECOM's request, naval units steaming to strike against the Inch'on-Seoul area were turned back.

Once again, as so often during the long, hot days of summer, Walton Walker had a critical command decision to make. Since the night before his Perimeter had been broken in two places—in the 2nd Division zone and in the 25th Division area in the south. In the south, the 25th had deep trouble, but in the Naktong Bulge the enemy was almost at Yongsan, only twelve miles west of Miryang and the main highway and rail lines linking the Perimeter.

This day and the next few were to test Walton Walker to the utmost. Walker was short and snappish, but under tremendous pressure he was a bulldog of a man. He was not demonstrative and had absolutely no flair for the dramatic, no personal traits that could make him beloved or admired as with a Patton or a Ridgway.

He was facing a situation that no American high commander had faced for a long time. He was fighting a last-ditch defense, largely with troops who would have been glad to depart Korea, and with commanders under him who in many cases were profoundly defeatist. Very few American generals understood the true condition of the Inmun Gun in early September. Behind Walker the Korean civilians of wealth and prominence were preparing to depart for Japan, and the Chinese merchants—those barometers of the Orient— were disposing of their property hastily and booking passage for Taiwan.

Walker, under pressure, never relented in his determination to hold the Pusan Perimeter. He spoke to his field commanders pungently and often sharply, and was not popular with them. He gave the troops stand-or-die orders, and lessened his popularity in that quarter. He had no use for the press, who got in his way, and was not adverse to letting the press know it. But whatever Walton Walker's popular image, his military reputation for the defense of the Perimeter must remain secure. And his pugnacious temperament, whatever it did to those around and beneath him, added to the defense the one thing it needed most at this point—stubbornness.

On 1 September Walker had in Army reserve only three weakened regiments, but compared to earlier times this was a princely force. He had the 5th Marines near Masan, the 27th Infantry, and the reconstituted 19th Infantry near Taegu. All these units he alerted. Then understanding that the salient in front of the 2nd Division was the most critical threat, he ordered General Craig to prepare the Marine Brigade to move into the Bulge area.

Afterward, at noon, Walker proceeded to the 2nd Division front, and riding up and down in his jeep with its special guard railing—fitted so that Walker could stand while traveling—and carrying an automatic shotgun in case of ambush, Walker told the 2nd Division to stand or die.

14

The Turn of the Tide

I never intended to withdraw. There was no place to go.

—Colonel Henry G. Fisher, commanding 35th Infantry, 1 September 1950.

TO FACE THE CRISIS in front of Yongsan, Friday, 1 September, General Keiser had only a few elements of E Company, 9th Infantry, the 2nd Engineer Combat Battalion, the Division Reconnaissance Company, and elements of the 72nd Tank Battalion. These other divisional units he attached to the 9th Infantry, and during the day they engaged the NKPA in the low hills and broad, rolling rice paddies surrounding the town.

The engineers, fighting as infantry, inflicted heavy casualties upon the enemy north and south of the town, but by night North Korean soldiers had entered Yongsan. By the morning of 2 September the edges of Yongsan and the hill south of town were littered with enemy corpses and burning equipment. The engineers also suffered. In D Company, 2nd Engineer Battalion, only one officer remained on his feet at dawn.

Meanwhile, the 9th's C.O., Colonel Hill, had gathered together the scattered remnants of the front-line companies that had been overrun 31 August. Among them were Muñoz's G Company, and F Company, which had also escaped the brunt of the enemy attack. By midafternoon these troops had been reconstituted into the 2nd Battalion, 9th Infantry, and, supported by the 72nd's tanks, they received orders to attack through the hard-pressed lines of the 2nd Engineer's Able Company south of Yongsan.

Before the attack, Frank Muñoz had been sent a great number of South Koreans, and ordered to integrate them in his squads. Muñoz didn't like the idea. The ROK's spoke no English; he couldn't communicate with them; and they seemed to have no clear understanding of which end of a gun the bullets came out.

But, desperate for manpower, the Eighth Army had decided to try to utilize the thousands of able-bodied young South Koreans that could not be readily absorbed in the ROK Army within its own ranks. The concept was never successful. The language barrier remained, and the cultural gulf between Korean and American was impassable. Lacking understanding of their allies, American troops refused to trust them; lacking training, the behavior and performance of the Koreans was spotty at best.

Muñoz protested, but was told to make the best of it. He put the KATUSA—Korean Augmentation United States Army—to work the way all other commanders put them to work, on labor details.

The attack jumped off through the engineer lines about one mile south of Yongsan. The NKPA had occupied the town, but had made no serious attempt to move farther east. Spreading out widely across the broad rice fields, Muñoz led his men toward the wattle-walled, grass-roofed city, which was already afire.

At the edge of Yongsan, they were hit by small-arms fire.

Muñoz brought a tank forward, and moved two squads in behind its armor protection and firepower. With the tank grinding ahead, the small spearhead broke through the edge of Yongsan, and now the fighting devolved into house-to-house combat.

Yongsan was a small town, hardly more than a village. Two principal streets crossed it, one running east, the other north-south. The other streets were mere alleyways or paths. The thatched houses were mostly one-storied, and made of wattle, which burned smokily. The single solidly built structure in Yongsan was the schoolhouse, which faced the park and trees of the town square.

In the reeking smoke and confusion of house-to-house combat, Muñoz's boys quickly ran into a new kind of trouble. Firing into burning houses, they moved along the sides of the streets, now and then tossing hand grenades into likely nooks. Occasionally, they stepped across Korean corpses.

In three instances, the "corpses" rose and shot one of Muñoz's men in the back. Another man, picking up a hand grenade lying beside a dead enemy soldier, blew himself up. The real corpses were booby-trapped.

"Make sure the stiffs are dead!" Frank Muñoz ordered.

George Company may have wasted a little ammunition, but now each "corpse" was thoroughly riddled as George passed by.

Ahead of the squads rumbled the 90mm-gun tanks of the 72nd Tank Battalion. Halting now and again to fire, the tanks blew apart whole houses. Bit by bit, Yongsan was being removed from the face of the earth, a fate which, tragically, was to befall almost every town and city within Korea during the coming months.

The tanks and following infantrymen reached the center of town. Already one American tank had been hit by an 85mm round from a T-34. The crew evacuated before the tank burned; another American tank passed around the crippled one and blasted the T-34, standing three hundred yards beyond. The T-34 went up in a burst of smoke and flame.

There were more North Korean tanks in Yongsan, but the 72nd, and men with 3.5 bazookas, took care of them. The enemy tanks and their infantry were well trained and well coordinated, moving closely together. But when the United States tanks engaged the T-34's, in every case the 90mm rounds penetrated the enemy armor. With their tanks blasted and burning, the North Korean infantry dispersed.

By late afternoon 2 September, Yongsan—or what was left of it—was free of enemy. By dusk, the NKPA had been pushed back into the chain of low rolling hills to the west.

For the moment, the enemy drive into the Perimeter had been stopped.

* * *

While the 2nd Battalion, 9th Infantry was clearing Yongsan, General Keiser, the Deputy Chief of Staff, Eighth Army, and General Craig of the Marine Brigade were holding conference at the 2nd Division CP. It was decided that the Marines would attack down the Yongsan-Naktong Road toward their old battleground, the Cloverleaf–Obong-ni hill mass, while the 2nd Battalion, 9th Infantry attacked just to their north, trying to make contact with the 23rd Infantry, in trouble up that way.

G and F of the 9th Infantry, with A Company, 2nd Engineers, held the line of hills west of Yongsan during the night. At 0855 on 3 September, the 1st and 2nd battalions of the 5th Marines opened their attack to the west.

During heavy fighting all 3 September, the Marines slowly backed the enemy into the Bulge. At nightfall they were on a line two miles west of Yongsan. They had taken casualties: 34 dead, and 157 wounded.

That night, 3/5 Marines were ordered to pass through 2/5 and continue the attack. During the hours of darkness torrential rains began to fall, making both Marines and soldiers miserable throughout the night.

In the next two days, they were going to make the North Koreans much more miserable.

* * *

The sun on Sunday, 3 September, came up like fire, and soon the pitiful band of survivors on the knob of Hill 209 beside the Naktong, the remnants of Dog and How companies, 9th Infantry, were broiling in the breathless heat. They had a few C rations, but they had long since run out of water, and the cries of the wounded men tightened the drawn and bearded faces of the men still holding out. The enemy fire blasting the hill never ceased.

The North Koreans on the ridge above the knob directed accurate mortar fire into the ragged foxholes. Enemy infantrymen crawled close up the slopes and tossed grenades. One man was forced to leap from his hole a half-dozen times to avoid bursting grenades; on the sixth attempt, he was killed.

The wounded Edward Schmitt never gave up. He had been promised help from his battalion, and he intended to hold the hill until it arrived. Under his leadership and quiet example, the men on the knob, suffering terribly, held together. He was still directing the defense when killed by a mortar round.

Lieutenant McDoniel, the next senior officer, took command. With darkness, it seemed as if the prayers and entreaties of the wounded and dying men had been answered; great gouts of water rained from the skies.

Men turned their blistered mouths upward, gasping to drink the falling drops; they wrung water from their filthy shirttails, and drank, half-sobbing. Lieutenant McDoniel spread out two woolen blankets, and from these he wrung enough water to fill a five-gallon can. As the rain continued, most men were able to fill their canteens.

In the rain and dark, the enemy left them alone.

But the night passed too quickly, and in the dawn, again warm and clear, only half of the men who had climbed the hill were still living. The enemy still lurked about them. Their ordeal was not done.

* * *

At 0800 on 4 September, the day dawning clear and warm after a night of chilling rain, 2nd Battalion, 9th Infantry, on line with the 5th Marines, jumped off again in the counterattack against the Bulge. During the rainy night the enemy had been oddly passive, and now, during the day, the advancing Americans began to come upon scenes of indescribable confusion and horror. Bodies of North Koreans, victims of American air and artillery, lay scattered all about along the roads, unburied. The advancing Americans passed abandoned equipment, including two undamaged T-34's. They came upon tents still standing, apparently the former command post of the enemy 9th Division. Now it seemed that the men of the Inmun Gun, asked to go to the well once too often, were beginning to break apart.

Keeping up continuous pressure, the Marines and infantry advanced three miles before digging in for the night. But the 9th Division was not finished—not yet. Moving onto his night defensive position by late afternoon, Frank Muñoz of George Company could see enemy troops assembling just out of effective rifle range to his west. They were moving into a number of small villages, and his request for artillery fire upon them was refused. From somewhere, Battalion had received instructions not to fire upon Korean villages, even if they held enemy.

The American way of street and town fighting did not resemble that of other armies. To Americans, flesh and blood and lives have always been more precious than sticks and stones, however assembled. An American commander, faced with taking the Louvre from a defending enemy, unquestionably would blow it apart or burn it down without hesitation if such would save the life of one of his men. And he would be acting in complete accord with American ideals and ethics in doing so. Already, in the Korean War, American units were proceeding to destroy utterly enemy-held towns and villages rather than engage in the costly business of reducing them block by block with men and bayonets, as did European armies. If bombing and artillery would save lives, even though they destroyed sites of beauty and history, saving lives obviously had preference. And already foreign observers with the United States Army—not ROK's—were beginning to criticize such tactics.

Observers from France and Britain, realizing that war was also highly possible in their own part of the world, were disturbed at the thought of a ground defense of their homelands. For the United States Army, according to its history and doctrine, would choose the lives of its men over the continued existence of storied cathedrals. These observers wrote news releases—and soon Frank Muñoz could get no artillery on the enemy assembling in plain sight in the villages below him. When he asked Battalion to fire on the village, and burn it down, Battalion replied it could not. Fortunately, such orders in Korea were soon changed.

Muñoz passed along his thinly strung line at dark, telling his boys to prepare for a night attack. "Those people are getting ready," he said.

At 2200 his outposts came back into his perimeter. "We hear something coming out there—" they reported.

At the moment, all hell broke loose. Coming up the hill quietly, without their usual screaming and yelling, two companies of North Koreans leaped into George's lines. The perimeter erupted in fire, and within a few minutes the enemy withdrew.

Then, without flares or other signals, they drove into George once more. And this time George Company sprang a leak. With the NKPA all over them, Muñoz's people were pushed from the forward slope of the hill, retreating over the crest. Muñoz had given no order to fall back—but the enemy pressure was too strong.

On the reverse slope George Company had dug no holes—but it had positioned its supporting tanks there. And the tankers who had served with Frank Muñoz had learned one thing: unlike some infantry commanders, he did not desert his tanks in the dark, leaving them to fend for themselves until morning. The tanks opened fire, blasting the crest of the hill with machine guns and high explosive from their cannon. They blasted the enemy off the hill.

Under their fire, Muñoz was able to get his company back up into their holes. But again the Koreans swarmed up the hill at him. He had no flares, and no artillery support at this time. Again the enemy drove George back over the crest. And again the tanks tore the North Korean charge to mincemeat. If the tanks could have climbed to the crest, they could have ended the battle there. But the hill was too steep, and the armor could only support by fire when the enemy came over the crest.

With his men on the reverse slope once more, Frank Muñoz decided to use his own judgment, throw the book away. He shouted for his men to *banzai* back over the hill. He went first.

George followed him.

They went in and shook hands with the North Koreans. Screaming, shouting, shooting, they crashed into the surprised NKPA. Bayonet duels flashed along the crest. Some of Muñoz's boys went down; some of the sturdy small brown men shrieked and died. It was like a melee in a crowded street for a few moments. Men crashed into each other in the dark, fell down. Others bumped into unseen attackers, and rolled down the slopes fighting.

The countercharge threw the NKPA off balance. Scared and yelling as Muñoz's men were, they scared the enemy more. The NKPA broke off and disappeared into the night.

Panting, Muñoz got on his SCR 300 and talked to his platoon leaders. "Join me." He knew the enemy would hit again, and he wanted to pull all of his men together so that no repetition of the earlier loss of his 3rd platoon would occur. It had begun to rain heavily once again.

One of his officers, Lieutenant Murphy, was new, and in his first fight. Murphy worried Muñoz; he had told him to be guided by his experienced platoon sergeant. Now, closing in on Muñoz's CP from his position farther down the ridge, the platoon sergeant, Loren Kaufman, led the way up ahead of Murphy. Coming through the dark, Kaufman lurched heavily into a sweating NKPA scout.

Before the man could react, Kaufman bayoneted him, Then, yelling, "Fire! Fire!" Kaufman threw grenades at the dark shadows of the enemy soldiers behind the Korean groaning on the ground, and opened up with his rifle. The enemy group dispersed, and the platoon came on into George's main position.

This was the way it went till morning. Fighting, clawing viciously at the enemy when he got too close, George held the hill. In hand-to-hand fighting, Kaufman himself put his bayonet into four more North Koreans, wiped out a machine gun that had been moved forward, and killed the crew of an enemy mortar.

And finally, heavy artillery-fire support crashed down about the company, as Muñoz found the time to call for and adjust it. The shellfire kept the enemy off George's back until daylight, when other units of the 9th Infantry attacked to the west, using George's hill as a line of departure.

* * *

As the sun of 4 September sank low over the muddy Naktong west of Hill 209, Lieutenant McDoniel realized that he had come to the end of his rope. He and his remaining officer, Lieutenant Caldwell of Dog Company, discussed an attempt to break through to friendly lines. It was obvious that the weary men atop the knob could hold no longer.

Some of the men were in a state of shock. Even the more alert ones had the thousand-yard stare, looking blankly into the dusk. Several men, half crazed by their long ordeal, had leaped out of their holes and dashed at the enemy. The enemy quickly shot them down.

As night fell, each man had only about one clip of ammunition; McDoniel knew he could repel no attack pressed in any determined fashion. But no attack materialized, as the darkness deepened. McDoniel could hear an enemy officer screaming *"Manzai!"* at his men, but there was no charge against the feeble perimeter.

For four days and nights the enemy troops surrounding the knob had left the bodies of their men stinking in the broiling sun, as attack after attack failed, and the heart had gone out of the besiegers, too.

McDoniel and Caldwell agreed to split the remaining EM, less than thirty, into parties of four men and try to scatter through the hills.

They had one problem—Sergeant Watkins, still alive, still paralyzed from the waist down from a machine-gun slug.

The Arkansan told them to leave him; he did not want to be a burden to those who still had a chance of getting away. The man who had done more than anyone to defend the hill before he fell was still brave, still cheerful.

They left him. Before they went, someone gave Watkins, at his request, his loaded carbine. They laid the stubby weapon on the paralyzed sergeant's chest, the muzzle pointing to his chin. Watkins put a hand around it and grinned at the men standing about.

"Good luck," he said.

A long time later, when the men who had been on the knob told their story, Watkins was awarded the Congressional Medal of Honor.

All but seven of the men who left the hill reached their own lines—mostly in the 25th Division Sector to the south. Caldwell was captured. A couple of NKPA took his boots and identification from him, then struck him in the head with a rock. Callously, supposing him dead, they threw his body into the Naktong. But Caldwell reached shore, and miraculously, four days later, stumbled into friendly lines.

Three weeks later, some men of the 9th Infantry climbed Hill 209. White-faced, they tried to separate and identify the decomposing corpses lying in the muddly holes; most had been blown apart or mutilated.

With this, they had little luck. Many of the men who had died on the lonely knob, like countless others who fought on the far frontier, went into nameless graves.

5 September 1950 was a day of heavy battle everywhere along the Perimeter. In the Naktong Bulge, the Marines and 9th Infantry fought their way back to the slopes of their old nemesis, Obong-ni Ridge, in the driving rain. Here they halted their counteroffensive. While they could see the enemy digging in on the ridge, it was apparent that the combat power of the enemy 9th Division had been destroyed, and the supporting 4th had lost its ability to fight long before.

Furthermore, General MacArthur had other plans for the Marine Brigade, and FECOM was waiting impatiently for Walker to release it. The next day the Marines marched back to Pusan for embarkation.

The NKPA had made a dramatic breakthrough in the Bulge on 1 September—but now it had revealed what was to be a continuing weakness of the Communist armies in Asia. They could break through the U.N. lines, but they could not exploit their local successes. With poor communications and even poorer systems of supply, dependent solely upon manpower to move their resupply, the enemy could not move quickly enough to exploit, particularly in the teeth of superior airpower, armor, and artillery. To put it simply, faced with breakthrough, the U.N. forces could retreat, and counterattack faster than the Inmun Gun could press their advantage. Whenever the heavier-armed United States Army could form continuous battle lines and withhold a reserve, the Communist tactics were doomed to failure.

If the NKPA had had a mechanized force capable of moving on Miryang, and an air force able to keep the Fifth Air Force off their backs, their tough and aggressive infantry might easily have split the beachhead and precipitated a U.N. disaster.

North of the Bulge, the 23rd Infantry had been separated from its parent 2nd Division, and pushed back. But it engaged in heavy battle with the NKPA 2nd Division, fighting it to a standstill, even though its 1st Battalion was pushed back against a lake, and isolated. Its sister regiment, the 38th, moved to support the 23rd from the north, and gradually the enemy threat was contained. By 9 September, the 23rd Infantry had been reduced to a strength and efficiency of only 38 percent, but the enemy 2nd Division shattered itself in fruitless attacks to break through.

One of the great mysteries of the Korean War occurred while the 23rd was making its stand. The North Korean 10th Division, over seven thousand strong, was in position to move either against the beleaguered 23rd or to drive east toward Taegu. If the 10th Division had added its weight to the assault, the pressure might well have been more than Eighth Army could stand. But the 10th Division, either through misunderstanding or ineptitude of its command, did not move at all against the Perimeter.

On the south, in the 25th Division zone, disaster had threatened from midnight 31 August onward. But the 35th Infantry, surrounded by two NKPA divisions, the 6th and 7th, with at least three enemy battalions in its rear, held fast. The 35th's Colonel Fisher, an experienced West Pointer, explained:

"I never intended to withdraw. There was no place to go."

The 35th fought the enemy into the ground, and won a Presidential Unit Citation. Colonel Fisher, viewing the paddies strewn with North Korean dead, remarked that even the slaughter at the Falaise Gap in World War II, where ten German divisions had been trapped, could not match the horrible sights along the Nam River.

Flies buzzing over the unburied corpses of Korean dead were so thick in some areas as to obscure the sun.

South of the 35th Infantry, the enemy broke through toward Haman. The 24th Infantry broke and streamed for the rear. Colonel Check's 1st Battalion, 27th Infantry, counterattacked, and with great slaughter halted the North Korean drive, and restored the 24th's positions. Again the 24th, reconstituted, did poorly; however, the splendid fighting ability of Fisher's 35th and Michaelis' 27th regiments with the attached 5th RCT, brought the enemy threat to nothing in the south.

On the east coast, the ROK divisions came under heavy pressure on 2 September. Some ROK units were driven back, others crumbled. But again, as in August, the mountains, and supporting American air and armor, tipped the balance. The NKPA could come over the ranges, but it could not fight its troops or keep supplied within the Perimeter. The eastern front held, in spite of local breakthroughs in several areas.

And while the ROK's in the east, the 25th Division in the south, and the 2nd Division in the Bulge were fighting and dying to stem the tide, in front of Taegu the 1st Cavalry Division held a front of thirty-five miles.

And along this front, for two solid weeks, raged some of the most vicious fighting of the war. The 1st Cavalry Division lived in a constant state of crisis. The terrain was hilly, split by many small and isolated valleys, and over these hills and through the rain-fogged valleys swirled incessant combat similar to that in the Bulge.

By 5 September the threat along three-quarters of the Perimeter had eased, but in front of Taegu the situation worsened. Eighth Army moved its HQ and signal equipment—irreplaceable if captured—south to Pusan, along with that of the ROK's. General Walker, however, remained in Taegu, prepared to fight as Bill Dean had fought two months earlier.

By 8 September, the enemy 1st and 13th divisions were only eight air miles from Taegu. The Cavalry Division was so depleted that one battalion commander said that any company that could muster one hundred men immediately became his assault company for the day. And a critical shortage of ammunition was developing. The expenditures of 105mm artillery shells had to be sharply curtailed, and from Tokyo General MacArthur urgently trumpeted requests that ammunition ships en route to FECOM proceed at all speed consistent with safety.

By 12 September, the 13th Division, Inmun Gun, had occupied the critical Hill 314, known as the key to Taegu. From this ridge, the enemy could see the vital city, and commanded the terrain about the Taegu Valley. The hill mass surrounding 314 was a mile in length, characterized by steep slopes on all sides. Against the enemy troops on this hill, at least 700, 1st Cavalry Division threw Lieutenant Colonel James Lynch's 3rd Battalion, 7th Cavalry.

The effective combat strength of the 3/7 stood at 535. Because of the shortage of 105's, there could be no artillery preparation preceding the attack. In an earlier attack, against another hill, the 3/7 Cavalry had failed badly.

Colonel Lynch, however, massed his companies so that maximum rifle fire could be thrown against the enemy ridge. After an air strike against 314, at 1100 on 12 September, the battalion moved out in the attack.

L and I companies, leading, ran into immediate 120mm mortar fire. The huge mortar shells burst among their thin ranks with great gouts of greasy black smoke as they walked forward; then the air was alive with the green tracers of NKPA machine guns and the snap of rifle bullets.

Many of the two companies' officers went down. But Captain Walker of Love Company, and Lieutenant Fields of Item, without regard for their personal safety, reorganized the two companies and led them on. And under the brilliant example, many men kept on on their own initiative even after their platoon officers were gone.

The officers and men of the 7th Cavalry were not happy with their behavior under their first baptism of fire, when many men had shown shock and fear against Hill 518. Each of them knew that the situation in front of Taegu was desperate and that around Taegu South Korean policemen were moving to the outskirts of the city and digging foxholes. And, as in the south, "There was nowhere left to go."

On 314, the 3/7th Cavalry, which had failed its first test, wrote one of the more splendid pages of American military history.

They fought their way up the steep slopes under heavy fire. Officers and N.C.O.'s, wounded, refused to relinquish command and retire. Many men, with minor hurts, refused treatment. As Love and Item neared the crest of 314, still under heavy mortar fire, the enemy rushed out at them in violent counterattack. Hand-to-hand fighting raged along the high slopes of the ridge; twice men of Love and Item reached the crest and were thrown off.

A new air strike roared in, blasting and searing the enemy on the top. When the planes went high again, Captain Walker of Love led a small group to the crest for the third time. Here he stood and shouted down the hill:

"Come on up here! You can see them here. There are lots of them, and you can kill them!"

All the officers of Item were down, including Fields. But the men sprang up the steep slope with those of Love Company; they ran into the North Korean positions, shooting, bayoneting. They swarmed over the face of the hill, and the enemy disintegrated.

At 1520 Captain Walker reported Hill 314 secured. He had forty men left in Love Company, and about the same in Item, and no officers. In the first two hours of combat, 3/7 had taken 229 battle casualties.

On the hill Love and Item found more than 200 enemy dead, wearing American uniforms, boots, and helmets, holding American M-1s and carbines. They also found the bodies of four American GI's, hands bound, shot, and bayoneted. And they found one officer, tied hand and foot, lying charred and blackened beside an empty five-gallon gasoline tin. He had been burned alive by the retreating enemy.

There was no place left to go, and all across the thin Perimeter Line American soldiers were stiffening. Hatred for the enemy was beginning to sear them, burning through their earlier indifference to the war. And everywhere, the first disastrous shock of combat was wearing off. Beaten down and bloody from the hard lessons of war, troops were beginning to listen to their officers, heed what their older sergeants told them.

A man who has seen and smelled his first corpse on the battlefield soon loses his preconceived notions of what the soldier's trade is all about. He learns how it is in combat, and how it must always be. He becomes a soldier, or he dies.

The men of the 1st Cavalry, the 2nd, 24th, and 25th divisions in Korea were becoming soldiers. For underneath the misconceptions of their society, the softness and mawkishness, the human material was hard and good.

There had been many brave men in the ranks, but they were learning that bravery of itself has little to do with success in battle. On line, most normal men are afraid, have been afraid, or will be afraid. Only when disciplined to obey orders quickly and willingly, can such fear be controlled. Only when superbly trained and conditioned against the shattering experience of war, only knowing almost from rote what to do, can men carry out their tasks come what may. And knowing they are disciplined, trained, and conditioned brings pride to men—pride in their own toughness, their own ability; and this pride will hold them true when all else fails.

After 12 September 1950, though heavy fighting continued, the situation about Taegu and elsewhere never seemed so black again. Now it was the enemy who was beginning to crumble, as Americans learned their lessons, and learned them well. Erwin Rommel had written that he had never seen any troops so inept at first as Americans in battle—or any who learned the hard lessons more quickly once the chips were down.

And while the most desperate hours of the men within the Perimeter were passing, a second battle had been raging in their rear, back in the continental United States. When American soldiers went into action, it had become customary to provide them with a free issue of candy, cigarettes—and beer. In the places American troops fought, there were rarely any handy taverns or supermarkets.

Reported to the home front, the "beer issue" rapidly became a national controversy. Temperance, church, and various civic groups bombarded the Pentagon and Congress with howls of protest against the corruption of American youth. One legislator, himself a man who took a brew now and then, tried a flanking attack against the complainers, saying on the floor of the House, "Water in Korea is more deadly than bullets!"

But no one either polled the troops for their opinion or said openly that a man who was old enough to kill and be killed was also old enough to have a beer if he wanted it.

Unable to shake the habit of acquiescence, the Army leaders bowed to the storm of public wrath. On 12 September, the day the 3rd Battalion, 7th Cavalry, lost half its strength securing Hill 314, Far East Command cut off its beer ration. The troops could still buy beer, but only when and if the PX caught up with them.

One soldier, asked his opinion of the move, said, "Let them people come over here and do the fighting if they don't like it."

A high-ranking officer cautiously said that in his opinion "one can of beer never hurt anyone."

The other remarks that have survived are not printable.

* * *

Through the middle of September, U.N. and North Korean forces were still locked in close combat all around the Perimeter. But the tempo of fighting was gradually easing; both sides were showing signs of exhaustion. Neither combatant had sufficient men to pass troops in reserve for any length of time.

By 14 September the issue had still not been decided. The NKPA had overrun all South Korea except one tiny toehold in the southeast corner—but this toehold had given it unexpected trouble. Its timetable calling for the Communization of all Korea by 15 August had been wrecked. Worse, the Inmun Gun, the People's Army, had left the bones of its best men scattered along the Naktong River, and the survivors were rapidly bleeding themselves to death against American guns on the broiling hills and in the fetid valleys.

The People's Army had almost shot its bolt. Less than 30 percent of the old China veterans remained, and these were dirty, tired, hungry, and in rags. Now only frequent summary executions and the threat of death could hold the newly drafted trainees in line. Now it was not American officers, but men like Senior Colonel Lee Hak Ku, who had come down from II Corps to serve as the 13th Division's chief of staff, who began to wonder how it all would end.

The Inmun Gun had made its supreme effort, and failed—and the Americans were just beginning to fight.

By the middle of September, a decision could not be long delayed.

15

Seoul Recaptured

Few operations in military history can match . . . the brilliant maneuver which has now resulted in the liberation of Seoul.

—President Truman to General MacArthur, September 1950.

A s AMERICANS discovered during 1861–1865, sustained land warfare is extremely costly in blood, and there has been a pronounced American distaste for such since. It is probably no accident that no great American tacticians have evolved since the War Between the States, while at the same time American strategical thinking has been superb. Having been once in the forest, United States military men tended to see it rather clearly—they had trouble with the trees, but rarely got lost in them.

During 1941–1945, on the whole, German tactical execution of battle was superior to American; German officers and N.C.O.'s on unit level exhibited particular excellence in fighting. But throughout the war, American strategical planning remained first rate. While the *Wehrmacht,* under Hitler, floundered about from one crisis to another, American strategists never lost sight of their ultimate goal of destruction of the enemy.

Because Germans considered battle itself important, their technique was bound to be good, but they became lost in the trees, winning battles, losing the war. After the fall of France, Germany's rulers never gave the *Wehrmacht* a clear, concise, strategical goal, because German planning never went beyond winning the West.

In the East, German planners again and again wasted their substance on transitory gains, while the Red Army never lost sight of its ultimate aim, which was to win the war politically as well as militarily. Significantly, while in 1942 Hitler struck deep in the Caucasus for oil, Russian military men always planned offensives for political effect, and for the control of populations. And while the *Wehrmacht* won many a tactical victory on the 1,800-mile Russian front, by 1942 it had no hope of controlling the Russian people, or of ultimate triumph.

Since the end of the Civil War, the United States has never been a massive land power. The ninety-two divisions raised in World War II never came close to matching either the almost four hundred of the *Wehrmacht* or the truly enormous field forces of the Soviets. But because the United States had Allies, such as Russians and Chinese, to keep the enemy heavily engaged on the ground, it was able to keep its commitment on land to a minimum.

If war is to have any meaning at all, its purpose must be to establish control over peoples and territories, and ultimately, this can be done only as Alexander the Great did it, on the ground. But because after the Civil War America's Allies again and again took the terrible losses required to bleed the enemy, Americans gradually developed a belief in cheap victory.

In World I, after Britain had suffered over 900,000 dead, and France more than 1,000,000, the United States threw her forces into the fray, to tip the scales at a loss of 50,000 killed in action.

In World War II, Russia lost more than 20,000,000 both military and civilian. Even agonized, stumbling France, in six weeks of 1940, lost more combat dead upon the field of battle—almost 500,000—than did America during the entire war.

Without this sacrifice of our Allies all over the world, World War II could not have ended as it did, with the United States relatively unscathed.

More Americans died in thirty minutes at Antietam than died in thirty days of the Normandy beachhead.

But by concentrating to a large degree on sea and air power, the United States was able to add the strategic punch that knocked the Axis out of the war. Japan, particularly, as an island empire was peculiarly vulnerable to air and sea attack. And the main body of the Imperial Japanese Army, on guard against the Soviets in Manchuria, was never engaged by the United States.

It must never be forgotten that without the enormous holding power of American Allies, American industrial capacity of itself would not have been a determining factor. Even in 1944–1945, when the United States Army engaged an already strategically defeated *Wehrmacht* upon the ground of Europe, the effort strained the relatively small land combat power of America to the limit.

By early 1945, men were being diverted in large numbers from the air forces and services into the infantry. No one had anticipated the replacements necessary once the *Wehrmacht* had been engaged.

Thus, again, it cannot be considered accident that in 1950 the dominant power of the world was barely able to contain the ground attack of an almost illiterate nation of nine million—nor could it have done so without the enormous manpower sacrifices of its Korean ally.

And thus, in the summer of 1950, General MacArthur, possessed of limited tactical ability on the ground, but with wonderful mobility of air and sea forces, instantly began to think in terms of strategic goals and sweeping maneuver rather than grinding infantry warfare across the face of Korea.

As early as the first week of July, MacArthur instructed his chief of staff, General Almond, to begin planning for an amphibious operation against the west coast of Korea. MacArthur planned to use his preponderance of air and naval forces, plus the unique ability of the United States Marines to go ashore against a hostile beach, to take the enemy in the rear and, by cutting his lines of communications, destroy him.

On joint Army, Navy, and Air Force levels, under the code name Blue-hearts, work began immediately for this operation. Almond initially scheduled Bluehearts for 22 July. But the continuing collapse of the Korean front, requiring that virtually all available troops be committed to save the diminishing Perimeter, rendered Bluehearts impossible by 10 July.

But, despite postponement after postponement, MacArthur never wavered in his belief that a sweep by sea around the enemy's flank was the most practical way to end the war. It was a concept MacArthur had used in humbling Japan, and it put United States strength to its best use, while minimizing American weaknesses.

The Joint Strategic Plans and Operations Group, FECOM, had to discard plan after plan during July and August. The 2nd Infantry Division arrived from Fort Lewis, Washington; it had to be committed on the Naktong. The Provisional Marine Brigade—which MacArthur had requested particularly for the amphibious operation—had to be diverted to the peninsula to help save the Eighth Army. Only the 7th Division, already cannibalized by the demands of the understrength committed divisions, remained in Japan as nucleus.

Of a number of plans postulated by the Joint Strategic Plans and Operations Group, MacArthur favored the one labeled 100-B: an amphibious landing at the port of Inch'on, coupled with a breakout from the Pusan Perimeter by Eighth Army. MacArthur chose Inch'on as a landing site because it was the second port of Korea, Intelligence reported it lightly defended, and it was only eighteen miles from Seoul, the nerve center of the Inmun Gun in South Korea.

Seoul in U.N. hands would leave the North Koreans isolated from their bases in the north, and encircled by hostile forces. It was the ancient hammer and anvil concept, and MacArthur felt that a successful operation would result in the complete disintegration of the invaders.

But Inch'on posed enormous difficulties. Between Inch'on and the open sea were expanses of mud flats, crossed by a tortuous channel. The tides at Inch'on were extreme—from 31.2 feet at flood to minus .5 at ebb. Landing craft could approach the harbor only during certain hours of the day. In the middle of September 1950, the Marines would have to land against the sixteen-feet-high seawalls surrounding Inch'on with only two hours of remaining daylight.

By 20 July, however, MacArthur had decided on the Inch'on operation, and neither the outright opposition of the Navy and Marine Corps, nor the Joint Chiefs' lack of enthusiasm—even Army General Collins was dubious—could sway him. Admiral Doyle, who would command the naval forces, told MacArthur, "The operation is not impossible, but I do not recommend it."

Marine General Lemuel Shepherd called on MacArthur and tried to argue him into a landing near Osan, below Seoul.

But MacArthur, fighting from behind his five stars and his enormous prestige as America's leading field commander, was adamant. There were better landing sites in other areas, true, but none that could so quickly pinch the vital nerves of the enemy. MacArthur was willing to take risks, provided the campaign could be brought to a rapid close.

In Washington, he received solid support from Secretary of Defense Johnson, who also wanted the war over as quickly as possible.

He moved ahead with planning for Inch'on, and he bombarded the JCS with messages stating his position in highly eloquent terms. On 6 September he confirmed his verbal orders for the operation in writing; 15 September was set as D-Day. When the JCS again asked him for reconsideration, he told them in part:

"There is no question in my mind as to the feasibility of the operation and I regard its chance of success as excellent."

Finally, in a reply contrasting oddly with MacArthur's long and literate discourses, the JCS allowed him the green light:

"We approve your plan and President has been so informed."

Meanwhile, the landing forces were being assembled. A new corps HQ, the X, was activated to command them. When Ned Almond suggested that a corps commander should be found, MacArthur smiled and said, "It is you."

But Almond was also to retain his other hat as FECOM chief of staff. MacArthur figured that the Korean fighting would come to a speedy close once the enemy were taken in the rear.

Almond took command of X Corps. A blue-eyed, gray-haired man nearing sixty, and a VMI graduate, Almond possessed both a driving energy and a contempt for incompetence at any level. He was both respected and feared throughout FECOM. He drove all men hard, but drove himself as well. He could evoke the thunders if crossed, but he was a man completely loyal to Douglas MacArthur, and one whom MacArthur trusted implicitly.

Around him, Ned Almond gathered a great number of handpicked staff. While many of Walker's staff had been thrown together in Korea under hasty conditions, Almond wished to avoid any obvious pitfalls.

For ground troops X Corps would have the 7th Infantry Division in Japan and the newly assembled and arrived 1st Marine Division, Fleet Marine Force. Both these units had been put together almost from scratch.

Each of the Marine regiments, the 1st and 7th, had been reactivated. Marines had been called from all over the world. Sixth Fleet in the Mediterranean was stripped of one battalion. Half of the ranks were filled with recalled reservists. While the first-arrived 5th Marines fought in the Naktong Bulge, the 1st and 7th Marines continued to debark in FECOM in bits and pieces.

The 7th Division was in worse shape than even the Marines. As the weakened occupation divisions had been alerted for Korea, they had slowly cannibalized the 7th by drawing on it for fillers. During July, more than 100 officers and 1,500 key N.C.O.'s and men had been taken from the 7th; at half-strength, it was even weaker in cadre positions.

For a number of days of August and September, despite the Eighth Army's shrieks of dismay, the entire infantry and artillery replacement pipeline was channeled into the 7th Division. And at MacArthur's order, Walker shipped 8,000 Koreans over from Pusan as KATUSA for the division. These unfortunates were all civilians, swept up from the streets and refugee camps of Pusan. They poured ashore in Japan bewildered, scared, and sick; many wore only sandals and shorts. Understanding no English, they were herded to American companies and batteries in packets of one hundred, where they were regarded with no high enthusiasm by American commanders.

Only in the quality of its artillerymen and infantry weapons crews did the 7th Division stand out. The Artillery School at Sill, Oklahoma, and the Infantry School at Benning had been stripped of veteran N.C.O.'s to fill these posts.

While the 7th Division gradually swelled to combat strength, the Marines and Eighth Army were having a jurisdictional squabble over Murray's 5th Regiment. Major General Oliver P. Smith, 1st Marine Division CG, wanted the 5th back before Inch'on.

But Walton Walker, pressed for the Provisional Brigade's release, snapped, "I will not be responsible for the safety of Eighth Army's front if I lose the 5th Marine Regiment!"

The Navy and Marine Corps informed MacArthur that without the return of the regiment they would not participate in the Inch'on landing.

MacArthur said, "Tell Walker he will have to give up the Marines."

The Marine Division sailed from Kobe, Japan on the 11th of September. The Army 7th Division embarked at Yokohama the same day, and on the 12th, and 5th Marines departed Pusan for a rendezvous somewhere at sea. Thirty minutes past midnight on 13 September, with MacArthur and party aboard, the command ship *Mt. Mckinley* weighed anchor at Sasebo.

The X U.S. Army Corps, 70,000 men, was at sea. It had been formed from scratch, operating against time, manpower, and every known logistic difficulty, and its very conception embodied the best of American military capability. No other nation in the world had the means and knowledge to put such a force together in so short a time. No other nation would have attempted what MacArthur had planned from the first.

Riding into rough seas from a near typhoon off Kyushu, the convoy steamed toward the most brilliant stroke of the Korean War.

Because the Inch'on landing was so completely successful, and achieved at such light cost, there has been a tendency to discount both the hazards involved and Douglas MacArthur's courage in holding fast to his original plan. Whatever the early American participation in the Korean conflict had been, amphibious assault by X Corps was no small operation. It involved more ships and men than most of the island operations of the Pacific War, and it could be accomplished only because of the skills and knowledge acquired by the Navy and Marine Corps during that war.

The Navy and Marine Corps had never fully accepted the plan; yet they carried it out to perfection. As MacArthur had said, "The Navy has never turned me down yet, and I know it will not now." And the first hours and days of Inch'on were strictly a Navy-Marine affair. Until a beachhead was secure on the peninsula, the Army was merely along for the ride.

Because of the extreme tides on 15 September 1950, the assault had to be made in two phases. Wolmi Island, connected to the mainland by a causeway, guarded Inch'on Harbor. There were troops and guns on Wolmi-do, and it had to be reduced before landing craft could crash against the seawall of Inch'on itself. It had been decided to land a battalion of Marines on Wolmi-do early in the morning; they would secure the island and hold it while the falling tide forced the fleet to retire. Then, in late afternoon, the fleet would surge back into the harbor, throw its landing craft against the sixteen-foot seawalls surrounding the city of a quarter-million people. The amphibious assault could not begin until past 5:00 P.M., when the tide was high enough to float landing craft over the slimy mudbanks of the harbor, and this left the attacking Marines only two hours' daylight to land and secure their beachhead.

If the Marines on Wolmi-do ran into serious trouble, there would be no way the fleet could help them, other than gunfire and air support, until the tide turned.

At approximately 0630, under an overcast sky, Lieutenant Colonel Taplett's 3rd Battalion, 5th Marines, followed a heavy naval gunfire and air preparation onto the beaches of Wolmi-do. Three LSV's landed tanks in support of 3/5. It took Taplett's men exactly one hour and twenty-five minutes to overrun and secure the rocky, caverned, 1,000-yard wide island.

The 5th Marine veterans killed or captured some 400 North Koreans of the 226th Independent Marine Regiment on Wolmi-do. They suffered total losses of 17 wounded.

Then the tide began to gurgle over the mud flats toward the Yellow Sea, and the fleet had to retreat down muddy, tortuous, Flying Fish Channel. For long hours Taplett's Marines were all alone on Wolmi-do, in the face of a now thoroughly alerted enemy.

But from offshore the big rifles of the fleet belched a curtain of fire and steel around the Marines, and Naval and Marine air ranged freely over Inch'on and twenty-five miles beyond, interdicting any possible enemy move. Then, in the rain that had begun to slash down into the smelly mud bottoms, the fleet steamed in with the resurging tide.

At 1733 the first landing craft of the 5th Marines grated against the seawall just north of Wolmi-do, near the center of Inch'on. Marines piled over the wall on scaling ladders or poured through holes blown in the barrier by naval gunfire. Within minutes they were in Inch'on's streets. After a brief, vicious fire fight along the wall, the enemy broke. Twenty minutes after touching shore, a Marine flare ascended into the sky, signaling the capture of Cemetery Hill, an initial objective.

At almost the same instant that the 5th Regiment went ashore, the 1st Marines struck toward Blue Beach, south of the built-up areas of Inch'on. After climbing the high seawall, the 1st Regiment moved north around the outskirts of the city to cut the Seoul-Inch'on highway. The rapidly falling darkness proved the most serious obstacle in their path.

There had been only 2,000 North Korean troops in the Inch'on area. By 0130 on 16 September, the Marines had completely ringed the city and taken each of their initial objectives. They had lost only 20 killed, 174 wounded, and 1 missing. Unfortunately, many of these casualties had been inflicted by trigger-happy naval gunners aboard LST's, who had fired into the 2/5 Marines.

Once Inch'on had been encircled, ROK Special Marines were allowed to enter the city to mop up. This they accomplished with such a vengeance that for a number of hours no man, woman, or child of Inch'on, friend or foe, was safe.

Now X Corps held a secure beachhead only eighteen miles from the vital nerve center of Seoul, thanks to the Navy and the 1st Marine Division. On 16 September, Murray's 5th Regiment and Puller's 1st pushed inland rapidly. By 18 September they had Kimpo Airfield. American air support now could fly from land bases. By nightfall of the 18th, Marines reached the banks of the Han.

On the same day, elements of the 7th Division went ashore. On the 19th, the 2/32 Infantry had relieved the 2/1 Marines south of the Seoul-Inch'on highway.

But the enemy had time to react. The NKPA 18th Division, bound for the Naktong, turned and engaged the 1st Marines. The NKPA 70th Regiment hurried into Seoul from Suwon. American air reported large numbers of troops moving toward Seoul and Yongdungp'o from the north.

But the enemy simply did not have the means to meet X Corps. He had been taken by complete surprise, and he was already stretched too thin in the south. The 20,000-odd soldiery he could throw into the battle for Seoul could stem the tide, but not reverse it.

MacArthur had told Ned Almond, "You will be in Seoul in five days."

Almond, however, was not so sanguine. "I can't do that—but I will have the city within two weeks."

On 20 September, elements of Murray's 5th Marines crossed the Han on LVT's. They moved to within three miles of the great Yongsan railroad station in Seoul, then settled down to a bloody struggle along a line of low hills ringing Seoul on the west. To their right, and south, Puller's 1st Marines moved against Yongdungp'o. On the far south, toward Suwon, 7th Division secured the flank.

On 21 September General MacArthur, feeling confident of success, returned to the *Dai Ichi* in Tokyo.

For four days the Marines and infantry locked the stubbornly defending NKPA in close combat along the western approaches to Seoul. The largest unit opposing them, the NKPA 25th Brigade, was newly activated. But its commanding general, Wol Ki Chan, had studied in Soviet military schools, and the majority of its officers and N.C.O.'s had seen battle with the Communist Chinese. The low hills and caves of the area gave them a good area for defense, and they had sufficient artillery and automatic weapons.

On 22 September and 23 September, both U.S. and ROK Marines engaged in heavy fighting along the ridge lines, with little gain. The 7th Marines, under Colonel Litzenberg, came ashore and entered the battle.

On 24 September, D Company, 2/5 Marines, assaulted Hill 66 in the center of the enemy line of resistance. Dog company's skipper, First Lieutenant

Smith, was killed at the start of the final charge; his men pushed on over him and reached the crest of 66. The enemy fought, then panicked, running from the hill, leaving dead everywhere. Hill 66 cost Dog Company 36 killed and 142 wounded out of 206 officers and men—but its capture broke the back of the NKPA defense. The next day the entire North Korean hill line broke. The NKPA left 1,200 dead behind them in their positions.

On 25 September, the Marines were inside Seoul, and 7th Division held South Mountain. Just prior to midnight, because he wanted to send the message exactly three months from the date of the North Korean aggression, General Almond announced the liberation of Seoul.

He was a little premature. Less than half of Seoul was in U.N. hands, and while certain enemy forces were evacuating, others had been ordered to stay behind for a last-ditch stand.

While fighting still raged from barricade to barricade, and from street to street inside the Korean capital, MacArthur issued U.N. Command Communiqué Number 9 on 26 September. MacArthur stated that Seoul was recaptured.

However, for two more days inside the city, from Seoul Middle School to the Kwang Who Moon Circle, from the Circle to the Court of Lions in front of Government House, the Marines had their hands full mopping up. Official communiqués studiously ignored this action.

In the process the city of Seoul was badly scarred. When MacArthur arrived at Kimpo from Tokyo on 29 September, parts of Seoul were still burning—but crowds of Koreans by hundreds of thousands lined the streets between Kimpo and Government House, cheering hysterically as MacArthur and ROK President Syngman Rhee drove to the National Assembly Hall.

At high noon, MacArthur and Rhee entered the Hall, which was packed with selected Korean officials and American military. On the platform sat Walton Walker and other American ranking officers, and Rhee's Austrian-born wife. MacArthur spoke, briefly for him, but in his usual sonorous and dramatic style:

"Mr. President: By the grace of a merciful Providence our forces fighting under the standard of that greatest hope and inspiration of mankind, United Nations, have liberated this ancient capital city of Korea. . . ."

After a mention of the horrors of war visited upon the land, and of the spiritual revulsion against Bolshevism, he faced Rhee, saying:

"In behalf of the United Nations Command I am happy to restore to you, Mr. President, the seat of your government that from it you may better fulfill your constitutional responsibilities."

While MacArthur concluded with a recital of the Lord's prayer, in which the assemblage joined, glass from the battle-shattered roof tinkled down. MacArthur paid no attention.

Little, stooped, wrinkled Syngman Rhee rose to speak. The man who had spent the greater part of his life in exile, now aging badly but still active and courageous, for a few seconds could not speak for emotion. He held out his hands in front of him, clenching and unclenching his fingers, and blew on their tips. Only those who knew Syngman Rhee well understood why his hands worked when he was under emotional strain—over fifty years before, Japanese officers had tortured him by lighting oil paper pushed up under his fingernails, and had finished by smashing his fingertips one by one.

Men who knew nothing of Syngman Rhee's harsh years in exile, or of the Japanese torments during the Protectorate, tended to be impatient with Rhee's stubborn anti-Japanese stand in relations between the two countries. But when Rhee merely considered the notion of Japanese fishing boats approaching Korean water, his fingers hurt.

Now Rhee turned toward the Americans in his audience, and said:

"How can I ever explain to you my own undying gratitude and that of the Korean people?"

The ceremony ended, MacArthur returned to Tokyo to receive plaudits from the President, the Joint Chiefs of Staff, and from all the non-Communist world.

In the ensuing days, Marines and Army pushed out from Seoul, establishing blocking positions south toward Suwon, and taking Uijongbu. On the high ground in front of Uijongbu the 1st Marine Division met its last organized resistance on 3 October.

Before abandoning the ROK capital, however, the NKPA and Communist officialdom had wreaked a frightful revenge on the helpless bodies of the old men, women, and children of the families of South Korean policemen, government employees, and soldiers. Thousands had been shot or otherwise executed. And from this time forward, learning what had been done in their captured cities and towns, the ROK Army and Government showed no mercy to any Communist, whether NKPA, guerrilla, or sympathizer. To a certain extent, Communist frightfulness was repaid in kind.

ROK officials were adamant in their determination never again to allow a Communist-sympathizing underground to exist in South Korea.

Meanwhile, the United States X Corps was in the enemy rear, seated firmly astride his lines of communications with his homeland. The anvil was in place. Now all that remained was for the hammer to fall.

16

Revenge

The last time we saw Taejon, it was not bright or gay,
Now we're going back to Taejon, to blow the goddam place away!

—Song sung by members of the 24th Division attacking back into Taejon,
27 September 1950.

ENERAL MACARTHUR's master plan for ending the Korean conflict
envisioned a massive offensive by Eighth Army to coincide with the
landings at Inch'on. The United Nations troops within the Pusan
Perimeter would break out, drive north, and link up with X Corps in Seoul,
while the enemy forces were smashed between the two friendly armies.

To take advantage of the morale boost word of the successful landing would
bring to U.S. troops, Eighth Army's offensive was delayed until 0900 on 16 September 1950. It was also hoped by FECOM that the enemy would be demoralized by the news, but evidence indicates that the North Korean High Command
concealed word of the landing from their men fighting on the Naktong.

On 15 September, most staff officers of Eighth Army were far from sanguine of their prospects. There was an ammunition shortage, especially critical
in 105's. All units of Eighth Army had been fighting continually for many
days, and there was no chance to concentrate a large offensive force for a
breakout. And the Intelligence estimate of enemy strength was more than
100,000 combat troops, with 75 percent equipment.

The same estimate indicated that the enemy still held the initiative and was
not likely to lose it in the immediate future. Eighth Army, however, had been
on the defensive too long. Defense had become almost a state of mind with
high officers; they found it hard to adjust to taking the offensive.

The NKPA was in far worse condition than American Intelligence dared
guess. Enemy losses in early September had been enormous; they will never
be known with complete accuracy. Some idea of what was left to the People's
Army in middle September can be gleaned from a captured daily battle report

that showed one battalion of the 7th Division at the following strength: 6 officers, 34 N.C.O.'s, 111 privates, armed with 3 pistols, 9 carbines, 57 rifles, and 13 automatic rifles. There were 92 grenades left to the battalion, and 6 light machine guns, with less than 300 rounds of ammunition for each.

All in all, the People's Army could not have numbered more than 70,000 officers and men by 15 September, of which less than 30 percent were the original veterans of Manchuria and Seoul. Morale among the new inductees was low—only the fact that anyone who showed open reluctance to fight was shot held the army together at all. Almost all divisions were suffering badly from hunger. But the fact that the men of the Inmun Gun knew that their own fanatic officers and N.C.O.'s would shoot them kept the South Korean conscripts from surrendering.

The thirteen divisions ringing Pusan retained no more than half their original guns and equipment.

The forces they ringed numbered now more than 150,000—60,000 of them heavily armed United States combat troops. However, these figures do not show a factor that continued to haunt American commanders throughout the war—the weakness of the rifle companies, the units that actually bore more than 90 percent of the fighting. While there were at least 10,000 men in or attached to the three new corps HQ's formed in early September, many rifle companies stood at 25 percent strength.

Throughout the war, the logistic tail continued to wag the fighting dog. While certain commanders complained and warned, none ever took any effective steps to amend the front-to-rear ratio, which of course could not be done without drastically altering the logistical practices and standard of living of the United States Army. In fact, as the war progressed, the amount of supplies required to support the American troops increased. PX goods were assigned to every company, creating both a transport problem and a headache for some company officer who had better things to worry about.

Throughout the war, because of the continuing lack of motivation of U.S. personnel, every effort was made to raise morale by the supply of goods and luxuries to the troops. Unit PX's carried tons of soft drinks and candy bars from battle to battle; they sold watches, cameras, and radios at tax-free prices, though the demand for these always exceeded the supply.

Actually, it was impossible to support overseas combat troops at anything like a decent American standard of living. The very nature and necessities of war forbade it. But every effort was made. Discussing the dozens of ships carrying fresh meats, poultry, and other goods from the States to Korea, one FECOM commander later wrote, "We can never again afford to support troops in battle with such logistic luxury." But this commander took no steps to halt the trend.

Because of the large numbers of service troops required to support American forces, the odds at platoon level were not quite so disparate as they would seem. Many United States battalions had only a few hundred effective fighting men.

Combat losses in September 1950 had been heavy among United States troops—heavier than they would be at any other time in the war. Already

American battle casualties totaled almost 20,000. And while 60,000 of the entire 70,000 men of the ROK Army were disposed on line, the ROK's were in about the same condition as the NKPA. Many of their trained men were gone, and the new recruits had no training or inclination for fighting.

Still, the United Nations had two-to-one superiority in manpower, and at least a five-to-one edge in firepower—the dominant factor in battle. They held the sea, and had complete control of the air, and could deliver the frightful combat power that control of the air implies.

All that was needed to break out of the Pusan Perimeter was a change of attitude.

The Eighth Army plan of attack was simple. It called for the Eighth and ROK armies to attack from their present bridgehead, with main effort along the Taegu-Kumch'on-Taejon-Suwon axis, to (1) destroy the enemy on the line of advance; (2) effect a junction with X Corps.

The newly activated I Corps, General Milburn, was to make the major effort in the center of the Naktong Line. Its route of advance lay roughly over the same roads and through the same towns through which Eighth Army had been pushed south in July and August.

Major General Frank Milburn's I Corps was given the 1st Cavalry Division, the 24th Infantry Division, 1st ROK Division, 5th Regimental Combat Team, and the British 27th Infantry Brigade, plus supporting troops. The U.S. 2nd and 25th divisions on the south were to remain under Army control until 23 September, at which date they would come under a newly organized IX Corps HQ.

The ROK divisions remained under their own corps HQ, although they were now fighting under almost complete United States direction.

At 0900 on 16 September, H-Hour for the breakout, there was little change in the battlefront. Under dark skies and heavy rains American divisions and People's Army were still locked in close combat, and in many places the North Koreans were yet attacking. Instead of jumping off in assault, many American units were on the defensive, repelling assaults of the enemy.

Then, suddenly, the front began to break apart.

* * *

George B. Peploe, a few weeks from being fifty, commanded the 38th Infantry, the 2nd Division's Rock of the Marne Regiment. Stemming from a family of fruit farmers near Waterport, New York, Peploe was a graduate of the Military Academy in 1925. In Europe he had served as G-3 of XIII Corps in Simpson's 9th Army, and he was within fifty miles of Berlin when the war ended.

A medium-sized, soft-spoken officer with thin gray hair and blue eyes, Peploe was still a colonel in 1950. He was unassuming, without the slap and dash of some professionals—but he had a consuming belief in the importance of hard training for soldiers.

Peploe felt soldiers should train in peacetime exactly as they trained in wartime. For an army has only two functions, to fight, or to prepare to fight. But Peploe faced the basic problem all officers who thought his way faced in the postwar years—hard, realistic training was unpopular, and it sometimes resulted in injuries.

While everyone admitted realistic training resulted in fewer dead upon the field of battle, a man injured or killed by accident on the training field soon had Congress down about an officer's ears. And the people up above showed no willingness to back their juniors up. Many a general who would have walked up a hill blazing with enemy fire without thinking twice quailed in his polished boots on the receipt of a congressional letter.

Under the Constitution of the United States, Congress holds the power of life and death over the military, and no one would have it otherwise. History has shown very clearly that for democracy to continue, the people, and not the generals or even the executive authority, must have control over the military. The people must dictate its size, composition, and its use—above all, its use. But control does not imply petty interference.

The problem seems to fall eternally upon the ground forces. While few men, legislators or otherwise, have felt down the years that they could command ships of the line or marshal air armies without specialized training, almost any fool has felt in his heart he could command a regiment.

And throughout history, the men in the ranks have been the ultimate victims of such philosophy. In the eighteenth century, when the British Navy, hard-bitten, professional, and competent, ruled the waves, His Majesty's regiments—"The thin red line of heroes, led by fools"—left their bones scattered across the world.

In the summer of 1950, while 80 percent of the officers of Peploe's 38th Infantry had seen combat in World War II, many of his new fillers had never so much as thrown a live grenade. Some of them were not even infantry by branch. Immediately and energetically, Peploe went to work. He put his men in the field, and he was always in the field with them.

The Division CG, General Keiser, was frequently annoyed because he could not find Peploe in his office or near a phone.

The 9th Infantry went to Korea first, then the 23rd, and the 38th had an opportunity for a few days' additional preparation. When they sailed, the 38th had been told they would stage in Japan, but they arrived in Pusan instead, bound for Naktong. Here Peploe abandoned a mountain of baseball bats, footballs, and other peacetime athletic equipment, and marched for the Perimeter. In late August he relieved the 34th Infantry, 24th Division, on the northern edge of the Nakton Bulge.

The front was 30,000 yards, many times that which a regiment could adequately hold. Peploe put all three battalions on line, kept only his regimental tank company in reserve. Fortunately the 2nd Division, unlike the first-committed occupation units, came over at full strength.

In August and early September, the 38th missed the desperate fighting that engulfed its sister regiments. 1/38 had a few scraps, and the tank company helped pull a battalion of the 23rd out of a hole, but on the whole the regiment went through the worst of the Naktong battles unscathed.

And 16 September, when the orders came to move west, the 38th was ready.

At this time the Air Force was not flying planes out of Korean bases—they had withdrawn their fighter squadrons to Japan. This meant that the supporting aircraft could remain over the front for only limited times—and Peploe figured that the man who asked first got the air support.

The Air liaison officer with the 38th became resigned to being kicked out of the sack an hour before dawn. But when the planes arrived over the Naktong, he was ready with his requests, and the strafing, rocketing, and napalming ahead of the 38th cleared the way for its advance.

The 38th began to push forward rapidly against crumbing resistance. South of them, the 23rd and 9th met heavy resistance and moved slowly, but in front of the Rock of the Marne the NKPA 2nd Division moved westward in disorder.

Once a flight of Australian pilots flying American F-51's roared in so close to his leading company that Peploe was concerned. The lead company commander disagreed.

"Leave 'em alone," he begged Peploe.

With the fighters spreading havoc ahead of them, Peploe and the 38th suddenly found themselves at the Naktong. All along the roads they had passed abandoned AT guns and enemy dead.

Looking at the wide, twelve-foot-deep Naktong before him, on 18 September Peploe called Lieutenant Colonel Swartz, Division G-3. "Where are the boats?"

Swartz said, "There aren't any boats."

Peploe ordered Skeldon's 2/38 to send patrols across the river and to secure a bridgehead on the west bank. A dozen of 2nd Battalion's hard, eager young men stepped forward, volunteering to swim across and secure the far shore.

These men stripped, and under the guns of their comrades went into the muddy brown water. Halfway across, one of the volunteers floundered and had to be rescued by another soldier. Hauled gasping back to the bank, he admitted he didn't know how to swim.

Moving cautiously along the west bank, the patrol found no enemy. And hidden in a large culvert beside the river, they found a cache of NKPA weapons, several collapsible boats, and one large boat capable of carrying thirty men.

Two squads went across in the two-man rubber reconnaissance boats, while Peploe talked to Division HQ again: "Let me go across in force."

At noon, Colonel Epley, Division Chief of Staff, gave him permission to cross one battalion.

Within three hours E and F and 2/38 had crossed and had taken the high ground a mile west of the river. Behind them, combat engineers built rafts to float over the heavy weapons, then a bridge for the regiment's vehicles.

Striking the disorganized enemy by surprise, the advance companies took more than a hundred prisoners, including a major and seven other officers. They also captured more than a hundred tons of ammunition, and many arms.

After an ordeal of six weeks, American forces had at last broken out of the Pusan Perimeter.

* * *

North of the Bulge, in I Corps zone, the 5th RCT moved against crucial Hill 268 on 16 September. In a vicious two-day battle, the hill was overrun, and the town of Waegwan flanked. Leaving hundreds of their dead on 268, and on the terrain between the hill and the Naktong, the NKPA 3rd Division showed signs of imminent dissolution.

Like a rubber band that has been stretched one time too many, the People's Army suddenly began to go slack.

In five days of savage fighting, the 5th RCT smashed the enemy's line in front of Taegu, and secured a crossing site on the Naktong for the 24th Division.

On the phone to Tokyo, Eighth Army's Chief of Staff, General Allen, told MacArthur's HQ, "Things down here are ripe for something to break."

* * *

Corporal James B. Mount, Medical Corps, was at Letterman General Hospital, San Francisco, when the Korean War broke. From Detroit, Mount had been a rifleman scout in the 10th Infantry in World War II, and he had seen enough fighting to keep him happy for the rest of his life. When the replacements for Korea began to sail through the Golden Gate from Fort Mason, Mount went down to the Presidio of San Francisco and waved the boys goodbye.

It was a nice gesture, but wasted. He beat most of them to Korea.

For when he reported back to the hospital, his C.O. asked him, "Can you think of any reason why you shouldn't go to Korea?"

For the first time in his life, Mount, a stocky, bespectacled man with thick sandy hair and a pungent manner of speech, regretted he wasn't faster on the draw. A few hours later, on 20 August 1950, he was on a Pan American clipper to the Far East.

The Army was scraping up men from everywhere, but Mount wasn't particularly worried. He was thirty-five years old, and he figured he'd end up in a hospital in Japan, as a medical technician.

Stopping at Hawaii, the replacements were fed in the Sky Room at Honolulu. Once, when Mount went to the door to take a look about, an MP tapped him on the shoulder. "You're going the wrong way, Corporal."

He didn't see much of Hawaii.

Then it was down at Wake, and Wake to Haneda. From Tokyo he was put on a train to Sasebo, and at Sasebo a ship bound for Pusan. After the usual Army milling about in Pusan, he was put on a train headed west, assigned for the 24th Division. By this time, he had given up all ideas about getting duty in a nice clean hospital.

At 24th Division HQ, he was assigned to Item Company, 21st Infantry, as a company aid man. Unlike most of the other new men coming in with him, he knew what it was all about, and he wasn't looking forward to it one bit.

Nobody knew what was going on in Korea, however. On the train from Tokyo to Sasebo, an officer had set up a blackboard and given a lecture trying to motivate the new men for combat. But it was a little too late for that; most of the men with Mount kept asking, "Why me?"

At Pusan, Mount was able to get his hands on a San Francisco paper. He couldn't find anything on the front page about Korea, though there was something on Page 2. Apparently, the pennant race and the upcoming World Series were more interesting to the people at home. The men around him didn't like that one bit—if they were going to get killed, they wanted it done with bands playing, girls crying, and great men telling them how they were going forth to save the world.

After all, that was the way war should be, wasn't it?

At the 24th Division, all the new men heard was, "Naktong—Naktong, everybody killed on the Naktong."

They also heard a new phrase, one Mount had never heard: "Bug out." "Bug out, bug out, everybody bugged out."

The division was getting ready for a push to the west, out of the Perimeter, and the troops were a little less than eager. The 21st's C.O., Colonel Richard Stephens, assembled all the men for a pep talk.

"There's only a shell of resistance in front of us," the bluff, rugged Dick Stephens told them. "When we break through that, we're on our way."

Oh, brother, Jim Mount thought, *that's the old rah-rah.*

But, as it turned out, the colonel was right.

The 21st went forward, into a little town torn apart and taken by the 5th Regimental Combat Team on its way to the Naktong. As Item Company went through, Mount saw a ROK soldier lying deserted by the road. He fell out and went over to check the man.

He knew from the smell even before he looked that the ROK had gangrene in a wounded leg. He gave the man a shot of morphine. "Nothing more I can do for you, fella."

The ROK tried to smile at him, and said something, so he packed the wound with cotton, and went on. On the other side of town, wounded GI's were beginning to stream back. Mount went into business.

But as soon as they saw his armband, or the red cross marking an aid station, Korean civilians came out of the ruins and the woods and the fields. There were crippled old men, and women with sick, wailing kids, begging for treatment. *What the hell, they think I'm the International Red Cross?*

But he was a medic, and he did what he could, when he could. His first job was to help GI's—but it was soon apparent who the real losers of this war were going to be. Hundreds of thousands of Koreans had been torn from the land as each army marched through, fighting, killing, burning. Nobody really wanted to hurt the civilians, but they were in the way. Nobody could help it if they got hurt.

When he could, Mount did whatever he could for them.

The 21st Infantry pushed up to the Naktong and went across in assault boats. Artillery was falling in, and I Company lost a few men. Mount had four Korean KATUSA's assigned to him for litter bearers, and he put these men to work. He couldn't talk to them, but he could make do with sign language and a lot of cussing.

Assembling to cross the river, Item had taken cover in an apple orchard. Mount, from his own experience, could have told them that apple trees splinter under shell fire. By the time he had dug out a few splinters, everyone in the company knew it.

By the time the company was across the Naktong, Mount had his wounded all to the rear. He himself crossed, but ran into a GI hit in the leg. Taking this man back across the river, he returned to find Item Company gone.

A new outfit came into the area, and Mount asked a lieutenant if he knew where Item was. The lieutenant took out a map and showed him where I should be. Mount took off, and followed a path across the hills for two hours before rejoining his company.

A few minutes afterward, the company received orders to return to the river. But they had broken through the shell, and the enemy was retreating. Now, it meant a long march each day to make contact, if contact was made at all, and then up on the high ground at night to dig in.

At dawn, it was up and away again.

The enemy was on the run.

* * *

For the first three days of the United Nations offensive, with the exception of the 38th's crossing of the Naktong in the south, there were no material gains. Everywhere the NKPA battled stubbornly, and everywhere—in the 5th RCT, in the 1st Cavalry Division north of them, and the 1st ROK still farther north, friendly forces suffered heavy losses in desperate, seesaw battle.

And then, suddenly, on 19 September, the day after Peploe's 38th crossed the Naktong, the Korean front began to fall apart. The single biggest factor, undoubtedly, was the knowledge of the Inch'on landing in the NKPA's rear. The North Korean High Command could conceal the disaster no longer; the news was out, spreading chaos and panic among the men around the Perimeter.

During the hours of darkness 18–19 September, the enemy 6th and 7th divisions in the far south, the farthest from North Korea, began a precipitate withdrawal.

On the east coast the 3rd ROK retook P'ohang-dong, while the enemy 5th Division retreated northward. Just west of the coast, in the rugged mountains, the ROK's suddenly found they could advance, and did.

On 19 September the 5th RCT took Waegwan. On the same date General Paik Sun Yup's 1st Division discovered a gap between the lines of the enemy 1st and 13th divisions. The hard-fighting ROK 12th Regiment shot through thirteen miles into the enemy's rear.

Only the 1st Cavalry, meeting stubborn, fanatical resistance in the hills around Taegu, could not advance. The Cavalry took frightful losses among its rifle units; but at the same time it was wreaking worse havoc on the enemy. And the enemy, with the knowledge that the 1st ROK Division had made a penetration, suddenly retreated north to Sangju.

And, retreating, the enemy came apart. The 3rd Division went from 5,000 men to less than 2,000 in two days. Entire units were caught on the roads by American air, or ground to pieces by American infantry and armor. The retreat became a slaughter.

The 13th Division, bled white in the hills by the 1st Cavalry, had already shown signs of internal distress. A regimental commander had surrendered voluntarily, claiming unfair treatment by the division commander. Faced with failure, the Communists were beginning to snap and bite at each other. Officers were being relieved; men were being summarily executed.

Pushing ahead, the 1st Cavalry Division units passed scenes of terror and devastation, burned-out tanks, dead and bloating animals, cannon pushed off the roads into ditches, tons of abandoned ammunition. Complete units of the enemy 1st, 3rd, and 13th divisions now fell prey to panic, and virtually disintegrated.

By 23 September the Inmun Gun was everywhere in full retreat. And on 22 September Walton Walker issued an order long awaited by the Eighth Army: *Pursue and destroy the enemy.* The time had come for revenge.

* * *

In the pre-daylight murk of the morning of 21 September, a senior colonel of the Inmun Gun walked down a narrow dirt road four miles south of the village of Tabu-dong. In full uniform, rank badges gleaming on his shoulder boards, a soft cap over his dark hair, the colonel quietly approached American lines and waited until daylight.

The colonel's name was Lee Hak Ku, and his exact motives this dawn of 21 September will never be completely known. But behind him the 13th Division, of which he was chief of staff, was in utter dissolution. It numbered only 1,500 men. Its HQ had lost communication and control over its regiments. The division held no line, and its survivors were now fleeing over the hills toward Sangju. It was *sauve-qui-peut,* and the men were no longer waiting to be shot down by their officers. The officers themselves were throwing away their guns.

The Koreans, North and South, are by any standard a brave people, but they are mercurial, rising one moment to extremes of exaltation, dropping quickly back into despair. They can be martyrs on any given day, and traitors the next. They have been called, not without reason, the Irish of the Orient. And in some cases, not even rigid Communist training, with its denial of basic human nature, can eradicate the nature of the Korean peasant.

When it became daylight, Senior Colonel Lee Hak Ku walked softly up into a small village held by the 8th Cavalry Regiment. Ironically, he had to awaken two sleeping American soldiers carefully in order to surrender. When they took him to the rear, the young, hard, square-faced North Korean was very cooperative with his interrogators.

He supplied them with whatever information they desired about his division. It did not matter, whatever he told them, because the division had been destroyed as a fighting force. Other prisoners, though of lesser rank, had told the same story.

His surrender so impressed General Walker that, when he heard the news, he phoned Tokyo from Taegu. Senior Colonel Lee Hak Ku was the highest-ranking Communist prisoner to be taken by the U.N. during the Korean War.

And in captivity, he would do more damage to the U.N. cause than he had ever accomplished while serving in the Inmun Gun.

* * *

Opposite the old Naktong Bulge, three NKPA divisions, the 2nd, 4th, and 9th, streamed westward in retreat. And streaming after them, like hounds in full cry, came the United States 2nd Division.

On 23 September the 2nd Division reduced the stubborn roadblocks the fleeing enemy had thrown up about the town of Ch'ogye. And then, on 24 September, the 38th Regiment swept north, the 23rd circled south, and both regiments linked up beyond the old NKPA command post at Hyopch'on.

Northeast of Hyopch'on, Peploe's infantrymen erected a roadblock while two enemy battalions still held the city. Then the 23rd fought into Hyopch'on from the south, driving the defenders out and north.

Running into Peploe's roadblock, the North Koreans met a storm of fire. That afternoon, after the killing ceased, Peploe's men counted more than 300 corpses along the road. The survivors, sloshing across the paddies in panic, were struck by American planes and shot to pieces. The few who got away ran into the hills without arms, ammunition, or food.

Now, in late September, it was North Koreans instead of Americans who straggled through the hills, broken, demoralized, shoeless, and hungry.

And grimly, without exultation, American soldiers found the taste of revenge sweet and good.

On the 25th, on order, the 38th Infantry moved northwest toward Koch'ang. In a few hours it had broken through the thin defensive crust of the enemy 2nd Division and was in the NKPA artillery areas, overrunning guns, vehicles, and heavy equipment.

General Choe, commanding the enemy division, was sick and worn out. He ordered all his vehicles and artillery abandoned, and then, his men carrying him, Choe and the remnants of the NKPA 2nd melted into the hills, where they became guerrillas.

On 25 September the 38th Infantry killed more than 200 enemy soldiers, captured 450 more. They amassed a total of 10 motorcycles, nearly 20 trucks, 9 mortars, 14 AT guns, 4 howitzers, and 300 tons of ammunition.

At dusk, 2030, the regiment had advanced thirty miles.

The American forces, well supplied with vehicles, with many good roads in this part of Korea, were advancing faster than the enemy could flee. General Walker's orders for the pursuit and exploitation had instructed the divisions to forget about their flanks, to press ahead against a beaten enemy, and this tactic was paying off.

Tanks rolling ahead, moving over an open road, with encircling hills far to either side, the 38th again and again overran the now desperate enemy. At Koch'ang the regiment captured a North Korean field hospital. Now Peploe received orders to strike across the peninsula to Chonju, a town near the west coast.

The 2nd Battalion leading, the 38th entrucked at 0400 28 September. Nine and one half hours later, after advancing 72 miles, the regiment closed in on Chonju. Here there was a brief fight. One hundred North Koreans were killed, and twice as many surrendered.

Inside the town, Peploe threw up a perimeter defense. He was far inside enemy territory; thousands of North Koreans had been bypassed along the road.

But the enemy was also confused by the slashing American movements. During the evening a North Korean truck tried to pull into the town. It was loaded with crates, and seemed to carry about twenty soldiers.

An outpost of the 38th along the road fired a single bazooka round at the truck as it approached. Then the men of the outpost cowered in the ditches as the truck disappeared with a horrendous explosion, raining fire and fragments over a wide area. The crates had been filled with ammunition.

Concerned by the terrific detonation, Peploe came out to see what had happened. Viewing the reeking crater in the road, he could find no remnants of either the truck or the men who had been upon it.

Coming into Chonju, the regiment had exhausted its motor fuel. Fortunately, a far-ranging 2nd Division liaison plane passed over them before dark. The pilot was confused, and incredulous. "Are you 2nd Division troops?" he kept asking over the radio.

"Yes, and we're out of gas," he was told. The plane buzzed back to its field, and soon both Division HQ and IX Corps had fresh gasoline trucks on the road.

While Peploe marked time in Chonju, waiting for resupply, the assistant commander of the 24th Division flew in. He seemed disappointed at the sight of the Indianhead patches on the sleeves of the men holding the town; he had hoped to find the taro leaf of his own division in the vanguard. Rather unhappily, he asked permission for units of the 24th to pass through Peploe's lines.

The next day, gasoline trucks reached Chonju, and once again the 38th Infantry moved north and west.

This time they went to the south bank of the Han, in sight of Seoul.

The hammer had fallen. It had met the anvil, and what had been in between was no more.

17

The Taste of Triumph

I see the most serious fault . . . to lie in . . . the legalistic-moralistic approach to international problems . . . the inevitable association of legalistic ideas with moralistic ones: the carrying into the affairs of states the concepts of right and wrong . . . whoever says there is a law must of course be indignant against the lawbreaker and feel a moral superiority to him. And when such indignation spills over into military contest, it knows no bounds short of reduction of the lawbreaker to the point of complete submissiveness—namely, unconditional surrender.

—George F. Kennan.

IN THE CLOSING days of September 1950, the Unites States seemed to be in an invulnerable position in the Far East. In the space of a few short days, the entire balance had turned; with almost shocking suddenness an American and ROK army that had been fighting for its life turned and destroyed its tormentors.

Trapped between the anvil of X Corps on the north, and the hammer of Eighth Army smashing upward from the south, not more than 25,000 survivors of the Inmun Gun were able to retreat north of the 38th parallel.

And as American field commanders could at last relax, as the men under them could savor the sweet taste of chasing and killing an enemy that had chased and killed them earlier, in Washington, where early confidence had turned to concern and then apprehension, confidence returned, strongly.

For a moment, the world had seemed to shake, to go awry—but now all was as it should be, as Americans felt it must always be. Men smiled, and vaguely wondered why they had allowed themselves to doubt the inevitable victory.

And with victory, as it had always come to Americans after a war, came the determination to force their will on the enemy, to punish them for the crime of aggression, for starting the war. If the fighting, with its resultant death and destruction, its loss of American lives, resulted only in the return of the *status quo,* then almost all Americans would feel cheated.

War could never be part of a system of checks and balances; the view seemed immoral. War must always be for a cause, a transcendental purpose: it must not be to restore the Union, but to make men free; it must not be to save the balance of world power from falling into unfriendly hands, but to make the world safe for democracy; it must not be to rescue allies, but to destroy evil.

Americans have always accepted checks and balances within their own system of government, but never without, in the world. Because in the world such checks have never been achieved with votes or constitutions but with guns, and Americans have never admitted that guns may serve a moral purpose as well as votes.

They have never failed to resort to guns, however, when other means fail.

It was inevitable that the United States should take the position that the North Korean Communist State must now be destroyed for its lawlessness and that all Korea should be united under the government of the Taehan Minkuk.

Actually, the Communist world had not broken the law, for one of the continuing tragedies of mankind is that there is no international law. The Communist world had tried to probe, a gambit, and had been strongly checked.

And the Communists would regard an American move to punish the "lawbreaker" not so much as justice but as a United States gambit of its own.

The question was not whether the American desire to reunite Korea under non-Communist rule was a proper goal for the United States, but whether the Communist world could sit by as the United States in turn ruptured the *status quo ante.*

The desire to join the two halves of Korea under Syngman Rhee was unquestionably proper, and in the best interests of the United Nations—if the U.N. had the power to accomplish it.

On 27 September 1950 the Joint Chiefs of Staff instructed General MacArthur as follows:

1. His primary objective was to be the destruction of all North Korean military forces.

2. His secondary mission was the unification of Korea under Syngman Rhee, if possible.

3. He was to determine whether Soviet or Chinese intervention appeared likely, and to report such threat if it developed.

With the third instruction appeared signs of an elementary weakness in American policy—a decision by the powerful Communist nations to intervene or not to intervene was a political question, on the highest level. The indications would be apparent—or nonapparent—not on military levels but through the channels of political intercourse.

FECOM, a subordinate command, was a collective agency only, not an evaluative one. Yet throughout the fall of 1950 Washington continued to permit

FECOM to evaluate not only its own intelligence but also that collected in other parts of the world as well. The eternally dangerous lack of insight into the aims and aspirations of hostile governments was to continue in Washington.

Military intelligence, quite competently, can determine the number of divisions a nation has deployed. Military men can never wholly competently decide, from military evidence alone, whether such nation will use them.

Such decision is not, and will never be, within the competence of military intelligence.

Following the directive of 27 September, two days later General George C. Marshall, the new Secretary of Defense—Louis Johnson, who had given the public what it wanted, had been the scapegoat of the public's error—sent MacArthur a personal communication—JCS 92985—"for his eyes only"—that he was free both tactically and strategically to proceed across the parallel and that President Truman concurred.

Meanwhile, the Republic of Korea had never seriously intended to halt at the old border. It is very doubtful if Syngman Rhee, who lived to reunite his country, would have obeyed a U.N. order to stop short of the parallel, any more than Abraham Lincoln would have favored an order from foreigners to stop the Grand Army of the Republic on the Potomac after Gettysburg. Rhee issued orders to his field commanders, now serving under American command, to move north no matter what the Americans did.

Whatever the ploy and counterploy of the great powers, it was in the vital interests of the Taehan Minkuk to expand to the Yalu.

On 1 October, MacArthur demanded the surrender of North Korea. Kim Il Sung made no reply.

At noon, 7 October, American units of the Eighth Army went across the parallel at Kaesong. ROK troops had already gone north days before.

* * *

On a clear, crisp October day, Captain Worsham Roberson, assistant surgeon of the 6th Tank Battalion, 24th Division, pulled his battered, dusty old jeep to a halt alongside the highway leading north. A hastily erected sign—the trademark of the passing of American troops anywhere in the world—told him that he was crossing the 38th parallel.

He looked at Captain Harvey Phelps, battalion surgeon, sitting beside him, and the stocky, round-faced Roberson fumbled in his kit, removing a carefully hoarded bottle of Seagram's 7 Crown.

Roberson and Phelps had arrived during the bad days, when the crumbling 24th held onto the Perimeter by a nail. They would never forget their arrival into the lines of the division with the new M-46 90mm-gun tanks, shipped hastily from Detroit Arsenal.

It had been hell to get the big tanks to Oakland, aboard ship, and on land again at Pusan. At Pusan there had been no port facilities to handle a 92,000-pound tank; the ship's officers had groaned and turned pale while the ship's winches and cargo booms strained under the extreme load. But lives, after all, were more valuable than winches, and one by one the 76 tanks had crashed down on the dock.

When the armor growled and roared up to the Naktong, men from the Taro Leaf Division ran forward to meet them, many of them openly sobbing. They crowded around the ugly steel monsters and patted them as if they had been blooded horses.

Under Lieutenant Colonel John Growden, West Point 1937, who had been with Patton, the 6th Tank soon had its baptism of fire.

To Growden came a radio flash from a leading tank: "We have sighted enemy. What are our orders?"

Growden radioed back: "Are they definitely enemy?"

"Affirmative!"

"Then fire—that's why the hell we're here!"

In each and every war, Americans must learn the hard way.

It had been a long, hard road. And when they had broken out, and the shooting was good, they had passed a little knoll, on which had been dug fifteen or sixteen trenches. Hearing the men talk, Captain Roberson went up to look.

Buried waist-deep, hands wired behind their backs, agony imprinted on their stark faces, were 500 ROK soldiers and 86 GI's. Some had been bayoneted to death; some had been clubbed; some mercifully, shot.

Doc Phelps, looking ill, determined the men had been killed the evening before the battalion passed.

Now, thinking of the long, dusty, bloody road, Roberson pulled the stopper on the bottle. "Doc, this calls for a drink."

Phelps was a teetotaler. Furthermore, he was married to the daughter of Dr. Godbold, famous pastor of the St. Louis First Baptist Church, who had strong opinions on alcohol. Doc Phelps hesitated, then took the bottle.

"To heck with Dr. Godbold—this calls for a drink—"

Worsham Roberson figured Dr. Godbold would understand, this once.

* * *

When it had voted, 7 to 0, with 3 abstentions, 1 absence, to form a unified command in Korea, to permit the United States Government to appoint the U.N. commander, and to use the U.N. flag, the Unites Nations on 7 July 1950 had in effect given the United States something very close to carte blanche for the conduct of the war.

The U.N. Commander, MacArthur, was requested to send, through his government, appropriate reports on whatever action he took.

At this time, the majority of the United Nations were either Western nations or pro-Western; only a handful of the so-called neutrals had been admitted to membership. And, shocked by the overt Communist action, these nations realized that only the United States was capable of effectual opposition to Communist power.

When the Inmun Gun collapsed, the U.N. was prepared to continue its backing of United States policy. The United States was riding a crest of success, and in October 1950 Americans were happily discovering that world opinion, for whatever it is worth, tends to follow power and success. Later, after Hungary and Tibet, they would again rediscover the fact, this time less happily.

As long as the United States was winning, and its aim did not seem to lead to general war or to sacrifices for the war-weary friendly nations, the U.N. as then constituted was content to follow.

But this was the last time the United States was to find general agreement.

There is every indication that, just as they had not expected that the United States would intervene in Korea in June, the North Koreans did not anticipate the U.N. offensive over the parallel. The shattered Inmun Gun had not been reconstituted after its retreat, and the extensively prepared positions along the border were not heavily defended.

When the Eighth Army smashed across Kaesong in the west, and the ROK's galloped northward to the east, formal resistance almost dissolved. Within a week, despite small pockets of violent resistance here and there, there no longer existed an organized North Korean front, and only remnants of the North Korean Army fled toward the Yalu.

Kim Il Sung's broadcast to his forces 14 October is highly revealing. He stated that the new disaster was due to his government's expectation that the U.N. would not move north and that "many of our officers have been thrown into confusion by this new situation. They have thrown away their arms and left their positions without orders."

Kim Il Sung further proclaimed resistance to the last. Traitors and agitators were to be shot on the spot, regardless of rank, and a new "Supervising Army" of politically reliable veterans was to be formed.

When it dragged its bleeding forces hastily back across the parallel, the Communist world had apparently been ready to accept a temporary defeat. It was Communist doctrine to exploit success, but it was also considered folly to support failure.

The move in Korea had failed; now they would drop it, wait till a better day. In New York on 2 October the Soviet delegate to the Security Council proposed a cease-fire along the parallel, and a withdrawal of all foreign troops from the peninsula.

Instead, he had a new American challenge thrown into his teeth.

* * *

On a balmy Sunday, 15 October, just as the Korean War was turning into a sort of American fox hunt, a star-studded group conferred on Wake Island. Peppery, sharp-eyed President Truman had flown halfway across the Pacific to discuss the final phases of the action with his patrician proconsul of American power in the East, Douglas MacArthur.

Oddly, a fact much noted, it was almost a meeting of two sovereigns rather than of Chief of State and field commander.

The architects of American policy were represented, from homely, keen-faced Omar Bradley, Chairman of the Joint Chiefs, talking in the same Missouri Valley twang as the President but the finest Army group commander America had produced, to quiet, self-effacing Dean Rusk of the State Department.

The conference was high-level, and five-star General Bradley took its notes.

There was very little talk about the fighting. It was taken for granted that the conflict was almost over and that now the main concern was the rehabilitation of Korea, north and south, most of which lay in ruins.

MacArthur said he expected formal resistance would end around Thanksgiving. He hoped to have the Eighth Army back in Japan by Christmas.

General Bradley, with problems around the world, wanted to know when MacArthur might be able to release a division for Europe.

Then the talk came around to a different matter. "What," asked Harry Truman, "are the chances for Chinese or Soviet intervention?"

Sonorously, MacArthur replied, "Very little."

He went on to say that had they interfered during the first or second months it would have been decisive. "But we are no longer fearful of their intervention. We no longer stand with hat in hand."

He mentioned that the Chinese had 300,000 men in Manchuria, of which not more than 200,000 were along the Yalu River. Of these, not more than 60,000 could be got across.

"The Chinese have no air force. If the Chinese try to get down to P'yongyang there will be the greatest slaughter."

No one, civilian or military, disagreed with MacArthur's view.

But it was not what was said, but what was left unsaid on Wake Island, Sunday, 15 October, that would change the course of history.

General MacArthur was operating on purely military assumptions that the Chinese did not have the ability to intervene. And one of these assumptions was that, if the Chinese dared oppose the righteous march of U.N. forces, the United States would retaliate with all its righteous wrath and fury—that American air would strike at China, interdict its long and painfully vulnerable supply lines across Manchuria, destroy the fledgling industry of which the Chinese were so proud.

He firmly believed such a fear would deter the Chinese from action. He firmly believed, also, that upon a Chinese move, America would cry havoc and loose the dogs of war. China, even with its millions, could not hope to gain by general war with the West.

These things he believed, but did not mention.

Quiet, modest Omar Bradley, with one of the best military brains in the business, was thinking of the massive Soviet divisions—at least 175 in the Satellite countries alone—positioned in Europe. To him, all-out war with China would be war with the wrong enemy, at the wrong place, at the wrong time. The United States had to bear the load in Asia, true, but its vital interest lay in Europe, and its greatest danger in Soviet Russia.

There was no occasion to discuss the matter.

And President Truman, with his civilian advisers, the architects of containment, had his own ideas. He saw no hope of, or profit in, America's trying to subdue the endless land masses of Russia and China. It could only be done—if at all—by such holocaust as mankind had never known.

Harry Truman was ready to defend his country at all costs. If the enemy attacked the United States, or its treaty allies, America would go to war, at once. But Harry Truman would do nothing to precipitate Armageddon.

It was one thing to attempt to prevent the further expansion of Communism, even at the cost of blood, but quite another to seek a global victory over world Communism. Harry Truman doubted that victory would be worth the price.

There was talk, high-level talk, at Wake Island, Sunday, 15 October, but there was not enough communication.

And while these men talked, unknown to any of them, the hordes of Red China, marching by night, wailing the minor keys of Sinic music, were streaming across the Yalu into the high and barren wastes of North Korea.

* * *

The punishment the U.N. and its agent, the United States, proposed to visit upon the Communist world was greater than the Communist world was willing to accept. Just as the United States had not been able to stand idly by in June as a friendly dependency was overwhelmed, in October the men of Peiping and the Kremlin felt they could not permit the forcible separation of North Korea from their own sphere.

One gambit had failed; now they must attempt another.

In 1950 Soviet Russia wanted general war no more than did the United States. Stalin and his associates held no illusions that the United States could be conquered. Russia's own wounds from World War II were hardly healed, and the nuclear balance of power in American hands was as yet overwhelming. But the Soviets were still willing to accept grave risks.

If the U.S.S.R.'s stance were different from America's, if it could not cease pushing, probing, and risking, it was because Soviet foreign policy was aggressive and expansionist. Communist ideology was far more than a tool to such expansion. It remained a taskmaster forcing the Soviets to it. Unless, with time, Communist ideology could be diluted, or diverted from the narrow precepts of Lenin, there could never be any true peace between Communists and the West. Westerners, tending to be pragmatic and liberal in viewpoint, often miscounted the driving reality of Communist dogmatism.

Russians, determined to oppose the American action in Korea, saw clearly that a confrontation of American troops with Russian, a direct clash, must inevitably escalate into general war, whether the governments wanted it or not. But the West had accepted Soviet arms in the hands of a satellite people; even though they had been drawn into the bloodletting themselves, the Americans had tacitly accepted war at secondhand with the Communist center of power. To substitute another Communist people, the Chinese, for the North Koreans, was not to change materially the tenuous rules of the game. And because of China's contiguous border with North Korea, even some sort of moral case for Chinese intervention could be made.

The Communist leaders, desperate to save both their face and North Korea, felt that if new forces were hurled into the Korean cockpit, so long as the move did not seem to be a direct confrontation of the major powers, the conflict could still be limited to the peninsula.

And on the peninsula they felt they still might win.

Equally important, Red China was ready and spoiling for war.

The Chinese Communists, newly come to power, were driven by that dynamic puritanism that accompanies all great revolutions. Like the French in 1793, they not only desired conflict with the "evil" surrounding them; they needed it. Their hold on the millions of the sprawling Middle Kingdom was far from consolidated, and a controlled, limited war would consolidate it as nothing else could do.

However lacking in Communist enthusiasm the hordes of China might be, there was both a sullen sense of grievance against the West and a passionate national pride in China's millions. Both these passions have been too often overlooked by foreigners.

Just as the northern states of the American Union have overlooked and forgotten their occupation and reconstruction of the southern states, the West has dismissed the painful humiliations repeatedly visited upon the ancient Sinic culture in the past hundred years.

Neither the South nor the Middle Kingdom has forgotten. The Chinese, a proud and very ancient people, never willingly accepted their domination by foreign powers. They never accepted the extraterritoriality, the quartering of foreign troops on their soil, the control of their commerce. Unable to fight the gunboats the foreign powers sent to quell their resentment, they could only smolder, and await the day when the Middle Kingdom was again a world power.

Even Chinese who detested Communism would thrill if the Middle Kingdom emerged from its long impotence, and the men in Peiping understood this.

If they could engage the West, defeat it, or fight it to a standstill, they would gain face as no Chinese rulers had gained for generations.

When the United States had entered the war in Korea, the Chinese had well understood the inevitable result. After all, China had supplied the hard core of the Inmun Gun; the Chinese were hardly blind to that Army's weaknesses. Early in September Chinese forces began the long march from the south, where they had been deployed against Taiwan, to the mountains along the Yalu. The early successes of the Inmun Gun had surprised the rulers of China—and now those successes gave them renewed confidence.

If the "imperialists" moved north, the Chinese would have a severe shock awaiting them.

On 1 October 1950 Mao Tse-tung stated publicly:

The Chinese people will not tolerate foreign aggression and will not stand aside if the imperialists wantonly invade the territory of their neighbor.

Red China had no relations with the United States, but on 3 October small, grave-faced Chou En-lai ordered the Indian ambassador, Sardar K. M. Panikkar, to his office. Here the foreign minister told Panikkar, "If the United States, or United Nations forces cross the 38th parallel, the Chinese People's Republic will send troops to aid the People's Republic of Korea. We shall not take this action, however, if only South Korean troops cross the border."

Panikkar was deeply impressed. He called New Delhi at once, and the Indian Government passed this word both to New York and to Washington. The Indian delegate to the U.N. announced that his government felt U.N. forces should remain south of the parallel.

Washington took no action except to inform MacArthur's HQ in Tokyo.

Meanwhile, other Chinese officials dropped pointed hints to members of the few Western missions in Peiping. All these views were reported to Washington, which in turn forwarded them to Tokyo.

On 10 October, Peiping Radio broadcast Chinese intentions precisely as Chou-En-lai had stated them.

* * *

On 14 October, from Tokyo, Major General Charles Willoughby, Far East Command Intelligence Officer, issued a detailed study of the question of Soviet or Chinese intervention in Korea. The question had long been one of concern to FECOM Intelligence, and already reams of reports, analysis, and estimates had been written. There was a great deal of evidence—pointing either way.

Evidence, however, signifies nothing unless evaluated, and evaluation is always more difficult than collection.

It was Willoughby's view on 14 October that the Soviet Union, in any case, had no military advantage in intervention, and such intervention could be discounted. Then Willoughby took up what the Chinese would do, which was the real problem.

The Chinese had at least 38 divisions in 9 field armies garrisoned in Manchuria north of the Yalu. Of these, 24 divisions were disposed along the border in position to intervene. This estimate of CCF strength was reasonably accurate.

But FECOM knew that 14 October the U.N. forces in North Korea stood very close to total victory. The Inmun Gun had deteriorated into remnants. The ROK's had seized the important port of Wonsan on the east coast, and in FECOM there was a definite feeling that the moment for fruitful Chinese intervention had passed. Most of the vital areas of North Korea had been overrun.

Willoughby's analysis described the open failure of the North Koreans to rebuild their forces, and suggested that this indicated the CCF and Soviets had decided against further investment in a losing cause. Willoughby's views unquestionably reflected those of his chief, and portions of his intelligence analysis are revealing:

> *Recent declarations by CCF leaders, threatening to enter North Korea if American forces were to cross the 38th parallel are probably in a category of diplomatic blackmail. The decision, if any, is beyond the purview of collective intelligence: it is a decision for war, on the highest level.*

Charles Willoughby, while devoted to MacArthur, had always been personally unpopular in the American Army. The time would come when the storm would break over his head—because General Willoughby, in truth, was wrong.

But it should never be overlooked that FECOM's views, as stated by Willoughby, were never contested by Washington. *The decision, if any, is beyond the purview of collective intelligence.* FECOM was at best a collective agency, not an evaluative one for matters of international policy; if Washington permitted FECOM both to collect and to make decisions, then whatever happened the fault was Washington's.

It was true that Washington had no pipeline—not then, not later—into the Kremlin. It was true that the CIA had become woefully spotty in East Asia since the Communist takeover. It was true that the picture of both Peiping and Moscow remained vague, distorted, and open to argument in Western capitals. Nevertheless, the responsibility to evaluate intelligence touching the highest political levels remained in Washington.

Yet throughout the whole uneasy fall of 1950, Washington kept relaying information to Tokyo. And Tokyo, very early, had made up its mind, as expressed by MacArthur: *The Chinese would not dare to intervene.*

Because Washington permitted soldiers to make and to act on decisions that were beyond the purview of the military, because it forced them to bring purely military thinking into matters that remained in essence political—in short, because Washington still sometimes acted as if there could be a separation between war and politics, the United States, intoxicated with the heady taste of triumph, was heading for disaster.

18

In the Never-Never Land

We should not assume that Chinese Communists are committed in force. After all, a lot of Mexicans live in Texas.

—Lieutenant General Walton W. Walker, Commanding Eighth Army, Korea, November, 1950.

A s OCTOBER waned, and the winds blowing off the roof of the world down into the mountains of North Korea turned dry and cold, American and ROK forces advanced steadily northward. Beating its drums, proclaiming its every objective and movement to the world, its every detail, composition, and minute location reported faithfully by its war correspondents, the United Nations Force raced to the Yalu. The war that was not a war continued, but everyone agreed that it was almost over. Somehow, even the men had read MacArthur's words at Wake Island, and everyone expected to be home—or at least in Japan—by Christmas.

But behind the open book of the armies' progress, behind the glowing communiqués, were controversy and confusion.

When the Eighth Army had approached the Han in September, General Walker had begun to worry about the future of X Corps, which had been created to command the Inch'on invasion forces. He felt that it should now cease to report separately to Tokyo and come under his command. But while Walton Walker expressed himself to his staff, he did not formally put his ideas in writing to MacArthur's GHQ.

But on 26 September MacArthur dashed whatever hopes the Eighth Army commander may have had, by informing him that X Corps would pass into GHQ reserve and ready itself to proceed with a GHQ-directed mission, of which Johnny Walker would be apprised in due course.

Instead of merging X Corps with Eighth Army, MacArthur decided to employ it on the east coast of Korea, and to keep it subordinate not to Walker but to himself in Tokyo. The X Corps was embarked for Wonsan, an important port of North Korea on the Sea of Japan—though the ROK Army, moving overland, beat it there—and then went into action, marching toward the far reaches of the north, where the Yalu roared through its gloomy gorges, and where Korea touched Manchuria and the maritime province of Siberia.

No decision was to come under such controversy as this splitting of the U.N. Command on the ground. For as Schlieffen had written, "It is better to surrender a province than to split an army." But MacArthur felt he could coordinate the advance of each column, Eighth Army in the west, X Corps in the east, better from Tokyo than could Walker from Korea. MacArthur's reasoning was based, simply enough, on the Korean terrain.

Above the Seoul-Wonsan Corridor, there is only one good lateral route of communication running across Korea—the P'yongyang-Wonsan road and rail line. North of this, the Taebaek Mountains rise to dizzy heights. Running north and south, they cross the land with rugged crests and vast, dark gorges, forming a trackless waste across which even Koreans do not go. Until the valley of the Yalu is reached, there is no lateral road connecting east and west.

The only routes of advance to the north are in the valleys on either coast. Up these, Walker on the west, Almond on the east, the main bodies had to advance, with junction possible only on the Yalu itself.

Because of the horrendous mountains in east central Korea, contact between the two forces was tenuous, at best. Japan, remaining the staging base, supplied both forces.

Whatever the order of battle, X Corps and Eighth Army were forced to live, advance, and fight in virtual isolation from each other. No matter who had been given command, the mountains would have remained.

As the U.N. advanced to the Yalu, this mountainous gap, approaching sixty miles in places, drew apprehension from the JCS and military men all over the world. But it was never important. The enemy, already in Korea, never utilized it in his plan of action, because the terrain was virtually impassable.

More important than the gap separating Eighth Army and X Corps were the maneuver formations of the armies themselves. The farther north they marched, the more nonexistent roads became. The advance had to proceed up single dirt roads, along parallel valleys. Nothing like a contiguous line or solid front could be maintained. Within regiments and battalions, units began to live and move in virtual isolation, separated by the ever-present hills. As they neared the Yalu, divisions were strung out, as Ned Almond put it, from hell to breakfast.

What the U.N. did, it did in the light of the restricting terrain, and in the view that no real enemy opposed it. And above all else, it was the terrain and a complete failure of Intelligence that brought disaster. Marching north, the U.N. trumpeted to the world its composition, its battle plan, and even the hour of its execution.

Without effort, the enemy knew everything there was to know about the U.N. forces.

The U.N., in turn, never knew the enemy existed—until it was much too late.

For more generations than men could count, soldiers in the Middle Kingdom had ranked low in the orders of society, far down the scale from the scholar and the poet. And for more generations than men could count, China had had no skill or success in war. For more than a hundred years, Chinese military forces had been objects of contempt, possessing neither skill, means, nor the will to fight.

Meanwhile, China had been humbled by one foe after another. Japan and the Western powers took from her what they wanted, as they pleased.

On 1 August 1927 the newly formed Communist Party of China began the fight against Chiang Kai-shek's Kuomintang. This date is still carried on CCF battle flags as the date of the Communist Army's founding.

For decades the battle raged across China. In 1934, when it seemed that the Nationalist Army had the CCF ringed, approximately 100,000 CCF soldiers retreated north for Kiangsi Province into Shensi, to far Yenan. It was a march without parallel in history, and one almost without parallel for hardships.

One year later, after crossing 6,000 miles, eighteen mountain ranges, twenty-four rivers, and twelve provinces, 20,000 survivors under a general named Lin Piao made juncture with other Communist forces in Yenan.

During the actual time of march, Lin Piao's forces had averaged twenty-four miles per day, on foot.

In Shensi Province, far removed from the Nationalists and the eyes of the world, the Communist Chinese began to rebuild their base of power. They began to wage guerrilla warfare against the Nationalists.

They were led by men who were now hardened soldiers, men who wanted above all else for China to be again a great power, and who felt that Marxism held out the only hope for its accomplishment.

The vast areas of China were still feudal; there had never been any true capitalism except that administered by foreigners in the coastal cities. And the pattern of Sinic culture had frozen five thousand years earlier.

The new Communist military leaders understood clearly that the pattern of Chinese culture must be thoroughly broken before China could again assume authority in the world. With cunning, courage, and great skill, aided by a centuries-old tradition of corruption that lay across China like a gray shadow, they began to break it.

During the time of war with Japan, the Communists sought not to drive out the Japanese, but to survive. When the Japanese departed, they had an army of 600,000 entrenched across North China. Now they began to war in earnest, fighting not only the Nationalists but also for the peasants' minds. From the first, the Communists understood that in a nation almost wholly peasant, only peasants have any political importance.

Within two years, they won not only the war but the peasants' minds. For the peasants would not understand, until too late, that the Communists wanted not justice for them, but to overthrow the entire fabric of Chinese life.

The popular morality of what the Communist Chinese have done will probably be judged only in the light of whether or not they made China a great power, and only the future will tell that. If they fail, history will condemn them for the enormous suffering they inflicted upon their land; if they succeed, their own history will largely regard them as heroes, even as Soviet history regards Peter the Great of Russia as a hero, or as the French revolutionists or the Irish Sinn Fein, who resorted to naked force and political murder, are looked upon favorably by millions of their countrymen.

* * *

In June 1950, the CCF Fourth Field Army, some 600,000 men, Lin Piao commanding, marched to the Korean border to stand ready for any eventuality. During the summer and early autumn, other field armies followed.

Shortly after United States troops crossed the 38th parallel at Kaesong, on 13 or 14 October, elements of the Fourth Field Army began to move south across the Yalu.

The 39th and 40th armies—the Chinese term "Army" is roughly equivalent to the U.S. Corps; a CCF Army contained three divisions of approximately 10,000 men each—crossed from Antung, Manchuria, to Sinuiju. The 38th and 42nd crossed from Chi-an to Manp'ojin. Over these armies Lin Piao placed the CCF XIII Army Group Headquarters. Artillery and horse cavalry regiments crossed behind them in support.

Three of the Chinese armies deployed in front of the Eighth Army; the fourth took a position in front of the Changjin Reservoir to the east.

Thus, on 15 October, when MacArthur and President Truman conferred at Wake, 120,000 Chinese veterans were already inside North Korea.

Ten days later, two more CCF armies crossed the Yalu, adding six divisions to Lin Piao's forward forces. Five armies were in the U.S. Eighth Army zone, one to the east in X Corps' zone.

Night after night, all during October and November, CCF armies continued to stream across the Yalu, moving into the deep Korean valleys south of the river.

By rail from Shantung Province came the IX Army Group, Third Field Army, comprising nine divisions. It was reinforced with three extra divisions, giving it a strength of 120,000 men. The IX Army Group moved across the mountains to the Changjin Reservoir area.

By the middle of November, 1950, approximately 180,000 Chinese waited in front of the Eighth Army, while 120,000 lurked in the mountains surrounding Changjin Reservoir on X Corps' flank. From Mukden, in Manchuria, Peng Teh-huai, Deputy CCF Commander, assumed direction and control.

While China broadcast to the world that Chinese "volunteers" would enter the Korean fighting, under Kim Il Sung, the leaders of the CCF never relinquished control of their forces. And it would have been considerable news to the 300,000 Chinese soldiers massed in the cold valleys of Korea to learn that they had volunteered. Many of them did not even know in what part of the world they waited.

Lin Piao, and the major leaders of the Chinese Communist Forces, were not simple peasant leaders. The vast majority of the CCF generals were graduates of Whampoa Military Academy or of Russian schools. They had studied Clausewitz and Jomini and the battles of Cannae and Tannenberg as thoroughly as any West Pointer, and they had been engaged in war for all their adult lives. But if they did not act upon the field of battle as Western generals did, it was because they did not command a Western army.

The hordes of the Red Army were tough and battle-hardened, but they could not read or write. They had no radios, nor did they have much telephone equipment. They had no air force, or any massive artillery. They were weak in motor transport. Their arms were a miscellany of United States, Japanese, and Russian equipment. They had very few of the things a European or Western army required for war.

But the hordes of the Chinese Communist Forces were deployed on an Asian battlefield, not Europe. Peng Teh-huai and his field commanders Lin Piao and Sung Shih-lun proposed to use their forces in a manner calculated to take advantage of their own strengths while discounting those of the enemy.

They had three immense advantages: their own minds, trained to war in the vast reaches of the Middle Kingdom, which instinctively thought in terms of fluid maneuver, without regard to battle lines; the hardihood and sturdy legs of their peasant troops, who could travel long miles on very little; and the enemy's complete lack of belief in their own existence.

Many have found it incredible that American Intelligence would never accept the fact that the Chinese were in Korea in force during October-November 1950. There were reasons. Neither MacArthur nor Willoughby believed the Chinese would intervene in force; both believed the Chinese threats were purely diplomatic blackmail. All evidence that they were in Korea broke against this preset belief. Nor was it easy for subordinate officers to go against the ideas of the FECOM commander.

More important, no concrete evidence that the Chinese were in Korea could be put forth. Americans believed it incredible that any army of significant size could cross the Yalu and deploy in Korea without observation by their air forces. Daily American aircraft flew over all North Korea; and no armies were ever sighted.

Above all, in formulating his plan of maneuver to the Yalu, MacArthur believed his air cover could destroy the Chinese if they tried to intervene. This belief dominated his thinking; he expressed it many times. Upon this foundation he laid his whole campaign. Too late, he would find out what Lin Piao already knew—against a Communist army, in primitive terrain, air power could be important, but not decisive.

The example of one Chinese army, which marched from Antung, Manchuria, to its assembly area in North Korea almost three hundred miles away, explains much: after dark, not sooner than nine o'clock, the Chinese troops began to march. Singing and chanting in the manner of all Chinese, they plodded south, night after night, for eighteen nights.

And each night, between nine and three, they covered eighteen miles.

When light came, every man, every gun, every animal, was hidden from sight. In the deep valleys, in the thick forests, in the miserable villages huddled on the forlorn plateaus, the Chinese rested by day. Only small scouting parties went ahead by day, to reconnoiter the night's march, and to select the bivouac for the morrow. If aircraft were heard, each man was under orders to halt, freezing in his tracks, until the noise of the engines went away.

In bivouac, no man showed himself, for any reason. Discipline was firm, and perfect. Any man who violated instructions in any way was shot.

It was not only cunning and hardihood, but this perfect march and bivouac discipline that caused U.N. aircraft to fly over the CCF hundreds of times without ever once seeing anything suspicious. Even aerial photography revealed nothing.

It was a feat that Xenophon's hoplites, marching back from Persia to the sea, could have performed. Julius Caesar's hard legions could have done it, and more—the Roman manuals stated that the usual day's march for a legion was twenty miles, to be covered in five hours.

It is extremely doubtful if any modern Western army, bred to wheels, could have matched it. It was almost impossible for Western generals, even those who knew of Xenophon and Caesar, to credit it.

Half contemptuously, American military men spoke of "elusive" Lin Piao, and of the "poet" Mao Tse-tung. Mao Tse-tung, Premier of China, had already revealed to the world how his Communist armies operated—how they flowed from place to place, fighting when fighting was profitable, biding their time when it was not. What Mao Tse-tung had written was instructive, and intensely practical for a war in Asia—but because the Chinese wrote in poetic language, not in the military terminology popular in the West, no ambitious second-year ROTC cadet would have dared quote him seriously.

After November 1950, many men would grudgingly learn that the thought behind words is more important than the phrases in which the thought is couched. The time would come when every leader in the world would read the writings of the Chinese Communists—for it was barely possible that the war they waged was not so anachronistic as Americans believed. Quite possibly, it was the pattern of all future land wars.

In November 1950, then, one army, in open array, loudly proclaiming its every move to the world, marched against a phantom foe. For the CCF, all that month, was a ghost; now you saw it, now you didn't. It marched by night, under a foggy moon; it sideslipped into the mountains in front of the advancing U.N., and lurked, biding its time.

When he was ready, the "elusive" Lin Piao would let the Americans find him.

* * *

On 25 October, 1950, the 1st ROK Division captured near Unsan an odd individual. Unlike all adult Koreans he spoke neither Korean nor Japanese. But he was quite voluble, however, in a tongue that could only be a dialect of northern China. He was flown to Eighth Army Advanced HQ in P'yongyang, and the top Intelligence brass interviewed him. Within a few days, he was followed by more of his kind.

Up to Thanksgiving, almost one hundred identified Chinese prisoners of war were taken. Yet their interrogation proved strangely unsatisfying.

Only much later would Americans understand there had been something odd about many of the POW's. Some had been deliberately planted, with deliberately misleading tales. They spoke of being from this and that "unit"— which Americans identified as regiments rather than what they were in actuality: CCF armies.

There was a great deal of confusion about the POW's and the way in which they were captured, indicative of a certain confusion among the enemy. American Intelligence began assuming that the North Korean Army had been reinforced with certain small groups of Chinese from Manchuria. But in the face of Tokyo's steadfast refusal to accept any Chinese intervention in the war, neither Eighth Army nor X Corps openly suggested there could be any massive CCF units south of the Yalu.

For the Chinese had slipped into the rugged land like phantoms, now creeping forward, now hiding from the light of day. Deliberately, Lin Piao was seemingly picking about in confusion, units here, units there, none clearly seen or identified. Chinese troops were deliberately misschooled on their own order of battle, so that, captured, they might tell weird tales. There were clashes between Americans and Chinese "volunteers" in odd places—obviously to draw American attention from where the Chinese planned to strike.

Then, in late October, because the Americans were pushing forward too fast, before he was ready, Lin Piao struck, with what the Chinese called their "First Phase Offensive."

Lightly armed but veteran and well-trained Chinese troops struck against the 1st Cavalry Division pushing northeast from the Ch'ongch'on bridgehead, toward the Chinese area of concentration. Others, in heavy strength, moved against the ROK 6th Division on the Cavalry's right.

East of Unsan, the ROK Division broke. On 1 November the Chinese sprang a carefully prepared trap against the 3rd Battalion, 8th Cavalry Regiment. The battalion was surrounded, a roadblock thrown up in its rear. Chinese, fighting hand-to-hand, swarmed over the battalion's command post. Only 10 officers and 200 men escaped; all told, the 8th Cavalry lost more than 600 men. On the Cavalry's right, ROK II Corps losses were extreme.

Along the Ch'ongch'on River, the 5th Cavalry ran into heavy opposition and had to fight sharply to hold the bridgehead across the river.

To the east, X Corps was also struck by Chinese. Moving toward the Kot'o-ri plateau, 1st Marine Division was heavily engaged.

For several days fighting flared savagely—then, as suddenly as they had come, the Chinese broke contact and melted into the shrouding mountain masses ahead of the U.N. advance. For the "First Phase Offensive" had succeeded. The first contact between Americans and Chinese had been inconclusive and bewildering. No one knew what the contact foretold.

Walker, of Eighth Army, in sudden alarm, as Chinese were positively identified as having entered the war, realized the extreme vulnerability of his strung-out divisions. The 2nd and 25th were to the south, beyond supporting range of the van of the army. The 24th had passed into the far northwest corner of Korea, near the mouth of the Yalu—where it could be cut off if the

Chinese interdicted the main coastal highway near the Ch'ongch'on bridge-head. The ROK 7th Regiment was already on the Yalu north of Unsan—but significantly, the enemy had boiled up from the hill masses fifty miles south of the border, on the Eighth Army's flank.

He ordered the advance halted, while the Eighth Army consolidated. The 24th Division and the ROK 7th Regiment were ordered to return south of the Ch'onghch'on. While the 1st Cavalry Division held the Ch'ongch'on bridge-head, the 24th returned without difficulty. The ROK's, more exposed, ran into heavy weather getting back.

The ROK outfit lost more than five hundred men, retreating, but they brought back a bottle of Yalu water for President Syngman Rhee.

Walker ordered the 2nd Infantry Division to move north, onto line. He was now experiencing logistical trouble; the Army as a whole was far north of its permanent bases, and it was in difficult terrain.

Tokyo was immediately on his neck for stopping the advance—but, reluctantly, Tokyo agreed to his consolidation and supply buildup before continuing the offensive.

In the east the Chinese had not been so successful with their spoiling attacks—but the Marines, of their own volition, slowed their painful advance toward the Changjin Reservoir. General Almond expressed his dissatisfaction with Marine progress, but Marines, from General Smith down through the regimental commanders, Murray, Litzenberg, and Puller, were highly dubious of what they were marching into.

Winter came early, in the second week of November, with subzero winds howling down from Siberia. Moving over tenuous, ill-defined roads, facing bitter weather, climbing thousands of feet into high hill masses, the Marine division, strung out in a long and vulnerable column, had trouble enough if they never saw a Chinese. For the Marines were as roadbound in North Korea as the Army.

Only in the far northeast corner of Korea did the advance push forward during November. Here there were no Chinese, and the ROK's and elements of the 7th Division marched against failing NKPA resistance to the Yalu.

The Chinese, by attacking sharply, then disappearing, threw confusion into the U.N. commands on the ground in Korea. Eighth Army staff began to have grave doubts as to what lay hidden in the mountains on their right flank; 1st Marine Division wondered what lay in wait for them north of the Changjin Reservoir. But day after day passed, and no further action by the enemy was apparent.

Air patrolling over the mountains revealed what it had always revealed—nothing. Only heavy, aggressive ground patrolling into the hills could have revealed that the main bodies of two massive Chinese army groups lurked in those deep valleys and forlorn villages, and this action the U.N. never attempted.

In the frightful terrain such patrolling was dangerous. It could not be supported by wheels, and where wheels could not go, neither could sizable units of Americans. And in such horrendous terrain a vast army could be—and was—hidden in a very small area, observing perfect camouflage discipline, waiting.

The weeks of November were a time for worry, snarling, and argument among the Eighth Army and X Corps staffs, whatever official face was put on. General Ruffner, Chief of Staff of X Corps, told General Willoughby, FECOM G-2, that he was increasingly concerned with the large numbers of Chinese units identified by ROK, Eighth Army, and X Corps troops. Willoughby insisted that no full divisions of Chinese were in Korea, but only elements of such divisions.

On one occasion, General Willoughby, with General Doyle Hickey, Acting FECOM Chief of Staff, visited Almond's X Corps HQ in Wonsan. After hearing reports of POW interrogations, Hickey turned to Willoughby.

"If, as General Almond says, these people turn out to be Chinese—"

Ned Almond roared, "What do you mean, 'if'? They are Chinese!"

Willoughby tried to allay their fears. He stated that only a few volunteers were in Korea, and it was most likely that only a battalion of each identified division was actually across the border.

To which Ned Almond asked bluntly, "What happened to the 8th Cavalry over in Eighth Army?"

Willoughby was of the opinion that the regiment had failed to put out adequate security, and had therefore been overrun by a small, violent attack.

As the month progressed, however, FECOM came more and more to the conclusion that there were Chinese troops in Korea. Their numbers were placed at between 40,000 and 70,000. Whether "volunteers," as the Chinese Government claimed, or otherwise, the big question remained as to what they were doing in Korea.

There seemed to be three possibilities, all of which were suggested:

1. The Chinese had come over in limited fashion to help the NKPA hold a base south of the Yalu;

2. They had entered as a show of force to bluff the U.N. into halting south of the river;

3. At the worst, they were a screening force to cover the advance of the main Chinese armies.

No one, either in FECOM or the two commands in Korea, suggested that the CCF were already in Korea in massive force.

But as November passed, and the Chinese did not appear again, gradually American fears and suspicion died. More and more, intelligence officers at FECOM reached the conclusion that the Chinese action was limited, and confined to a mere bluff to deter the U.N. final victory. Willoughby and his chief never wavered from their conviction that the Chinese threats were a form of political blackmail. Their influence on the Eighth Army—which was not so sanguine—was naturally decisive.

Time magazine reported in a November issue, as its own view, that the CCF action in Korea might really be in the nature of political blackmail to win

U.N. recognition for Red China at Lake Success—where a delegation of Chinese Communists was already headed, by way of Moscow, to complain of United States "imperialist" policy in North Korea.

Washington did not interfere, whatever information it may have had. Washington still had not learned that while war itself is best left to the generals, international politics are much too important to be so left. But while Washington had numerous political evidences of Chinese intervention, in effect both the CIA—weak in Asia—and the Administration concurred in MacArthur's views. At least they permitted MacArthur to proceed as he saw fit.

Eighth Army consolidated along the Ch'ongch'on; its supply situation, while not good, got better. The first two Marine regiments, the 5th and 7th, moved south and west of Changjin Reservoir. Both left and right wings of the United Nations command were now in position fifty miles south of Manchuria; all that seemingly remained was the final pinching out of a small bit of enemy territory. Once on the Yalu, or a few miles south of it, the U.N. could form a solid defensive line and hold all Korea, come what may.

MacArthur, left with the decision, had the U.N. forces deployed halfway through North Korea. He felt he could not sit still, and allow U.S. troops to be tied up for the winter. The CCF plan might be to make Korea a permanent running sore, and to tie up more than a hundred thousand U.S. ground troops indefinitely. With winter already howling down out of one of the coldest spots on earth, he had to retreat or attack. He attacked.

MacArthur ordered the offensive resumed on 24 November, the day following Thanksgiving. He flew to Korea, and sent a message to the troops, assuring them that the war was almost won and that a final effort would see them home before Christmas. In fact, plans were now being laid to redeploy some of the divisions to other theaters.

High in the bitter land, Americans ate Thanksgiving dinner. Depending on their tactical position, they ate well or plainly—but most received turkey and all the trimmings, brought into this savage country at great effort.

Morale was high, not because they relished the final offensive but because everyone thought they would soon be homeward bound.

Because he had used the magic word "home," the troops believed MacArthur implicitly. Even the staffs and commanders, who had seen harsh evidence of Chinese interference in the "First Phase Offensive," were reasonably confident—after all, for nearly three weeks the enemy had not been seen.

And nothing is more revealing of Douglas MacArthur's frame of mind than the messages and communiqués he released as the new offensive jumped off. To the JCS he wrote:

"I believe that with my air power, now unrestricted so far as Korea is concerned . . . I can deny reinforcements coming across the Yalu in sufficient strength to prevent the destruction of those forces now arrayed against me in North Korea."

His communiqué of 24 November read:

"The United Nations massive compression envelopment in North Korea against the new Red Armies operating there is now approaching its decisive effort. The isolating component of the pincer, our Air Forces of all types, have for the past three weeks, in a sustained attack of model coordination and effectiveness, successfully interdicted enemy lines of support from the North so that further reinforcement therefrom has been sharply curtailed and essential supplies markedly limited."

To the U.N. in New York he sent:

"The giant U.N. pincer moved according to schedule today. The air forces, in full strength, completely interdicted the rear areas, and an air reconnaissance behind the enemy line, and along the entire length of the Yalu River border, showed little sign of hostile military activity."

It is obvious that MacArthur's reliance on air power was almost absolute. Whatever the weaknesses of his ground forces, whatever their difficult and exposed positions, U.N. mastery of the skies was complete, and air would be the decisive arm. It was a typically American viewpoint.

MacArthur and the men around him had a great deal to learn about Chinese Communist armies.

*   *   *

In the hidden fastness of his screening mountains, Lin Piao knew almost everything there was to know about American fighting men. He did not despise American power. He knew the strengths of the American Army, and Chinese officers read these in a pamphlet distributed to the "Chinese People's Volunteer Army":

"The coordinated action of mortars and tanks is an important factor. . . . Their firing instruments are highly powerful. . . . Their artillery is very active. . . . Aircraft strafing and bombing of our transportation have become a great hazard to us. . . . Their transport system is magnificent. Their rate of infantry fire is great, and the long range of that fire is even greater."

Americans, Chinese Intelligence said, had machines and knew how to use them well.

Then the pamphlet, entitled "Primary Conclusions of Battle Experience at Unsan," talked of the men behind the machines:

". . . Cut off from the rear, they abandon all their heavy weapons. . . . Their infantrymen are weak, afraid to die, and have no courage to attack or defend. They depend always on their planes, tanks, artillery. . . . They specialize in day fighting. They are not familiar with night fighting or hand-to-hand combat. If defeated, they have no orderly formation. Without the use of their mortars, they become completely lost. . . . They become dazed and completely demoralized. They are afraid when the rear is cut off. When transportation comes to a standstill, the infantry loses the will to fight."

The Chinese, knowing they could not slug it out with American planes, tanks, and artillery, in which they themselves were weak, planned to tailor operations to fit what they considered were American weaknesses. They would plan attacks to get in the enemy rear, to cut escape and supply roads, and then to flail the enemy with pressure from both front and rear. They would use what they called the *Hachi-Shiki*—a V-formation, which moved open and against the enemy, then closed about him, while other forces slashed through to his rear, engaging any unit that tried to relieve the trapped enemy.

Simple tactics, they were suited to the violently broken Korean terrain—and they could be coordinated with flares and bugle calls, the only means of communication the Chinese possessed.

"As a main objective, one of our units must fight its way quickly around the enemy and cut off his rear. . . . Route of attack must avoid highways and flat terrain in order to keep tanks and artillery from hindering the attack operations. Night warfare in the mountains must have a definite plan and liaison between platoon groups. Small, leading patrols attack and then sound the bugle. A large number will at that time follow in column."

The Chinese soldiers to whom the instructions were read were well fed, well clothed, and sturdy. They wore warm quilted jackets of white, mustard-brown, or blue; many had fur-lined boots. They were tough. They did not fear to leave their own lines; they carried their supply and food, even mortar rounds, with them, over hills, through valleys. Their minds were conditioned by the vast, flowing landscapes of China itself; they would move over the land as if it were the sea, caring little whether they were before the enemy or behind him, for on the sea all position is relative.

They possessed courage, and they would obey orders unto the death.

But they were illiterate, simple peasants, and they had almost none of the things a modern army required to make it a scientific instrument. They had no radios, no tanks, very little artillery, and that little they were inept in using. They had no mechanized system of supply, nor any vast stockpiles of goods or equipment; their food and their ammunition they were forced to carry on their backs.

They could move, in any direction, no faster than their legs might bear them. They could not shift rapidly to meet a changing situation, nor could they at once exploit a breakthrough.

In open battle, openly arrived at, an American army might have slaughtered them. On the fields of Europe, or in the deserts of North Africa, they would have died under the machines and superior firepower of a mechanized host. But now, Lin Piao's hosts were not going to engage in open battle, openly arrived at, with the West.

They would fight, in their own way, in their own mountains, and they would inflict upon American arms the most decisive defeat they had suffered in the century.

19

Kunu-ri

Lordy, Lordy, listen to me,
While I tell of the battle of Kunu-ri!
We're buggin' out—
We're movin' on!
—From the "Bugout Boogie," a folk ballad preserved in the 2nd Division despite its proscription by the powers that be.

SOUTH OF THE broad, shallow Ch'ongch'on, some thirty miles northwestward from the Yellow Sea, the forlorn village of Kunu-ri—on some maps shown as "Kunmori"—sat drably across the junction of the north-south road from Sunch'on and the lateral road running from Huich'on to a connection with the main coastal highway at Sinanju.

To the east, or right, of Kunu-ri the mountains rose, high and terrifying in a foggy sky, becoming virtually impenetrable at Huich'on. And to the east, along the road, on both sides of the river, spread the 2nd Infantry Division, from Kunu-ri to Kujang-dong to Sinhung-dong. On their right were deployed the two divisions, the 6th and 8th, of the II ROK Corps. West of them the rifle regiments of the 25th Division held the line, on a front generally facing northwest toward Huich'on and the forbidding mountains.

Generally behind the 2nd Division's rifle regiments, facing eastward, the artillery dug in its supporting base on the only flat terrain they could find, an exposed flat draw near Kujang-dong.

The battalions and companies were scattered along the river in weird array, for this was no country for a modern, mechanized army. The hills were not high here, but they were endless. There were no side roads, and no flat spaces anywhere, where command posts, medical aid stations, or anything else could be set up. The hills ran into each other; they overlapped; they blocked vision and hearing in every direction.

Because the terrain was compartmented by the hills, some units stood too close to others; others were out of sight and hearing of those supporting them.

Wire often did not reach; the ancient radios did not work. The units of the 2nd Division were not far from each other in yards and miles—but each moved, fought, and worried in almost complete isolation, in a tormented vacuum of its own.

Men who have never walked these hills will never adequately understand what happened to the 2nd Division. Because among these endless ridges the 2nd Division was brought to battle the day after Thanksgiving, 1950, and it was, in detail, defeated.

During the next five days every unit of the division, combat and support alike, would know its moments of danger, of fear and death and destruction. All would suffer, some more than others. What each company, each platoon suffered, is a story in itself.

Enough of the whole, perhaps, can be glimpsed from the ordeal of a few.

> *The 2nd Division sat on the hill,*
> *Watchin' Old Joe Chink get set for the kill—*

Captain Frank E. Muñoz, commanding George Company, 9th Infantry, knew that his division was attacking across the Ch'ongch'on. He had no idea that across that same river another, hostile, army was also poised to attack.

In ninety days all the faults of the American Army had not been corrected—there were still men in the ranks who were poorly trained, and replacements who had no stomach for Korea, north or south. The old men had learned, the hard way, but many of the older men were gone. The inexorable law of combat is the disintegration and replacement of rifle companies, and the pool from which replacement came was the same as that which had furnished the first men into Korea.

Because the fighting had lessened in recent weeks, because all believed the war was ending, the hard-won discipline in the ranks had lessened, too. Men had discarded their steel helmets, because they were heavy and awkward over their pile caps. Disdaining their use, most men of the 9th Infantry had tossed aside their bayonets. Few carried grenades, or much ammunition. There were few entrenching tools, and not much food, because in these goddam hills, man, you had to go light.

Because most men equated discipline with the infrequent nonsense of digging six-by-six trenches to bury cigarettes, or scrubbing coal bins white, practices the Army had wisely discarded, many men had discarded discipline, too. They—those who lived—would have to learn again that discipline means keeping a full bandoleer of ammunition and a full canteen, despite their weight, and all the equipment men wiser than they had issued to them.

Over George Company Frank Muñoz and his trusted deputies, such as Sergeant Long, worked to exercise their will. It was a never-ending and a thankless job.

But George Company had good clothing: OD trousers, with field cotton pants to go over them, field jackets, parkas, combat boots with overshoes, and arctic sleeping bags. They were eating good food as yet, and they had no real trouble with the bitter weather.

Muñoz knew very little of the tactical situation. He knew the Chinese were in. He thought: *We'll have to fight them. We'll push them back to the Yalu, and there we'll draw a line to keep them out.*

He figured the enemy units in front of George were only a screening force. For that matter, so did Colonel Foster, the Division G-2.

On the night of 25 November, 9th Infantry's front began to come apart, but Frank Muñoz and company didn't know it. Baker was hard hit; King and Love virtually wiped out. Chinese were pouring into the 2nd Division along the natural corridors by night, seeking the American rear. Where they met no opposition in the dark, they flowed through; where they hit, sometimes by accident, an American unit, they flailed it from all directions. Some, decimated and shaken, held; some broke.

Men could hear the firing, but not even the regimental commanders, with no communication, knew what was happening.

At dawn, 26 November, 9th Infantry, except for 2nd Battalion, which was separated from the other units by the river, was ready for the scrapheap. The 23rd and 38th regiments were heavily engaged in their own areas. And 2nd Battalion's turn was coming.

Dug in along a high hill beside the river, George and Fox companies had been missed by the Chinese as they streamed through. With daylight, the dawn cold and clear, they made contact. Fortunately, George saw them first.

In the first, shadowy winter's light, Master Sergeant William Long, leading George's 3rd Platoon, saw a body of men walking openly along a creek from the area where K and L of the 3rd Battalion should be. Because the troops moved in the open, with no attempt at concealment, the men with Long decided they must be Americans, and ignored them.

Warned by the sixth sense old hands develop in battle, Long kept his eye on the approaching men. They closed to within three hundred yards, and suddenly Long yelled, "Chinks! They're Chinks!"

Quickly, men holding rifles and BAR's swiveled toward the visitors. Long let them come within two hundred yards; then he leveled his own carbine, and let fly.

The first burst of fire knocked down nearly half the Chinese. The remaining jumped behind rocks of the creek bed or plunged into the half-frozen rice paddies. There was a small village nearby, and a few Chinese raced for cover among the huts.

Quickly, a furious fire fight built up.

Muñoz tapped his runner. He sent the man scurrying to First Lieutenant Kavanaugh of Fox, dug in farther along the hill, to get Fox to hit the Chinese in the flank.

Kavanaugh sent one of his supporting tanks rumbling down toward the village. The tank opened fire, killing at least ten Chinese. Others came out with hands up.

Meanwhile, Sergeant Long led his platoon around the ambushed men and struck them in the rear. In a brief, sharp fire fight, Long wiped out the enemy column: seventy-odd killed, and twenty captured.

Frank Muñoz and Long looked over the dead Chinese carefully; they were the first they had seen. The corpses were clean-looking, solid, muscular. Each soldier had carried a pack complete with entrenching tool, blankets, and extra ammunition; they had had a miscellany of weapons—American, Japanese, Russian—and plenty of stick grenades. Some of them had carried a pot and a great quantity of rice—their rations.

Because they had thought all the American line companies had been wiped out during the night, the Chinese had walked blithely into a trap.

Muñoz and Long had no time to celebrate their easy victory. Now, bloody, exhausted survivors of K and L companies straggled in, and learning what had happened to his front, regimental commander Colonel Sloane moved his remaining companies from the east to the west side of the Ch'ongch'on, to reinforce his intact 2nd Battalion. Then Sloane ordered all his units, including 2nd Battalion, westward down the river, forming them again approximately two miles downstream.

They held the west side of the river; across from them the 23rd Infantry held the eastern bank.

The day passed swiftly with the moving about, but without significant action. No one knew what was happening elsewhere in the division zone.

Then, not long after dark, a strong enemy column from the north burst into the 23rd's perimeter. The regiment's CP was overrun and the Headquarters Company shattered. Its 2nd and 3rd battalions retreated several hundred yards downriver before they were able to get hold of themselves once again.

Sloane, learning this, immediately realized the Chinese might wade the Ch'ongch'on from the east and take Fox and George in the rear. He called Major Barberis, the 2nd Battalion C.O., and told him to move his battalion to the east side of the river, onto the ground where the 23rd had been.

The river was not deep, but it was swift, and Sloane ordered Barberis to move his men across on all available vehicles.

Barberis relayed the message on to Fox and George, dug in on high ground about six hundred yards west of the river. Fox left its holes, beginning to trail down to the river, while George remained on the high ground, covering, and How, the Weapons Company, kept its mortars emplaced to support in case of trouble.

Precisely at this moment, from three sides, rifle fire blazed up at George's hill. Unseen in the dark, Chinese skirmishers had crawled less than fifty yards from George's foxholes.

Muñoz had positioned the company for all-around defense. His 1st Platoon faced toward the Ch'ongch'on; his 2nd was on the crest of the rise, looking north. The 3rd Platoon, Sergeant Long, was on line with the 2nd, to its right. On a slightly lower rise, some hundred yards distant, a platoon of Easy Company had been stationed to protect the company's west, or left, flank.

The first fire fell on the left, on Easy's platoon, then bounced all along the line, around the hill. A blaze of gunfire and sound came from F Company, nearing the river. They had been hit, too. The Chinese seemed to know the location of each of George's strongpoints.

Then, weirdly, the bugles began to blow. Having pinned the enemy, the Chinese were talking to each other. The shrill sounds, riding the cold night wind, puckered Muñoz's boys a bit. Second Lieutenant Danny Hernández, his 2nd Platoon leader, ran over to where Muñoz stood.

"Captain, the Chinese are all over us!"

Coolly, the short, dark Muñoz said to him, "Let's see what happens."

Suddenly a red flare soared high over the ridge, rising from the west.

"Well," Muñoz said, as calmly as he could, "here they come!"

He was right. The Chinese attack, perfectly planned, coordinated, and executed, burst against George's hill. The hill slopes flamed and roared with the sounds of firing.

"Notify Battalion we're under attack—" Muñoz said. But his radio operator could no longer raise Battalion; they were across the river and out of range.

The firing slackened momentarily, and Muñoz got to one of Lieutenant Haywood's supporting tanks. He contacted Regiment, and ruined whatever peace of mind Colonel Sloane had briefly enjoyed, over the tank radio.

Then the enemy brought their small 57mm mortars up on the fingers of the ridge, firing into George's positions. With a mighty rush forward, Chinese burst over the lower parts of the hill and leaped into the holes of the 1st and Easy's platoon. In a wild melee, the two American platoons disappeared.

George's rear was now unprotected.

Meanwhile, George's 2nd and 3rd platoons had not yet been engaged. Up on the crest, they could see and hear the uproar in the other platoon areas, but could not tell what was happening.

Then men ran toward Long's 3rd Platoon, shouting, "GI's! GI's! Don't shoot, GI's!"

Long figured that stragglers from the overrun platoons were trying to join the men on the crest. He shouted, "Don't shoot—don't shoot!"

His men couldn't have shot anyway, because so far they had seen nothing in the dark to shoot at. But now, oddly, Long thought he heard the same voices that yelled not to fire yammering in unmistakable Chinese.

While Long strained his eyes into the night, a bugle rapped sharply. *Tatatata— tatatata*. Whistles blew.

One of Long's men yelped: "I can see 'em! I can see 'em! Here they come!"

He hadn't told William Long anything—Long could see them, too. Hunched over, moving up the hills with their centers of gravity low to the sloping ground, the Chinese were coming silently through the night.

Long and his men opened up. Immediately, grenades burst among his holes. Under heavy pressure, Long remembered what Captain Muñoz had told him—if he got in heavy trouble, to join up with the 2nd Platoon, because in the final extreme the 2nd Platoon's area was better for last-ditch defense.

Under Long's shouted command, his men dashed to their left, along the ridge toward Danny Hernández's platoon. Just as they joined, fire from a machine gun tore through 3rd Platoon's line, knocking many of Long's men down.

Now all Muñoz's men were together, what was left of them, but the Chinese kept coming. Three big waves of Chinese boiled up out of the dark, hammering at George's men with rifles and submachine guns, hurling dozens of grenades. Muñoz's men needed grenades now, badly, but they didn't have them. As the Chinese poured up the fingers and fell into their holes, they needed bayonets—but they didn't have these, either.

Captain Muñoz, meanwhile, was on the phone, talking to Kavanaugh of Fox Company. "I'm being hit heavily—I'm in danger of losing the hill—can you help?"

"God, Frank, I need help, too!"

Fox was waist-deep in Chinese, trying to fight its way to the river.

The mortars of How, the Heavy Weapons Company, had been throwing up a continuous curtain of fire in support of the beleaguered riflemen. Now the tubes ran out of ammunition. The mortarmen dropped thermite grenades into their tubes, and ran for the protecting tank platoon that was covering by the river.

Muñoz, down in the ravine beside his CP, could see the action on the hill in silhouette. He could see the dark shadows of hunched-over Chinese coming over the ridge, only to be chopped down. But others jumped the crest and tumbled into the foxholes of his men. He could hear screams and shouts, punctuated by the occasional blast of a grenade.

From the positions that had been overrun, Chinese machine guns began a crossfire over the remaining company area. Now Muñoz's men were pinned down.

Muñoz realized the battle could not go on much longer. George was being overwhelmed. The friendly mortars had ceased fire. The tank platoon, down by the river, could not support in the darkness.

One of the tankers called to him; there was a radio message from his Battalion S-3, Major Woodward: "What's happening?"

Muñoz filled him in. He told him the company was almost shot, and the position ready to give way.

"Okay, Frank, bring your men back across the river—tell Fox to do the same. The 23rd Infantry's on line behind you, somewhere—be careful!"

Muñoz passed the word to Kavanaugh at once.

"I'm with you!" the Fox Company commander said.

But Muñoz never gave the order to pull out; he had no need to. The platoons on the hill had thrown their last grenade; most of the small-arms ammunition was gone. Sergeants Long shouted for his men to try to roll off the hill back into the protecting saddle, and under heavy fire the survivors scrabbled down.

Only some twenty minutes had elapsed since the first shot, but George had lost more than seventy men.

Several men did not get off the hill—one private named Smalley and two ROK KATUSA's were swarmed upon by Chinese, who put rifles in their backs and forced them to surrender.

In bits and pieces, Fox and George companies straggled to their vehicles waiting behind the hill. The supporting tanks and Quad .50's threw up a hail of fire now, to keep the Chinese off their backs. But the enemy did not immediately pursue. They paused to reorganize on their newly won ground.

Behind Fox and George the river was fordable by vehicles only. Ice-rimed and swift, it was four feet deep, with enough current to sweep a wading man from his feet. Muñoz ordered all the wounded who had been salvaged, some thirty to forty, to be put on the tank decks. Then, the tiny column started to move back to the Ch'ongch'on. As they moved out, mortar shells began to whistle down on them.

One tank, sighting the enemy tubes up on the hill, fired a 76mm shell into them and put them out of action.

In the darkness, all was confusion and terror. Trying to round up his men, Muñoz heard sobbing sounds coming from a wood shack—there were a number of shabby Korean dwellings scattered along the river by the crossing site. Muñoz went into the hut, saw an American soldier sitting on the floor, tears streaming down his stubbled face.

"What're you doing in here?" Muñoz shouted.

"I don't know—I don't know!" the soldier sobbed.

"Come with me."

"Captain, I don't want to go out there—"

Muñoz grabbed the man, dragged him to his feet. He was rough and impatient. "Get your ass on one of those tanks!"

Outside, another enlisted man, shot through the foot, was whimpering with pain. "Hang on, you'll be all right," Muñoz told him. The soldier shut up.

Muñoz still had ten to fifteen POW's they had captured earlier. Not knowing what to do with them, he had forced them into one of the Korean huts. Now, pulling out, an H Company officer shouted to Muñoz that they'd better kill these prisoners right away.

On this, Frank Muñoz put his foot down. When the company pulled back, the POW's were left unmolested in the hut.

Under scattered fire, seeing Chinese crawling over the small ridges like ants in the gun flashes, the column ground slowly toward the river. Suddenly, a rocket launcher flared in the night, and the lead tank stopped, started to smoke. The men riding it leaped off; the crew bailed out, and both groups dashed wildly toward another vehicle.

The stopped tank caught fire, its engine flaming up with a loud whoosh. In this light, and behind the cover the steel hull afforded, Muñoz gathered five or six of his men. "Stay here! Fire on the Chinks! We'll cover the others; then they'll cover us—"

There were two more tanks, and most of Fox company, still behind. Now, under the covering fire Muñoz's small party threw against the hills, the others streamed through. But they did not stop to cover Muñoz's withdrawal—they kept on going.

Bullets whined off the damaged tank as the Chinese in the ridges kept up a steady fire, and the gasoline in the tank engine blazed up so high Muñoz began to worry that the tank might explode.

"Let's get out of here," he said to the men around him. "Stay close to me—there's safety in numbers!"

But one of the men, First Sergeant Lester Heath, had been shot in the foot, and crippled. He could barely walk; he could only hobble along, leaning on Muñoz's shoulder.

The little party could not run for the river; hampered by Heath, it moved along at a snail's pace.

The Chinese rushed. Firing coolly with his .45, Muñoz knocked five of them down, while the other men used carbines and M-1's. There was no hope of bringing out the dead, Muñoz knew—but he was not leaving any wounded behind. They brought Heath out.

For this action Frank Muñoz would be decorated.

By the time Muñoz and his party reached the river, the Quad .50's had burned up all their ammunition, and could be used only to ferry men across. The tanks, also, took the wounded across the icy river, then returned to carry more.

From the other side of the river, an artillery battalion was firing now in support, but the fighting was so confused in the dark, and so close-in that the howitzers could not be effective.

Having made the east bank, both the tank officer, Lieutenant Haywood, and Kavanaugh of Fox Company returned to scour the hostile side for wounded and stragglers. The tanks made several trips, and gradually the remnants of the 2nd Battalion formed west of the river. Muñoz and his men were brought across—but many men, despairing of crossing on a tank, waded into the Ch'ongch'on and splashed to safety. In the ten-degree weather, most of these men immediately became weather casualties.

On the east bank, trying to reorganize his company, Frank Muñoz could at first find only twenty men. And it was here he first discovered that his own trousers had been cut by bullets in two places. He had neither heard nor felt the bullets' passage.

At daylight, after losing two more tanks to enemy action, Lieutenants Kavanaugh and Haywood finally came back across the Ch'ongch'on. They were the last men to cross, except one.

Captured up on the hill, Private Smalley had been ordered into his sleeping bag. There, exhausted, he had fallen asleep under Chinese guard while the battle raged. At dawn, a slender Chinese officer shook him awake. Speaking perfect English, the officer began to question Smalley and the two ROK soldiers who had been taken with him.

Smalley refused to open his mouth. Seeing his example, the two KATUSA's were silent, also. At last the Chinese officer snapped his fingers. While Smalley watched, horrified, the Koreans were marched a few paces away and shot down.

Then the officer said to Smalley, "We know all about you." And he did—down to Smalley's unit, and who commanded it. "Now go back and tell your commander not to use fire bombs—napalm—against us. Your outfit is over there"—he pointed to the river—"take off!"

Fully expecting a bullet in the back, Smalley ran for the river. Though he was forced to hide twice to avoid Chinese patrols, he reached the Ch'ongch'on and splashed across.

During this time the Chinese released many such prisoners as Smalley, undoubtedly for propaganda reasons. In Private Smalley's case the propaganda backfired. Finding Captain Muñoz, he said bitterly: "I saw what they did to those ROK's. Gimme a machine gun!"

During the day, George and the other units received dry clothing and hot food. But the 9th Infantry was rapidly becoming disorganized. The night before, 2nd Battalion had been its strongest remaining force. Now 2nd battalion could account for only nine officers and slightly more than two hundred men.

During the day the Chinese lurked in the valleys, burying their dead, cooking their rice. Frank Muñoz and Company could use the respite, but there were limits to what it could do, even with a few hours.

So far, however, there had been no talk of retreat.

* * *

While the left and middle of the 2nd Division line had undergone their nights of fire, and were getting chopped up badly, on the right, or eastern, flank sheer disaster had struck, as yet unknown to either division HQ or Eighth Army.

The II ROK Corps, guarding the 2nd Division's right, had come under the heaviest attack. Badly trained, weapon-poor, the frightened ROK's had been split apart, and were fleeing southward in complete panic.

There were KMAG officers with the ROK's, and as many of these as possible were flown out by American liaison planes. But the complete picture of the disaster was slow in coming through the American staffs in the west.

On the 2nd Division right, Colonel Peploe's 38th Infantry had been strung out south of the Kunu-ri–Huich'on road, in contact with the ROK II Corps. Very soon, the Chinese were all over the Rock of the Marne. Again, this action followed that in the middle of the line—Chinese units prowled down the natural corridors by night, slashing through to the American rear. In some areas they collided violently with American companies on line; in others there was no contact.

There was massive American weapon power among these hills. There were regiments, battalions, a whole division. But only companies fought, and each company fought alone, out of sight, often out of knowledge of any other American unit. The battle boiled down into how long individual companies, singled out and enveloped on all sides by overwhelming numbers, could hold out.

It was weird fighting, such as the United States Army had not seen since the days of Fort Phil Kearney, the Washita, the Little Big Horn. And what the Army had learned on those fields had long since been discarded on the battlefields of Europe. Unable to maneuver where its wheels could not go, unable to emplace and effectively use its big guns, unable to see or communicate in these hills, the United States Army was being bitten to death rather than smashed down by numbers.

While on 26 November Colonel Peploe was having trouble finding out what had happened to his front-line platoons, he soon learned what had transpired in the ROK sector, on his right flank. A little past noon, an entire ROK regiment, the 3rd, came wheeling across his lines, causing great confusion among American riflemen unable to tell friend from foe.

The ROK colonel, his own division dissolved, had sent his men retreating into the American sector in an effort to save them.

Peploe called Major General Keiser at once. "I've got a whole ROK regiment coming into my area. What the hell shall I do with these people?"

Keiser, along with Division HQ, was unquestionably suffering from a certain amount of shock. Against the 2nd Division's own abortive offensive, an enemy blow had landed with stunning speed and ferocity; communications were disrupted, and the inevitable friction of war was slowing Division's reactions. Keiser, worried with other problems, told Peploe, "Take command of 'em and use 'em, dammit!"

This, Peploe was most happy to do. In these hostile hills friendly faces were scarce. He also adjusted his flank against the new menace.

But Keiser, who earlier had pointed to Eighth Army's east flank and said: "Goddam it, that's where they'll hit! That'll be their main effort, off our flank and against ROK II Corps!" along with his staff was slow to react to the tidings of disaster. His own division was in deep trouble, the extent of which he could so far only imagine. His own running sores required such attention that the slings and arrows falling upon the ROK's seemed far away and hardly felt.

So that when IX Corps, concerned with the ROK collapse, sent the newly arrived Turkish Brigade up the Kunu-ri road to Tokch'on to guard 2nd Division's flank, the Turks were left dangling. Their mission required close contact and coordination with 2nd Division, at the very least. Furthermore, the Turks, seeing their first action in Korea, had at this time no idea of which side was up or down, or even where the ball park was.

Beset by the crisis within his own front, the 2nd Division commander left the Turks to shift for themselves; no ranking American officer visited them or briefed them.

Floundering about in a morass of uncertainty and a fog of ignorance about everything that was happening, the Turkish Brigade, 5,000 strong, marched east. Near the village of Wawon the Turks became engaged in battle, and ringing reports soon came back that they had routed the enemy, taking many prisoners.

But, tragically, they had blundered into fleeing ROK's, and the "victory" was over these miserable, panic-stricken remnants of II Corps.

Then, still at Wawon, the main strength of the Chinese burst over them. The detail of what happened will probably never be reported; the essence has been: The Turkish Brigade was destroyed.

Tall, pale-eyed men with dark faces, in heavy greatcoats, wielding long bayonets, the Turks refused to fall back. There were observers who said some officers threw their hats to the ground, marking a spot beyond which they would not retreat, and, surrounded by the enemy, died "upon their fur." There were others, all else failing, who threw cold steel at the enemy in bayonet charges. Rarely has a small action, dimly seen, sketchily reported, sent such intimations of glory flashing across the world.

But the Turks died. On 28 November, when the Turkish Brigade at last fell back southwest and linked with the 38th Infantry, only a few of its companies were combat-fit.

It was deeply ironic later, when the American Government, badly concerned with Turkish public opinion concerning their losses, sent quiet apologies to Turkish authorities. The Turks hardly knew what the Americans were talking about. The Turks, however badly used, had come to fight, and above all else Turks were proud of what their men had done.

Americans had forgotten that only a generation before one of their own generals, Pershing, could stand on the soil of France and say to Clemenceau: "We are here to fight and be killed. Do with us as you will, without counting."

Colonel Peploe, meanwhile, sooner than Division HQ, had seen the way the tide was running. The first of battle he had four line companies broken, and a reserve company badly battered. His only real error as to the gravity of the situation was that he thought his 38th was standing off the enemy's principal strength. He did not really understand that the ROK's and Turks were meeting that, or that the Manchu Raiders were suffering far worse in the middle of the division zone than was his Rock of the Marne.

Only gradually he learned that he had no right flank at all and that the Chinese were south of him.

He wanted to rearrange his units so that his right flank was refused to the enemy, and concerning this he again called Keiser. Unless Peploe pulled back to the southwest, the Chinese would be in position to cut the American main supply route running south.

Keiser, though not really understanding the seriousness of the situation, told him to use his own judgment. Peploe's move, while it could not break the web of fate closing in about 2nd Division, diverted complete disaster.

Rolling with the punch, fighting a battle royal, the men of the 38th pulled back astride the Ch'ongch'on during the night. As Brigadier General S. L. A. Marshall put it, writing of this night of battle, "It is . . . a pity that young Americans have to die bravely but inconspicuously on a foreign hillside in a national cause and have no better words than these spoken of them."

Slowly, the 2nd Division was contracting back toward Kunu-ri. While the 38th was being pushed back on the right and south, the 9th, across the Ch'ongch'on, was also being sprung backward. Strung out along the river and road, the division hourly neared being taken by a double envelopment, a fact that was only slowly being appreciated in higher headquarters.

To the north and east, 25th Division, also bloodied, though not to the extent of the 2nd, was falling back toward the Kunu-ri junction.

For once, things were actually worse on the ground up front then on the maps at Division HQ.

> *When the mortars started falling 'round the CP tent,*
> *Everybody wondered where the high brass went.*
> *They were buggin' out—*
> *Just movin' on . . .*

While the men of the rifle companies had no idea of the enemy's grand scheme of maneuver, or what their own leaders planned, they could look about them, see the missing faces, and know the extent of their hurt. Battalion and regimental staffs, looking for fresh units with which to plug the gaps left by broken ones, were scraping the bottom of the barrel.

East of the Ch'ongch'on and after its first savage night of battle, 2nd Battalion, 9th Infantry, did its best to recoup. Easy Company, Lieutenant Joe Manto, was in bad shape. Fox was down. Frank Muñoz's George was a mass of doll rags. Only the Weapons Company, How, was more or less intact.

But hearing that the enemy had slipped into his rear, establishing blocking positions west of the river, Colonel Sloane had to send the battalion back across the Ch'ongch'on opposite Kujang-dong.

Sloane ordered Major Barberis to move George, How, and Fox into a blocking position against the Chinese, and to try to make contact with the 24th Infantry, 25th Division, which was supposed to be wandering about on the division left.

Muñoz's men moved west of the river again, and took a small hill, driving away a squad of Chinese. But they saw neither hide nor hair of the 24th Regiment. In these hills, across the valley was the same as being in the next county. And the men of the 2nd Battalion, shivering in ten-degree cold, hungry, without sleep for several nights, were reaching the point of exhaustion.

Worried, Sloane called Division HQ. He wanted to know what the further mission of the 9th Infantry would be. "I can't keep these men going till dark, then give them orders to consolidate ground where they stop. They need a decent chance."

The officer at the other end of the line told Sloane not to get his bowels in an uproar; Division had problems, too.

After dark, what was left of Lieutenant Colonel Hill's 1st Battalion was hit and pushed back across the icy river. The wet, freezing men were given dry clothing, then put back on line immediately.

The 3rd Battalion, 9th Infantry, fighting a die-hard action, was driven back into Major Barberis' battalion. All at once, some of the supporting 105's were running short of shells. Painfully, a new day passed.

Frank Muñoz, on the hill west of the river, received a radio message from the battalion exec, Pete Birmingham. "Go to Easy Company CP where we can talk by phone."

Muñoz walked back to Manto's command post, which had wire, a more secure means of communication, strung back to Battalion HQ. Here Birmingham ordered George Company to come back across the river and to take up new positions. "We're beginning an organized retrograde movement."

Muñoz could figure that out. For a great many hours, as far as he was concerned, all signposts had been pointing south.

After dark, he moved back across the river, and with Easy on his right, Fox on his left, began leapfrogging back some two miles toward Kunu-ri. And on this movement began the next-to-final act of the continuing tragedy.

Retreating toward Kunu-ri to the southwest, the companies heard the ring of Chinese bugles from the direction of the river, five hundred yards away. The enemy was already across, in regimental strength.

Something went into the air, bursting redly like Roman-candle balls. Exactly sixty seconds later, behind heavy firing, long waves of Chinese charged frontally against the retreating 2nd Battalion.

Working their weapons desperately, Muñoz's boys knocked the onrushing Chinese back. Just short of his line, the Chinese charge was broken—but some of Muñoz's men were beginning to get the shakes. He saw several get up to try to run to the rear.

"Hold it! Hold it!" he bellowed. At his side, Lieutenant Hernández was trying to help, but Hernández had had it. A brave man, the lieutenant had been commissioned in the field, but he was so worn down by cold and exhaustion he was almost through.

Then the weirdest experience of Muñoz's career took place—suddenly, the battleground was lighted with a brilliant white light, much more intense than that of an artillery flare. He never knew where the light came from, but in it both he and his men had a panoramic view all the way to the Ch'ongch'on. And framed in the white light were more Chinese, in coffee-colored quilted tunics, then Muñoz could count.

The low ground along the river was swarming with thousands of enemy, all headed toward him. It was the most terrifying sight Frank Muñoz was ever to see.

He saw some of Easy's people start to run from their positions. Later, he learned that Joe Manto had been hit, and was left to be captured. The two tanks supporting Muñoz had seen the Chinese sea, too. Now, their engines roaring, they took off to the rear.

Muñoz knew it was hopeless. He shouted for his people to move down from their high ground, and to move back through the valleys. His commo was out. He had no idea where Battalion HQ was.

The Chinese hordes did not press them as they fell back, though they drew some fire. Stumbling through the dark, Muñoz led his men back more than two miles, and at last came into his Regimental post, quite by accident.

Here he reported to the regimental adjutant. He told him what was happening, and Muñoz said that it looked as if the whole line was gone. He then went back into the tent to report to the S-2, the Intelligence Officer, Captain Murphy.

Regiment began to talk with Division via radio, one phrase Muñoz overheard being that "the situation is fluid all over."

Then men started to take the big CP tent down.

"What are my orders?" Muñoz wanted to know.

He was told to attach his command to the 23rd Infantry, "just down the road."

Muñoz went back to his company, seething. What the hell was this, every man for himself? He located some ambulances and put his wounded aboard; he found he had about a hundred men still with him. He moved down the road until he located a battalion command post of the 23rd. The battalion commander ordered him to hold his men there until morning.

At 0400 he was able to get breakfast for his people—dry cereal and black coffee—from the 23rd. The night before the battle began west of the river, Muñoz's men had ambushed and butchered a Korean steer. Rangy and tough as the animal had been, it was their last good meal for a long time.

Muñoz reported to Colonel Paul Freeman, C.O. of the 23rd, at daybreak. Freeman said, "Take up a position on our right flank." But then a staff officer from 2nd Battalion, 9th Infantry, bumped into some of George's people along the trail, and this officer ordered George Company to rejoin.

The 2nd Battalion CP was just up the road.

Muñoz went back to Freeman, who accepted the loss of these unexpected reinforcements cheerfully. "Go on, rejoin your outfit," Freeman told him.

Moving up the frozen dirt road, Muñoz saw Major Barberis standing beside a clump of vehicles. The tall, slim battalion commander's eyes lighted as he saw Muñoz lead George by.

"God, Frank, I'm glad to see you! I thought you were gone."

Barberis, one of the most capable infantry officers in Korea, had somehow got most of his battalion back together—all that was left of it. Now he started these men on the final march back toward the road junction at Kunu-ri.

That day, while the 23rd held the door, the shattered 9th pulled back around Kunu-ri. When night came, it was bitterly cold, but the men were allowed to light no fires. When ordered to stop, men fell down on the frozen earth and lay stiffly in little clumps, unmoving. Most of them had been fighting incessantly for more than forty-eight hours.

That night the firing on all flanks died away, and after midnight it grew strangely peaceful across the frozen wastes. Gratefully, the cold and exhausted survivors did not question the peace and quiet.

But had they remembered the history of the United States Army in their own West, they might have guessed the next step in this anachronistic war. Taking a leaf from the Cavalry's book, the enemy was flowing past the 2nd Division, to cut them off at the pass.

The final horror was yet to come.

20

Into the Valley of Death

Just as in classical Greek tragedy events move toward their predestined course, so the actors in this drama, however courageous and selfless were powerless to change the result.

—S. L. A. Marshall.

IN THE BITTER, foggy dawn of 29 November, while the 2nd Division was locked in battle across the endless hills and corridors along the Ch'ongch'on, a Turkish motor convoy drove north from Sunch'on, some thirty road miles below Kunu-ri, bound for the division rear. The trucks carried supplies intended for the Turkish Brigade, already smashed, and it proceeded north on the single road into the division area.

The convoy never arrived. Near the straggling little village of Yangwan-ni it met a storm of fire from both sides of the road. Trucks exploded and slued off the road. Others stopped, burning. Men fell from the cabs, riddled by machine-gun bullets fired at close range. Some died in the ditches beside the road; a few ran or crawled north into the 2nd Division lines.

Because of language barriers, perhaps because of shock, the Turkish survivors were not able to get their story fully across—and one fact of extreme importance was omitted from their story altogether: two miles south of the area where they had been ambushed, the supply trucks had rolled by the corpses and burned-out vehicles of an even earlier ambush.

The evidence, then, was that a vast area of the division's lifeline south was already interdicted, but the evidence did not get into the right hands. Such of it that did, in the fury and desperation of the moment, seemed to indicate only one more small pinprick among the proliferating wounds from which the division was already bleeding.

Two squads of the 2nd Division MP's were dispatched south on the road. They never returned.

However, a platoon of tanks, from IX Corps reserve, went down the road in complete peace. Near Sunch'on they joined elements of the British Brigade moving north—code name "Nottingham"—and radioed back that the road was clear.

The 2nd Division Reconnaissance Company next went over the same route at midafternoon. Nearing the wreckage of the Turkish convoy, it drew heavy automatic-weapons fire, and radioed back to Lieutenant Colonel Foster, Division G-2, that it was unable to move. A platoon of tanks from the 72nd Tank Battalion and one company of the 38th Infantry was sent south to clear the area. This force was brought to battle along the road, and got nowhere.

At dark, Division HQ ordered it to break off the fighting. From the evidence it now had, Division assumed approximately a thousand yards of the road were interdicted, around Yangwan-ni. The division staff was not unmindful of the threat, but felt it to be more in the nature of an annoyance than a disaster.

Meanwhile, General Keiser had become fully apprised of the major surgery the Chinese had inflicted upon his rifle units. For five days he had been falling back slowly along the Ch'ongch'on, never breaking contact, never with a chance to straighten the division out or to get it back into a firm holding position. The division had been poised to attack against crumbling resistance—not to withstand the *café-au-lait*-colored hordes that poured out of the hills against it.

Now, wanting to pull back a considerable distance, to reorganize and get a breathing spell, Keiser was forced to argue with IX Corps, who did not relish retreat at all. The point was not easily won.

It was not until after the Turks' trucks were already flaming along the division's main supply route that Corps reluctantly agreed to 2nd Division's withdrawal to Sunch'on. Corps left it up to Keiser to come out on whatever route he chose.

There were only two possibilities: the north-south road between Kunu-ri and Sunch'on, and the lateral road leading west from Kunu-ri to junction with the main coastal highway at Sinanju.

Keiser talked by radio with General Milburn, CG of I Corps, who was situated west near Sinanju. Milburn wanted to know how things were with Keiser, Bad, Keiser told him—the 2nd was even drawing fire on its CP.

"Well," Milburn radioed, "come out my way." To the west, all was clear.

But Keiser was not under Milburn's Corps, and he was concerned about becoming enmeshed with the 25th Division, which was retreating along the westward route.

He then drove to the IX Corps CP, which was a few miles west of Kunu-ri, toward Sinanju. Here the Corps G-3 gave him the boundaries of I and IX corps, but again did not specify how Keiser was to bring his division out of the trap being formed about Kunu-ri.

Debating how he was to move, Keiser flew back to his own CP in an L-5 liaison plane. From the plane's height he was able to see many miles across the low hills to the south. He saw hundreds and thousands of men moving southwest along the tiny trails and corridors, and he took these for Korean refugees.

And he thought that if refugees were still fleeing from the enemy in that area, the enemy must still be considerably to the east. Seemingly, he had time to move the division due south rather than into I Corps' zone to the west.

Only later was the evidence to show that these moving men, many wearing captured ROK uniforms, must have been Chinese hastening to block the division's withdrawal.

Keiser was aware of the roadblock on the Kunu-ri–Sunch'on road, but did not consider it yet of major importance. However, after dark 29 November, most of the supply and service trains, including a Mobile Army Surgical Hospital with thirty female nurses, were sent along the west road to Sinanju. These trains passed just after the 25th Division, and experienced no difficulty. With them went the trains of the 38th Regiment, and most of the wounded.

Other service elements, including those of 9th Infantry, went out by way of the lateral road to safety.

Now, on the evening of 29 November, the 23rd Regiment was still north of Kunu-ri, while Peploe's 38th was grudgingly fighting backward from the east. With Peploe were still more than a thousand men of the ROK 3rd Regiment, who were becoming increasingly difficult to control. And with him also were the 155mm howitzers of the 17th Field Artillery.

The 23rd was ordered to move south to the road junction, and to hold the gate open while the division prepared to move south. Peploe was ordered to bring his regiment in, and be prepared to lead the movement toward Sunch'on.

Pulling his units back toward the CP, Peploe told the 17th's C.O., "You'd better get out of here, because now there is nothing in front of you." The artillery commander refused; he had no orders for a move.

Colonel Sloane, of the 9th, was called into Division CP tent and informed that as soon as possible on the next morning, the 30th, his regiment must attack along the Sunch'on road and wipe out the blocking force around Yangwan-ni.

Sloane was far from cheerful at the news. He told Lieutenant Colonel Holden, the division operations officer, that his men were worn out and that his supposed regiment now consisted of only two battalions—each of which had the strength of a rifle company. There were two hundred men in the 2nd, and only slightly more in the 3rd. The 1st had disappeared amid the lonely hills.

Holden, backed up by Colonel Epley, the division chief of staff, told him he had plenty of strength to do the chore. "You will be fighting not more than two Chinese companies."

Sloane asked, "Who's in contact down there with them now?"

The division officers admitted that no one was, at the moment. Sloane grew less cheerful. He was given, finally, a platoon of tanks from the 72nd, in support.

Then, by feeble candlelight, Lieutenant Colonel Holden wrote out the fateful operations order for the retreat. The order was not typed, but scratched out on a scrap of paper in red crayon. It read, simply:

"When R/B [roadblock] is open, follow this priority for movement south: (1) 38th Inf (2) 2nd Recon Co, Div HQ, MP Co, 2nd Signal Co (3) Divarty [divisional Artillery] (4) 2nd Engr Bn (5) Rearguard—23rd RCT (23rd Inf, 15 FA Bn, 72d Tank B—Co C, Battery B of 82d AAA."

Events were rushing toward a conclusion. Soon they would be beyond the control of anyone, in Division HQ or elsewhere.

* * *

Formed up in chilly moonlight, before the cloying fog rolled in from the Yellow Sea, the remnants of 9th Infantry marched south toward Sunch'on on the main supply route. Under Sloane's orders, 2nd Battalion was to clear the ridges west of the main supply route, while 3rd Battalion moved on its east. Just beyond the division CP, flanking patrols left the road and clambered through the dark onto the surrounding ridges.

To the left of the route, Frank Muñoz's George Company moved across hilly, ridged ground. While the hills to the right of the road seemed to be bare, those in front of Muñoz were lightly timbered.

Moving down a dry riverbed, in the dark, George came under fire more than a mile north of where Muñoz had been told to expect the roadblock. Stung by orange streaks blazing from the ridges, George Company piled into the ditches or sought cover along the roadway.

Sloane, badly startled to find enemy here, called his battalion commanders in for hasty conference. As the sky turned light in the east, and the fog thickened, an attack line was formed, and once again the regiment went forward. Surprisingly, they met thin air; the enemy had withdrawn.

By 0800, after an air strike had been called on the ridges up ahead on either side of the road, Muñoz's men had advanced in skirmish line to the high ground whence the Chinese fire had ripped the road the day before. Even though the men were tired, all was proceeding according to plan. A platoon of the supporting tanks were ordered to advance down the road, to see if it were now clear.

The tanks rumbled south, following the twisting, turning route for some six miles down to an area called "the pass," a narrow defile a quarter of a mile in length where the road cut between fifty-foot-high rock embankments. South of this defile, they made contact with elements of Nottingham. They radioed back; the way seemed clear.

Colonel Sloane ordered his units to push on down either side of the road. It was now midmorning. He reported the good news to Division. But immediately, all members of the 9th came under fire from both machine guns and mortars. The heretofore silent hills crawled with Chinese.

Muñoz's company was able to make no progress. The others did no better. The ROK's who had been attached to the 38th marched down to aid them. Colonel Chung, the ROK commander, was asked to attack and clear the ridges on the west. Chung said he would be ready to begin at 1030. Chung, like Soane, had no real idea of what he was getting into.

The ROK's attacked. At first they made good progress—then, quite by accident, American tanks supporting from the road fired into them. And by this time Colonel Chung also must have understood he was attacking more than a simple roadblock; he had a bear by the tail. His men ran into swarms of Chinese on the hills.

The ROK attack failed; as some of the ROK's fell down the ridges they threw their arms away in disgust.

General Keiser had come up in time to see the failure of the ROK effort, but he still thought, as did Colonel Sloane, that he was facing only a shallow roadblock, extending south not more than a thousand yards. While Sloane's tired men were having trouble blasting across it, no real volume of fire had so far fallen on the road.

Meanwhile, to the north, Chinese pressure on the rearguard 23rd RCT was mounting steadily. Colonel Freeman could not hold the door indefinitely; Keiser feared the division would soon be overrun from the north and east, regardless of what lay to its south.

It was this pressure to the north that loomed most heavily in Keiser's mind. Also, while no radio contact had been established, he believed that the Nottingham force was only a short distance south of linkup.

Watching the abortive attempts of Sloane's infantrymen to fight their way across the ridges, Keiser suddenly made his decision. He said, "We've got to get out of here before dark."

It was noon, and the short winter day was fading.

Even if the ridges could not be cleared, Keiser believed his motorized columns could slam through over the road. To Colonel Peploe, standing beside him, he gave a verbal order to begin moving his regiment toward the pass. The division had already struck its camp around Kunu-ri, and the long lines of vehicles stood waiting for the word to move.

Most of the trains and noncombat vehicles of the 2nd Division had been sent out over the road to the west, toward Sinanju. The 25th Division, which had been on the 2nd Division's north, was retreating down this route. With the right—east—flank of the 2nd Division gaping because of the destruction of the ROK II Corps, it was imperative now for the division to fall back to the area of Sunch'on to the south, to make contact with the British brigade there, and to reconsolidate the U.N. line. With unknown numbers of Chinese flowing down the eastern flank, Keiser realized his division was momentarily in danger of being enveloped and cut off.

He thought, however, that the road south to Sunch'on was relatively clear, and fearing imminent increased pressure from the north, he chose to move over the shortest road to Sunch'on. Also, by moving along the other route to the west, there seemed danger of entangling the 2nd with the retreating 25th Division.

The one thing neither Keiser nor anyone else at 2nd Division HQ knew was that the CCF had already sideslipped a full division south and east and had already enveloped the Kunu-ri–Sunch'on road. The British brigade, brought to full battle twenty miles to the south, was in no position to move north to assist.

The division had to come out. It was in serious peril of being trapped. But in sending it down the Sunch'on road, not disposed for battle but organized only for a motor march, General Keiser, unknowingly, was sending it unprepared into the gauntlet.

Most of Peploe's organic vehicles had been sent out with the trains to the west; he had his men mounted on what were left, some artillery vehicles, and the supporting tanks. Peploe had no intimation that the roadblock was not clear at the time he mounted his regiment; therefore he loaded up for a motor march, not for combat.

Tanks were not kept together, but scattered up and down the long truck column, to give support to the thin-skinned vehicles. Since at least one battalion of the 38th—all of which averaged now about two hundred men—had to ride out on the tank decks, Peploe's command immediately lost all tactical integrity. Companies were split apart as they loaded on many separate vehicles; even squads and platoons split up as the men crowded aboard whatever truck or jeep still had room.

Once mounted thus, even senior officers had command and control over only a single vehicle, the one in which they rode. Peploe's regiment, approaching the interdicted area, was now prepared and disposed to do only one thing: ride out.

At the head of the column went the lead tank of Captain Hinton's 38th Regimental Tank Company. With this tank, commanded by Lieutenant Mace, were eighteen infantryman and three officers of the 2/38, including Lieutenants Knight, Rhotenberry, and a young man eager to get the show on the road, Lieutenant Charley Heath.

Now, as the tanks gunned their engines, Sloane came up to Captain Muñoz's thin skirmish line on the ridge and told him two companies of Turks were to attack through George, in a final attempt to clear the ridges. And now, with the plan of maneuver radically altered, the 9th Infantry, including George Company, would have to catch a ride on the convoys as they came through.

Thus 9th Infantry, also, dissolved as a fighting force.

The Turks, in flapping greatcoats, carrying American rifles with fixed bayonets, marched through Muñoz's line of riflemen. These two companies were the last of the Turkish expeditionary force. They assaulted the ridges east of the road while Muñoz watched.

As they attacked, over the radio came the word to Lieutenant Mace's lead tank at the head of the 38th's column: "Haul ass!"

Ponderously, like a great snake uncoiling, the miles-long column thrust its head between the hostile hills, picking up speed. Now the action was irretrievably begun. With the fighting elements of the division fractionalized, scattered over dozens of vehicles, and the vehicles on the road, there could be no change of plan. Officers, even General Keiser, could no longer influence more than a few men close to them, and they, like Keiser, would come out not leading a rearguard action but as individuals speeding for their lives.

The first tank roared ahead, while Mace on the .50-caliber machine gun and the riflemen aboard sprayed the surrounding hills with fire. Machine-gun bullets spattered the tank hull from time to time, but no one was hurt. This tank was to be the luckiest of all that came through.

Then, approximately three thousand yards from where they had started, the tank slued to a sudden halt. Directly ahead, blocking the road, were a damaged tank, a truck, and an M-39 carrier, all pointed north. As the tank stopped, machine-gun fire poured upon it from all sides.

The infantrymen ran for the ditches and began to fire back, as Mace pushed the truck and tank to the side of the road with his own tank. But the M-39 vehicle would not budge. Lieutenant Heath ran for it, to see if the brakes were set. As he boarded it, a bullet struck his rifle, knocking it from his hand, and beside the stalled carrier he saw and heard a desperately wounded man.

This soldier, holding out an empty canteen, pleading, gasped, "Me Turk— me Turk!" Heath had no water; no one in his party had any. All he could do was to shake his head and point to the north, from whence help was coming. The Turk had been shot in both the stomach and shoulder.

And then Heath saw something that struck like a dagger of ice in his own bowels—the blood surrounding the Turk's wounds was clotted and dark; he had been lying beside the road many, many hours.

Instantly, Charley Heath knew that instead of holding a shallow block along the main supply route, the enemy held these ridges at least three miles deep, and they had held them for a long time. Long enough to emplant machine guns, long enough to set up and register mortars. In a single sickening second, Heath knew the division was speeding into a trap.

But it was too late to stop, too late to do anything except to try to barrel through. Heath leaped onto the carrier and released the laterals; Mace's tank shoved the now loosened vehicle off the road. Only a few minutes had been lost, but these were enough to stop the entire convoy behind them.

And from this halt, it would never completely recover.

In motion once more, Mace's lead tank roared ahead, picking up speed again to fifteen miles per hour. Firing, fired on, the tank clanked south another three thousand yards, and entered the narrow defile of the pass. Coming at such speed, Mace surprised the Chinese assembled there; he even saw one group leap up from their noon meal as he went by. Grinding down from the pass, he saw more wrecked vehicles with Turkish markings, and he rammed across a makeshift roadblock the Chinese had set up. The heavy tank barreled across the obstacles; the jeeps immediately following had no such luck; they piled up against it.

Spurting onward, throwing up clouds of dust, Mace's tank cleared the pass and swooped around a bend. High in the turret, his hand on his .50-caliber machine gun, Mace stiffened as he saw a tank in the road.

But it was an American tank, one of those that had broken through earlier. Beyond it was the British brigade, brought to battle south of the pass and being knocked about. The British would not be able to close the gap this day.

Mace's tank, miraculously, had come through without loss among either crew or riders—the first and last vehicle to do so. Surprise, and their momentum, had served them well. And as they went through the British lines, these men knew the worst: that instead of holding only a small stretch of the road under light fire, a full Chinese division had locked itself over six miles of the route, covering it with small arms, mortars, and forty machine guns. Nor could Mace and party give warning; like those of the British, his radios wouldn't carry over the pass.

At any rate, such warning would have come too late. Behind the lead tank, with a roar of flame and singing steel, the huge trap closed.

21

Terror by Night

If you have a son overseas, write to him. If have a son in the Second Division, pray for him.

—Walter Winchell, 1950.

I N THE DARK days of December 1950, certain American commentators became very bitter over the performance of American troops in North Korea. American armies were, after all, being pushed about by those of a third-rate power.

Whatever its skill or courage, it cannot be argued that the United States Army still suffered from deficiencies in discipline and training. A "fair weather" attitude cannot be wiped out in a day. It was not until the Korean War was many months old that new Army trainees began to live half their time in the field, and to undergo a third of their training by night. Slowly, commanders then began to restore the old hard slap and dash that had characterized Grant's men in Virginia, Pershing's AEF, and Patton's armored columns.

This would be a bitter battle, fought against both men in the ranks and the public behind them. It would never be completely won.

But the principal reason that the Eighth Army was defeated along the Ch'ongch'on was that the men marching north had no more idea of what awaited them than had Lieutenant Colonel Custer riding toward the Valley of the Greasy Grass.

There had been the same arrogance in the march north that had characterized Braddock's movement against the French and Indians, Dade's demonstration against the Seminoles, and Custer's ride to the Little Big Horn. And it was the same conditions of terrain, low cunning, and barbarian hardihood that brought all these forces to defeat by an intrinsically inferior enemy.

It was almost as hard for minds trained on the fields of Europe to adjust to Korea as it had been for British generals to learn to fight colonials—who threw the book of civilized warfare away.

But the most ironic thing, in those bitter days of December 1950, was that the commentators who cried havoc the loudest were the very men who had done most to change and destroy the old 1945 Army. These were the men who had shouted for the boys to be brought home, who had urged the troops to exert civil rights. They were the ones who had hinted that leaders trying to delay the frenetic demobilization, or the reform of the Army, were no better than the Fascists.

And these were the men who screamed most shrilly when some young Americans on the field of battle behaved more like citizens than like soldiers.

* * *

Once irrevocably committed in motion, the single forlorn hope of the 2nd Division's motor column to clear the gauntlet sprung about it rested on its momentum. Once begun, there was gigantic power in the mechanized onrush difficult even for machine guns to stop.

But the single M-39 carrier, which forced Mace's tank to halt for half a dozen minutes, dealt this slender hope a fatal wound.

For as the long, serpentine column braked to a halt behind Mace, a hail of gunfire beat against its exposed sides like rain, killing men, exploding trucks, driving riders into the ditches. Still moving, stricken vehicles could have slued off the right of way. Destroyed while at the halt, they plugged the narrow road for those pressing on behind.

Brought under sweeping automatic fire, the tactically disorganized riflemen of Peploe's battalions could only tumble off their tanks and trucks and fight back from the roadside. But officers were separated from their platoons, and battalion commanders had lost touch with their companies upon entrucking. No organized action could be started and pushed home against the enemy firing from the flanking ridges. The movement had begun as a motor march, and a motor march it remained until the last.

When the tanks finally pushed wrecked vehicles out of the road, after each accordion-action halt, the armor and trucks, spurred by the flailing steel beating against them, often roared ahead without pausing to reload their passengers.

Wounded and dead clogged the ditches. Some lay apathetically, while others ran along in the column's dust, desperately trying to hitch a new ride. Officers had not anticipated trouble, and now, committed, they could only bore ahead, trying to bring through the few men riding in the same vehicle with them.

Some vehicles stopped, loaded hale and hurt alike. Men grabbed hold of others as they raced by, only to be kicked off by the already overcrowded riders. And each stop, when it occurred, only delayed the column more.

There could be no turning back. As the Light Brigade had ridden into the valley of death, so the 2nd Division rode into six miles of hell. The greater part of the leading serials came through safely, though blooded. Their momentum and the furious strafing of the encircling hills by the Air Force took them through. Then, as the road became more clogged with broken and burning vehicles, and Chinese fire increased at the final defile, the movement became more and more sluggish. Finally, about midafternoon, the pass itself was blocked and closed.

The major trouble, all that bloody afternoon, was that a strung-out motor convoy could have no unity of command. Tankers, who could move freely up and down the road, had no orders. Some stopped to fight; others blared through to the south. Senior officers filled their own vehicles with wounded and walked out. Some fought off encircling Chinese with rifles. No one had command; no one had control.

Colonel Peploe, his own jeep filled with wounded men, roared into the last defile before the road closed. In the pass a great heap of debris from exploded trucks lay across the road; Peploe, holding on with all his strength, felt the jeep would never clear it.

But his driver, a young lieutenant, poured on the gas like a madman, careening and sluing across the road. The jeep bounced through. Whining down the last ridge, Peploe's quarter-ton raced around a curve and up over a wooded hill, and suddenly there were men about the truck. A friendly British voice yelled, "You can slow down now—you're safe!"

Behind Peploe, the pass closed in a fury of fire and death. Still to the north of it was the greater part of the 2nd Division.

The British, fighting their way north, were in contact with a Chinese division, stalled. A force might have been put together from the men who had first cleared the pass, and such force might have gone back and swept its sides of enemy guns—but the men who reached British lines had been fighting their own separate Little Big Horns for five days and nights. As an observer remarked, these survivors were men, not gods. No relieving force was ever organized from the south.

Within the gauntlet, each vehicle, each man, lived through an individual Hades. There were acts of immense courage, and of heartbreaking solicitude, as well as of stupidity and cowardice. As in all battles, all that reflected good or bad for the race of man took place within the pass.

These tales have been well told, elsewhere.

* * *

On the northern lip of the gauntlet, after the column started through, Colonel Sloane's 9th Infantry had run into new trouble. As the Turks, cut to pieces, reeled back from the surrounding slopes, mortar fire crashed down on the men holding the shoulders of the road.

Barberis was hit, a litter case. The 2nd Battalion S-3 was hit. Captain Frank Muñoz, senior surviving officer, took temporary command.

The 2nd Battalion, like all the units of 9th Infantry, had been told to come out any way it could. And most of the men of the 9th secured places in the convoy as individuals as the trucks came by, so losing their lives or coming through, as their fortunes read.

Muñoz tried to keep his own men together. On the road he found some stalled vehicles, abandoned when they were stopped. Their tires had been shot away, their radiators perforated by bullets. Using the native mechanical genius of his men, Muñoz put an artillery ammunition truck in running order. Then, throwing out the heavy stuff, he loaded aboard all the small-arms ammunition he could find.

He told George Company: "We're going to fight our way through. We're going to evacuate our wounded on this truck. Anyone who can't walk, rides—"

His men were worried and shaken, but they listened to him.

A .50-caliber machine gun was in a ring mount on the repaired truck, and with his firing at the enfilading hills, Muñoz and his company started south, picking up stragglers, fighting their way through.

Some time after three o'clock, they arrived at the pass. Coming below the high slate cliffs, they walked into a swarm of Chinese bullets. The pass itself was blocked with wrecked vehicles, and from the high ground to either side of it enemy machine guns blazed incessantly at the vehicles piling up to the north.

Men had to leave their vehicles and make for the rocks and ditches, while gunfire cut them down. In the ten-degree weather, soldiers were becoming exhausted and apathetic. Americans, ROK's, and Turks lay on the ground, shocked, uncaring, while Chinese fire beat the earth about them. Their faces were dust-grimed, their eyes watering, their jaws slack.

Muñoz saw a scene of incredible confusion. The dead lay about in droves. Now and again a hurt man croaked aloud for water. Only a few men were trying to fight back at the enemy holding the hills.

On the other side of the road, meanwhile, across from Muñoz, General Keiser arrived in his jeep. He left the truck and walked up to the edge of the fatal log jam in the defile. Here he tried to bring some sort of order to the dazed men on the ground.

"Who's in command? Who are you? Can any of you do anything?"

The ROK's and Turks couldn't understand; the Americans kept silent.

Then Major General Keiser, division commander, walked on into the pass, to see what he could do. He found a few men fighting, and he saw men helping the seriously wounded. But he found no officers, and he went back to the northern edge, while bullets chipped the rock behind him.

On the way out, he accidentally stepped on the body of an American lying in his path. The man suddenly moved and said, "You damn son of a bitch!"

Surprised, General Keiser could only say, "My friend, I'm very sorry." Feeling very old and tired, he went on.

He knew that infantry parties had to be formed to attack and clear the ridges lipping the defile. Until this was done, there was no hope of clearing the obstacles in the road.

* * *

Over the pass now, Air Force jets were strumming in full fury, rocketing, napalming, stinging the rocks with machine-gun fire. They did a great deal to ease the burdens of those below, but they could not do the job alone. Still, they tried.

A plane whined in so low that the spent .50 caliber cartridges from its wing guns tinkled off Frank Muñoz's helmet. The flame from a napalm blast seared his face.

Muñoz, pinpointing a machine gun on the right side of the pass, got five men together. Frozen, exhausted to the point of hardly caring whether they lived or died, men moved as in molasses. It was almost impossible for anyone, officer or man, to do the slightest task—but Muñoz moved up the slope, and the Chinese pulled the gun away.

Meanwhile, the man who could get the job done had arrived.

Lieutenant Tom Turner, exec of the 38th's Regimental Tank Company, had had an incredible afternoon. Earlier, while directing fire against attacking Chinese, a rocket blast from friendly air knocked him unconscious in the ditch, where he lay for more than an hour as the motorcade ground past.

Coming to, bruised and shaken, he had walked more than a mile south, moving along stopped vehicles whose drivers and riders were down in the ditches, fighting. At the head of this mile-long column he found a small truck standing idle, clear road opening before it, while its crew engaged in rifle duels with the Chinese in the hills.

Turner got this truck on its way—then, under heavy fire, he moved back along the road, getting men into their trucks and moving again. It took tremendous effort, and great courage. Finally, with the trucks moving, he leaped on the running board of a two-and-a-half ton, only to fall into the ditch again as the bit of metal to which he clung was carried away by a machine-gun slug.

Again Turner blacked out.

When he crawled from the ditch once more, he saw the column had braked again approximately a thousand yards to the south. But as he stood erect, he felt a Chinese rifle in his back.

He was in the midst of a Chinese squad, some of whom were rendering first aid to American wounded lying along the road. Limping from a badly sprained ankle, Turner was told by the Chinese leader, in good English, to sit down.

Then, after a few minutes, the Chinese asked him if his ankle was good enough for him to walk back to his own lines. Surprised, Tom Turner answered, "I think so."

The Chinese then searched him—but politely, asking if he objected. They took two letters from him, leaving his money intact. More important, they missed the bottle of I. W. Harper that Turner had stowed in his jacket.

Then the Chinese leader ordered him to move down the road, collecting American walking wounded as he went. Limping, his ankle afire with pain, Turner walked away, fully expecting to be shot in the back. Instead, the Chinese faded into the hills.

Turner began to collect American wounded men who could walk, and he passed his bottle around. With three other men, all hurt, he approached the north end of the pass. Here a machine gun opened fire on the little group, and they hit the ditches. Resting, Turner passed the bottle once more.

There were wounded men all around, crawling, groaning, trying to move south into the pass. Tom Turner took another swig from his bottle, then got up. Hardly feeling his ankle, he trotted forward, under the embankment. And here American soldiers shouted to him to get down; a Chinese gun was dug in only twenty-five yards above him, spraying the road.

Turner asked for a grenade, but none of the men near him had any. Shaking his head to clear it, he then asked, "Who'll join me in rushing that gun?"

The suggestion went over like a lead balloon. One soldier told him, "You want it, you go take it, Lieutenant."

Somebody else said, "Take it, and shove it up your ass."

Giving up on the Americans, Turner went back the way he had come, shouting for any ROK or Turk who could talk English to come forward. He found one ROK who could. The man brought more than thirty other ROK's with him. Turner explained what he wanted—and the ROK's agreed.

He set some of them up as a base of fire to pin down the enemy gun, while he explained to the others that they would attack it behind him. Then he moved out. Looking back, he was shocked to see the whole group coming with him—they had not understood his orders.

Operating on his own genuine courage and the stimulus of the liquor, Turner figured what the hell. He yelled, *"Banzai—Banzai!"* and ran up over the covering embankment toward the enemy gun.

Turner's group swamped the gun crew before they could swivel it to meet the charge. Eager to go on, Turner's ROK's wanted to rush another gun, but he held them back, trying to get them into some kind of fighting order first.

At this moment an aircraft whistled low over the ridges, firing into them. A rocket exploded, and once again Tom Turner, bruised and concussed, lost consciousness.

But while he lay on the cold dust, other men were beginning to take charge.

The low-flying planes, howling angrily over the pass, had knocked over gun after gun as the sun sank. And both General Keiser and his assistant commander, General Bradley, now where organizing rifle parties to sweep over the enfilading ridges. Other officers, Muñoz from the 9th, and several from the 38th, got together small groups to move across the hills.

By now it was within minutes of becoming dark. The Chinese fire seemed to slacken a bit, and Muñoz moved his ammo truck with the .50 caliber forward along the road. Eight or ten Chinese suddenly appeared in front of the truck, apparently trying to surrender. But these men carried weapons, though their hands were high.

A Korean lieutenant yelled at Muñoz: "Don't trust them—they're trying to get in close!"

Muñoz and the Chinese opened fire at almost the same time. The Chinese went down, but now somebody ran up the line yelling, "Cease fire! Cease fire! The Chinese are trying to surrender!"

Farther ahead, General Keiser heard the shouts. He began yelling, "Stop that! These Commies know English! They started this—we're beginning to get them on the run!"

Now two light tanks from the 2nd Recon Company came into the defile, and with them an officer of the 38th was able to push the blocking debris out of the way. Suddenly, painfully, the serpentine column began to wind once again through the narrow pass, around the curve, and up onto the wooded British ridge beyond.

Muñoz heard Keiser say, "We've got to get through here before dark—" and the general hopped into his jeep and started through the pass. Behind him, Muñoz and the others followed.

The movement broke the will of the hovering Chinese. The ravaging fury of the American air, blasting out guns, spilling the enemy hordes trying to move up onto the hills to reinforce the defenders, the courage of a few ROK's and Americans, and the impact of a bottle of I. W. Harper had all added up to clear the pass.

As it grew dark, Tom Turner, once more on his feet, led a column of mixed allied troops through draws to the southwest on foot, reaching friendly lines at last.

Muñoz lost twenty-five of his people in the gauntlet, but coming into Nottingham, he found—miracle of miracles—his company kitchen truck. At that moment he would rather have had it than diamonds.

As the sun flared redly in the west and went out, the long jam at the pass was broken—but a great part of the 2nd Division was still north of the defile when the sun went down.

When General Keiser had first encountered the stoppage at the pass, he had tried to raise Colonel Freeman's 23rd Regiment, holding the gate north of Kunu-ri. Keiser had hoped for help from the embattled 23rd—but he could not make contact because of the hills and distance.

But Colonel Sloane, 9th Infantry, was in contact with both headquarters, and he relayed the messages.

Freeman, to the north, was under pressure equal to that of Keiser at the pass. Minute by minute, the volume of fire falling on the rear guard was increasing; Freeman could hear the ominous bugling from surrounding hills as Chinese massed for the kill. Both he and the commander of his attached artillery, Keith, agreed that if the 23rd RCT did not soon withdraw it would never get the chance.

Freeman, sending messages through Sloane to Keiser, was thinking about his own withdrawal. He wanted permission to move out by way of the Sinanju road to the west instead of coming through the pass. In the sending and relay of messages, both Freeman and Keiser, thinking of different problems, became somewhat confused. To Freeman came the message, "Go ahead, and good luck."

Later, neither Keiser nor his ADC, Bradley, could remember having authorized the change of plan. But as Keiser told Freeman, "Thank God, Paul, that it all worked out for the best."

For upon getting the relayed message, Freeman and Keith at once decided to fire all ammunition on the ground, and to abandon the heavy guns. The road west was unfit to move howitzers by night on a fighting withdrawal.

As the riflemen of the 23rd began to leave their positions on the high ground about Kunu-ri, the cooks, clerks, and drivers of the 15th Field Artillery formed daisy chains from the ammunition dumps to the guns. Only a few thousand yards beyond, Chinese were pressing down from the hills in column. With every man in the artillery bearing a hand to bring up the ammunition, the gunners opened fire.

In twenty minutes, the battalion sent 3,206 rounds through the tubes; the earth before the advancing Chinese trembled and exploded in fire and death. Paint burned and peeled from the guns; breechblocks went dark from heat. Then, the ammunition gone, Keith's gunners' removed the firing locks and sights and thermited the tubes, and made for their trucks.

But the hail of explosives had saved the regiment. Running into such unprecedented fire, the Chinese stopped—and believing they were about to be counterattacked, they dug in. Though they would come out again later and attempt pursuit, they would never be able to catch up with the motorized column on foot.

As dark fell, Freeman's command started west, to the main coastal road, and came through intact. The last men and vehicles did not clear Kunu-ri till midnight—and after these came still the hard-pressed rear guard of the 25th Division, elements of Corley's 24th Infantry.

At 0200, 1 December, Blair's 3/24th still held Kunu-ri. While Blair was reporting to Colonel Corley by field phone, Chinese swarmed into his CP. By dawn, the 3/24 had dissolved as a fighting force, and it was every man for himself.

Ironically, the Chinese allowed those who ran toward the west to escape, and in many cases actually helped these men along by picking them up and carrying them until they were close to American lines.

Those who stayed and fought were not seen again.

The 2nd Division Artillery, less Keith's 15th Field, was the last element of the division to come through the gauntlet on the south. They had been waiting all afternoon. Because Freeman went west, the artillery became not an element in the column, but fighting rear guard for the division. Thus, the gunners had the terrible chore of moving, trying to support the column by fire, and defending the guns all at once. For a while, the artillery was in a quandary as to what to do.

Just at dark, the pass cleared, and seeing the vehicles ahead of the artillery move out, Brigadier General Haymes, Divarty Commander, realized his decision had been made for him. He ordered the artillery columns to proceed through the pass.

With the artillery came engineers, MP's, and dozens of stragglers from the infantry serials that had gone through earlier. It was a blazing fight for most of the way. Some batteries were forced to deploy and man their guns; some were overrun. All were badly shot up.

On the night march, under fire, the road became clogged with blazing vehicles. Swerving to avoid the blocks, other vehicles overturned. The first artillery battalions in the column came through best. The 17th leading, came out in good shape. The 37th, following, lost ten guns. The 503rd fought most of the night to save its 155's, finally losing them. The 38th Field, at the end of the column, lost every gun and truck, and its men came out as stragglers over the hills, if they came out at all.

Because the guns were undeniably lost, there were men who cried discredit upon the artillerymen. But the men who came through with them, of whatever arm or service, are firm in the belief that the guns were served with honor until the last.

The last men of the division to come through, arriving within the British lines of the moring of 1 December, could remember very little of what they had experienced. There comes a time when the conscious mind accepts no more; as with women experiencing childbirth, even the memory of pain is blotted out.

On that morning, thousands of allied wounded filled every field aid station and hospital even beyond Sunch'on. British and American surgeons worked until they dropped, then got up and worked again. Men lay on the frozen ground for hours, waiting for treatment.

But aside from the dead, there were still men more unfortunate than these.

All of 2nd Division did not come out.

* * *

One of the persistent myths of American arms in the middle of this century is that technicians somehow are not and should not be soldiers. But when a man dons the uniform whether he wears crossed muskets, the wheel, or the caduceus, events are apt to prove the falseness of such belief. For any man who wears his country's uniform, of whatever service, should be prepared to suffer, and if need be, to fight.

Sergeant Charles B. Schlichter, 2nd Medical Battalion, 2nd Infantry Division, had been soldiering most of his life. At eighteen, in 1939, tall, slim, and green-eyed, he had enlisted in the Pennsylvania National Guard. Later, during the war, he had served forty-three months overseas with the Coast Guard, as part of a beach party with the Fleet Marine Force. He had seen Kwajelein, Eniwetok, Saipan, and Tinian, among others.

But, somehow, after the big war, he found himself married and selling furniture for a living. The service, he figured, was nothing to inflict upon a new wife. But some men are fortunate in their choice of mate—Elizabeth Schlichter had been raised in the Army, and day by day, month by month, she knew what ailed her man.

One night, while Charles was sitting in the bathtub, washing his long brown hair, Elizabeth lay on their bed, reading the evening paper. Suddenly she said: "I see here the Army needs men. Why don't you go back into the service?"

Schlichter washed soap from his ears. "What?"

She repeated her question.

He said, "I'd love to—but it's not fair to you—"

"I like to travel, anyway."

The next morning, Schlichter called at an Army recruiting office. Looking at his records, the Army gave him sergeant's stripes on enlistment. In June, 1950, he was a surgical technician at Madigan General Hospital. When the news of the outbreak in Korea came over the air, Charles Schlichter had a premonition. In the middle of the night he told Elizabeth: "Something is going to happen to me—I don't know what, but something is going to happen. No matter what, stay where I leave you—because I'll be back." Neither he nor Elizabeth slept much that night.

In a few days, something did happen. He was diverted to the 2nd Division on 16 July, and restricted to post. He asked about a chance to make arrangements for his wife, and was told, "After you leave for Korea, she can find a place to live."

The 9th Infantry, his new unit, went aboard ship for the Far East. It was a ship diverted from civilian trade, and N.C.O.'s had staterooms, with bath and clean linen. But at sea, Schlichter and the medics of his unit received no real briefing on the Korean situation. Korea was described to them as a minor police action, which might be cleared up before they arrived. But listening to the radio, Schlichter visualized the vanishing American Perimeter.

When the regiment debarked at Pusan, the medics were issued rifles. As Schlichter put it later, this caused a certain amount of consternation in the ranks. For here they were told that the North Korean enemy considered any man in uniform fair game, whether he wore medic's armband or the chaplain's silver cross, and they should govern themselves accordingly.

Soon, in the fighting that followed along the broiling Naktong, Schlichter went to the division collecting company. He followed the division from the Naktong to the Ch'ongch'on. And here, on Thanksgiving Day he wrote his wife, like many others, that he would be back in time to buy Christmas presents in the States.

Then, suddenly, the medical collecting company was busy along the Ch'ongch'on. And just as suddenly, Major Bert N. Coers, the C.O., told the men: "We're withdrawing south. This is not a retreat, but an organized withdrawal."

In the confusion that was overwhelming the division on 30 November, Schlichter figured the medics were lucky to be told anything.

In a serial of some twenty vehicles, the company formed up on the Sunch'on road south of Kunu-ri. It was the last element of the regimental convoy, and here there was some argument. The vehicles already held 180 wounded men. Should the medics be last, so as to aid future wounded, or should they proceed out early, to take care of those they already had?

It was finally resolved that the medics would go last. After all, Coers had been told it was to be an orderly withdrawal, and no one expected trouble.

At dusk on 30 November, the medical convoy was still stopped on the road miles north of the pass. Sitting in a truck with Kenneth Beadke, the company field first sergeant, and Sergeant Wright, Schlichter could hear heavy firing ahead, see the pink and red tracers bouncing off the hills. All three wondered what was happening, and why they were stopped, but they were not really worried. They felt that the combat units ahead of them would fight through and clear the way.

It grew darker, and the thermometer fell. The firing reverberated among the hills, and in the convoy men became tired and cold and scared.

"What's the matter? Why don't we move out?"

There were many young men in the company who had come to Korea with no concept of war. Panic began to sprout.

Then an officer—for there were young men wearing bars among this convoy who were never soldiers, either—ran along the stalled line of trucks, shouting: "It's every man for himself! We're trapped! Get out any way you can!"

Men got down from the trucks and began to run for the circling hills—and the officers and sergeants followed. *Here,* thought Sergeant Schlichter later, *we committed a grievous error. Here we broke faith with our fellow soldiers, and fellowmen.*

There were 180 wounded men in the trucks, and no one said anything to these men as they were abandoned.

The two hundred-odd men of the company spread all over the hills. Schlichter and Ken Beadke were in one small group. All knew they had to move south to reach safety—but now none of them knew where south was, in the dark. No one had any idea of how to move, or how to orient themselves. Men ran into the hills until they dropped from exhaustion; they ran as long as the panic held them and their legs would carry them.

Others climbed hills, to try to see about them. Some saw moving men in the dark, and opened fire with their rifles and carbines. Sometimes agonized voices answered the shots in English.

All night the medics, none of whom possessed any infantry training, wandered aimlessly through the hills fringing the road.

At dawn of 1 December, Schlichter's small group of fifteen men rested on a cold plateau three hundred yards in length. Looking over the lip of the ridge, Schlichter could see Chinese on horseback riding through the valley. Hugging the ground, Schlichter and the men with him realized the Chinese were all around them in these hills.

To Schlichter's hill came an infantry officer named Hill; he was a major or lieutenant colonel from the 9th Infantry. This officer tried to organize a defense of the ground, positioning the half-frozen men about. He had an air panel, and as an American plane flew over, searching the ridges for Chinese in the dawn, he waved this up and down, trying to attract the pilot's eye.

The pilot saw, and radioed for help—but the Chinese also saw Hill as he exposed himself. A rifle bullet struck him in the belly, passed through, and tore a hole in his lower back.

Hill fell down and said softly, "Oh, my God!"

Schlichter ran to him, tore open his bulky winter clothing. Hill said, "My God, boy, get down—they'll kill you!"

"Hell, the SOBs can hit me," Schlichter muttered. He put a bandage across Hill's wounds, gave him morphine. There was nothing else he could do.

As he treated the officer, the Air Force roared in, slamming the ridges and valleys with rockets and machine guns. They drove the circling Chinese cavalry away.

Now, in the strengthening light, Schlichter could see he was on a ridge only a little way from the abandoned vehicles on the road—during the night his party had circled about like a running hare, ending up almost where they had begun. And here, suddenly, Charles Schlichter decided that those wounded men down below belonged to him. With the men about him, he held a short powwow.

There were Chinese moving on ridges to the far side of the road; but the senior soldiers with Schlichter's party—but not all of those senior in rank—agreed that their wounded had to go out with them.

They started back down the slope toward the vehicles standing forlornly beside the debris-littered road. But the decision of what to do for those hurt men was taken from them.

Undamaged, the vehicles stood starkly by the road, in column, easily visible from the air. Before Schlichter's party reached them, Air Force planes screamed out of the south, shooting, bombing. It was standard practice for the Air Force to destroy abandoned equipment before the enemy could profit from it. The pilots could not know what cargo those deserted trucks still held.

Schlichter was too far away to do anything, but close enough to hear the wounded men aboard the vehicles scream. Then the Air Force dropped napalm, the drums bouncing from the frozen ground and engulfing the dusty trucks in flame.

In the zero weather, Charles Schlichter's face was suddenly wet with sweat. Some of the men with him closed their eyes.

And then they all ran back into the hills. They went in small groups. There was no unity. The C.O. was unable or unwilling to do anything. Some of the men were now wounded from Chinese fire, and many had thrown their weapons away.

Yet there were many who still walked as men. One, Captain Struthers, M.C.—to whom a general had offered a job in Japan, and been refused—died in a machine-gun burst, trying to aid a wounded soldier.

But most were neither heroes nor cowards. They were ordinary men, and they went with the tide, wherever it carried them.

Within a short time, a North Korean patrol had pinned them on a hill, holding them down with submachine-gun fire. Major Coers and a second officer talked. Coers said, "It's futile to resist." He stood up, and surrendered himself and his men. There were fifteen in the little group, including Schlichter.

The North Koreans marched the captives over a ridge, then halted them before a long, narrow slit trench that had been dug in the hill. They turned the muzzles of their Russian-made submachine guns on the group, and in a blinding moment of fear Schlichter realized the Koreans were going to shoot them.

In that moment, the men holding those guns cut his line to home. The power and the glory of the United States were suddenly far away, impotent, as he stood facing death on a frozen, windswept hill ten thousand miles from home.

He had carried a small Bible in his jacket because his people had been religious, and they had brought him up in the same way. But until now he had hardly glanced at it. In the seconds he had left, Schlichter drew the book from his jacket, and it fell open at the Twenty-third Psalm.

He did not have to read it, he knew it from childhood.

The North Koreans did not fire. An officer, apparently Chinese, ran toward them, shouting orders in a high voice; sullenly, the troops lowered their weapons. The Chinese officer barked again, and with motions of their gun barrels the soldiers herded the captive Americans into motion. They headed north.

They staggered north, numbed, silent, cold, and exhausted by their ordeal. But in the little group, Charles Schlichter suddenly felt he would never again be so afraid of tomorrow. And of these men, only he would live to see again his native land.

22

Changjin Reservoir

Easy Company holds here!

—Captain Walter Phillips, commanding E Company, 7th Marines, on a hill above Yudam-ni.

THREE DAYS after Walton Walker's Eighth Army found the hostiles along the Ch'ongch'on, X Corps met a Chinese buzzsaw in the east. Here again occurred some of the most savage actions in the long history of land warfare. In many respects, the fighting in the east resembled that in the west—U.N. forces were flanked, some brought to battle while others remained unscathed, and the whole position rendered untenable.

But there were differences, too.

While Eighth Army attacked on a broad front, Almond's X Corps advanced north in four main columns. On the eastern side of Korea there were no relatively flat valleys, only deep and tortuous corridors fingering their way through bare and brutal mountains. The roads—such as there were—were dirt. In many places the arteries of communication were only cliff-hanging trails leading along the mountainsides.

Because of the terrain, contact even between the various units of X Corps was fragile. On the left, trying to close the gap with Eighth Army, advanced the American 3rd Division. Above them, the 1st Marine Division marched northwest, toward the Changjin Reservoir. The U.S. 7th Division, east of the reservoir, went straight north for the Yalu. On the far right, the ROK I Corps of two divisions moved along the coast.

It was not a steady line advancing across the savage reaches, but rather four separate fingers thrusting upward into the narrow mountain corridors. The progress made during November by each column varied greatly.

Attacking against crumbling remnants of the NKPA, the ROK Corps galloped freely toward the maritime province of Siberia. In the ROK zone no Chinese ever appeared.

The 7th Division, on the ROK's left, met scattered opposition. By 21 November Powell's 17th RCT of that division reached Hyesanjin on the Yalu. The village's connecting bridges with Manchuria had been shattered by U.N. Air, and it was a ghost town. The wattle huts were deserted, and cold cattle, abandoned, lowed in misery in the frozen fields.

The Marines, marching northwest from Hungnam toward the Changjin Reservoir, met Chinese in force first week of November. But these Chinese, part of Lin Piao's First Phase Offensive, were defeated in sharp fighting, and pushed back. By 8 November they too had melted into the looming mountains to the north. But General Oliver Smith, of the Marine Division, and his regimental commanders, Litzenberg, Murray, and Puller, were now highly dubious of what might lie ahead of them in the mysterious north.

Deliberately, the Marines slowed their advance, even though Ned Almond fretted at their lack of progress. The Marines felt that, strung out as they must be in such terrain, a pellmell rush to the Yalu was highly dangerous. The whole Corps plan of maneuver was ill advised, if more than broken, remnants of the NKPA faced it.

But, like Walker, Almond had his orders from Tokyo: push on, and end the campaign. Under Almond's prodding X Corps, including the reluctant, exposed Marines, pushed on.

North from the Korean port of Hungnam on the cold, gray waters of the Sea of Japan, a narrow, dirt and gravel road snaked into the hills. For some forty-three miles—the distance from Hungnam to Chinhung-ni—the road contained two lanes and moved across reasonably rolling ground.

But at Chinhung-ni, the aspect changed. The remaining thirty-five miles north by west to the sordid little hamlet of Yudam-ni became a multiple nightmare.

Beyond Chinhung-ni the road rose 2,500 feet into cold, thin mountain air. The second lane disappeared; now the road crept ribbonlike into the soaring wastes, a yawning abyss on one side and a precipice on the other.

It climbed and climbed, struggling upward to the Kot'o plateau, on which sat the single, miserable village of Kot'o-ri. From Kot'o-ri the road crept through mile-high hills to the city of Hagaru, straggling near the southern tip of the thirty-mile-long Changjin Reservoir.

Hagaru, an important center before the war, but now broken and blackened by U.N. Air, huddled in a bleak bowl of frozen earth some three miles across. Here the road forked.

One fork, the right hand, passed north and east into equally miserable terrain. The other skirted the reservoir and turned west; it climbed the 4,000-foot peaks of Toktong Pass, and after fourteen miles through sullen gorges it devolved into a broad valley ringed by five great ridges.

Here, in this valley, sat the lowly village of Yudam-ni, 3,500 feet above sea level, hardly sheltered from the bitter winds and snows of Siberia by its mile-high ring of peaks. Here, and along the whole length of the road from Hungnam, the land is barren and bleak in winter. The grass dies, and rustles sere and brown in the sharp winds; snow falls repeatedly, and ice covers the gorges and craggy ridges.

And here, in November 1950, winter came early, howling off the roof of the world, screaming across the frozen Yalu, the worst winter the world had seen for a decade. There was nothing on Marine and Army maps to indicate such weather—but Korea is not sheltered by the surrounding seas from the cold that sweeps the northern land mass of Asia. On a parallel with climes that are moderate in Europe or America, Korea is arctic when winter comes.

Moving up this road, fighting sharply to reach the Kot'o-ri Plateau, winter struck the men of the 1st Marine Division the night of 10 November. The mercury dropped to ten below. At the first shock, men became dazed and incoherent. Some grew numb, others cried with pain. No amount of clothing, even good GI issue, could entirely keep the cold out.

Many Americans were used to much worse weather—but not to fight in, without fires, shelter, or warm food. Water froze solid in canteens; rations froze in their cans. Plasma froze; medical supplies could not be stored more than eight feet away from a roaring stove at any time. Vehicles, once stopped, would hardly run again. Guns froze solid—all oil had to be removed from them; and many automatic weapons would fire but one shot at a time.

While the first, worst shock of winter soon wore off, the problem of the cold continued. It was to be an enemy as much to be feared as the Chinese lurking in the dark hills and passes. Feet and hands of the men exposed on the ridges turned white with frostbite, and a man who was wounded suffered agonies. The cold, through the bitter days of December, would destroy as many American fighting men as enemy bullets.

The ground froze eighteen inches down. To dig a hole with chapped, numb hands was prolonged agony; each night each man had to dig his shelter nonetheless, and lie shivering in its shallow length through thirteen hours of darkness.

Into this bitter land in November 1950 marched the Marines, and sundry Army troops. They called the road the MSR—the main supply route. To those who lived, there will never be any other.

They could not move together; on this MSR there was not room. The 5th and 7th Marine regiments pushed far ahead, reaching Yudam-ni, securing its ringing ridges. Behind them they left a battalion and its supporting troops in Hagaru, to build and defend an airstrip. Fox Company, 7th Marines, held high ground in Toktong Pass between the towns to protect the road. Far behind, Puller's 1st Marines held Kot'o-ri, and sections of the road below.

And up this MSR came the 1st Battalion, 32nd Infantry, Lieutenant Colonel Don G. Faith. At Hagaru on 25 November, Task Force Faith, numbering 1,053 officers and men with attached troops, turned right, marching east of the reservoir. Plans called for Faith to push to the Yalu on the right, while the Marine effort moved left, to sweep each side of the now-frozen stretch of water.

A few miles north of Hagaru, Faith detrucked his men, and allowed them to warm up in special tents. The troops of the 32nd Infantry were numb, but morale was high, because all knew the war was almost over. The next day, 26 November, Faith relieved Marine units in this area, and on the 27th he pushed north. The relieved Marines informed Faith they had heard that three Chinese divisions were in the area.

These regiments and battalions, Marines and Army, were spread over many miles of bleak terrain, joined only by a fragile thread, the road. There was no one on their flank to east, no one to west. Eighty miles beyond the horrendous peaks lay the Eighth Army. What lay in between no man knew.

*   *   *

On 25 November, men of the 1/7 Marines took a prisoner, a subdued, wounded Chinese, who said he was a private soldier. Under interrogation, this humble POW became a fount of information. Among other things. he described the CCF plan of battle:

In the mountains above the reservoir were two CCF armies, of three divisions each. When the Americans reached Yudam-ni, this was to trigger an attack. Three divisions would strike at Yudam-ni; one from the north and one from the west were to attack the two regiments there, while the third flowed around to the south and cut the road to Hagaru-ri. A full division would throw itself against Hagaru and its defenders, while a fifth broke the road between that city and Kot'o to its south, and also isolated Kot'o from Chinhung-ni.

Marine field grade officers hardly knew as much of their own battle plans, and the Chinese' information was greeted with suspicion or ironic amusement. It was never credited. Unfortunately, it was correct.

And while this sufferer from delusions of grandeur was being questioned in a hut at Yudam-ni, General Sung Shih-lun was briefing his senior officers in the shadow of Paemyangji Mountain, ten miles to the north. Sung Shih-lun was just forty years old this 1950, the Chinese Year of the Tiger, and he had led men in battle for most of those years.

One of the bravest men in the Chinese Communist Forces, Sung had tired of formal instruction in the Whampoa Military Academy at the age of seventeen. Since then he had had his training in the field, with the Communists. In November 1950 he commanded the CCF IX Army group, twelve divisions of 120,000 men, and beside the fingers of Changjin Reservoir he had poised six of these divisions.

Hardheaded and quick-tempered, Sung had driven his men across the terrible mountains from the Yalu in fourteen nights of marching. By any standards, it had been a prodigious feat for the Chinese hordes to clamber across the icy mountains unseen. Unable to bring across his heavy artillery, Sung gambled. He drove the men, with rifles, mortars, and machine guns, on ahead, leaving his big guns behind.

At Paemyangji-san, General Sung Shih-lun had perfect intelligence of each movement of his enemy. He knew where they were and what they would do. He knew that the massive blow against Eighth Army had already been launched in the west, and he himself was ready to move.

He described to his senior officers how the divisions would infiltrate across the mountains, to take Hagaru and Kot'o-ri from both flanks and rear. The road, the American MSR, was to be cut in a dozen places. Chinese troops then would dig in above the road beside the American supply and escape route. As for the two regiments near Yudam-ni, they would be flailed to pieces once isolated.

It was a very good plan, trading on the strengths of Sung's Chinese hordes and on the supposed weaknesses of the American enemy.

"Kill these Marines as you would snakes in your homes," Sung instructed his officers.

As the moon, swollen and gibbous, rose over the harsh, frozen peaks on the night of 27 November, the hills beside the Changjin Reservoir swarmed with dark figures. Long, antlike columns of men, their gloveless hands huddled in the sleeves of their mustard-green quilted jackets, marched down the corridors toward Yudam-ni. At first they chanted and sang in wailing minor keys, the music of all Chinese on the march. Then they fell silent, waiting for the horns and bugles to summon them to the kill.

*   *   *

On the eastern fingers of the frozen reservoir, Lieutenant Colonel Don C. Faith had dug in his rifle companies in a perimeter facing north. The road ran through them, and on all sides there were reasonably good fields of fire. Dark came early here on the roof of the world in winter; and with it came intense cold. Huddling in their miserable, icy holes, the men of 1/32 Infantry shivered, waiting.

Shortly after nine, the first Chinese reconnaissance patrols touched the fringes of their perimeters.

Chinese advanced until they drew fire, then retired. One officer, realizing that the enemy was trying to smell out American positions, ran up and down shouting, "Don't fire—don't fire!" But he was too late. Nervous, the men had fired at the slightest sound, and the Chinese learned what they wanted to know.

By midnight, the enemy was in position. Suddenly, Faith's company's perimeters erupted in orange-purple streaks of fire, resounded with the clatter of machine guns. Striking head on into the American lines, the Chinese also kept trying to probe a soft place between units, and to slip men past into the rear areas.

Some platoons held; others were forced out of position. Meanwhile, the supporting 57th Field Artillery came under small-arms fire; the wire to the front-line companies went out. With its own worries, the 57th was unable to continue its support mission with any authority.

At dawn Task Force Faith was still in place, but it was grievously hurt. There were gaps in the line, and the men were badly shaken. The night had been stingingly cold, and everyone now realized that something new was in the wind.

The attacks had not been those of a defeated, fleeing enemy.

The sun came up, but it did not warm. Men pulled their sleeping bags around their feet, and kept hands on guns, shivering in their holes. Later, on Colonel Faith's order, some of the higher ground lost to the Chinese during the night was retaken—only to be lost again. Through the day, more than sixty casualties were gathered at the battalion aid station.

In the afternoon, a helicopter whirled down out of the skies, settling beside the hut that was Faith's command post. General Almond stepped out. Faith reported to him, and the two men talked to one side for several minutes.

Then Almond mentioned that he had three Silver Stars with him. One was for Faith himself—and Almond wanted Faith to select two others for the award.

What Faith did next indicated something of his frame of mind. He snapped to a wounded young officer, Lieutenant Smalley, sitting on a five-gallon water can and waiting evacuation, "Smalley, come over here and stand at attention!"

Bewildered, Smalley obeyed.

The next man to pass by was Sergeant Stanley, a mess steward. Faith called, "Stanley, come here and stand at attention next to Lieutenant Smalley."

A dozen men, clerks, wounded, and the like, were assembled to watch, while General Almond pinned Silver Stars on Faith's and the other two men's parkas. Almond then shook each man by the hand. He said:

"The enemy who is delaying you is nothing more than some remnants of Chinese divisions fleeing north. We're still attacking—and we're going all the way to the Yalu. Don't let a bunch of Chinese laundrymen stop you!"

Then Ned Almond got into his waiting copter and whirled away over the snow-covered hills. Almond was neither a fool nor an ass—he had orders from Tokyo to move to the Yalu—and he intended to comply, whatever his own doubts.

Lieutenant Smalley went back to his seat, muttering, "I got a Silver Star, but I don't know what the hell for."

As soon as Almond's copter disappeared, Faith ripped his own decoration from his parka and hurled it into a snowbank. His S-3, Major Curtis, approached him and asked obliquely, "What did the general have to say?"

Faith looked at him. "You heard him—remnants fleeing north!"

When darkness fell across the bleak, icy landscape, Task Force Faith began another night of battle. Alone, exposed to the full weight of the Chinese assault pouring against its front, flanks, and rear, after more than one hundred hours of incessant combat Task Force Faith dissolved. Colonel Faith was killed by a hand grenade.

The Chinese tide had risen everywhere; X Corps could not help; the Marines at Hagaru were undergoing their own nights of fire. But the bitterness of the men who fought east of the reservoir, hoping for rescue, would never be erased.

Survivors stumbled back over the frozen road to Hagaru. Others were seen by Marines wandering across the ice of the reservoir; they had fled across the lake itself. Of the original thousand officers and men, less than two hundred returned. The others, killed, captured, or frozen, had been swallowed up in the frigid wastes.

Late on the evening of 28 November, General Almond flew to Tokyo at General MacArthur's request. Almond reported to the *Dai Ichi* one hour prior to midnight, and at this time he was told to break off the corps offensive, to withdraw, and to consolidate his forces.

For Task Force Faith, already isolated, the order came too late.

* * *

The Marines, admittedly advancing reluctantly into the unchartered wastes, had paused to consolidate after each move forward. The terrain made it impossible for the division to remain intact, but at each successive plateau along the MSR, units were consolidated at regimental or battalion strength, with supporting artillery able to fire in any direction.

While the road link connecting the units was tenuous, the broad valleys at Yudam-ni, Hagaru, and Kot'o-ri allowed the Marines space to form solid perimeters. The ground, while higher than that in the west, was not characterized by the endless washboard of hills that had broken the United States 2nd Division into a hundred separate fragments.

This consolidation, and the fact that most Marine officers had had experience with Oriental warfare, learning the importance of keeping tight, steel-ringed perimeters by night whatever happened in the rear, did much to save the division.

On 27 November, as the 7th Marines attacked westward from Yudam-ni, the 5th Marines moved west of the reservoir and joined them. It had first been planned to move only two battalions through Toktong Pass, following with the third on 28 November, but at the earnest suggestion of the motor transport officer, the entire regiment moved together. Thus, at nightfall on 27 November, two full regiments of Marines, less one company holding high ground above the pass, and a weapons company left at Hajam, were able to operate in conjunction at Yudam-ni.

Before the night passed, both regiments were deep in crisis.

Again, the story of one company, one platoon, tells the story of all.

At dark, the seventy men of First Lieutenant John Yancey's platoon of Easy Company, 7th Marines, was dug in frozen earth facing north along the brushy, rocky slopes of Hill 1282. Each foxhole, painfully scrabbled out of the frozen shale, held two men, and machine guns protected the flanks. Yancey's platoon was in the middle of the hill, with Bye's to his left, Clements' to his right. Behind Yancey's position the company skipper, Captain Walter Phillips, was positioned with his exec, Lieutenant Ball, to fight the company.

The moon came up, huge and swollen, rising clear and bright over the swirling ground mists. It came up behind Easy Company, silhouetting the company positions for the enemy, but not throwing enough light along the dark corridors to reveal the lurking Chinese. On the hill, the temperature had dropped to twenty below.

Easy's men heard monstrous shuffling sounds through the dark, as of thousands of boots stamping in the snow. They heard sounds, but they could see only ghostly moon shadows.

Yancey asked Ball, on the mortars, to fire star shells.

Ball had little 81 ammo, but he tried. The flares wouldn't work—lifted from crates stamped "1942," they fizzled miserably.

"Oh, goddam," Yancey said. Yancey, a reservist, had been a liquor-store operator in Little Rock when the war broke. He had a baby, born on the day he went ashore at Inch'on, whom he had never seen. He had a Navy Cross from Guadalcanal, and he had washed off the mud of Okinawa. He did not consider himself a fighting man. But he had learned his own lessons in a hard school, the hardest there was.

The ranks of the Marines were now diluted with reservists, at least 50 percent. Few of them were mentally prepared to fight, or physically hardened to war. Inch'on, luckily, had been easy.

But now, on the frozen hills above Yudam-ni, the Marines, regular and reservist alike, faced reality.

Because their officers were tough-minded, because their discipline was tight, and because their *esprit*—that indefinable emotion of a fighting man for his standard, his regiment, and the men around him, was unbroken—weak and strong alike, they would face it well.

The enemy mortars fell first, bursting with pinpoint precision among the foxholes on the forward slope of Hill 1282. Then, in the moonlit hills, bugles racketed; purple flares soared high, and popped. The shadows suddenly became men, running at Marine lines.

The Chinese did not scream or shout, like North Koreans. They did not come in one overwhelming mass. They came in squads, yards apart, firing, hurling grenades, flailing at the thin line across the hill, probing for a weak spot across which they could pour down into the valley beyond.

Again and again they were stopped; again and again Chinese bugles plaintively noised the recall. The icy slopes were now littered with sprawled figures in long white snow capes.

Again and again, while the Marines' guns grew hot, they came back to flail at the hill. Looking down into the shadowy valley, John Yancey could see hundreds of orange pinpoints of light, as the enemy sprayed his hill with lead.

The night seemed endless. A grenade exploded close to Yancey, driving metal fragments through his face to lodge behind his nose. Many of his men were hit. Those who could stand continued fighting; those badly hurt were dragged some twenty yards behind the company position, where a hospital corpsman worked over them in the snow.

There was no shouting or crying. Now and then a man gasped, "Oh, Jesus, I'm hit!" or, "Mother of God!" and fell down.

The attacks whipped the hill. By the early hours of morning, most of Easy's men had frozen noses or frozen feet in addition to their combat wounds. Yancey's blood froze to his moustache, dried across his stubbled face. Snorting for breath through his damaged nose, he had trouble breathing.

Slowly, painfully, day began to spread over the bleak hills. Now, Yancey thought, surely it must get better, with daylight.

Instead, things grew worse.

A fresh wave of Chinese, in company strength, charged the hill. Yancey's men fired everything they had—rifles, carbines, machine guns. The Chinese fell in rows, but some came on. At his line of holes, John Yancey met them with as many of his men as he could muster, including many of his wounded. Somehow, he threw them back.

The platoon, all Easy Company was in desperate straits. Captain Phillips, who had carried ammunition to Yancey's platoon during the night, and who had said again and again, "You're doing okay, men; you're doing okay!" took a bayoneted rifle, and ran out to the front of Yancey's line.

"This is Easy Company!" Walt Phillips said. "Easy Company holds here!" He thrust the bayonet deep into the snowy ground; the rifle butt swayed back and forth in the cold wind, a marker of defiance, a flag to stand by.

The wounded lay helplessly behind Easy Company; there was no way to get them out. And Easy Company was not going to leave its own.

The Chinese came again. Now they stumbled over their own dead, scattered like cordwood a hundred yards down the slope. And on the hill, Americans also fell over their own dead, moving to plug the leaks in the line. Small leathery-skinned men in quilted jackets leaped into the perimeter, and overran the command post.

For over an hour, close-in fighting raged all over the hill. The Chinese wave was smashed, but Chinese dropped behind rocks, in holes, and fired at the Marines surrounding them.

John Yancey realized that some sort of counteraction had to be taken to push them out. He ran back of the hill, found half a dozen able men coming up as replacements. "Come with me!"

With the new men, he charged the breach in Easy's line. His own carbine would fire only one shot at a time; the weapons of two of the replacements froze. The other four dropped with bullets in their heads—the Chinese aimed high.

Beside the CP, Lieutenant Ball, the exec, sat cross-legged in the snow, firing a rifle. Several Chinese rushed him. Ball died.

Now Yancey could find only seven men in his platoon. Reeling from exhaustion and shock, he tried to form a countercharge. As he led the survivors against the broken line, a forty-five caliber Thompson machine-gun slug tore his mouth and lodged in the back of his skull. Metal sliced his right cheek, as a hand grenade knocked him down.

On his hands and knees, he found he was blind.

He heard Walt Phillips shouting, "Yancey! Yancey!"

Somebody he never saw helped Yancey off the hill, led him back down the rear slope. He collapsed, and woke up later in the sick bay at Yudam-ni, where his sight returned.

Behind him, on 1282, Captain Walt Phillips stood beside his standard until he died. Late in the afternoon, a new company relieved Easy; of its 180 men only twenty-three came off.

But they held the hill.

Everywhere it had been the same. Dog Company was driven from its hill three times, and three times it charged back. Captain Hull, Dog's skipper, had fourteen men left, and he himself had as many wounds.

To the east, above the pass, Barber's Fox Company was in like shape. Barber was down, but still directing the defense.

Reality had caught up with the Marines, as with all men, but they had faced it well. Everywhere, the Marines had held.

The shock of tactical defeat struck the Marines as hard as it had the Army—for tactical defeat it was, despite all the noises that went up later. Three Chinese divisions had enveloped Yudam-ni. The road to Hagaru, except where Barber's Fox Company held fast, was cut. Hagaru was surrounded, its supporting artillery firing to the four winds until paint peeled from the guns. The main body of Puller's 1st Regiment was unable to push forward from Kot'o-ri. Everywhere the road was cut; everywhere the Marines were surrounded.

Lieutenant Colonel Ray Murray, of the 5th, summed it up: "I personally felt in a state of shock, the kind of shock one gets from some great personal tragedy, the sudden loss of someone close. . . . My first fight was within myself. I had to rebuild that emptiness of spirit."

For the Marines at Yudam-ni were now ordered to retreat. It would be called an attack to the south—and attack it would be, all the way—but the field had to be left to the enemy.

There was great toughness, however, in the Marine commanders, and no sense of panic. Homer Litzenberg, of the 7th, a senior colonel already posted for brigadier, and the younger Ray Murray, a junior lieutenant colonel, men who on paper held equal commands, conferred. Together, the two men worked very well.

First, their perimeter was consolidate. Their thousand wounded were brought down from the bitter hills for care. Then they discussed getting out.

Litzenberg felt Fox Company must be relieved; it was the key to Toktong Pass. But he knew the road across the sullen cliffs was infested by Chinese. He wanted to send one battalion attacking across the hills themselves, above the road.

"I don't think the Chinese will expect us to move overland. They think we're roadbound. They think we'll have to stay with our vehicles; furthermore, they think we won't attack at night. I want to prepare to move out tomorrow—"

To which Ray Murray replied, "Make it so."

With the temperature standing at twenty-four degrees below zero, Ray Davis' 1/7 Marines moved out into the horrible mountains. Each man was given rations for four meals—mostly canned fruit and biscuit, which could be thawed by body heat—and each man, in addition to his weapons, ammunition, and sleeping bag, was ordered to carry one 81mm mortar shell.

As one Marine said, "If the Chinks can run the goddam ridges, so can we."

Tired, frozen, weakened from poor diet and shot through with raging dysentery, the battalion went over the hills, while a second, the 3/5 attacked along the MSR itself. All day the battered men fought, to clear one hill after another.

When night came, Colonel Davis knew his men, tired, sweaty, listless after a day of hard combat, might never get up again if he allowed them to bed down.

For most of the night, Davis marched his men through the hills. At dawn, they attacked again, and broke through to Barber's beleaguered company, carrying their twenty-two wounded with them. When contact was made, neither Davis nor Barber could talk coherently.

Barber still held, after five days of fighting, but he had only one officer, and he had suffered 26 killed, 89 wounded, and 3 missing. All his survivors had either frostbite or dysentery.

Behind them, and on their flank, Taplett's 3/5 Marines carried the pass in heavy fighting. With Davis' men running the ridges, knocking the Chinese back, enough of the pressure was removed for the Marines of Yudam-ni to break through.

When Davis had joined Barber on his lonely hill, word came from Litzenberg: "Assume the point and lead the way to Hagaru."

At Yudam-ni only the wounded and those who could not walk were placed aboard vehicles; many men who were hurt had to walk. Then, the infantry battalions leading the way, the regiments came out through Toktong Pass.

They came out intact, with their jeeps, guns, tractors, and trucks. Strapped to the fenders and hoods of vehicles lay bloody, half-frozen Marines. Others lay across gun barrels, or were carried in ox-drawn sleds taken from Koreans.

It was not a motor march. It was a tactical battle most of the way, against Chinese who held the hills in depth. But the Marines came out, for three reasons:

One, Davis' and Taplett's men were able to climb the encircling mountains, knock the enemy off the ridges, drive them across the high timber. Moving by night, attacking cross-country in savage terrain and savage weather, these Marines took the Chinese in the flank, and by surprise. In the face of incredible hardship, the Marines were able to mount offensive action—and Barber's Fox Company, 7th Marines, had been able to hold off two enemy regiments for six days, preventing the Chinese from closing their ring. If Barber had not held, the way would have been much more difficult.

Two, Marine air from the 1st Air Wing near Hamhung, carrier pilots from *Philippine Sea* and *Leyte,* and Air Force supply planes flew constantly over the column. Marine aircraft strafed, bombed, and napalmed as close as fifty yards from the leading elements. Marine air, flying so low as to touch the mountains, knocked out roadblock after roadblock, as fast as the Chinese assembled them. Marine pilots volunteered to fly night missions in the dangerous mountains.

Hour after hour, the sky above the American troops was black with friendly aircraft, and without them, in spite of their courage, in spite of all else, the ground troops would never have come out.

Third, General Sung Shih-lun had gambled. In the horrendous terrain, he had never been able to bring his full manpower to bear on the embattled Marines, outnumbered though they were. By pushing his men across the mountains from the Yalu in fourteen days, he had had to leave most of his supply and artillery behind—and as the battle continued day after day, stinging night after night, even Sung Shih-lun's sturdy peasants neared collapse.

The Chinese had come into Korea well fed and well clothed, but they were without supply, depending on the countryside for future livelihood.

Near-starvation and dysentery hit them, too. The hardy Chinese peasant, while brought up to hardship, was no superman. As the Marines neared Hagaru, weary CCF units deserted their peaks under air attack. The Marines found some who had thrown away their arms and who lay huddled together in the snow, freezing and apathetic, trying only to stay alive.

But others fought to the end, and it was not until the morning of 3 December, a morning obscured with a stinging curtain of snow, that the advance guard fought in sight of the Hagaru plateau. By late afternoon, the main column reached the summit of the mountain ridge separating Yudam-ni from Hagaru, and suddenly men could see the friendly perimeter, and the airstrip, eleven miles away.

Now it was downhill all the way. Brushing aside roadblocks, snipers, and attempted ambushes, the two regiments crashed down toward Hagaru. Coming toward the friendly lines, some of the Marines tried to sing. Others marched in, erect, in column, picking up a cadence without order. Men so tired they could hardly stand, who had fouled themselves repeatedly from raging dysentery, who had frostbitten faces and fingers, and who were weak from hunger, made one final effort—and marched in like Marines.

More than one grown man broke down and cried as the Marines of Yudam-ni came together with those of Hagaru.

From their encirclement at Yudam-ni, Litzenberg and Murray had brought out all their wounded—six hundred of them stretcher cases. They brought out all their equipment, with the exception of one quarter-ton truck and four medium howitzers that had slid from the icy road into a chasm.

But an airstrip had been completed at Hagaru, and the thousands of wounded could be flown out. Ammunition and supply could be flown in. Without this, the retreat would have become a debacle, for 5,400 men were flown from Hagaru, all of them too hurt to march.

Relieved of his wounded, issuing all his stocks of candy and food to the troops, Marine General Smith ordered the march south to Kot'o-ri on 6 December.

Nine heavily defended roadblocks barred the road; bridges were gone, the road mined. But Marines and Army troops—the survivors from east of the reservoir—swept out from the road, clearing a frontage of seven hundred yards right and left, from which distance even Chinese machine guns could not fire accurately. The Marines would not repeat the tragedy of Kunu-ri.

It cost the column twenty-two hours of agony to cover the nine and one-half miles from Hagaru to Kot'o-ri. On arrival, there were six hundred more wounded.

At Kot'o, these wounded were flown out, and the dead were buried in shallow graves torn out of the frozen ground by bulldozers.

On 8 December, the column moved south again. The air cover droned over them by day, scouring the hills, but even the hospital units were sometimes attacked by sporadic Chinese assaults, marching out.

But air, ground action, and hunger had taken their toll from the attackers, and now many Americans saw isolated units of Chinese, often merely wandering along the American flanks, making no determined effort to stop the column.

On 9 December the advance guards of the men from the reservoir and the forces trying to move north to relieve them linked up on a windswept ridge north of Chinhung-ni.

Now no power on earth could prevent the Marines and Army from coming out. Marching down the frozen road, men picked up a song, roaring, as one observer put it, until the North Korean hills rang like bells of ice. It was a parody of the old British Indian Army song "Bless 'Em All":

> *Bless 'em all, bless 'em all,*
> *The Commies, the U.N. and all:*
> *Those slant-eyed Chink soldiers*
> *Struck Hagaru-ri*
> *And now know the meaning of U.S.M.C.*
> *But we're saying goodbye to them all,*
> *We're Harry's police force on call.*
> *So put back your pack on,*
> *The next step is Saigon,*
> *Cheer up, me lads, bless 'em all!*

Down into the level ground beside the Sea of Japan came the Marines; from the north the 7th Division left the Yalu and hurried south, and the ROK I Corps scurried back from the fringes of Siberia. With the enemy massed in force on the left flank, any other course would have been madness.

Before the ports of the gray-blue Sea of Japan, X Corps massed, under the cover of its air and far-reaching naval guns. The Chinese, starving in the hills, made no attempt to push them into the sea. Such an attempt would have failed, and Sung Shih-lun and his generals knew it.

But X Corps was now isolated in North Korea. To its west, the Eighth Army was in full retreat; it had already abandoned P'yongyang and was moving south toward the parallel. While General Almond and the Navy said they could hold their beachhead indefinitely, Tokyo saw no point in this.

It was a new war, and already men in Tokyo and Korea were beginning to think in terms of a solid line of defense somewhere south of the 38th parallel.

To X Corps came orders to embark from Hungnam and Wosnan for redeployment in South Korea. Under an encircling ring of artillery, tanks, and naval rifles, X Corps went aboard ship, taking its equipment and supplies, even its gasoline, with it. It was not a Dunkirk—there was no pressure against the embarkment.

Thousands of North Koreans, anti-Communist and desperate to leave with the Americans, were taken aboard. Hungry, freezing, with little medical aid or facilities, hundreds of these unfortunates died during the embarkment and passage to Pusan.

Day after day, the corps perimeter shrank down to the icy sea. At last the field pieces were firing at the hills from the wharf area; then they turned and were trundled aboard ship.

Hungnam was blown up, and the city set afire. Even the docks were destroyed. On Christmas Eve, with the coastline a mass of flame and billowing dark smoke, the convoys stood to sea, leaving the shore to the enemy.

A gallant page had been added to the history of American arms from Yudam-ni to the reservoir, from Hagaru to the cold plateau of Kot'o-ri.

But though thousands upon thousands of his frozen corpses dotted the hills, and the survivors would be long without effective combat power, as in the west the enemy had won the field.

Ominously, the precarious balance on the remote shores of Asia had turned again.

23

Chipyong-ni

Goddamit, get back up on that hill! You'll die down here anyway—you might as well go up on the hill and die there!

—Lieutenant Thomas Heath, G Company, 23rd Infantry, Chipyong-ni.

B Y 1 DECEMBER 1950, Walton Walker, MacArthur, and Washington knew what the front-line riflemen had been painfully aware of for some days—they had an entirely new war on their hands. MacArthur was outraged at the Communist defiance. With entire sincerity he branded the Chinese intervention a criminal act, and with equal sincerity, from this time on, he desired to unleash the lightning upon the transgressors.

The Chinese criminals should be punished; they should be bombed, interdicted, and harassed, and their warmaking potential destroyed for decades to come. Despite the sharp tactical defeat on the ground of North Korea, the United States had sufficient power to do so, if such power were to be thrown into the war.

It was a time of confusion once again in the United States. Men in government met, while newspapers and periodicals spread a finely distilled gloom across the land. From their arrogance of October most media came full circle; now the action on the Ch'ongch'on and at the reservoir was described as the greatest defeat in American history; even as the Marines marched out, heads up, and the Eighth Army, once more in order, pulled back from P'yongyang, newsman and analyst cried disaster, and that the troops were lost.

Time, in its 11 December 1950 issue editorialized: *The United States and its Allies stood on the abyss of disaster. The Chinese Communists, pouring across the Manchurian border in vast formations, had smashed the U.N. Army . . . caught in the desperate retreat were 140,000 American troops, the flower of the U.S. Army—almost the whole effective Army the U.S. had. With them, fighting to establish a defensive position were 20,000 British, Turkish, and other allies, and some 100,000 South Korean soldiers.*

It was defeat—the worst defeat the United States had ever suffered. If this defeat were allowed to stand, it would mean the loss of Asia to Communism.

To place the defeat in North Korea in perspective, American casualties during the entire time of action did not come to half one week's total in the Ardennes campaign, when Germans killed or wounded 27,000 Americans in one seven-day period.

The 2nd Division, in the west, bearing the brunt, lost its equipment and some 4,000 men; the Marines lost slightly less. And after the first week's fighting, American retreat was a matter of policy. It was decided in FECOM, by the military. American forces had never been positioned to fight the CCF. When its intervention was a known reality, the American tactical and strategical position was untenable.

But the U.N. Army, pulling south faster than its tired, decimated pursuers could at first follow, was basically intact. It was in no danger of being overwhelmed, although there was some appearance of gloom and doom among commanders and staffs.

The problem that worried Washington was not what was happening in the frozen wastes of North Korea, but what was happening in the chancelleries of Communist nations. Now, as in summer, Washington could never be sure the thing it feared most—the start of World War III—was not occurring.

At a mass briefing of all officers stationed at Fort Knox, Kentucky, concurrent with such briefings all across the world, an Army spokesman stood before a map of the earth, pointing out the location of Soviet divisions, Soviet air armies. He pinpointed the hordes of the CCF; discussed the at least 175 divisions—one-third of them armored—Russia had assembled in East Germany alone. He talked of Soviet nuclear capability, and most of the assembled Americans, knowing their own strengths and weaknesses, were shaken. In the event of a major Soviet move, only the American nuclear deterrent could stave off disaster.

But after the divisions were placed on the map, and all the possible moves of the potential enemy analyzed, a twenty-five-year-old lieutenant seated in the middle of the theater stood up.

"Sir," he asked the briefing officer, "but what do we figure the Communists will do?"

The briefing officer touched his pointer to the floor, looked down. Then he met the lieutenant's eyes and smiled wryly.

"Son, I don't have a living clue."

In Washington, General of the Army Omar Bradley could have said the same. He was certain of only one thing: That a war with the Chinese, on the mainland of Asia, was the wrong war, at the wrong time, with the wrong enemy. The more important men in government tended to agree with him.

Time shrilled, for all the world to read in its 18 December 1950 issue: *The policy of containment was dead. There remained only the policy of retaliation and positive action by the U.S. and its allies to damage Communist power at the sources from which aggression flowed.*

But what the editors of *Time* believed, and what was truth, were, as it so often is, two different things.

Harry Truman had not altered his basic belief that the United States might engage in general war with the Communist bloc, but it had no reasonable hope of forcing its will over the vast expanse of immense humanity of Eurasia. In defense of its vital interests America would still fight such a war—but Harry Truman saw no profit in it, and he would avoid it as long as he could do so with honor. Truman and his advisers could only hope that the Eighth Army could avoid complete debacle.

In the last days of November 1950, MacArthur wired Washington: *We face an entirely new war . . . this command has done everything humanly possible within its capabilities but is now faced with conditions beyond its control and strength.* MacArthur now wanted to accept Chiang Kai-shek's offer of Nationalist Chinese troops, but Washington told him such a move would have to be cleared with the U.N.—which was obviously hostile to the idea.

On 28 November, in a Security Council meeting, Omar Bradley informed President Truman that the JCS did not think the situation in Korea was "such a catastrophe as our newspapers were leading us to believe." At the same time George Marshall, Secretary of Defense, stated that in his opinion it was essential for the United States to go along with the United Nations and that all the service secretaries had agreed that neither the U.S. nor the U.N. should become involved in a general war with Red China if it could be avoided. Dean Acheson, Secretary of State, said that the nation should try to find some way to end the conflict.

He added that if the United States went into Manchuria and bombed bases and airfields there as part of a successful action, "Russia would cheerfully get in it."

The United States' entire foreign policy rested on the containment of Soviet Russia—not bringing her to battle.

Averell Harriman thought careful consideration had to be given to the opinions of the rest of the free world. Truman himself said it was going to be hard to convince the free world that United States policy was going to remain calm in the face of the cries of alarm and distortions of "three of our biggest publishers."

The Cabinet, the next day, agreed with the Security Council.

The United States must continue to fight in Korea, hoping for the best, but it would not send orders to MacArthur to bomb Manchuria or in any way carry the war to the Chinese mainland. The conflict would still be an attempted police action.

The Korean conflict—it would still not be dignified by Washington by the name of war—had escalated, but perhaps not fatally. South Korea must still be held. The holding would take more time, money, and men than anyone had realized, but the mission had not changed.

To MacArthur went no orders to attack the criminals in their lair; the prohibitions upon his air and sea power were not lifted. As before, he was to hold the far frontier. He might punish the Chinese all he desired—as long as he did so within the confines of the Korean peninsula.

If World War III were to begin, it would be by Communist initiative.

* * *

Now, at Christmastime, a new wave of apprehension swept over the American people, for unlike the old wars on the frontier, this one was reported daily by electronic means.

Time magazine stated: *The nation received the fearful news from Korea with a strange calmness—the kind of confused, fearful, half-believing matter-of-factness with which many a man has reacted on learning he has cancer . . . . The news of Pearl Harbor . . . pealed out like a bell. But the numbing facts of Korea seeped out of a jumble of headlines, bulletins, and communiqués.*

The people could not remain indifferent in the face of incessant newscasts. Again scare buying was in progress, and even dealers of unpopular makes of automobiles sold out their stocks.

Millions resolved to enjoy one last great Christmas before the deluge, and for hundreds it was the last Christmas, as the holiday traffic toll rose to a record level.

There was still no problem of money or machines, guns or butter, despite the increased effort Chinese intervention now required. But the problem of the men—never solved—remained. President Truman called the militia of Minnesota and Mississippi, the Viking and Dixie divisions, into Federal service, and induction calls soared. Thousands more reservists were ordered to the colors, of all services.

Still the clarion call to arms was not sounded to the people, who waited in confusion. Men were again taken from each city, town, and village, but the bugles did not blow, the drums did not resound, for there is no glory to a war on the far frontier.

This kind of war, however necessary, is dirty business, first to last.

It took, perhaps, more courage for Harry Truman not to sound the angel's trumpet than to mobilize the nation, for the people would never understand.

* * *

It must be emphasized that the decision to withdraw from North Korea was a strategic one. Once contact had been broken both in east and west, American and ROK forces were under no immediate pressure forcing them backward. But the stance in the mountains of North Korea was exceedingly perilous with unknown numbers of Chinese in the war. The supply situation had never been good, and the transportation network was completely incapable of standing up under the needs of a large-scale campaign. MacArthur wanted to pull back.

And there was always the haunting fear that a bigger war might start, elsewhere. If the Russians came in, fully, all the men in Korea might be cut off as Russian submarines and air interdicted their lifeline; and forgotten in the general chaos, they might be slaughtered at leisure.

On 3 December 1950 MacArthur sent a message to the Joint Chiefs of Staff that the Eighth Army situation was "becoming increasingly critical. . . ." He stated that he and General Walker agreed, as part of a very long and thoroughly gloomy report, that a withdrawal to the Seoul area was necessary. He wrote of the weakness and tiredness of his command, and of the freshness, complete organization, and splendid training of the Chinese divisions. He ended: *The directives under which I am operating based on the North Korean Forces as an enemy* [no bombing of Manchuria, and so on] *are completely outmoded by events. . . . This calls for political decisions and strategic plans in implementation thereof, adequate fully to meet the realities involved. In this, time is of the essence as every hour sees the enemy power increase and ours decline.*

The evidence is very strong that the continually gloomy reports that MacArthur regularly sent from this time forward were written with the motive of influencing United States policy. MacArthur wanted "political decisions and strategic plans" that would permit him fully to engage the Chinese enemy, and he continued to hint and ask for them. His own feelings on what should be done were closer to those of the publisher of *Time* than to those of the United States Government—but the President of the United States, and neither *Time* nor public opinion, was General MacArthur's boss.

On receipt of MacArthur's message on 3 December, Truman approved the following terse reply: *We consider that the preservation of your forces is now the primary consideration. Consolidation of forces into beachheads is concurred in.*

Truman had decided that until the United Nations clarified its position, or decided to support a major United States move, it seemed best not to sacrifice men trying to hold a tenuous position in North Korea.

The new U.N. Command plan now was to try to hold a line across South Korea north of Seoul—or if worse came to worst, to hold two beachheads, one in the Seoul-Inch'on area, the other the old Pusan Perimeter.

With more than a quarter-million Allied ground troops in Korea, heavily mechanized and possessing all supporting weapons, the JCS felt the Chinese could be contained despite their seeming advantage in numbers.

But over a defeated—even though not shattered—army lies a grayness of spirit. A retreat, once started, is the most difficult of all human actions to reverse. Most of the thousands who had come to Korea had never been interested in the action; now, most of them would have willingly departed the peninsula forever.

The grayness spread upward, to staffs and even to commanders. Men who had burned their fingers were now wary of the flame.

* * *

After coming through the CCF gauntlet on the Kunu-ri–Sunch'on road, the movement south was nothing but a truck ride for George Company, 9th Infantry, 2nd Division. The division was shattered, its equipment gone. It would be rebuilt and rebuilt well, but the process would take time.

On 5 December 1950, disgusted and in a low mood, Captain Frank Muñoz and his company reached Seoul. He realized the Chinese had not been supermen; in many instances they hadn't even been good. Frank Muñoz would always believe that if the division could have maintained battalion integrity, set up mutually supporting strongpoints, and held on to them until hell froze over, the Chinese would have been beaten. But what was done was done.

Arriving in Seoul, Muñoz found the AP cable offices were still open. He sent a wire home. It was something of a puzzle what to send—there were security regulations, and he didn't want to frighten anyone. Finally he sent the wire in his daughter's name. "Happy Birthday. I'm fine."

He figured that took care of everything.

Then his unit went to stage and recoup at the old ASCOM City, between Seoul and Inch'on, where it rebuilt from the ground up until Christmas Eve. Now it was getting warm in Seoul, as thousands of CCF pressed down, and the divisions holding the line were backing up. Muñoz went to Ch'unch'on, and finally, his company once again reconstituted, to a hill north of Wonju.

* * *

Moving south from the vicinity of the Yalu, Corporal James B. Mount, aid man with Item Company, 21st Infantry, had been too busy to worry much over where the company was going, until he saw a stopped tank doused with gasoline and set afire. Now he thought, *There's more to this than they're telling us.*

There was. The 24th Division was going south, a long way south. As far as the eye could see, long columns of trucks threw up frozen dust on the coastal roads, and beside the roads every village burned smokily as the Americans retired. *Scorched-earth policy,* Mount understood they called this.

By New Year's Eve, Mount's Company was dug in along the 38th parallel some fifteen miles north of Seoul, a broad valley stretching out before them. It was as cold as hell, and nobody was in a celebrating mood.

In front of them were more Chinese than Mount or anyone else liked to think about.

Mount was aid man with the 2nd Platoon, Lieutenant Pritchard. Pritchard was a West Pointer, of the recent class that had been pretty well decimated already in Korea. Mount understood that the losses in this class had been a matter of argument at home—as if the public thought the function of a military academy was to make future generals rather than men capable of ably leading platoons in action.

Mount himself knew that battle was a series of platoon actions, each of which went toward deciding the battle as a whole. The best general in the world couldn't succeed without good men in his small units, however high the loss of skilled manpower. And realistically, Mount knew that the men who survived platoon combat would make better generals, however many were killed.

The 2nd Platoon was centered on high ground to the right of the Seoul highway. Across the road, on the left, stood some old Quonset huts that had been used by the occupation forces years ago.

About dark, artillery began to search Item Company's lines. Fortunately, most of the incoming stuff fell behind them. But snipers had moved in close, under the shelling, and two enlisted men of 2nd Platoon had been killed. As Mount and an aid man from an adjoining platoon struggled with a third man, shot through the shoulder, a bullet clipped the other aid man in the heel. Then Mount had two casualties on his hands.

Captain Porter, who had taken the company upon the former commander's breakdown, was hit in the leg by the first round that came in. Porter refused to stop long enough for an aid man to look at him, hobbling up and down furiously.

As dark deepened, all the company could hear heavy firing off to the left, where the 19th Infantry held their flank. It sounded like the 19th was getting clobbered.

The company radio man reported, "I've lost all contact with the 19th—"

Porter sent out patrols to try to contact the units on his left flank. The patrols went as far as they dared, came back to report no contact. "Hell," said Porter, "get in your holes and stay there. Shoot anything that moves!"

Mount, sticking tight now with Pritchard's platoon, heard one report come to the lieutenant from company HQ. "There's 50,000 Chinks out there. Stay loose!" The boys at Company were getting puckered.

The night grew colder. With Pritchard, Mount helped check the outposts. In the bitter weather, the sentries were having trouble staying alert. It was cold enough to keep a man's teeth chattering all night long—but Pritchard had learned a lesson earlier in the campaign. At first, every man had been issued a sleeping bag—and this had proved a mistake, fatal for a lot of Americans who could not resist the temptation to crawl in the bag, even on guard, and fall asleep.

The Chinese had learned the expensiveness of bugling and tootling their way into American lines. Now they came quietly, padding on rubber-soled feet. The only way for the outposts to have a chance was to issue only one arctic sleeping bag to each two men. This way, one man would be too miserable to go to sleep, and he would damn well see to it that his buddy didn't sleep too long.

It was not a popular ruling, but it saved lives.

Shivering but alert, Item Company held during the night. At daybreak, Porter found that the units adjacent to him had pulled out. He checked for a reading with Battalion, and was ordered to pull back, too.

The company moved out after New Year's Day dinner, which for the line companies was a fiasco. Mount got no dinner, but did grab a handful of cigars, which he preferred. Now the regiment pulled back to a line five miles north of Seoul, from which it was ordered to retreat no farther. A thorough defensive position was completed—holes, wire, minefields.

But immediately the regiment was hard hit by Chinese. Neither air nor artillery could completely stop them from scrambling over the ridges, dropping down into the valleys. Mount saw that some attacking Chinese had no rifles; as they advanced, they waited until a companion was hit, then took his weapon.

But they had plenty of manpower, and manpower—and the grayness that was sinking over Eighth Army—pushed them out.

They held north of the Han exactly four days. When they withdrew, they went back thirty miles.

* * *

On a gray day in December 1950, riding in his jeep with its handrail and autoloading shotgun, Walton Walker was spilled and killed in a collision on the dusty road.

Walker, dying on the frozen dirt, was spared a worse fate. For days a whisper had run through command channels of the Eighth Army that Walker was through.

The reverse of the coin that nothing succeeds like success is that in battle there is no prize for second place.

Walker, an armored leader of some note in the big war, had done his best, against great odds, in Korea. He fought in a way completely new to his experience, with an army passionately preferring not to fight. Before Pusan, his blunt, bulldog outspokenness and stubbornness had much to do with the successful defense of the Perimeter.

Given his plan of maneuver in the North, it is doubtful that any leader, with the same troops, could have done much better. But the one thing a democracy has in common with a dictatorship is that when there is military failure, heads must roll. Perhaps, as Voltaire remarked, it is not a bad policy, since it tends to encourage the remaining leaders.

Some days before, Lieutenant General Matthew B. Ridgway, CG in the Canal Zone, had been briefed for Korea. But with Walker's death, this would never be publicized.

But the man who could dissipate the grayness arrived in Korea, to assume command of the Eighth Army.

History has tended to prove that, like bishops, generals need a certain flamboyance for public success. Walker had none; he could never have been a public figure, win or lose.

Flamboyance in itself is worth nothing, but when it is coupled with genuine ability, history records the passage of a great leader across the lives of men. It is no accident that the names of Clausewitz, Jomini, von François, or Gruenther—brilliant minds all—are known only to students of warfare, while all the world remembers Ney and his grenadiers, Patton's pearl-handled pistols, and Matt Ridgway's taped grenades.

For while Karl von Clausewitz, Henri Jomini, and Kurt von François influenced the history of warfare, Patton and Ridgway made an indelible mark upon the hearts of men.

Ridgway, a well-built, bald soldier with the look of eagles about his strong-nosed face, was the kind of leader the Eighth Army needed. For as the commandos say, "It is all in the mind and in the heart," and battles, more often, are won not on the drawing boards but in the hearts of men. Ridgway was a strong man, and an articulate one. He could think, and he could put his thoughts across with pen and tongue.

He was possessed of such personal courage that, caught in artillery shellfire, he was always the first man out of the ditch—a habit that caused his aide, a Medal of Honor winner, once to remark, "Oh, Jesus, I wish the Old Man would wait a little longer!"

Ridgway came to an army gray with the habit of defeat, strong but no longer sure of itself. He said to his staff, who had caught enough brickbats to last them a lifetime in the past weeks, and had grown cautious: "There will be no more discussion of retreat. We're going back!"

But habits are hard to break. Shortly after this, Ridgway's G-3, Dabney, said, "Here, General, are our contingency plans for retreat—"

Ridgway relieved him upon the spot.

The staff got the message. It took only a little longer for it to seep down to the ranks. Seventy-five miles below the 38th parallel, the U.N. line got "straightened out." It would never move south again, except under local pressure, for the balance of the war.

* * *

Into Frank Muñoz's new George Company flowed dozens of replacements, many of them recalled reservists from the States. These last, as Muñoz said later, didn't want to be there.

He integrated and oriented his newcomers. He told the N.C.O's and old men: "No war stories to scare hell out of these people. I don't want a bunch of scared rabbits. Let's get 'em trained and on the team."

When he was fully manned again, one half of his company, including N.C.O.'s, had never seen combat. He had some new officers, some of them recallees. These men were not eager. They were patriotic men, with good records. But listening for the trumpet, they had received instead orders to Korea, telling them to go and serve, not saying why.

They had little interest in holding the far frontier. They were citizens, and each of them had better things to do.

South of Wonju, there was patrol action, and George Company got into more than one skirmish. Once, knocking, some Chinese off a hill, Muñoz saw several of his EM run up to enemy dead, pause, searching, then move on.

Long, now made lieutenant in the field, smiled wryly at him, when Muñoz asked what the hell they were doing. "One old hand teaching two new ones how to loot, Captain."

Fortunately, the old hands were teaching the new ones how to fight, too. The old hardness they had had after the Naktong returned. Again, all thoughts of going home soon had vanished; everybody realized that they were going to have to stay in Korea to fight. And the veterans of the early fights had forged in each company of the division a solid core of strength.

But there were still some problems. Thousands of Korean refugees in January 1951 were pouring southward, streaming through U.N. lines, and with them came disguised NKPA. Muñoz, like all the old hands, had grown wary of infiltrators.

One day he ordered his roadblocks, "Let no more civilians through."

A sergeant, a recallee who had had to leave his new business and was understandably bitter about it, said, "Captain, I'm not about to shoot civilians."

Muñoz put hard black eyes on this man. "Sergeant, I realize you're new. We've had experience with this. Some of these 'civilians' have inflicted casualties on us, and unless you want to be killed, you'd better watch it."

One night, while on roadblock guard, the sergeant disappeared. Muñoz figured some "civilians" had probably thrown his body into the deep snows along the road. In spring, thousands of skeletons were found all over the roadsides of Korea, but few of them could be identified.

Then, in early January 1951, the 2nd Division was ordered to attack north. At the same time, Muñoz was offered a job up at Battalion, but turned it down.

Wading in snow up to their waists at times, crossing ridges so high that they could clearly see the pilots of supporting aircraft in their cockpits, George Company attacked toward Wonju. They had sharp fights with enemy in the hills, and enemy interdicting the roads from deep railway tunnels. They took Wonju, and news photographers took their pictures in the square of the damaged, burning city.

But now Colonel Messenger, the new C.O. of 9th Infantry, had learned that Frank Muñoz was the senior company commander of the regiment. He felt Muñoz had had enough line time from the Naktong to the Ch'ongch'on to the hills about Wonju. And there was an opening on Division G-4—supply—staff.

Major Birmingham called Muñoz in, offered him the job. "Frank," Pete Birmingham said, "last night I had a dream that you were KIA—"

Young Muñoz, normally not a superstitious man, was convinced. A man had only so much luck. On 17 January he reported to Division G-4, and was made supply liaison officer between that HQ and the regimental supply officers.

* * *

The Chinese hordes that had burst the U.N. Korean bubble did not number more than 300,000 at the time of their intervention, and of this number, probably not more than 60,000 actually went into close combat with the advance ROK and American divisions.

While in overall numbers the allied forces nearly matched the Chinese, at the point of impact the disparity was overwhelming. It had been the plan of maneuver of the U.N., plus the Chinese tactics—not the relative size of the two forces—that resulted in U.N. defeat.

At the crucial moment, only two American divisions had been in contact with the Chinese in the west, while in the east a large part of the combat power of six CCF divisions engulfed one Marine division.

Had the U.N. Command been able to employ the main body of the Eighth Army, or to throw the entire X Corps against the CCF IX Army Group, there is good reason to suppose the Chinese might have failed. But the terrain made it a series of Indian fights. While one American division was cut to pieces, others a few miles across the mountains enjoyed relative peace and quiet.

Understandably, American commanders were eager to get out of the horrible mountains and back to where they could fight once more in modern, civilized fashion.

The first withdrawal, to the 38th parallel, would have accomplished this. But the retreat once started was difficult to halt. The U.N. line, with X Corps redeployed in the center of South Korea, finally came to rest along the 37th parallel in January 1951.

Contact, except for scattered patrol actions, was broken. The mechanized U.N. forces had been able to move south faster than the footsore, ill-supplied, and badly coordinated CCF could follow.

Now geography began to exert its influence in reverse. In South Korea the terrain was still broken, but passable to vehicles. In a narrower part of the peninsula, Americans and ROK's could throw a continuous line from coast to coast, with a refused flank to either side. And while U.N. supply lines were shortened and improved, the CCF inherited a logistic nightmare.

The CCF's guns, ammunition, and supplies had to be brought down from the Yalu under constant air attack, over poor roads, and on a limited amount of transport. The CCF had manpower, including thousands of Korean laborers, and could live on very little, but there is a limit to the operations of an army that has to bear its ammunition hundreds of miles over mountains, principally by muscle power.

Now, rebuilt, reequipped, in maneuverable terrain, the U.N. forces needed more than anything else the will to fight. The means they had.

Matt Ridgway supplied the will.

By the end of January, as a result of firm and unmistakable orders from the new ground commander, the Eighth Army moved north to reestablish contact, and to bring the enemy to battle.

Everywhere Ridgway went, he talked of attack. Soon, nothing more was heard of the whispers that had been bruited about, over a gray-spirited army, that Korea might have to be evacuated.

And soon there was renewed battle.

The first United Nations counteroffensive, beginning 5 February 1951, was short-lived. On the night of 11 February, the CCF struck south again, this time in the center of the line, against Ned Almond's X Corps, which now contained the United States 2nd Division. The CCF attacked with two main columns pointed toward Hoengsong and Wonju. As usual, the Chinese first put pressure against the weaker firepower of the ROK's.

They slashed through two ROK divisions, forcing friendly lines southward from five to twenty miles.

Leading the U.N. offensive, Paul Freeman's 23rd Infantry had been well ahead of the van. On 3 February the regiment had moved into the road junction village of Chipyong-ni, already half destroyed by air and artillery, and in the small valley about the town Colonel Freeman threw up a tight mile-long perimeter. To the northwest of Chipyong-ni the 23rd dug in across a section of frozen rice paddies, and on the other sides of the valley the line lay across a series of low hills. Here the 23rd, including a French battalion, supported by the 37th Field Artillery, a battery of 155's from the 503rd, a Ranger company, and engineers, were still positioned when the CCF released the flood.

The front lines to either side of Chipyong-ni washed back, and Freeman, his patrols reporting Chinese on all sides of him, conferred with General

Almond on 13 February. Freeman wanted to pull back fifteen miles to prevent encirclement; the 2nd Division commander approved.

Almond agreed, and submitted the request to the Eighth Army.

Matt Ridgway's comment can be summed up in one printable word: No.

The word went north to Freeman, who immediately strengthened his perimeter and called his various subordinate commanders in. He advised them, "We're going to stay here and fight it out."

That night, the fight began.

Soon after dark, there was skirmishing, and a few violent close-in brushes on the south of the perimeter, where 2nd Battalion, 23rd Infantry, the French, and Battery B of the 503rd defended.

Then, two hours past midnight, Chinese blew bugles and whistles and ran forward toward the lines of the French battalion.

The French nation, already heavily engaged in war with the Communists in Vietnam, had supplied only one battalion of infantry to the Korean effort. But throughout the conflict the battalion was a good one. Professionals all, the unit contained many half-wild Algerians, to whom no war was complete unless a little fun could be had out of it, too.

As the first platoon of Chinese rushed them, a Frenchman cranked a hand siren, setting up an ungodly screech. A single squad fixed bayonets, grabbed up hand grenades, and when the enemy was twenty yards away, came out of their holes and charged.

Four times their number of CCF stopped, turned, and fled into the night. The Frenchmen went back to smoking and telling jokes.

But in another part of the line, Heath's George Company was hit four times. With some difficulty, the company held till dawn.

With light, the Chinese withdrew to the circling hills, and the defenders had a breathing spell. The Air Force came over to search the hills with rockets and napalm, and cargo planes made two-dozen ammunition drops. Other than this, nothing occurred on 14 February.

But after nightfall, flares soared high all around the southern rim of Chipyong-ni, and the brassy noise of bugles beat on the defender's ears. Chinese began to infiltrate over the low hills, carrying pole and satchel charges. They poured into George Company, killing many men by dropping explosives in the fox-holes. McGee's 3rd Platoon was riddled, and in bad shape by midnight. He asked the company commander, Heath, for help. B Battery offered men to plug the infantry line.

Heath assembled fifteen men from the supporting artillery, and sent them forward. These men were not trained as infantrymen, and when they drew mortar fire they ran back down the hill, without making contact with the hard-hit 3rd Platoon.

As they ran, the enemy poured across the 3rd Platoon area, and the hill was alight with grenade blasts and pinpricks of rifle fire.

Lieutenant Heath himself stopped the artillerymen at the base of the hill, screaming and raging at them. He re-formed them, and led them toward the blazing fire fight up above. Again the group came apart when fired on, and the men ran away.

Still on the hill, furious, Heath grabbed men by the collar and tried to make them go forward. When they refused, he came back off the hill with them. By now Chinese flares were throwing weird light over the hill and its rear slope, and the air was filled with reddish tracer. The artillerymen tried to hide themselves in the ground, and Heath ran back and forth, urging them to get up and fight.

An artillery liaison, Captain Elledge, heard Heath's yelling. Elledge was the rare breed who loved a fight. He went back to the firing positions, grabbed about a dozen men, and forced these up to the rifle platoons' defense line. Elledge himself carried up a .30-caliber machine gun. He heard the Chinese whistling and hooting to one another in the dark, and he went forward over the hard snow to investigate. He met Chinese face to face. He killed two with his carbine in a hand-to-hand fight, before a grenade blast numbed his left arm and he retired.

Now, while the entire perimeter of Chipyong-ni was under pressure, the main CCF blow fell against weakened George Company. George was piling up the dead by the hundreds, but too many of the enemy were getting in close with explosives and hand grenades. The artillery fired star shells and HE alternately, riddling the Chinese, but still they came on.

The CCF washed up on the low ridge again and again, fighting a determined battle for each foxhole. Little by little, against violent resistance, they were chipping the ground away from the American defenders.

Heath, behind the hill, went to the 503rd's battery commander for more men. He was determined to counterattack and thrust the Chinese out of his position. He yelled over and over, "We're going up that goddamned hill or bust!"

Again the artillery C.O. gave him all men not needed on the guns. But neither officer could force these men onto the hill.

The 2nd Battalion commander, Lieutenant Colonel Edwards, sent a squad from Fox Company to help fill the gaping holes in George's line. Heath sent these men into the hottest part of the fight, the saddle between 1st and 2nd platoons. Within minutes, every man of this squad was killed or hurt. Still, G Company held its precarious perch on the ridge.

The 2nd Platoon's platoon sergeant, Bill Kluttz, yelled at Lieutenant McGee, "Lieutenant, we've got to stop them!"

The Chinese kept pressing in. They did not try to overwhelm G with one vast rush, but continued to creep through the night, knocking out hole after hole. The 1st Platoon, near three o'clock in the morning, was pushed back out of position. Now without the support on his flank, McGee was down to a few able-bodied men.

And the fires of his spirit ran low, too. He said to Kluttz, over the field phone, "Looks like they've got us—"

On another portion of the hill, Kluttz snapped back grimly, his voice carried by its own power over the wires, "Let's kill as many of these sons of bitches as we can before they get us!"

Meanwhile, to the rear, George's 4th Platoon leader commanding the company mortars, discovered a group of artillerymen huddling together inside one of the battery's canvas tents. Fire from the hills was beginning to spray over into the valley now, and mortarmen and gunners were being hurt.

"Hell!" this officer barked at them. "A squad tent won't stop bullets!"

Despite this officer's urging, none of these men would go up on the hill to give the riflemen a hand. Faced with being overrun, they seemed to feel that because their primary military occupational specialty did not include handling a rifle, no one had the right to make them use one.

A few minutes later, McGee's last machine gun jammed. The 1st Platoon, under its surviving sergeant, was coming off the hill; McGee and Kluttz realized they could gain nothing now by dying in place, for even their ammunition was low.

McGee, Kluttz, and four other men backed off the hill. They were all who were left.

The 23rd's perimeter was broken. The Chinese had a pathway into the vitals of the regiment. All they had to do was to exploit it.

And now, at Chipyong-ni on the night of 14 February 1951, the battle took in miniature the form it would have for the next few months: The Chinese by prodigally throwing men against fire and steel had wiped out a defending unit. Any ground commander, given men and willing to spend them, can break any ground defense, in time, at any chosen place.

The CCF had punched through George Company, on the south, but that in itself availed them nothing. Everywhere else they were still battling a solid line that could not be flanked.

And the heartbreaking effort to spring George Company had left the Chinese spent, too. Their ammunitions was low, and their supply center far behind. Their communications—horns and bugles—could not pass the word fast enough, coherently enough, that the bung had been started and that the Chinese wave might now flow through into the hollow of Chipyong-ni.

The Chinese now demonstrated what would be proved again and again upon the Korean Field of battle: they could crack a line, but a force lacking mechanization, air power, and rapid communications could not exploit against a force possessing all three.

Lieutenant Heath was on the phone to Colonel Edwards, telling him George was through. Edwards, alarmed, promised help. But all Edwards had available as reserve was one platoon of Fox Company, already minus the squad previously committed.

Edwards called Freeman—but Freeman was also scraping bottom. The 3rd Battalion was under heavy pressure, and Freeman was afraid to commit his entire reserve—one Ranger company. He granted Edwards one platoon of the Rangers and one tank.

Edwards ordered the Fox platoon and the Ranger to the G Company zone. He placed a staff officer, Lieutenant Curtis, over the two-platoon force. But at first the Ranger C.O. made trouble; he refused to take orders from anyone but Freeman. Hearing this, Edwards sent down a captain from his staff, Ramsburg, to take control and get the Rangers straightened out.

As the new force arrived in George's sector, Heath's line was only a group of men stretched thinly along a furrow of earth in front of the artillery-fire direction center. Fire was pouring down upon these men from the shadowy line of hills they had lost.

But to either side the flanks were holding firm, and the artillery was firing a continuous crescendo of flame and noise into the gap.

Ramsburg organized his small force quickly and sent them forward in counterattack. The Rangers, screaming and yelling, led the way back onto George's old hill.

In the near-dawn chill, the blazing fire fight raged across the hill. Both Americans and Chinese massed on the crest, desperately trying to throw the other off. The Ranger platoon leader was killed. Ramsburg was injured by a grenade. Heath, coming up the hill to take Ramsburg's place, was shot through the chest. One of his men, his own arm almost severed from his body, dragged Heath back to safety.

In a brief, savage action, the Americans were knocked off the hill. Fox's platoon lost 22 men of 28; the Rangers suffered equally. Curtis, who had remained to the rear, now tried to take charge of the survivors, and to throw up some kind of line in back of the hill to protect Chipyong-ni.

The CCF, stung by the counterattack, could not reorganize quickly enough to advance against the dozen wounded men barring their way. Ramsburg reported to Edwards by phone, who shouted to hold on, more help was on the way.

Freeman, realizing that whatever happened elsewhere, this hole must be plugged, gave Edwards the remainder of the Ranger force.

In a few minutes Curtis and Ramsburg, having now no able-bodied riflemen, began falling back slowly.

Captain Elledge, the artillery liaison officer, took up the slack. Realizing he was not badly hurt, and having no command, Elledge returned to battle on his own. In the ditch beside the road into Chipyong-ni he found an abandoned Quad .50 ack-ack gun mounted on a half-track, and this he got a tank crew to help him swing around until its muzzle faced the enemy.

Elledge was able to get the track's motor started and the power turned on the gun mount. He leveled the gun and sprayed the hill in front of the retreating Americans. Four .50-caliber machine guns, firing in unison, went over the hill like a vacuum cleaner, sucking it dry of Chinese life.

A Chinese squad sneaked close to him with a 75mm recoilless rifle they had captured on the hill. But it was now light, and Elledge saw them. As they loaded the rifle, he swung the gun and cut them down with one burst.

Now three American tanks moved down the road, blasting the hill with cannon fire. The artillerymen, still on their guns, leveled their huge howitzers and covered the area with bursting white phosphorous.

Colonel Edwards rushed forward with the Rangers, and B Company, which Freeman had released to him at daylight. Soon, overhead, there was the comforting whistle of friendly aircraft.

The Chinese tried to come through, to reach the soft belly of the regiment. They failed; a wall of steel had been moved in front of them. They tried to hold what they had taken, George's hill, fighting stubbornly all day during 15 February against air- and tank-supported infantry attack, while American artillery pounded them.

But air, armor, artillery, and redeployed infantry had plugged the hole. The Chinese had not been able to move swiftly enough during the crucial hours of darkness. All day the best they could do was to hold the single hill they had taken at such cost, and with dusk their spirit broke. Those Chinese who could yet walk faded into the hills.

After dark, a soft snow fell, covering thousands of Chinese corpses lying in a ring about Chipyong-ni. Hundreds lay in front of George Company's hill, and others dotted the hill itself, intermingled with American dead.

At Chipyong-ni on 15 February 1951 a massive Chinese offensive had been blunted. On this date the CCF suffered its first tactical defeat at American hands.

The CCF would try again, and again, but now a new pattern had been set. Eighth Army had risen from its own bitter ashes.

It would not fall again.

24

Vae, Caesar

I was left with one simple conclusion: General MacArthur was ready to risk general war. I was not.

—Harry S. Truman, President of the United States.

THE FIRST WEEKS after the massive Chinese intervention in Korea were a time of crisis not only upon the frozen battlefields of that tragic peninsula but in virtually every chancellery in the world. In New York the United Nations was a ferment of agony, doubt, and indecision. U.N. delegates, as reported by the *New York Times,* refused to be quoted officially, but now sudden doubt was expressed over future United States policy.

The Truman press statement of 30 November 1950 brought things swiftly to a head. Truman, while making a temperate statement, in response to a reporter's question, touched upon the sorest nerve of the mid-century. As reported in the *Times,* Truman said:

" 'Recent developments in Korea confront the world with a serious crisis . . . we have committed ourselves to the cause of a just and peaceful world order through the United Nations. We stand by that commitment.

" 'We shall meet the new situation in three ways. We shall continue to work in the United Nations for concerted action to halt the aggression in Korea. We shall intensify our efforts to help other free nations to strengthen their defense . . . we shall rapidly increase our own military strength.

" 'We shall exert every effort to help bring the full influence of the United Nations to bear on the situation in Korea.' "

As it had already been decided in Cabinet and National Security Council, Truman made it very clear that further moves such as attacks on the Chinese mainland, blockades, or bombing, depended on U.N. reaction.

Then, in response to a question, Truman affirmed that the atom bomb still remained in the United States' arsenal of weapons. In its summary of news 1 December 1950, the *New York Times* said: *The Truman press statement said the United Nations will fight . . . for justice and world peace, and we will if necessary use the atom bomb.* He would give the authorization, and MacArthur would pick the targets, in accordance with U.S. military policy: *CCF bases in Manchuria would be attacked, he added, if the U.N. brands Red China an aggressor. The President showed impatience with the slowness of Western Europe to rearm.*

Within three hours, there was resulting explosion.

The *Times* of 1 December remarked: *The President's mention of an atom bomb caused consternation and alarm in Britain and brought from France official disapproval. Most U.N. delegates were agreed that it would be politically disastrous to use the bomb in Asia.*

Nothing so awakened the French Assembly as mention of the bomb. To the fear of the bomb lately has been added a fear of General MacArthur, who is regarded as impulsive and reckless in his reported desire to bomb Manchuria and risk extending the war.

A headline read: *Britons dismayed by Truman's talk—Atlee will fly to Washington to discuss crisis with President.*

The *London Times* editorialized: [*Truman*] *touched upon the most sensitive fears and doubts of this age.* . . .

Winston Churchill, in Commons, warned the West against involvement in Asia at the expense of Europe. The House cheered Prime Minister Atlee's announced flight to Washington.

In Melbourne, Australia, where there were few friends of Red China, newspapers expressed the hope that diplomatic skill would avert a conflict with Communist China. The *Melbourne Herald* wrote: *The Chinese can no longer be despised militarily. Their revolutionary leaders obviously command unity and loyalty which Chiang never attained.*

Italian Communists and anti-Communists alike expressed deep fears of general war.

And papers all over the world stated that MacArthur should have halted the U.N. armies no farther north than the middle of North Korea, leaving a buffer between them and Manchuria.

Whatever else the press statement may have done, it cleared the air: the United States Government understood immediately where its major allies— indeed, the greater part of the world—stood on the China question. Above all else, the world wished to avoid general war, and atomic war in particular. That United Nations and allied thinking was not brought home forcefully to millions of Americans was due to the fact that apart from the Atlantic-seaboard area, few newspapers or other media printed or reflected foreign views.

For the first time the U.N. cloak that the United States Government had so expeditiously woven for its action in Korea became not a support, but a hindrance. The U.N. in June had been almost wholly responsive to American leadership, and the United States had chosen to implement its national policy under the aegis of the U.N., at the time a great moral victory. With the entry of Red China into the fighting, the sharp U.S. setback in the north, and the prospect of an enlarged war yawning ominously, the nations composing the U.N. suddenly became restive. American leadership, unfortunately, had lost a great deal of its prestige on the battlefield.

After 1 December 1950, the allies who had tripped unquestioningly into the never-never land would never again allow the United States an unlimited credit card, moral or otherwise. For by 1 December the vast majority of the member nations of the U.N. wanted "out" of the Korean debacle. Whatever the moral issues, few saw any profit in a continued war with Red China over the eventual fate of divided Korea. The smaller nations had been willing to follow the United States into a small conflict—a police action—against an aggressor as long as the fighting had a clear moral purpose and demanded few sacrifices of them. Now the earth was on the brink of general war, and the moral purpose of defeating Red China was not at all clear in European minds.

Five years after the close of the most destructive war in history, few nations were willing to risk atomic war for any reason short of immediate self-preservation.

The British prime minister, deeply worried, called at Washington to reassure himself of American policy. Other leaders did the same.

In the U.N., thirteen Arab-Asian nations sponsored a resolution asking for a cease-fire in Korea. On 14 December the General Assembly adopted it overwhelmingly. A three-man deputation—Pearson of Canada, Rau of India, and Entezam of Iran—tried vainly to make contact with the Chinese, who at that time were unwilling to discuss the matter except on their own terms.

But the smaller nations of the U.N. continued to press the matter. India's Sir Benegal Rau suggested that "Peiping was for peace"; India refused to consider any strong measure against Red China. The United Nations had been envisioned—however it was sold to the peoples of the world—not as a parliament of earth but as a controlling body on the questions of peace and war. Real power, through the institution of the veto, remained where it was in reality, in the hands of the great powers: America, Britain, China, the Soviet Union. The problem, as well as the tragedy of the United Nations organization, was that it had never been anticipated that the great powers at the end of World War II would have no community of interest.

The first U.N. action utilizing force was, in essence, against itself, for the Soviet Union, sponsor of North Korea, continued in membership. Only the fact that the U.S.S.R. was absent in June 1950 permitted the Security Council to take effective action.

American planners, painfully aware of this accident, strove to overcome such an impasse in the future. The powers of the Security Council—the voice of the big nations—were diluted to the extent of permitting the General Assembly to bypass the Council on certain grave issues. With U.S. sponsorship, such changes were made in the framework of the U.N.

In effect such changes meant that eventually the U.N. would pass, with constantly increasing membership, completely from big-power control. American planners, unfortunately, could not see they were tugging at the lid of Pandora's box. Some of them, probably, did not understand the political—and power—realities of the world they lived in.

In 1951, having wrapped its policy in the U.N. cloak, the United States could not, without being branded with hypocrisy, throw off what were now hampering folds. American policy would have to be worked out within the myriad conflicting policies of the U.N.

The majority of the U.N. wanted an end to the war, as soon as possible. The United States, whatever its own desires, would be forced to listen. Who calls the tune often has to pay the piper, whether he likes the music or not.

When President Truman made the decision to intervene in Korea—with general support—Dean Acheson said to him that the decision "might not always be so popular as it seemed at the moment."

Secretary of State Acheson, a much-maligned man, was soon proved to be a prophet, though his status resembled that of most prophets as far as honor in his own land was concerned. Acheson, always intensely anti-Communist, had always to be intensely practical. In the months following Korea, any American Secretary of State in addition to other qualifications needed the abilities of a door-to-door salesman of insurance. Acheson, an aristocrat, a brilliant mind, and a practical man, could never be an effective salesman of policy.

His policy was Truman's policy, as Truman said, but Acheson became the butt of all the frustration felt by the mass of the American people. The truth was that what the American people wanted was no longer—could be no longer—paramount in the world, once the United States chose to work in conjunction with the U.N. and its allies.

Someone had to sell this understanding to the people. The Truman Administration could never do so.

In Washington, in December 1950, there was political crisis.

On 15 December, after lengthy consultation and much argument, Truman declared a national emergency. For some American leaders, such as Senators Taft and Wherry, this was too much. For others, it was not nearly enough.

For as Representative Taber of New York told Truman, "The people were confused and upset."

What the people could not understand was, Was the United States at war or not?

It had massive forces in the field, killing, being killed, but life went on much as before. Men were being called from factory and field, but there was still "peace." There was war, obviously, but still there was not war as Americans had come to understand it.

Americans had been brought up to avoid war as the plague, but once in it, to pull all the stops. It had been almost a hundred years since they had fought a war on the far frontier or held the border for civilization, and the taste of those campaigns was still foul in their mouths.

They had been taught for generations that the use of war for reasons of national policy was wrong, and now that their government followed such a course, in the path of imperial Britain, they felt only anguish and frustration.

One of the men who felt the agony and the frustration most deeply was America's proconsul in the Far East, Supreme Commander Douglas MacArthur.

* * *

It is given to the President of the United States, with the advice and consent of the Senate, to conduct the foreign policy of the Republic. From the time of Athens and Republican Rome, no representative parliament has ever had much success with dealings beyond the water; there have been historians who claim that continued involvement of a people beyond its own frontiers inevitably produces Caesarism.

The jury on this question must be reported to be still out. At least, no Caesars were produced by the Korean conflict. Both potential Caesars were, in fact, humbled, one at the hands of his superiors, the other by his people. But first they collided, and the shock was felt around the world.

Douglas MacArthur, one of the most brilliant military minds America has yet produced, graduated from West Point at the turn of the century. He stemmed from a distinguished military family; his father was a lieutenant general and proconsul—of the Philippines—in his own right.

MacArthur was a product of the old, alienated American officer caste, but, like Dwight Eisenhower, he was never typical of that group. While Eisenhower came to embody all the virtues—and vices, to some—of the old-American bourgeoisie, remote from the hard-bitten cavalry of the sun-blasted plains, MacArthur's mind and heart, at the age of thirty-eight, were forged in the horror of the trenches of World War I.

At an age when most professionals looked forward to leaves or eagles, Douglas MacArthur wore general's stars. Yet, from the ghastly slaughter of 1917–1918 he retained a profound horror of the effects of war, as well as a never-faltering belief in the idealism that lay behind that war.

That slaughter he saw at close hand. He was decorated seven times by an awed government and people for valor in the field.

After what he had seen in the trenches, war could never again be a mere profession to Douglas MacArthur. He would continue to be a professional soldier, but forever afterward war to him would be an awful act, to be entered on only for the most transcendental of purposes.

In this feeling MacArthur was one with most of the nonmilitary intelligent men of his age. He had a profound hatred of war, but any war upon which he embarked must henceforth be a crusade. In no other way could the suffering be justified.

It would occur to few of that generation that wars fought for a higher purpose must always be the most hideous of all. It is desperately hard for men to accept that there is a direct path from the highest ideals to the torture chamber—for no man who accepts with his whole heart can fail equally to reject with his whole being.

In his feeling for war, MacArthur was a typical American of his school. He was one with Woodrow Wilson, whose pronouncements deeply influenced him, and he was one with Franklin Roosevelt. War was to be entered upon with sadness, with regret, but also with ferocity.

War was horrible, and whoever unleashed it must be smitten and destroyed, unto the last generation, so that war should arise no more.

When war is entered upon for the highest moral purpose, there can be no substitute for victory, short of betrayal of that purpose, and of the men who die.

In 1918, and 1941, and even in 1951, probably most Americans felt as felt Douglas MacArthur. Yet MacArthur, raised to the highest honors of the Republic, would remain an uncertain hero in the public mind. He was an aristocrat, if military, and he was a devout Christian—not a social Christian, but a weight-of-centuries Anglican to whom God stood close at hand; and near such men most Americans have always felt uncomfortable.

It was no accident that of all American military men, only MacArthur and Eisenhower, untypical of their caste, should be seriously considered for the Presidency, and that of the two only Eisenhower, more in the mainstream of American social tradition, should receive the office.

MacArthur, the oldest and the ranking of the hierarchy of generals, was not one of them. And though his thinking was close to that of the people, he was not one of them. It was ironic—and again no accident—that a generation unborn when MacArthur won every significant decoration on the field of battle that could be given by a grateful Republic should come to call him "Dugout Doug."

It was as well. Right or wrong, had Douglas MacArthur been a man of the people, and so minded, he might have overturned the Republic.

For now, in early 1951, two points of view concerning war entered collision course. One, MacArthur's, was that of Wilson, Roosevelt, George Marshall, and most of the older generation. War must never be an extension of politics; it must be jihad.

Such men recoil at the thought of nuclear war, but in general prepare for nothing else. A crusade, by its very nature, cannot be limited.

But in Korea, in 1950–1951, the United States was not fighting a holy war. Momentarily, and at MacArthur's urging, it had lost sight of its original goal and proceeded into the never-never land.

President Truman and his advisers, wrapped tightly now in the embracing U.N. cloak, would not enter the twilight zone again.

Now troops were being used as a counterpawn on the broader table of diplomacy, for a specific, limited purpose: the holding in check of expansionist Communism. The troops remained, fighting, because State argued that abandonment of Korea would be a political error irredeemable in Asia, even while the Pentagon, concerned for Europe, scraping the bottom of its strategic troop barrel, talked of ways to end the war "with honor."

To each group, the men about the President, and the men about MacArthur, the viewpoint of the other seem immoral. Collision was inevitable and necessary.

In December, Harry Truman dispatched Army Chief of Staff J. Lawton Collins to the Orient. Shortly afterward, Lightning Joe Collins returned and reported MacArthur's views to his chief.

The Supreme Commander, Collins said, saw three possible courses of American action.

One was to continue the war in Korea as before, under limiting restrictions. This meant no large-scale reinforcement of U.N. troops, no retaliatory measures against Red China, such as bombardment of Manchurian bases, naval blockade, or the use of Nationalist Chinese forces.

A second course was to enlarge the conflict by the bombing of the Chinese mainland, blockading the coast, and setting Chiang Kai-shek free, with American support, to fight both in Korea and in South China, giving Communist China more than it had bargained for.

The third course would be to get the CCF to agree to remain north of the 38th parallel, and to make an armistice upon that basis, under U.N. supervision.

MacArthur then told Collins he personally favored the second course. The first course, to him, was identical with surrender. He would, however, agree to the third, if it could be managed.

Harry Truman was deeply disturbed. His thinking and that of MacArthur were in wide divergence. Truman felt that Course Two would inevitably lead to general war—not only with China but also with Russia, which could not sit idly by while its Asian ally was humbled.

Truman wanted a combination of courses One and Three—the door would be held while a collective political agreement was hammered out.

He recognized that MacArthur, however, had a perfect right to make his own views known to his chief. But the problem soon arose that MacArthur began to make his views known to everyone.

On 19 December, MacArthur requested four additional divisions, for the defense of Japan. He began to ask for more and more, to prosecute the war. The requests were impossible, short of mobilization. The U.S. Army had one division, the 82nd Airborne, in strategic reserve. NATO was just getting underway in Europe. It was unthinkable that U.S. troops be stripped from that area.

There were hardly any allied divisions in Europe worthy of the name, and they dare not be moved, even had their governments been willing—which they were not.

About the only move that could be made was to increase the ROK Army by from 200,000 to 300,000 men, armed with rifles, BAR's, carbines, and submachine guns. About this, MacArthur was not sanguine. He preferred to arm the Japanese.

On 29 December MacArthur sent a message to the Joint Chiefs, as he had before, that he desired permission to blockade the China coast and attack airfields in Manchuria. He stated he did not fear the Chinese would be provoked—MacArthur considered the United States already at war with China. He also stated that if his wishes were not granted, the Korean peninsula should be evacuated.

Summed up, Douglas MacArthur held that the U.S. should attempt to win, and win big, or get out.

On 9 January, after carefully clearing it with the President, the JCS sent MacArthur the following directive: to continue to defend in Korea, to continue to inflict losses on the CCF, and to withdraw only if essential to save his command.

MacArthur asked for clarification. He said he could not hold in Korea and protect Japan at the same time. He stated that U.N. troops could not continue to operate under the limiting restrictions without prohibitive losses. If international political reasons forced a continuance on the present terms, then the JCS—and the President—should be prepared to accept grave consequences.

General of the Army George Catlett Marshall hand-carried this message to Truman.

Truman became very disturbed. What MacArthur was telling him, in essence, was that the policy decided upon by the National Security Council, the JCS, and the President was not feasible.

Events were to prove MacArthur wrong, but at this time Truman could only give the general's views grave consideration. He called a meeting of the National Security Council on 12 January. What was decided here, mainly, was to inform MacArthur of the international political realities of the world situation. The United States had embarked on a course of collective security, through its allies and the U.N., and it had no intention of "going it alone."

Feelers among allies and U.N. had revealed not one government willing to back MacArthur's course.

On 13 January 1951 Truman wired to MacArthur:

"I want you to know that the situation in Korea is receiving the utmost attention here and that our efforts are concentrated upon finding the right decisions on this matter of the gravest importance to the future of America and to the survival of free peoples everywhere.

"I wish in this telegram to let you have my views as to our basic national and international purposes in continuing the resistance to aggression in Korea. We need your judgment as to the maximum effort which could reasonably be expected from the United Nations forces under your command to support the resistance to aggression which we are trying rapidly to organize on a world-wide basis. This present telegram is not to be taken in any sense as a directive. Its purpose is to give you something of what is in our minds regarding the political factors.

"1. A successful resistance in Korea would serve the following important
   purposes:

   "(a)   To demonstrate that aggression will not be accepted by us or
   by the United Nations and to provide a rallying point around which
   the spirits and energies of the free world can be mobilized to meet
   the world-wide threat which the Soviet Union now poses.

   "(b)   To deflate the dangerously exaggerated political and military
   prestige of Communist China which now threatens to undermine
   the resistance of non-Communist Asia and to consolidate the hold
   of Communism on China itself.

   "(c)   To afford more time for and to give direct assistance to the
   organization of non-Communist resistance in Asia, both outside
   and inside China.

   "(d)   To carry out our commitments of honor to the South Koreans and to demonstrate to the world that the friendship of the United States is of inestimable value in time of adversity.

"(e)   To make possible a far more satisfactory peace settlement for Japan and to contribute greatly to the post-treaty security position of Japan in relation to the continent.

"(f)   To lend resolution to many countries not only in Asia but also in Europe and the Middle East who are now living within the shadow of Communist power and to let them know that they need not now rush to come to terms with Communism on whatever terms they can get, meaning complete submission.

"(g)   To inspire those who may be called upon to fight against great odds if subjected to a sudden onslaught by the Soviet Union or by Communist China.

"(h)   To lend point and urgency to the rapid build-up of the defenses of the western world.

"(i)   To bring the United Nations through its first great effort on collective security and to produce a free-world coalition of incalculable value to the national security interests of the United States.

"(j)   To alert the peoples behind the Iron Curtain that their masters are bent upon wars of aggression and that this crime will be resisted by the free world.

"2.   Our course of action at this time should be such as to consolidate the great majority of the United Nations. This majority is not merely part of the organization but is also the nations whom we would desperately need to count on as allies in the event the Soviet Union moves against us. Further, pending the build-up of our national strength, we must act with great prudence in so far as extending the area of hostilities is concerned. Steps which might in themselves be fully justified and which might lend some assistance to the campaign in Korea would not be beneficial if they thereby involved Japan or Western Europe in large-scale hostilities.

"3.   We recognize, of course, that continued resistance might not be militarily possible with the limited forces with which you are being called upon to meet large Chinese armies. Further, in the present world situation, your forces must be preserved as an effective instrument for the defense of Japan and elsewhere. However, some of the important purposes mentioned above might be supported, if you should think it practicable, and advisable, by continued resistance from off-shore islands of Korea, particularly from Cheju-do, if it becomes impracticable to hold an important portion of Korea itself. In the worst case, it would be important that, if we must withdraw from Korea, it be clear to the world that that course is forced upon us by military necessity and that we shall not accept the result politically or militarily until the aggression has been rectified.

"4.   In reaching a final decision about Korea, I shall have to give constant thought to the main threat from the Soviet Union and to the need for a rapid expansion of our armed forces to meet this great danger.

"5. I am encouraged to believe that the free world is getting a much clearer and realistic picture of the dangers before us and that the necessary courage and energy will be forthcoming. Recent proceedings in the United Nations have disclosed a certain amount of confusion and wishful thinking, but I believe that most members have been actuated by a desire to be absolutely sure that all possible avenues to peaceful settlement have been fully explored. I believe that the great majority is now rapidly consolidating and that the result will be an encouraging and formidable combination in defense of freedom.

"6. The entire nation is grateful for your splendid leadership in the difficult struggle in Korea and for the superb performance of your forces under the most difficult circumstances.

"[s] HARRY S. TRUMAN"

In brief, Truman informed the FECOM commander that United States policy was based on the premise that the peace of the world could be attained only through collective security and that, while continuing the war in Korea under the present circumstances, the world was getting a clear and realistic picture of the dangers it faced despite some wishful thinking in the U.N.

The United States, Truman told MacArthur in essence, must continue to defend South Korea, while at the same time it consolidated the defense of Europe. The major potential foe was still Soviet Russia, and Europe still the world's great prize. Any measure that provided relief for the United States forces in Korea, but set back United States support or strength in Europe, would be imprudent. If the United States began a unilateral war with Red China, it stood an excellent chance of fatally rupturing the embryonic North Atlantic Treaty Organization which for some years had been a goal of its policy.

MacArthur was told to hold the frontier so that the tribes of the interior could continue to organize, and to forget about carrying the war to the barbarians.

Truman's policy was not only dictated by the reliance upon collective security and the reluctance of the United Nations, but by Western weakness. America had the bomb, but no divisions. There was no barrier in middle Europe that could prevent its being overrun by the massive Red Army.

Until such a barrier could be built, under NATO, Washington would never breathe easy. It would never favor involvement in Asia. It would continue to eye such involvement suspiciously, looking for a Russian trick.

MacArthur might disagree with such a policy—but he could hardly fail to get the message.

And there, for many days, while the Eighth Army righted itself and began to batter its painful way back up the peninsula, the matter rested. Oddly, it was U.N. success that brought the divergence between MacArthur and the Commander in Chief to a head.

By March 1951, the CCF had been halted, hurt, and forced back. It was apparent that it would soon be forced completely out of the Taehan Minkuk. The lines would then stand where they had in June 1950, and where they had stood in October. But this time there was no exaltation in Washington, no confidence in cheap victory. With each of its allies screaming for an end to the war, now deeply aware of the dangers involved in humbling China, Washington was willing to negotiate.

The *New York Times,* which in December 1950 had reported *Paris and London Unite to Seek Curb on Korean War,* in February 1951 carried a highly significant headline: *U.S. to Seek Peace, Spokesmen Say—A Reversal of Policy.* Well-placed men in government, who could not be named, stated to reporters that the old policy of October 1950, seeking the defeat of the aggressor, was dead.

Military reports indicated that there was a strong possibility that the CCF in Korea could be brought to ruin by continued offensive action. But would the collapse of the CCF, and the resultant loss of face in Asia, force the U.S.S.R. to act?

The answer will never be known, for the United States had had enough of challenges.

On 20 March Truman, Dean Acheson, Marshall, and the Joint Chiefs discussed the possibilities of peace in Korea, and then informed MacArthur:

"State Department planning a Presidential announcement shortly that with clearing of bulk of South Korea of aggressors, the United Nations now preparing to discuss conditions of settlement in Korea. United Nations feeling exists that further diplomatic efforts toward settlement should be made before any advance with major forces north of the 38th parallel. Time will be required to determine diplomatic reactions and permit new negotiations that may develop. Recognizing that parallel has no military significance, State has asked Joint Chiefs of Staff what authority you should have to permit sufficient freedom of action for next few weeks to provide security for United Nations forces and maintain contact with enemy. Your recommendation desired."

MacArthur sent a message back that no further restrictions should be placed on his command, since those already in force—no bombing of Manchurian bases or diversions against the Chinese mainland—precluded the possibility of clearing North Korea anyway, in his mind.

Then Truman, with members of State and Defense, drew up a presidential announcement. In draft it read:

"I make the following statement as Chief Executive of the Government requested by the United Nations to exercise the Unified Command in Korea, and after full consultation with United Nations Governments contributing combat forces in support of the United Nations in Korea.

"United Nations forces in Korea are engaged in repelling the aggressions committed against the Republic of Korea. . . .

"The aggressors have been driven back with heavy losses to the general vicinity from which the unlawful attack was first launched last June.

"There remains the problem of restoring international peace and security in the area in accordance with the terms of the Security Council resolution of June 27, 1950. . . .

"There is a basis for restoring peace and security in the area which should be acceptable to all nations which sincerely desire peace.

"The Unified Command is prepared to enter into arrangements which would conclude the fighting. . . . Such arrangements would open the way for a broader settlement for Korea, including the withdrawal of foreign forces. . . .

"The Korean people are entitled to peace. They are entitled to determine their political and other institutions by their own choice. . . . What is needed is peace, in which the United Nations can use its resources in the creative tasks of reconstruction. . . .

"A prompt settlement of the Korean problem would greatly reduce international tensions in the Far East and would open the way for the consideration of other problems. . . ."

The announcement said, in effect, that the United States, acting for the U.N., was willing to settle, without threats, recrimination, or talk of punishment. The Communists had tried a gambit, and failed. The U.N. had tried one of their own, and had also failed. No one had really lost—but no one had really won. The United States said that the *status quo ante* was quite all right with it, if the Communists agreed.

Thousands upon thousands of men, women, and children, civilians and soldiers were dead, crippled, or homeless. But the frontier had been held. After all the fighting, and suffering, and dying, all was as it had been. Nothing had been settled—except that now each side knew the other had the will to fight, in defense of what it considered vital interests.

The West better understood the East. It was to be hoped that the reverse held true. At least that much had been accomplished.

The Truman Announcement was the product of a new group of men in the American Government, whose like had not been in government since the War Between the States. These men had no hope of, nor interest in, making the world safe for democracy, or of destroying evil. They were vitally concerned with the continued good of the United States, and with preserving some semblance of order in the world, if not democracy.

In the seventh year of the Nuclear Age, they accepted the fact that each of the two opposing power systems held an effective veto over the other. They would not, except as a last extremity, accept general war.

They would fight; they would reluctantly spill the blood of their nation's young men, but if possible, only in limited fashion, and only to prove a point to the enemy.

They tended to be level-headed, pragmatic, cynical of sweeping conclusions in any direction, with complete awareness of the dreadful complexities of the modern political world. They did not envision surrender. But they also saw no clear-cut answers, in a world that held only awesome problems.

It was typical that many of these men, like Dean Acheson, wore London suits, for they had inherited the mantle the British Lion had worn a hundred years earlier.

Many of them, strangely, often had the name of Woodrow Wilson on their lips, as they talked to the public. This was ironic, because a Wilson would have vomited them forth from his Administration. Like a great many of the American people, the crusader Wilson would never have understood them.

Nor did General of the Army Douglas MacArthur, who had come to full maturity in Wilson's time.

The Truman Announcement was coordinated with every friendly government on the globe, but it was never issued. For General of the Army MacArthur, America's Supreme Commander in the field, in a statement almost unprecedented in American history, beat Harry Truman to the punch.

On 24 March 1951, with no word first to Washington, he issued his own pronouncement from Tokyo:

"Operations continue according to schedule and plan. We have now substantially cleared South Korea of organized Communist forces. It is becoming increasingly evident that the heavy destruction along the enemy's lines of supply, caused by our round-the-clock massive air and naval bombardment, has left his troops in the forward battle area deficient in requirements to sustain his operations. . . .

"Of even greater significance than our tactical successes has been the clear revelation that this new enemy, Red China, of such exaggerated and vaunted military power, lacks the industrial capacity to provide. . . crucial items necessary to the conduct of modern war. He lacks the manufacturing base . . . he cannot provide . . . tanks, heavy artillery, and other refinements science has introduced into the conduct of military campaigns. Formerly his great numerical potential might well have filled this gap, but with the development of existing methods of mass destruction, numbers alone do not offset . . . such deficiencies. . . .

"These military weaknesses have been clearly and definitely revealed since Red China entered upon its undeclared war in Korea. Even under the inhibitions which now restrict the activity of the United Nations forces and the corresponding military advantages which accrue to Red China, it has shown its complete inability to accomplish by force of arms the conquest of Korea. The enemy, therefore, must by now be painfully aware that a decision of the United Nations to depart from its tolerant effort to contain the war to the area of Korea, through an expansion of our military operations to its coastal areas and interior bases, would doom Red China to the risk of imminent military collapse. These basic facts being established, there should be no insuperable difficulty in arriving at decisions on the Korean problem if the issues are resolved on their own merits, without being burdened by extraneous matters not directly related to Korea. . . .

"The Korean nation and people, which have been so cruelly ravaged, must not be sacrificed. This is a paramount concern. . . . Within the area of my authority as the military commander, however, it would be needless to say that I stand ready at any time to confer in the field with the commander in chief of the enemy forces . . . to find . . . means whereby realization of the political objectives of the United Nations in Korea, to which no nation may justly take exceptions, might be accomplished without further bloodshed."

Right or wrong, this was a remarkable statement to have been issued by an American proconsul in the field. It was more than a statement of military policy; it was a political act. It disregarded Washington's instructions for FECOM to abstain from declarations on foreign policy. It flouted the announced policy of the U.N.

MacArthur had delivered Red China an ultimatum. He had hinted that the full power of the United States and its allies might be brought to bear against the Chinese homeland; threat was redolent throughout the discussion of Chinese weakness, and it was a threat that MacArthur obviously relished.

When Truman read it, he went white. MacArthur's announcement was a challenge to the authority of the President, under the Constitution, to make foreign policy.

Considering MacArthur's high office, his pronouncement crashed into allied chancelleries like eight-inch howitzer shells. The wires began to burn to Washington. Was a shift in American policy imminent?

Had the United States decided to punish Red China?

The Norwegian ambassador called at State, demanding to know what lay behind this "pronunciamento."

At noon, Saturday, 24 March, Truman conferred with Acheson, Robert Lovett, and Dean Rusk. It was undoubtedly a bitter and passionate conference, even among men not given to stampede.

On 6 December, when the U.N. had begun to grow restive, Truman had sent a directive to FECOM, instructing that all public statements be cleared through Washington. Truman now read this order, and asked Rusk and Acheson if there could be any doubt as to its meaning.

They agreed there was none in their minds.

Truman then told Lovett to get a priority message to FECOM, telling MacArthur to shut up. Truman had long understood that MacArthur disagreed with him, but he had not understood the extent.

Nor could Truman really understand MacArthur. Truman could not be sure but that the general was playing for the gallery, trying to embarrass the President, and as political leader of the nation Truman found this intolerable. MacArthur was challenging traditional civilian supremacy in government, and Truman was not at all certain but that Caesar was speaking from beyond the Rubicon.

MacArthur was no Caesar, with immense political ambitions. He was a servant of the Republic who felt so strongly that the course of the Administration, eschewing triumph over the transgressor, was immoral that he had put himself into public opposition. He was trying to influence policy.

Under the Constitution of the Untied States, no soldier has that privilege.

Soldiers are brought up to tell the truth, and to take positive action. Since politicians, in the main, regard neither of these with great affection—they must forever please the people, regardless of what is true or what needs to be done—soldiers and political men are often in conflict.

A political leader who takes strong action, who does not equivocate, dally, or try the impossible task of pleasing everyone, has usually nothing to fear from soldiers, even in authoritarian lands. It is the leaders of the Fourth Republic, the Frondizis, the Roman Senate, the men who try to walk a tightrope, who have been intolerable to the soldiery.

Military men, who are willing to risk their lives, have small sympathy with anyone unwilling to risk his office. While politics may be the art of the possible, war is often the art of the impossible.

Douglas MacArthur, as American as Woodrow Wilson or Cordell Hull, had not purposely decided to challenge civilian control of the military—but the result of his act could be that this institutional safeguard was in danger.

Harry Truman, however history will regard him, was one of the most unpopular and unrespected of Presidents. If the people and the Congress rose behind MacArthur, supported his views, Harry Truman and his Administration were in trouble.

Sometime between 24 March and 5 April 1951, Harry Truman resolved to relieve MacArthur of his command. When the next evidence of MacArthur's insubordination arose, Truman's mind was already made up—but what occurred on 5 April 1951 in effect allowed Truman no other course.

On that date Joe Martin, the leader of the opposition in the House, rose and read a personal letter from MacArthur. Martin, of Massachusetts, had long been an isolationist, clinging beyond 1941 to the old school of American thought, much like Taft and Wherry in the Senate.

The old school of thought was honest and sincere, but contradictory. Its major premises were that America should avoid trouble overseas—but that if it arose, should smash it, without counting any cost. No entangling alliances should be made; there should be no involvement in foreign politics; but if the United States were confronted with evil opposition, if it were attacked, then it should rise in righteous wrath.

The old school was highly suspicious of the military, and preferred to cut arms spending to the bone.

There was nothing wrong with this school of thought—Americans had cleaved to it for generations, and as late as 1941 more than 70 percent of them had been against entry in world affairs—except that there was now no one to hold the far frontier. There was no Army of France, no British Navy, to strive, morally or immorally, for order in the world.

Representative Joseph W. Martin, a sincere man, stood before the House on 5 April 1951. He had written MacArthur in early March, saying, among other things, that he considered it sheer folly not to use Nationalist Chinese troops in Korea. He had asked for MacArthur's comments, and now he read them aloud:

" 'I am most grateful for your note of the eighth forwarding me a copy of your address of February 12. . . .

" 'My views and recommendations with respect to the situation created by Red China's entry into war against us in Korea have been submitted to Washington in most complete detail. Generally these views are well known and understood, as they follow the conventional pattern of meeting force with maximum counterforce as we have never failed to do in the past. Your view with respect to the utilization of the Chinese forces on Formosa is in conflict with neither logic nor this tradition.

" 'It seems strangely difficult for some to realize that here in Asia is where the Communist conspirators have elected to make their play for global conquest, and that we have joined the issue thus raised on the battlefield; that here we fight Europe's war with arms while the diplomats there still fight it with words; that if we lose this war to Communism in Asia the fall of Europe is inevitable, win it and Europe most probably would avoid war and yet preserve freedom. As you point out, we must win.

" 'There is no substitute for victory.' "

Thus, two views of war, the traditional American, the view of Wilson, Roosevelt, Marshall, and MacArthur, clashed head on with that of the new, the Great Power American, the view of Acheson, Rusk, Harriman, and Bradley.

George Catlett Marshall, one of the most splendid of men, had once said, discussing the possible entry of American troops into the Balkans rather than Western Europe in 1944, that such a move would be political rather than military in nature, might cost 100,000 more casualties, and would delay the destruction of the *Reich.* He would not allow political considerations to change the course of military operations.

And America met force with counterforce, devoting all her energies to the destruction of evil as embodied in the *Reich,* and her troops did not meet those of her Russian ally on the Vistula or the Danube. A generation of American statesmen have had to wrestle with the result.

Field Marshall Erwin Rommel once said he had no real interest in logistics. He would do the fighting; how the gasoline, tanks, and ammunition reached him was somebody else's concern.

Both Marshall and Rommel, splendid men, did not really understand the world they lived in. A war can no more be successfully fought without political concerns for the future than a panzer can roll without gas.

In 1951, defeat of Red China, whether it would have brought on general war with Russia or not, would have alienated the world. In such a world, America could then have led as Hitler led, or not at all.

History, unfortunately, is never concerned too much with where morality lies.

Wherever it lay, whoever was right, and who was wrong, MacArthur's letter to Joe Martin was insubordination.

Truman hit the ceiling. He called a meeting with Acheson, Bradley, Marshall, and Harriman. On 6 April he asked these men bluntly what they felt should be done. All were agreed that the Administration faced a serious threat.

It took an hour to hammer out the decision.

Averell Harriman, head of the Mutual Security Agency, stated that MacArthur should have been relieved two years ago. Harriman was unhappy with MacArthur's handling of some occupation matters in Japan, where he had also opposed Washington policy.

Acheson, moustached and deliberative, said he believed that MacArthur had to be relieved but that he thought it should be done very carefully. "If you relieve MacArthur, you will have the biggest fight of your Administration," he said.

Omar Bradley, head of the JCS, looked upon the question as a matter of military discipline. A true centurion, Bradley saw a clear case of insubordination; he felt MacArthur deserved relief.

Secretary of Defense George Cattlett Marshall counseled caution. He was reluctant to discipline MacArthur; it might make trouble with Congress.

President Truman let these men talk, then and later. He did not advise them that he had already made up his mind and that the "ayes had it." MacArthur would be relieved. Truman advised Marshall to reread the file of communications between Tokyo and Washington.

On 7 April Marshall reported back to Blair House that he now felt MacArthur should have been fired long ago.

On Sunday, 8 April, the Joint Chiefs of Staff concurred.

On Monday, with everyone in agreement, Truman then told them that he had made his decision after MacArthur's "pronunciamento" of 24 March. At 3:15 that afternoon, the President signed an order relieving MacArthur of all his several commands, and replacing him with Lieutenant General Matthew B. Ridgway.

Truman's intention was that this notice of relief be given MacArthur through Secretary of the Army Frank Pace, then in the Far East. Dean Acheson sent the orders through Korean Ambassador Muccio, with instructions that Pace was to proceed immediately to Tokyo, to deliver them in person.

But Pace could not be reached; he was up near the Eighth Army front, firing a howitzer in the company of General Ridgway. One of the traditions of modern war that had grown up was that distinguished visitors be taken to a firing battery of heavy artillery, suitably behind the front, and there be allowed to fire "one at the enemy," which made for a good picture and gave a feeling of active participation, all without untidy risk.

Pace could not be reached, and the message was too hot to be bandied about in lesser hands.

Later, Matt Ridgway, who had spent all afternoon in Frank Pace's company without ever learning that he was already Supreme Commander, Far East, remarked that Mr. Pace had an odd sense of humor. It did not occur to General Ridgway that Mr. Pace was as ignorant of the fact as he.

Truman then sent word to John Foster Dulles to go to Japan and inform the Japanese Yoshida Government that the change would affect them in no way. While Dulles prepared to emplane, Omar Bradley dashed into Blair House, visibly excited.

There had been a leak, Bradley said, and a Chicago paper was going to print the story of MacArthur's relief the next morning, the 11th.

A President—any President—hates to be scooped almost more than anything else. More than once such a fear has changed the course of history, and now Harry Truman decided that courtesy be damned, he could not wait until Frank Pace finished getting his kicks gallivanting around the front.

MacArthur would get his notice over the wire, at the same time everyone else in the world got it. And so he did.

At 0100, 11 April, Truman's press secretary gave a group of grousing, sleepy-eyed reporters a presidential release:

"With deep regret, I have concluded that General of the Army Douglas MacArthur is unable to give his whole-hearted support to the policies of the United States Government and of the United Nations. . . . I have, therefore, relieved General MacArthur of his commands and have designated Lieutenant General Matthew B. Ridgway as his successor.

"Full and vigorous debate on matters of national policy is a vital element in the constitutional system. . . . It is fundamental, however, that military commanders must be governed by the policies and directives issued to them . . . in time of crisis, the consideration is particularly compelling.

"General MacArthur's place in history as one of our greatest commanders is fully established. The Nation owes him a debt of gratitude for the distinguished and exceptional service he has rendered. . . . For that reason I repeat my regret at the necessity for the action I feel compelled to take in his case."

In the free chancelleries of Europe there was joy. As an indication of how deeply and consistently almost all of America's allies felt on the subject of MacArthur, at the front in Korea British battalions staged an impromptu celebration, and other U.N. units fired their guns in the air.

In the United States, most of whose people were not sure what was going on, there was shock.

That night Truman went on the air, explaining his course to the American public: "The free nations have united their strength in an effort to prevent a third world war. That war can come if the Communist leaders want it to come. But this nation and its allies will not be responsible for its coming."

There is no question but that there was an element of wishful thinking even in Truman's stand. Collective security had a fine sound, but it was still little more than a word; it would still be the United States, and the United States alone, that held the far frontier. No one else had the will or the power.

China would not be punished for its transgression. Evil would continue to exist; it would even be allowed to prosper, if it could. Peace, if and when it came, would not be moral but pragmatic.

The door would be held, and men would continue to die, not for victory, but for time.

There are men who said that the task was merely postponed and that it would be far harder in the future. There are men who said the United States should have won, or got out. History may prove them right.

But while a civilization lives, it may hope—as long as the far frontier, whether it be Korea or Berlin, is held.

* * *

General of the Army MacArthur took the news, which came to him as a slap in the face, calmly, and with good cheer. When Matt Ridgway reported to him at the *Dai Ichi* on 12 April, he was quiet, composed, and entirely helpful and friendly. Ridgway could ascertain no trace of bitterness.

Matt Ridgway personally did not feel a drive to the Yalu, or an enlargement of the war, was worth the cost. As a soldier, he did not question the President's right to do what he had done. But out of the loyalty he held in his heart for MacArthur, he was angry that the dismissal had been done so summarily.

No general, even those who disagreed with, stood in awe of, or disliked MacArthur, could feel happy at the outcome of the Case of the Haberdasher and the General.

But even these, who were with MacArthur, and even Truman, only the nation's servants, had to agree that the Republic never stood stronger.

On 11 April a violent storm broke over much of the front in Korea. It snowed, hailed in some sections, and a howling wind blew, leveling tents and stinging the eyes of the soldiers who now heard the news of the historic dismissal.

As the sky darkened and the earth seemed to shudder, one soldier remarked, "Say, do you suppose MacArthur was God, after all?"

Everybody smiled, and then the storm was gone. The war went on.

But MacArthur was not God. He was not even Caesar, as Truman had half feared. Caesar, recalled, brought his army back to Rome; MacArthur, an erect, brilliant, but an old, old man, returned across the lonely Pacific almost alone.

And the storm broke across America, violent, emotional, and as indecisive as the one that had whipped the Korean front. Where MacArthur went, millions cheered him. But even those who screamed in the crowds were not sure what they were screaming for, or against.

Men wrote Congress by the thousands, but from the letters came mostly emotion, and not much sense. Sometimes it is necessary for men to scream against a world they never made, and cannot control.

The general went before the houses of Congress, and there he spoke. Men from Fresno to Piccadilly, who had never heard MacArthur speak, who knew him only as a legend, stood transfixed at his eloquence, as it was broadcast across the world.

It was here, perhaps, that General of the Army Douglas MacArthur, soldier, aristocrat, man of God, had his greatest moment. He spoke, and he stated his case, but he did not sound the tocsin of revolt. What might have been public disgrace to a lesser man he turned into personal triumph.

There are such things as great men. Some are born, or make themselves, as Douglas MacArthur, and some, like Harry Truman, are made by the Constitution.

The storm broke, and then, like MacArthur, it faded away.

Power, after all, still stood on Pennsylvania Avenue. There was never any real possibility of congressional revolt centering around the general. The President, after all, was leader of the Democrats. They might gleefully slaughter his domestic program—after 1948 Truman got not one Fair Deal measure through Congress—but these same men had no desire to tear their party in shreds, however they felt about China.

And the leaders of the increasingly powerful Republican opposition—Bob Taft, Wherry, and Joe Martin—could hardly rally behind the general, even had he raised the standard of revolt. More than anything else, these men really wanted to get out of Korea entirely, not to expand the war into Central Asia.

It was ironic that those who screamed the loudest on MacArthur's relief were the former isolationists, and those who had consistently voted down or pared every military budget.

There was frustration in the spring of 1951, but no change of policy. The world had changed, and America was being forced to change with it. Containment, as developed by the Truman Administration, was not a satisfying answer. Millions disliked or distrusted it, but could put forth no better course. There were frustration and trauma.

The majority could no longer accept isolation as a way of life. And only the paranoid saw a true solution in atomic war.

There was nothing left but to return to the checkerboard, and to play the dangerous game.

MacArthur faded away in retirement; Ridgway soon proved, bluff paratrooper that he was, that he would not be a bull in the China shop of the *Dai Ichi*.

In the soggy, just-turning-green hills of Korea, the war went on.

* * *

First Lieutenant Leonard F. Morgan, of the Army 1st Base Post Office, arrived at Hungnam, North Korea, 12 December 1950. Morgan was an Adjutant General's Corps officer who had enlisted in 1938 and worked his way through the ranks. And over the years he had come to regard the flowing of the mails as seriously as any postman.

But at Hungnam, with the Marines and soldiers of X Corps streaming down out of the frozen hills for evacuation, Morgan was told politely but firmly that this was no time to set up in business. And just as firmly, he was ordered onto an LST for shipment to Pusan.

At Pusan, the 1st Base Post Office was billeted at the old Agricultural College Building, called universally by the troops "Pusan U." And here the P.O. had to wait until the lines got straightened out once more, and the mails could flow.

Then, on 5 February, Morgan, a small, dark, serious officer, at thirty-eight a bit grizzled for his rank, was told to take twelve enlisted men up to Suwon by air. He was to take tents and stoves and a minimum amount of postal equipment, mostly fixed credit—postal stamps.

He got into Suwon seventy-two hours after the Chinese had cleared it. It was cold as hell, with snow all over the ground, and now Morgan found out what it was like to be in what the Army called a bastard unit.

He arrived with a few tents but no mess facilities, no vehicles, or anything else. And there were no combat men in the Army Postal Unit; it strained their ability to get the tents up.

Fortunately for Morgan, he ran into Captain Bond of the 25th Division Quartermaster Company, in whose area the new APU was to be located. And Bond was a good man to know.

"I've got a big squad tent for your men, and I can feed you," Bond said. "We'll get you some litters from the Medical Company to sleep on."

Shivering in their borrowed tent, the boys of the APU decided war was hell. But as Leonard Morgan told them, "The mail must go through."

Morgan himself carried $5,000 worth of postage stamps, which he kept chained to his cot post.

But at Suwon, he dragged out some fifty-five-gallon oil drums, made a platform, and put up a sign that he was open for business. There were some 88,000 American troops in the area, from the 2nd, 3rd, 1st Cavalry, and 25th divisions, plus the Air Force. The mail came in, in truckloads.

Day and night now, handling mail and the *Stars and Stripes,* Morgan's men were kept busy. Things might be tough in the rear areas, but the mail went through.

* * *

For several hours after capture at Kunu-ri, the troops guarding Sergeant Charles B. Schlichter and the other men from his medical company marched the exhausted prisoners north. Finally, they herded them into a North Korean farmhouse, where they were allowed to rest till dark.

The men who were wounded had received no medical treatment, except for the little they could give themselves. One of the surgeons with the party, an American major, declared he had been an administrator for so long he was not up on the latest treatment. He was able to do very little to help.

With dark, the chilled, miserable men were forced outside. And now, from sundown to sunup, they were marched north. At dawn they staggered into another Korean farmhouse, where they were allowed to lie soddenly until the sun sank once more.

They received one meal a day, a handful of corn boiled in water. But all of them had been eating good United States rations, and as yet the cold and hunger hadn't really bothered them.

The single daily meal was fed to them in their canteen cups. Some men had lost or thrown their mess gear away. These ate out of their caps, or from their cupped hands, like animals.

And each day at dusk they were forced out into the stinging, freezing wind, to march north until light broke in the east. The Communists moved them by night, because they feared the United Nations air power, which still ranged over the whole of North Korea despite the retreat of the land armies; and they kept the prisoners on the road because they had taken far more POW's than had been anticipated, and they did not know what else to do with them.

For more than twenty nights, until Christmas 1950, they kept the POW's from Kunu-ri and other points marching over the hills, in circles, gradually bearing toward the Manchurian border.

Under the terrible pressure of those night marches, the meager diet, and the brutal cold, some of the American soldiers began to give up. Soon all were exhausted; many were sick.

On Christmas night, while people back home were recuperating from Christmas dinner and drinking eggnog, the men with Schlichter—now grown to several hundred—were marched over what seemed like the longest, highest mountain in Korea.

Worn out, miserable, hopeless now, several of the American POW's started to cry. One young boy gave up completely. He told Schlichter, "Sergeant, I can't go on."

Schlichter tried to argue him into continuing. But the boy refused to move. The guards came—and they were very considerate. They did not shoot or bayonet the boy, but brought a sled.

All night long, up the mountain and down its far side, other men took turns dragging the man who refused to march.

In the dawn, when the stooped, limping party halted under the harsh command of their guards, the face of the man who had been pulled on the sled was white with frost. He had frozen to death during the night.

The next day, the group of POW's arrived at a bleak, deserted bauxite mine. Here, in the little squalid huts that made up the old mining camp, the Americans were sequestered, some forty men to a hut. The valley was in no sense a true POW camp, with barbed wire, sentry posts, and the like. But it was surrounded by cruel mountains, and the guards stood about with ready guns.

As the long, bedraggled, stubble-faced column weaved its way into the mining valley, men falling out at each hut a lean collie dog ran up and down the column, barking happily. As the dog came up to sniff the strange Americans, Charles Schlichter held out a hand to the friendly animal, soothing it.

That night, Schlichter and the men in his hut ate roast dog. The other men let Schlichter, who did the honors, have the largest piece.

Later, huddled in the tiny huts, the Americans found they had to lie down twenty to a side, with their booted feet interlaced. There was so little room that they had to lie hip to hip, pressed tight against each other.

Their hips and elbows became raw before the night was over—and they also discovered something else: if a man wanted to shift his position or turn over, he could not do so without waking every other man on his side of the room.

They slept. Men who had been marched forty miles a night for almost a month, who had been fed only a ball of boiled cracked corn once a day, and who had had only fistfuls of dirty snow to drink as they stumbled along, fell down, pressed against each other, and went to sleep. Most of them were ill—with malnutrition, dysentery, untreated combat wounds. Most of them were hopeless. Some of them were already a little crazy.

Still, they were Americans, and still men. It was here, in this dirty mining camp that came to be called Death Valley, that the Chinese accomplished a terrible thing.

Here, little by little, the Communists took away their manhood.

25

Proud Legions

We was rotten 'fore we started—we was never disciplined;
We made it out a favour if an order was obeyed.
Yes, every little drummer 'ad 'is rights an' wrongs to mind,
So we had to pay for teachin'—an' we paid!
—Rudyard Kipling, "That Day"

During the first months of American intervention in Korea, reports from the front burst upon an America and world stunned beyond belief. Day after day, the forces of the admitted first power of the earth reeled backward under the blows of the army of a nation of nine million largely illiterate peasants, the product of the kind of culture advanced nations once overawed with gunboats. Then, after fleeting victory, Americans fell back once more before an army of equally illiterate, lightly armed Chinese.

The people of Asia had changed, true. The day of the gunboat and a few Marines would never return. But that was not the whole story. The people of the West had changed, too. They forgot that the West had dominated not only by arms, but by superior force of will.

During the summer of 1950, and later, Asians would watch. Some, friends of the West, would even smile. And none of them would ever forget.

News reports in 1950 talked of vast numbers, overwhelming hordes of fanatic North Koreans, hundreds of monstrous tanks, against which the thin United States forces could not stand. In these reports there was truth, but not the whole truth.

The American units were outnumbered. They were outgunned. They were given an impossible task at the outset.

But they were also outfought.

In July, 1950, one news commentator rather plaintively remarked that warfare had not changed so much, after all. For some reason, ground troops still

289

seemed to be necessary, in spite of the atom bomb. And oddly and unfortunately, to this gentleman, man still seemed to be an important ingredient in battle. Troops were getting killed, in pain and fury and dust and filth. What had happened to the widely heralded pushbutton warfare where skilled, immaculate technicians who had never suffered the misery and ignominy of basic training blew each other to kingdom come like gentlemen?

In this unconsciously plaintive cry lies buried a great deal of the truth why the United States was almost defeated.

Nothing had happened to pushbutton warfare; its emergence was at hand. Horrible weapons that could destroy every city on earth were at hand—at too many hands. But pushbutton warfare meant Armageddon, and Armageddon, hopefully, will never be an end of national policy.

Americans in 1950 rediscovered something that since Hiroshima they had forgotten: you may fly over a land forever; you may bomb it, atomize it, pulverize it and wipe it clean of life—but if you desire to defend it, protect it, and keep it for civilization, you must do this on the ground, the way the Roman legions did, by putting your young men into the mud.

The object of warfare is to dominate a portion of the earth, with its peoples, for causes either just or unjust. It is not to destroy the land and people, unless you have gone wholly mad.

Pushbotton war has its place. There is another kind of conflict—crusade, jihad, holy war, call it what you choose. It has been loosed before, with attendant horror but indecisive results. In the past, there were never means enough to exterminate all the unholy, whether Christian, Moslem, Protestant, Papist, or Communist. If jihad is preached again, undoubtedly the modern age will do much better.

Americans, denying from moral grounds that war can ever be a part of politics, inevitably tend to think in terms of holy war—against militarism, against fascism, against bolshevism. In the postwar age, uneasy, disliking and fearing the unholiness of Communism, they have prepared for jihad. If their leaders blow the trumpet, or if their homeland is attacked, their millions are agreed to be better dead than Red.

Any kind of war short of jihad was, is, and will be unpopular with the people. Because such wars are fought with legions, and Americans, even when they are proud of them, do not like their legions. They do not like to serve in them, nor even to allow them to be what they must.

For legions have no ideological or spiritual home in the liberal society. The liberal society has no use or need for legions—as its prophets have long proclaimed.

Except that in this world are tigers.

*   *   *

The men of the Inmun Gun and the CCF were peasant boys, tough, inured to hunger and hardship. One-third of them had been in battle and knew what battle meant. They had been indoctrinated in Communism, but no high percentage of them were fanatic. Most of them, after all, were conscripts, and unskilled.

They were not half so good soldiers as the bronzed men who followed Rommel in the desert, or the veterans who slashed down toward Bastogne.

They were well armed, but their weapons were no better than those of United States design, if as good.

But the American soldier of 1950, though the same breed of man, was not half so good as the battalions that had absorbed Rommel's bloody lessons, or stood like steel in the Ardennes.

The weapons his nation had were not in his hands, and those that were were old and worn.

Since the end of World War II ground weapons had been developed, but none had been procured. There were plenty of the old arms around, and it has always been a Yankee habit to make do. The Army was told to make do.

In 1950 its vehicles in many cases would not run. Radiators were clogged, engines gone. When ordered to Korea, some units towed their transport down to the LST's, because there was no other way to get it to the boat. Tires and tubes had a few miles left in them, and were kept—until they came apart on Korean roads.

In Japan, where the divisions were supposedly guarding our former enemies, most of the small arms had been reported combat unserviceable. Rifle barrels were worn smooth. Mortar mounts were broken, and there were no longer any spare barrels for machine guns.

Radios were short, and those that were available would not work.

Ammunition, except small arms, was "hava-no."

These things had been reported. The Senate knew them; the people heard them. But usually the Army was told, "Next year."

Even a rich society cannot afford nuclear bombs, supercarriers, foreign aid, five million new cars a year, long-range bombers, the highest standard of living in the world, and a million new rifles.

Admittedly, somewhere you have to cut and choose.

But guns are hardware, and man, not hardware, is the ultimate weapon. In 1950 there were not enough men, either—less than 600,000 to carry worldwide responsibilities, including recruiting; for service in the ranks has never been on the Metropolitan Life Insurance Company's preferred list of occupations.

And in these 600,000 men themselves the trouble lay.

There was a reason.

Before 1939 the United States Army was small, but it was professional. Its tiny officers corps was parochial, but true. Its members devoted their time to the study of war, caring little what went on in the larger society around them. They were centurions, and the society around them not their concern.

When so ordered, they went to war. Spreading themselves thinner still, they commanded and trained the civilians who heeded the trumpet's call. The civilians did the fighting, of course—but they did it the Army's way.

In 1861 millions of volunteers donned blue or gray. Millions of words have been written on American valor, but few books dwell on the fact that of the sixty important battles, fifty-five were commanded on both sides by West Pointers, and on one side in the remaining five.

In 1917 four million men were mustered in. Few of them liked it, but again they did things the way the professionals wanted them done.

The volunteers came and went, and the Army changed not at all.

But since the Civil War, the Army had neither the esteem nor the favor of public or government. Liberal opinion, whether business-liberal or labor-liberal, dominated the United States after the destruction of the South, and the illiberal Army grew constantly more alienated from its own society.

In a truly liberal society, centurions have no place. For centurions, when they put on the soldier, do not retain the citizen. They are never citizens to begin with.

There was and is no danger of military domination of the nation. The Constitution gave Congress the power of life or death over the military, and they have always accepted the fact. The danger has been the other way around— the liberal society, in its heart, wants not only domination of the military, but acquiesence of the military toward the liberal view of life.

Domination and control society should have. The record of military rule, from the burnished and lazy Praetorians to the *juntas* of Latin America, to the attempted fiasco of the *Légion Étrangère,* are pages of history singularly foul in odor.

But acquiesence society may not have, if it wants an army worth a damn. By the very nature of its mission, the military must maintain a hard and illiberal view of life and the world. Society's purpose is to live; the military's is to stand ready, if need be, to die.

Soldiers are rarely fit to rule—but they must be fit to fight.

The military is in essence a tool, to be used by its society. If its society is good, it may hope to be used honorably, even if badly. If its society is criminal, it may be, like the *Wehrmacht,* unleashed upon a helpless world.

But when the *Wehrmacht* dashed against the world, it was brought to ruin, not by a throng of amateurs, but by well-motivated, well-generaled Allied troops, who had learned their military lessons.

Some men, of kind intention, are always dubious because the generals of the *Wehrmacht* and the men of West Point and V.M.I. and Leavenworth read the same books, sometimes hold the same view of life.

Why not? German plumbers, Americans plumbers, use the same manuals, and look into the same kind of water.

In 1861, and 1917, the Army acted upon the civilian, changing him. But in 1945 something new happened. Suddenly, without precedent, perhaps because of changes in the emerging managerial society, professional soldiers of high rank had become genuinely popular with the public. In 1861, and in 1917, the public gave the generals small credit, talked instead of the gallant militia. Suddenly, at the end of World War II, society embraced the generals.

And here it ruined them.

They had lived their lives in semibitter alienation from their own culture (What's the matter, Colonel; can't you make it on the outside?) but now they were sought after, offered jobs in business, government, on college campuses.

Humanly, the generals liked the acclaim. Humanly, they wanted it to continue. And when, as usual after all our wars, there came a great civilian clamor to change all the things in the army the civilians hadn't liked, humanly, the generals could not find it in their hearts to tell the public to go to hell.

It was perfectly understandable that large numbers of men who served didn't like the service. There was no reason why they should. They served only because there had been a dirty job that had to be done. Admittedly, the service was not perfect; no human institution having power over men can ever be. But many of the abuses the civilians complained about had come not from true professionals but from men with quickie diplomas, whose brass was much more apt to go to their heads than to those of men who had waited twenty years for leaves and eagles.

In 1945, somehow confusing the plumbers with the men who pulled the chain, the public demanded that the Army be changed to conform with decent, liberal society.

The generals could have told them to go to hell and made it stick. A few heads would have rolled, a few stars would have been lost. But without acquiescence Congress could no more emasculate the Army than it could alter the nature of the State Department. It could have abolished it, or weakened it even more than it did—but it could not have changed its nature. But the generals could not have retained their new popularity by antagonizing the public, and suddenly popularity was very important to them. Men such as Doolittle, Eisenhower, and Marshall rationalized. America, with postwar duties around the world, would need a bigger peacetime Army than ever before. Therefore, it needed to be popular with the people. And it should be made pleasant, so that more men would enlist. And since Congress wouldn't do much about upping pay, every man should have a chance to become a sergeant, instead of one in twenty. But, democratically, sergeants would not draw much more pay than privates.

And since some officers and noncoms had abused their powers, rather than make sure officers and noncoms were better than ever, it would be simpler and more expedient—and popular—to reduce those powers. Since Americans were by nature egalitarian, the Army had better go that route too. Other professional people, such as doctors and clergymen, had special privileges—but officers, after all, had no place in the liberal society, and had better be cut down to size.

The Doolittle Board of 1945–1946 met, listened to less than half a hundred complaints, and made its recommendations. The so-called "caste system" of the Army was modified. Captains, by fiat, suddenly ceased to be gods, and sergeants, the hard-bitten backbone of any army, were told to try to be just some of the boys. Junior officers had a great deal of their power to discipline taken away from them. They could no longer inflict any real punishment, short of formal court-martial, nor could they easily reduce ineffective N.C.O.'s. Understandably, their own powers shaky, they cut the ground completely away from their N.C.O.'s.

A sergeant, by shouting at some sensitive yardbird, could get his captain into a lot of trouble. For the real effect of the Doolittle recommendations was psychological. Officers had not been made wholly powerless—but they felt that they had been slapped in the teeth. The officer corps, by 1946 again wholly professional, did not know how to live with the newer code.

One important thing was forgotten by the citizenry: by 1946 all the intellectual and sensitive types had said goodbye to the Army—they hoped for good. The new men coming in now were the kind of men who join armies the world over, blank-faced, unmolded—and they needed shaping. They got it; but it wasn't the kind of shaping they needed.

Now an N.C.O. greeted new arrivals with a smile. Where once he would have told them they made him sick to his stomach, didn't look tough enough to make a go of his outfit, he now led them meekly to his company commander. And this clean-cut young man, who once would have sat remote at the right hand of God in his orderly room, issuing orders that crackled like thunder, now smiled too. "Welcome aboard, gentlemen. I am your company commander; I'm here to help you. I'll try to make your stay both pleasant and profitable."

This was all very democratic and pleasant—but it is the nature of young men to get away with anything they can, and soon these young men found they could get away with plenty.

A soldier could tell a sergeant to blow it. In the old Army he might have been bashed, and found immediately what the rules were going to be. In the Canadian Army—which oddly enough no American liberals have found fascistic or bestial—he would have been marched in front of his company commander, had his pay reduced, perhaps even been confined for thirty days, with no damaging mark on his record. He would have learned, instantly, that orders are to be obeyed.

But in the new American Army, the sergeant reported such a case to his C.O. But the C.O. couldn't do anything drastic or educational to the man; for any real action, he had to pass the case up higher. And nobody wanted to court-martial the man, to put a permanent damaging mark on his record. The most likely outcome was for the man to be chided for being rude, and requested to do better in the future.

Some privates, behind their smirks, liked it fine.

Pretty soon, the sergeants, realizing the score, started to fraternize with the men. Perhaps, through popularity, they could get something done. The junior officers, with no sergeants to knock heads, decided that the better part of valor was never to give an unpopular order.

The new legions carried the old names, displayed the old, proud colors, with their gallant battle streamers. The regimental mottoes still said things like "Can Do." In their neat, fitted uniforms and new shiny boots—there was money for these—the troops looked good. Their appearance made the generals smile.

What they lacked couldn't be seen, not until the guns sounded.

There is much to military training that seems childish, stultifying, and even brutal. But one essential part of breaking men into military life is the removal of misfits—and in the service a man is a misfit who cannot obey orders, any orders, and who cannot stand immense and searing mental and physical pressure.

For his own sake and for that of those around him, a man must be prepared for the awful, shrieking moment of truth when he realizes he is all alone on a hill ten thousand miles from home, and that he may be killed in the next second.

The young men of America, from whatever strata, are raised in a permissive society. The increasing alienation of their education from the harsher realities of life makes their reorientation, once enlisted, doubly important.

Prior to 1950, they got no reorientation. They put on the uniform, but continued to get by, doing things rather more or less. They had no time for sergeants.

As discipline deteriorated, the generals themselves were hardly affected. They still had their position, their pomp and ceremonies. Surrounded by professionals of the old school, largely field rank, they still thought their rod was iron, for, seemingly, their own orders were obeyed.

But ground battle is a series of platoon actions. No longer can a field commander stand on a hill, like Lee or Grant, and oversee his formations. Orders in combat—the orders that kill men or get them killed, are not given by generals, or even by majors. They are given by lieutenants and sergeants, and sometimes by PFC's.

When a sergeant gives a soldier an order in battle, it must have the same weight as that of a four-star general.

Such orders cannot be given by men who are some of the boys. Men willingly take orders to die only from those they are trained to regard as superior beings.

It was not until the summer of 1950, when the legions went forth, that the generals realized what they had agreed to, and what they had wrought.

The Old Army, outcast and alien and remote from the warm bosom of society, officer and man alike, ordered into Korea, would have gone without questioning. It would have died without counting. As on Bataan, it would not have listened for the angel's trumpet or the clarion call. It would have heard the hard sound of its own bugles, and hard-bitten, cynical, wise in bitter ways, it would have kept its eyes on its sergeants.

It would have died. It would have retreated, or surrendered, only in the last extremity. In the enemy prison camps, exhausted, sick, it would have spat upon its captors, despising them to the last.

It would have died, but it might have held.

One aftermath of the Korean War has been the passionate attempt in some military quarters to prove the softness and decadence of American society as a whole, because in the first six months of that war there were wholesale failures. It has been a pervasive and persuasive argument, and it has raised its own counterargument, equally passionate.

The trouble is, different men live by different myths.

There are men who would have a society pointed wholly to fighting and resistance to Communism, and this would be a very different society from the one Americans now enjoy. It might succeed on the battlefield, but its other failures can be predicted.

But the infantry battlefield also cannot be remade to the order of the prevailing midcentury opinion of American sociologists.

The recommendations of the so-called Doolittle Board of 1945–1946, which destroyed so much of the will—if not the actual power—of the military traditionalists, and left them bitter, and confused as to how to act, was based on experience in World War II. In that war, as in all others, millions of civilians were fitted arbitrarily into a military pattern already centuries old. It had once fitted Western society; it now coincided with American customs and thinking no longer.

What the Doolittle Board tried to do, in small measure, was to bring the professional Army back into the new society. What it could not do, in 1946, was to gauge the future.

By 1947 the United States Army had returned, in large measure, to the pattern it had known prior to 1939. The new teen-agers who now joined it were much the same stripe of men who had joined in the old days. They were not intellectuals, they were not completely fired with patriotism, or motivated by the draft; nor was an aroused public, eager to win a war, breathing down their necks.

A great many of them signed up for three squares and a sack.

Over several thousand years of history, man has found a way to make soldiers out of this kind of man, as he comes, basically unformed, to the colors. It is a way with great stresses and great strains. It cannot be said it is wholly good. Regimentation is not good, completely, for any man.

But no successful army has been able to avoid it. It is an unpleasant necessity, seemingly likely to go on forever, as long as men fight in fields and mud.

One thing should be made clear.

The Army could have fought World War III, just as it could have fought World War II, under the new rules. During 1941–1945 the average age of the United States soldier was in the late twenties, and the ranks were seasoned with maturity from every rank of life, as well as intelligence.

In World War III, or any war with national emotional support, this would have again been true. Soldiers would have brought their motivation with them, firmed by understanding and maturity.

The Army could have fought World War III in 1950, but it could not fight Korea.

As a case in point, take the experiences of one platoon sergeant in Fort Lewis, Washington. During the big war he had held sway over a platoon of seventy-two enlisted men. The platoon was his to run; the officers rarely came around the barracks.

The platoon sergeant was a reasonable man, in charge of reasonable men, who knew why they were in the Army. Their average age was thirty-two; one-fourth of them, roughly, were college trained. Almost all of them were skilled, in one trade or another.

This kind of man cannot be made to dig a six-by-six hole to bury a carelessly dropped cigarette, nor double-timed around the PX on Sunday morning.

The platoon sergeant relieved a multiple-striped young idiot—as he termed the man—who tried just this. The platoon, as platoons can, ruined the former sergeant.

The new platoon sergeant told his men the barracks needed cleaning, but if everyone would cooperate, each man clean his own area each day, he could get a few men off detail to clean the common areas, such as the latrine, and there need be no GI parties.

The platoon cooperated. There were no GI parties, no extra details. A few men went off the track, now and then; the older men of the platoon handled them quietly, without bothering the platoon sergeant.

This was discipline. Ideally, it should well up out of men, not be imposed upon them.

The platoon prospered. It won the battalion plaque for best barracks so often it was allowed to keep the plaque in perpetuity.

Even after VJ-Day, every man fell out for reveille, promptly, because the platoon sergeant explained to them this was the way the game was played. And the platoon was proud of itself; every man knew it was a good outfit, just a little better than the next.

Then, one by one, the men went home, as the war ended.

The platoon sergeant now was promoted to first sergeant, six stripes, an enlisted god who walked. He got a new company of several platoons, all filled with the new, callow faces entering the Army to be trained.

The war was over, and every man coming in knew it.

The first sergeant, wise now in the ways of handling men, as he thought, carefully explained to the newcomers that the barracks must be cleaned, but if everyone would cooperate, each man clean his own area each day, there would be no GI parties, and there would be passes.

On Saturday the barracks were dirty.

The sergeant, who thought that men needed only to understand what was required to obey, carefully explained what he wanted. Friday, with a great deal of hollering, shouting, and horseplay, the new men cleaned the barracks.

On Saturday, the barracks were still dirty, and the captain made a few pointed remarks to the sergeant.

The sergeant got everyone together, and told them how it was going to be. These men on the mops, these men on the brooms, these men with the lye soap. No hollering or sloshing of water or horseplay—just clean the goddam barracks.

It took most of Friday night, and the men had to stay in the latrines to clean their rifles, but they cleaned the barracks. A few of them got out of hand, but there were no older hands who could—or would—hold them in check. The sergeant handled each of these himself.

The platoon prospered, but it wasn't easy, particularly on the sergeant. Gradually, he came to realize that seventeen- and eighteen-year-olds, mostly from the disadvantaged areas of society, had no feeling of responsibility to the Army or to the Republic for which it stood. They were not - self-disciplined, and they tended to resent authority, even more than the college men and skilled artisans he had commanded before. Probably some had resented their parents; definitely most resented the sergeant, even as most of them, back in their home towns, had instinctively resented the police.

There is no getting around the fact that cops and sergeants spoil your fun.

The platoon prospered, as a sort of jail, until someone wrote to his congressman. After that the captain spoke to the sergeant, telling him that it was peacetime and that perhaps the real purpose of an Army was not to learn to use the bayonet, but to engage in athletics and take Wednesday afternoons off.

The sergeant, now a confused young man with six stripes who walked, left the Army, and graduated from college. If the Army was going to hell, it was a lot more pleasant to watch it go to hell from the Officer's Club than from the Orderly Room.

A decade after Korea, the military traditionalists still grind their teeth. The sociologists still keep a wary eye on them. Both still try to use the Korean battleground, and its dreary POW camps, to further their own particular myths of human behavior.

Probably, both are wrong.

The military have the prepondence of fact with them as far as Korea was concerned. Korea was the kind of war that since the dawn of history was fought by professionals, by legions. It was fought by men who soon knew they had small support or sympathy at home, who could read in the papers statements by prominent men that they should be withdrawn. It was fought by men whom the Army—at its own peril—had given neither training nor indoctrination, nor the hardness and bitter pride men must have to fight a war in which they do not in their hearts believe.

The Army needed legions, but society didn't want them. It wanted citizen-soldiers.

But the sociologists are right—absolutely right—in demanding that the centurion view of life not be imposed upon America. In a holy, patriotic war—like that fought by the French in 1793, or as a general war against Communism will be—America can get a lot more mileage out of citizen-soldiers than it can from legions.

No one has suggested that perhaps there should be two sets of rules, one for the professional Army, which may have to fight in far places, without the declaration of war, and without intrinsic belief in the value of its dying, for reasons of policy, chessmen on the checkerboard of diplomacy; and one for the high-minded, enthusiastic, and idealistic young men who come aboard only when the ship is sinking.

The other answer is to give up Korea-type wars, and to surrender great-power status, and a resultant hope of order—our own decent order—in the world. But America is rich and fat and very, very noticeable in this world.

It is a forlorn hope that we should be left alone.

In the first six months America suffered a near debacle because her Regular Army fighting men were the stuff of legions, but they had not been made into legionaries.

America was not more soft or more decadent than it had been twenty years earlier. It was confused, badly, on its attitudes toward war. It was still bringing up its youth to think there were no tigers, and it was still reluctant to forge them guns to shoot tigers.

Many of America's youth, in the Army, faced horror badly because they had never been told they would have to face horror, or that horror is very normal in our unsane world. It had not been ground into them that they would have to obey their officers, even if the orders got them killed.

It has been a long, long time since American citizens have been able to take down the musket from the mantelpiece and go tiger hunting. But they still cling to the belief that they can do so, and do it well, without training.

This is the error that leads some men to cry out that Americans are decadent.

If Americans in 1950 were decadent, so were the rabble who streamed miserably into Valley Forge, where von Steuben made soldiers out of them. If American society had no will to defend itself, neither did it in 1861, at First Manassas, or later at Shiloh, when whole regiments of Americans turned tail and ran.

The men who lay warm and happy in their blankets at Kasserine, as the panzers rolled toward them in the dawn, were decadent, by this reasoning.

The problem is not that Americans are soft but that they simply will not face what war is all about until they have had their teeth kicked in. They will not face the fact that the military professionals, while some have ideas about society in general that are distorted and must be watched, still know better than anyone else how a war is won.

Free society cannot be oriented toward the battlefield—Sparta knew that trap—but some adjustments must be made, as the squabbling Athenians learned to their sorrow.

The sociologists and psychologists of Vienna had no answer to the Nazi bayonets, when they crashed against their doors. The soldiers of the democratic world did.

More than once, as at Valley Forge, after Bull Run, and Kasserine, the world has seen an American army rise from its own ashes, reorient itself, grow hard and bitter, knowledgeable and disciplined and tough.

In 1951, after six months of being battered, the Eighth Army in Korea rose from its own ashes of despair. No man who was there still believes Americans in the main are decadent, just as no man who saw Lieutenant General Matt Ridgway in operation doubts the sometime greatness of men.

> *He who supposes all men to be brave at all times . . . does not realize that the courage of troops must be reborn daily, that nothing is so changeable, that the true skill of a general consists of knowing how to guarantee it by his positions, dispositions, and those traits of genius that characterize great captains.*

—From the French of Maurice de Saxe, REVERIES ON THE ART OF WAR.

When Lieutenant General Ridgway left Tokyo to assume command of the Eighth Army on 26 December 1950, he asked MacArthur in parting, "General, if I get over there and find the situation warrants it, do I have your permission to attack?"

MacArthur's aged face cracked wide in a grin.

"Do whatever you think best, Matt. The Eighth Army is yours."

These were, as Ridgway said later, the sort of orders to put heart in a soldier. And Ridgway's own first task was to put heart in the Eighth Army.

Matt Ridgway came to Korea convinced that the United States Army could beat any Asiatic horde that lived to its knees. He quickly found that on this subject he was a majority of one.

The Eighth Army was not only pulling south; it had no great desire to meet the Chinese. Contact over much of the front was broken. There was almost no patrolling.

When Ridgway asked where the Chinese were, and in what strength, he was shown a vague goose egg on the map to the north of the Eighth Army in which was inscribed the figure 174,000. More than this no one knew, and no one was making concerted efforts to find out. The Eighth Army had had its fill of Chinese-hunting in the north.

But if the Eighth Army expected General Matt Ridgway to be satisfied with that, they had another think coming.

Ridgway began to hammer away. At first, realizing the problem, he talked of simple things: aggressive patrolling, maintaining contact at all costs, supply, and firepower. He talked of the most basic thing of all, leadership. He was as blunt or as gentle as the situation called for.

He told his senior commanders the simple truth that America's power and prestige were at stake out here, and whether they believed in this war or not, they were going to have to fight it. He would help provide the tools, but they would have to provide their own guts.

If the American Armed Forces could not beat the hordes of Red China in the field, then it made no difference how many new autos Detroit could produce.

Everywhere Matt Ridgway went, however, he found the same question in men's minds: *What the hell are we doing in this godforsaken place?*

If men had been told, *Destroy the evil of Bolshevism,* they might have understood. But they did not understand why the line must be held or why the Taehan Minkuk—that miserable, stinking, undemocratic country—must be protected.

The question itself never concerned Matt Ridgway. At the age of fifty-six, more than thirty years a centurion, to him the answer was simple. The loyalty he gave, and expected, precluded the slightest questioning of orders. This he said.

But to a generation brought up to hold some loyalties lightly, and to question many things, this was not enough. To these men Ridgway said:

The real issues are whether the power of Western Civilization, as God has permitted it to flower in our own beloved lands, shall defy and defeat Communism; whether the rule of men who shoot their prisoners, enslave their citizens, and deride the dignity of man, shall displace the rule of those to whom the individual and his individual rights are sacred; whether we are to survive with God's hand to guide and lead us, or to perish in the dead existence of a Godless world.

Under General Ridgway's hammering, the Eighth Army took the offensive within thirty days. After 25 January it never really again lost the initiative. At Chipyong-ni, the battle that presaged what was to come all spring, it was the Chinese who melted away into the snow-draped hills, leaving their dead behind.

Under a new, firm hand, and with the taste of Chinese blood, the Eighth Army found itself. Ridgway made legions.

The ranks were salted now with veterans, men wounded and returned to duty, and were led by men like Ridgway, Captain Muñoz, and Lieutenant Long, who had been through the drill before, who had been from the Naktong to the Yalu, and had learned, as Americans had always had to learn, how to fight this new-old war.

They had learned the Chinese could be cunning, but also stupid. Failing to meet quick success, he could not change his plan. Often he continued an operation long after it had turned into disaster, wasting thousands of his troops. Lacking air cover, artillery, and armor, his hordes of riflemen could be—and were—slaughtered, as the Eighth Army learned to roll with the punches and to strike back hard.

Again and again, with the prodigal use of men, he could crack the U.N. line at a given point. But the men at the point had learned to hold, inflicting terrible losses, and even if the line gave, the Chinese could not exploit, while U.N. reinforcements, mechanized, rushed to deploy in front of them and to their flanks.

In the terrain of South Korea, battle was more open, and in open battle no amount of savage cunning could substitute for firepower. The Chinese could not even apply superior combat power to the 135-mile line. The truth, that a backward nation can never put as many well-armed men into the field and support them as can even a small-sized industrial country, became apparent. Chinese replacements, even with Russian aid, were often ill equipped and ill trained.

The press still reported human seas and overwhelming hordes, but except where they massed for a breakthrough, the Chinese remained apart and in moderate numbers on the line. Front-line soldiers began to joke: "Say, Joe, how many hordes are there in a Chink platoon?" Or, "We were attacked by two hordes last night. We killed both of them."

But the Chinese retained the will to fight.

The drive northward was not easy.

As many years earlier, when the cavalry fighting on the Plains had developed leaders such as Miles, Crook, and Ranald Mackenzie, men who rode hard, made cold camps, threw away their sabers, and moved without bugle calls, putting aside all the things they had learned in the War Between the States—but who had driven the Indians without surcease, hammering them across the snows and mountains until their women sickened and their infants died and they lost their heart for war, so the Army developed men who learned to fight in Asia.

Soldiers learned to travel light, but with full canteen and bandoleer, and to climb the endless hills. They learned to hold fast when the enemy flowed at them, because it was the safest thing to do. They learned to displace in good order when they had to. They learned to listen and obey. They learned all the things Americans have always learned from Appomattox to Berlin.

Above all, they learned to kill.

On the frontier, there is rarely gallantry or glamour to wars, whether they are against red Indians or Red Chinese. There is only killing.

Men of a tank battalion set spikes on the forward sponsons of their tanks, and to these affixed Chinese skulls. This battalion had come back from Kuniri, and the display matched their mood. They were ordered to remove the skulls, but the mood remained.

In Medic James Mount's company, there was a platoon sergeant named "Gypsy" Martin. Martin carried a full canteen and bandoleer, but he also wore a bandanna and earring, and he had tiny bells on his boots. Gypsy Martin hated Chinese; he hated gooks, and he didn't care who knew it.

In anything but war, Martin was the kind of man who is useless.

In combat, as the 24th Division drove north, men could hear Gypsy yell his hatred, as they heard his M-1 bark death. When Gypsy yelled, his men went forward; he was worth a dozen rational, decent men in those bloody valleys. His men followed him, to the death.

When Gypsy Martin finally bought it, they found him lying among a dozen "gooks," his rifle empty, its stock broken. Other than in battle, Sergeant Martin was no good. To Jim Mount's knowledge, he got no medals, for medals depend more on who writes for them than what was done.

It made Jim Mount think.

The values composing civilization and the values required to protect it are normally at war. Civilization values sophistication, but in an armed force sophistication is a millstone.

The Athenian commanders before Salamis, it is reported, talked of art and of the Acropolis, in sight of the Persian fleet. Beside their own campfires, the Greek hoplites chewed garlic and joked about girls.

Without its tough spearmen, Hellenic culture would have had nothing to give the world. It would not have lasted long enough. When Greek culture became so sophisticated that its common men would no longer fight to the death, as at Thermopylae, but became devious and clever, a horde of Roman farm boys overran them.

The time came when the descendants of Macedonians who had slaughtered Asians till they could no longer lift their arms went pale and sick at the sight of the havoc wrought by the Roman *gladius Hispanicus* as it carved its way toward Hellas.

The Eighth Army, put to the fire and blooded, rose from its own ashes in a killing mood. They went north, and as they went they destroyed Chinese and what was left of the towns and cities of Korea. They did not grow sick at the sight of blood.

By 7 March they stood on the Han. They went through Seoul, and reduced it block by block. When they were finished, the massive railway station had no roof, and thousands of buildings were pocked by tank fire. Of Seoul's original more than a million souls, less than two hundred thousand still lived in the ruins. In many of the lesser cities of Korea, built of wood and wattle, only the foundation, and the vault, of the old Japanese bank remained.

The people of Chosun, not Americans or Chinese, continued to lose the war.

At the end of March the Eighth Army was across the parallel.

General Ridgway wrote, "The American flag never flew over a prouder, tougher, more spirited and more competent fighting force than was Eighth Army as it drove north. . . ."

Ridgway had no great interest in real estate. He did not strike for cities and towns, but to kill Chinese. The Eighth Army killed them, by the thousands, as its infantry drove them from the hills and as its air caught them fleeing in the valleys.

By April 1951, the Eighth Army had again proved Erwin Rommel's assertion that American troops knew less but learned faster than any fighting men he had opposed. The Chinese seemed not to learn at all, as they repeated Chipyong-ni again and again.

Americans had learned, and learned well. The tragedy of American arms, however, is that having an imperfect sense of history Americans sometimes forget as quickly as they learn.

26

Gloster Hill

They will remember for a little while in England. The soldier does have his day. I want to remind you this afternoon that it is not enough to remember now. We've got to show what we think of their sacrifice in the way we conduct ourselves in the days ahead.

—The chaplain of the 1st Battalion, Gloucestershire Regiment, at a memorial service in Korea, April 1951.

I N THE SUMMER of 1914 the nations of Europe sprang to arms in an uproar of popular hysteria. The French Republic raised a hundred divisions in ninety days. The German Empire had its reservists in Belgium within weeks, and the United Kingdom soon sent millions of men onto the battle-fields of Flanders, where nine hundred thousand of them lie buried beside more than a million French comrades-in-arms.

In 1940, with less enthusiasm but with equal will, Europe again waged internecine war. The Third Republic lost half a million dead, and went down to humiliating defeat and captivity. The British Empire lived its finest hour, but put its manpower and resources to such strain that they would not soon recover.

Victory, each time, was a will-o'-the -wisp.

Americans, who were largely spared these bloodbaths, often cannot understand why, when the jaws of hell yawned once more in 1950, few Europeans showed much inclination to rush into them.

Twice in a generation Europeans had "defended themselves," and now, while America blew an urgent trumpet, urging them to prepare to defend themselves once more against the Bear, response was slower and much more uncertain than Americans desired.

The famous British Navy was a shell in 1950. France, which had levied a hundred divisions in a matter of days, could not raise twenty-five given a decade. It was as much as an alarmed United States could do to persuade these nations, with their smaller allies, partially to rearm in defense of their own homelands, under NATO.

Slowly, painfully, under the menace of overt Communist aggression, the armed forces of NATO became reality, but America's North Atlantic allies were not willing to fight in remote Korea. They were, actually, already fighting part of that struggle in other places.

The British had troubles in Malaya, and other areas.

In Vietnam, De Vigny's centurions, hamstrung by a weak and hesitant government that had neither the courage to support nor to withdraw them, were fighting the Communist Vietminh to the death.

Inevitably, illuminating the woes that America had fallen heir to, the burden of the fighting in Korea fell upon the United States and the Taehan Minkuk.

The maximum military support rendered by members of the United Nations to the Republic of Korea was as follows:

Nation	*Armed Forces Committed*
United States of America	7 Army divisions; 1 Marine division; army and corps HQ's, almost all logistical and support forces. 1 tactical air force and supporting elements; 1 combat cargo command, air; 2 medium bombardment wings. 1 complete naval fleet, including a fast carrier task group, blockade and escort forces, reconnaissance and antisubmarine units, supply and repair units; military sea transport services.
United Kingdom	2 army brigades of 5 infantry battalions; 2 field artillery regiments; 1 armored regiment. 1 aircraft carrier, 2 cruisers, 8 destroyers, with Marine and support units.
Canada	1 army brigade of 3 infantry battalions; 1 artillery regiment; 1 armored regiment. 3 destroyers, 1 air transport squadron.
Turkey	1 army brigade of 6,000 men.
Australia	2 infantry battalions; 1 fighter squadron; 1 air transport squadron; 1 carrier, 2 destroyers, 1 frigate.
Thailand	1 regimental combat team of 4,000 men; 2 corvettes, 1 air transport squadron.
Philippines	1 regimental combat team.
France	1 infantry battalion; 1 gunboat.
Greece	1 infantry battalion; 1 air transport squadron.
New Zealand	1 artillery regiment; 2 frigates.
Netherlands	1 infantry battalion; 1 destroyer.
Colombia	1 infantry battalion; 1 frigate.
Belgium	1 infantry battalion.
Ethiopia	1 infantry battalion.
South Africa	1 fighter squadron.
Luxembourg	1 infantry company.

In addition the Scandinavian nations, with Italy, furnished hospital units. India, conspicuously neutral, sent a field ambulance unit. Other nations furnished food, or money, in limited amounts.

The United States' contribution was ten times that of all other nations combined, excepting the Republic of Korea. The Taehan Minkuk received wholesale American aid, of course—but it suffered the devastation of most of its territory; its cities were destroyed, and it lost 1,312,836 men, women, and children, soldier and civilian alike, during the course of the war, more than one in twenty of its total population.

But while the troops sent by U.N. members were small in number, they were usually high in courage and effectiveness. Most of them, from the six-foot Imperial Guardsmen of Haile Selassie, to the half-wild Algerians of the French battalion, were professional soldiers. Some, like the British, were recalled reservists. Almost all came from units of long history and proud tradition in their native armies.

Most of them, from the bayonet-wielding Turks to the knife-swinging Thais, earned the admiration of American troops.

A few of them wrote proud history.

At the first of April 1951, the U.N. forces, now half a million strong, had crossed the parallel in most places. The CCF, bleeding badly from multiple wounds inflicted by air, sea, and ground action, were hurrying more and more troops into North Korea, until their strength reached three-quarters of a million.

The Chinese still had numerical superiority, and they thought they had the initiative, too. They began to plan what they called First Step, Fifth Phase Offensive. This offensive would concentrate on the western portion of the battle line, and its objective was the Korean capital of Seoul, thirty-five miles to the south.

In the meantime, the Eighth Army kept making limited attacks, until in the third week of April its forces were ten miles above the parallel everywhere except at Kaesong. In the center of the line U.N forces were striking toward the Ch'orwon-Kumwha-P'yonggang complex, an imp and supply area called the Iron Triangle.

The original Iron Triangle—so called because the ste cities formed a rough triangle on the map—had had Hwa when Hwach'on fell to the Eighth Army, the corresponde that the town of P'yonggang, farther north, was put in Hw

The U.N. probe was confident, but cautious. Ridgway attack, but he was determined to see how far the Eighth

Spring had come to Korea, with spring rains, and briefly beautiful with grass and flowers. But the skulls of winter snows, loosened by the thaw, rolled down the hi the azalea and forsythia just bursting into bloom.

With spring there came to Korea not rebirth but furthe

The United States 3rd Infantry Division struck towar road running from Seoul, and on 21 April was some ten and ten miles north of the Imjin River. On its right, IX Corps, consisting of the Marine Division and one ROK division, prepared to attack along the line running from Kumwha to the Hwach'on Reservoir. On the 3rd Division's left stood the British 29th Brigade, with a front-line strength of four thousand, and the 1st ROK Division.

The British Brigade was just south of the Imjin, and had sent exploratory patrols across. Crossing an area of flinty two-hundred-foot cliffs and rocky gorges, the patrols reported nothing much to bar the way.

But here, some thirty miles northwest of the ROK capital, was fought the fourth battle for Seoul.

On 22 April the Chinese struck the 17,000-yard front of the British Brigade with six divisions, more than fifty thousand men.

* * *

On the eve of St. George's Day, the 29th Infantry Brigade consisted of the 1st Battalion, Royal Northumberland Fusiliers, just south of the Imjin, an attached battalion of Belgians, the 1st Battalion, Gloucestershire Regiment, on the brigade left, and the 1st Battalion, Royal Ulster Rifles, in reserve. In brigade support were the 45th Field, Royal Artillery, equipped with 25-pounders, and the 8th King's Royal Hussars, who had once charged on horseback at Balaclava but who now rode fifty-ton Centurion tanks.

Each of these was a unit long known to history, and steeped in glory.

The Fusiliers began in 1674, and wear the badge of St. George and his dragon on their berets. The Gloucestershire Regiment—"Glosters"—dates to 1694, and their battle standards stream with the names of Waterloo, Quebec, and Gallipoli, on 22 April 1951 forty-four in all, more than any regiment of the British Army.

Since the time English bowmen wore red crosses on their breasts, the day of their patron, St. George, has been sacred to English arms. For 23 April the British Brigade planned festivities, both gay and solemn. The Ulsters, who had lost more than two hundred dead along the Imjin in January, planned to dedicate a monument. The Fusiliers had readied a turkey dinner, and had made from colored paper the red and white St. George's Day roses for their caps. The Royal Artillery, not to be outdone, had even flown in real roses from Japan.

There would be no festivities this St. George's Day, but the men of the 29th Brigade would wear their roses all the same. They would wear them into battle as desperate as any their forefathers had seen, from Acre to Agincourt.

For on the eve of St. George's Day, at 6:00 P.M. the Chinese struck.

The Belgians, across the Imjin, were surrounded first. Then, the Northumberland Fusiliers were brought to battle, but without concern at Brigade HQ. Efforts were made to relieve the Belgians; first a column of the Ulsters tried, then a patrol of tanks, without success.

While concern for the Belgians mounted during the night, they went relatively unscathed, though cut off. On the 23rd they were able to sideslip across the Chinese lines on their right, and withdraw.

It was on the brigade left, where the Glosters held four miles of rugged front, that the main blow fell, when St. George's Day was one hour old.

The Chinese, their horns and bugles raucous in the clear cool night, came across the Imjin in wide, massive waves. The very first washed screaming into A Company, in front, and swamped it. The Able Company commander went down, with two of his officers. The company command post was overrun.

The company radio operator fired his rifle until it went dry, then used it as a club to beat off the Chinese swarming out of the dark. Then, as the Chinese split around him in the fire-prickled night, he crawled to his radio.

"We are overrun. We've had it. Cheerio."

The other companies held, while the entire brigade, from one end of the 17,000-yard front to the other, was now locked in close combat. By dawn the 1st ROK Division, on their left, had been forced back, and by midmorning Chinese crawled over the flinty hills on the Glosters' flank and rear.

The battalion supply offices were overrun, and the battalion split away from the brigade, while a full regiment of Chinese fixed them from the front.

By radio, the Glosters were told to hold their high ground, where they were, and this they did.

The 45th Field fired in their support until gun tubes shimmered. In all, the 25-pounders fired more than a thousand rounds per tube, more even than the average at Alamein. They fired until almost every round of British ammunition in Korea had been exhausted, and at times they fired into Chinese riflemen less than one hundred yards away.

They protected the guns, and continued the mission. More than that cannot be expected, or said, of any artillery.

But as 23 April lengthened, then waned, the Glosters, fighting on, began to run out of supply. They needed ammunition, fresh guns, medicines. They had no food, except some bread and a few hard-boiled eggs.

American air tried to drop supply to them, but the battle was too close about the beleaguered hills. The air drops had poor success.

But all the air power that could be thrown into the battle swarmed down from the sky, rocketing, blasting, searing the Chinese-dotted hills with napalm.

In spite of the continuous rumble of the artillery, in spite of air power, the CCF trickled behind the two other battalions. The Ulsters and Fusiliers were cut off, too. The Brigade HQ was under small-arms fire. A number of green replacements just in from England for the Fusiliers were fired on, and some were killed before they could join.

All day the 23rd, and all that night, the Glosters beat off swarming infantry attacks, holding their precious high ground. At dawn of the 24th, the Glosters' situation was serious.

Able Company had been swamped by the first wave, and insistent pressure had worn Baker Company down to an effective strength of one officer and fifteen other ranks. The remaining men fought back from deep foxholes, into which sleeted unceasing machine-gun fire. It was impossible to move without being hit.

Commanding the original 622 officers and men of the Glosters was Lieutenant Colonel J. P. Carne, a tall, normally reticent officer who had been with the regiment twenty-six years. Carne, calm and pipe-smoking, drew the companies back onto the hill on which he had placed his own CP. Despite the heavy fire, the maneuver succeeded; now the Gloster line had shrunk from four miles to a few hundred yards, but the line still held.

Carne, in weak radio communication with Brigade, asked only for helicopters to carry away his desperately wounded. But the fire was too close and too intense for the copters to come in. Carne was asked if he thought a relief column through the hills could reach him.

"No," he said, with complete honesty.

But on the afternoon of 24 April a battalion of Filipinos led by American tanks was ordered toward Gloster Hill. The column ground to within less than two thousand yards of the British before the lead tank caught fire and blocked a defile. Lashed by unbearable fire, the column retreated.

Later, the Filipinos tried again, now accompanied by Belgians, some Puerto Rican infantrymen, and tanks from the 8th Hussars. They ran into thousands of Chinese in the hills and gorges, and fell back.

The American 3rd Division, which had fallen back south of the Imjin now and which was not yet under heavy pressure, abandoning its own probe toward Ch'orwon, tried to break through with tanks and infantry.

They were not able even to get close.

On the hill, the Glosters held fast, as the sun sank. By now a gap of seven miles had been opened between them and the other units of the 29th Brigade.

All night they fought off Chinese, now coming at their hill in desperation. The Glosters were spoiling the First Step, Fifth Phase Offensive, at its very start. Before them already lay several thousands of dead Chinese, and they still had teeth.

But at dawn they had only some three hundred men fit to hold a gun, and ammunition was so low that officers whispered to hold fire until the assaulting infantry was fifteen yards away.

And at dawn of the 25th, the brigadier commanding the 29th received new orders: fall back. The Fusiliers and Ulsters were badly hurt, and with the front holding solidly elsewhere, and supporting units behind them, it was senseless slaughter to keep the decimated British on line.

Those Fusiliers and Ulsters who were on their feet came out in good order. Their wounded, two hundred of them, were loaded onto tanks. Coming out, the tanks were brought under fire. The decks and sponsons ran slick with blood, and the dead and dying lay so thickly across the tanks the gunners could not traverse the tubes. But the hurt and dying were brought out, and the 29th Brigade, two-thirds of it, fell back.

Miles deep in Chinese territory now, the Glosters were on their own.

And they were almost done, this 25th of April.

At Alexandria, Egypt, during the battle for the Nile, the Gloucestershire Regiment had approached the French in two long ranks, one to kneel and fire, one to hold off the enemy with the bayonet while the second row reloaded. They were surrounded.

Their officers shouted, "Rear rank—right-about-face! Fire!"

Back to back, the Glosters fired and repelled charges until the French retired.

Ever since, the Glosters, alone in the British service, have been entitled to wear two cap ornaments, one in front, one in back.

On Gloster Hill, Korea, one hundred and fifty years later, the Glosters fought back to back again. These were no longer the mindless automatons of Wellington's legions; many of them were reservists called to the colors upon the Korean emergency. Most of them were past the age of thirty; a great many of them had left wives and children behind in Britain.

But whatever else they might be, they were men of the Gloucestershire Regiment.

Just before daylight, the Chinese bugles made the rocky hills eerie with music, as they marshaled to charge again. There were three hundred Glosters on the hill, and a bugler. The bugler put his own horn to mouth and blew *long reveille.*

The sound of the Chinese horns died away.

Then, as the Chinese listened in amazement, the Gloster bugler sounded *short reveille, half-hour dress,* and *cookhouse.* While the brassy music died, in the still before the firing began again, the Glosters cheered.

At 0605, by radio, their brigadier told them they had his permission to leave Gloster Hill.

Lieutenant Colonel Carne said he was surrounded and could not break out. He asked for air support.

He got it. Dive bombers shrieked down upon their hill, blasting the ground only thirty-five yards beyond their holes. Individual Gloucesters threw smoke grenades to mark the spots they wanted hit. It was close, desperate work, but it sent the CCF reeling back.

At 0755, after fighting continuously for almost sixty hours, Carne reported to Brigade that his radio batteries were almost gone. He asked for the air and artillery to continue pounding in close.

Then Carne talked to his acting company commanders, sheltered by a fold of ground near the CP where the wounded litter patients, some five dozen of them, lay about. He told them the battalion was done. They had a choice of surrendering or trying to fight their way out in small groups.

The commanders of Able, Baker, Charlie, and Dog said they would try to fight their way through.

There was no hope of taking the seriously wounded through. With these volunteered to stay Colonel Carne, Regimental Sergeant Major Hobbs, the doctor and chaplain.

Hobbs and Carne had lived their entire adult lives within the Glosters; it was unthinkable to them to desert their own. The surgeon and chaplain, brave men each, could in no other way fulfill their callings.

The remnants of A, B, and C companies started off the hill in the respite the savage air attacks had given them. On the hill Colonel Carne and the leader of the fourth party, Captain Michael Harvey of Dog Company, watched these dirty, hungry, unkempt, staggering, proud men march away into oblivion.

Harvey got his own party, about a hundred, ready to move out.

As they started down the hill, Carne asked quietly, "Any of you chaps happen to have a spare twist of tobacco?"

Captain Harvey, not yet thirty, was a reserve officer and a veteran of the Hampshire Regiment. Until this moment, he had considered himself a Hampshire man strayed from the fold. On the 25th of April, Michael Harvey, with no discredit to the Hampshires, became a Gloster.

A somewhat untidy man wearing large horn-rimmed glasses, Harvey ordered his group not to follow the three other parties moving south toward friendly lines, but to do the unexpected—head due north for at least a mile then bear west and south toward the Americans.

He told all hands, "We must travel fast. There can be no stopping to aid anyone who is wounded."

Amazingly, for several miles, moving north and then west, they neither saw nor encountered Chinese. Harvey, knowing the CCF liked to run the ridges, crept cautiously down the deep gorges. When they turned to head south again, they bumped into a CCF patrol; they killed these men, and kept on.

Mile after mile the exhausted, stumbling Glosters crept along the rocky corridors.

At last they entered a valley, almost a canyon, with clifflike sides and a stony floor almost a quarter-mile wide. A stream flowed through the valley, and Harvey's men proceeded down this for nearly a mile.

And then, suddenly, the cliffsides swarmed with the black dots of Chinese, and automatic weapons ripped at them from right and left. Harvey estimated forty guns opened up on them. Some Glosters fell, but the others leaped into a narrow ditch that ran along the valley. Under heavy fire, leaving men behind, they crawled along the rocky, foot-deep ditch on bleeding hands and knees.

The ditch disappeared in places, and more men were hit running to new cover. American planes came over them, recognized them, and poured fire into the surrounding cliffs, without much effect.

Desperately, they crawled on, moving south.

At last, more than five hundred yards ahead, Harvey saw tanks he recognized as American spread across the valley, firing. Still under heavy fire, but joyous now, the Glosters crawled rapidly toward the American Shermans.

The tanks were receiving fire from the Chinese, and the American lieutenant in command had no inkling that any friendly troops could be to the north. As the first Glosters rushed forward, he gave the order to open fire.

Cannon and machine guns lashed the stumbling Glosters, and six of them fell.

An American liaison plane, directing air support over the escapees, knowing them for British, went into aerial convulsions. The pilot swooped low over the tanks, waggling his wings at them, waving. The lieutenant, puzzled, continued to direct fire at the ragged men trying to close with his tanks.

Harvey, lying panting on the ground, found a stick. He tied his kerchief to this, stuck his cap on it, and crawled forward, waving it like a pitiful flag. The stragglers of his column, their ammunition gone, were screaming as Chinese slipped down from the ridges and bayoneted them.

The liaison pilot, sensible now, flew low and dropped a frantic note. At once, the Shermans ceased fire.

The remnants of the Gloster Battalion crawled into their line and crouched behind the meager protection of the armored hulls.

Together, then, the tanks sweeping the hostile hills with fire and steel, they retreated down the valley until the protection of the ground allowed the British to climb up on the tanks.

The American crewmen were frantic at their error. One, almost in tears, took off his shoes and gave them to an English soldier who came up on the tanks with bleeding feet.

The American officer said over and over again to Harvey, "My God, how many of your people did we hit?"

None of the Glosters would say.

For more than three miles, still surrounded by the CCF, the tanks fought back, bringing the remnants of the Glosters through. The tank lieutenant was hit, but they kept the swarming enemy off the Glosters' backs. They came out.

At the end, in the American lines, there were only thirty-eight men with Harvey. His was the only party that came through.

* * *

To the right of the 29th British Brigade, the American 3rd Division had dropped back to the Imjin River at the start of the CCF offensive. It had good positions and, better yet, it had confidence.

The Chinese, many of whom wore new, clean clothing, and carried bright new weapons, hit them.

On an outpost one N.C.O. yelled: "They're coming! They're coming! Millions of 'em? They're going to *banzai* us!"

They came, and they were met with fire and steel. When outposts and rifle companies had to give ground, they gave it in good order, and at high price. Men, ordered to hold and fight, showed what soldiers who have learned new discipline and know how to wield their weapons can do.

One triumphant shout from a fire-swept, bloody hill that was recorded 25 April 1951 sums up the actions of many brave men:

"We're holding them! By God, we're holding them!"

Farther east, in the Marine and ROK Zone of IX Corps, Chinese poured into the perimeter of Lieutenant Colonel L. F. Lavoie's 92nd Armored Field Artillery Battalion, a self-propelled 155mm howitzer outfit supporting both the ROK and 1st Marine Division.

The CCF had burst through the weaker firepower of the ROK's, scattering a ROK regiment, then turned to strike the United States Marines in the flank. Two ROK artillery units were in their way and were overrun, losing all equipment.

On 24 April the CCF found the 92nd Field in their way. They struck while the battalion was still at mess.

Colonel Lavoie's first warning was the sudden appearance of a bullet hole in his mess tent. He leaped outside, yelling, "Man battle stations! Man battle stations!" to HQ Battery, and ran to his CP to get in touch with his firing batteries.

All the batteries were under close attack. But Lavoie had made each officer and man spend long hours on dry runs, and men sprang to the guns. With both small arms, machine guns, and heavy howitzers, the battalion fought back with viciousness and enthusiasm.

The commander of Charlie Battery reported to Lavoie, "Sir, Battery C has Chinks all through its area."

"Dead or alive?" Lavoie asked.

"Both!"

"To hell with the dead ones—take care of the live ones and make every bullet count!"

The initial, freezing panic of being attacked lasted only minutes. The artillerymen, well trained, tightly disciplined, and superbly led, suddenly realized they could hold their own, and they fought almost cockily, as Lavoie walked about the perimeter, dodging bullets.

One very young soldier saw some Chinese crawling toward the fire direction center. "Look at those sons of bitches! They think they're going to make it—"

He jumped up, fired. "I got one!"

Other men joined him, and the Chinese died.

Within a few hours, the battalion, intact, pulled back to safer positions beyond sniper range, as Marine tanks growled in to relieve them. They hadn't asked for help; they hadn't needed it.

Lavoie, all told, had lost 4 men killed and 11 wounded, and no equipment. Around the battalion perimeter the Marines reported they found 179 Chinese dead.

The First Step, Fifth Phase Offensive, was failing.

It was a long, long way from Kunu-ri, not in time or distance but in the hearts of American fighting men.

* * *

Because of British hearts and bayonets, the thrust at Seoul had failed. At least fifteen thousand Chinese were killed along the Imjin; the best their offensive could achieve was a realignment of U.N. lines.

In the west, U.N. troops pulled back, and more units were sent to reinforce the vital Seoul corridor. Ridgway was not interested in real estate; he gave up ground to ensure that no units would be exposed or trapped.

A new line was formed, still north of the parallel in the east, but running just above Inch'on, Seoul, to south of Ch'unch'on in the west. It was heavily fortified.

But by dark of 30 April, the CCF, exhausted, turned and crept north once more. This time, the CCF had met the tiger.

* * *

Each year, for the decade following the Korean conflict, on St. George's Day units of the British and Australian armies have sent telegrams of thanks and appreciation to certain units of the United States Army.

Each of the units so honored helped the British in a sticky place.

Each year, a telegram comes to one American tank battalion that gained great tradition and prestige in the bloody hills, whose men, like those of the Glosters, learned to walk the hills with confidence and pride. Because of them, certain men now living in England and elsewhere are still alive.

When the message comes to this battalion, however, the people in the Pentagon do not know what to do with it. On the rolls of the Pentagon, where slowly human hearts and the legends men live by are being replaced by computers, this unit no longer exists.

The Gloucestershire Regiment, now with forty-five battle honors and an American citation, will never understand.

27

Death Valley

The United States does not claim to have the key to human wisdom or success. But we do claim the right to be judged on facts and not on fiction.
—General of the Army George Catlett Marshall.

F ROM THE TIME man first raised fist to man, the lot of prisoners of war has been hard. The ancient peoples sometimes crucified captives; they invariably enslaved them, for life. From the time of Peter of Dreux, who burned out the eyes of prisoners, with hot irons, to the captives of Stalingrad and the hell camp of Cabanatuan, it has often been better for men to die fighting than to be taken by the enemy.

No nation, no culture has an unblemished record in what is merely a part of the long story of man's inhumanity to man. Germans have starved Russians; Russians have worked Germans to death. Napoleon's seamen rotted, chained like beasts in English prison hulks. A Swiss-American in the uniform of the Confederacy turned other Americans into snarling animals at a place in Georgia called Andersonville.

In recent years Western Civilization has begun to give the moral and ethical questions of the treatment of prisoners of war agonized consideration. The Geneva Conventions, as part of the hopeless task of making war more humane, specified that a prisoner of war must be treated in the same fashion as a nation's own prisoners.

But while Western Civilization has tended to grow more humane in the treatment of its prisoners of all kinds, the balance of the world has not. In World War II it was found that the Geneva Conventions did not adequately cover the subject. The problem was one of culture and chemistry.

An American, or other Westerner, will starve and die on a diet that Japanese peasants or prisoners may live on almost indefinitely. And it is patently impossible to force a belligerent to treat foreign prisoners of war better than, say, its own political detainees.

The question of toughness or decadence aside, American body chemistry has undoubtedly changed in the past two hundred years. A by-product of the rising Western standard of living has been larger bodies, the need for more food, and a psychological inability to readapt easily to the animal-like existence normal to much of the world.

In postwar Japan, Americans imprisoned by the Japanese Government for various reasons have been given a special diet, heated cells, and recreation facilities—none of which are given to Japanese prison inmates.

This has been done because the Japanese Government, since the signing of a peace treaty in 1952, has been peculiarly sensitive to American opinion and pressures.

During World War II the Japanese handled Americans and Britons in the same brutal fashion with which they treated their own miscreants and other Asians. Thousands of Americans and English died or went mad in the POW camps. Almost all the lives of the men in the bamboo camps were shortened, even if they survived.

Yet, in many cases, putting aside the unmistakable brutality of the Japanese guards, the Japanese were able to demonstrate that they had fed the POW's as well as they had fed their own Korean laborers.

The Germans had a peculiarly defined system of standards in handling their own POW's, based on Nazi notions of race. Westerners, including British and Americans, were not coddled, but were generally well treated. Other races, particularly the Eastern European, were handled in a way to suggest that the Germans felt extermination was the final solution.

Americans treated their own POW's, Japanese, Italian, and German, as they vainly hoped they themselves would be treated.

The Soviets treated the Nazis and Japanese in kind. Most of the men who were taken in Russia disappeared behind the iron curtain and were never heard from again. Survivors have written of the wholesale degradation and death in Communist prison camps.

The problem is one of chemistry, and culture.

Americans who felt, and still feel, that their soldiers taken by a power of different culture and lesser standards of humanity should be, or will be, treated in accordance with decent Western standards are naïve.

They were naïve in 1950, since no American fighting men were prepared in any way to face what they could be expected to face. The Army, as well as government and society, was at fault. All had known for some years of Communist methods of indoctrinating POW's—the world knew of Colonel General Paulus' experiences after Stalingrad—and knew what Asian Communist culture was like. But just as they had not prepared their young men to fight, they had not prepared them to go into captivity.

In the first six months of Korea, American arms faltered on the battlefield because of a lack of American material and psychological preparation for bloodletting, and in those first six months almost all the American POW's were taken.

Whatever failures there were, in the bleak and dreary prison camps of North Korea, were no more than a continuation of the failures on the battlefield, by the same men.

For some reason, the POW camps have been much more widely publicized than the battlefields. What happened in them has become an emotional issue, and for that reason will probably never be clarified.

Let one thing be clear, however.

What happened in those camps was not unique. It had been known to history before. If it was new to Americans, who pride themselves on being informed, the fault was their own.

In Andersonville, Americans fought each other for scraps of food, and let each other die. Tough panzer grenadiers of the *Wehrmacht,* whom no one has accused of being overly fat or soft, went listless in Communist pens, and died "for no reason." Americans and Britons in Japanese prisons retreated into dream worlds, and some informed on their buddies.

A human being in a prison camp, in the hands of his enemies, is flesh, and shudderingly vulnerable.

On the battlefield, even surrounded, he still has a gun in his hand, his comrades about him, and, perhaps the most important thing of all, leadership. If he has training, and if he has developed pride, he can stand as a man.

In a POW cage, he is flesh, however strong the spirit. He has no gun, he has no leader, and his comrades are flesh, too.

Americans often forget there are millions of brave men and women behind the iron curtain, living in virtual prisons. They have no love for Communism, yet they accommodate. The Roman Catholic primate of Poland—whom no man accuses of Communism—"collaborates."

In a prison, most men, if their jailor wills, may be broken.

Men there are like all men, everywhere, in that some will never do wrong, and some will never do right. The great majority will lean the way the wind takes them as most men have since the dawn of time.

There were utterly reprehensible acts committed by Americans in the prison camps. These have been recorded, and punished. There were also acts of incredible courage, which have been rewarded, in some cases.

The average man was neither courageous nor cowardly.

Young, untrained, with the iron most men expect in soldiers not yet forged in him, he was forced to face the tiger as best he could.

* * *

In the snow-covered bauxite mining camp they would call Death Valley, Sergeant Charles Schlichter and the other Americans taken at Kunu-ri were gathered into an old school building.

Here a slender Chinese officer addressed them in broken English.

He told them that the People's Volunteers had decided to treat them, not as war criminals, but under China's new Lenient Policy.

Though the officer did not say it, the average Army POW would be treated much like an average Chinese felon or class enemy. No great pressures would be put on him, other than those of starvation, lack of medical care, and a certain amount of indoctrination.

This was the Lenient Policy. All American POW's, however, were not subject to it. Airmen, in particular, who were bombing North Korea to rubble, rousing the hatred of both Chinese and Koreans, were criminals from the start. Later, when the typhus carried across the Yalu by the CCF hordes spread to the civil population, airmen would be accused of germ warfare, giving the CCF both an out and a chance at a propaganda coup.

Airmen, and some others, would be put under acute stress to confess alleged war crimes. Some were put in solitary. Some were physically tortured. All were starved and interrogated until their nerves shrieked. They were treated in almost the identical way that political prisoners had been treated by Communists for a generation.

Even under the Lenient Policy, no relief parcels were allowed to be delivered to Communist POW's, nor were any neutral observers, at any time, allowed to inspect the prison camps.

Communists saw no reason why Americans should have special privileges not given to their own people.

When he had told them of the Lenient Policy, the officer told the shivering, tired, fearful POW's one thing more:

"Everybody here is the same. No officers, no N.C.O.'s here. Everybody is equal!"

It has always been customary to separate officers from sergeants, and sergeants from other ranks, in POW camps. It is the most effective way of breaking down possible resistance and cohesion in any group of prisoners, American or Hungarian. But the Chinese tried a new twist.

"No one here has any rank—you are all the same," the Chinese said. To Sergeant Schlichter's horror, this had an immediate appeal for many men.

One soldier went up to an officer and slapped him on the back. "Hey, Jack, how the hell are you?" He thought it was very funny.

The Chinese smiled, too.

In this way, and in others, such as putting ranking POW's on the most degrading jobs, the Chinese broke what little discipline remained in the POW ranks. The officers themselves did not quite know what to do. To many of them, it seemed self-aggrandizing, almost totalitarian, to insist upon their right to command, since they were only captives, too. Most of them did nothing.

The officers and sergeants, as well as the young men, faced a new situation, for which they were wholly unprepared.

Morale, among the captives, was already gone. Now the last shred of discipline went, and with it went many Americans' hope of surviving.

There was no one to give the POW's direction, except the Chinese. Among the Americans, it could not be anything but dog eat dog, hooray for me, and to hell with you.

The disciplines that hold men together in the face of fear, hunger, and danger are not natural. Stresses equal to, and beyond, the stress of fear and panic must be overlaid on men. Some of these stresses are called civilization. And even the highest of civilizations demands leadership. There has to be a Chief Executive of the United States, with the power to bully and chivvy both the Congress and the people, sometimes into doing what is necessary for their own good.

In Death Valley, there was no one to bully and chivvy the wretched prisoners but the Chinese, who had no American's welfare at heart. Men did not hold together, but came apart, dissolved into individuals, governed only by their individual consciences. And as fear, cold, sickness, and starvation deepened, conscience shallowed.

The controls of civilization make men, often against their will, become their brother's keepers. When the controls are taken away, it is but a step to becoming their brother's killers. The veneer of civilized decency is much thinner than most Americans, even after seeing Auschwitz and Belsen, think.

Civilization is a fragile discipline, at best. In Death Valley it disappeared.

The prisoners, in subzero weather, were huddled into filthy huts where there was not room enough even to sleep comfortably. Men lay on the odorous ground, pressed tight against each other at night, week after week.

The food they received daily, in a bucket, was not enough to keep the average American in decent health. Rapidly, they began to starve.

A number had combat wounds that had received only cursory treatment. Infection and dysentery seared them, making the huts even more horrible.

What medical care they received was pitiful by any standard.

Sergeant Schlichter, rather than an Army doctor, was placed in charge of the camp hospital, in accordance with the CCF policy of humiliating officers. The hospital was an old North Korean school building, high-roofed, heated by two pot-bellied stoves, without pipes.

The stoves had only green wood to burn, and the smoke lay across the room like a blanket of death. Sergeant Schlichter and his surgeon, Captain Shadish, had to crawl about on their hands and knees to keep from choking.

The crude "hospital" had pallets for only sixty men, among the hundreds who had untreated combat wounds, dysentery, pneumonia, jaundice, and psychic disorders. The Chinese allowed Shadish exactly enough medicines to give four men one sulfa tablet four times a day.

Each day, Shadish and Schlichter, crawling from man to man, had to play God. To the four men who had the best chance to live, they administered the sulfa. The worse off, Schlichter said later, "We committed to God's care."

Men died.

Each morning Charles Schlichter came into the hospital and said, "Sit up." Then he said, "If the man next to you can't sit up, shake him. If he doesn't move, call me—"

Then, after those who could sat up to be counted, Schlichter and Shadish carried out the dead. The ground was frozen, and they had no tools, but at first, while they still had strength, the bodies were buried in shallow graves. Later, when their strength began to fail, they turned the bodies over to a detail of South Korean prisoners. The ROK's threw the emaciated bodies on the ground outside the camp.

The prisoners remained in Death Valley from the day after Christmas until 12 March 1951, and each day men died. They died of war wounds, of infection, pneumonia, dysentery. In most cases malnutrition was a contributing factor.

The prisoners continued to receive only a diet of millet and maize, boiled in a pot, delivered in a bucket, supplemented by dog. But the dogs grew more wary, and the prisoners weaker. Without salt, greens, or essential minerals, they sickened.

The sick and those with war wounds died first. Then the men without faith began to die, often, seemingly, of nothing at all.

The youngest men, oddly, died first.

Schlichter, who never lost his determination to live to return, or his faith in God, believed that most who died didn't have to die. For the first time in his life, he wondered if the will to die, when men's worlds have been turned upside down, was not stronger than the urge to live.

There were men who had grown up with no strong belief in anything; they had received no faith from parents, school, or church. They had no spiritual home or haven. Exposed to horror and misery, when the man with the gun cut the line to home, destroyed every material reason for living, they could not adjust. They no longer wanted to live.

Schlichter saw men who refused to eat the meager slop he was eating, in his own effort to stay alive. He heard men mumble fantasies, living in a dream world of their own warm, protected past. One boy angrily told him, as he urged the youth to eat, "My parents never made me do things like this!"

Another told him one night, sobbing, "I know my mother is bringing me a pie tonight—a pie, Sergeant."

In Charles Schlichter grew a feeling, which he never lost, that some American mothers had given their sons everything in the world, except a belief in themselves, their culture, and their manhood. They had, some of them, sent their sons out into a world with tigers without telling them that there were tigers, and with no moral armament.

Most of those who could adjust, who wanted to live on, lived. It helped if a man could hold to something. Some lived simply because they came to hate the Chinese so much.

And there were some, determined to live, who took food from the sick and dying, and there was no one to say them nay.

Not all the quitters were youths. The older men went, too. One night a decorated officer said, simply. "I'm going to die." He lay in his hut, neither eating nor drinking, unspeaking, until he did.

Without discipline, without a chain of command, there was no effective way to help the dying or aid the faltering. There were men who needed to be cheered, helped, cared for. No man would obey another, and no organized effort was ever made. Organization had broken down completely. It must be reported that few officers showed any willingness to take command. The failures were not of the few, but of the many.

Each day Shadish and other doctors went to the filthy, crowded, lice-ridden, fecal-smelling huts, taking the sickest to the hospital.

Each night Sergeant Schlichter reported to the Chinese commandant the number who had died. There were some Turks and ROK's with the Americans. To Schlichter's knowledge, not one Turk had died.

On 12 March 1951, while winter still howled through North Korea, the enemy closed down Death Valley. There were fewer POW's now, and they could be consolidated in fewer camps. The men of Death Valley were assembled from their huts and marched north.

Charles Schlichter closed out the hospital by burning the straw pallets on which the sick had lain. When the straw went into the fire, the floor and shimmering sides of the stoves were black with lice, trying to jump away. Schlichter loaded some twenty patients, pale with jaundice and too ill to march, onto a mule cart and rode north with them. He was the last to leave the valley.

As he left, he stood up in the cart, looking back. The last sight he had of Death Valley was of three starving Korean dogs, snuffling warily in from the hills to feed on the bodies of the young Americans they had left behind.

On the 17th of March he arrived at Camp Number 5 on the Yalu River. Here the officers, N.C.O.'s, and other ranks were separated.

And here, now that they had been starved and sickened into a disorganized, slack-faced mob, more animals than men, their education began.

* * *

The island of Koje, approximately the size of an American county, lies in the Korea Strait a few miles southeast of Pusan. Koje-do is only a mile and a half from the southern tip of the Korean peninsula, but it is five hours from Pusan by boat, twelve hours by twisting road, which in early 1951 was connected to the mainland by an ancient ferry.

Koje-do rises green and lovely from the sea. It is a land of lush hills, clear streams, and delicately tinted paddies. The hills hold wild deer, and the streams run with trout. Korean farmers and fishermen have lived upon it since the dawn of history, and in 1951 the island was further populated with refugees from the north, diverted from teeming, crowded Pusan.

Up close, the beauty fades, and the odor of Koje-do is indistinguishable from that of the mainland.

To Koje Island, in early 1951, were sent the 80,000-odd prisoners of war taken so far by the United Nations during the Korean War. The Eighth Army was in full retreat, and there were rumors on the wind that all Korea might have to be evacuated. The thousands upon thousands of POW's gathered around the Pusan area were in the way; worse, they were a potential hazard. On Koje, it was felt they would be both secure and out of the Eighth Army's hair. In early 1951 all Eighth Army, from General Matt Ridgway down, was monumentally uninterested in the POW's it had taken. The Eighth Army had more pressing concerns.

The problems of handling the POW's, of feeding, clothing, guarding, and disciplining them, was delegated to the 60th General Depot in Pusan, which later was to become the 2nd Logistical Command. The mission of the 60th General Depot was to supply the troops fighting in Korea, and they were doing a superb job of this. The fifteen technical service officers, under their

Quartermaster Corps C.O., were proficient in the way that only American supply officers can be proficient.

They had to be, for United States troops are prodigal on the battlefield.

But however efficient these men might be at supply, none of them knew anything about the handling, care, and feeding of Asian Communist prisoners of war. They were logisticians, not cops.

But in their defense, it must be said that nobody else in the United States Army knew any more than they did. When the shattered conscripts of the Inmun Gun began to surrender in droves in the fall of 1950, the United States found itself facing a new situation.

In World War I America's Allies had assumed control of all POW's.

In World War II the United States came in late, and took over an existing British system. And the Germans and Italians captured after North Africa had proved to be a fairly tractable lot. In spite of Fascism there was no great cultural gulf between captors and captured; they understood each other, adhered to the same general code. Several hundred thousand POW's were sent to places like Montana and Texas; at the end of the war they were shipped home without incident.

In spite of protestations at the time, World War II was never an ideological war, for Fascism and Nazism were fundamentally inexportable. The German Reich never stood a chance of winning a political victory in Europe; it stood and fell by arms alone.

Ideology never raised its ugly head in the prisoner-of-war camps outside Russia in World War II.

The Japanese POW's taken in the Pacific were so few as to be insignificant. The Japanese-Americans herded into detention camps after Pearl Harbor showed a remarkable restraint toward the intolerance of their native land.

When the Korean War began, therefore, the United States had no experience in the handling of hostile prisoners of war. It had developed no real doctrine; it had trained no personnel. And worse, the United States Army understood Asians imperfectly, and Communists not at all.

When the thousands began to flow into the POW cages in Korea, U.S. authorities were certain of only one thing: they did not want to bring almost 100,000 Orientals to the homeland for detention.

The prisoner-of-war compounds on Koje-do were born of expediency. And like so many measures so adopted in the modern age, the temporary solution became permanent. Once rid of the POW's, General Ridgway, and his successor, Van Fleet, never wanted them back.

It was up to the logisticians at Pusan to make out as best they could.

Major William T. Gregory, Corps of Engineers, was engineer supply officer of the 60th General Depot on Christmas Day 1950. Bill Gregory was a career reservist, tall, redhaired, and skinny. He held a Regular Army warrant as master sergeant, and he intended to return to his North Carolina home only when the Army made him go.

As a part of rounding out his career, the Army sent young Major Gregory to Koje-do. The C.O. of the 60th General Depot called him in and said: "Bill, the POW's are coming to Koje Island. You are appointed Procurement Officer for them. Go buy food—all you can find."

The C.O. didn't know just how many were coming, or just when they would arrive—all he could do was to send Bill Gregory and a small party on ahead to the island.

LST's crossed the choppy strait from Pusan, dumping thousands of small, miserable, brown-skinned men on Koje's beaches. Soon there were 40,000 prisoners, mostly Koreans, herded together in the open rice paddies up from the sea. There were less than two hundred U.S. personnel to guard them, and not even a barbed-wire fence to wrap around them.

Cold, hungry, and apathetic, the POW's sat in the fields, and waited. They gave no trouble. They expected to be badly used, after the way of all captives in the Orient. At the best, they expected to wear their lives away in labor battalions, slaving for their captors. At the worst, they expected to be shot.

On Koje-do there were no combat troops, no HQ, no organization. There were no compounds. Fortunately, the POW's gave no trouble.

Bill Gregory ranged the island, buying rice. He was the first of the big spenders come to Koje; all he could find, he bought. Soon he had tons and tons of rice stored on log foundations some of his engineers had built over the marshy soil.

But as fast as Gregory bought it, the POW's ate it. Koreans and Chinese ate a hell of a lot of rice, together with fish, vegetables, and other items. Finally, just before the economy of Koje-do collapsed, Gregory got authorization to purchase supplies directly from Japan. Now, with the competent Japs securing mountains of fish and rice for shipment across the strait, Gregory was relieved of food procurement.

He was ordered to begin constructing compounds. The POW's could not live in the fields forever. The Neutral Nation inspection teams were raising hell. A few more American troops came in, plus the 93rd Engineer Construction Battalion and two battalions of ROK's.

The ROK troops weren't much help, but with the U.S. Engineers Gregory began building barbed-wire compounds. These were jerry-built affairs, for time and labor were limited; even wire was scarce. Inside the wire, Gregory constructed living quarters—huts—and sewer lines running down to the sea, for the forty thousand POW's were consuming rice by the ton, with no place to dispose of it.

One source of labor was indigenous personnel. In a very short time, most of the inhabitants of Koje discovered there was such a thing as the U.S. payroll. For all of them it was a very happy discovery. The half of the island that was unable for some reason to get on the payroll was able to sell or otherwise do business with those who had.

The Chinese and North Koreans were moved into the new, hardly secure compounds, already overcrowded as more and more POW's reached Koje. But the comptrollers were screaming over the expense: good or bad, there was to be no more money for POW camp construction.

Through it all the POW's remained subdued and quiet. They made no trouble.

Five weeks after the first captives had landed on Koje, a specially trained Military Police Detachment arrived from Camp Gordon, Georgia, to assume direction of the island. This unit, from its commander down, had been given careful instruction on how to handle POW's, which was, after all, an MP function.

There was only one problem—the instructors hadn't known anymore than the people they taught. But they had given them some ideas.

Colonel Fitzgerald, the MP commander, took charge at once. He called all officers on the island to a staff meeting.

"These people are our equals," he said, strongly. "Our job is to teach them democracy." However dimly, someone in the States had recognized the essentially ideological nature of the conflict with Communism. "We're going to treat these people as human beings. I want you to understand that if a POW is abused, or refuses to work, and a U.S. guard strikes him, the guard will be court-martialed. We are here to teach these people democracy, and we can't do it by being a bunch of bullies."

The inescapable Anglo-Saxon sensitivity to race—all the captives belonged to the colored races—tended toward a certain overcompensation on the part of the American guards. It was not enough to stress that the POW's were human beings, to which there could be no argument; it must be brought out that they were fully equal human beings, which was debatable.

However, the assembled officers shifted their feet and got the message. The prisoners were to be equals, and not to be bashed, no matter what. They were also to be taught democracy. That was clear enough.

Nobody asked Colonel Fitzgerald, however, the approved method by which democracy was taught, which was probably just as well.

As it turned out, the method seemed to consist in giving the POW's anything they wanted. As Bill Gregory put it: "We told 'em we're here to serve you. If you want anything, you let us know, boy. We're going to show you what democracy means. You're all damn fools to be Communists—you do the way we do, and you'll be living on top of the world."

It was a materialistic approach. The main idea seemed to be that democracy was better than Communism because it produced a life richer in the goods of this world.

Colonel Fitzgerald had plenty of help. In addition to the Americans, there was the International Red Cross, informing the POW's of their rights, and a U.N. Commission on Korea, called UNCORK by the GI's for reasons having nothing to do with their announced mission.

The POW's were furnished books on democracy, and copies of the United States Constitution. That took care of the theory, for those who could read.

For the rest of it, tons of athletic equipment, much of it abandoned by U.S. units in Pusan, were shipped in. A new hospital was built, with sick call daily. North Korean and Chinese doctors treated the POW's; these men were allowed all the drugs and medicines they desired.

Mess halls were constructed. The POW's own cooks worked in stone and baked clay kitchens, with new Korean utensils. They were given more rice, fish, and vegetables than nine-tenths of them had seen in their lifetime.

They were inspected for cleanliness and health by a special Medical Sanitation Company.

They were given new clothing, some of which, like socks, they didn't know how to use. Because most of the U.S. supply of fatigue uniforms had been diverted to surplus sales and relief work around the world and now with a new war were scarce, the POW's were issued new officers' pinks and greens, straight from QM depots. Each man received new boots and a clean mattress cover.

Major Gregory saw many men inside the barbed wire walking about in better uniforms than he owned. American officers had to pay for their uniforms, and Bill Gregory had a family in the States.

Now the POW's were screened, to determine their sentiments. Already it was becoming known that many of them were not true Communists. Of the nearly 80,000 Koreans, many were conscripts taken in South Korea, or men torn from their homes in the North, with no interest in or inclination toward politics or the war. Of the nearly 6,000 Chinese, many were soldiers of Chiang Kai-shek forcibly incorporated into the Chinese Peoples' Volunteers; many had suffered, or their families had suffered, from the Communist conquest.

Already, there was ferment in the compounds between the fanatic Communists and the non-Communists, as different factions jostled for control. This ferment was dimly seen by the guards, and not understood at all. Communists and non-Communists were treated alike, as equals.

But the screening did have one result. The worst Communists, officers and men alike, were segregated into compounds like the soon-to-be-notorious 76. The segregation did not have the desired result; instead, it concentrated Communist talent.

Now, a certain senior colonel of the Inmun Gun, the ranking POW in Compound 76 and on Koje-do, had a staff at hand. All Lee Hak Ku had to do was use it. But while the Russian-trained Lee remained the senior officer on paper, the real power among the captives was probably in the hands of a small, evil-faced officer called Hong Chol.

Lee Hak Ku, by surrendering, had shown himself capable of weakness, and the inner cadre would never again wholly trust him. And Hong Chol was where he could keep an eye on Colonel Lee.

Together, these two began to organize and control the compounds. When the Americans told the prisoners to elect representatives from each compound, Lee and Hong were ready. The campaign was brief, violent, and secretly bloody.

Occasionally, the guards would find a corpse in the latrine, or a body stuffed down the sewer line. Now and then a roll call turned up someone short, and the POW's would seem to be uneasy, talking and muttering in small groups.

The missing men were often listed as escapees.

And the Lee-Hong slate was elected. Whatever the non-Communist POW's had learned from reading the U.S. Constitution, the Lee-Hong forces were better organized at the precinct level.

Meeting with U.N. representatives, the new representatives of the prisoners slowly became more confident. The new chief *honchos,* or head knockers, met daily with the guards, and began to demand things.

To their delight, they were never disappointed.

They asked for whitewash, and got it. Soon, pretty rock designs of Chinese, Korean, and U.S. flags adorned the compound yards. They asked for record players, paper, ink, mimeograph machines, and work tools.

Because the U.N. Commission felt it was good therapy to let them work, they got everything they asked for, at U.S. expense.

There was no appropriation for extra barbed wire, or for more compounds to ease the crucial housing shortage, which made the existing compounds so large as to be almost unmanageable. But there was money for sheet metal, saws, hammers, and nails for the prisoners, who went studiously to work, making things. Some of the items they made they buried underneath the floors of their huts before the Americans had a chance to admire them.

Happy with their work, a certain amount of spirit returned to even the most apathetic Communist POW. Now some of them ignored their guards when ordered to work for their own benefit, such as in the kitchens, and spat in the guards' faces if the Americans became insistent.

One day a sergeant approached Bill Gregory. The sergeant was an old Army man, wooden-faced with his consciousness of duty. "Sir, you told us to let you know if anyone hit a POW—"

"Well?"

The guard wiped his face. "Major, I just hit one myself."

"Don't tell me, boy—don't tell me," Gregory said quickly.

The N.C.O. saluted and went away.

This kind of crisis Bill Gregory had to learn to live with.

One day, the flags went up, blue and yellow and made of clean new mattress covers donated by the U.S. Army. Seeing the myriad banners flying over each compound, each with its Communist propaganda slogan, a GI remarked to Gregory: "Boy, aren't they pretty sir? These people are sure artistic!"

"They sure are," Gregory said.

Since the POW's seemed to enjoy putting them up, the flags were allowed to stay.

Bill Gregory had other things on his mind, however. He was busy installing automatic flushing commodes in the four-holers that served the compounds.

And he had a problem on the beach, where one of his sewer lines emptied into Korea Strait. The mouth of the line, made of 55-gallon drums, ran out three hundred feet beyond the water's edge—but Korean tides were extreme, and at low tide the sewer mouth was exposed.

The problem was caused by rice. The prisoners ate rice as if they had never eaten before, and kept the new toilets busy. And rice feces, among the various kinds, are unique. They come out as small hard balls, tough as cement, insoluble in water. They will not float, nor will they wash away. They lay by the hundreds of millions on the beach, like dark, ugly snails.

The beaches of Koje-do, at low tide, were a sight to behold.

It was one engineering problem Bill Gregory was never to solve.

With the prisoners learning about democracy in lectures, and happily at work the remainder of the time, turning out mimeographed newssheets or banging away in the metal shops, Colonel Fitzgerald could turn his attention to the U.S. personnel on the island. It had come to the C.O.'s notice that many of the POW's looked better than his own troops.

He ordered officers to wear pinks and greens on duty, and all personnel were to don ties. After all, the eyes of the world were on Koje-do.

And with the compounds slapped together, he ordered work commenced on the officers' club. This went up quickly, a huge, barnlike structure of sheet metal and native island timber. While it was built, somebody arranged for Korean barmaids, in freshly starched dresses, to be imported from Pusan.

Things were looking up all over.

There was even a rumor that the Eighth Army was now winning the war on the mainland.

During this period, Major Gregory noticed that the population of Koje-do, aside from the POW's, was increasing. More and more Koreans showed up, to get jobs as servants, houseboys, laundrymen, barbers. The U.S. payroll, after the manner of such rolls, continued to increase geometrically each month. In Colonel Fitzgerald's HQ there were more Koreans than GI's.

The Koreans who still hadn't made the payroll were opening new business ventures, selling souvenirs to both GI's and POW's. Each day tradesmen surrounded the compounds, doing a brisk trade through the barbed wire.

It would have been cruel, and a blow to the local economy, to interfere with them.

The ROK's of the two guard battalions were doing well, too. Most of them had brought in their families. Some had also opened up new businesses. All were busily engaged in erecting new quarters, complete with landscaping.

Two alert Koreans noticed that the traffic between Pusan and Koje had increased tenfold since 1950. They dug up two diesel barges to supplement the official ferry on the end of the island, and they soon grew rich.

A great many of the young women refugees from North Korea, who had been dumped on Koje by the ROK government, found steady employment, at compensation formerly undreamed of in East Asia.

Colonel Fitzgerald inspected the officers' club daily, and it was coming along real well.

The POW's continued to make things in their shops. They put out more flags, some of them artistic triumphs. They sang and chanted in their compounds, and seemed content. Now and then a battered body blocked one of Bill Gregory's sewers, which was a hell of a nuisance until they removed it.

But it was understood that the Asians weren't too well checked out on modern plumbing, and no one worried.

The POW press turned out more and more newssheets, flooding the island. Many began to turn up in Pusan, as the paper ration was increased. One evening Major Gregory found one in his quarters. He asked his houseboy what it said.

He was told, "Oh, the Communists are telling the people what fools the Americans are."

28

May Massacre

It is a necessary to provide soldiers with defensive arms of every type as to instruct them in the use of offensive ones. For it is certain men fight with greater courage and confidence when they find themselves properly armed for defense.

—From the Latin of Vegetius, MILITARY INSTITUTIONS OF THE ROMANS.

AFTER THE MASSIVE failure of the CCF First Step, Fifth Phase Offensive, the front, which now almost evenly divided the Korean peninsula, enjoyed two weeks of uneasy quiet.

May Day came, but the CCF had turned to limited retreat on 30 April, and the expected blow did not fall. Always, during the Korean War, U.N. observers tensed at the approach of May, fearing action on the traditional pagan holiday, sacred both to ancient Anglo-Saxons and modern Communists. But the Communists showed no more disposition, if conditions were not right, for action on 1 May than the Americans did to start their own ruckusses on July Fourth.

But U.N. intelligence, warned by aerial observation of troop and supply movement, felt that a new CCF offensive was brewing and that this time it would fall against General Ned Almond's X Corps, in the center.

Air power, in the mountains of North Korea, could not stop the continuing reinforcement of the CCF front any more than it had been able completely to choke off the German armies in Italy during World War II.

The CCF, relying on night movement and muscle power, were always able to move sufficient supply forward. Air interdiction could cripple the forward flow from time to time; it could not kill it.

The CCF, as others before then, had learned to live with a hostile sky. They clung to hills and mountains, and they dug deep. They moved by night, when it was difficult even for the night-flying fighter-bombers to seek them out in the bristling terrain.

It was only—as in Italy, at Anzio and other places—when ground action put inexorable pressure on enemy ground forces, forcing them to move or to displace, that conventional tactical air could come into its own. Massed to attack, the CCF became vulnerable. When they broke through U.N. lines, and their artillery and supply were forced to move out into the open, to displace forward in support, U.N. air could pounce upon them and chew them mercilessly. When they were forced by U.N. ground pressure to retreat, to stream down the roads and corridors of escape, air again could inflict deadly wounds.

Conventional air action, in Korea, could be decisive only when coupled with decisive ground action. It is impossible to interdict the battlefront, in mountains, of an army that eats only a handful of rice and soya beans and carries its ammunition forward piggyback.

But when the Chinese came down out of their brooding hills, either to attack or retreat, U.N. air, armor, and artillery, all vastly superior in the spring of 1951, more than offset their advantage in manpower.

For the first two weeks of May, feeling the enemy would strike again, Lieutenant General Van Fleet kept Eighth Army on the defensive, dug in behind its "No Name Line." As it turned out, this was an eminently sensible maneuver.

In the center, behind prepared positions, crouched the CCF's old friend, the United States 2nd Division.

The division's line ran along the crest of a huge hill mass in East Central Korea, separating the Hongch'on and Soyang rivers. The main line of resistance ran in most places a mile or more beyond the ends of the nearest supply roads, and all matériel of war had to be hand-carried up the thousand-foot slopes.

The 38th Infantry held the left of the division line, and on the regimental left, firmly fixed on a hill mass known as Hill 800, the 3rd Battalion, 38th, dug in.

Lieutenant Colonel Wallace Hanes, the C.O. of the 3/38, gave explicit orders to cut fields of fire, to dig bunkers, and to build covered positions for every man of the rifle companies.

Colonel Hanes discovered what many had discovered before and since— that while the American soldier is among the best in the world at getting his tents up and his socks dry, he has no love for digging in the earth. Inspecting, Hanes found that most men had merely dug a foxhole, put a poncho over it to keep out the cold spring rain, and a few leaves over the poncho as concealment. American troops always despise physical labor.

Hanes roared at his company commanders: "Damn it, I want solid bunkers with cover to protect you from artillery fire!"

Under Hanes' lashing, the 3/38 cut down trees, to build solid bunker walls. On top of these they put earth, and rock as a bursting pan. They dug deep trenches from firing position to position, and they dug great holes in the mountainsides in which to hide their bunkers.

Still, some positions stuck out, and Hanes insisted on their being covered over with sandbags, by the thousands. He wanted positions that would stand under enemy artillery—or friendly, if the 3/38 were overrun.

With the deep positions ready after a week of Hanes' prodding, wire was strung across the front, and mines emplaced along the forward hill slopes. All of the matériel was carried up the steep slopes on the backs of Korean laborers and laboriously emplaced by the grudging U.S. troops.

When Hanes had first explained to them what he wanted, many had thought him joking.

When Colonel Hanes was satisfied, they had used up 237,000 sandbags, 385 rolls of barbed wire, more than 6,000 steel wire pickets, and 39 *fougasse* drums. A *fougasse* was an improvised land mine, consisting of a 55-gallon POL drum filled with napalm, a small explosive charge, usually white phosphorous shells, and a detonator. When exploded, the crude mine threw a mass of 3,000-degree Fahrenheit flame over an area ten by thirty yards long, with extremely salutary effects on any CCF who might be nearby.

In addition to fortifications, the 3/38 had to carry its water, food, and ammunition up the hill. It took three to four hours for a round trip.

The only way Colonel Hanes found to get his heavy 4.2-inch mortars up was by the use of Korean oxen.

With his front completely wired in, Hanes now insisted on trip flares and AP mines being strewn over the forward slopes, and his wire communications being placed underground.

The 3/38, which already figured it knew how to fight, now learned how to work. On 12 May Hanes was halfway satisfied.

And the 2nd Division knew that something was in the wind. Enemy patrols were thick out along the Soyang River; refugees and line crossers were pouring in; air reported vehicular traffic and new bridges deep in the enemy mountains.

Waiting in their deep positions, Hanes' men were now proud of their handiwork, and confident. It had dawned on them, that while they had never had positions half so good, they had seen some the Chinese had made that were as good, or better. Once the work was over, they were at last glad they had done it.

Hanes, talking to Major General Ruffner, the division commander, said, "I'm worried about only one thing now, General—I'm afraid the bastards won't hit us!"

Wallace Hanes need not have worried. On 16 May, after nightfall, the bastards launched their Second Step, Fifth Phase Offensive, which the United Nations Command designated the "The Second CCF Spring Offensive," X Corps called "The Battle of the Soyang," and the soldiers of the 2nd Division remembered ever afterward as the May Massacre.

* * *

On 16 May 1951, the III and IX Army groups, comprising the 12th, 15th, 60th, 20th, and 27th armies, CCF, moved 137,000 Chinese and 38,000 North Koreans southward like a muddy, coffee-colored sea. The sky was heavy and overcast, and American air blind and impotent.

The Chinese "volunteers" had been told of great victories in the offing. They knew they faced the ROK's, of whom they were contemptuous, and the U.S. 2nd Infantry Division, whose blood they had tasted before.

The long, undulant, columns chanted and grunted and sang, after the manner of all Chinese at work or on the march, until the hills were hideous with their noise.

At night, on the flare and bugle call, they went into the ROK's holding No Name Line to the east of the 2nd Division. The ROK's, outnumbered, outgunned, and badly led, came apart.

Like a door swung sharply inward, the line east of the 3/38 fell to the southwest, toward Wonju. The ROK's did not run, at first. They fought; they were overwhelmed. They fell back.

By 17 May once again, as at Kunu–ri, the 2nd Division was gaping and exposed on its right flank.

By daylight, the Chinese had struck into the 1st and 2nd battalions of the 38th, and had run full into Task Force Zebra, a 2nd Division force whose steel tip was the 72nd Tank Battalion.

They struck fire such as they had never faced before.

Infantrymen held to their hilltops; tanks moved along the valley corridors with machine gun and cannon. Tank gunners and artillerymen fired until they were exhausted from loading shells, and tubes were close to burning out.

On the right flank of the division, finally, the advance was stopped.

The CCF, hurt, milled and coiled about, seeking an easier way. Striking farther to the west, on the left flank of the 2nd Division, the Chinese threw a division against the 38th Infantry's solid hills.

By the prodigal spending of men against wire and flame, C Company of the 38th was overrun. East of Colonel Hanes' positions, 1/38 pulled back to the left, and 2/38 also moved back.

The French Battalion was sent forward to plug the gap between Task Force Zebra and the 38th Infantry caused by the loss of C Company. The French could not restore the line, but they held the Chinese at bay until the 72nd Tank moved back, and the 23rd Infantry assumed their mission.

Now the Chinese went for the apex of the U.N. defensive line, the hills held by 3/38, which were rapidly assuming the character of a salient, with enemy on either side of them.

The CCF route of approach led them directly into Hill 800, the anchor about which the 3rd Battalion was centered. Dug in atop 800, which they already called Bunker Hill, was Company K, Captain Brownell.

The men of Bunker Hill were deep inside more than two dozen bunkers, the positions Colonel Hanes had forced them to build so painfully a week before.

Shortly after dark, 17 May, waiting in a cold mountain fog, King Company heard the sound of bugles. Soon, then, the men on Bunker Hill heard the Chinese at their first wire barrier; several mines exploded, and the Chinese opened fire on the hill.

Gradually the firing increased as the Chinese neared; some of King's men could even hear querulous Chinese words shouted back and forth. The attackers slipped around the side of the hill, cut the wire, and climbed up the steepest part, where few mines had been laid.

Now King opened fire, with a crackling roar.

Brownell, however, owing to poor communication, was unable to call down artillery fire. A shell landed directly on his command bunker, damaging his radio; and a number of men from Mike, the supporting Weapons Company, under a new, green lieutenant, had left their positions and were falling back across the hill.

Other men joined them. In a thunderous small-arms fire fight, Chinese and Americans were wandering about all over Bunker Hill in the dark.

Captain Brownell, in a superb defensive position, was suddenly in command of complete confusion, for men heard that the line was falling back, and began to pull out.

Colonel Hanes met some of these at the bottom of the hill. "Get back up on the hill—we don't give up a position until we're beaten, and we're not beaten if every man does his share!"

The men went back. The green lieutenant who had started the pull-out got back into his position with several wounds.

Meanwhile, Captain Brownell had organized his reserve platoon for a counterattack to hurl the Chinese off the hill—many of them were already in some of the abandoned bunkers. They waited for artillery to fall in support—but commo was still spotty, and the artillery did not arrive.

"Hell with it," one of Brownell's officers snapped. "We can take the damned hill ourselves!"

Forming a long skirmish line, they advanced through the dark, firing rifles and carbines. They had many white phosphorous grenades, and they hurled these into bunkers and trenches as they passed. As each grenade exploded on the hill, advancing infantry stood out sharply in the ghastly light; then the men went blind again.

After sharp, close-in fighting, Brownell threw the scattered, disorganized Chinese off his hill. Sometime after midnight, the position was restored.

But numerous Chinese had flowed around King Company, and were heavily engaged with I in its rear. With daylight some two hundred of them burrowed into bunkers between K and I, and Colonel Hanes realized this force had to be reduced before nightfall 18 May, or his entire line might break.

Hanes personally led the counterattack under extremely heavy mortar fire from his supporting 4.2's. The Chinese broke and ran. Many were killed fleeing, while Hanes lost no one.

During the day, King Company strengthened its defense once more, while on its right the entire X Corps line was swinging southwest, to prevent a possible CCF envelopment.

Bunker Hill was becoming more exposed by the moment. With dark, Brownell and his men crawled deep into their strong holes. And with dark, they heard the sound of horns again.

Not like the British at Boston, marching arrogant and erect, but padding catfooted, hunched over, their buttocks near the earth, the horde of Chinese ran forward to Bunker Hill.

Brownell called for artillery. This time he had communication.

But the enemy walked in over his own dead, and reached King's bunkers. Brownell told his platoon leaders what he planned to do, then asked for variable-time shells directly on the hill.

The shells whooped in, bursting a few feet above ground, spraying the area with sizzling shards. It was recorded in the Division Operations Journal that 2,000 rounds of 105mm shell burst over Bunker Hill within eight minutes.

Gradually, it grew quiet. Then Chinese artillery began to probe the hill; the CCF was not yet ready to accede.

The Chinese, climbing over their dead, came again.

When they were firmly on his hill, Brownell called for every inch of 800 to be seared with fire. The 38th Field Artillery, that night, fired ten thousand rounds alone, and other artillery units supported, too.

Nothing above ground could live. Brownell and his men, who had built well, were untouched. At dawn, the CCF broke and streamed north, leaving only their dead behind.

King company was king on Bunker Hill.

It was not easy for Hanes and Brownell to give up, on 19 May, when orders from General Almond forced the 3/38 to move south out of what had become a dangerously exposed position, as part of a general consolidation of the corps lines.

* * *

By 21 May, Ned Almond realized that the massive CCF thrust against Ruffner's division had been contained. By swinging wide the door but holding the hinges, the X Corps had led the CCF into a bottomless pit; it rushed into the valleys, ran short of ammunition and supply, and died in windrows under the pounding of U.N. air, artillery, and armor.

It had no chance of cracking the whole line, or of exploiting. It had struck against a division very different from its old acquaintance of the Ch'ongch'on.

Understanding that the CCF had been stopped and was faltering, Almond ordered X Corps to counterattack. He talked Van Fleet out of an additional division and the 187th Airborne RCT, and on 23 May, attached to the 2nd Division, he sent the paratroopers north.

The first attack proved that the U.N. now held the initiative. Almond ordered the 187th, with the 72nd Tank Battalion, to form Task Force Gerhardt—named for the C.O. of the paratroopers—to advance to the Soyang, seizing the bridges there and killing as many Chinese as possible on the way.

While the Chinese still defended from roadblocks, and their men still wandered armed through the hills, the main body of the Chinese armies was in full retreat. As Task Force Gerhardt pursued them, the Chinese displacement became a rout.

U.S. tasks roared past abandoned supply, pack animals, ammunition. They went by burning villages and dead Chinese lying beside the roads, killed by tank fire or air strafing.

The CCF, which had come across the Soyang singing, fled back in disorder. On 28 May, Inje fell.

By launching a powerful counterattack almost before the end of what was to be the most spectacular defensive stand of the war, X Corps had suddenly, sharply, changed the course of war. The Chinese had now completely lost the initiative; worse, they had been hurt almost beyond recovery.

Against the 2nd Division had been committed at one time or another ten CCF divisions, and during the month of May an estimated 65,000 Chinese and North Koreans had died under its guns.

In one valley, alone, where the artillery had done its work, 5,000 corpses were counted.

At the end of the May Massacre, the Eighth Army again moved north.

When it stopped, it would not be stopped with guns, but with words.

PART III

Blundering

29

Truce Talks

To my mind it is fruitless to speculate on what might have been. If we had been ordered to fight our way to the Yalu, we could have done it—if our government had been willing to pay the price in dead and wounded that action would have cost.

—General Matthew B. Ridgway.

O N 1 FEBRUARY 1951 the U.N. branded Red China as an aggressor, and at the same time passed a resolution in effect abandoning the objectives it had set forth on 7 October 1950, for it now stated such objectives should be accomplished through peaceful means.

Since action in the Security Council had been blocked by a Malik veto, the General Assembly voted 44–7, with 9 abstentions, that, *noting the Central People's Government of the People's Republic of China has not accepted United Nations proposals to bring about a cessation of hostilities in Korea with a view of peaceful settlement, and that its armed forces continue their invasion of Korea and their large-scale attacks upon the United Nations Forces there:*

[The General Assembly] Finds that the Central People's Government . . . has engaged in aggression in Korea;

Calls upon the Central People's Government . . . to cause its forces . . . in Korea to cease hostilities . . . and to withdraw from Korea;

Affirms the determination of the United Nations to continue its action in Korea to meet the aggression;

Calls upon all states . . . to continue to lend assistance to the United Nations action in Korea;

Calls upon all states to refrain from giving any assistance to the aggressors in Korea;

Requests a committee composed of the members of the Collective Measures Committee . . . to consider additional measures to be employed to meet this aggression . . . ;

Affirms that it continues to be the policy of the United Nations to bring about a cessation of hostilities in Korea and the achievement of United Nations objectives in Korea by peaceful means, and requests the President of the General Assembly to designate forthwith two persons to meet with him . . . to use their good offices to this end.

The U.N. refused to impose sanctions or other punitive measures against the Communist Chinese.

The United States, facing at the time a very poor tactical situation in Korea, finding the U.N. action backed by each of its European allies, had begun to explore the means of ending the fighting that brought Truman into conflict with MacArthur.

But while the Western world was willing to talk peace, and from this time continuously put forth feelers to the Communist bloc, the Red Chinese still hoped for a favorable decision on the battlefield. When they would hint of terms at all, these included withdrawal of all foreign troops from Korea, leaving North and South to settle their own affairs, withdrawal of U.S. protection to Taiwan, and admission of Red China to the U.N., all of which were strategically and politically impossible for the United States.

Here the matter rested during March, April, and early May, while a violent war of maneuver flowed up and down the middle part of the Korean peninsula. Encouraged by their success in the North, the CCF briefly engaged in open battle with the U.N. forces, in one massive assault after another, in February, April, and again in May.

Each time the CCF were spectacularly unsuccessful.

At the end of May 1951, the CCF had proved they could not prevail in open warfare in the more maneuverable ground of southern and middle Korea. But the U.N. Command had no burning desire to push and pursue them back into the horrendous terrain girdling the Yalu. Unless Manchuria could be interdicted, the CCF would fight here from a base of strength, while the U.N. would again be restricted and far from its sources of supply.

On the Yalu, the U.N. defensive line would be four hundred miles long, almost four times the distance it covered in the area of the 38th parallel.

In the spring of 1951 a movement against Red China itself was politically unfeasible in the U.N. As Winston Churchill, soon to return to power in Great Britain, put it, the thought of an Anglo-American army mucking about through Manchuria gave him nightmares. Ridgway, well aware of the processes that had brought him his fourth star, was content to take his direction from Washington.

Washington was seeking any means out of the Korean conflict that might be achieved without surrender, and with honor.

The fighting had escalated from a small limited war to a very large— though still limited—war, and it had poised the world on the brink of a general holocaust.

On 26 May, Lester Pearson of Canada, President of the U.N. General Assembly, stated that surrender of the aggressors might not be required to end the war; the U.N. would be satisfied if the aggression could be brought to an end. On 1 June, Trygve Lie, understanding completely the mood of his charges, mentioned that the time seemed right for stopping the bloodshed, since on this date the Chinese and North Koreans had been driven back across their line of departure. If a cease-fire could be made along the 38th parallel, Lie said, the Security Council resolutions of 25 and 27 June, and 7 July 1950, could be considered carried out.

On 2 June, Dean Acheson publicly agreed with Lie. He said there were actually two problems, one political, one military. While the long-term political approach of the United States, desiring a united, free, and independent Korea had not changed, the immediate problem of concern to Washington was the stopping of the shooting, with assurances it would not begin again. On 7 June, in response to vigorous grilling by a Senate committee, Acheson further stated that any reliable armistice based on the 38th parallel would be acceptable to the United States.

The United States had come full cycle, back from its position of October 1950, to its position of the previous June. The goal was containment, not victory.

And in June, with the CCF very close to real disaster in Korea, Communist thinking altered, too. The Soviet Union wanted neither defeat nor a big war, whatever the firebrands in Peiping desired. The battle lines, except in the west, where they neared the parallel, already stood well above the old line of demarcation, and the situation for the Communist powers was worsening.

It was very clear to Soviet observers that the CCF could not win a decision in South Korea; they could not now even halt the slow, steady U.N. advance northward.

It was also clear that the continuing hot war in the Far East was jangling Western nerves and hastening the slow rearmament of Europe under NATO. The West obviously desired peace—but continued Communist intransigence could tend only to unite the Western allies in the long run.

When Communists cannot win by force, they are prepared to negotiate. If, in 1951, they could stop the U.N. advance by talking, they would firm an increasingly fluid and dangerous situation and in effect achieve a tactical victory.

On 23 June, almost one year from the hour that the Inmun Gun deployed above the parallel, Soviet delegate Yakov A. Malik made a remarkable speech before the U.N. He claimed not to be speaking for the real belligerents, North Korea and Red China, but as a sort of *amicus curiae* for everyone. He made certain his speech was carried by radio to the gallery at large, the Western public.

The greater part of the speech was the usual Soviet reiteration of charges and complaints—but Malik ended on a new note:

"The problem of armed conflict in Korea could . . . be settled . . . ; as the first step, discussions should be started between the belligerents for a cease-fire and an armistice providing for mutual withdrawal of forces from the 38th parallel . . . provided there is a sincere desire to put an end to the bloody fighting in Korea."

If the government Malik represented was sincere, it had apparently now agreed to the present goals of the United Nations Command.

He was immediately challenged by the United States delegate to put up or shut up. Truman repeated the American position in a broadcast. And on 30 June General Ridgway, as U.N. Commander in Chief, radioed the commander of Communist Forces in Korea as follows:

I am informed that you may wish a meeting to discuss an armistice providing for the cessation of hostilities and all acts of armed forces in Korea, with adequate guarantees for the maintenance of such armistice.

It was a remarkable statement for an American commander, triumphant in the field, to make to an as yet unhumbled enemy. It occurred less than a decade after an American pronouncement of a goal of unconditional surrender of its enemies, but it revealed an aeon of diplomatic and political change in American thinking on the matter of war.

And here, on 30 June, a certain amount of love between the United States and the Taehan Minkuk ended. For the Republic of Korea saw no honor in the proposed cease-fire, which left its people ravaged and still divided. A settlement along the 38th parallel, for all the American and U.N. protestations of continuance of the goal of uniting Korea by peaceful means, meant the separation of Korea into two blocs for as long as man could count, possibly for centuries.

Syngman Rhee was spurred not only by economic and national reasons to oppose peace now, but also by those same reasons that bound Europe's leaders into an emotional straitjacket in 1916–1917, when the Great War stalemated and it seemed sensible to end it. The Taehan Minkuk had gone into the war with its whole heart; it had been devastated, and one in twenty of its people killed or injured. Millions of orphans and homeless wandered its ruins.

To end the war after such wholesale sacrifice with nothing but the *status quo ante* was more than aging Rhee or the Koreans could bear.

Dr. Rhee issued a statement on 30 June 1951.

The Republic of Korea's conditions for peace were as follows: the CCF must withdraw north of the Yalu; all North Korean Communists must be disarmed; Soviet and Chinese arms assistance to the North must end, under a U.N. guarantee; full ROK participation in any settlement; and no settlement conflicting with the sovereignty or territorial integrity of the Republic of Korea.

From this time on, Syngman Rhee continued to be a patriot or became a major nuisance, depending on the vantage point from which he was viewed. Rhee never materially changed his demands, and he was to experience a continually worsening press in both Europe and America. Rhee, threatening again and again to block an armistice desired by most, became less and less a heroic old resistor of Communism and more and more a stubborn, opinionated old tyrant, determined to keep the West from getting what it wanted.

Actually, both Rhee and Korea were largely helpless. Not a U.N. member but a ward of that body, completely dependent upon American arms, fuel, munitions, and economic aid, the Taehan Minkuk had no chance of materially influencing U.S. policy. Willingly or not, Dr. Rhee had to continue as an American puppet or cease to exist.

But a certain amount of love was lost. With divergent aims, neither Washington nor Seoul now fully trusted the other.

Kim Il Sung, Supreme Commander of the Inmun Gun, and Peng Teh-huai, Commander of Chinese Volunteers—whose name until that day was unknown to U.N. intelligence—radioed on 1 July 1951, agreeing to a meeting, not at sea, as Ridgway desired, but at Kaesong.

Kaesong was three miles below the parallel and a few miles inside Communist lines; north of Seoul, it lay athwart the main north-south corridor through western Korea, along the main invasion route.

The United Nations Command, not caring to be technical, accepted Kaesong. It was to learn that Communists propose nothing, not even truce sites, without an eye to their own advantage.

On 8 July Colonel James C. Murray, USMC; Jack Kinney, an Air Force colonel; and Colonel Lee Soo Young, ROK Army, representing the U.N. command, met with a Colonel Chang of the Communists at a teahouse on the outskirts of rubble-strewn Kaesong. All agreed that the principals to negotiate a possible cease-fire would meet at Kaesong at 1100 on 10 July.

On that date, Vice Admiral C. Turner Joy designated by General Ridgway as the Senior UNC Delegate, said to newsmen as he left Munsan-ni:

"We, the delegates from the United Nations Command, are leaving for Kaesong fully conscious of the importance of these meetings to the entire world. We are proceeding in good faith prepared to do our part to bring about an honorable armistice, under terms that are satisfactory to the United Nations Command."

The seventeen nations with fighting forces in Korea had already met, and agreed on terms, which in essence were to freeze the fighting and forces where they stood, form a demilitarized zone in the vicinity of the parallel, exchange of prisoners, and the establishment of an international commission with access to supervise any truce.

The Joint Chiefs of Staff, meanwhile, had explicitly instructed Ridgway not to discuss any political or territorial questions with the enemy. Not to be discussed were the seating of Red China in the U.N., Red claims to Taiwan, or any permanent division of Korea, or the 38th parallel as a political boundary.

From the American and U.N. point of view, the sole purpose of the meetings at Kaesong was to end the bloodshed, and to create some sort of machinery to supervise such an armistice. This done, an entirely separate body would sift the political and territorial questions posed by the Korean situation, in an atmosphere of peace.

Americans, even the knowledgeable Dean Acheson, had once again tried to separate peace and war into neat compartments, to their sorrow.

Assembled with Admiral Joy were Major General Laurence C. Craigie, USAF; Major General Henry I. Hodes, USA; Rear Admiral Arleigh A. Burke, USN; and Major-General Paik Sun Yup, ROK Army. Not one of these men was other than a military commander; not one was in any respect a diplomat or politician. They were soldiers, come to forge a military agreement to end the killing.

On the other side of the famous green table at Kaesong was a formidable array of Communist talent: General Nam Il, North Korea Senior Delegate; Major General Chang Pyong San, North Korea; Major General Lee Sang Cho, North Korea; Lieutenant General Tung Hua, Chinese Volunteers; and Major General Hsieh Fang, also Chinese. Several of these men were graduates of Soviet universities, and not one was a fighting man.

All had held political posts, and with typical Communist deviousness, seemingly the junior man at the table in rank, Hsieh Fang, was the man who actually held the Communist cards.

Immediately, it became apparent that the Communist delegation intended not only to discuss the proposed cease-fire but everything up to and including the kitchen drain. Immediately, they would not agree to an agenda. Immediately, they made sharp protest at Turner Joy's use of the word "Communists"—there were no "Communists" in Kaesong, but only Inmun Gun and Chinese Volunteers; on the other hand, they used such terms as "that murderer Rhee" and "the puppet of Taiwan" quite freely.

They insisted that the 38th parallel must be the new line of demarcation, although the U.N. armies in most places stood well above it—and the parallel, as had been proved, was hardly a defensible line—and that unless the United Nations Command ceased actual hostilities in Korea at once they could not discuss the armistice. They at once refused demands to permit the International Red Cross to inspect North Korean POW camps.

And from the selection of the site at Kaesong—in Communist hands, yet still below the parallel, one of the few spots in Korea where this condition obtained—the forcing of U.N. negotiators to enter Communist territory displaying white flags, as if they were coming to surrender, to the seating of Admiral Joy in a chair substantially lower than Nam Il's, the enemy showed that nothing was too small to be overlooked, if it accrued to his advantage.

As best it could, without sabotaging the truce talks, the U.N. Command began to fight for its own ends. Its delegates had come in good faith, to make an honest end to the killing, with the settlements to come later.

The tragedy of the talks was that the Communists intended merely to transfer the war from the battlefield, where they were losing, to the conference table, where they might yet win something.

The United Nations' desire for peace was genuine—almost frantic. Nothing else could have kept their negotiators, subjected to harassment, stinging insult, and interminable delay, at the green table after the first few sessions.

On 8 July, when Colonels Jack Kinney and Chang Chun San arranged the first Plenary Session, the world had displayed conspicuous joy. Only the United States Government sought to dampen the enthusiasm a bit: the *New York Times* reported on that date that "fighting for several weeks is foreseen by Washington."

Washington was still not seeing clearly. No one dared guess that it would take 159 plenary sessions and more than two years of haggling to end the killing.

Turner Joy, determined to succeed, said: "Unless you come prepared to spend time you only shortchange yourself and those who depend on you. Time is the price you pay for progress."

But time, above all, was what the Communist world needed in Korea in the summer of 1951.

And time, thirty fatal days, while the U.N. forces paused and marked time in expectation of immediate peace, was what they got.

Sometimes the price of progress comes high.

* * *

After the start of talks—first at Kaesong, then transferred to Panmunjom, in a neutral zone ten miles east at U.N. insistence—every action on the checkerboard of the Korean War would be made with one eye on the state of the front and one on the conference table.

Very soon, the U.N. Command was in quandary.

It wanted peace; the governments it represented wanted peace. The Communist world was willing to talk, even though it obstructed day to day, and while the talks went on there was always the hope of peace, eventually.

As Winston Churchill said, "It is better to jaw, jaw, than war, war."

But yet, with both armies in the field, lurking within gunshot of each other, with nothing settled, war could not wholly end.

The U.N. Command no longer looked for victory in the field. It had already been committed to settlement in the vicinity of the 38th parallel, though it insisted upon the present line of contact, not that indefensible, imaginary line of demarcation on the ground. If it flailed ahead now, made great gains, these would have already been compromised and might well be lost at the conference table. Ridgway and Van Fleet and Washington were loath to spend lives for nothing. Yet Ridgway and Van Fleet dared not sit still, letting their forces stagnate, despite Washington.

As summer ripened, there was no progress at the table. The Communist delegations seemed willing, even eager, to delay forever. They had transferred their war largely to the truce table, and now were as happily waging it as before, while they put the time they had bought to good use, if another round at arms should come.

As summer deepened, and the hopes of the world slowly withered, another round at arms was bound to come. In the green and muddy hills of Korea, the war had not ended. It had begun a new and terrible phase.

30

Bloody Ridge

The capture of this hill is worth ten thousand men!
—Remark by a French general on the Western Front, 1916.

Generous bastard, isn't he?
—Quote from the French general's first assault battalion commander.

F OR ALL PRACTICAL purposes the Korean War ended 30 June 1951, when United Nations Supreme Commander Matthew Ridgway radioed his willingness to discuss truce terms with the Communist forces. The end was stalemate.

At heavy cost, the original aggression and the fresh intervention of the Chinese had been contained. The aggressor in each case had suffered frightful losses and had gained nothing material.

Having eschewed the goal of victory, the United States had nothing further to gain from continued fighting. It had accomplished its original purpose in going into Korea, the salvation of the Taehan Minkuk.

The Communist World had gained no territory, wealth, or peoples—but by opposing American arms, by defying the United Nations, with some success, Red China had undoubtedly neared great-power status. Her prestige among Asian peoples, still smarting from Western humiliations, was enhanced, whatever moral questions were involved.

A nation that had been continually harassed and humiliated by all powers since 1840 had actually defied the world, and fought it to a standstill. It was this Asian feeling of solidarity with China that Americans found so hard to understand, as typified by the statement of one Captain Weh, of the Nationalist Chinese Army on Taiwan:

"We listened to the radio, and the Communists were defeating the Americans. All of us in this room were officers who had fought with the Generalissimo for many years. Most of us had fought the Communists all our adult lives. One officer had been captured and tortured by them. In a world the Communists won, there could be no place for any of us, or our families.

"It was very bad for us to have the Communists win. But we had very queer feelings, listening to the news of disaster in Korea. It was almost like a certain exaltation. I do not know how to explain it to you Americans.

"For our Colonel, who hated Communists with all his soul, kept saying: 'The Americans are being beaten by *Chinese.* The Americans are being beaten by *Chinese.*'"

It was this feeling, shared by most Asians, that China, though unable now to conquer in battle, wanted to exploit. As long as China could hold a U.N. Army at bay, she stood to gain enormous prestige in Asia.

And because the United States Government took a certain naïveté and almost total lack of understanding of Asian Communism to the conference table, the Korean War, stalemated June 1951, would go on for two more years, and half as many men again as were maimed and killed in its first twelve months had yet to suffer and die.

* * *

During the fourteenth plenary session at Kaesong, 30 July 1951, all parties agreed that hostilities should continue even while negotiations were in progress.

But it was from this time forward that political reality in Korea diverged from military, and from this time forward the frustration of American soldiers grew. From now till the end of fighting, political considerations, both international and domestic, would shadow all combat operations.

An army in the field, in contact with the enemy, can remain idle only at its peril. Deterioration—of training, physical fitness, and morale—is immediate and progressive, despite the strongest command measures. The Frenchman who said that the one thing that cannot be done with bayonets is to sit on them spoke an eternal truth.

Unwilling to strike for victory, but equally unable to clutch the elusive dove of peace the Communists tantalizingly held forth and then withdrew, time and again, American commanders and American government leaders began to writhe in frustration.

The situation was hard on the generals, for it was the very antithesis of the American tradition of generalship, cutting across everything it had been taught to believe and do. Their new orders seemed to read: *Fight on, but don't fight too hard. Don't lose—but don't win, either. Hold the line, while the diplomats muddle through.*

These were directives desperately hard for men brought up to take positive action, and quickly, even if wrong.

But it was harder still for the riflemen and tankers and weapons squads dug in along the scarred, dirty hills. Now they knew less than ever why they dug their holes or why they died. Hoping for the war to end at any moment, they kept one eye on Kaesong or on Panmunjom. When they were ordered to defend a hill or to take one, they knew the action was a limited one, and they

knew in their hearts, whatever brave words were said, that such action probably would not affect the outcome of the war at all.

No man likes to give up his life for an inconsequential reason, and there is
no honor—only irony—to being the last man killed in a war.

Still the Eighth Army, dug in along what they called the Kansas Line, could
not sit idle forever.

When the advance had stopped in June, it had not been along any carefully
preplanned battle line. There were bulges, salients, and vague areas of no
man's land along the whole front. From a military standpoint, corrections
were needed. In many places the Eighth Army held disadvantageous ground.

As the talks droned on at Kaesong, the U.N. Command became more convinced the enemy was stalling. And U.N. commanders agreed that a little
pressure, judiciously applied, might have wholesome effect. The decision was
made in FECOM, but approved by Washington.

By the first of August, they were ready to apply such pressure. There was
no intention of striking for the Yalu or of opening up the battlefront for a new
war of maneuver.

The new attacks would be limited in zone, for limited objectives, a hill here,
or to erase a bulge there, or to deny enemy observation in yet another place.

The attacks would serve two other purposes—to pressure the enemy into
sincerity at the peace table, and to keep the Eighth Army on its toes.

It was not an ambitious program, or an unreasonable one, in the situation.
Policy was guided by restraint, and limited.

The only thing that would not be limited were the casualties.

* * *

In any democratic society, equality of sacrifice is a cherished ideal. Yet in
war nothing is more difficult of attainment.

Soldiers know that it is never possible to share the load completely. One man
went to Korea; another—who equally served—never went west of San Francisco. While American units were decimated in the Far East, others went through
training in the European Command, without hearing a shot fired in anger.

Soldiers know the reasons this must be so, and accept them. But they also
like to think they are getting an even break.

In modern war, short of ending the fighting, combat troops have only three
means of escape from incessant action: death or injury, insanity, or rotation.
In modern war there are no winter quarters or lengthy withdrawals from
action until the harvests are in. In Korea by early 1951, thousands of wounded
men had been returned to action, and more thousands of unwounded risked
their lives daily, month in and month out.

In the spring of 1951, with no end to what had been considered a short
campaign in sight, the United States Government began to consider ways of
equalizing the burden, for it was manifestly unfair, in a free society, to ask a
few to bear the entire burden.

Troops on line began to hear rumors of a rotation policy. Already there had
been set up R&R—Rest and Recuperation—a five-day rest period back in
Japan. R&R at first worked wonders. Men came off line, away from incessant
danger and hardship, for a flight to Tokyo, Yokohama, or Kyoto. They board-

ed planes at Seoul and elsewhere, gaunt, unshaven, some with the thousand-yard stare. Five days later they returned, new men, rested, bathed, refreshed. R&R gave the troops something to look forward to; it was a morale factor without equal.

It was only later, when the pressure in Korea was not so great, that men going to Japan turned R&R into the great debauch that came to be known as I&I—intercourse and intoxication. Men coming out of weeks and months of hard combat are too tired and beaten down to seek trouble.

Men leaving months of filthy living and screaming monotony tend to seek something else again.

But R&R, then and later, was only a stopgap. Soon there rose talk of Big R—rotation to the United States.

On 1 May, Captain Muñoz's boss, the 2nd Division G-4, called him in and said, "Frank, you're going home!"

Muñoz was the second officer to rotate from the 2nd Division. The first quota had been for only one, and the man who got that quota had received the Distinguished Service Cross. Muñoz, who had more infantry-line time than any other officer, had only the Silver Star. He made the second draft.

He went from the area of the Soyang to Pusan, and boarded the *General M. M. Patrick* for States-side. A few hours after the "Mickey Mouse" docked, he was on a plane for Tucson. Frank Muñoz's war was over.

All over Korea, those who were left of the early men to arrive began to go home in little dribbles, as new men came in to replace them.

A point system was set up. It took thirty-six points to rotate. On line, a man received four points a month; anywhere in the combat zone, from the firing batteries back through regimental headquarters, three.

Any man in Korea got at least two, which meant rear echelon and service troops rotated at eighteen months. Tankers went out in ten months, the average infantryman within a year.

Now, if asked why they fought, many men would say, "To get my time in." The point system had great merits—and great disadvantages. No man liked to risk his neck—and thirty points.

The handling of high-point men was a continuing problem of commanders from this time on.

Some men, with enough points, did not rotate. James Mount, who had come to Korea a corporal, was made second lieutenant in the medical service. The promotion delayed him till November.

One colonel, who had had long and arduous service since the beginning, was ready to leave. On the eve of his departure he received his brigadier's single star. He felt it a crowning accomplishment to his service in Korea—until he was informed that as a general officer he was on a new rotation list; he was now the general officer with the least overseas service in the Far East. Dedicated man that he was, the new brigadier's remarks were pungent and heartfelt.

After the beginning of truce talks, the primary interest of every man in Korea was going home. It could hardly be otherwise.

And with rotation, the complexion of the Army changed. Now the men and officers coming in were largely reservists, National Guardsmen, draftees. The percentage of regulars in most line units sank to forty or less, as more and more men were recalled from business and farm to man the line. Few of the new officers and men arrived with any enthusiasm, then or later.

For whatever enthusiasm the American people might have had for the Korean conflict had died in childbirth, up along the Ch'ongch'on.

Worse than lack of enthusiasm, the new troops were green. The kind of lessons troops needed to fight this kind of war could be learned only in Korea. In a period of a few months the complexion of the American Army changed, more even than the generals realized.

New troubles were inevitable. But, under the circumstances, it was not remarkable that they occurred—what was remarkable was that the new men, unready, unmoved, and coming from a society that was beginning to hate this war, did so well.

* * *

On 1 July, approximately 750,000 Chinese and North Koreans held the Communist battle line, against half a million U.N. troops. The CCF and the Inmun Gun had changed, too.

The cream of the Communist armies had been destroyed, from the Naktong to the Imjin, and from the Imjin to the Soyang.

Replacements coming down the mountains were recent inductees, impressed from rice field and village, untrained, in some cases unarmed and badly clothed.

But though they might not be expert at war, these men were used to hard work and hardship all their young lives. Their leaders set them to work, digging. From the Sea of Japan, on the east, to the Yellow Sea on the west, they burrowed into the earth. They entered mountains from the rear slope, tunneling through to make gun positions opening on the front. They dug bunkers in which a company could safely and warmly bivouac. They dug so deeply into the earth that no conventional gun or cannon could reach them.

They dug bunkers and trenches and firing steps.

And when they had dug these, they went backward and dug a new defensive line, and one beyond that, stretching into the north. They dug a line such as the world had never seen—ten times the depth of any in World War I.

They dug positions that could—and might have to, their leaders reasoned—stand against nuclear explosion.

With their mountains, hollowed out, the training of the new CCF and Inmun Gun could begin. They were taught all the tricks the older men had learned: to move and attack by night, when the terrible American air was impotent; not to rush down valleys, as the CCF had learned to its sorrow on the Imjin and across the Soyang, but again to become phantoms, lurking in the hills, never letting the enemy see them until they chose.

They learned to use their bright new weapons, carried laboriously down from the Yalu, and to load, aim, and fire the huge numbers of cannon with Cyrillic inscriptions on their tubes, now coming into Korea for the first time.

They were sent on patrol, to learn to move quietly and effectively, and to learn the taste of blood.

Over the months, beginning in the summer of 1951, the tough, squat peasant boys from China and Korea learned well.

In the Communist armies there was no rotation.

* * *

In February, when MacArthur had again and again pressed for reinforcements for FECOM, Washington had authorized him to arm and train some 200,000 to 300,000 more ROK's.

More than 100,000 South Koreans were in arms, and other thousands served with United States forces, as KATUSA—a program that was quietly being abandoned; the cultural gulf between Korean and American was too great for them to use the buddy system—or laborers.

Each American battalion and company had its indigenous personnel, from barbers to houseboys, paid in native currency and eating Korean rations furnished by the Army. They might add little to the effective fighting ability of the units, but they helped a great deal with the laundry problem.

But American planners were still looking forward to the day of their eventual displacement from Korea, and the twice-shattered ROK Army had to be once again rebuilt. Men—tough, patient, hill-padding Korean peasants—there were in plenty. Surplus weapons from the big war, food, and money to pay them, America could easily furnish.

What neither Korea nor America could furnish was leadership.

A nation that for forty years had been made into hewers of wood and haulers of water could not put forth competent, educated officer material overnight. What little the Taehan Minkuk had enjoyed had mostly died north of the Han in 1950.

Thousands of new Korean officers were sent to the United States, to Army schools like Benning and Sill. But these schools could not graduate enough men to officer an army quickly.

And there was another problem, aside from the lack of officer material, common to most imperfectly democratic societies. Military preferment in the ROK Army often followed political preferment. The politicians in primitive societies want no generals they cannot trust. They prefer a politically reliable man at the head of a division to a competent one who may happen to belong to the wrong family or team.

In almost all non-Communist Sinic countries, armies tend to be paternal, also. The discipline and punitive code of the ROK Army was severe, in large part inherited from the Imperial Japanese Army—but it was another form of paternalism that constantly gave American KMAG officers gray hairs.

A ROK general was paid 60,000 *won* per month; a ROK private 3,000. With the *won* varying between 4,000 and 6,000 to the dollar, no ROK soldier could offer much to his family. His pay included a U.S.-bought ration of 3,165 calories, canned fish, biscuit, barley, kelp, rice, and tea; but his family had to eat, too.

Frequently when the transport of a ROK division was vitally needed to haul ammunition at the front, the trucks were back in the interior carrying firewood for soldiers' dependents, or on private hire to build the divisional welfare fund. Gasoline disappeared regularly into the civilian economy.

KMAG fought a losing battle against five thousand years of Oriental custom. Most of them, it must be admitted, developed a frustrated respect for the Chinese Reds who overnight destroyed the "silver bullets" tradition of the Chinese Army—the old situation when Chinese generals fought not with bullets of lead, but silver, meaning they could be bought—and who delivered supplies from Canton to Mukden, and from Mukden to Korea without pilfering, tampering, or diversion to private use according to sacred custom. But the Chinese Communists, puritan like all human revolutionists, had means not available to KMAG.

In the CCF it was very easy to have a man shot.

KMAG itself had difficulties. Traditionally, a nation instructing another should send its best men abroad, traditionally, from Athens to the America of 1950, nations do not. There was little prestige, promotion, or hope of glory in serving with the Korean Military Advisory Group. The United States Army tended to forget these men. Most officers who could avoid KMAG duty did so, preferring to serve among their own troops, where food, companionship, and the chances of recognition were all considerably improved.

Unfortunately, a certain number of KMAG, understandably, became more interested in Korean *seikse* and the whiskey-run to Seoul on Saturday night than in the future of the Republic of Korea Army.

But with all its deep-seated troubles, the ROK Army grew. Eventually it would stand at 600,000 men, and man two-thirds of the Korean line, and take more than two-thirds of the total casualties.

It would remain weak in combat support, such as engineers and communications men. Korea produced no trained men. And it would remain weak in artillery; it would have no armor, and almost no air.

It would depend upon transportation built in Japan on American order, and it would totally depend on American munitions, fuel, and supply, other than food.

The United States wanted an army that could defend its homeland, but not one grown so independent it might follow its own course, or listen to its own leader, Syngman Rhee.

As the Korean War lengthened, the ROK Army would, as Rhee said, "hold fifty-one percent of the stock," bought with its blood.

But its U.N. and American directorate, firmly united on the point, would never allow the Korean majority stockholders voting rights, from now to the end of fighting.

* * *

Brigadier General Haydon L. Boatner, United States Army, arrived in Korea in August 1951, just at the time the Eighth Army had decided, with irrefutable military logic, to lean on the CCF and NKPA before it occurred to the otherside to lean on them.

It took Haydon Boatner four and one-half days to come from the Commandancy of Texas A&M, where he had picked up the odd sobriquet of "The Bull," to Bloody Ridge.

Boatner, a Louisianan, was a professional soldier from a family of professional soldiers. Some observers, eyeing the undeniable hereditary cast of American generaldom, have voiced fears that this tendency may become in time a caste—but the fact that sons follow the career of their fathers in the military is no more unusual, or deplorable, than the fact that lawyers' sons become lawyers, or a Ford makes autos in Detroit.

And just as family-owned corporations in the main are as well-managed as others, a Douglas MacArthur or a young Van Fleet, missing in action in Korea—both the sons of generals—make as good soldiers as the next fellow.

There is nothing wrong with a caste so long as it remains open-end, and competent.

Haydon Boatner had graduated first in the West Point Class of 1924. In 1928 he went to the Far East, beginning what was to be a long career on the China station. Young Boatner, of an active mind, began the study of Chinese on the boat, and continued it while on duty with the mounted scouts of the old 15th Infantry at Tientsin.

After two years there, he transferred to Peking, where he took a Master's degree in Chinese at the Evangelical Missionary Language School. His thesis, naturally enough, dealt with war: the Manchu invasion of the Middle Kingdom in the seventeenth century.

In 1942, it was natural enough that old China Hand Boatner should end up in Burma, on General Stilwell's staff. Here he was among the first of his class to make brigadier, and here he spent thirty-eight months, going finally up to China, where he drew up the original surrender terms for the Japanese Army in China.

But with Stilwell, he was run out of Burma in 1942, and serving with Vinegar Joe—who, like Krueger, was sometimes given to referring to the commander in chief as a horse's ass—was not the most advantageous place to be in World War II. Europe, not the CBI, was where the guns, glamour, girls, and fresh new stars were. Men who were junior to Boatner, and who got a transfer to the European Theater, ended up with more stars than the single one he still wore in 1945.

In 1951, still a one-feather chieftain, he returned to the Far East.

With ten years of service in the Orient, with Asian troops, Boatner figured he would go with KMAG. He was deeply gratified, however, when General Milburn, FECOM G-1, told him in Tokyo, "You're being assigned to the 2nd Division."

Later, he heard that Van Fleet had been told Boatner should go to Koje-do as commandant of the POW compounds. Haydon Boatner would always thank God he did not. The time to go into a ball game is when the last pitcher has cleared the bases—not when he has walked them full. Though in August 1951 General Boatner had only vaguely heard of the island of Koje-do.

At 2nd Division, Boatner became Clark Ruffner's Assistant Division Commander.

As part of the leaning operation, the Eighth Army was making what were designed as limited attacks here and there along Battle Line Wichita, which

Eighth Army had prepared when the talks began at Kaesong. The objectives of these attacks were a hill here, such as Fool's Mountain or the Punchbowl of the 2nd Division zone, or to deny vital ground to the enemy, such as Million Dollar Hill in the 24th's area.

But the mountains, here in east-central Korea were growing steeper. The North Koreans, defending here, had, like the Japanese of World War II, gone underground.

In these hills armor could normally only support by fire, and air was not wholly effective. And here, abruptly, the war of maneuver ended.

In a four-day battle for Hill 1179, both sides lost heavily. And when 1179 fell, beyond it lay one more hill, or rather three, 983, 940, and 773, forming a steep ridge several thousand yards long.

This ridge, parallel to the battle line, lay directly athwart the U.N. advance. It had little value to anyone, except as a vantage point for superior observation over the defensive line hostile to whoever held it.

But it was there, and that seemed reason enough to take it.

And it seemed an excellent opportunity for the ROK Army, newly revitalized, to show the world what it could do.

To the 36th ROK Regiment, 7th Division, supported by the tanks of B Company, 72nd Tank Battalion, American air, and 2nd Divarty, came orders on 17 August, to assault and seize this ridge.

As liaison with them, Clark Ruffner detached his Chief of Staff, Colonel Rupert Graves, to give the ROK's all the help they needed to convince the world that they had come to maturity.

Behind the 36th ROK's stood Colonel Lynch's 9th Infantry, ready to support by every means of fire available to an American regiment.

The ROK's were brave, and they tried hard.

They advanced onto steep slopes plowed by a maze of deep trenches, thorny with hidden bunkers. The bunkers were fortified to withstand air and artillery pounding, and some had room for two platoons of NKPA. Others sheltered small cannon and mortars. Dug into a rubble of partially wooded slopes, obscured by morning mists, the North Korean positions were almost impossible to detect.

Until it was too late.

The ROK's were brave, and tried hard, and in ten days the 36th took a thousand killed and wounded. They also took the middle peak, 940, and spread over the ridge that by now ran freely with their blood, on 25 August 1951.

Seeing the decimation of the ROK's, and the desperateness of the NKPA defense, American observers reported to Major General Ruffner that the ROK's needed help. Ruffner called Lieutenant General James Van Fleet for permission to move 9th Infantry onto the ridge with the ROK regiment.

Van Fleet was furious. He had made the rehabilitation of the ROK Army a personal project, and he was determined to demonstrate the project's success to the United Nations and the world. He told Ruffner, "You're trying to hog the glory from the ROK's!"

A few hours later, a massive NKPA counterattack rolled out of the east and sent the ROK survivors of the 36th Regiment stumbling from the hills.

Now there was nothing to do but commit the 9th. The demonstration was shot to hell, but at least the Americans could come in and save the ball game. On 27 August the 2nd Battalion, 9th Infantry, attacked toward Peak 983 of the ridge. It went forward with utter confidence that somehow the ROK's had managed to blow an easy one.

It went into the maze of trenches, hidden bunkers, and stubbled trees along the slope, and it was stopped cold.

Bleeding, the battalion pulled back, out of range.

The 3rd Battalion struck from the east, toward Peak 773. The 3/9 failed to reach even its initial objectives. When night came, the North Koreans counterattacked, and 3/9 fell back on top of 2nd Battalion.

As 1/9 prepared to make its own attack, no part of the hill mass was in friendly hands. And a number of people in high places were becoming distinctly annoyed.

On 30 August, 1/9 and 2/9 attacked the spiny ridge frontally, determined to overwhelm the stubborn resistance quickly. In recent months Eighth Army had grown unaccustomed to this kind of difficulty, and there was complete determination up above to end it at once. The four organic battalions of 2nd Division Artillery, supported by three additional howitzer battalions, two heavy-mortar companies, two regimental tank companies, and a company from the 72nd Tank, registered in on the ridge, and stood ready.

In all, artillery fired 451,979 rounds. The ridge turned into a flaming hell of whining steel and searing flame. The trees were splintered to stubs, and fresh earth gaped where communications trenches were tumbled.

North Koreans died, by the hundreds. But many were deep in bunkers where no shelling could reach them, until they came out to close with the advancing Americans. And they had artillery of their own, too, firing to protect the ridge—more than any American had so far seen in Korea.

And something else had happened. While the enemy had dug into the hill, the U.S. Army had gone down it. Rotation had removed too many men who had learned the answers; companies were shot through with new, green men and, worse yet, new green officers.

The 9th Infantry was no longer a team. And even the All-Stars, most days, can be licked by any team in the league.

Attacking onto the ridge, the situation grew worse. Able Company, 1/9, was 100 percent casualties three days running. New replacements were fed into the shattered companies while they were still in action, and teamwork and cohesion became even more sporadic.

Conventional supporting weapons have not been invented that can dislodge a stubborn enemy from deliberately prepared positions. The only way to reduce the long ridge was bunker by bunker, at close range, with rifle and grenade. It was horrible, bloody work.

And each night, from ridges running to the north, the NKPA sent fresh men pouring into the disputed positions. Soon, 9th Infantry identified corpses from six separate regiments of the Inmun Gun.

All the artillery, and most of the energy, of an American division and an NKPA corps, were being focused on one small area of bloody earth. Here, at what the correspondents were now calling Bloody Ridge, a new pattern of Korean warfare was being set—one that resembled more than anything else the hideous, stalemated slaughter on the Western Front in World War I.

The 9th Infantry was being decimated. Ruffner sent "Bull" Boatner forward, up to the 9th. Ruffner felt that perhaps the difficulty with the regiment lay with its C.O., and one job of an assistant division commander is to act as hatchet man for his chief. Besides, General Ruffner was eager to promote the executive officer of the 38th Infantry, and was not loath at having a chicken-colonel vacancy in the division.

All this Bull Boatner, a light-haired hooked-nose man, small for a general, whose pale eyes could stab like ice daggers from behind his glasses, and whose high voice could cut like a whip, understood.

Boatner found trouble, and lots of it.

Pushing against Bloody Ridge, the men of 1/9 and 2/9 were being cut to pieces. The troops and leaders were often green. They were brave and, like the ROK's, they were trying hard. It wasn't enough.

They needed flamethrowers to reduce the deep enemy bunkers, and they didn't have them. Worse, few if any men knew how to use them. Boatner set up a school in the use of the flamethrower, and ran men through, quickly. Now, deep in hitherto safe bunkers, soldiers of the Inmun Gun died shrieking in searing flame, as American infantrymen crawled close under fire and sprayed them with newly issued weapons.

Replacements were wandering up to engaged units, and getting killed the first hour, before they could report in. Boatner ordered replacements to be kept in the replacement company at least one day, and to have five or six days' special training before being sent into combat. Men new from the States were often soft. They were to get conditioning exercises, and it was mandatory that they zero their weapons.

This practice the Eighth Army later made mandatory for all divisions.

Boatner met with each group of new replacements. He talked with them calmly, and joked with them. And then, his eyes hard, he told them:

"Let there be no question: it will be tough. You had better do what your N.C.O.'s tell you, if you want to stay alive. And remember three things: when you're on the hill, if you stand up you'll get your ass shot off; if you get off the paths, or roam, you'll get your ass blown off by mines; and when you take a hill, you'll be tired as hell, you'll want to poop out, slap your buddies on the back, and take it easy—but remember, as soon as you take a hill, just as water comes out of a spigot, the mortars come in on you, and blooey!—it's too goddam late then!"

The 9th Infantry tried hard, but it was shattered against Bloody Ridge. The entire 2nd Division was reshuffled. On 2 September there was no attack—and then the brutal, frontal attacks were stopped. Since the action had been conceived of as limited, units had been committed piecemeal, into a small area. Now the 23rd Infantry was sent around the flank, to envelop Bloody Ridge from the side and rear, while the dazed companies of the 9th, filled again with new officers and men, probed once more to fix the enemy.

On 5 September, having lost an estimated 15,363 men, 4,000 of them dead, the NKPA voluntarily relinquished Bloody Ridge. The ROK 35th Regiment went onto 773, and Colonel Bishop's 1/9 occupied peaks 940 and 983 without opposition.

The enemy had not fled. He had merely pulled back to positions on the next prominent ridge line that ran perpendicular to Bloody Ridge, some 1,500 yards to the north.

It had cost the ROK's more than a thousand men, and the 2nd Division almost three thousand, to secure three insignificant knobs among the hundreds that thrust up along the line.

Now the ROK's and 2nd Division rested several days, licking their wounds and eyeing the gloomy peaks to their north. Soon they would move forward against those peaks.

And there the hearts of some men would break.

31

Heartbreak Ridge

The peace talks had been going on for months. The heart to fight though not gone, was not the bright light it had once been.

—Captain Raymond E. Webb, 72ND TANK BATTALION IN KOREA 1950–1952, Toppan Printing Co., Ltd., Tokyo.

T HE ACTION ON Bloody Ridge, the principal activity along the Korean front at the time, drew attendant publicity to the discomfiture of some military leaders. Correspondents, watching the hellish fighting along the blasted spurs and ravaged slopes of 773, 983, and 940, wrote florid descriptions of the struggle. It was a correspondent from *Stars and Stripes* who first named Bloody Ridge, and during one action a group of men of 9th Infantry, on the ridge, read his account. For reasons of security, the exact location of Bloody Ridge was never mentioned in the papers.

"Jesus," one soldier said, after reading the article, "them poor bastards are getting clobbered, wherever they are."

And the publicity had other, more unfortunate side effects. Bloody Ridge—though the Army need never feel shame for what it did there—had not been the kind of demonstration General James Van Fleet had in mind when he authorized it. Washington did not receive the casualty reports with anything like enthusiasm. Matthew Ridgway, in Tokyo, showed no indication of being pleased.

It was during this time that Tom De Shazo, a classmate of Boatner, and the Brigadier Commanding 2nd Division Artillery told the Assistant Division Commander:

"Haydon, don't you know people are expecting you to relieve John Lynch?"

"Sure," Boatner said. He had had more than a few leading questions and insinuations on that score. "Sure, that'll wash all our linen. That'll solve everything!"

Haydon Boatner knew that Colonel Lynch had assumed command of the 9th Infantry while it rested along Line Kansas, idle, while many of its best men rotated home. What failures, what disappointments had occurred in the 9th had not been due to command, but to a breakdown of team effort. And it was doubtful if any United States regiment, in August 1951, given the same assignment, could have done much better.

Haydon Boatner, a man not noted for tenderness, who believed with Jefferson Davis "that tender consideration for those who are ineffective kills the good," refused to recommend the relief of the 9th's C.O.

But he had found something lousy in 9th Regiment—the 3rd Battalion.

During the desperate days of Bloody Ridge, the 3/9 had done nothing. It had failed miserably in the only real attack it had attempted, and its C.O., Boatner knew, had been on the bottle.

The 3/9, in contravention of new Army policy at the insistence of a former corps commander, was wholly colored.

Boatner recommended that the battalion commander be reclassified or eliminated. The battalion could not be depended upon, which left the 9th with only two effective battalions in any fight, and Boatner said so.

He stabbed deeply into a subject that the Army, let alone Washington, preferred never to discuss.

There had been continual difficulty with the all-Negro units sent into Korea, in the 25th Division and elsewhere. The 503rd Field Artillery—"Get out of the way, here comes the Nickle Oh Tray!"—and others, through the present 3/9, had sometimes written less than glorious history on the battlefield.

But other colored soldiers had done splendidly, as well as any Americans had ever done.

A Columbia sociologist, quietly making a survey for the Army, had some reasons, which had long been understood by United States Army leaders: An essential ingredient in any fighting man is pride—pride in himself, pride in his unit, and the men around him. The seemingly nonsensical swagger of paratroopers, their special insignia, their carefully nurtured arrogance, seemingly in conflict with most decent, democratic practices, make sense only when what paratroopers must do is considered.

At the final moment, when a man must leap from a speeding aircraft into what is normally the most hazardous of military missions, an airdrop behind enemy lines; when his chances of serious injury or death are always high, even routine, a special *esprit* is required.

Unless spurred by a fearful pride and belief in themselves and their comrades, men do not willingly "join hands and jump out of aeroplanes."

It is this final, basic pride—*what will my buddies think?*—that keeps most soldiers carrying on, beyond the dictates of good sense, which screams at them to run, to continue living, and to hell with war.

American society had permitted Negroes little chance to develop pride. American society tends to give its colored segments an inferiority complex, almost from birth. And in the military service, placed solely among other colored men, there is developed not mass pride but mass neurosis. Few colored men, understandably, feel the urge to prove themselves in front of other colored men.

The problem is not one of race or color, but of a minority group, anywhere, which has had much of its essential pride as human beings stripped from it. The strongest urge of any minority group, Armenians, French-Canadians, or Untouchables, is to survive. They have no other effective way of fighting.

The old jokes about the military courage of certain minority groups has some basis in fact. Turks joke about the fighting ability of Turkish Christians. The indigenous Christians that Turks know are submerged, wily folk, sharp with money, slyly sticking together against the Moslem world, absolutely uninterested in going out to fight and die for the Turkish State. They see absolutely nothing to be gained by it—nor is there.

A diplomat from Istanbul, several centuries ago, remarked it was odd that Franks in the Western kingdoms were much more like Turks than like Christians. If this Turkish gentleman had visited the medieval ghettos, he might have begun to understand.

Jews in Eastern Europe often went to the gas chambers without a protest, without lifting a hand. The young men of the same human stock raised in Israel are among the toughest, hardiest folk in the world.

To most people, this proves something.

Any group of human beings that has known long persecution is soon winnowed down to survival types. The brave and the bold in a persecuted society are soon lopped off.

And no army has ever been successfully forged wholly from survival types. Survival, in an army, is only incidental to the mission.

The Columbia professor, and others, discussed practical means of ending the Army's trouble. They saw only one solution: desegregation.

In front of white men, the sociologists claimed, colored soldiers would feel an urge to prove themselves, and have a chance to develop pride they could never achieve in a segregated unit. They recommended one per squad, or two, no more—because the tendencies of the persecuted are to group together against the world.

With much disagreement in some quarters, the Army bought the idea. There was also the hope, as one unbeliever mentioned, that if the one man in a squad was guilty of malfeasance, the others would take care of him.

Under Boatner's urging, the commander of the 3/9 was relieved, and 534 men were transferred from 3/9 to the other combat regiments.

The 534 themselves were not wholly happy. They had a thousand and one bugaboos, from possible loss of rotation points to fear for their ratings.

Some of the old first sergeants of the receiving companies conjured up every procedure in the book to delay the transfers.

But they went through.

The troops were integrated, at 10 percent throughout the companies.

And the United States Army's combat problem with colored troops was largely ended. Filtered through the white units, they did well. Three weeks after its fiasco on Bloody Ridge, 3/9 performed with excellence.

The social problems, of course, were not solved. A solution to these can be anticipated only when all men look alike, hold the same views, or are so apathetic that it no longer matters.

And some time later, General Bull Boatner heard that the Eighth Army had relieved the corps commander because of the trouble on Bloody Ridge.

There are times, not only in the Army, but in Washington and General Motors, when somebody, somewhere, simply has to go, to take off the heat.

* * *

On 13 September 1951, with the harsh heat of summer fast fading this high on the eastern coast of Korea, the 23rd Infantry and its attached French Battalion moved against the seven-mile-long hill mass running perpendicular to Bloody Ridge, on its north. The high parts of this ridge, running north and south, pointed daggerlike into enemy lines. It was felt its capture would knock the enemy back some ten miles, and deny him use of a road net even farther back.

Because of the terrain, the assault was frontal, piecemeal, and bloody.

Again it was work for riflemen, grenadiers, and flamethrower operators. Tanks could support by fire only from the base of the hills, and artillery alone could not demolish the deep NKPA fortifications, though the 2nd Division Artillery fired 229,724 rounds.

The 23rd Infantry moved due north, then attacked the ridge line from the east. It struck for the knobs rising bare and ugly along the spine, and on this gloomy ridge the 23rd Regiment, as had the 9th Infantry the month before, brushed a hornets' nest.

Whatever the new ROK Army was like, the reconstituted Inmun Gun was fanatic, tough, and stubborn. The contested ridge line could easily be reinforced from a series of hills still farther north, near the town of Mundung-ni, and the Inmun Gun seemed willing to pour men onto the smoking, reeking slopes from a bottomless well.

The 23rd, whose show this battle was until its last stages, left its blood along every step of the way up the ridge. Again the fighting was close-in, brutal, dangerous, while mortars and artillery punished each side without respite. Again and again American companies of the 23rd fought their painful way up the slopes, blasting bunkers, killing enemy in their trenches—and again and again, reaching the crests exhausted, decimated, and low on ammunition, they were knocked off by a howling charge of fresh North Koreans.

Companies sometimes stood at less than thirty men, before the fresh-faced replacements came in from Japan. They were killing the enemy at a ratio of close to nine to one because of the superior American artillery—but to the men dying along the ridge there was small satisfaction in that. Few of them were really interested in killing North Korean peasants.

The fate of one American company characterized the whole action. Captain Pete Montfort's men attacked toward the northern knob of the ridge under blazing automatic fire, continually slammed by enemy artillery.

They went up the hill painfully, leaving dead and wounded behind all the way. Just at dusk, with a mighty effort, Pete Montfort and company overran their objective.

But Montfort's men were almost out of ammunition, and in the dark, and under the curtain of fire, no more could be brought up the mountainside to him. Montfort reported back by radio. He was determined to stay.

The division could support only by fire. General De Shazo ordered Divarty, "Put a wall of steel around those men!"

All night Divarty fired; the wall of steel went up. But that night Pete Montfort was overrun and his weakened company wiped out, to the last man.

Later, when a new company fought its way up to the position, they found the Americans sprawled stiffly all along the crest. Pete Montfort lay across a machine gun that had run dry. There was not a round of ammunition remaining in any dropped rifle or in any bandoleer.

Again and again the division commander received reports that a crest or knob was taken. Again and again the report proved false, as the attackers were knocked back down the slope.

By now, the reporters were writing of a place called Heartbreak Ridge.

Each time a group of one hundred or more replacements entered the division, Brigadier General Boatner, the ADC, met them, and talked with them. It was little enough to do.

These men who came in now were selectees, for the most part. They knew there was a war on; they knew it would be hard, which was a help. Most of them knew very little else. A great many of them did not last long enough to learn more.

Boatner, personally, began to feel a deep regret for the recalled reservists who were now filling the junior-officer slots of the division. Many of them were overage, lieutenants in their thirties, captains near forty. They had accepted commissions in the big war; they had done a job that had to be done, and gone home. Most of them had not remained active; they had new businesses, new families, other concerns.

But the Judge Advocate General had ruled that any man who had once held a commission, whether he had kept it active or not, could be legally recalled. And the Pentagon, when the Chinese poured across the Yalu, had made an incalculable error, one that would damage the Army Reserve Program for a decade. Never certain that a big war would not start any minute, the Pentagon called, not the officers and men in Table of Organization units, receiving pay and training, but the bulk of the inactive reservists, men who had received neither, and whose interest was less. The inactive individuals could be called up for fillers; the units were kept in reserve for a bigger war, which never came.

Most of the forty thousand Reserve officers recalled involuntarily and sent to Korea had never expected service short of all-out war. They never quite understood why they were taken, when hundreds of thousands of National Guardsmen and others, organized in units, were kept at home.

Guardsmen and many Reserve units were called, but according to the needs of the moment. The six Guard divisions called to federal service, a handful of the many, often felt they had been in the wrong place at the wrong time.

And because of rotation, few new units were sent to Korea. Hundreds of thousands of officers and men were sent as individual replacements. They arrived in their new divisions friendless and alone. Most of them never developed any feeling for a division in which they had not trained, in which they merely put in their time, until they could rotate out once more, again as individuals.

There have been few reunions of veterans of the Korean War.

And there was a final tragedy, affecting many of the recallees. Reserve officers, recalled from jobs and businesses for two years, on top of the loss of time during 1941–1945, often had no career to return to. Many elected to remain in the Army. But when Korea ended, and Washington, determined once again never to fight a ground war, shrank the Army back below a million men, the Army had no place for these men.

Thousands would have to return to civilian life, short of qualifying for pensions, to seek new jobs after the age of thirty-five or forty.

Of all the officers Haydon Boatner met on entering the division, only one asked to be sent on line. What they asked made no difference; it was division policy that all newcomers went forward—the rear-echelon jobs were filled from survivors of the line. Ironically, the one man who asked to fight, a West Pointer, Boatner had to relieve.

Brave enough himself, eager to advance his career, this officer was a moral coward. He could not be tough enough on his men.

For twenty-seven days the 23rd Infantry assaulted Heartbreak. They took knobs, and lost them. They took stretches of the hill mass, but they could not secure the ridge.

For the NKPA poured in men from the north, without counting.

A new pattern, the one that would characterize most of the following hill battles, was being set. On the disputed terrain, generally a small area, the fighting was hell itself. Artillery fire such as the world had never seen was massed against single hills, day after day. Because of the limitation of the fighting area, units were committed piecemeal, and the committed units were generally quickly cut to pieces, and replaced.

A few miles to either side of the disputed hill, the front lay quiet and brooding, without more than routine activity. And behind regimental headquarters, few men even knew there was a war on.

Action of this kind was contrary to all American military doctrine. The solution to success on Heartbreak, as later on Baldy, Pork Chop, Arrowhead, T-Bone, and a dozen others, would have been to hit the enemy elsewhere, knock him off balance in a dozen places, punch through.

But the United Nations Command had no authority to put massive pressure on the enemy along the whole line. They had no authority to reopen the wholesale fighting; the United Nations did not want military victory; they wanted truce.

And the enemy was perfectly willing to fight to the death over a small piece of ground, seemingly forever. The fought-over hills assumed propaganda and political values out of all proportion to their military worth.

It was a case of the children's game of King on the Mountain, played with blood and bullets.

Whoever lost a hill lost face.

After weeks of fighting for Heartbreak, it was clear to 2nd Division that the ridge would have to be flanked. The 2nd Engineers worked day and night, clearing a route through a blocked defile north of the hill mass over which the 72nd's tanks could pass. On 9 October the trail was ready.

At 0600 on 10 October, the M-4A3E8 tanks of Baker Company, the old Shermans, workhorses of World War II, fitted with new high-velocity 76mm cannon, broke through the hills into the clear, and raced for Mundung-ni.

The 23rd was kept on Heartbreak, still fighting for pieces of the ridge. The 9th Infantry moved left, and the 38th struck behind Heartbreak to get a grip on the hill from which the NKPA reinforced.

This hill, called Kim Il Sung Ridge, the division struck in mass, from 5 through 15 October, and overran it. Now the enemy could be reinforced on Heartbreak only through the passes around Mundung-ni.

The tanks of Baker Company, 72nd Tank, meanwhile had raved up the Mundung-ni Valley, running a gauntlet of fire. The hills and defiles swarmed with NKPA, and every available gun was turned on them.

But the tanks went through Mundung-ni, and four thousand yards beyond. From 10 October to 15 October, the 72nd ran two excursions per day through the hostile valley, ripping up the enemy rear as they passed. They branched out on the meager dirt roads, blasted dumps and concentrations of troops and bunkers, and then withdrew before dark.

They destroyed more than 600 troops, one SP gun, 11 machine guns, 350 bunkers—with uncounted casualties—three mortars, and several ammunition dumps, at a total cost of three killed, five wounded, and eight tanks lost to enemy action.

By 15 October both maneuvers had broken the back of the defense of Heartbreak Ridge.

The NKPA Corps that had held Heartbreak would not again be fit for action. There, with those lost on Bloody Ridge, it had suffered more than 35,000 casualties. The 2nd Division had leaned on the enemy, heavily.

But atop Heartbreak, the men of the 23rd Infantry could see ten miles to the north. They could see mile after mile of dark hills, growing gradually higher, hills in which lurked hundreds of thousands more Chinese and North Koreans. It was a long way to the Yalu and the Tumen, and these men knew in their hearts they were not going there, no matter how many hills they took.

On 25 October, at a new site, Panmunjom, the truce talks had begun again in earnest.

An officer writing in a battalion history, which was published in Japan, summed up their feelings: "The heart to fight though not gone, was not the bright light it had once been."

On 25 October the men who had taken Heartbreak came down off the hill, replaced by the United States 7th Division.

Their real heartbreak lay not in their dead and maimed, 5,600 of them, some of whom the men of 7th Division found still wedged in bunkers and crevasses, but in what had been accomplished by it all.

32

Stalemate

A diplomat's words must have no relation to actions—otherwise what kind of diplomacy is it? Words are one thing, actions another. Good words are a concealment of bad deeds. Sincere diplomacy is no more possible than dry water or iron wood.

—From the Russian of Josef V. Stalin.

O N 22 AUGUST 1951, the Communist negotiators had broken off the talks at Kaesong on the pretext that the U.N. had dropped bombs in the demilitarized zone declared about that town. For two months there were no plenary sessions, but the proceedings did not wholly end.

Liaison officers from the two camps met continually, to try to find a basis for new negotiations.

And in the meantime the U.N. Command carried out its line-straightening operations, leaning on the enemy. The U.N. Command, to the strident screams of the other side, refused to agree to the 38th parallel as a new line of demarcation, even though Secretary of State Acheson had mentioned this in a speech in June. The parallel was not easily defensible in most places, and the U.N. Command preferred the line of contact as a territorial basis for a cease-fire. In the meantime the Eighth Army proceeded to improve the line from the U.N. viewpoint, punching out bulges, knocking the enemy back off high ground, at heavy loss to both sides.

The losses at Bloody Ridge, Heartbreak, and elsewhere had some result. On 22 October the enemy offered to meet in full plenary session once again, and to accept the U.N. preferred site of Panmunjom for future discussions.

Panmunjom was not in Communist territory, but a tiny village of deserted huts along a dirty road in true no man's land, between the opposing lines. Here incidents or accidents, like the alleged bombing of Kaesong, could easily be avoided; the new neutral zone was tiny and easily marked by captive balloons; and the Communists could no longer gain propaganda value by bringing U.N. negotiators through their lines. Here no one was host.

On 25 October 1951 Major General Lee Sang Cho, Inmun Gun, faced United States General Hodes across the bargaining table. Item Two—where the cease-fire line would be drawn—was still as they had left it in August, undetermined.

"Now we will open the meeting," Lee said.

"Okay," Hodes said.

"Do you have any idea about the military demarcation line?"

"We ended the last conference before the suspension by asking for your proposal. Do you have one?"

"We would like your opinion first."

Hodes said wearily. "We gave our opinion many times, and asked for your proposal based on our proposal. As it was your proposal to have the Subdelegation meeting, we expected you to have a proposal. Let's have it."

"You said you had made a new proposal, but we have heard nothing new that would break the deadlock."

"That's right," General Hodes said. "You haven't."

After almost an hour of this, a recess for fifteen minutes was called.

And finally, in desperation, the U.N. proposed a four-kilometer-wide demilitarized zone for the cease-fire line, to be based on the current battle line at the time of signing.

The other side went into a propaganda tirade. They wanted the cease-fire line drawn now, before the firing ceased.

"You . . . are trying to escape the righteous solution and trying to shirk the duty which has been specified in the agenda item. You use in these discussions and also in your press and radio the sophistic argument that the time of signing is unknown. By doing so you have truly revealed your true color. . . . I sincerely hope and think that you and we are bound in duty to show our sincerity to the peace-loving people of the world by your acceptance of our proposal of establishing a military demarcation line. . . ."

What the enemy wanted was to fix the armistice line irrevocably before the remainder of the agenda was solved. This, of course, would effectively relieve the Communist powers of any further military pressure while the negotiations continued; the United Nations Command could hardly launch an offensive for ground it had already agreed to relinquish.

It would enable the Communists, as Admiral Joy saw and mentioned, to talk forever if they chose, with freedom from the grinding pressure they had been experiencing at Bloody and Heartbreak ridges.

He was loath to agree, unless he had to.

* * *

The limited attacks of the Eighth Army during August, September, and October 1951 had unquestionably improved its military stance, and had unquestionably inflicted deep wounds on the enemy forces.

But as Boatner said, "Everybody was sick to death of the casualties."

Men die to make others free, or to protect their homeland. They do not willingly die for a piece of real estate ten thousand miles from home, which they know their government will eventually surrender. Nor do the generals appointed over them, nor the governments they elect, willingly spend them so.

As the thousands of notification telegrams to next of kin went out, so soon after the high hopes raised by the negotiations, Washington grew more and more concerned. The public had accepted the end of the war, but continued casualties were rapidly becoming unacceptable.

In Tokyo, General Ridgway was so informed.

And Matt Ridgway had to put his foot firmly on Lieutenant General James Van Fleet's neck.

Now field commanders writhed under a new restriction: *Fight the war, but don't get anyone killed.* Such orders were never issued—but they were clearly understood.

The United Nations Command had learned a great deal from Heartbreak and Bloody ridges. They had learned that, with the new enemy fortifications and the newer, greener troops in the Eighth Army, effective pressure on the enemy could be achieved only at a cost in blood unacceptable to Washington.

On 17 November 1951, the U.N. Command agreed to accept the Communist position on the cease-fire line, provided the armistice was signed within thirty days. The Communists eagerly assented.

They had a thirty-day reprieve. They utilized it by reinforcing their defensive lines in depth until they were almost impervious to attack. With a flank firmly anchored on each side by the sea, in broken ground, it would now require an effort equivalent to that of the Somme, or Verdun, to dislodge them, short of use of nuclear weapons.

Three hundred thousand French and British troops fell trying to breach the German fortifications at the Somme in 1916. No Western power had the heart for such useless slaughter, ever again.

On 27 November the cease-fire line, the present line of contact, was formally ratified by each side. Initialed maps were exchanged.

The Communists had a great part of what they had wanted from the first hour they had requested peace talks. They had dissipated the danger of a U.N. march to the Yalu, or a disastrous defeat in the field.

From this time forward, smarting under the losses they had taken in the abortive attacks of later summer, having agreed to a firm line, and despairing of breaching the enemy lines anyway, the U.N. took no more large-scale offensive action.

At the end of thirty days the enemy was no nearer signing the armistice than he had been in July. He now felt free to delay as long as he pleased, and it was soon apparent he intended to do so, reaping whatever propaganda coups he could.

In Korea the U.N. had granted a sort of cease-fire, but there was no peace.

It was now, not openly, but in mess tents and private gatherings along the brooding lines of entrenchments, that some men began to say, "MacArthur was right."

* * *

Captain Arthur B. Busbey, Jr., a slightly built, dark-hazel-eyed advertising executive with thinning black hair and faint East Texas accent, was recalled to the Army in September 1950, at the age of twenty-eight. He had served from 1941 through 1946, before becoming a partner in an agency in Wichita Falls, and now, with his orders, Busbey decided the hell with it.

He decided to try to stay in the service. He would be one of the more fortunate ones who took this course, since eventually he would be integrated into the Regular Army.

He had always done Public Information Officer work in the Army, but had never particularly cared for it. When in March 1951 he received orders for Korea, he resisted all attempts of his commanders to keep him in this slot, insisting he be given a rifle company.

Because Busbey had never had combat in World War II, like many such men, he had a faint feeling of guilt. In Korea, he was one of the few who asked for line duty.

He joined the 7th Infantry Division in June, in the east-central sector north of the Hwach'on Reservoir, near Kumwha. He took command of Baker Company, 32nd Infantry, just as the 7th Division was finishing Matt Ridgway's Operation Killer against the Chinese.

And, like all newcomers, at first the hills bushed him. A man who has never climbed the thousand-foot slopes of the Taebaek Range cannot appreciate their steepness, or the difficulties they caused an army used to mechanization.

Almost as soon as he arrived, there was rumor of peace talks. He spent July dug in, in a combat situation, while the Eighth Army marked time.

Then, in August, Baker of the 32nd became involved in the line-straightening designed by the Eighth Army in the Punchbowl area.

On 27 August, Lieutenant Colonel Woods, 1st Battalion C.O., briefed the officers for the operation: it was conceived as a battalion attack against light resistance, to erase a bulge.

"A Company will jump off, take this first hill—then B Company will take the ridge line on its east, up to this high point on that larger ridge. After these are secured, A and B will furnish fire support for C, which attacks to seize the final ridge beyond."

On its face, it was simple infantry operation. The 32nd Infantry had been doing things like it all spring, with great success.

But Busbey, looking at the map, pointed to a huge hill mass just beyond his own objective: "Who will take care of that monster?"

Woods said, "Division's worried about that, too."

But intelligence estimates stated that few enemy were in the area and that the battalion would meet only weak resistance. Intelligence was not aware that these hills were held by five enemy battalions and that the easy days were almost over.

Early in the misty morning, the attacks jumped off. A Company took its objective within the hour, and Busbey's crowd shoved off. For the first three hundred yards, moving along steep slopes, they encountered nothing, and they advanced in a column formation of platoons.

They arrived at a very steep rise at the base of their objective. And halfway up, Lieutenant Petsche's leading platoon drew fire.

It drew fire such as the battalion had not seen in Korea. The whole ridge was covered with artillery fire, an experience new to 32nd Infantry.

Dirt from a near miss by a Russian-made 76mm covered Busbey, as he dived into a hole.

Petsche's platoon was stopped cold. Approximately half its men went down. The platoon leader's ankle was broken, and his messenger killed standing beside him.

Busbey, just behind, ordered the company to advance. But he quickly realized he was stretched out along a long ridge, attacking into a "T"—the worst position possible for a rifle company. He could put little fire down on the enemy, while they could enfilade him from each side.

He requested C Company be committed to assist him. Battalion wouldn't buy that, and finally told him to hold where he was, and to consolidate for the coming night. "Hold every inch you've got!"

B Company was in a lousy position to form a perimeter, strung out along the sides of a steep rise. But Busbey dug in, deciding if he were hit hard he would have to pull back.

Across the small valley from him, A Company dug in, also. So far, Able had had no troubles.

Under shelling, Busbey held until nightfall.

At 2300 the men of Baker Company heard firing and saw flares ascending from Able's ridge. Fire seemed to rush at Able's perimeter from three sides. Soon things in Able were a mess. The C.O. was killed, the perimeter broken. Then the firing died away, while Busbey's men waited tensely.

At exactly 0200 it was his turn. The enemy rolled out of the night at him from three sides. He called his outer platoon to come in, and for the artillery to fire flares over him for the rest of the night.

As the big artillery flares, throwing whitish light, popped over him, giving his men light to shoot by, someone at the artillery position complained that this was expensive.

"Who the hell cares?" Busbey told them, by radio.

With light and gunfire, Baker Company held off the attacks till dawn. Then someone wanted to know how many Busbey and company had killed.

His answer was, "How the hell would I know?"

With daylight, he was ordered to attack.

But the big hill he had been concerned about was feeding Chinese down onto the ridges he assaulted, faster than the friendly artillery could destroy them. Baker took a very bloody nose trying to move up the T-bone, and finally, Busbey received orders to pull back before dark.

He was lucky to get out. A sergeant from the supporting Weapons Company D, firing from a supporting finger ridge, realized his machine gun could not hold off the enemy long. This N.C.O. sent his crew back, while he fired to give them cover, staying on the gun.

As the Chinese pressed in, the machine gun snapped empty. Unable to load a fresh belt in time, the sergeant emptied his .45 at them. His body was found later; the Chinese had left it and taken the gun.

The sergeant, whose name Busbey thought was Henderson, got a posthumous D.S.C., while Busbey and his men, under heavy pressure, got out.

Later, both the corps and division commanders came down to the battalion, apologizing for the operation. They had had no intimation that they were sending 1st Battalion into a buzzsaw.

During September, Busbey replaced his casualties and held the MLR around Artillery Hill—so named because enemy shells always fell at chow time. Then, in October, a battalion of Colombians relieved his battalion, and the 32nd Infantry took over from the 2nd Division on Heartbreak Ridge.

During the last days of October, the 7th Division tried to police up the litter left at the scene of that battle. Equipment and material lay everywhere; enemy dead were strewn across the hills. And even some American dead still lay in the ditches beside one road. How they came there Busbey never knew.

Tied in with the ROK 7th Division, Busbey's company was given the mission of covering the valley beyond Heartbreak, a two-hundred-yard-wide defile through which flowed a small stream, and up which American tanks patrolled each day.

By day Busbey could cover the valley by fire, but at night it was a matter of setting up ambush patrols near the stream and on the fingers of the covering ridge to prevent the enemy from mining the valley floor and stream bed.

On the third night, one of Busbey's patrols hit the jackpot.

Several of his men with a light machine gun manned by an assistant gunner who had never fired in combat were sitting close by the stream. They heard the stealthy noises of approaching men, and through the dark were able to make out a mining patrol, 2 NKPA officers, and half a dozen enlisted men carrying AT mines.

"Wait till they're closer," the machine gunner whispered.

To fully load a round into the chamber of a light machine gun, the bolt must be pulled to the rear and released twice. The assistant gunner, who had pulled the bolt back once, thought the gun full loaded—until the pressure on the trigger produced only a terrifyingly loud *click*.

By the time the patrol figured out what was wrong, the North Koreans were six feet away. The first shot tore off the top of an NKPA lieutenant's head. Swiveling the gun rapidly, the blond young man who had waited just a bit longer than he had intended cut down all of the surprised unfortunates before they could escape.

Next morning Major General Claude Ferenbaugh, the division commander, who visited front positions regularly, was shown the stiff and blasted Korean corpses. "By God," Ferenbaugh said, "I get these reports all the time, but this is the first time anyone has had the bodies to prove it!"

He decorated the blond gunner before he left.

Now there was no offensive action taken against the enemy—but an army could not sit still. It had to patrol, even as the enemy had to patrol, to keep contact, to see what the other side was doing, and to attempt to keep the other side honest.

It was this patrol action, this continual flirting with danger and death, for reasons many of the enlisted men thought flimsy, that soldiers all across the Eighth Army's line came to hate. But there was no help for it.

And while the front was still, except for patrols, there was the shelling. The enemy, who had to bring his precious ammunition under air attack over many miles, did not care to waste it. But he was not loath to shoot it, if he had a target.

One of Busbey's platoon leaders, Jack Sadler, was restive at the inactivity. "How about letting me snipe at them over there with my 75mm recoilless?"

"Hell, you'll make 'em mad, Jack," Busbey told him.

"Aw, just one round, anyway—"

Sadler fired one round at the enemy lines, with indeterminate effect.

Then, immediately, the enemy shelled his platoon, heavily. Two of Sadler's men were killed—and forever afterward Sadler held himself responsible. After that, a sort of gentlemen's agreement held—each side left the other alone during the day.

It was a weird war now, not so dangerous, but more frustrating than ever. Now and then, by night, the enemy made limited attacks.

The U.N. almost never returned them.

It began to grow quite cold by night, as winter neared. And since the men had to be alert at night—everything in Korea happened at night, whether the Americans liked it that way or not—orders came down for each man to get his sleep during the day, so that he could remain alert at night without hardship.

There was nothing else for the troops, holding a line of foxholes and bunkers until the boys of Panmunjom could come to agreement, to do. Bored and restless, they didn't like the schedule, particularly the standing guard each night.

One night, as the temperature dropped to near zero, Lieutenant Sadler called Busbey's CP by phone at 0200. "Captain, I have a fully armed NKPA here who has turned himself in—"

Quite a few North Koreans, from time to time, when they could slip past their officers, came voluntarily into U.N. lines. This was nothing new.

But Sadler continued. "He surrendered to the tanks back of me—"

Busbey snapped, "How'd he get past you?"

"By God, I hadn't thought of that—I don't know, Captain."

"Well, think about it!" Busbey told him, hanging up.

Sadler roused his platoon sergeant, Trexler, and they got a ROK to query the enemy soldier. He had walked down the road in the valley—right through an area where Sadler had two standing patrols, two foxholes containing three men, with absolute orders that one man remain awake at all times. Sadler and Trexler looked at each other, and went out into the night.

Jack Sadler went up one side of the trail. Trexler the other. On both sides they found all men zipped up in their bags, sound asleep.

If the Inmun Gun had probed that night, they could have walked to Seoul for the weekend, as Busbey said.

After listening to the lame, stumbling stories, Busbey, furious, preferred charges against four enlisted men.

And two nights later, while the four were awaiting trial, the NKPA attacked down through the same valley. The outposts were alert; they were repulsed at the main line.

A 76mm artillery round killed Sergeant Trexler, however; and the Division Judge Advocate General said he would have to drop the case against the two men Trexler had caught sleeping on outpost—there was now no witness against them. The two were released.

But the remaining two, with Sadler's testimony, were convicted by a general court-martial at Division HQ. Each was given ten years at hard labor, and dishonorable discharge.

Because of their stupidity, and their lack of responsibility, hundreds of their comrades might have died. During the American Civil War they would have been shot.

But it was a long time since the Civil War, and with the Korean War a new factor had entered American military justice: during a crusade, or a war with fervent popular support, a soldier's malfeasance is almost always regarded severely by civilians. Whatever the effect on his comrades, the public then regards his failure as treason, or close to it.

Vengeance, indeed, is futile. It is not the purpose of justice. But when—as happened—an officer or man refused to go into combat, or threw away his weapon, crying, before ever a shot was fired at him, and then was permitted to resign, with honor, or had his sentence rescinded and his rights restored on petition at a later date, the nation is playing with disaster. There is a certain percentage of men who will always do their duty, just as there is a small percentage who will never do it, or even recognize it. The majority of men, however, will do unpleasant duties only if their society makes them, whether it is the study of English as children or service with the colors as men.

Busbey's two men received ten-year sentences—in itself unfair, since equally guilty men got off—but the matter did not rest there. For the father of one of these men was a man of some political influence in an Eastern state. Learning that some got off, while his son did not, this gentleman understandably raised hell.

The papers picked up the case, from Newark to Dallas.

An INS man came down to 32nd Infantry from Tokyo, looking for a story. He interviewed the men of B Company, still licking wounds from the night attack. Every man he talked to told him, "Those men didn't get half what they deserved." B Company had learned its lesson.

The INS man went back to Tokyo and phoned his chief. But he didn't have the kind of story his chief wanted. Many editorials were taking the tack that ten years for sleeping on sentry go was rather rough, even barbaric.

One year later, the son of the Eastern man was granted a new trial. The Civil Court of Military Appeals had discovered a flaw in the original proceedings. The president of that court had asked the law officer, present at all general courts-martial, "What is the maximum sentence that can be given?" while neither the accused or counsel was present, a violation.

The new trial was held in Fort Meade, Maryland. The witnesses were now the other enlisted men who had been in the hole with the accused.

Jack Sadler, at this time in Baltimore, was not called, then or later. The verdict, understandably, and to everyone except Captain Busbey's relief, was reversed.

In itself, this case was nothing new. Justice, either military or civilian, can never be perfect.

But inevitably, sooner or later, a people will get the kind of justice and military service they deserve.

* * *

Before Arthur Busbey returned to the States on emergency leave—on the death of an infant child—with too many points to be returned again to FECOM, one incident occurred that he would never forget.

In the valley behind Heartbreak, where his company had now built fairly decent living bunkers for the winter, his patrols were just eating a hot meal at dusk before going in front of the ridge, down into the no man's land under enemy surveillance. He noticed a short soldier, unknown to him, trudging up the hill, a heavy pack on his back.

"Hey, soldier," he called, "come here."

The man, just a kid, reported to him.

"Where're you going, soldier?"

"To the front lines."

"What unit?"

"Any unit, sir!"

"Well," Busbey told him, "if you go around that ridge line you will be in the gooks' front lines. What's your outfit?"

The young soldier told him the 187th Airborne.

"Now I know you're lying, kid. The outfit's in reserve in Japan."

But the young man was not lying. The 187th had made a practice jump near Pusan—and some men had immediately taken off for the front. The 187th—paratroops are a sharp but fragile tool, which, since they cannot be used and then put back into the bottle, are best reserved for special missions—had been out of action a long time, and these men wanted to fight. Any fight, anywhere, would do.

Busbey called Battalion. Battalion informed him he couldn't keep the young man, who was AWOL. But before he was sent back to the rear, Busbey gave him a letter of acceptance to B of the 32nd Infantry, in case the paratrooper's C.O. would release him.

Just before Arthur Busbey went home, in December 1951, he got a letter from another man in the 187th Airborne, wanting to know if this man could have a letter too.

33

Behind the Wire

The true test of civilization is, not the census, nor the size of cities, nor the crops—no, but the kind of man the country turns out.
—Ralph Waldo Emerson, SOCIETY AND SOLITUDE.

A S THE LINES stabilized and the year lengthened, Army Postal Office 971 also began to get things stabilized at Yongdungp'o, on the outskirts of Seoul. First Lieutenant Leonard Morgan received a new C.O., First Lieutenant Forrest Patrick. An ex-infantry officer, Patrick was blood and guts all the way, which was sometimes out of place in an APO.

He tried to get the four officers and eighty-five enlisted men shaped up, with lectures, and other exhortations, while the mail went through.

One day, he had the men assembled outside the shoe factory beside the Korean brewery, discussing the problem of the five-gallon water cans always being filled with native beer. At another time Patrick discussed proper conduct in the host Republic of Korea, in compliance with a directive put out by the 2nd Engineer Brigade in Inch'on.

"We've got to be friendly, and make a good impression," Patrick said. "I don't like this going into the local houses and carrying off the possessions, as some of you have been doing. I want it stopped."

While he talked, two GI's walked past behind him, carrying a large antique dresser on their backs. Even though they were from another outfit, Patrick's show was ruined.

Finally, a new C.O. came in, Major Harry Steinberg, Adjutant General's Corps. And Steinberg, called "Dollar Sign" because his initials on a piece of paper looked like one, was an operator. He got things done.

The first month, he got a shower for the EM.

The second month, the water ran dry. A careful investigation proved that Kim, the Korean factotum who took care of the officer's tent, had been an engineer, and had diverted the water from the shower pipes underground to the Korean houseboy quarters.

Kim went, the water came back, and the mail continued to move.

Business was good.

During the third month there was an arrangement with the officers and men flying in now and then from staff jobs in Tokyo—who wanted to see how things were doing in Korea, earn a shiny new campaign ribbon, and qualify, if they came often enough, for the $200 per month income-tax exemption granted to all serving there—to smuggle in Air Force liquor.

And so the months went by.

It took a hell of a long time to accumulate thirty-six points this way, but as the boys of APO 971 knew, there were ways much worse.

* * *

On 17 March 1951 Sergeant Charles B. Schlichter's group from the Valley closed in at Prison Camp Number 5, near Pyoktong, on the Yalu River. The officer and N.C.O. ranks were separated from the others, and a physical count revealed 3,200 POW's of all grades present.

Between March and October that number was reduced by 50 percent.

American doctors were allowed to continue with sick call and treatment, but they were given nothing to work with. Medicines were almost nonexistent. The food continued below the caloric content necessary to keep an average American's flesh and spirit together.

One American doctor in the camp told Schlichter the 400 to 600 grams of boiled cracked corn and millet—with occasional dabs of soya beans and Chinese cabbage—issued each day could not contain more than 1,600 calories, and sometimes the content was only 1,200.

While under this diet extreme weight loss was inevitable, the worst was the diet's lack of mineral and vitamin content. In East Asia soya is almost the sole source of protein for the poor. But the Americans did not understand how to cook the beans; usually half cooked, these were often indigestible, and their sharp edges tortured men already suffering from starvation-induced diarrhea. Many men refused to touch the soya—cattle fodder in the States—and ate the starches alone. Few of these men lived.

The Geneva Conventions, revised after Western experience in Japanese POW camps in World War II, state:

> *To keep prisoners of war in good health, and to prevent loss of weight or the development of nutritional deficiencies, account shall be taken of the habitual diet of prisoners.*

But to expect an Asian nation accustomed to famine to feed its prisoners of war better than its own half-starved peasantry was and remains wishful thinking on Americans' part.

The evidence does not suggest that the Chinese deliberately tried to starve the POW's with the end of extermination in mind, in the footsteps of the Nazis. When in late winter the death rate climbed alarmingly, to twenty-eight men each day, the Chinese commandant of Camp 5 showed signs of concern; he ordered the American doctors in the camp to stop the deaths, at once.

More medicines were made available—but the commandant angrily resisted the Americans' demands for more food.

He admitted the POW's were fed worse than the guards—but they were receiving the same diet that class enemies of the Chinese state received, who not only had to undergo two or more years of reorientation on such rations, but hard labor, too. It was only with the coming of spring and summer, when most of the deaths had already occurred, that the Chinese improved the POW's diet. It was again improved, late in the war, for obvious reasons of world opinion. The Chinese did not wish to repatriate tottering skeletons.

And one fact that stands out starkly among the pieces of evidence is that while 50 percent of the American POW's died, and a percentage of British that caused grave concern later to her Majesty's Government, few South Koreans experienced much difficulty, and not one Turkish prisoner of war died.

Chemistry and culture killed the Americans.

The disciplines, attitudes, and organization that Americans brought into captivity killed many of them.

Only an extremely cohesive group, with tight leadership and great spiritual strengths, coupled with inner toughness and concern for one another, could have survived the shocks visited upon their minds and bodies.

The British sergeants stood like rocks, and did well. The British other ranks, largely National Servicemen drafted from the factory towns, with little sense of purpose or cohesion, did less well.

But it was the Turks who did best of all.

The Turks were a completely homogeneous group, with common background and common culture, and with a chain of command that was never broken.

They remained united against the enemy, and they survived.

The Turks did not come from an admirable society. Only a few decades back in time, Turks were slaving in Egypt, and conducting vast pogroms in Armenia. In the last century Turks still blew living men from the mouths of cannon for minor crimes and punished more serious ones by impalement—a peculiarly horrible form of execution, in which a man was seated on a sharpened tapered stake, toes off the ground, and his body weight, and movements, slowly drove him downward.

There had never been anything approaching freedom, or democracy, in Turkey. Elections have been held, but the losers normally wind up in jail.

Turkey had journeyed partway into the twentieth century only under the iron fist of Kemal Atatürk and his successors, who were just as determined as the Chinese Communists to destroy an ancient, backward, Oriental way of life.

Atatürk was determined to Westernize his people by force. He broke the power of the Moslem clergy, revised education, changed the traditional headgear and alphabet.

But in the middle of the century the Turkish soldier who served his country's colors was still a fanatically devout custom-ridden peasant, close to the soil and survival, accustomed to the fiercest discipline all his life, from father, state, and army—but with a barbarian's pride in himself and his people.

He would take baths only with his clothes on in the prison camps, or allow a nonbeliever friend such as Schlichter to view his Koran only through the seven veils, and he went white with outrage if venereal disease were even discussed.

But he was completely aware of what he was—he was a Turk, and a Turk was unquestionably the finest of all possible things to be, even as there was no God but Allah. These matters he felt no need to prove or argue; he had imbibed them with his mother's milk, and his mind had not been cluttered with other notions since.

He knew Russians were Communists, and he knew Russians were enemies, always had been, always would be. He hated Russians; he hated Communists. The matter was not arguable.

He was close to the soil, and knew hardship; he ate what Allah or the dogs of Communist Chinese provided, without complaint. He also knew enough to eat any scrap of greenery he could place his hands on, and in the camps many better-educated Americans watched him eat weeds in amazement.

Later, many of them followed suit.

He was barbarian-proud of his manhood and his fighting ability. He knew, dimly, that his ancestors had been the backbone of Near Eastern armies since the Empire of Roum and that their courage with cold steel had rarely been equaled. He knew, dimly, that firepower had vanquished his vaunted empire and that economically he was backward, but this had not lessened his faith in Turks or Turkdom. What schools he had attended used no economic arguments in teaching the greatness of Turks.

Even after thirty years of state anticlericalism, his faith in his God was childlike, ignorant, and complete.

He had enlisted for a minimum of six years, and he could not hope to become a sergeant until after that first six years. He had served long with the men about him in these camps, and he expected to serve beside these same men again, if Allah willed him to survive. He could not understand these Americans who often acted like strangers to one another, and as if they would never see one another again.

His senior enlisted man took command in the prison camp, because he was senior. Neither he nor the British N.C.O.'s held an election, as did the Americans—who elected in Camp Five a corporal masquerading as a sergeant who was popular with the Chinese guards.

His senior enlisted man ran a detail roster daily. There was never any question of who would chop the wood, haul the water, or care for the sick—while American N.C.O.'s and doctors and chaplains often begged men to feed the sick, wash the unconscious, or go outside for firewood—and were told, "Go to hell, you're no better than I am!"

When his senior enlisted man was threatened by the guards for defiance, it did them no good to remove him. The second, the third, even the hundredth senior man took over, and nothing changed.

When one Turk was too friendly with the Chinese, court was held, and Sergeant Schlichter was invited to observe. The senior N.C.O. sat as judge, and trial was held, with argument and testimony. When one Turk was found guilty of amiability toward the enemy, he was severely beaten. His defense counsel was beaten, too, for daring to extol such a traitor.

When Schlichter asked, "What happens if he does this again?" he was told, "Then we shall kill him."

It was a rigid society, far from admirable by Western standards. Disturbingly, it had the best record of any group in Communist captivity.

Americans should remember that while barbarians may be ignorant they are not always stupid.

The sociologists, soldiers, and doctors will argue long why Americans died in Communist prisons, why some broke, and why others lived. The evidence has been fed into hearts, not computers, and the answers are unclear.

* * *

In Prisoner of War Camp 5, at Pyoktong, the Chinese tried to reeducate their captives. The methods were much the same as those of all Communist reeducation—reiteration, argument, lies, confusion, and the application of force and fear with varying degrees of subtlety.

It came to be called brainwashing, but it was nothing new. The Soviets had employed the same means against men they took at Stalingrad, with about the same degree of success.

Men behind wire are always afraid of their captors. Only by tight inner discipline and complete cohesion can they hope to resist completely what their captors will do to them. Inevitably, when pressured, some men collaborate.

Turks were asked to collaborate. They did not, because each Turk was firm in what he believed, and he knew implicitly that his group—the Turks—would never permit any individual lapses. A Turk who aided the Chinese was signing his own death warrant—and knew it.

There was no such cohesion to the body of Americans within the wire. In any group of human beings, of whatever nationality, there are criminals, fools, and potential traitors. American policy within the wire remained disapproving of such—but tolerant.

A certain number of Americans did criminal acts, against their own. A very few committed treason. A very few resisted fanatically.

The great majority, although disorganized, confused, and completely uninstructed as to how to behave in this new situation in which they were asked to sign petitions and state anticapitalist opinions, resisted passively. They did not condone collaboration, though they made few moves to stamp it out, as did the Turks. They preferred to shun it.

The Chinese educators were not diabolically clever; at times they were incredibly stupid. But they had the prisoners in their power, and they had them continually off balance. The POW's never understood the Communists, and never caught up with them.

As Charles Schlichter reported, almost all POW's were under the misapprehension that they might be tortured at any time. They were threatened with it, though it did not materialize.

Day after day, the POW's attended forced classes. They sat on hard wooden benches for six to eight hours a day, while Chinese lecturers hammered at them, over and over, about Okies, Roman Catholics, and Negroes in America, that all officials of the Republic were rich men, that all congressmen were college-trained, and that not one workingman had any say in the Republic's affairs, in American accents ranging from that of the deep South to Brooklyn.

The POW's were never excused from class for any reason. Men fainted, and were left where they lay. There was no excuse to visit latrines, even for men with dysentery. These fouled themselves, and were forced by guards to continue sitting.

The Chinese instructors found the POW's knew almost nothing of civics or the mechanics of American government, and of this they made big play. The fact that American soldiers knew so little, they said, proved that the ruling interests wanted it so.

The fact was that the majority of the very young men taken in the early months of Korea had little education—averaging not much beyond eighth grade. They had imbibed very little, also, with their mother's milk, as to what they were and what they stood for.

They knew the Communist lecturers were wrong—but they did not know how to refute them. American youth, during a grade-school education, or even beyond, do not learn the status of American Roman Catholics vis-á-vis the Constitution, discuss the plight of Okies, or hold debate on the ramifications of the Negro in American life.

Under the hammering, some of these men began to feel they did not even know who or what they were, or what their place might be in the grand design of the universe, while the Turks—fortunately protected by the language barrier—no Chinese spoke Turkish—sat happily aware that a Turk was a Turk, unarguably better than any pig of a Chinese Communist, educated or otherwise.

It was apparent to some men in Camp 5 that in order to permit Americans to live more amicably together, American education had done a great deal of damping of the flaming convictions men live and die by.

The men who had in one way or another come to hold strong, unswayable beliefs—such as Schlichter's reborn faith in his God, or some old infantry sergeant's belief in his service and Colors, or even some men's firm convictions on the superiority of Anglo-Saxon institutions—were the men who were untouched, whom the Chinese soon classed as reactionaries, and segregated.

Fortunately, after lectures, the POW's talked among themselves, and sometimes came up with answers to the provocative questions of their tormentors. Sometimes, they could not, although few believed in their hearts the Chinese had the right of it.

And, oddly, it was with the Okies, Catholics, and Negroes that the Communists, on the whole, had small success. Many of the disadvantaged understood the dream of America better than those who had enjoyed its benefits.

Sitting in the lecture room, Sergeant Schlichter, like so many others, was taken sick. He was sent to the crude Chinese hospital with pneumonia.

He almost died.

But here, as he said, he saw the greatest example of faith he had ever seen, in the actions of Chaplain Emil Kapaun, who had been taken at Unsan. Father Kapaun, ill himself, stood in front of the POW's, prayed, and stole food to share with others. By his example, he sometimes forced the little bit of good remaining in these starving men to the fore.

But Chaplain Kapaun could not take command, and he soon grew deathly ill, probably as much from sorrow as from his own starvation.

Schlichter saw him put in a room, without food or medicine. No other American was allowed to treat the priest, and he soon died.

He was not alone. Schlichter heard that no other chaplain survived the prison camps of Korea, the only class or group to be wiped out.

The Communists had no great fear of capitalist production; they hoped to surpass it. But as the proponents of what is certainly a secular religion, they feared and hated any sign of non-Communist spirituality, and showed it no mercy. They understood clearly that religion—not necessarily organized religion—was among the greatest stumbling blocks they faced.

They feared no church, as such; some of these they had come to control, in East Europe and elsewhere—but they were deeply apprehensive of forces such as neither Nero, Gallienus, nor Maxentius could destroy.

Also in the hospital was Dr. Kubenick, ill, like Schlichter, with pneumonia. Kubenick called to Schlichter, "Sergeant, I want you to do me a favor."

"Anything—"

"See my things get home to my wife—"

"Why do you think I'll live and you won't?"

"Sergeant, I know—that's all. I want you to promise."

Later, Schlichter gave Kubenick's poor effects to Graves Registration. And later still, he visited Kubernick's wife, who asked him only if he had seen her husband die.

Among the families of men who died in the prison camps, there remains much bitterness. And there have been no reunions of POW's either.

On 3 October 1951, his thirtieth birthday, Charles Schlichter was released from the hospital. The next day the last man died in Camp 5 at Pyoktong.

Immediately after the deaths ceased, the Chinese saw a chance for propaganda. American doctors were removed from sick call, and more medical supplies were made available. The Communist Green Cross took over sick call.

Schlichter was made camp sanitation officer. "What can we do to help living conditions?" the Chinese asked him, with apparent sincerity.

"Replace the American M.D.'s, if only for psychological reasons," Schlichter told them.

"Ah, we can't do that—why, the American doctors didn't care whether you lived or died. Look how many died while they took care of you—"

It was the big-lie technique; the American doctors had held sway while the diet was at its worst, while men with wounds died without drugs, and with no cooperation from the guards. Only after the worst were they removed.

Yet many POW's believed this lie. Some never relinquished it, even after repatriation.

But prison life was not all horror. The Chinese announced a huge clean-up campaign of the camp. To get it rolling, they offered a pack of cigarettes for each two hundred dead flies caught, or three smokes for a rat.

Each evening Sanitation Officer Schlichter picked up the dead flies and rats, counted them out, and marked them down in his notebook. Then, with a guard, he marched in front of a camp official, who determined if the count was honest with a broken chopstick.

No one objected to Schlichter's handling the tobacco; he did not smoke.

One sergeant, who had been active as a Scout, devised a gauze flytrap, and placed it over the reeking latrine. When he had about 1,500 flies enmeshed in it, he took them to the Yalu and drowned them.

That night, when Schlichter turned in flies for cigarettes, the Chinese officer's eye popped. He said, "So many flies—good! Good!" Then his eyes narrowed. "How come no squash?"

But he paid off.

The Turks, closer to the soil than Americans, sought out pregnant rats, caught them, and slit them. Sometimes they got twenty-one smokes per rat.

There were libraries available, stocked with books from Communist countries, extolling the beauties of collectivism and exposing the fallacies of the capitalist system. From boredom, everybody read them.

The only newspapers available were old copies of the New York *Daily Worker* and the Shanghai *Daily News,* English-language sheets that gave only the Communist side.

The sole English or American books in the library were Steinbeck's *Grapes of Wrath,* and Dicken's *A Christmas Carol,* a story the Communists have never quite understood.

Life, through 1951 and 1952, was composed of details, now, in addition to the constant education. Men cooked, cut firewood, and wondered about the war.

There was almost no news. Newer prisoners, taken after the big hauls during the summer and winter of 1950, were never allowed to mingle with the older prisoners.

There was free enterprise, even in a Communist camp. The troops had been paid just before Kunu-ri, and almost everyone had a great deal of MPC. Money was useless; besides, all knew that the Military Payment Certificates had been changed, and doubted if the government would make the old ones good. An old watch went for $200. A cigarette cost $10, or sold at a volume price of three for $25.

Some men gambled. Schlichter saw as much as $1,000 rest on the turn of a card—though men seldom bet their food or sugar ration.

Inevitably, some men in Camp 5 soon had all the money there was to be had.

That was also part of free enterprise, any way you cut it.

For recreation, the POW's were taught to sing the "Internationale," and "The Chinese People's Volunteers' Marching Song." Sometimes, by a particularly hearty rendition of these, they could get extra chow.

Slowly, bitterly, even though the dying had ended, the months dragged on.

Finally, on 12 August 1952, Schlichter and many others, classified as reactionaries unfitted for further education, were sent to Camp 4, at Wewan. This was a camp reserved for sergeants; there were three POW companies: Number 1 contained three French N.C.O.'s, Puerto Ricans, Niseis from the 5th RCT, 35 British sergeants, and 23 Turks. Number 2 was wholly American and white, while Number 3 was filled with colored soldiers.

Here, one man asked Schlichter, "Do you think a POW-camp promotion will be permanent?" The man was a private who had told the Chinese he was a sergeant.

Schlichter answered him that, unlike a posthumous promotion, he didn't think it was.

* * *

On Koje Island, the U.N. compounds were now filled to bursting with Chinese and North Koreans. The 2nd Logistical Command in Pusan, under whose command Koje-do remained, continued to cope as best they could.

Actually, all seemed to be running very well.

The POW's were busy in workshops, making placards, flags, and newssheets, with which they flooded the island. They were making other things, too, but these they hid.

Each day one American N.C.O. with a couple of POW trusties made routine inspections of the compounds housing the 80,000-odd captives. There was no question that food, clothing, and housing were adequate, although the number of POW's in each compound made control difficult, and close inspection almost impossible.

POW's still disappeared or turned up dead; there still seemed to be dissension in the compounds. But none of the guards thought it was their business, or of any great concern.

In the absence of concern, or pressure, the control of the camps tended to grow lackadaisical.

And certain of the POW's tended to grow more and more arrogant.

The command of Koje-do changed rapidly, now, as Colonel Fitzgerald became a sort of permanent executive officer to various officers sent in by 2nd Logistical Command in Pusan. In all there were thirteen different commanders, none with any experience with POW's—and none with any backing from higher up.

Certain nations of the U.N. were hypersensitive over the treatment of the POW's, whether because of common geographical background or fear of American discrimination, or whatever. These, and the International Red Cross, and the Neutral Nations Inspection Teams—called NITS by all Americans—harassed the POW Command regularly regarding POW rights and privileges.

None of these agencies could enter North Korea because of the blunt refusal of the Communists, but they compensated by being twice as officious on Koje-do. Because of their vigilance and constant complaints, higher headquarters in the Eighth Army and FECOM made it quite clear that no force of any kind might be used against the POW's, regardless of their actions.

Colonel Lee Hak Ku and the mysterious Hong Chol were spreading their network of control through the compounds day by day. Certain American officers knew this, but their hands were tied. As Major Bill Gregory said: "No commander could get any backing from General Yount in Pusan, General Van Fleet, Ridgway, or anyone else. Ridgway himself never seemed to care a hoot in hell about what happened in Koje-do."

There were certainly no appropriations for new compounds, new wire, new construction materials. Eighty thousand potential tigers milled behind the flimsy, jerry-built wire pens that had been erected in early 1951; no better ones were ever built. Such requests were promptly rejected.

One big reason so little concern was shown for the POW camps was that higher headquarters, with the start of truce talks, was convinced the war would end any day, automatically ending the POW problem by repatriation.

There were matters that needed straightening out within the compounds— but each commander on Koje-do knew clearly that if the hair of one POW were bruised, if one guard bashed a prisoner, neither Van Fleet nor Ridgway would lift a finger to aid during the ensuing hue and cry.

It is very clear that if Washington and Far East Command had been less concerned with world and neutral opinion and more with internal order, the near tragedy that was to come to Koje-do could have been averted.

By late 1951 it was already clear to both Americans and neutrals that there was intense political ferment within the compounds. The POW's were dividing into Communists and non-Communists—and amazing to the neutrals, who would not at first believe this—many POW's began to petition the U.N. not to allow them to be repatriated.

The treatment of the POW's, and their glimpses into non-Communist life, had had some results. More fundamental, however, was the fact that many Koreans and Chinese had been forcibly pressed into the Communist armies, and many of these had no political belief and even, in thousands of cases, a genuine hatred of their rulers.

The U.N. was slow to capitalize on this fact. The situation called for fair and impartial screening of all POW's, as Swiss Delegate Lehner reported. There was an unspoken reason behind the United Nations' reluctance to become involved in the POW's loyalties, however.

After agreement on the cease-fire line in November 1951, hopes appeared bright for a quick end to the fighting in Korea. The only really knotty question remaining was disposition of each side's POW's. The Communists—who had boasted of having taken 64,000 POW's, mostly Koreans—now claimed they had only 11,000 available to return. This disclosure caused anguish among the ROK's, who wondered at the fate of 50,000 of their countrymen, but did not seem an obstacle in the way of the U.N.'s desire for peace.

But in March of 1952, at Panmunjom, the U.N. negotiators were forced to admit to the enemy that apparently a great many of the POW's held at Pusan and Koje-do did not wish to return to their homelands. Surprisingly agreeable, the Chinese and North Koreans suggested these men be screened.

For two days, beginning in April 1952, loudspeakers blared in every U.N. POW camp, telling the prisoners that each man would be individually interviewed to determine which desired repatriation, and which, for various reasons, did not.

No promises were now issued to those who might not want to return. In fact, the prospects held out were almost grim. After so many happy months of trying to indoctrinate the POW's, it had suddenly occurred to Americans that if a substantial number refused repatriation, the end of the fighting could be long delayed, with the further delay of repatriation of American POW's in the north.

One Captain Harold Whallon, the son of American missionaries born in China, a recalled Reserve officer, was ordered to Koje-do to assist with the screening. Arriving at the island, he found a number of other officers and men, all with backgrounds similar to his.

The screening began. It was a difficult job; most of the Orientals could not conceive of truly free choice without strings.

But amazingly, of the Chinese, it soon turned out that not more than one in five wanted to go home. Most of the Chinese POW's claimed to be old soldiers of Chiang Kai-shek, forcibly inducted into the Communist Forces, who now considered themselves political refugees.

In the Korean compounds it was different. Here Communist leaders had imposed tight control in many compounds, and a virtual war was being waged between Communist and anti-Communist groups. American guard officers knew of this control, but they also knew that bloodshed would be required to break it. With world opinion focused on Koje-do, and with an armistice hanging in the balance at Panmunjom, higher headquarters would not listen to suggestions of strong measures.

But the screening went on, and U.N. figures showed that only 50 percent—about 70,000—of the total POW's and civilian internees held by the U.N. Command would return voluntarily to Red China or North Korea.

It was one of the greatest propaganda coups against world Communism ever recorded, but it brought only gloom to U.N. officials, who by now wanted only "out" of the war.

President Truman, informed, declared that "forced repatriation was repugnant to the free world" and that Americans would not force human beings to return to Communist slavery.

He was not wholly applauded, though editorial comment was favorable. It was deeply feared that this development would delay the return of the hundreds of thousands of American soldiers now in Korea.

And at Panmunjom, as feared, the Communist representatives dropped dialectics for once and exhibited sheer rage. Publicly to admit defection from their ranks was an unthinkable loss of face. The Communist delegation shrieked that all captured personnel must be returned, whatever their politics.

They stated flatly the U.N. would get no peace, unless at least 110,000 POW's were forced to return. On 25 April 1952, they angrily recessed the meetings.

Faced with stinging defeat in an unexpected quarter, the Communists now planned a diversion—one that would prove to the world that the U.N. was actually coercing its POW's into the stand so many had taken.

The fact that the diversion would be bloody and cost hundreds of lives—North Korean and Chinese lives—bothered Nam Il, the man who conceived it, not at all.

* * *

Jeon Moon Il, or Pak Sang Hyong, the name he went by, was the child of Korean refugees in the Soviet Union. He was a Young Communist, a graduate of the University of Khabarovsk in 1937, and his rise was rapid.

In 1945 he had the honor of being one of the thirty-six Soviet citizens of Korean ancestry ordered to enter North Korea, change citizenship, and organize the Chosun Minjujui Inmun Kongwhakuk, in company with Kim Il Sung and Nam Il. He became Vice Chairman of the North Korean Labor Party.

In 1952 Jeon Moon Il, a short, evil-faced man, was officially listed as a Private Pak of the Inmun Gun in the U.N. prisoner-of-war camp on Koje-do. Good Communists go where they are ordered, and serve wherever they may be.

Certain POW's, newly captured along the battle line and sent to Koje-do, reported to Jeon, head of the Communist Political Committee, once inside the camp. These brought news from the North, and fresh orders from Nam Il, otherwise busily engaged at Panmunjom.

In April of 1952, Jeon received special orders. They came to him in a special way, through the major.

The major, whose real name and identity were as difficult to ascertain as that of all Communist bigwigs, had received several months' special training and instruction. He was taught to rehearse his story of the murder of his family by the Communists and of his secret hatred for the regime. When he was thoroughly prepared—even to a clear understanding of the dangers of his task—he was reminded once again of the promotion and decoration his work, successfully completed, would bring, and he was assured that if he did not return his family would receive a pension for forty years.

Then the major was given a dirty, ragged, front-line private's uniform, with a stained U.N. surrender leaflet in its pockets.

It was dangerous, but no great problem, to walk into U.N. lines with his hands up, spouting his story, and brandishing the surrender leaflet with its announced safe conduct.

From there on, the U.N. did the rest. They saw that he arrived at Koje-do. Inside the wire, it was no great problem to contact the Communist grapevine and pass Nam Il's word to the head of the Political Committee.

Further screening and separation of Communists and anti-Communists must now be resisted to the death, the major informed Jeon. Further, a high-ranking American officer must be captured. With his life at stake, then a promise against further screening might be exacted—if not, then the enemy without the wire might be provoked into such violence that the Communist claims of U.N. brutality would be proved to all the world.

Jeon, the political officer, had a senior colonel and a full division of men under his tight command. He had compound colonels, captains, corporals. The senior officers, Lee Hak Ku and Hong Chol, felt they could capture Koje-do, if necessary, though they then had no place to go; they saw no great difficulty in capturing the newly arriving Brigadier Francis T. Dodd, the first general officer ever sent down to command the island.

Nor did they, on 7 May 1952.

34

Frustration

There is a certain blend of courage, integrity, character and principle which has no satisfactory dictionary name but has been called different things in different countries. Our American name for it is "guts."

—From Louis Adamic, A STUDY IN COURAGE.

T HE MONTHS AND years that began with the peace talks at Kaesong and Panmunjom were the most frustrating the American Republic, and more particularly its Army, had endured.

While all citizens could feel frustration at the continued thwarting of American policy, and at the continued failure to achieve either military or political results from continuing expense and sacrifice, while political leaders, in or out, fretted and worried over public reaction and tried to trim their sails accordingly, the period was hardest of all upon the military services.

American military leaders, of all services, are brought up in the belief that vigorous action saves the day, and it is always better to do something, even the wrong thing, than to take no action at all.

History proves that on the battlefield he who hesitates is usually lost.

But in the early 1950's the United States had at last decided that the battlefield could no longer be separated from the political arena—and in politics, domestic and international, the rules are different.

Fools rush in, while success often comes to him who cleverly bides his time.

Seeking a substitute for MacArthur's victory, the United States was forced to bide its time, while its treasure poured into arms, and millions of its young men were forced into hard and painful service they detested.

It was hard for all services. The Navy, forced to blockade and patrol, had lonely, cheerless duty in the China seas, unrelieved by much action. Its carrier pilots flew dangerous patrols, and sometimes its landing parties went ashore on North Korea—but the rest of the time the Navy sowed mines, or harvested them, and merely stood on station in the gray waters off Korea.

Without its utter control of those seas, there would have been no U.N. stand in Korea—but it was made to stand watch only. It was not allowed to blockade the real enemies, nor had it any enemy fleet to engage. Still, despite this frustration, the Navy was fulfilling its primary mission—keeping control of the seas, and holding the sea lanes open.

The Air Force, out of Japan and Korea, flew in support of ground operations of Eighth Army. It bonded, strafed, rocketed, and napalmed, and without it the very presence of the U.N. in Korea would have ended early. Day by day, night by night, over the long months and years, it leveled each city, each shop and factory and mine in North Korea. It had quickly gained its primary goal of air superiority over the skies of Korea, and never lost it.

Yet the Air Force knew frustration, because it could not interdict this kind of battlefront, could not destroy a Chinese ground army that was a lurking phantom, and it could not do what was in so many of its leaders' hearts—strike the enemy where it hurt him.

North Korea it could reduce to rubble, but North Korea did not contain the enemy's warmaking potential. In this anachronistic type of war, the Air Force had been reduced almost to what it had been in World War I—an adjunct, not the decisive arm.

Except for brief moments, the Korean War had always been old-style, down in the mud. There were only two new developments in this conflict, both of which were in the air: the general use of jet aircraft, and the widespread use of rotary-wing craft for evacuation, transport, and reconnaissance.

In the first days of the war, American Far East Air Force had knocked down the antiquated YAK-9 and YAK-15 fighters of North Korea. It was not until 31 October 1950 that a new phase of air warfare began.

On that date Russian-built MIG-15 jet fighters appeared in strength over North Korea. They raised havoc with the lumbering B-29's bombing the Yalu bridges, and threw a fright into American pilots flying World War II F-51's and Corsairs. On 8 November an American F-80 shot down the first MIG-15, but the Air Force was forced to rush its newest and best fighters, the F-86 Sabrejets, to the Far East.

And here began the incessant air-to-air combats, which without significant change went on until the end of the war. The Communist aircraft, although field after field was constructed in North Korea, and as quickly bombed out, never were based south of the Yalu. They remained, silvery in plain sight on broad airdromes just north of the river, in privileged sanctuary, coming now and again across the river to engage patrolling American aircraft above the Valley of the Yalu—the famous MIG Alley.

American aircraft were never permitted to cross the Chinese or Russian boundary, even in hot pursuit.

On the other hand, although the Communists built up a large numerical superiority, they never attempted to carry the air war to South Korea, or even to the battle lines along the parallel. Both sides enjoyed their "privileged sanctuary"—and the resulting air combat resembled that of 1916–1918, or even the jousting of the knights of old.

American flights of Sabrejets, day after day, spread contrails high over MIG Alley, watching both sky and ground.

Often, across the river, they could see the MIG pilots leisurely walking to their parked and waiting aircraft.

American pilots talked to each other, as they rode by at great altitude and high mach in the sky.

"Dust at Fen Cheng—the clans are gathering," from Blue Leader.

"Thirty-six lining up over at Antung," from Black Leader.

"Hell, only twenty-four coming up here at Tatungkou," from another flight leader.

"Don't bitch—here come fifty from Takushan. That's at least three for everybody!"

Aided by their close ground control radar, the Communist craft rose high, preferably waiting until American fuel ran low before striking. Then at rates of closure as high as 1,200 MPH, the two formations came together.

Immediately, the formations dissolved into individual dogfights.

It was air war with a code more out of the Middle Ages than of twentieth century combat. Yet day after day, always outnumbered, too far away from their own bases to glide to safety, as could the enemy, American airmen accepted mortal combat.

The MIG-15's flashing upward from Manchurian bases were faster than the Sabrejets, and could outclimb them. The Russian-built planes carried twin 20mm cannon and a single 37mm against the .50-caliber machine gun armament of the F-86s. The MIG-15 was a superb aircraft, superior to any U.N. craft except the Sabrejet, which proved to be the only United Nations plane able to live in the air with it.

The appearance of the MIG-15 caused many people deep concern. These men had not accepted the fact that culture and weaponry, or even culture and plumbing, are not synonymous, and while a society may lag a hundred years behind in comforts and ethics, it may catch up in hardware in a human lifetime.

But the F-86 that flew daily down MIG Alley was an exceedingly rugged plane, extremely maneuverable, flown by competent pilots sifted for the "tiger" instinct—the quality that makes a man bore in for the kill—and above all, it carried a radar-ranging gunsight superior to anything owned by the Communists.

Because of that radar sight, as the Air Force admitted, American pilots destroyed enemy jet aircraft at a ratio of 11 to 1. At sonic speeds the human eye and hand were simply not fast enough—but more than 800 MIG-15's were sent spinning down, to crash and burn over North Korea.

The MIG-15's, flown by North Korean and Chinese pilots, were never handled with a skill matching that of American airmen.

Yet, overall, considering the hours of combat, few jets fell. The high altitudes, the high speeds, the toughness of the planes, which almost required a hit on engine or pilot to cripple, combined to keep losses small in comparison with earlier air combats.

This was to be an interim air war, a testing and a learning phase for both American and Communist. Tactics and weaponry could be put to test, and the answers—radar gun controls, air-to-air rocketry, automatic cannon—reserved to the future.

Through it all, American skill, courage, and ingenuity remained preeminent.

And even though the Air Force could not utilize its cherished strategic power in this war, though it fought under a maze of hampering restrictions, it could still fulfill its mission, like the Navy. It held control of the skies, and could work actively at its secondary missions.

It was the Army that knew the worst frustration, from July 1951 to the end of the war. The mission of the Army is to meet the enemy in sustained ground combat, and capture or destroy him.

The Army was indoctrinated that strength lay not in defense but in attack, and that the offensive, as Clausewitz wrote, always wins.

The Army not only could not win; it could not even work at the task. Yet it was locked in a wrestler's grip with the enemy, suffering hardship, taking losses, even after the peace talks began.

It was the first time that American generals, as well as Supreme Court judges, were forced to study the election returns. At home, the people and government, with certain exceptions, wanted peace, not costly victory. Abroad, American generals were closely watched by jittery allied governments who regarded them as irresponsible jingoists, and their every initiative as a reckless provocation that might lead to World War III.

It is understandable that some American Army generals chafed a little at the bit.

* * *

While certain units remained on line, the bulk of the U.S. 2nd Infantry Division proceeded to bivouac near Kap'yong on 25 October 1951. Here replacements were fed in; specialists schools set up; a one-week course run for replacement officers. Bloody and Heartbreak ridges had shown that again basic weapons instruction and small-unit tactics—the seemingly eternal weaknesses—were the chief needs of the division, as they were of every United States division manning the Korean battle line.

Training in the Zone of the Interior was just not thorough or tough enough to prepare men for ground combat.

While schools were set up, and battle drills organized, some elements of the division were detached to the south, where guerrilla activities had once again come to the fore.

When the Inmun Gun had collapsed along the Naktong, in September 1950, approximately twenty thousand North Koreans had neither been killed nor captured; they had faded into the rugged hills surrounding Pusan, and made contact and common cause with the guerrillas in the region.

When the frontier was violated, two ROK divisions had been deployed on counterinsurgency missions—and during the course of the war the problem was never completely solved. While the great majority of South Koreans were loyal to the Syngman Rhee government, elements in the mountainous South continued in armed opposition, with the support of some of the peasantry. Because of this support, and the broken terrain, where each valley remained almost a world to itself, the survivors of the NKPA and the guerrillas melted into the population. They were seemingly peaceful agriculturists by day, becoming armed marauders by night.

U.N. convoys continued to be fired on; individual soldiers were sometimes killed. The troop and hospital trains running between Pusan and Taegu—in spite of frequent railside patrols, sentry posts, and flatcars filled with infantry on each train—were fired on almost daily, sometimes with casualties.

A favorite trick of the insurgents was to slip close to the rails by night, set up a machine gun, wait until a well-lighted hospital train—its passengers strapped helplessly in berths—puffed by. Then, in a matter of seconds the train could be sprayed with bullets, the gun dismantled, and the guerrillas, in white peasant garb, gone into the night.

The mountain villagers knew which men went on these nocturnal excursions—but it was no simple matter to make them talk. The ROK Government, with American advice, grappled with the problem, but never completely solved it. There had always been a sort of banditry in the southern hills, and probably always would be.

It could not affect the war, but it could be a nuisance.

In December, the 2nd Division moved back into line north of Kumwha, on the central front in the area known as the Iron Triangle. Hopes at this time for a negotiated peace were high, and the mission was to hold the line, no more. The division relieved the 25th, which now passed into Army reserve for rest and training.

By now, the lines had been stable for months, and improved positions were constructed. Units, on relief, left their positions intact, and overhead cover was constructed for every position on the MLR, and heated shelters and mess tents protected all men from the fierce winter weather.

As General Bull Boatner said, "Aside from being cold as hell, it was as easy and plush a winter as could be expected in combat. The division took an average of only two casualties a day, and that was peanuts."

And by any standard of actual war, peanuts it was—yet human lives are not potatoes, and it was now almost 1952, an election year. A good argument could be made that men who died now on line in Korea died for nothing, and Washington was adamant that none must die, if it could be so ordered.

While patrols had to be run nightly, and the enemy shelled, and kept off balance if possible, no attacks above platoon size were permissible short of Corps' approval. And Corps was very chary with its approval of anything that might result in soldiers being hurt.

With one eye always on Panmunjom, the old noncoms running the patrols grew wise, too. They quickly understood the nature of this new war, and of all the thousands of patrols run by the division—some for the express purpose of capturing prisoners—few ever made contact with the enemy. Each night there were hundreds of Americans and Chinese slipping out of the hills into the

broad valleys that ran between the two main lines of resistance, listening, waiting, each supposed to ambush the other.

The operation journals record that contact, and resultant fighting, occurred
with remarkable irregularity, and when it did, it was often by CCF initiative.

General Boatner and the new division commander, Major General Robert
N. Young, knew these things, just as the company and battalion commanders
knew them; but there are some things, like this and one's relations with one's
wife, that gentlemen do not discuss.

When the 23rd Infantry took over the 27th Infantry, 25th Division's sector,
the Wolfhounds had told Colonel James Y. Adams, commanding the 23rd
and the son of the Army adjutant general, that the Chinese up on Papa-san
to the north would not shoot unless three or more vehicles got on the roads
near the front. The CCF, while it had plenty of artillery, continued to show a
marked reluctance to fire on any unprofitable target, or any target its
observers could not see. It had to bring its ammunition over a long and
painful route—thus, while U.S. artillery shelled Communist areas behind the
lines regularly, American areas back of the immediate front were normally as
safe as San Francisco.

The Wolfhound officers explained that it was fine to run two jeeps or trucks
down the road, anytime—but three or more pulled the plug.

Colonel Adams thought he knew a line when he heard one. A few days
later he went down the road under Papa-san in a convoy of three jeeps.

During the resulting uproar, Adams' buttocks were made a bloody sieve.
The exec of the 23rd took over the regiment. This officer was told to make no
personnel changes for the moment, since he was junior to one of the battalion
commanders. Unheeding, the exec moved a senior lieutenant colonel up to his
old job, probably feeling he was getting rid of a potential rival—and four
hours later, Brigadier General Boatner was sent down to assume control of
the regiment, until a new eagle colonel could be rounded up.

Christmas came while Boatner still commanded the 23rd. There had been
talk of a Communist attack on the 25th, and during the morning, in a light
snowfall, Boatner went out to inspect his forward lines.

At 1000 hours, he couldn't find a man on line in one area.

He went into a platoon CP, dug into a heated bunker, and found one enlisted man by the phone. "Phone your platoon leader," Boatner barked.

"Yes, sir—only the phone's out of order, sir—"

Boatner, mad as a snapping turtle, placed the platoon leader under arrest.
That young man, as so many others, had not had the moral courage to force
his men to stay alert and ready out in the snow on Christmas Day.

A little later, Boatner was on the phone to the lieutenant's battalion commander. "You hear about this, Colonel?"

"Hear about it? Hell, the whole regiment's heard about it, General! Don't
come up here—everybody's running for their holes!"

Boatner growled, "All right, I want you to chew that platoon leader out,
and when you have, take him off arrest. I don't want him KIA while under
arrest—"

He had made his point, and it was still Christmas Day.

A few days later, Boatner was inside a bunker with the same second lieutenant, under heavy shelling. When the enemy fire eased, the young officer started for the exit.

"Where the hell are you going?"

"Sir, I've got to make up my shellrep—" After shelling, regulations required a report of the number and caliber of shells that had come in, and the craters had to be inspected.

Now, that was the last thing Bull Boatner wanted to do—but to keep up appearances he had to accompany the young officer outside.

The lieutenant was wounded, and Boatner was wondering if he hadn't almost been hoisted by his own petard.

A continuing problem of this static war was that senior officers did not have enough to do to make them keep their hands off their junior's affairs. Or they had time to think up new projects, from painting fire buckets red to promulgating the color of name tags on enlisted fatigues.

Just before Clark Ruffner turned over the division to Bob Young, he had told Boatner: "Haydon, we ought to get out a division history. Since I'm leaving, you take it over."

As clearly as Boatner could remember later, his own comment was, "Jesus Christ!"

"Now, I want you to do it."

"Yes, sir," Boatner said. Fortunately, in the 72nd Tank Battalion was an officer who had been editor of the Texas A&M newspaper, and Boatner was able to get rid of this jewel fast.

And then there was the problem of the new corps commander. This general had been in the CBI with Boatner and Stilwell, and had been junior to Boatner. But he had had the good fortune to be transferred to Europe, and now returned to the Far East as lieutenant general. Bob Young, the 2nd Division commander, considered it great fun to kid Boatner about this.

And this new corps commander had been brainwashed as he came in, as they all were in Tokyo, and in Seoul. Ridgway still had his foot firmly on Van Fleet's neck on the matter of casualties, and Van Fleet made sure his corps commanders got the word.

Just before Colonel Adams was wounded, he had got permission to stage a limited tank attack across the frozen paddies—actually, a hit-and-run raid with two sections from the regimental tank company.

The raid, with a total of five tanks, started off on schedule.

But out in the Kumwha Valley, the schedule blew up, along with the AT mines the right two tanks rolled over. While Boatner watched from a hill within friendly lines, the crews of the two disabled tanks, between three hundred and four hundred yards in front of their own positions, abandoned their vehicles and ran to safety, before the enemy could zero in on them.

Then the platoon leader in charge led his remaining tanks to within about twenty-five yards of them, and proceeded to blow them to hell with his 76mm cannon. They were left out in no man's land, ruined and smoking.

Now, Bull Boatner was no politician. If he had been, he would have written his own regimental situation report for the day. As it was, the sitrep went forward, listing the events of the day with appalling clarity.

That night, General Young called him on the phone. "Haydon, your friend"—Young's inveterate manner of referring to the corps commander—"is madder than hell!"

"Who's he mad at?"

"He's mad at you!"

"What the hell's he mad at me for?" Boatner wanted to know.

"You lost two tanks—and Bill says his corps does not lose tanks!"

Boatner fortunately remained silent.

"Haydon, you're in for it—you're in a hell of a jam. He's madder'n hell. I mean it, Haydon!"

Though Bull Boatner was no politician, he was no fool, either.

"Bob," he said, "what are you talking about? What's this about my having two tanks destroyed?"

"Goddamit, that's what your sitrep says!"

"Oh, hell, that's a mistake. Those two tanks were disabled, not destroyed. Hell, I can turn 'em in. Please scratch out that part on the sitrep about 'destroyed' and make it 'disabled.'"

After Young hung up, Boatner thought, *Well, hell. Here we are, fighting a war, and—now, maybe some auditor of General Motors would say I'm crooked, or a liar—but dammit, I'm not a liar about anything that amounts to anything.*

He got the Regimental Tank Company C.O., Captain Juno, in front of his desk, next morning.

"Juno, we're in a jam. We've got to go recover those two tanks we left out there. Now, I'll give you all the support you need—mortars, engineers, division artillery—"

"General," Juno said, "those tanks are no goddam good!"

They were obsolete M-4A3E8's, and there were thousands of them rusting in depots in the States, from Detroit to Red River. And these two had exploded and burned to black hulks when their basic load of ammunition blew under the tank officer's shelling.

"Juno, you tend to your goddam business and I'll tend to mine—I'm telling you you got to go get those two tanks back! Now, I don't want anybody hurt—I'm going to get you all the support you need. You go rack up a plan—but it's got to be this afternoon."

"This makes no sense to me, General," Juno said.

"It's not supposed to—just do it," Boatner snapped.

It made plenty of sense to him.

Juno did it. He took out his tank retrievers under a curtain of friendly fire and dragged the burned-out hulks back smoothly and efficiently, without a casualty. The CCF were too surprised to shoot. It was no sweat at all.

As the two blackened hulks were pulled within the edge of his main line of resistance, Bull Boatner was on the horn to the division ordnance officer. "Come get these goddam disabled tanks out of my area—"

What the division ordnance officer said or what he did with the "disabled" tanks is not recorded.

But it was one way to satisfy a newly arrived corps commander who tried to get down and operate on tank-section level.

As the winter wore on, General Van Fleet, feeling continual pressure, continued to raise hell with the divisions for losing too many men.

And the 2nd Division, while it inflicted more casualties during the Korean War than any other, always had the misfortune of losing 50 percent more men than other divisions.

There was the matter of the 38th's platoon raid.

Colonel Rowny's regiment was authorized to stage a one-platoon raid on the extreme left flank of the division, toward a hill that had been firing into the division lines. From a friendly hill, General Boatner, Ed Rowny, and the battalion commander of the selected infantry platoon watched the attack proceed. From this hill they could see clear to P'yong-gang, in enemy hands.

The platoon assaulted the hill, which was neither completely within one MLR or the other. And it ran into a hell of fire from machine guns and mortars, and was pinned down, helplessly.

Eighth Army orders, all across Korea, read that no more than one platoon could be committed without express approval from jurisdictional Corps HQ. The company commander of the pinned-down platoon, however, ordered a second platoon into action, and finally his whole company, to bail his first platoon out.

To do so, he had to take the disputed hill and knock the enemy off it. Then, his boys relieved, he had to relinquish the hill, since it was too close to CCF lines to be tenable. No one wanted to start a new Bloody Ridge.

And in saving his platoon, he took heavy casualties.

Boatner, Assistant Division CG, Rowny, the regimental commander, and the battalion commander saw the whole operation, watching in an agony of suspense. Not one of them jumped into the action, however—to do so would have been the best way in the world to destroy the confidence and command ability of the junior officers, who, like children, have to learn to make their own mistakes however desperately it pains their parents.

However painful it is to contemplate, officers have to learn in battle. There simply is no other feasible way to learn experience commanding men in battle, except in battle.

Whatever else he had done wrong, the company commander had done the right thing by committing his full company to extricate the men in trouble. But the next day, when the casualty reports reached higher HQ, all hell broke loose. Major General Young called Boatner in.

"Haydon, what's this all about?"

Boatner explained the whole matter to him.

"Well, go up to the 38th and make a complete investigation. We'll have to make a report."

Boatner did so, and reported back. The raid had been a mistake. It never should have been undertaken—but then who could tell beforehand what would have happened?

The company C.O. involved had made some mistakes—but his decision to commit his entire company had been the only one. How could he have stood by while his one platoon was cut to pieces before his eyes?

Maybe Bull Boatner was out on a limb, for not taking over as he watched—but what kind of brigadier general or regimental commander would it be that got down on company level and started commanding platoons?

The whole trouble stemmed from one thing: in the year 1952 the division had got men killed, during offensive action, and in this year if anything was anathema to the men running the Republic it was that.

Now, here they were. They had lost men, and that was that. Young asked, "What're we going to do about it?" He was concerned over Ed Rowny, who was a fine officer, and could be ruined if the ball bounced the wrong way.

In higher echelons the urge to seek scapegoats was slowly becoming irresistible. As Boatner said, what was often not understood about the Army was that while it threw someone to the wolves frequently, it was civilian pressure that was often the cause.

Now, Boatner told Young, who the hell was more interested in those young men—besides the parents—than their immediate officers, the officers who knew these kids, who lived and ate with them? Some staff officer, some corps or army commander, or the theater commander in Tokyo?

"It's simply goddam ridiculous and absurd for a combat man to be put in a position where his own subordinates that he's known—youngsters that he's eaten with—get killed or wounded, and someone thousands of miles back puts the bite on him, as though he were callous about it!"

Boatner wrote a formal report. He refused to hang anyone and he made his refusal strong—so strong the matter ended there.

To Bull Boatner, it was a shining example of people in the rear being damned cowards. On line, there was no such thing as a "limited" war—when the shooting started on line, no man a thousand miles away could tell the man in combat what or what not to do.

And anyone who believed that American officers were callous underneath their hard exterior poses about the men who died in action under their command had simply never commanded a platoon or higher unit in action, or ever had to write a tragic letter home. But there is no such thing as war—even limited war—without losses.

As the months passed, and 1952 deepened, and there was no peace at Panmunjom, the war that was not a war went on endlessly. Every night the guns on each side cannonaded; every night the patrols went out, for no army may sit entirely still, except at its peril.

Every night, men died.

Frustration grew, in government, in generals, and in the men on the line, while the guns sounded and the talks about the peace table droned on.

And, caught in a Communist trap, the moral courage of some leaders grew less. The pressure on Tokyo to hold down the loss never ceased. In Korea, on the ground, it intensified. It was no longer possible to permit juniors any latitude, or any possibility for error.

What Boatner foresaw happened. Soon battalion commanders led platoons, and general officers directed company actions, for the loss of one patrol could ruin the career of a colonel. In one way, it was an efficient system. It worked, for the lines were stable, and no senior officer had enough to do.

But the damage done to the Army command structure would be long in healing. If a new war came someday, there would be colonels and generals—who had been lieutenants and captains in Korea—who had their basic lessons still to learn.

35

Koje-do

Let none presume to tell me that the pen is preferable to the sword.
—From the Spanish of Miguel de Cervantes Saavedra, DON QUIXOTE.

O N THE MORNING of 7 May 1952, on the Island of Koje, word arrived at the headquarters of Brigadier General Francis T. Dodd through the normal and proper channels that the spokesmen of Korean Officer Compound Number 76 immediately and earnestly desired his presence for a powwow.

To Frank Dodd, completely unaware of Communist complexities or the recent orders given to NKPA Private Pak Sang Hyong, the shortest distance between two points seemed to be a straight line.

He put on his cap, with its single silver star, and went to see what was wrong with Senior Colonel Lee Hak Ku and the boys in 76.

At the gate to the flimsy wire compound, he got down from his jeep and met the clustered Communist delegation at the wire. The gate was opened, while U.N. guards stood by, idly watching, manifestly bored by the island and their duty.

At a sudden signal, the POW's, who had carefully rehearsed the maneuver, formed a press around Frank Dodd; he was seized and dragged within the compound; a flying wedge pushed the startled guards back, and the gates were closed.

Their shouting did no good. Dodd was pulled deep inside Number 76, inside a hut, and the men around him suddenly had sufficient homemade workshop items, made from spare metal and the slivers within GI shoes, effectively to release him from his earthly existence long before a guard detachment could knock down the wire and fight its way through to him.

This, as the officer now in charge of the island, Colonel Bill Craig, realized, was one hell of a mess. He passed the buck, quite properly; though he did not realize that the buck would move idly across Koje Island, bounce about in Pusan, wing its way to Tokyo, then shriek its way across the ocean, only to come sizzling back, within a period of three days.

Americans, snorting their disbelief, forgot that few of them had believed the rumors about Belsen and Dachau, either, until they were proved. Russians, who had in 1941 considered Germany among the most civilized of nations, whatever their Fascist politics, undoubtedly believed, as did devout Communist everywhere. But the real loss of face was before the neutrals, who did not know what to believe.

And some of the United States' staunchest allies rather politely queried, "Just what the hell *is* going on over at Koje-do?"

The truth was that Ridgway, Clark, Frank Pace, and his boss, Harry Truman, were all wondering the same thing.

These things General Colson did not know, although for three days the wires everywhere were burning. He did know that Frank Dodd, ill and scared inside Number 76, had talked to him with a shaken voice, and he wanted to rescue his brother general as soon as possible.

During this period Charles Colson got very little help from Pusan, or higher up. It was his ball game. Ridgway and Clark were up at Panmunjom, where Major General William K. Harrison, Jr., was replacing Admiral Turner Joy as chief American whipping boy.

Colson talked to 2nd Logistical Command in Pusan, thought he had its concurrence, got the POW's to tone down their demands a little—though he agreed, in essence, that "the U.N. Command would stop beating its wife"—which confession he discounted, since he felt everyone knew such allegations were silly—and signed on the dotted line, to get Dodd out.

It was a tremendous Communist propaganda victory.

On 10 May 1952, Frank Dodd walked out of Compound 76, and was whisked away to Tokyo. Here he would learn that Army Secretary Pace, hot with anger and embarrassment, had decreed that he "should have brought the spokesmen to his office under guard."

There could be little argument with Frank Pace's view on that.

Dodd was reduced to the grade of colonel, and retired. That left Colson.

When a man has done nothing conspicuously or flagrantly wrong, and yet has embarrassed his chiefs, whether he is an Army officer or an executive of Travelers Insurance, the current American phrase is "exhibited lack of judgment." It is a wonderfully enveloping phrase, like the 96th Article of War's ". . . and all other acts prejudicial to good order," and can be fitted to almost any situation.

Whether in the Department of Agriculture or Department of the Army, anyone who causes acute embarrassment must go, or the lack of judgment is considered to be even higher up.

Charles Colson's neck was being stretched for the block, too, unknown to him.

Meanwhile, a sort of anarchy had come to Koje-do. POW's shouted and chanted and waved banners and placards inside the wire, while the guards stood helplessly by outside. There were riots, and it was questionable who controlled the camp.

In Compound 76, where the North Korean brass plotted, detailed plans were being drawn.

Craig held the buck until Brigadier General Charles F. Colson arrived to take charge. Charlie Colson was a quiet, reserved, mannerly gentleman, who came over to Koje-do quite unaware that half the world was laughing at the fiasco of who was guarding whom, that General Matt Ridgway was deeply annoyed, that General Mark W. Clark, who was taking over from Ridgway in Tokyo—to James Van Fleet's annoyance—was worried about the stink, and that in Washington Army Secretary Frank Pace, Jr., was tearing out his hair.

A field telephone was fed into Compound 76, over which Colson and the Communist leaders engaged in collective bargaining. Colson had troops, guns, and tanks—in small quantity, but present—but Compound 76 had Frank Dodd. The POW's made it quite clear that any attempt to relieve him by force would result in one brigadier with slit throat.

They presented Colson, who had walked into Koje-do cold, knowing nothing of the POW and propaganda situation there or anywhere else, with a long string of demands. Among them was confession of past crimes against POW's, a pledge to recognize Communist organizations and control of the POW's, and agreement "to stop torturing and mistreating prisoners to make them say they are anti-Communist."

It was the old "have you stopped beating your wife?" technique, and Charlie Colson walked into it.

Colson knew the Communist demands and allegations were ridiculous; he was completely aware that no such torment or abuse of POW's had ever taken place. He was not aware that when the demands, repeated by the newsmen now deserting the barren front for Koje-do in droves, were wired across the world, millions of people said, "Where there is smoke there must be fire," and that Nam Il in Panmunjom was shrieking, in joyous and righteous rage:

". . . These criminal acts committed by your side under the name of voluntary repatriation thoroughly violate the Geneva Convention relating to prisoners of war and repudiate the minimum standard of human behavior!"

And, "Your side must bear the full and absolute responsibility for the safety of our captured personnel!"

The editor of *Pravda* in Moscow came forth with full and somber wrath:

> *Koje Island! Again the gloomy shadow of Maidenek (a Nazi extermination camp in Poland) has come upon the world, again the stench of corpses . . . the groans of the tortured . . . we learn that "civilized" Americans can be yet more inhuman, yet more infamous than the bloody Hitlerites. Dachau was a death camp, Maidenek was a death factory; Koje is a whole island of death. The American hangmen are torturing, tormenting, and killing unarmed people here. They are experimenting with their poisons on them . . . .*

Communist press and spokesmen were having a propaganda field day, while the plaintive demands coming over the single strand of thin wire from inside Compound 76 seemed to back up everything they claimed. "Please stop torturing us, and we'll give you your general back."

These plans, if carried through, would make Koje an island of death indeed.

* * *

When spring came, the 2nd Infantry Division had its turn off line again, while the 40th—one of the two National Guard Divisions sent to FECOM in 1951— and the 7th took over its zone below the Iron Triangle. The division returned to Kap'yong, and from here it spread to many places, fulfilling the typical missions of an American division in reserve. The 9th Infantry, minus 3rd Battalion, took up blocking positions west of the Hwach'on Reservoir, meanwhile carrying on aggressive training. The entire 38th Regiment, plus 3/9, embarked for Koje-do, which was reported to be rocked by riots and insubordination. The 2/23, meanwhile, marched to Sangdong to guard valuable tungsten mines. Several individual companies went to provide security for IX Corps HQ, and for a guerrilla-beset radio station. Divarty went over to support the 9th ROK Division, and the 72nd Tank moved back on Heartbreak Ridge, under X Corps.

On line or off, there was little rest in Korea. The division had received 4,466 replacements for rotated men, and these must trained.

The top command changed; the high brass played musical chairs, too. General Young left and Brigadier General James C. Fry took command on 4 May, with full pomp and ceremony at the division airstrip.

With the easing of combat pressure at the front, pomp and ceremonies were rapidly returning. Units remained stable for long periods now, and everywhere flagpoles went up, rocks were painted, and areas policed and improved. Divisions built show-type war rooms out of plywood, and stationed MP's with burnished stainless steel helmets outside them. Bands, no longer needed to carry wounded and the like, could indulge in concerts, while more and more troops, with less and less to do, could be kept busy on the fiddling details normal to garrison life.

The Army fatigue uniform, in World War II a work and combat uniform, utilitarian and unadorned, became a wonder to behold. Starched, pressed with creases, complete with sewn unit patches and colored name tags, it became more colorful than the OD semidress. Soon, even in the combat zone, the old, sloppy fatigue cap was taboo—now caps had to have stiffeners to make them like that of General Ridgway. For one buck American, GI's and officers could buy a locally made stiff fatigue cap, which was simpler than trying to put a stiffener in the GI-issue kind.

Sometimes, when an army cannot go, it turns to show. At any rate, the Korean economy benefited.

It was at this time that Brigadier General Boatner went to Japan on R&R. He had word that his son, Second Lieutenant James G. Boatner, was coming to FECOM—"Destination Evil," as the coded orders read.

In Tokyo, Boatner talked to the personnel people. He wanted to make certain his son did not come to the 2nd Division; that would be unfair. But he didn't want young James to end up in the 40th or 45th, one of the National Guard Divisions either. The personnel people laughed at that, and asked, "Well, where?"

James Boatner had been born in the 15th Infantry, in Tientsin. It was finally decided to send him to the 3rd Division, one of the Army's proudest units, and parent of the 15th Regiment.

On 11 May, Boatner was in the Tokyo Main PX, when he was paged over the store loudspeaker. "Brigadier General Boatner, please come to the office—"

There he was informed that his presence was earnestly desired at the *Dai Ichi*. He went at once to the Assistant Theater G-1—Personnel Officer—and asked what was up. Dick Key, an old friend, told him, "Haydon, they've decided to send you to Koje-do."

Now, what had been going on at Koje-do had been in all the papers for some days. The Bull was deflated. "My God, how do I get out of it?"

"You don't. General Clark is ready to see you immediately—and a plane is standing by to take you there in one hour," Key said. "Can you make it?"

"If those are my orders," Boatner said morosely, "of course I can make it."

It was the lunch hour, but he was ushered in to see General Mark Wayne Clark, the new FECOM commander, who had just replaced Ridgway, who was off to Europe to command NATO.

Wayne Clark, long-nosed and schoolmasterish in appearance, had had the Fifth Army in Italy, and now, coming into Japan, he was absolutely flabbergasted by what had happened at Koje-do. He told Boatner he felt the American Army had been disgraced. He had just visited the island with the departing Ridgway, and he had been horrified at the lack of discipline and control over the rioting POW's

"I'm putting you there, and you take command!" he said. He was very clear.

He made no mention of General Van Fleet, who had expected to take over Tokyo from Eighth Army, à la Ridgway, and who was reputed to be somewhat cool toward Clark. He made it clear that Boatner was to take his direction straight from the top.

Finally, he said, "Any questions?"

Bull Boatner, no politician but also no fool, was well aware that the great trouble with Koje-do was that the hands of all previous commanders had been tied. He said: "Yes, sir, I fear the situation is so bad over there, the POW's out of control to such an extent, that it will require bloodshed to restore control."

Clark said, "I agree absolutely. I expect bloodshed, and I'll support you."

Boatner then asked for a competent law officer who was thoroughly conversant with the Geneva Conventions, and Clark said he would order the G-1 to provide such.

Outside Clark's office, Boatner went immediately to Lieutenant General Doyle Hickey, the Chief of Staff. It was customary that any officer coming from the commander's office briefed the Chief of Staff on the substance of the conversation—and Boatner had his special reasons, too.

He made very certain that Hickey understood that Clark had agreed to bloodshed on Koje-do.

Then he talked with the next two men in line, Major General Whitfield Sheperd and Major General Ryan, to have them on record that strong measures were called for.

That night, he arrived by plane in Pusan, and was hosted by Brigadier General Paul F. Yount, CG of the 2nd Logistical Command, which had jurisdiction over Koje-do. Frank Dodd was in Pusan, in Yount's HQ, on his way to Tokyo and Mark Clark. Dodd, ill with ulcers, was drinking milk sent over from Japan—there was no fresh milk in Korea—and he seemed a shaken man, heading for disgrace and demotion.

Yount briefed Boatner as best he could, though Boatner didn't get too much out of him. The main thing Yount was angry about, in all this uproar, was that friendly aircraft had recently strafed Koje, and Yount was furious over this.

Staying at Pusan overnight, Boatner went on to the island, and was ushered into General Charlie Colson's office the next day. Boatner had never met Colson, but Colson had been a classmate of his older brother, and now Colson was very solemn, very courteous, and very decent.

Colson, it appeared, was in no way feeling under tension or pressure. He had no idea that his actions were under question or that they had stirred up a raging hornets' nest in Washington and Tokyo.

Talking to Boatner, he was like the old officer of the day passing on the special orders to the new, quite dry and relaxed.

Boatner, newly come from the press and propaganda storm in Tokyo, was amazed.

Colson asked, "By the way, have you seen Clark?"

"Yes, I saw him yesterday, and he's mad as hell."

"Why, what's *he* mad about?"

"About the agreement you made with the prisoners of war."

"Why, Clark approved it—Clark approved all that agreement—how can he be mad about it?"

Boatner, amazed, asked, "Colson, can you prove he approved it?"

"Why, yes. I've got it right here in my desk." Colson pointed to his upper right-hand drawer.

"What's that?"

"Those are stenographic notes of my conversation with Pusan."

Boatner said slowly: "Well, stenographic notes of a conversation with Pusan don't prove that General Clark approved anything. I'm afraid you'd better take those with you to Tokyo—you're going to have to prove all this."

It was certain that Charlie Colson never realized he was under any criticism or fire whatever, and whatever this said for his judgment, many people, including Bull Boatner, regarded his subsequent demotion to colonel and retirement to verge on the criminal.

In democratic societies as well as totalitarian it never pays to embarrass the powers that be.

But Boatner, coming in at the lowest ebb of the ball game, was under no illusions as to how Washington and Tokyo felt. He also knew that higher HQ, willy-nilly, had to support him, in spite of NITS, IRC, UNCORK, or the Associated Press.

General Yount had moved the International Red Cross from the island on 7 May, and he was making it hard for newsmen to cross over from Pusan. But

Boatner knew it was not in publicity that the trouble lay. He rather wanted the Red Cross and newsmen about; he wanted witnesses.

He was not going to seek trouble, but he was going to meet it head on when it came, firmly but fairly.

Now the correspondents asked him, "Are you glad to have us here?"

Boatner said, "Christ, I'm not that stupid—but I know I've got to have you here—so tell General Yount I have no objections."

He sat now at Colson's desk, and within two hours the Military Police executive officer of the command, who had been on Koje throughout the entire tenure of Boatner's fourteen predecessors, came in and asked: "General, what uniform do you want to prescribe for the cocktail party we're having for you?"

Boatner looked at him. "What cocktail party?"

The colonel said, "Sir, we give a cocktail party for every newly arriving general officer—"

"I'm not so sure about this," Boatner said.

The colonel smiled, figuring Boatner was thinking of the cost. "General, this won't cost you a thing. We make so much money at the Officers' Club out of liquor that this is one way we have of using up our excess profits."

Boatner thought, *My God.* He had just come from Japan; he'd been reading the papers; and everyone was furious at the propaganda beating the U.S. had been taking—and here on Koje-do they were worrying about cocktail parties!

"Colonel, there'll be no cocktail party."

Meanwhile, Boatner had noticed that everyone on the island was in different uniform. His exec was wearing tropical worsted semidress; some men were in fatigues. The uniform for the guard detachment specified combat fatigues. "Fitzgerald, speaking of uniforms, why are there so many different kinds around?"

"General, you wouldn't want your own headquarters wearing the same uniform as the troops!"

Boatner, who had been on Heartbreak Ridge, was speechless. But only for a moment. "Dammit, that's exactly what I want! Furthermore, some of the troops are wearing side arms, some aren't. Put everybody under arms."

"Oh, please, General, don't do that. You'll be sorry."

"Why?"

"There'll be so many accidental discharges around here, somebody's going to get hurt."

"Goddamit!" the Bull roared. "Goddamit, if a soldier can't handle his weapons, what the hell kind of outfit have we got? Put 'em under arms!"

"General, I wish you'd reconsider—"

The summation of Boatner's further remarks was No.

Boatner looked around his HQ. There were combat troops down the road, the 38th Infantry, one battalion of the 9th. But everywhere else there were MP troops, engineers, quartermasters, most of whom were unaware there was a war on. Nor were many of these service troops typical of their services— many officers relieved on the line as unfit had been sent to Koje-do as POW guards, and the replacement pipeline had funneled some of its worst into the island, considering the need there the less.

Boatner loved the Army, and he loved the American soldier, though he had a firm belief that the American soldier was only as good as his officer made him. A man unconsciously profane, Boatner thought, *Jesus Christ, what a mess!*

Some of his old boys from the 38th and 9th had told him what a lousy, snotty, overbearing HQ he had inherited, in their opinion. The feeling between the regular service troops party on Koje and the combat battalions sent in to supplement them was like that between the blue and the gray.

Charlie Colson had taught him a lesson, too, about getting it in writing. He began to write letters and send telegrams: *In all my experience I have never seen such a poor group of American soldiers. . . .* He asked permission to screen out four hundred of the worst troops for return to the mainland.

Pusan, angry, had to agree. Boatner's wires, and his strong stand, had them on the spot. It was a shot in the arm to the good troops.

The problem on Koje and at Pusan was that none of the people on the ground there seemed to realize how prominent they had become, that the eyes of the world were focused on them, and that what happened here could affect the whole course of the war.

And Boatner sensed that he was not in command of the island, though he sat at the commandant's desk. Somewhere, in secret, hidden within a hard core of Communist officers behind the wire, sat the real commander of Koje-do, with the initiative in his grasp.

Boatner had seen the flimsy compounds, had seen the thousands upon thousands of rioting, singing prisoners crammed into a few square yards surrounded by one apron of wire and a handful of armed troops, and he had seen what had to be done.

In his mind, he broke his job down into three phases: Phase I, to show the will to command, to let the POW's know who was boss, and to get more armed strength on the island; Phase II, to build new, secure compounds to hold the prisoners; Phase III, the actual movement of the POW's into their new wire prisons.

Boatner was sitting on a volcano, in danger of a mass break at any hour. The resulting slaughter would be a black eye from which the U.N. Command might never recover. The POW's had been encouraged to argue, to assert their rights, and this had played into the hard-core Communists' hands. Boatner knew he had to let these men know the old days were over; he had to beat their arrogance down, but little by little, or risk explosion.

There was almost no time left. How little time there was, even Bull Boatner did not guess. In Compound 76, a date had already been set for wholesale slaughter.

Boatner did what any competent commander might have done, had he Boatner's two priceless assets: Boatner had backing from above, and Boatner knew Chinese.

He asked Clark for more power, quickly. From Japan he got the 187th Airborne Regimental Combat Team, and from Eighth Army a Canadian company, a British company, some Greeks, and a company of Turks, and tanks to display on the hills above the compounds. The sending of the Commonwealth troops raised a stink; Van Fleet caught hell for ordering them to Koje, and the Canadian Brigadier, whose nation had never accepted the enmity of Red China, was relieved. Van Fleet figured the POW's were just as much a U.N. problem as the battle line, but few U.N. governments wanted any part of the mess at Koje-do.

With the combat power came more engineer construction troops. The purse strings had been loosened, and Boatner was to spend $3,500,000 in a matter of days to secure the island. The old compounds were filled to bursting; the watchtowers were inside the perimeter of fences, where they could be rushed, and the compounds were enclosed by only a single apron of barbed wire, held fast by already rotten saplings instead of solid timber.

Everything was makeshift, insecure. The towers would have to be moved without the wire, three aprons of wire stretched, more machine guns placed, and stronger fences laid.

The day after the new engineer troops arrived, Boatner inspected them. The entire battalion was prettifying their area, painting rain barrels, and building a PX to store their goodies. When Boatner ordered the Engineer commander to report to him, that officer was far from defensive.

"General, I've got to take care of my men."

Boatner told him: "You're not here to make a model camp, police the area, paint rain barrels, or anything else—you're here to build compounds. You start doing it on a twenty-four-hour basis, as of now, with maximum use of your equipment. If you have any question about this, ask me now. The next time, I'll relieve you."

The colonel got the point.

Boatner hated to talk to the Engineer in this fashion, but he just didn't understand these people. Not understanding the enormous pressures created in Washington and Tokyo, they were still determined to make life as pleasant as possible and to carry on business as usual.

Now he could begin Phase I in earnest, the beating down of the POW's, even while Phase II was in progress.

During the first days, Boatner was worried all the time by the prospect of a mass break. If this happened, hundreds would be killed, and the uproar would shake the world. He knew that, coldly and confidently, the Communist leaders were planning a break. They had no hope of getting off the island; they wanted a mass atrocity with which to brand the United States.

Haunted, Boatner drove his own troops, both infantry and engineer, with the whip of his own barbed tongue, with the lash of his threatening voice. Slowly he got his own urgency across to them.

But when he took over, on 12 May 1952, not even the Texas A&M Mothers' Club, who had come to know him, would have bet on the Bull.

36

Twenty Rolls of Toilet Paper, One Quart Mercurochrome

Knowledge is power.
—Francis Bacon, Meditations Sacrae, de Haeresibus.

Brigadier General Haydon L. Boatner, who had graduated from the care and handling of a few thousand Texas A&M cadets to the full responsibility for more than eighty thousand Chinese and North Koreans on Koje-do, was well aware that the United States was not wholly without blame for the riots and bloodshed that had already swept the island.

The American Army had been ineffective at Koje-do, and the reasons lay in the background of the POW question. The United States had never faced handling massed POW's since the War Between the States, and both sides had botched it then; in World War I the Allies shouldered the burden; and in the last war it was not until 1943 Americans had any prisoners, and these were from a foe of the same basic culture, who sensed they were already beaten.

There had never been enough Japanese POW's to matter.

But in Korea the United States not only had taken thousands of POW's of alien culture; it faced an alien psychology also. The "specially trained" guard units sent out from the States understood neither Orientals nor Communists.

And fighting a limited war, which was expected to end at any time, no long-range provisions had been made for POW's. There had been set up no real POW guard troops or equipment; every dollar spent on these had been begrudged.

When General Walton Walker had been in retreat, and plans drawn up for a possible evacuation of Korea in December 1950, the POW's had been sent to Koje Island so that they could not hamper an evacuation from Pusan. Once on Koje, every higher commander preferred to keep them there, for out of sight was out of mind, and every higher commander had better things to worry about, especially when the peace talks began.

Also on Koje-do were dumped thousands of refugees from Wonsan, and among these were enemy agents, to keep a pipeline open between North Korea and the island. And to the dedicated Communist, such as Nam Il, a POW of his own blood was as much a potential weapon as a gun—or word.

With such a situation, with such a lack of understanding of the real problems, or of the men they held, it seemed almost criminal to blame men like Charlie Colson for fumbling the hot potato dumped into their laps.

General Boatner, the old China hand, had the good fortune of every other commandant's experience. And he was wise enough to seek help.

He knew that in Japan was General Sung Shih, a Nationalist officer graduate of V.M.I., who had been an aide to Stilwell in Burma.

Once, when Boatner, some two miles behind the lines, had been sprayed with American psychological warfare leaflets from an aircraft, he had called Eighth Army Psych War Branch, saying caustically, "The 2nd Division has no intention of surrendering to the Eighth Army!"

"What the hell are you talking about?" The Psych War officer asked.

Boatner informed him of where the Chinese lines were, and furthermore, told him the leaflets were no damned good. They had been written in high literary Chinese, and wouldn't motivate a common soldier with a full gizzard to take a crap.

Rather abashed, the officer, who had studied only high literary Chinese, came up to visit Boatner, and asked for help. Boatner had given him the name of Sung Shih, in Japan.

Now Boatner remembered this officer, whom he knew well, and requested him to come to Koje-do.

General Sung—who had no official business with the American Army, and whose presence made the Chiang-hating U.N. allies scream with rage— arrived on Koje, but unfortunately the correspondents got to him before Boatner. They printed the fact that he had come, and forthwith Sung had to go—but not before Boatner asked his advice on how to handle his CCF POW's.

You must not, Sung said, say no to a Chinese bluntly. It was always best to give a minor point or two, to permit him to save face. But at the same time, you must always show a Chinese very plainly who is master. He would, General Sung Shih indicated, understand nothing less.

It was advice that was to stand Boatner in good stead.

On his second morning on Koje-do, he got word by telephone that all hell had broken loose in the Chinese compound of 6,500 POW's.

Boatner had seen Frank Dodd, sick and strained on his way to Tokyo, and he knew what had happened to that officer when he visited a compound, and he thought, *I'm not going to get involved.*

This mood lasted two seconds. But Boatner realized he was in command, and he could not command from a desk, whatever Frank Pace thought about it.

He went to the Chinese compound by a circuitous route, without fanfare, with only his aide. Though he did not sneak about, neither did he seek to attract attention. Up ahead, he could hear a terrific commotion.

At the CCF compound, he saw an incredible sight.

Inside the compound, lined up in ranks, with perfect discipline, stood 6,500 Chinese, each with a blue and yellow banner in his hand, all chanting and singing and waving the flags in a concerted drill, all within an area of some three hundred square yards.

Outside the wire were literally thousands of U.S. soldiers—all the men off duty and some who weren't—who had flocked to the uproar as if it were a fire or sideshow. These men were waving fists at the Chinese, and shouting insults at them, like "Blow it out, ya dirty bums!" and worse.

Boatner, watching, saw a great mass of people in front of the main gate. He sent his aide, Warrant Officer Robert B. Mills, a man of very great judgment and coolness, over there with this instruction:

"Go over, get the U.S. officer in charge, and bring him back to me, with the head Chinese and an interpreter. Don't let anyone else come—and don't let the mob see you."

Boatner's first piece of good luck was that the senior U.S. officer was Lieutenant Colonel Robert W. Garrett, C.O. of 3/9 Infantry, whom he was both fond of and respected highly. Woody Garrett—so-called because it had taken him five years to get through the Point—reported to Boatner. A balding, moustached infantryman, he also knew and understood the Bull.

The second piece of luck was that the senior Chinese representative, a CCF lieutenant colonel, about thirty-five, was a Northern Chinese whose dialect Boatner understood and spoke perfectly. As it turned out, the Chinese officer was the son of a Yenan landowner near the town of Fenjo-fu where Boatner had hunted during his service with the 15th Infantry.

An educated man, he had been forced into the Communist Army to save his father's life. He was not a dedicated Communist, but he was a dedicated Chinese.

First, in English, Boatner asked Garrett, "Goddamit, who's in command here?"

"I am," Woody Garrett said.

"Then act like it, goddamit!" Boatner snarled. "Run every goddam American soldier who hasn't any duty around this compound out of here!"

Garrett did so. He and Boatner understood each other, as was evidenced by Garrett's having made, a few days later, a reversible sign for Boatner's parking space, one side of which was painted *General Boatner,* and on the other *Colonel Boatner,* in case the Bull went the way of Dodd and Colson.

Boatner had a similar sign made for Garrett, which said *Major* on one side. Without doubt, all the junior officers got the point.

While the shouting, sight-seeing crowd of Americans was run off, Boatner let the CCF officer speak through the interpreter, though he could understand him clearly. And the Chinese went into a long spiel, about Panmunjom, prisoner repatriation, Geneva Conventions—nothing whatever to do with the riot at hand or why the Chinese were demonstrating.

This was the kind of thing they had been getting away with for months. It was sheer propaganda; as Boatner said, a line of bull.

When the Chinese colonel had completely run down, satisfied that he had done a good job of selling the new American commander a bill of goods, Boatner said, in Chinese, *"Nah shunar du wa na?"*

Literally, this meant "That is what kind of talk?" To a Chinese, it had the connotation, "What kind of bull are you handing me?"

Haydon Boatner spoke excellent Mandarin, and the Chinese have always had a high respect for any foreigner who can do so; they think that only an educated Chinese can handle the flowery tongue of the Middle Kingdom.

The Chinese officer's jaw dropped.

Boatner went on: "You're a soldier; I'm a soldier. You hear my language—I have lived long in China. My son was born in Tientsin; my son is Chinese." He did not mention that his wife was Occidental. "I fought with Stilwell"—who was well thought of in China—"and I am a friend of China." He mentioned the names of several prominent Chinese officers he knew well. "You do not know what has caused this riot, nor do I know what has happened. Now, you know very well the only thing I can do is to hold an investigation. This I will do, and when I know, I shall tell you."

Then Boatner looked at the young officer with complete assurance, "But don't think your soldiers, by their singing and chanting, are impressing me. I will do nothing while they sing, this also I promise you. Go back, tell them that the new commander is an old China hand and that I will report back to you the results of my investigation. But I will do nothing while you try to bluff me—have your men break ranks and return to their huts."

Crestfallen, the Chinese officer was led back into the compound.

Then, in front of thousands of eyes, Boatner said: "Woody, my guess is that it'll take an hour to get this group disbanded and back in their huts. Now, don't show any concern whatever—ignore 'em—act as though you know implicitly my orders are going to be obeyed—"

Looking neither left nor right, Boatner finished, "I'm leaving now, and goddamit, they're watching us for weakness. Now, you salute me, and I'll salute you, and you telephone me when they have dispersed."

Calmly, in front of the silent eyes, the American satrap walked for his jeep, and he and Warrant Officer Mills drove off.

Twenty-two minutes later, Woody Garrett phoned. It was all over.

But the investigation showed that the riot had been caused by the death of a Chinese; a POW had been killed, and the United States, in this particular case, was not without blame.

During the investigation the Chinese presented a long list of demands—a formal apology, permission for the whole compound to attend the funeral, and so on. This was what they had been getting away with for a long time—but Boatner, remembering what Sung Shih had said, knew what to do.

He wrote the Chinese a letter, telling them they might hold a military funeral—but that only a few representatives might attend.

He furnished the POW's a truck to take them to the cemetery and back, and sent a captain as his own personal representative. And the supply officer of Koje-do puzzled over a requisition for twenty rolls of toilet paper and one quart of mercurochrome.

Chinese make red and white flowers for funerals, and this Boatner understood. And while he was spending millions of dollars for new wire and watchtowers, Bull Boatner bought the peace of one compound, he thought, at quite a bargain.

Phase I had begun. Each day, each hour, General Boatner continued to show his authority. He was reasonable, he was human—but he was boss.

He had to move step by step, not to goad the POW's into angry reaction until he was ready, which would only be when the new compounds, going up night and day, were finished.

Now, statues and images of the Communist saints, national flags, and portraits of Stalin and Kim Il Sung were displayed in all compounds. Picking on the least dangerous compounds first, Boatner ordered these to come down, without result.

Boatner planned his next step with Woody Garrett. With the men of Garrett's battalion, they rehearsed a raid into a compound in secret, getting the timing down pat. There was no question that Boatner could march armed men into any compound he chose, and tear down the Communist symbology—but the purpose was to accomplish it without bloodshed.

The eyes of the world were watching for the next American fiasco.

Then, when an ultimatum to the Chinese to pull down their flags at 1200 was ignored, at that hour the sergeant of the guard threw open the compound gate, and two tanks roared in, followed by infantry with arms at high port. In five minutes, the flags and portraits were torn down, and all Americans back outside the wire—without incident, and before the Chinese could react.

One by one, Boatner did this to each compound.

Day by day, he drove his Sherman tanks past the roads near the compounds, and he marched his heavily armed infantry by, showing his force. Day by day he beat the POW's down, without laying a finger on them, without killing one of them.

Phase I took ten days, and time was running out.

General Clark flew into Koje-do, accompanied by General Van Fleet. Boatner briefed Clark, while Van Fleet had little to ask or say. When Boatner finished, Wayne Clark said: "Boatner, you're doing exactly what I told you. You can rest assured you'll never get hurt."

A few days after Boatner took command at Koje, Van Fleet had visited him. At that time the Eighth Army CG said, "You've got to tighten up on security." It was obvious to all that a grapevine ran from Panmunjom and P'yongyang down to Koje-do.

"Then, General," Boatner said, "I've got to move all these thousands of civilians away from the camps. There's the security problem."

But Van Fleet argued. "You can't do that."

So for a few more days the POW camps were surrounded by a raucous throng of hawkers, prostitutes, and probable Communist agents. It was common practice for civilians to throw notes back and forth across the wire with the POW's.

One day, the correspondents asked Boatner why he permitted this. He told them General Van Fleet's orders. Shortly afterward, Van Fleet's orders were changed.

Boatner had no legal authority to move the civilians away from the camp— but all it took was a little action. He gave orders that they must not be brutalized, and put trucks at their disposal; in one day and a half, all were moved far away, and not allowed to return. There was no further trouble from that source.

By this time, the brass studiously refrained from nibbling on Boatner; technically, there were a number of people in the chain of command between him and Mark W. Clark, but each of these, whatever his own notions may have been, was knowledgeable enough to keep his finger out of the pie.

Phase II, the building of the new compounds, took almost thirty days, while Boatner sweated out each day, expecting trouble to break at any moment. It was not until 10 June 1952 that he was ready to begin Phase III, the breaking up and movement of the existing compounds.

With this move, he would accomplish three things: the breakup of the tight Communist control organizations in some compounds, the placement of POW's into secure compounds from which they had little chance of escape, and the reducing of the huge, unwieldy compounds into smaller ones more easily managed.

This had to be done, but he also knew that the Communist leaders would resist it to the death.

Boatner planned and organized the moves as a military operation. Four weeks before, Phase III would have been impossible—but Boatner had used his month well. Not only had he beaten the will of the POW's down day by day; he now had also a completely disciplined, taut American military structure under his command, immediately and efficiently responsive to his order.

To begin Phase III, Boatner decided to crack the toughest nut first. Compound 76 held the hard-core Communist officers; it had captured Dodd. It was also closest to the U.S. hospital in which were American female nurses. In 76 were the meanest and most vicious POW's, and the best leadership.

Putting 76 out of operation first, Boatner felt, would go a long way to reducing the others.

The 187th Airborne and the 38th Infantry dug in two battalions along the road into Compound 76, in plain sight. Also in plain sight, the infantrymen and paratroopers set up machine guns and mortars, laid on the prison camp.

Then Boatner had the paratroops stage a mock advance into an empty compound next to 76, with fixed bayonets and flamethrowers, while the Communist prisoners watched. The demonstration went like clockwork; it had been timed and scheduled to the second, and every officer briefed on his part.

The demonstration was both impressive and frightening.

Then Boatner sent for the senior Korean officer of Compound 76. He told him that the POW's were to be moved, into better quarters. He took him to inspect the new compounds, and told him when and where he would be moved, in an attempt to forestall any panic among the prisoners.

But the Communist leadership could not be trusted to tell their people the truth. Loudspeakers were set up outside all compounds, and in English, Korean, and Chinese, the same word was put out for the rank and file. The compounds were bluntly warned that they were going to be moved, by force if necessary, and if there was any resistance the POW's would be responsible for the results. Compounds other than 76 were informed so that they would not panic when trouble began in the first one to be moved.

When the word was out, 9 June 1952, General Boatner's officers reported to him that instead of getting ready to move, the North Koreans in 76 were putting out pickets to see that no one attempted to obey his instructions.

Early the next morning, 10 June, Boatner and Brigadier General Trapnell, the paratroop commander, stood on a low hill outside Compound 76, watching.

The troops had their orders; everything had been planned and rehearsed down to the most minute detail. Phase lines within the compound had been drawn, and the troops were to cross them at given times. A large number of paratroops were to be used. Inside the compound, they would operate from a fixed base, sweeping movable forces through the compound to force the POW's out. The paratroops had bayoneted rifles, but no cartridges in the chambers. They could fire only on the express command of an officer.

With the compound completely ringed by men and steel, the paratroops who were to enter 76 massed. At 0615 they tore down the wire fence, and went in.

The Koreans fell back, to a preplanned defensive line within the compound. Suddenly, many of them brandished long spears and sharp knives, made in the workshops.

The paratroops reached Phase Line A, having covered one-eighth of the compound area, without contact, and without result. They moved on, slowly, deliberately, irresistibly, grinding the mass of POW's before them, pushing them around against the fixed base of men set up in one area. At Phase Line B—one half the compound—they began to throw concussion grenades.

Now the bulk of the POW's began to come apart, to flee before the grim Americans and out into the fields ringed by men and guns. They were pushed on into their new homes.

But behind a line of trenches they had dug in one section of the compound, 150 holdouts refused to surrender. They screamed and shouted defiance, and waved spears and knives.

The paratroops advanced, slowly, grimly, pushing them back. Now there was chaos. The POW's had set their huts afire, and smoke blanketed the area, choking men, obscuring vision. In the Korean press, a number of men panicked, and tried to run.

They were killed by their own people, with spears in the back.

Then the tough paratroopers met the lines of Koreans, and in a wild melee broke the back of their resistance. At a cost of 43 POW's killed, 135 wounded—half by their own officers—the 6,500 hard-core Communists in 76 were broken down into groups of 500 and placed behind new wire.

As the resistance ended, Boatner walked into the still-flaming compound, into which no American had gone for days. Not far within the circle of huts he recognized an odor familiar to all men who have intimately known the battle-field: the smell of death.

Inside a hut, he found a five-day-old corpse, hanging by its heels—a symbol of the Communist determination to dominate, placed there as an example by the leadership.

And in a ditch, cowering, the paratroopers found Senior Colonel Lee Hak Ku, of the North Korean People's Army; they dragged him out, roughly, and pushed him on his way. Colonel Lee, who had expected to be killed, never afterward gave much trouble.

Nor did the other compounds, some of whom had witnessed the reduction of 76, and some of whom heard of it on the grapevine, when their own turn came.

Buried in 76, Boatner's men found two sets of plans. One was the defense plan by which the North Koreans had resisted movement.

The other was the plan for a mass breakout by the dedicated Communists of all compounds, set for 20 June 1952.

The plans called for the POW's to cut the wire, make for the hills, and slaughter everything in their path.

The plans, however, were eight days too late. For on 12 June 1952, with the compounds broken up, Brigadier General Bull Boatner was at last in command of Koje Island.

37

Summer, Winter,
Spring, and Fall

The destiny of mankind is not decided by material computation. When great causes are on the move in the world . . . we learn that we are spirits, not animals, and that something is going on in space and time and beyond space and time, which whether we like it or not, spells duty.

—From a speech by Winston S. Churchill, Rochester, New York, 1941.

B Y SUMMER 1952, as the rice began to ripen in the muddy brown paddies, and as the Korean valleys, which had been glacial in December, turned into malarial swamps, the only serious obstacle to a cease-fire was the problem of prisoners of war. The armistice line had been drawn, and by that agreement each side had relinquished any wholesale designs on the other's territory.

But now, with the Communist POW's once again under firm control, the Communist powers could not refute the fact that not more than 83,000 of the 132,000 of their personnel in U.N. hands would voluntarily return to their homelands, and this was a loss of face that they could not accept.

At Panmunjom, General Harrison had to face every kind of devious tactic, including the most flagrant lies and virulent abuse bordering on the personal. The Communists, who had deeply shocked the U.N. Command with their admission that they themselves held only 12,000 men—leaving thousands of Americans and 250,000 South Koreans, the latter mostly civilians who had disappeared during the Communist occupation unaccounted for—in addition to claiming torture and slaying of their people, also claimed that the U.N. held 40,000 more Communist POW's in secret.

Whatever heinous act the Communists committed, or intended to commit, they considered it good tactics to accuse the other fellow first.

Because U.N. POW's had died or disappeared by thousands in their own death camps, it was inevitable that they must accuse the U.N. of the same. But with the failure of planned mass breakout on Koje-do—which might have confused and concealed the real facts forever—it had soon become apparent to the world where the truth lay.

The International Red Cross, banned from Koje while Haydon Boatner cleaned up the island, returned there on 2 July. And while the IRC handed General Clark a stinging rebuke over the death and injury of certain POW's in the cleanup—which Clark shot back in similar language—neutral observers such as the IRC continued to uphold the U.N.'s word.

The Communists tried side gambits—in what was now primarily a propaganda war—such as the germ-warfare accusations. While it was true that wholesale epidemics, mainly typhus, raged over North Korea, this was due to the ravages of war, the destruction caused by the continual United States air bombardment, and the passage of huge, unwashed Chinese armies across a land lacking sanitation and medical facilities—not deliberate seeding of virulent bacteria by Americans.

The Communists were able to back up their accusations with statements by American airmen shot down over North Korea. Under great physical and mental pressure, a number of Americans confessed or otherwise acquiesced that the United States engaged in germ warfare.

While quite naturally scoffed at in the West, these claims—and their written and pictorial documentation—had great effect in the East.

After all, every Asian nation was quite aware of who had dropped the first nuclear bomb—and on whom.

One of the ironic and deeply tragic trends of the middle of the twentieth century was that just as the Westerners were gradually abandoning their own racial shibboleths and awarenesses, the rest of the world was adopting a virulent racial consciousness, which would, however unspoken, color all international policy.

When hemorrhagic fever—a particularly dreadful and at first fatal disease, causing bleeding from skin and eyeballs—attacked U.N. troops in western Korea, and a research laboratory was set up on a hospital ship off Korea, the ship was branded as a germ-warfare factory. General Harrison, a member of an old and distinguished Virginia family, and a quiet, Christian gentleman, was once provoked to say "that when you deal with Communists, you deal with common criminals."

General Harrison was wrong—and his error pointed up the dangerous weaknesses of the West in dealing with Communism. The charge of criminal, flung at a Hitler or an Eichmann, clings—because by the ethos of the society in which these men were born, they were criminal—but Communist society does not have a common ethos with the West. It cannot be evaluated by the cultural standards common to the West.

These vital differences made General Harrison's job at Panmunjom desperately difficult.

For the United States and its U.N. allies, to be true to their own concepts, could not in conscience do what the Communists now demanded as the price of peace: force their unwilling captives home at gunpoint.

There was some grumbling inside the United States, and more in Europe, at continuing the war for the sake of a few grubby POW's in Korean stockades, who probably didn't even know their own minds. But the United States Government never wavered.

And as the State Department reported, regardless of the moral issue, to force the POW's to return would be a propaganda defeat of the utmost magnitude; it would be surrender, and the significance of such breach of faith would not be lost throughout Asia.

Offering to return only those POW's who desired to return, the U.N. Command reiterated:

> *You have been repeatedly informed of the finality of our 28 April proposal . . . our stand is unshakable. We will not make further concessions. We are, however, always ready to explain the elements of our proposal.*

The answer was no, but the door was still open.

Now the United Nations Command in Korea recommended to Washington that the POW's who refused repatriation be granted asylum as political refugees, and released in South Korea or on Taiwan, depending on their nationality. For as Edwin D. Dickinson, an authority on international law, wrote in the New York Times, . . . *in the absence of treaty, the competence of states to grant asylum is unlimited.*

States have unlimited right to grant asylum—but no obligation, if they do not choose. Washington rejected the proposal.

With both sides now intransigent, but still willing to talk, negotiations on the POW question droned through June and July.

The United Nations Command made further offers: to let the POW's be screened again by neutrals, and by the Communists themselves, in public. The Communist powers screamed foul to each proposal.

With growing discouragement, the U.N. negotiators began to recess frequently. In all, they threw out three alternative proposals, none of which, however, required an unwilling POW to return home if he did not so desire.

By early fall it became obvious that the Communist powers were not going to accede to anything short of return of all prisoners. And it had also become obvious that with the United States in the throes of a bitterly disputed presidential election, they preferred to stall, to continue the propaganda war.

On 8 October 1952, Harrison, now a lieutenant general, stated: "The United Nations Command has no further proposals to make. The proposals we made remain open. The U.N.C. delegation will not come here merely to listen to abuse and false propaganda. The U.N.C. is therefore calling a recess. . . . We are willing to meet with you again at any time you are willing to accept one of our proposals . . . which could lead to an honorable armistice. I have nothing more to say."

The United Nations Command, from Mark W. Clark on down, had had enough of lies, calumnies, sophistry, and flaming propaganda.

The talks of Panmunjom recessed. They would not begin again, except for liaison meetings, until the following year.

*   *   *

In the United States, as the day of presidential election neared, there was basic disagreement, not only between the parties but also within them. This conflict centered on Korea.

The problem was that the United States seemingly could not win victory, secure an armistice, or get out of Korea. It was a situation the American people had never faced before. It was one that their government had shown no skill for handling since the peace talks began more than one year before.

The United States was unwilling to accept the losses required in putting new pressure—other than air bombardment—on the enemy, and it was so desirous of peace that it hesitated to rock the boat in any fashion. Thus, the proposal to free the non-Communist POW's was denied, for fear of its effect on the enemy. And the U.N. cloak continued to bind United States operations tightly. To work within the U.N. the nation had to observe that body's wishes, and the U.N. wanted only peace.

By the fall of 1952, Americans could agree on one thing: that Dean Acheson's remark to Harry Truman in July 1950, "that your decision may not always be the popular one," was the understatement of the decade.

It was not the decision to intervene in Korea, however, that caused the frustration and anger and disquiet. It was the continuing stalemate. More and more people began to say, "Win it, or get out."

The anguish of the United States Government, politically unable to win, strategically unable to withdraw, can be easily understood. The government, from failure to understand clearly that Communists negotiate fairly only when it is in their interest to do so, or when unbearable pressure is placed upon them, had clamped itself in a Communist trap. The most difficult thing for all Western statesmen to learn was that there never had been, and probably never would be, a permanent community of interest between themselves and the Communist bloc. The understanding was so often rejected, no doubt, because its acceptance meant that the world was a checkerboard, the pressure unending, and that competition would prevail further than any man could see.

Oddly, in America, both pacifists and jingoes combined in anger against the Administration. Legislators who had never voted favorably on a single military budget cried for victory; while professional anti-Communists hinted that the POW's should be abandoned as the U.S. withdrew back into its own *Festung America.*

Inside the government there was considerable sentiment to accede to the Communist demands on the POW question in order to achieve peace before the election. All this sentiment was centered in the domestic, or "political," area of the Cabinet. The guts of the Cabinet—State and Defense—remained adamant that the United States would have to continue present policy, however politically unbearable.

The opposition was also deeply split. Some wanted peace at any price; some wanted complete victory at any price; some wanted escape into a world with less danger and fewer insolvable problems. But an opposition party—as each party discovers periodically in America—has certain shining advantages: it can carp and criticize all past and current mistakes without being too specific with its own remedies.

In the presidential election of 1952, the majority of words and arguments did not concern Korea. The majority of words and arguments—on both sides—had no relevancy to any current problem.

Men tend to repeat political slogans and arguments a generation after they have become obsolete. There were Democrats running against Hoover, and Republicans opposed to Franklin Roosevelt, though 1929 was a generation gone, and the New Deal had sputtered and died for all practical purposes in 1938.

Yet, there is little doubt that political historians will grant the Korean War, and its side pressures, such as fear of Communism both international and domestic, the principal credit for the Republican victory.

There were inflation and high prosperity in America; there were guns, autos, and margarine in high plenty; there were millions of people happily content, unconcerned with the Far East.

But there were too many millions, touched in some way by the men holding the grim and dangerous battle line, who were troubled.

On its foreign policy, as opposed to its domestic, the Democratic Administration still could not effectively communicate. It was not that so many people did not approve; it was that they did not understand what had to be done and what had been done. Within the Administration there had always been a reluctance to use the hard sell on its foreign policies; the government had preferred to act in secret where possible rather than submit delicate questions to public debate.

In the middle of the century, this course was impossible. Neither Metternich nor Talleyrand's various bosses had had to stand for election. Harry Truman's boy Stevenson did.

Perhaps a little blunt speech, a declassification of government communications prior to the first week of November 1952, when it was much too late, a certain amount of public screaming by the Secretary of State that Communism was the Antichrist—however he personally would have detested such an emotional display—and the throwing to the wolves of a few cronies and misguided officials who in the thirties and forties had mistakenly thought that Communists were human beings, would have saved the architects of containment.

But perhaps it was time for a change, and nothing could have saved them. As it was, they won the election everywhere in the free world except where the votes were counted.

* * *

The Republican attack was many-pronged, but in its van were men trumpeting the traditional American views toward war: never get involved if possible, but once you're in, give 'em hell.

The moral issue, which sounded metallic and out of place in the mouth of an Acheson, rang cold and righteous in the tones of a Dulles. Americans had always fought for moral issues since 1776, not for the balance of power, not to restore world order. And they had always struck hard for victory, not balance, even if such victory left the world in ruins.

The Republican leaders, saying and implying that they would either end the war, or in one great upsurge end the evil underlying it, struck much closer to the hearts of the public than had the framers of containment.

They called for a rolling back of the iron curtain, which the architects of containment knew to be patently impossible, short of general war, and emotionally satisfied millions, who accepted a Soviet veto on U.S. actions only with frustration and grave disquiet.

Their views and their calls to action were far more in line with those of Wilson and Roosevelt, Democratic saints, than those of the Democratic leaders of 1952. The new Democratic leaders were much more inclined to accept the fact that the outside world had changed, in 1952, than were the Republicans.

It was probably necessary for the opposition to win, in 1952.

Whatever the domestic issues, only a Republican Administration could have dragged the American liberal middle classes into world affairs—an entanglement they violently distrusted. Only a Cabinet of men who never once, not even in college, had seen anything attractive in the far left could have brought to Americans understanding that Communism must be lived with, even while it is opposed.

This Republican Administration would do damage—it would toy with solutions such as "massive retaliation," and it would seek cheap answers: "More bang for a buck." It would continue to dislike professional legions, and try to do away with them. It would find, painfully, that all the old ideas dear to business-liberal society would not work.

It would, after a year or two, adopt containment, and continue virtually unchanged, every foreign policy of the Truman Administration.

They found, as would a new Democratic champion in the future, that despite the call for new looks, new solutions, such looks still revealed only the stone face of Communism and Soviet power; and new solutions, however appealing, remained too dangerous.

And therein continued the tragedy of Americans of these years. Containment of Communism could never be a solution, of itself; it could be only a ploy for time, a stopgap, a pragmatic attempt to hold a dangerous line as long as possible.

But the destiny of America, hopefully, did not lie in pragmatism or stopgaps. The pragmatic man worries about today or tomorrow, never the day past tomorrow. He rarely seeks, and he seldom creates.

Pragmatists create no new ways of life; they found no new religions, nor do they become martyrs to them. They believe in balance, compromise, adjustment. They distrust enthusiasms; they trust what works.

They make good politicians, excellent bankers, superb diplomats.

They never build empires, either of the earth or of the spirit.

They often preside, wisely and temperately, over their liquidation.

Pragmatists did not land at Plymouth Rock, nor did they "pledge their lives, property, and sacred honor," at Philadelphia.

Containment, forged in the forties and carried through the fifties and into the sixties, was a pragmatic policy. It was necessary, for there is a time for defense, even as there is a season for all things. But it was sterile; it could afford only time, and time, of itself, solves some problems, but not many.

In the middle of the century, hopefully, as Democrat and Republican hammered at each other on the hustings, mouthing moth-eaten arguments, and as men held high and lonely hills along the battle line of civilization in Korea, a new policy might have come forth.

It seemed the hour, now, for a concept as brilliant as Wilson's world democracy—so glorious in vision, so utterly impossible of attainment—without Wilson's flaws, or a crusade with a base as practical as that of containment, without its emptiness of spirit. For the one thing no American might have, in the middle of the century, was the *status quo ante quem.* He could hold the far frontiers, with money, guns, men, or trade. He could try to soothe a worsening world as the hour demanded, day to day, year to year, from Acheson to Dulles, to Herter and Rusk.

But so long as he had no new policy, so long as he sought only to contain, the enemy without would always hold the initiative.

In Washington, in November 1952, there was a changing of the guard. There was nothing new, but that changing of the guard affected history. It did one thing good and one thing bad—it froze in men's minds the political dangers of sending men to hold the far frontier, and every future government would be reluctant to order it, but it hastened the end of the Korean War.

* * *

In Korea, it was stalemate.

Neither side could advance; neither side would retreat. Each side held its own hills and valleys in depth, but from November 1951 onward, the enemy continued to be more aggressive than the U.N.

He patrolled aggressively, and he launched limited attacks, again and again. He took hills, and he took the platoons and companies that had been on them. And he killed more men when the U.N. attacked to take its property back. Usually, the action was minor, except to the men hip-deep in swarming Chinese, or pounded by artillery fire falling at the rate of hundreds of shells per minute.

One division commander in Korea recognized that the warfare resembled that of the Western Front, 1915–1918. And like that trench fighting, it was more costly than those unfamiliar with it would think.

Exactly half as many men were killed and wounded during the stalemate as were lost during the violent war of maneuver that surged up and down the peninsula.

By summer 1952, the enemy had grown more aggressive. He waged a bitter struggle over a number of U.N. outposts from Mabang to Kumsong to Oem'yon. On 17 July at 2200 hours, after devastating artillery preparation, a

CCF battalion overran the U.N. outpost on Old Baldy, west of Ch'orwon, a hill neither completely inside one defensive system nor in the other.

For four days a seesaw battle raged for the blasted, denuded hill. The 23rd Infantry eventually had elements of E, F, I, L, B, K, and G companies on the hill at one time or another; it took hundreds of casualties. Its commander, trying to control the action day after day, without rest, lost control and had to be relieved.

The battle for Old Baldy, which the CCF eventually lost, proved that the enemy had as many, if not more, field guns as the U.N. He could not, however, switch their fires or employ them as effectively as the Americans.

It was not until 31 July that a full battalion attack of 1/23 retook the hill—a position that could accommodate comfortably only a single rifle company.

Here, and elsewhere, the U.N. defenders learned that they would have to dig deeper. Soon, more and more positions were completely underground, and all of the bunkers—which tended to collapse under rain or artillery—were reinforced with logs.

On 16 September the CCF tried for Old Baldy again. First, an estimated 1,000 rounds of artillery fell on the small hill in a ten-minute period; then a battalion of CCF surrounded it and assaulted it from all sides. They took Baldy, and K Company, 38th Infantry on it, with lightning speed, while a diversionary attack overran Pork Chop Hill, to the northeast of Old Baldy.

On the night of 20 September, after heavy artillery preparation, 2/38 attacked to retake their property. Plunging through a hail of enemy fire, the battalion cleared the crest and was in control 21 September. The attack was well coordinated and well-pushed home, and it killed or wounded more than a thousand Chinese.

But the American losses, overall, were nearly as high.

The pattern of this hill fighting, which resembled that of Heartbreak and Bloody ridges, was repeated again and again. Aggressive, the CCF would plaster a forward hill or outpost with tremendous concentrations of artillery, then assault it with large forces, and overrun it.

Soon, most of the artillery fires of two to four divisions would be falling into one tiny area, as a seesaw battle raged. The U.N. would not initiate such attacks, as a rule, but it would not permit the enemy to push it about. Given an inch, it was the custom of the Chinese to strike for a mile. The U.N. forces had to return the CCF maneuver, in spades.

During these immense artillery and infantry duels, in which thousands of men were hurt or killed, the crowning horror was that usually units on either side of them, or beyond regimental HQ on the front, were completely unaware there was a war on.

Again and again the CCF felt free to attack, into a limited area.

On 6 October they struck east of Baldy and Pork Chop, against Arrowhead and White Horse Mountain—now, with long occupancy, every hill along the battle lines had its own name—and the preparatory fires there exceeded anything yet seen. Jim Fry, CG of the 2nd Division, said they were beyond anything he had known in his previous considerable military experience.

The artillery fires laid down in Korea during the latter periods normally far exceeded anything fired in either of the two world wars, day after day. The average fire falling on U.N. lines was 24,000 per day.

The CCF sent two divisions piecemeal into White Horse and Arrowhead. The French Battalion held Arrowhead for four days, under incessant attack, losing no ground. White Horse, held by ROK's of the 9th Division, changed hands twenty-four times between 6 and 15 October. When the battle ended, all U.N. territory was back in friendly hands.

And the hillsides were dotted with the bodies of thousands of ROK's and Chinese.

On White Horse, and on the central front, around the Iron Triangle, the ROK Army now proved it had come of age. With only a few American tanks, and generally with American artillery in support, the ROK's were weaker in firepower than American units, and at first more easily overrun. The CCF preferred to hit them, given a choice. But the ROK's had had two years to prepare; they counterattacked with stubborn courage, and time after time threw the CCF back.

On the Kumwha sector, ROK's and CCF locked in heavy combat, all over limited objectives. On Sniper Ridge, changing hands daily during November 1952, the ROK soldier proved he had lost all his superstitious horror of his ancient masters.

He killed thousands of Chinese, while that fall he himself suffered forty thousand casualties. But the front hardly changed at all. In front of the ROK position, the ground was cleared of Chinese only to the extent of six hundred yards.

During these bloody battles there was some comment that KMAG was presiding over the slow death of the ROK Army, to preserve American lives.

The hill battles that raged all across the front, though mostly in the western zone, accomplished little, except again to provide revulsion in American ranks against the casualties suffered. When the totals reached Washington, there was a certain amount of despair. Quietly, some men began to talk of taking the offensive, and even more quietly, of the use of the atomic weapon.

The Chinese, seemingly, had no regard for the lives of their conscript soldiers; the West did.

But doing its best to preserve lives, the U.N. Command still had to defend its ground. And while men died, the names of blasted, forsaken humps of ground, outposts Reno, Carson, and Vegas, of the Marines; Baldy, Arrowhead, and Pork Chop of the 2nd Division; Triangle Hill and Sniper Ridge and Big Nori of the ROK's, and dozens of others, became infamous. U.S. and ROK divisions went on line and off it; they turned over their prize property to other units; then, weeks later, came back to reclaim it.

When enough men had died on a hill, their comrades began to hold a grim fondness for it. "Take good care of our Pork Chop," soldiers of the Thai Battalion wrote on their bunker walls when they turned it over to the 7th U.S. Division on relief.

The intense attacks on the U.N. outposts during 1952 were undoubtedly political in nature. The Chinese, balked on the POW question, took this means during an election year to pressure the United States out of the war. The policy was a costly failure.

The American soldier and officer who held the line in late 1952 and early 1953 was yet another breed from the man who had gone into Korea, who had fought during the massive battles of 1951, or who had watched the front during the second Korean winter.

The recalled reservists were largely gone now, their time—seventeen months for veterans, twenty-four for others—expired. The National Guardsmen of the 40th and 45th divisions had gone home, though these two divisions remained on the FECOM trooplist, as Army of the United States units, filled with other personnel.

The average man of the infantry companies was a selectee, and rapidly, he was becoming a special sort of selectee.

The first of draft call, in the summer of 1950, was a vacuum cleaner—sprung without warning, it took skilled and unskilled alike, high-school senior and college teacher together; there was no time to escape.

The Army got a great number of highly skilled men, which it badly needed. Throughout all history, only the pinch of poverty or the pressure of the draft board has made men in large numbers enter the ranks; this has always been the defensive weakness of a mercantile society, whether Carthage, Britain, or America. But by 1951, there was little poverty, and the draft pressures had relaxed.

Thousands of young men, with no stomach for infantry war, entered other services to avoid it, generally in the following priority: Coast Guard, which could pick and choose the best; then Navy and Air Force, where skills were more at a premium, and combat dangers—in this particular war—less. The Marine Corps, which had written some of its most glorious history at Changjin, and which kept its standards high, had difficulty recruiting up to authorized strength. For as one high-school student, who had been at the reservoir as a reservist, returned to his old school and said: "For God's sake, watch where you enlist—the Marines will kill you!"

There was exemption for students, and anyone who could get into college and keep his marks up, or join ROTC, had it made. Parenthood—even *ex post facto*—was a good out.

Understandably, with an unpopular war that had little public enthusiasm or support, the quality of men left over for the Infantry declined.

By May 1952, of over 5,000 new trainees entering the 1st Armored Division at Fort Hood, Texas, slightly over half had Army General Classification Test scores of 80 or under—by Army standards unfit for training at any Army school, including cooks and bakers. It seemed an unmistakable trend that only those too stupid to figure an out were coming into the ground forces.

Yet, these men proved they could fight, and fight well, when trained.

The involuntary Reserve officers who had fought on Bloody and Heartbreak had left, most saying *"Damnation memoriae"* to the service, and their places had been taken by the new products of the college Reserve Officers Training Corps.

Very few of these young men, though intelligent and better educated than almost any wartime American officer corps had been, had seen hardship before. They were keen and alert, but tended to be permissive with their men. They had a difficult time with platoon command, because ROTC had given them little practical experience with the rough and tumble of combat; but graduated to staff jobs, they gave the Army an indispensable balance of poise and education junior officers promoted from the ranks could not.

Ironically, the officer who is often best at leading small units of men, who can rough it in the earth, living in filth and danger beside his men, the familiarity breeding no contempt, often is helpless when put behind a desk.

The ROTC boys worried their battalion commanders while they were in command of platoons and companies, at ages ranging from twenty-one to twenty-four, but—if they survived—they were invaluable later up on staff, where the pen is always mightier than the sword.

Few of these men, either officer or soldier, had a strong belief in the reasons for which this war was fought. They came because they had to, they did what they had to do, with one eye on Panmunjom, and when their time was up, they went home.

Oddly, they were never sanguine about their own combat prowess. Most of them, officers and men, felt a deep respect for, and almost an inferiority before, the various professionals that comprised the other U.N. troops in Korea. Their praise of the allies—the French, Thais, Turks, and Abyssinians— was far removed from the grousing about allies that had marked most previous wars. Most Americans, privately, would admit the U.N. troops were better than they were.

Which was highly surprising, since until the last, captured CCF intelligence documents always indicated the Chinese considered Americans the best.

For, unassuming, unaggressive, with no desire whatever to kill the man they called Joe Chink, when backed into a corner, or assaulted on their hills, these men showed that the spirit of the Alamo was not dead.

They had had the benefit of what had gone before. They came to Korea knowing in some measure what it would be like. The word was out. Like Frank Muñoz, when offered George Company, they wouldn't volunteer—but what had to be done they would do.

If the job was pointed out to Americans, and they understood it had to be done, with no escape; if they were trained to do it, as they were from 1951 onward, Americans could do what had to be done.

If another war follows Korea, if American policy is threatened anywhere on the globe, it will not be years and months, as in the two world wars, or days, as in Korea, but only hours until American troops are committed.

In battle, Americans learn fast—those who survive.

The pity is, their society seems determined to make them wait until the shooting starts.

The word should go out sooner.

In May of 1952, a treaty of peace was signed between the United States and Japan. The Army ceased to occupy, and now became honored guests of the shrunken Empire of Japan.

Very little changed, except that now the Japanese were free to criticize their best customers, if they dared.

In Japan, the Korean War was always close, but always far away. While the Korean people were inevitably the real losers of the war, the Japanese became the true winners. The Korean War poured billions of American dollars into the Japanese economy.

Millions of Americans passed through Japan, moving to and from the combat zones. These had money in amounts unbelievable to the Nipponese—and the Japanese, among the world's most industrious people, soon found Americans would spend it for almost anything, if given the opportunity.

The Japanese, who view the nude human body with the same aplomb they view the naked dawn, soon found nudity was highly marketable. Farm areas were scoured for girls whose bosoms measured up to Western standards, to walk about in clubs without clothes. Some Americans, understandably, when buying tobacco from the strolling cigarette girl, picked up the wrong brands.

There were other business ventures. One young chaplain from a tank battalion, a Methodist with a family back home, was accosted by procurers fourteen times in 1952 while walking from his Tokyo hotel to a cab.

All Americans, passing through, found that good Canadian whiskey was $1.50 a fifth, and drinks a quarter U.S. a throw. As one officer said, happily, "At these prices I can't afford to stay sober!"

These things were inevitable in war. Men going to and from a battlefield, even in crusades, have usually sought the same things. The Japanese could not be blamed for turning their nation into a large red-light district, for what the customer with money wants, he always gets.

The big money, and the prosperity that flushed the Japanese economy, however, came from American arms expenditures. American military procurement officers found Japanese industry—far more capable and efficient than it is generally given credit for—could produce almost anything needed at the front—and much cheaper than it could be made in the States and sent across the Pacific.

Thousands of American military vehicles, damaged or worn out in Korea, were rebuilt in Japanese shops, some as many as three times, far more cheaply than they could have been replaced. The Japanese, under contract, could manufacture ammunition, tools, equipment, almost anything. They could produce millions of tons of food for Koreans and Americans in FECOM. All in all, the Japanese economy hummed. They made big money.

The benefits did not all accrue to the Japanese, however.

Without its solid industrial base in Japan, in privileged sanctuary from the battles, the United States would have found it as difficult to fight the Korean War as it would have been to land on Normandy on D-Day, had Britain not been there.

38

The Last Spring

. . . All of the heroism and all of the sacrifice, went unreported. So the very fine victory of Pork Chop Hill deserves the description of the Won-Lost Battle. It was won by the troops and lost to sight by the people who had sent them forth

—S. L. A. Marshall, PORK CHOP HILL.

COMPARED TO Gettysburg, Bastogne, or Verdun, the outpost battles that erupted across Korea from time to time were skirmishes, pinpricks next to the wounds of the world's great battles. But on the bodies of troops actually engaged the casualties were exceedingly high. When companies are reduced to forty men, and platoons to six or seven, to the men in them it is hardly limited war.

The hill battles along an unmoving line were costing the United States casualties at the rate of thirty thousand a year.

This number was still less than the annual traffic toll. But while Americans are well conditioned to death on the highways, they are not ready to accept death on the battlefield for apparently futile reasons.

The last spring of the Korean War, when it was apparent that peace was near, was one of the most horrible of all.

By 1953 almost every troop leader in the Far East held the opinion that continuance of the war under the present conditions was not only wasteful but verging on the criminal. It was all very well to say that sometimes the line must be held while nations muddle through—but there comes time when soldiers no longer see logic, when they are no longer willing to suffer while someone else improvises.

Now generals said freely that it had been a mistake to remove the terrible pressure from the Communist armies in 1951. They did not say the U.N. should have marched to the Yalu—though many believed it—but they agreed that a firm foot should have been kept on the Communist neck until a signature was on the dotted line at Kaesong.

In retrospect, it seems beyond question that because the West brought naïveté concerning Communist motives and methods to the conference table thousands more men than necessary were maimed and killed. If the U.N. had approached the table with a hard eye instead of a sigh of relief, in fighting stance instead of immediate relaxation, the chances are high that peace could have been attained in 1951.

Perhaps, as General Matt Ridgway wrote, it is futile to speculate. Perhaps it was necessary that the United States prove its own desire for peace. But to the men who for two more bitter years held the outpost line, and to the friends and families of those thousands killed and injured between July 1951 and July 1953, the question will forever remain.

* * *

One final bitterness, of all these people, was that much of the bitter struggle of the last spring went unreported. There were months when as many as 104 enemy attacks—from company to division strength—smashed against the U.N. outpost line, and days when as many as 131,800 rounds of Communist artillery fell on it within a twenty-four-hour period. Few of these events, buried deep in newspapers, caused a stir.

These were limited attacks, for the purpose of destroying outposts and killing men, similar to the bloody raids and counterraids on the Western Front during 1915–1918. None of them, by itself, could affect the war. In each of them men died.

Because the lines never move, trench warfare is not spectacular. The public and the home fronts soon lose interest in it; it seems to them that nothing happens. The lines do not move. But each day and night, men die, by the bayonet, grenade, or submachine gun, in violent night assaults down trenches and across bunkers and revetments, or by the deadly pounding of artillery, which falls again and again, without warning.

Between the times of dying, men wait. The waiting, seemingly endless, is perhaps the worst of all.

And one final bitterness was that this type of warfare was self-imposed. In 1915, developments in weaponry had stalemated the battle lines; no one knew any other course. In 1953, the men along the outpost line knew that the powers that had sent them forth apparently had chosen to play the enemy's game.

Fighting this anachronistic war, over the long months each of the armies changed.

The Republic of Korea Army grew better. While its high leadership was still shot through with weaknesses, its divisions had lost their horror of Chinese. Hit by waves of CCF, they no longer dissolved; they took high losses, but they held. The ROK Army was still far from "second best in the world," though it was now among the largest of the non-Communist world. Neither so good as the American or the Chinese, it still had little of which to be ashamed.

The American Army changed the least, from 1951 onward. The men came and went; the faces changed, for the United States divisions had one great disadvantage compared to the other combatants—they continually bled away their best men through rotation. Because of rotation, quality tended to remain static. The divisions retained the basic excellences developed in 1951: good weapon handling, superior communications, and superb artillery and superb artillery direction. But the troops were shot through with green men and remained somewhat clumsy and heavy-footed to the last, and their patrolling left something to be desired.

The new men arrived with legs unequal to the steep Korean slopes, and by the time they had learned to patrol the windy hills and deep valleys of no man's land, they had become casualties, or had enough points to go home.

It was the CCF, by all accounts, that changed the most. By 1953 the clumsy peasant armies, which had pushed masses of men through the valleys to the sound of horns and bugles, were no more.

There had been no rotation in the CCF, and the painful lessons of modern ground warfare had been pushed home.

In 1950, in the frightful mountains of North Korea, the CCF had won initial victories against a modern army beset by intelligence failures and deployed in an impossible scheme of maneuver, an army that had walked almost blithely into a trap. In 1951, from the Imjin to the Soyang, the CCF learned at great cost that they could not push home pell-mell attacks against a modern force that had both room to maneuver and the will to fight.

Unlike the old Imperial Japanese Army, the CCF understood the lessons of firepower, and did not repeat their failures.

After 1951, the Chinese soldier again became the phantom he had been in the North Korean hills. His fortifications and fieldworks, built with unstinted labor, almost always surpassed the American. Harassed by ever-present air power, he went completely underground, and he learned to move stealthily, and by night. He became furtive, fast, and skilled at deception.

He could pad noiselessly through the dark and assemble a battalion within U.N. lines before it was seen or heard, and fade away again before daybreak. He became adept at the ambush of American patrols, which could often be heard coming hundreds of yards away, and in the dark, deep valleys, more and more the honors went to him.

He rarely lost prisoners now, a matter of concern to American Intelligence. He proved he could slip small parties into U.N. lines and drag U.S. soldiers screaming from their bunks. While Americans continued to hate the dark, he loved the night as a friend, and made use of it.

He came onto the heavily defended U.N. hills and outposts like a phantom, and often took them within minutes. He could rarely hold them, however, under the quickly massed and superior fires of American artillery, and the grinding attacks launched against him by day, under artillery, air, and armor cover.

New American soldiers arriving in Korea were surprised to hear their officers tell them not to sell the Chinaman short, and that, man for man, the Chinese was as good a man as they. They were told of the vast improvement of the CCF; the Chinese had artillery and communications, now, supplied by Russia, and even more important, they had improved morale.

Corruption and desertion had disappeared. Rape and plunder, the old hall-marks of all Asiatic armies, were no longer reserved to field commanders or common soldiers, but to the state. Under continuous indoctrination, CCF soldiers fought more from pride and belief in their cause, and less from fear of their leaders. All ranks, down to squad privates, were briefed before operations to an extent no Western army attempted, because of security hazards.

There was no democracy in the CCF, or freedom of choice; the soldiers were still peasant conscripts, under harsh discipline. But the essential puritanism of the Communist leadership had seeped downward. As one Chinese POW proudly told Haydon Boatner on Koje-do, it was now possible to blow the whistle on a corrupt commander, and to make the charge stick.

The day of "silver bullets"—when a Chinese general could be bought—was done. Now, using machine guns, grenades, and other hand weapons with a skill they had not possessed on entering Korea, the CCF fired real bullets, with disturbing accuracy.

The erasure of the corruption that had marked Chinese life from top to bottom—and which still held sway in Korea—undoubtedly caused many individual Chinese, though they remained non-Communist, to support the new regime.

As both General Mark W. Clark and S. L. A. Marshall remarked, the two and a half years in Korea were priceless to the Chinese Army, "for on that training ground [the Chinese] armies became as skilled as any in the world in the techniques of hitting, evading, and surviving."

* * *

After the violent activity prior to the U.S. elections—about which Communists hold the same shibboleths as Westerners do about May Day—the action eased off during December 1952.

Then, by January 1953, the CCF was making life miserable again, now on Old Baldy, held by the 7th Division, now at Nori, against the 1st ROK, or at the Hook and Gibraltar, where the British stood firm.

During one small action as savage as that at Cold Harbor, the British lost a pipe major, which to the bewilderment of Americans and ROK's the British regarded as a blow against the Empire British soldiers stated, angrily, that it was easier to make a good colonel than a good pipe major, and the commander in question should have acted accordingly.

In January, shortly after Eisenhower's inauguration, the U.S. 7th Division launched one of the infrequent U.N. raids against the enemy, with the primary purpose of taking prisoners. Moving a company over frozen ground toward the bristling CCF fortifications, in open daylight, the 7th Division took a severe black eye from what it had code-named Operation Smack.

Because the move had been planned in advance, and a great amount of brass had come forward from Eighth Army and other places to observe, the press then charged that the whole operation had been staged as a show for the generals, and American boys had died for reasons somewhat similar to the early Christians in the Roman arena. While this was nonsense, it did point up three things: that the CCF had built their line to the point where any operation against it would be exceedingly costly; that any kind of losses were rapidly becoming unacceptable to the American public; and that the brass, admittedly, did not have enough to do.

On 11 February 1952, Lieutenant General Maxwell D. Taylor, who had dropped as CG of the 101st Airborne Division in Normandy, replaced Van Fleet as Eighth Army Commander. Van Fleet, disappointed at not moving up to FECOM command, retired.

Max Taylor, handsome, a paratrooper, and superb soldier, arrived understanding the situation perfectly. Among his first directives to the line was an order that every man wear his flak jacket—the new nylon or steel-plated body armor devised and issued as protection against shell fragments—at all times. Any officer, high or low, who suffered men killed was apt to find himself in painfully hot soup.

February passed, with continuing outpost activity. Over MIG Alley, between the Yalu and the Ch'ongch'on, the jet air war increased in intensity, with hundreds of Communist aircraft now sighted, though the U.N. retained complete dominance of the air. The U.N. air interdiction against North Korea went on, destroying what little was left of its economy, making life utterly miserable for its people, but affecting the dug-in Chinese and North Korean armies, supplied from privileged sanctuary across the Yalu, hardly at all.

March came, and the men of the front-line divisions heard increasing rumors of a political settlement of the war. They heard that after a long recess since October, men at last were going to talk again at Panmunjom.

But during March, the enemy became more vicious along the line.

He flailed at the Marine outposts of Carson, Vegas, Reno. Reno, a particularly exposed section outpost that had been fought over many times, had to be abandoned, though elsewhere the 1st Marine Division held firm. The Chinese also assailed Old Baldy again, now held by a Colombian battalion of the 7th Division, and in a flaming debacle, took it.

After a violent effort, after some retail spending of men in wholesale totals, Generals Trudeau—called Shaped Charge by the riflemen—and Taylor decided the price of Old Baldy was too high. The Chinese were left in possession.

Afterward, there would be fist fights and bitter words between men of the 2nd Division, which had shed the blood of thousands of its troops holding Baldy, and those who wore the hourglass patch of the 7th, who had lost it.

With Baldy gone, the Pork Chop was flanked and by military logic should have been abandoned, too. But gradually now, the U.N. Command was beginning to realize the political nature of these hill battles. The CCF was fighting, not for territory that had little value, and would be abandoned anyway according to the agreement already signed at Panmunjom in November 1951, but in a test of wills. While it seemed foolish to expose men to danger and death on worthless real estate, the U.N. Command was being forced to play King on the Mountain with the Chinese.

For it was becoming apparent that each relinquished hill only whetted the Chinese appetite, and made the Communists more intransigent than ever. In their own way, they were trying to force the U.N. to give up on the POW question, and to end the war on Chinese terms.

Stubbornly, the U.N. Command refused to give up Pork Chop, and here, in April, American troops engaged in their heaviest fighting of 1953.

* * *

Spring 1953 was a cruel time in Korea. Once again, behind the blasted stumps and explosive-churned earth of the outposts, the grass struggled upward through the shell shards and bones; the geese flew north, honking, for the Manchurian border, and the magnificent Mongolian green-necked pheasants pecked with renewed vigor among the long-abandoned rice fields behind the lines.

Springs, loosened by the thaw, trickled down the hillsides, and the smell of sap was in the air.

Behind the corps boundaries, beyond the sound of guns, behind the Farm Line, the odor of fecal earth that had vanished from the untilled and unfertilized fields to the north began again with raw freshness. And from here southward to the Japanese Strait, life was again much the same as it had always been: hard, painful, and never free of debt.

Though most of the American money, the new lifeblood of the Taehan Minkuk, stopped in Seoul where there were again motorcars and imported luxuries, the blasted and burned cities were being rebuilt. To them flocked the thousands of homeless and jobless, living in squalor, as at Tongduch'on-ni above Seoul, on the boundary of United States I Corps. Here squatted thousands of Korean prostitutes—women whose husbands and fathers had disappeared into the Communist maw—old men, orphans. Here, they lived in wattle huts and hoped to survive.

Frequently, they strayed from Tongduch'on-ni over into the forbidden corps zone. The American MP's always caught them and turned them back to Korean police, who let them straggle back to the place the Americans called "Little Chicago." The Korean National Police were devoid of sentiment, but even they understood that all human beings had the right to earn their bread, as best they could.

The women plied their trade; the old men made Ridgway hats for the big loud foreigners; the orphans begged and stole, with equal fervor.

Thousands of men who had come to Korea saying, "This war is for a bunch of lousy gooks," passed through Little Chi, and thousands of them contributed millions of American dollars to the missions and orphanages.

Some, like Colonel Ted Walker, who came to hate Communism to the point of incoherency, adopted Korean waifs, and sent them to school in the United States. In 1953 not all the shining deeds of the American Army were done on line.

Bitter, feeling forsaken, haunted by the fears of all men going into battle danger, the Americans who passed through Korea and Japan whored and drank with abandon, and the whoring and the drinking had its chroniclers.

Few men wrote of the orphanages supported by battalions, or the schools donated by divisions. Few people, perhaps not even the Koreans, will remember them. For there was never enough.

In the stinking paddies, free once more from the destructive passage of armed men across the land, the peasants sloshed in muddy water, praying to their gods that the rice might grow. In the Orient, there are no bad crop years—there are simply good harvests or disaster.

The crops of 1953 were already mortgaged, for even the Inmun Gun had not been able to find all the moneylenders. The farmers, hungry now in spring, had no hope of ever being free from debt.

The physical scars of the war in the Orient, where man had not greatly changed the face of the earth, were not long in healing.

The other scars, in the minds of men, were more difficult to see, for the Koreans, over the centuries, have learned to keep their miseries to themselves.

There were other men, this spring, who said little: small, dark-eyed, hard-bodied men who wore the uniform of the Taehan Minkuk. Of peasant stock, they had been to battle, and in subtle ways changed; they had learned to command men, and with them, respect. They had fought alongside the brash and bewildering Americans, and these men had learned many things.

Many of these small, hard men in the American-style tunics of officers of the ROK Army had been to *Mikuk*, the Beautiful Land, which the hated Japanese had called Big Rice. They had not found *Mikuk* beautiful, but scandalously empty, while they had learned to employ infantry in Georgia, and to aim cannon in Oklahoma—but they had learned that all men did not live as did those in the Hermit Kingdom.

In *Mikuk*, the Beautiful Land, it was possible for a peasant to own his own land, and to live free of crushing debt. In *Mikuk*, men of high office lived little above the commonalty, nor was it ordained that some lived as the favored of the gods, while others starved.

There were troubles in the Beautiful Land, as their American friends never tired of admitting, but men had not as yet accepted them as everlasting.

These small, hard men in new colonels' and generals' uniforms, who had come to high command when the city folk, the merchants' and officials' sons who once commanded the armies died under the blazing guns of June, had never learned to drink the whiskey-soda; they had never jokingly adopted the patronizing Western nicknames of Fat or Joe or Tiger Kim.

In *Mikuk* they had not learned golf—but unfortunately, neither had they learned the principles by which free men live. They had learned only that life could and ought to be, different from the way it was lived in the Taehan Minkuk. Someday, these men, who had learned also to command men and guns and armies, and to expect obedience, might strike to make it so, in the only way they knew.

South of the Farm Line, the granaries were low, the new crops not planted, and the waiting hard.

To the north, the waiting was also hard. Here, there were only the twill-clad hosts of the Eighth Army, making the roads rutted and dusty with their thousands of trucks. Eighth Army was firmly implanted now, its tents walled and floored with wood against the harsh seasons, its larger HQ's solidly timbered with an air of permanence. Its bright flags flew from tall poles, and the stones of its company areas were painted white.

Eighth Army had little to do, except put out more flags, and paint more pathstones, as months went by.

Still, the waiting was hard.

Still farther north, where the vehicles did not go, and the hills grew bare and dark, the waiting was hardest of all.

Here the untilled ground was dug in long furrows, and there were wire and sandbagged earth, and thousands of men lay in deep trenches and revetted bunkers.

And still farther north, among the outposts thrusting into the sullen Chinese hills, far in front of the main line of resistance, with spring at hand, men lay in cold, sleeting rain, and talked of peace.

Now and then artillery rumbled, and fire splashed the hills. Men's eyes, even while they talked of peace, kept to the north. Over there, in the black hills and misty valleys, nothing moved. The observation posts saw nothing; friendly aircraft hurtling overhead reported nothing.

Now and again, gunners fired, and in their hearts felt they fired at nothing.

Yet everyone knew that he was there—Old Joe Chink, Luke the Gook, the enemy. Unseen, he was real, massing in his deep tunnels and hollowed-out mountains. He had come before, slipping out of the night behind shrieking shell bursts, pouring into trenches and bunkers, shooting, killing.

He would come again, even while they talked of peace at Panmunjom.

* * *

On 16 April, while the eyes of the world and most of the correspondents were at Panmunjom, where the Communist side had just agreed to exchange sick and wounded POW's, the CCF struck to destroy the 7th Division's outpost line. The Chinese hit Eerie, the Arsenal, and swamped Dale.

The men on Pork Chop, an understrength company, E of the 31st Infantry, heard from the heights of enemy-held Hasakkol the wailing minors of Mongol music, the chanting with which Chinese liked to begin concerted action.

The sound was muted, as from out of deep tunnels. Listening as they ate supper, Lieutenant Thomas V. Harrold's riflemen cracked unhappy jokes. Numbering only seventy-six, they were in an extremely vulnerable place to play King of the Mountain.

The Division G-2 had word from secret line crossers of an imminent attack, and had informed Harrold. But somehow, in the inevitable mishaps of war, the word had not passed down to the outposts beyond Pork Chop.

With dark, these men strolled down to their listening posts on the outcroppings, and crouched down amid the flowering wild plums and other greenery. The night was clear, and starlit.

After 2200, two companies of heavily armed Chinese slipped out of Hasakkol and crossed the wide valley. They came on catfeet, and were onto Pork Chop, before the alarm could be given.

They broke over Easy's 1st Platoon in a wave of gunfire. Of 1st Platoon's twenty-odd men, seven survived.

Harrold fired one red flare, signifying he was under serious attack; then a second, requesting the artillery to flash Pork Chop. At 2305, 7th Divarty joined Chinese guns in firing on the hill, putting a horseshoe-like band of steel around its base, and firing proximity-fuse projectiles on top of it.

But the CCF were in the trenches and bunkers now, and close-in, hand-to-hand fighting erupted across Pork Chop.

Regiment sent two platoons to reinforce Harrold, one from Fox Company and one from Love. The Fox platoon became lost in the dark, and did not arrive; the men from Love, misunderstanding the situation, walked up the hill and came under Chinese fire. They had not understood the Chinese were already on the crest, and under surprise and shock of being taken under fire, they ran back down into the valley.

Pork Chop was overrun, but it was a maze of trenches, bunkers, and fortified positions. Harrold, and a number of his men, piling sandbags, ammunition boxes, and sleeping bags against bunker entrances and embrasures, fought the scattered parties of searching CCF off. With dawn, they were still holding, but for all practical purposes the hill had been lost.

Deep in his own bunker, Lieutenant Harrold hardly understood what had happened; the very nature of the fight had allowed him to view very little of it. From him his battalion commander had no clear picture of the situation on Pork Chop. Battalion thought the sending of one company forward to reinforce would be more than ample.

At 0330 Lieutenant Joseph Clemons, Jr., commanding K Company, was ordered to move his outfit forward just behind Pork Chop. From there he was to assault the hill, while two platoons from Love Company went up Pork Chop from the right.

From Joe Clemons' assault point, it was only 170 yards up to the fortified positions on Pork Chop—but the slope was steep, cratered, and rocky, and strung with wire.

It took King almost thirty minutes to reach the top of the ridge.

And there King's work began. The Chinese had burrowed into Pork Chop like rats, and their own artillery kept dousing the hill in regular timed patterns. In two hours the attack was carried forward only some two hundred yards, and the Americans' legs were exhausted. The length of the hill had crumbled into tumbled rubble under artillery fire, and each piece of rubble provided shelter for riflemen and grenadiers.

Meanwhile, the Love platoons, coming up on a narrow front on the right, had been chopped to pieces by the entrenched defenders on the crest. Ten men out of sixty-two who had attacked under Lieutenant Forrest Crittenden, came exhausted, under a sole surviving officer, into Joe Clemons' lines atop Pork Chop.

And by 0800 17 April, Joe Clemons was out of water and running short of both ammunition and men, a few feet away from the Chinese. The enemy was in poor shape, too, and if King Company could have mounted any kind of determined attack the Pork Chop battle would have been over—but the men remaining in King had almost no strength left. The steep Korean slopes wore men down faster than Chinese gunfire.

Shortly after eight, a few replacements came up the back slope of Pork Chop, joining Clemons' men. First Platoon, G Company, 17th Infantry, came in; the rest of George, 17th, was coming up the hill behind, under heavy artillery fire.

Clemons, seeing George's C.O., asked, "Now, what in hell are you doing here?"

The George Company commander, Lieutenant Walter Russell, was Clemons' brother-in-law, and the last Clemons had heard from him he was in the States. Russell said he had been sent to help King Company with the mop-up, and then to withdraw from the hill.

The people at Battalion and Regiment simply did not know what was going on. King, now composed of only thirty-five tired survivors, ten men from Love, and twelve men of Harrold's Easy Company rescued from the rubble, wasn't mopping up—it was trying to hold its own.

At the same time that Russell's men were struggling up the cratered slopes, a fresh Chinese company pushed onto the other end of the ridge. With fresh men on the hill, the battle suddenly blazed up again. But again, stumbling, shooting, and grenading about in the fantastic jumble of tumbled trenches, shattered bunkers, and shellholes on Pork Chop, neither side was able to make progress.

The fresh men were rapidly chewed up. The barrage fire on the hill was horrendous in weight of metal, and almost unceasing. Soon, Russell's George Company, 17th, was down to fifty-odd men.

At noon, Joe Clemons received a fantastic message from his battalion C.O., delivered by the battalion S-2, who stumbled into the bunker on Pork Chop from which Clemons was directing the battle. Clemons was ordered to send any and all survivors of Easy Company to the rear at once, and Russell was to take his company off the hill at 1500.

Exhausted, Joe Clemons told the S-2; "Take this message back. Tell them the crisis here is not appreciated by Battalion or Regiment. I have very few men; all are exhausted. Russell has only fifty-five men left. When they go out, it is not reasonable that we can hold the hill."

The S-2 went back. An hour later, while the crisis atop Pork Chop got no better, Battalion acknowledged receipt of Clemons' message—receipt, nothing more.

While men were being killed and wounded all about, elements of the battle for Pork Chop were almost ludicrous. Fifteen minutes before three, daring artillery fire, a Public Information Officer dashed into Clemons' bunker. The PIO, Lieutenant Barrows, had come up from Division with two staff photographers to write the story and get pictures of what was supposed to have been a glorious American action.

Clemons said, simply: "Forget the pictures. I want you to carry a message to Battalion." He wrote, only, *We must have help or we can't hold the hill.*

Barrows, seeing the death and destruction on Pork Chop, dashed back at once.

Again Battalion acknowledged, and nothing more.

But the battalion C.O., Colonel Davis, and Colonel Kern at 31st Regiment, this time got the message. The trouble had been simple—Clemons had sent a number of desperate messages to the rear, but he had never stated his losses.

Higher HQ had continued to believe he was fighting with a tired but still strong rifle company. With no loss figures, Division had been serenely confident of Clemons' ability to hold.

Now the balloon went up.

Still, Joe Clemons received no answer.

The answer was simple, and yet complex. A great many men had been thrown down the drain already on Pork Chop, relatively worthless, scabrous piece of earth, whose very presence in Chinese territory was a continuing affront to them. Intrinsically, Pork Chop was not worth the life of a single human being, American or ROK. And the fight was rapidly becoming another Bloody Ridge or Triangle Hill, where Americans had gone into the meat grinder at the rate of a battalion a day.

Neither Battalion nor Regiment could make the decision to throw more troops onto Pork Chop. They bucked it up to Division.

Division, which had been stopped by Max Taylor from pouring more men onto Old Baldy, was not about to accept the buck. Division recognized that if Pork Chop were let go, the CCF, encouraged, would strike for the next hill, and the next. But it could not make the decision to accept the losses that might be forthcoming. The 7th Division HQ ordered that Clemons should hold, but until it got instruction from higher up, he was to be given no help. Division HQ did not want to throw good money after bad, though they could hardly put it in such terms.

Major General Trudeau talked to I Corps by phone, then took a helicopter up close to the front, to wait in Colonel Davis' CP.

I Corps got in touch with Eighth Army. Eighth Army decided it had to talk with FECOM in Tokyo.

Pork Chop Hill was a battle of wills, and the U.N. was not winning.

At 1500, receiving no new orders, and having lost half his command in a few hours, Lieutenant Russell wished his brother-in-law luck and pulled his company back down the hill. Joe Clemons now had a total of twenty-five men left to him, of all who had climbed to Pork Chop since morning. He made a small island of defense on one of Pork Chop's knobs, and there he and his men waited, for whatever might come.

He and his men had been without water for many hours; their weapons were dirty and jammed; all were in almost trancelike exhaustion. Yet, under Clemons' command, they were still a disciplined body, and still had the will to remain. Small-arms fire plucked at them all afternoon, and the Chinese artillery sought them out. Only fourteen of these men would survive.

At about 1700, Joe Clemons, after fighting off a couple of snipers with a rifle, got on the radio to Battalion. He said, ". . . about twenty men here who are still unhit. They are completely spent. There is no fight left in this company. If we can't be relieved, we should be withdrawn."

Trudeau was in Battalion CP. Immediately he got into his copter, and flew to his phones at Division HQ. He talked to I Corps Commander Major General Bruce C. Clark. He wanted one promise: that if he threw more troops into the Pork Chop affray, the hill would not be given up at a later time.

It was at this time that the United States Army began to win its battle of wills. It might seem a nightmarish children's game, with ghastly stakes—but the United States Army was going to have to show the CCF who was King on the Hill, if it wanted success at Panmunjom.

Lieutenant Denton, of Love Company, was ordered to attack onto Pork Chop. He brought his men into Clemons' area when Clemons had just sixteen men left. And Denton, and the remnants of Love, would have as bad a time as Clemons, before the night was out.

Just before 1800, the 2/17 was attached to Colonel Kern's 31st Infantry, giving him two fresh rifle companies. Withholding E, 17th, he ordered King's Fox to assault Pork Chop and relieve Clemons. Sometime after 2100, Fox Company mounted the back slopes, and Clemons' survivors started to the rear.

Under the artillery pounding, and the desperate Chinese attempts to batter down all resistance on the hill, Fox Company was not enough. Easy, 17th Infantry, had to be committed, too.

Everywhere else along the line the front was cool. At Panmunjom prisoners were being exchanged. But around Pork Chop the life of a rifle company was measured in hours.

At dawn, Able Company, 17th Infantry, was committed.

In retrospect, both Easy and Able should have been committed earlier; the haunting fear of committing too many men, of taking too many casualties, which had begun with the terrible civilian pressure after Heartbreak, had resulted in piecemeal commitment and, ironically, more losses than were probably necessary.

For Able of the 17th, fighting beside the remnants of Fox and Easy all day of 18 April, against company after company of reinforcing Chinese, finally turned the tide.

Love, Fox, and Easy, relieving Clemons' King on the hill, each took almost as many casualties. But when the CCF finally understood that they could not have the hill—would not get it, even if they killed a thousand Americans, or fought it out all summer along this line—their assault ceased as quickly as it had begun.

After sunset 18 April, the sound of guns ceased, and the stars came out once more through the fading smoke.

The United States Army had expended more than 130,000 rounds of artillery ammunition within twenty-four hours, and had expended several hundred men. It was King on the Hill.

Sometimes the cost of games is high.

39

Cease-fire

It was very easy to start a war in Korea. It was not so easy to stop it.

—From the Russian of N. S. Khrushchev, speech before the Bulgarian Party leadership.

L ATE IN THE 1952 presidential campaign, Dwight D. Eisenhower, the Republican candidate, said, "If elected, I will go to Korea."

The effectiveness of this pledge, though it had little of promise in it, was adjudged by the agony of Eisenhower's opposition. While the pledge was immediately attacked as cheap politics, it undoubtedly swayed the votes of thousands of families with men in Korea. And it was a simple acknowledgment of a fact the incumbent Administration wished to avoid—that the Korean War was at the heart of the campaign and that its continuance under present terms was becoming politically impossible.

It was not the entrance of the United States into the war that came back now to haunt Harry Truman and his picked successor, Stevenson, but the continuing military and diplomatic standoff since 1951. The 2,500 American casualties per month the stalemate was costing were insignificant, except on the conscience of the American people.

During the last years of Napoleon's reign, his ministers calculated that the French nation could afford 100,000 casualties per month in the emperor's wars. The figures were based on the total French population, and the number of men coming of military age each year. What was not taken into account was that the French people, having left the bones of two million men from Lisbon to Moscow, were becoming completely unenthusiastic about stepping "into the breach" however valid the reasons.

Professional soldiers have been and may be used as pawns on the table of diplomacy. Impressed American citizens may not, without vast consequences. In November 1952, General Eisenhower carried the election by a landslide.

On 21 November General Clark in Tokyo received word that the President-elect was flying to Korea in early December, and wanted no receptions, diplomatic teas, and the like. He would make a tour of the front, which presented Clark with an enormous security problem. Eisenhower's movements in a hostile theater had to be kept secret as far as possible, and he must never be permitted to come within each of enemy guns.

The news of the President-elect's coming had a palpable effect on the men engaged in Korea. Ranking general and private alike, many of these men had been haunted by the sense of being forgotten. It had seemed to them that the United States was slowly adjusting to a situation in which Eighth Army held the far-off battle line forever, while life in the homeland went on as before. While public opinion was hostile to the war, there was also evidence that many people preferred to put the unpleasantness out of mind.

There was now very little of the hero's welcome for returnees of the Korean War. The American people did not quite know how to regard a war they had not won.

With news of Eisenhower's coming, generals began to speculate if soon they might be released from the restrictions that bound them to stalemate, while privates wondered if it meant they might soon go home.

Clark, who in company with most of FECOM generaldom, had felt deeply the same frustration as MacArthur, had prepared a detailed list of forces needed and planning required to achieve military victory in Korea. Clark was particularly sanguine about employing Chiang Kai-shek's idle and aging divisions on Taiwan—which had not been used primarily because of European repugnance to the idea.

Eisenhower flew into Suwon early in December 1952, bringing with him a large entourage—Charles E. Wilson, the Secretary of Defense Designate; General Omar Bradley, Chairman of the JCS; Admiral Radford, COMINPAC; Generals Ramey and Persons, Herbert Brownell, and his press secretary, Jim Hagerty.

He made a whirlwind tour of the areas in back of the battlefront, and met briefly with Syngman Rhee. He discussed very little business, and in that sense his trip seemed what his political opponents claimed—a cheap gesture, to pay off a campaign promise in even cheaper coin. But from this visit two highly significant facts stood forth.

Ike never saw Clark's list of requirements for winning the war. The matter was not even broached, and it was immediately apparent to Clark that the new Administration intended to press for an honorable peace rather than to broaden the fighting. In this sense, Eisenhower's trip seemed to solve nothing, accomplish nothing, except to inform the generals that there would be no immediate change of policy.

The other significant matter that was discussed lay buried under a cloak of security. For two years the enemy had battered the U.N. with a propaganda war, while the U.N. attempts to strike back had been somewhat fumbling. Now Eisenhower showed himself keenly interested in psychological warfare as it was being waged from Japan. For two years and more, the U.N. Command had shouted its every intention to the world—and to the enemy; now this was to change.

Eisenhower, and the men around him, rightly or wrongly, were of the opinion that the Soviet Union wanted no big war, and it was time for the United

States to take a certain amount of initiative—to keep the other side off balance, if possible. This tactic had been discussed before, and always discarded as too dangerous. Consequently, the policy had been always to tell the Communists exactly where the United States stood, while the Communists said nothing of their own intentions.

The new Administration was determined to step up the psychological pressures that could be applied to the enemy. The Communist world had many vulnerable areas. Some of these, like the captive European peoples, the Administration would find too sensitive; the United States could meddle behind the iron curtain only at the certain risk of war.

But there were other areas, such as the situation in Korea, that might be exploited. Now, certain measures were planned that would have an important bearing on the ending of the war.

While in Korea, Eisenhower was briefed by Clark on the reported ammunition shortage, which had become a major scandal in the American press. It was true that certain calibers of artillery and mortar ammunition were in short supply, and Clark had rationed them. But the line itself had never been hampered.

Part of the shortage was real. Rear-area ammunition dumps had been depleted by the unprecedented expenditure along the line; in the commendable effort to save lives American artillery had taken to hurling enormous quantities of metal during the hill battles. The barrages fired exceeded anything in either of the two world wars, and by 1953 more shells had already been fired during the limited war in Korea than in all of World War II. While the enemy had an estimated number of field guns equal to those of the U.N., it was the American volume of fire, hurled without stint or counting, and its superior placement, that enabled the U.N. to win almost all the hill battles from Heartbreak to Pork Chop.

The rest of the shortage lay in mismanagement by FECOM ordnance. A new ordnance officer was installed; accounting methods were improved; shipments from the States speeded up, and front-line troops ordered not to discuss any restrictions with reporters—and the question of the ammunition shortage died a natural death, while some divisions went on burning up as many as ten thousand rounds per night.

The briefings and discussions ended, Ike flew home; Christmas came. The war went on as before, and the expectations of troops and generals dulled.

But everywhere new pressures were mounting, and events were marching toward conclusions.

* * *

While hills along the uneasy battle line were disputed, now in the eastern mountains, now in the Marine zone near the estuary of the Imjin on the west, the American people's impatience with the war was matched in other places. And the impatience was colored by rising fear, for the longer the guns in Korea exploded, the greater the danger of a bigger conflict. The smaller countries of the U.N. had never ceased to explore ways out of the prisoner-of-war deadlock.

It was a difficult task. Steadfastly, the United States refused to order men to return to tyranny at gunpoint; here the moral issue was clear-cut. And just as adamantly, the Red Chinese and North Koreans declined to accept anything less than full repatriation.

This was the only deadlock preventing truce. The other questions, such as unification of Korea, and guarantees of its independence, the U.N. had put by the board in its resolution of February 1951, when it was decided that these problems were to be solved "through peaceful means" at a conveniently unspecified time following cease-fire.

At first, owing to the extravagant claims of Nam Il and the Communist leadership at Panmunjom, world opinion had remained confused on the POW issue. Among the neutrals, particularly, there had been much doubt that the United States told the truth, that there had been no coercion used on the POW's at the time the prisoners were rioting by the thousands on Koje. If a mass breakout had occurred, the United States would never have been able to convince these peoples of its truthfulness and morality.

But with the POW's under tighter control, and inspected by neutral teams, the truth of the American position slowly became self-evident.

And inevitably, from the time Haydon Boatner had control of U.N. POW Camp 1, the Communists began to lose the POW propaganda war. After all, their camps had never been opened to anyone, including the Red Cross.

Whether the Communists could publicly admit that many of their captured soldiers refused repatriation or not, the world was becoming aware of it. And more and more of the world, from Mexico to India, was becoming annoyed at Communist intransigence.

In November 1952, Indian Delegate V. K. Krishna Menon, avowedly no friend of the United States, proposed to the U.N. that the POW's of both sides be released to a neutral repatriation commission completely outside the control of either combatant, in agreed numbers and at agreed exchange points in Korean demilitarized zones. The commission would screen them, and if there were any POW's whose return was not provided for, these should then become the responsibility of the U.N.

The proposal was greeted with anger by the Communist side.

In December, with slight modifications, it was passed as a resolution by the U.N. Lester Pearson of Canada, Assembly President, presented the resolution to China and North Korea, requesting their acceptance in order to facilitate "a constructive and durable peace in Korea."

The two Communist governments termed the proposal "illegal, unfair, and unreasonable," and promptly rejected it.

South Korea, which was holding a large number of now decidedly anti-Communist POW's, also angrily denounced the Indian resolution.

The United States was cautiously—it had no great trust in Menon—agreeable.

Now the Communists, who cried over and over again their fervent desire for peace, were increasingly being backed into a corner in which it was apparent they preferred continued bloodshed to a propaganda defeat—and in so doing they were getting the defeat anyway.

Trygve Lie, U.N. Secretary General, stated publicly that it seemed those who had commenced the aggression in Korea were simply not willing to end it. He was widely quoted.

In late 1952, world opinion, for whatever it was worth, was turning slowly but definitely against the North Koreans and Red Chinese. Continued fighting by these nations could only intensify the swing.

* * *

When Eisenhower departed the Far East in December, General Clark was certain that the new Administration would opt for a negotiated peace rather than intensified war. Shortly after the inauguration, he was formally notified to this effect.

Then, on 19 February, he was advised by the Joint Chiefs of Staff that on 13 December 1952 the Executive Committee of the League of Red Cross Societies meeting in Geneva had voted fifteen to two that sick and wounded POW's of the Korean War be exchanged even before a truce was negotiated. Only Red China and Russia opposed, and the JCS understood that a similar resolution was pending before the U.N. With concurrence from the State Department, they urged Clark to put such a proposal before the enemy, in advance of the U.N. action.

This very thing had been proposed by the U.N. Command in December 1951; the Communists had rejected it.

On 22 February 1953, Clark wrote to premier Kim Il Sung of North Korea, and to Peng Teh-huai of the Chinese Volunteers: . . . *The United Nations Command remains immediately ready to repatriate those seriously sick and seriously wounded captured personnel who are fit to travel in accordance with provisions of Article 109 of the Geneva Convention. I wish to be informed whether you are prepared for your part to proceed immediately with the repatriation of seriously sick and wounded personnel. . . . The United Nations Command liaison officers will be prepared to meet your liaison officers to make necessary arrangements.*

The appeal was delivered through Panmunjom. For thirty-six days there was no reply.

During the first months of 1953, as the propaganda war began to turn against the Red Chinese, other pressures, both subtle and unsubtle, began to make themselves felt in Communist capitals.

Communist leaders, without success, had tried to assess the meaning of the American change of Administration. During 1952 it had been the Republican leadership that had cried the loudest for direct action against the Communists—which had threatened, in one way or another—the loosing of the lightning against the transgressor. It had been largely Republicans who proposed Douglas MacArthur for the Presidency; it had been largely Republicans who seemed to support him in the Congress.

Now the Republicans, a general, at their head, were in power. And generals were as worrisome to the Kremlin, in one way, as they were to Capitol Hill, for the Communist leadership was essentially civilian. It had occurred to the Communist leaders, too, that generals were much more likely to regard war as inevitable than either politicians or diplomats.

The Communist ruling circles knew that General MacArthur, oddly, had been idolized by the American "millionaire ruling cliques" and supported by Senator Taft, who was certainly at the very center of those cliques—and Communist rulers were now trapped by their own mythology, which they tended to believe more than the West gave them credit for. It was Communist dogma that capitalists desire war in search of profits, ignoring the fact that in any Western nation the wealthy probably wanted war less than any other group—since wars normally bring social upheaval.

It may have been, in 1953, that the Republican leadership didn't know exactly what it was going to do about the Korean War. So far, it had not exactly enlightened the American people. But, more important, it had failed to enlighten the Communist world, too, and the Communist world, just now developing new problems, was deeply concerned, and far from convinced that the United States, in a fit of frustration, would not strike out.

Certain pressures out of Tokyo fell on receptive ground.

In Nevada, at Frenchman's Flat, a bright flash and ugly mushroom cloud had signified a gigantic change in the tactical battlefield—a change that had not come about at Hiroshima, despite statements to the contrary. In its early years the atomic device had remained a strategic weapon, suitable for delivery against cities and industries, suitable to obliterate civilians, men, women, and children by the millions, but of no practical use on a limited battlefield—until it was fired from a field gun.

Until this time, 1953, the armies of the world, including that of the United States, had hardly taken the advent of fissionable material into account. The 280mm gun, an interim weapon that would remain in use only a few years, changed all that, forever. With an atomic cannon that could deliver tactical fires in the low-kiloton range, with great selectivity, ground warfare stood on the brink of its greatest change since the advent of firepower.

The atomic cannon could blow any existing fortification, even one twenty thousand yards in depth, out of existence neatly and selectively, along with the battalions that manned it. Any concentration of manpower, also, was its meat.

It spelled the doom of Communist massed armies, which opposed superior firepower with numbers, and which had in 1953 no tactical nuclear weapons of their own.

The 280mm gun was shipped to the Far East. Then, in great secrecy, atomic warheads—it could fire either nuclear or conventional rounds—followed, not to Korea, but to storage close by. And with even greater secrecy, word of this shipment was allowed to fall into Communist hands.

At the same time, into Communist hands wafted a pervasive rumor, one they could neither completely verify nor scotch: that the United States would not accept a stalemate beyond the end of summer.

The psychological pressures on Chinese Intelligence became enormous. Neither an evaluative nor a collective agency, even when it feels it is being taken, dares ignore evidence.

China, losing the propaganda war, had yet gained tremendous prestige on the Korean battlefield. It had engaged the armies of the West and seemingly fought them to a standstill; it had leaped into great-power status in the Orient in a day. But if the United States threw the weight of its industrial and nuclear power onto the scales, power which so far it had held back, the Chinese gains could vanish even more quickly.

While they still spoke boastfully, in the frozen gardens of Peiping there were men who worried. In addition to military concerns, it had been a bad year economically from the Elbe to the Yalu; in many areas harvests were light, spelling trouble in the months to come.

On 5 March 1953 Joseph Stalin died. And because Stalin, like all dictators, had never really dared plan for his own succession but had systematically destroyed anyone seemingly capable of replacing him, the monolithic structure of Russian Communism was doomed.

Before Stalin was eulogized and in his tomb, the struggle for power within the Kremlin began. Before it was over, far in the future, the foundations of the Soviet state would be shaken to their roots.

And with the news, the satellite states, plagued with shortages and famine, suddenly hopeful, seethed with revolt. In East Germany, restlessness would result in open defiance before summer.

The Soviet state could survive both internal power struggles and satellite revolt, but all factions within the Kremlin had no time now for foreign adventures. For a certain length of time, Russia, still not recovered from the ravages of the Second World War but pushed on by Stalin's steel will, would require a respite, for the steel will was gone.

On 6 March 1953, it was time for the sound of the dove in the land, and the invention of the Peace Offensive.

It was time, now, to tempt fate no longer, and to place certain subtle but unmistakable pressures on the Chinese comrades, who, though concerned, still hated to give up a good thing.

Many things, joined together, now moved the world toward great events. In the spring of 1953, the leaders of the United States and the non-Communist world wanted peace. The Communist leadership desperately needed it.

Suddenly, ironically, there was a community of interest in the world, however fleeting it might be.

In the middle of the night in Tokyo, 28 March 1953, Wayne Clark was called out of bed to receive a message from Peng Teh-huai and Kim Il Sung. As Clark groggily scanned the message, replete with the usual Communist complaint, abuse, and prevarication, one paragraph suddenly stood out.

Peng and Kim not only agreed that exchange of sick and wounded POW's was a good idea; they suggested that the plenary sessions at Panmunjom, in permanent recess since 8 October, be resumed at once.

Excited, but with much skepticism, Clark pushed the buttons that made it so. More than anything else, he was wondering what new trick the Communists had up their sleeve.

But on 30 March, Chou En-lai, Foreign Minister of Red China, announced publicly that China and North Korea might accept the idea of a neutral repatriation commission for the screening of all POW's.

At Panmunjom the liaison officers from the north suddenly exhibited an interest in progress never heretofore shown.

President Eisenhower said in Washington that the United States would accept every Communist offer at face value "until it was proved unworthy of our confidence." It was at this time that certain Communist leaders, who had been deeply concerned, began to wonder if Dwight Eisenhower might not genuinely be a man of peace. But the die was cast; in their secret conclaves the decision had already been made. The Communist world would try to salvage as much from Korea as they might, but they would withdraw. The adventure was over.

Because of the Communist salvage operations, the end would not come suddenly, but gradually. Men would still die on the gloomy hills, and fighting would still go on, while the Communists stubbornly tried to gain what they could from the POW debacle, for the Communists could never completely forego testing an opponent's will.

On 11 April, both sides agreed on terms for the exchange of sick and wounded captives. The U.N. would return 5,800; the Communists only 684: 471 ROK's, 149 Americans, and 64 from other nations.

For the first time, Americans had concrete evidence that not all of the 8,000 men they had lost into Communist captivity would return home. They did not yet understand the sickening fact that 58 percent of their men had perished in the dreary camps along the Yalu—and when they did, the moves toward peace were already far advanced, and no disclosures of atrocities could delay them.

Around the world, the hopes for a genuine peace rose. Newsmen flocked to Korea as they had not done since the summer of 1950. And it was while the hopes were highest, and newsmen gathered outside the demilitarized zone, that the Chinese tested the United States for the last time on Pork Chop, and made the dying there doubly cruel.

On 20 April, when Pork Chop had hardly cooled, Operation Little Switch began; the American sick and wounded came home, as Americans thought. It was only later, much after 26 April, when the exchanges ended, that Americans learned that the enemy had not played fair—many of the men exchanged on Little Switch were not hardship cases but those amenable to the Chinese, the "collaborators," whom the Communists expected to give a favorable picture of their captivity on return.

After the waves of sentimentality that poured from the press, any future attempts at wholesale punishment of these weaker prisoners was compromised at the start. The Chinese gambit was highly successful. The American public, understandably, gave its immediate forgiveness to the "sick and wounded," and rightly or wrongly, the military forces could not muster public support for harsh measures against those they claimed had been guilty of misconduct behind the wire.

The day after Little Switch ended, 27 April 1953, negotiations to end the fighting began in earnest. The Communists submitted a six-point proposal, the main points of which were:

1. All POW's desiring repatriation would be returned home two months following an armistice.

2. One month later, all others would be sent to a neutral state, where for a period of six months agents of their home countries would be allowed to make explanations to them.

3. Captives asking for repatriation from the neutral country would be released immediately.

4. If any POW's remained at the end of six months, the question of their disposal would be submitted to the political conference that was to follow the armistice.

May 1953 was spent in arguing modifications of the above—the United Nations wanted strict time limitations—and hammering out the selection of nations that might sit on the neutral commission. Late in the month the enemy became more active all along the line, but concentrated on non-American units. Several outposts were lost.

In June, the plenary sessions went into secret meetings, while the enemy launched 104 separate attacks on the U.N. lines, and 131,800 rounds of artillery fell on U.N. lines during a single day. During June, and later in July, the heaviest attacks and fire the enemy had launched in two years crashed against the front, and American opinion was divided. Some felt the Communists were out to wreck the peace talks; others thought they were merely firing up their painfully hoarded ammunition supplies before a truce was signed.

On 4 June the Communists effectively agreed to all major American counterproposals. The way had not been easy; they had fought a rear-guard action all the way, disputing each small point.

In final form, the POW question was settled as follows:

1. Within two months, each side, without hindrance, would repatriate all POW's desiring return.

2. A neutral commission would be set up within the demilitarized zone to accept custody of POW's of each side refusing to return. The commission and the POW's would be guarded by Indian troops.

3. Explanations might be made to reluctant POW's by agents of each side for a period of ninety days, then,

4. For thirty days, while the POW's continued in Indian custody, a conference would try to settle the eventual disposition of any who still refused to go home.

5. At the expiration of this time, any POW for whom no provision had been made would be released to civilian status.

6. The International Red Cross would assist those released to find new homes, if no other provisions had been made.

Now, with the Communists and the U.N. in agreement, only the Republic of Korea and aging Syngman Rhee stood in the way of armistice. And during the days of June, Syngman Rhee alternated between despair and defiance.

Emotionally and politically, Syngman Rhee could not accept the armistice terms. They left his nation and people divided; they left a million South Koreans dead seemingly in vain. Americans who grew bitter at old Syngman Rhee during these days, when it seemed he might wreck the peace, should have been able to imagine what Abraham Lincoln would have felt, or done, had Britain and France imposed an armistice upon the United States in 1863, leaving it forcibly divided, perhaps forever.

The tragedy of Syngman Rhee and the Taehan Minkuk was simple—while they could not go on fighting without American support, acceptance of the truce doomed the Korean people to permanent division, and the Taehan Minkuk to continued existence as a rump state, permanently incapable of supporting itself economically.

Every American pressure, from cajolery to blunt talk, was used to make Syngman Rhee come around. Rhee continued the same refrain in reply: Never, never, never.

Then, on 18 June, Rhee almost destroyed the armistice. He removed South Korean troops from Clark's command, and ordered the release of 27,000 anti-Communist Korean POW's held in camps in the Pusan area. Most of these POW's melted immediately into the Korean population, and many, inducted into the ROK Army, came back as guards for the few who had not escaped.

In Korea, American guards whose heads had been kept down by South Korean fire while the POW's broke out, as at Camp Number 5, Wonju, regarded the release as a big joke. Shortly after the mass uproar at Wonju, when thousands of POW's had run out, South Koreans and American sergeants threw a big party, using up the stock of the N.C.O. club.

But in Washington, for a time, there was consternation. Criticism of Rhee poured in from all over the world. The Communists screamed in self-righteous agony, even though none of the men released would have ever been returned to them. And the Communists asked some very disturbing questions: Could the United States control its Korean ally if Syngman Rhee refused to accept truce?

But, significantly, the Communists directed their anger and propaganda diatribes not at the United States but at the "murderer Rhee." They still wanted cease-fire.

Walter S. Robertson, Assistant Secretary of State for Far Eastern Affairs, was dispatched by the President to Seoul. He arrived in the Korean capital 25 June 1953, the third anniversary of the Communist invasion, and across every thoroughfare Walt Robertson saw antiarmistice streamers and printed slogans. Many of them cried, *Don't sell Korea,* in English.

Thousands of demonstrators, on order of the ROK Government, poured through the streets. They shouted *"Puk chin! Puk chin!*—Go north!"

Outside the correspondents' quarters, hundreds of schoolgirls sat in the dirt, and wept.

For twelve days Robertson and Rhee engaged in what came to be called the Little Truce Talks. For the United States now had to make peace also with its Korean ally. And the Taehan Minkuk's price was high, despite the fact that it had no hope of going north without the United States Army, and that the United States could sell it or not, regardless of how its young women wept.

However painful, Korea, a helpless nation, had to accept the fact that it was to be the principal loser of the Korean War. But in return Rhee got the promise of a U.S.–ROK Mutual Security Treaty, agreement to expand the ROK Army to twenty divisions, at American expense, and long-term economic aid, with a down payment of $200,000,000 and 10,000,000 pounds of food, worth $9,500,000, at once.

In exchange for peace along the parallel, the United States agreed to accept the Republic of Korea as its ward, perhaps forever. For without the United States the Taehan Minkuk could not exist.

In exchange, Syngman Rhee agreed not to obstruct the armistice. He would not sign—nor did South Korea ever ratify the eventual agreement—but he would now support a cease-fire.

While Robertson and Rhee bargained, the Chinese, angered, threw vicious pressure against the line, at a cost to the U.N. of nine hundred casualties per day. A massive offensive crashed against the ROK zones, rendering two ROK divisions unfit for further combat, though the fixed position of Chinese artillery, buried underground, and the quick maneuver of American divisions in support stopped any hope of a CCF breakthrough.

Though the pressure was against the ROK's, American and other U.N. units were caught in the backwash. American artillery units supporting the ROK's were overrun; American tankers with ROK infantry were lost in a Chinese sea. These men, those who survived, would never afterward be admirers of President Rhee.

But the CCF had proved its point, and perhaps taught the ROK's a lasting lesson—without outside aid, the Republic of Korea not only could not mount an offensive; it could not even hold its own frontier.

In this way, with the battlefront ablaze, with most Americans, the scent of peace entrancingly before them, uncaring of the gaping losses inflicted on the ROK's, the final negotiations went forward. The United Nations on 19 July gave the Communist powers solemn assurance that the Republic of Korea would not upset the terms already agreed upon.

Along the weary battle line, green and hot now with the midsummer of 1953, U.N. troops licked their wounds and wondered if they dared hope. A hundred times in two years the peace rumors had waxed strong; a hundred times they had been cruelly dashed. And while they wondered, the big guns continued to flame.

But the talking was done. Each side had accepted a situation that was virtually unchanged from what it had been on 11 July 1951, a truce line upon which they had agreed 27 November 1951, and a POW question that they had settled on 4 June 1953, after each of which dates thousands of men, on either side, had continued to be maimed and killed.

Each side had, perhaps, learned something: the Communists, that the will of free men is not easily broken, even when they are of peaceful intent; the West, that the Communist world holds human life cheaply, if there is aught to be gained.

For that knowledge, and little else, many men, of all nations, had died.

On Monday, 27 July 1953, Lieutenant General William K. Harrison, of the United Nations Command, and Nam Il, of North Korea, entered the wooden building the Communists had erected at Panmunjom during the long 1952 recess, from which the Picasso doves had been removed at U.N. demand. At 1001 they signed the first of eighteen documents prepared by each side. It took them twelve minutes to sign them all. Then, each man got up and left the building, without speaking.

Later, the documents, in English, Chinese, and Korean, were signed by Kim Il Sung, Peng Teh-huai, and Mark Wayne Clark.

Wayne Clark, putting away the golden pen the Parker Company had sent him specially for the signing, said: "I cannot find it in me to exult in the hour. . . . If we extract hope from this occasion, it must be diluted with recognition that our salvation requires unrelaxing vigilance and effort."

Now, to the units along the line came the words, "Shoot 'em up, boys—it's done!"

In a burst of wild enthusiasm—yet restrained, in many men, as it was in General Clark, by a certain sadness—the U.N. units burned up what ammunition they had on the ground.

For the last time—all men hoped—the dark Korean hills rocked with flame and noise.

Then, twelve hours after the pens scratched at Panmunjom, the hills lay quiet. At sea ships put back from the cold gray waters off North Korea, and the silvery aircraft stood silent on their fields.

There was no more war—but there was no peace. There was no victory.

It was called cease-fire.

*   *   *

At Prisoner Camp Number 4, Wewan, Sergeant Charles Schlichter had been handling sick call for POW Company 1 since August 1952. He had Turks, British, French, Niseis, and Puerto Ricans, with all of whom, in varying degrees, he had made friends.

With some of the Turks, especially Beli Hassan, and Hilmi Andranali, the sergeant who interpreted for him with the Turks, while Schlichter spoke to the Chinese doctors in English, he became very friendly.

He could never fail to admire the iron discipline and fierce pride the Turks exhibited in the face of the CCF. Years later he would still correspond with some of these men, and from both the Turkish and British governments he would receive commendations for his work with their nationals.

As the days went by, as each morning Turks came in to greet him gravely with, "*Nasa-san, Akadash*"—How are you, my friend?—it seemed that captivity would never end. There was no news—but living conditions had improved. Gradually, the Chinese were fattening the POW's up; most of whom were now approaching good health. Most of the POW's felt there must be a reason, and the reason had to be good.

Schlichter could not know that in California an officer had called on his wife to offer her Schlichter's GI insurance benefit, and his death gratuities. Schlichter had been listed as missing in action for two years, and the government was willing to pay. In tears, Elizabeth Schlichter refused.

She told the officer that her husband had told her to stay where he had left her, that no matter what, he would come back. In the absence of everything else, she had only this to cling to. Somehow, alone of all those who had known him, she would not believe him dead.

But suddenly, in April 1953, a number of prisoners were selected to be repatriated, on Little Switch. These were supposed to be the sick and lame, on each side—but the Communists selected mainly men who had no right to go out on those terms; a large number of them were "collaborators."

It was Communist policy to hold the "reactionaries"—of which Schlichter was one—to the last.

Schlichter and most of the men at Wewan knew nothing of what was happening at Panmunjom, and elsewhere, that long spring and summer of 1953.

And then, suddenly, out of a clear sky, they were told, "You're moving." They were taken south to a large collecting point, where hundreds of U.N. prisoners of war were being gathered.

Schlichter saw truckload after truckload of men hauled south from the collecting point—but he was told nothing.

On 6 September 1953, in the morning, he and the men about him were ordered to board a truck. One man suddenly had an intense anxiety reaction; he shouted and broke into a run, and ran headlong into a pole, knocking himself out.

Schlichter asked an English-speaking Chinese doctor to help this man. It was only when the Chinese shrugged and said his own people would take care of him that Schlichter realized what was coming.

He could never adequately describe how he felt when he knew he was going home.

At 1100 his truck pulled up at Panmunjom, the last convoy of American POW's to be exchanged. A huge, moustached Marine master sergeant walked up beside the truck, called out: "I will call out your last name. You will answer with your first name, middle initial, and Army serial number—"

"Schlichter!"

Schlichter barked out his response, and stepped down.

"Sergeant," the big Marine said gravely, "glad to have you home."

"Fella, you don't know how glad *I* am," Schlichter said.

One by one, the last 160 American POW's passed through Panmunjom. These were all men who had been marked as "war criminals" by the enemy— and each of these criminals, before he went on to the tables of fruit juice, milk, and ice cream, glittering in the background, in one way or another, on his knees or otherwise, thanked God that he had returned.

General Mark W. Clark was there to greet them.

In this way, Sergeant Charles B. Schlichter, United States Army, returned home. He had done his job. It had taken him 1,010 days to do it.

On 23 September 1953, with the Korean War already largely forgotten by the people, Schlichter's ship lay just outside San Francisco harbor. It was a cold and dreary day, the Pacific fog thick. But the POW's returning home crowded the decks, straining to see.

Then the Master's voice boomed over the horn: "Gentlemen, if you will all look forward, you will see something you never thought to see again—"

And the fog rolled back, and they saw the Golden Gate.

There was an Air Force band on the dock, playing "God Bless America." Men who had spent a thousand days and nights in Communist prison camps did not think it was corny. Every man Charles Schlichter could see through his own misty eyes was crying.

The whistles blew, and the band whumped and boomed, and on the dock he saw Elizabeth.

Some men, no matter how fate deals with them, are fortunate.

As the truce terms provided, within ninety days of cease-fire all POW's had to be screened and repatriated, or otherwise disposed of. After Big Switch was officially finished, evidence in American hands indicated that the Communists still held 3,404 POW's, 944 of which were Americans.

The Chinese said they would not repatriate 320, for various reasons. And for various reasons, twenty-three Americans chose to stay with their captors. In neither case was the American Government able to do anything.

Of the 132,000 Korean and Chinese military POW's taken by the U.N. fewer than 90,000 chose to return home. The Koreans were settled in the Taehan Minkuk, and some 13,000 Chinese went singing and chanting to Taiwan.

Each Chinese or Korean POW who refused repatriation was screened by a neutral commission at Freedom Village, Panmunjom, and his own people allowed to persuade him, while the Indian Army stood guard.

Watching the Communist tactics, the Indian Army became decidedly anti-Communist, whatever the notions of its government. The Indians had to fly in and out of the Demilitarized Zone—causing the U.N. Command considerable difficulty—since Syngman Rhee refused to allow one Indian soldier to set foot on South Korean soil.

Among the thousands of Communist POW's on Koje-do had been 474 North Korean female personnel, and the girls had been among the worst of the lot. At about the time Charles Schlichter and his comrades were coming home, these women were put on a South Korean train and sent north to Freedom Village for repatriation. On the way, they broke out Communist flags, and screamed and yelled at the gaping South Koreans alongside the tracks.

As they neared Panmunjom, they began to tear off their capitalist-made and imperialist-issued clothing, to return home in Communist purity. Then they screamed and shrieked and ripped and tore up the train seats. They urinated on what they could not destroy.

Finally, before they got off the train, a number of them defecated in the aisles. Men, and women, come home in different ways.

＊　＊　＊

From the silty Yellow Sea, on the west, to the cold gray waters of the Sea of Japan, on the east, the armies facing each other along the line of contact each withdrew two kilometers to establish the agreed demilitarized zone.

As the U.N. withdrew, its storied hills—scabrous Baldy, torn Pork Chop, Bloody, Heartbreak, Sniper, Arrowhead, White Horse, Kelly, Nori, The Hook, Gibraltar, and a hundred more—drenched in blood, hallowed by human courage, were abandoned. They lay in no man's land, blasted and reeking symbols of man's interminable collision with man. No monuments would mark them, and no pilgrims would visit their rubbled graveyards.

With another spring, or perhaps two, the pine and forsythia and wild plum might grow on them once more, thrusting upward green and fresh from the rusting rubble of wire, shards of shells, and moldering bones.

Except by the men who fought on them, they would be soon forgotten.

To the north of these hills the truce, hardly signed, had already been violated. New men, new arms, new modern aircraft poured across the Yalu, to new fortified bases deep within the mountains. No man knew when they might be used.

To the south, many men—only a few Americans, now, and many Koreans—stood uneasy watch, on a forgotten vigil whose end could not be foreseen. The Korean War, never declared, never ended.

More than two million human beings had died, forty thousand of them American soldiers and airmen, in what was a skirmish, nothing more. Nothing had been won, nothing gained—except that the far frontier had been held.

At a great price, a little time had been bought. The free peoples of the world might use it badly or well, as they saw fit.

40

Lessons

And ye shall hear of wars and rumours of wars: see that ye be not troubled:
for all these things must come to pass, but the end is not yet.
—Matthew, 24:6.

T HE KOREAN WAR ended inconclusively on 27 July 1953. Not until long
afterward was it even dignified by the name of war—the governmental
euphemism was Korean conflict—and it rapidly became the most forgotten war in American history. There was little in it, from near-disastrous
beginning to honorable but frustrating end, that appealed to American sensi-
bilities. Because they cannot look back on it with any sense of satisfaction, or
even the haunted pride that a defeated nation sometimes finds, Americans
prefer not to look back at all.

Yet men forget, as always, at their peril.

There have been millions of words written about the cold war, Communist-
Western competition, and Korea. Perhaps, as Major Hanson Baldwin wrote:

> *The angry voices speaking shrilly in the land—the carping arguments of*
> *men who contend the war was lost and of other men who term Korea "victo-*
> *ry"—will pass away. But the deeds of those who fought, the men who died*
> *and those who lived, beget their own posterity. Arguments and objectives,*
> *grand strategy and national policy, even Korea as a fork in the road of histo-*
> *ry, may come to have, in future generations, less meaning than the human*
> *drama of life and death in the stinking valleys and denuded hills of a penin-*
> *sula where wars have raged since man first raised fist to man.*

Somehow, the fateful moments when Task Force Smith first sighted the ominous approach of a powerful enemy from its green wet hills through the Korean
rain, or when the 5th and 7th Marines understood that they were cut off and
surrounded at frozen Yudam-ni or when General Matthew B. Ridgway asked
MacArthur if he had permission to attack "if things seemed right"—these

moments of life and death and human drama have more historic significance than all the words spoken in Cabinet, all the long communiqués, all the painful hammering out of the policy of containment.

For every time a nation or a people commits its sons to combat, it inevitably commits its full prestige, its hopes for the future, and the continuance of its way of life, whatever it may be. If the United States ground forces had not eventually held in Korea, Americans would have been faced with two choices: holocaust or humiliation. General, atomic war, in a last desperate attempt to save the game, would have gained Americans none of the things they seek in this world; humiliating defeat and withdrawal from Korea would have inevitably surrendered Asia to a Communist surge, destroying forever American hopes for a free and ordered society across the world.

A nation that does not prepare for all the forms of war should then renounce the use of war in national policy. A people that does not prepare to fight should then be morally prepared to surrender. To fail to prepare soldiers and citizens for limited, bloody ground action, and then to engage in it, is folly verging on the criminal.

This, from the scamper at Osan to the bloody withdrawal from the Ch'ongch'on to the heroic resistance at Chipyong-ni, the Imjin, the Soyang, and Pork Chop Hill, is a lesson Americans and others must take from Korea.

Because the Korean War was not, as most large wars were, the end of an era, but only a bloody skirmish in the middle of the post–World War II age, no definitive history can yet be written. The principal figures of the Korean War are still living, and many are still in power. The game still goes on.

Yet Korea set certain patterns for the future.

The Communist powers, notably Soviet Russia, would remember the rapid escalation from a small, almost civil-type conflict into a large-scale action involving most of the major powers of the world. After Korea, overt, brutal armed aggression, which had produced so violent—and unexpected—a counteraction from the West, would be avoided. Now the emphasis would be on infiltration, subversion, and insurgency to gain Communist ends in the fringe areas; the trick was never again, as with the South Korean invasion, to give the West a clear moral issue.

Communist planners, studying the lessons of Korea, could not help wondering what the result might have been could they have slipped several North Korean divisions into the South clandestinely, keeping them supplied across a fluid border. They might well wonder if the West would have then sprung to the defense of autocratic old Dr. Syngman Rhee, even though the interests of the West were equally imperiled.

The Red Chinese, impervious to human loss and suffering, gloried in their sudden leap to large-power status—for by defying the United Nations, and holding the Western armies in check, they became a great power in the East. They learned many of the lessons of modern ground warfare, and proved that Chinese armies could perform creditably in the field. They, more than the Soviets, would be eager to try again, for they had less to lose; but they still could not move without their industrial ally's aid and consent.

Neither power would desire general war, for both were realists, not perhaps in what they say, but in what they do.

They were balked, not defeated. Inevitably, they would try again, if not Korea, elsewhere. Within a year after Korean fighting ended, they would succeed in Vietnam, this time without overt aggression.

From the Korean War the United States drew troubled conclusions. American policy had been to contain Communism along the parallel, and in this, American policy succeeded. But not one realized, at the beginning, how exceedingly costly such containment would be. The war reaffirmed in American minds the distaste for land warfare on the continent of Asia, the avoidance of which has always been a foundation of United States policy. But the war proved that containment in Asia could not be forged with nuclear bombs and that threats were not enough, unless the United States intended to answer a Communist pinprick with general holocaust.

Yet the American people, Army, and leaders generally proved unwilling to accept wars of policy in lieu of crusades against Communism. Innocence had been lost, but the loss was denied. The government that had ordered troops into Korea knew that the issue was never whether Syngman Rhee was right or wrong but that his loss would adversely affect the status of the United States—which was not arguable.

That government's inability to communicate, and its repudiation at the polls, firmly convinced many men of the political dangers of committing American ground troops in wars of containment. Yet without the continual employment of limited force around the globe, or even with it, there was to be no order. The world could not be policed with ships, planes, and bombs—policemen were also needed.

Less than a year after fighting ended in Korea, Vietnam was lost to the West, largely because of the complete repugnance of Americans toward committing a quarter of a million ground troops in another apparently indecisive skirmish with Communism. Even more important, the United States, as the Joint Chiefs of Staff reported, simply did not have the troops.

Korea, from Task Force Smith at Osan to the last days at Pork Chop, indicates that the policy of containment cannot be implemented without professional legions. Yet every democratic government is reluctant to face the fact. Reservists and citizen-soldiers stand ready, in every free nation, to stand to the colors and die in holocaust, the big war. Reservists and citizen-soldiers remain utterly reluctant to stand and die in anything less. None want to serve on the far frontiers, or to maintain lonely, dangerous vigils on the periphery of Asia. There has been every indication that mass call-ups for cold war moves may result in mass disaffection.

The United States will be forced to fight wars of policy during the balance of the century. This is inevitable, since the world is seething with disaffection and revolt, which, however justified and merited, plays into Communist hands, and swings the world balance ever their way. Military force alone cannot possibly solve the problem—but without the application of some military force certain areas, such as Southeast Asia, will inevitably be lost.

However repugnant the idea is to liberal societies, the man who will willingly defend the free world in the fringe areas is not the responsible citizen-soldier. The man who will go where his colors go, without asking, who will fight a phantom foe in jungle and mountain range, without counting, and who will suffer and die in the midst of incredible hardship, without complaint, is still what he has always been, from Imperial Rome to sceptered Britain to democratic America. He is the stuff of which legions are made.

His pride is in his colors and his regiment, his training hard and thorough and coldly realistic, to fit him for what he must face, and his obedience is to his orders. As a legionary, he held the gates of civilization for the classical world; as a bluecoated horseman he swept the Indians from the Plains; he has been called United States Marine. He does the jobs—the utterly necessary jobs—no militia is willing to do. His task is moral or immoral according to the orders that send him forth. It is inevitable, since men compete.

Since the dawn of time, men have competed with each other—with clubs, crossbows, or cannon, dollars, ballots, and trading stamps. Much of mankind, of course, abhors competition, and these remain the acted upon, not the actors.

Anyone who says there will be no competition in the future simply does not understand the nature of man.

The great dilemma of our time is that, with two great power blocs in the world, each utterly distrustful of the other, and one, at least, eager to compete, we cannot compete with thermonuclear weapons. Competition, after all, is controlled action or controlled violence for an end, and nuclear weapons do not lend themselves to control. And in nuclear war there is apparently no prize, even for first place.

Yet men must compete.

It is still possible that one or both segments of mankind will embark upon what will be the last crusade. It is much more likely that they will collide again on lesser scale, as they have before. But even on a lesser scale the game can be lost, or won.

We can lose the game not only because of the nature of our enemies, but because of our own. We understand we cannot ignore the competition, and realize with frustration that we cannot end it by putting our competitor out of business with a bang, but we will not willingly face the fact that we may walk along the chasm, beset by tigers, for many years to come.

There will be more threats in fringe areas, like Korea, because Communist doctrine demands them. Here ends and even morality will be vague. There will be no cheap, easy, or popular answers to these threats. We may have the choice of limited, controlled violence for temporary ends—or of blowing the whistle on the game—and with the game, possibly mankind.

The enemy is no superman, as was proved on Pork Chop Hill. Anything he can do, we can do better—if we have the will. At Pork Chop men said we played the enemy game, not our own—but from Saigon to Berlin the enemy game may be the only one in town.

Korea showed, or should have shown, that all is not easy in this world, that for the rest of this century things may not get better but will probably get worse, and to talk despairingly of going up in smoke or frying in hard radiation is no answer. If the free nations want a certain kind of world, they will have to fight for it, with courage, money, diplomacy—and legions.

Korea showed it was time to tell the men who man our legions that there is nothing easy is this world, that there are tigers, and to furnish them not only with atomic life eradicators but tiger guns. Korea showed that a free government must be prepared to do the unpopular thing, even if it destroys itself. Governments are not important; nations and peoples and what they stand for, are.

It was time for free, decent societies to continue to control their military forces, but to quit demanding from them impossible acquiescence in the liberal view toward life. A "modern" infantry may ride sky vehicles into combat, fire and sense its weapons through instrumentation, employ devices of frightening lethality in the future—but it must also be old-fashioned enough to be iron-hard, poised for instant obedience, and prepared to die in the mud.

If liberal, decent societies cannot discipline themselves to do all these things, they may have nothing to offer the world. They may not last long enough.

Aristotle wrote, *Almost all things have been found out, but some have been forgotten.*

Americans have learned of Brad Smith, who first saw long, black T-34s rumble forward in the rain at Osan, of the late Company A, of Frank Muñoz and Company at the horror of Kunu-ri, of Mike Shinka on Obong-ni, John Yancey led back blind from the icy hills beside Chang-jin, and Joe Clemons' dozen men who were King indeed on Pork Chop Hill. These were the Korean War—the misery, the waste, the splendor, the courage, the trauma that lingers still. Millions of Americans can find no meaning in any of it.

It is while men talk blithely of the lessons of history that they ignore them.

The lesson of Korea is that it happened.

CHRONOLOGY

25 June 1950	NKPA invades South Korea.
	U.N. Security Councils calls for end of aggression.
27 June 1950	U.N. asks members to go to aid of ROK.
28 June 1950	Seoul falls; ROK Army destroyed.
30 June 1950	President Truman orders U.S. ground forces into Korea.
5 July 1950	First U.S. ground troops go into action at Osan.
7 July 1950	U.N. creates United Nations Command, under commander appointed by U.S.
5 July–4 Aug. 1950	U.N. Forces fight delaying action across South Korea.
4 Aug. 1950	Pusan Perimeter in southeastern Korea established.
5–19 Aug. 1950	First Battle of Naktong Bulge.
27 Aug.–15 Sept. 1950	Perimeter battles, heaviest fighting of war.
1 Sept.–5 Sept. 1950	NKPA great Naktong Offensive.
15 Sept. 1950	Inch'on landings.
18 Sept. 1950	U.N. breakout from Pusan Perimeter.
19 Sept.–1 Oct. 1950	U.N. pursuit and exploitation.
26 Sept. 1950	Seoul recaptured.
7 Oct. 1950	U.N. Forces cross 38th parallel.
	U.N. sanctions defeat of North Korea, reunification of country.
12 Oct. 1950	First Chinese Communist troops enter Korea.

15 Oct. 1950	Truman and MacArthur meet at Wake Island.
19 Oct. 1950	P'yongyang, N.K. capital, taken.
26 Oct. 1950	X Corps lands at Wonsan on east coast.
1 Nov. 1950	CCF ambush 1st Cav. Div. at Unsan.
10–26 Nov. 1950	X Corps advances toward Yalu in east, Eighth Army in west.
24 Nov. 1950	MacArthur's "final offensive" jumps off.
25 Nov. 1950	CCF strike Eighth Army along Ch'ongch'on River in west.
27 Nov. 1950	CCF strike 1st Marine and 7th Division at Changjin Reservoir in east.
26 Nov.–1 Dec. 1950	U.S. 2nd and 25th divisions defeated along Ch'ongch'on in west. Retreat.
27 Nov.–10 Dec. 1950	X Corps fights back toward port of Hungnam in east. Marines retreat from Kot'o-ri.
22 Dec. 1950	Walker killed; Ridgway to command of Eighth Army.
24 Dec. 1950	X Corps sails from Hungnam. North Korea evacuated.
4 Jan. 1951	Seoul captured by CCF.
14 Jan. 1951	U.N. lines rest along 37th parallel in South Korea.
25 Jan. 1951	U.N. reassumes offensive.
1 Feb. 1951	U.N. votes to end Korean conflict by "peaceful means."
14 Feb. 1951	CCF counteroffensive; CCF turned back at Chipyong-ni.
17 Feb.–17 March 1951	U.N. continues offensive, moves north.
18 March 1951	Seoul retaken.
11 April 1951	MacArthur recalled; Ridgway assumes command at FECOM, Van Fleet of Eighth Army.
22 April 1951	CCF offensive; Glosters hold on at Imjin.
30 April 1951	CCF breaks contact.
16–22 May 1951	U.S. forces halt CCF Soyang Offensive.
	May Massacre.
23 May–1 June 1951	U.N. drives north.

13 June 1951	U.N. on 38th parallel.
23 June 1951	Soviet Delegate Malik proposes truce in U.N.
10 July 1951	Truce talks begin at Kaesong.
1 Aug.–31 Oct. 1951	U.N. launches limited attacks to straighten lines: Bloody, Heartbreak Ridge battles.
27 Nov. 1951	Truce talks resume at Panmunjom; cease-fire line agreed upon, at line of contact.
Nov. 1951–April 1952	Stalemate along Korean battlefront during discussions at Panmunjom.
2 April 1952	Screening of U.N. POW's begins; Koje-do riots commence.
7 May 1952	General Dodd captured by Communist POW'S at Koje-do.
12 May–12 June 1952	Mark Clark replaces Ridgway at FECOM. General Boatner quells disturbances on Koje.
June 1952–Oct. 1952	Stalemate along battlefront while truce talks deadlocked on POW repatriation question. Hill battles rage on Baldy, Whitehorse, elsewhere.
8 Oct. 1952	Truce talks recessed at Panmunjom; complete deadlock.
Oct.–Nov. 1952	Heavy pressure on ROK's in center of line. ROK Army comes of age.
Nov. 1952	Indian proposal on POW's in U.N.
Dec. 1952	President-elect Eisenhower comes to Korea; intensification of U.N. psychological warfare.
Dec., Jan., 1953	Continuation of stalemate; hill battles.
11 Feb. 1953	Maxwell Taylor replaces Van Fleet at Eighth Army.
22 Feb. 1953	U.N. Command again proposes exchange of sick and wounded POW's.
5 March 1953	Death of Josef Stalin; struggle for power in Kremlin; disaffection in Soviet satellites.
28 March 1953	Communists agree to POW exchange proposed by U.N.C.
30 March 1953	Chou En-lai indicates Communists will accept Indian U.N. proposal of November, 1952. Resumption of truce talks at Panmunjom.

Chronology

16–18 April 1953	Battle for Pork Chop Hill.
20–26 April 1953	Exchange of sick and wounded POW's at Panmunjom.
27 April 1953	Resumption of plenary sessions at Panmunjom.
May 1953	Savage fighting along stalemated line while details of truce ironed out at Panmunjom.
4 June 1953	Communists agree in effect to all U.N. truce proposals.
25 June 1953	Robertson begins "Little Truce Talks" with Rhee to secure ROK acceptance of armistice; CCF launch massive attacks against ROK divisions.
7 July 1953	ROK agrees to truce terms.
27 July 1953	Cease-fire signed at Panmunjom. Fighting ends.
4 Sept. 1953	Screening and repatriation of POW's begins at Freedom Village, Panmunjom.

GLOSSARY OF PRINCIPAL WEAPONS

Because of the limited nature of the Korean War, all combatants chose to fight it largely with surplus weapons from World War II. No startling developments, either in weaponry or tactics, came out of the conflict. While the United States made innovations and great improvements in logistical techniques, cold-weather clothing, and medical service, the only wholly new developments were the use of helicopters for reconnaissance, transport, and evacuation on a large scale, and the employment of jet aircraft in combat. The most modern jet, the F-86 Sabre, was thrown into the aerial war only when Communist forces first employed a first-rate, modern aircraft, the MIG-15, in what was essentially a field test.

Throughout the entire course of the war, weapons, radios, and vehicles, on both sides, remained of World War II vintage, although newer series of each had either been developed or were in production. In this sense, the Korean War was definitely anachronistic, for not only were nuclear weapons withheld, but so were modern varieties of transport, communication, and conventional weapons. At the beginning, the United States had no modern conventional weapons, a great weakness due to the complete cessation of procurement for ground warfare following World War II; but the Communist bloc, fighting through its secondary powers, followed the same course in employing only old or obsolescent weaponry, though much of this was of more recent manufacture, and in better condition, than that in American hands in 1950.

One indication of Communist thinking toward the future of warfare lies in the fact that Communist nations have continued, after World War II, Korea, and up to the present time, to develop and place in production whole new series of conventional arms, in addition to nuclear devices and means of delivery. The United States in recent years has produced new conventional arms in scant supply and with marked governmental reluctance, preferring to base its strategy wholly on the nuclear deterrent.

The principal infantry weapons used in Korea (with the exception of Commonwealth forces, which used British issue), were the following, the majority of which are now obsolete.

United States

1. U.S. Rifle Caliber .30 M-1 (Garand): The basic shoulder weapon of United States, ROK, and many other U.N. rifle regiments. A vintage of the mid-1930's, it was gas-operated and semiautomatic, fired an 8-round clip, and weighed 9.5 pounds, 10.5 with bayonet. Its effective range was about 500 yards, and its rate of fire up to approximately 30 rounds per minute.

461

2.   U.S. Carbine Caliber .30: Produced as both a semiautomatic and full-automatic weapon, it fired a lighter bullet than the M-1 Rifle, with correspondingly less range, accuracy, and killing power. Fitted with a 15-round magazine, or 30-round or so-called "banana magazine"; gas-operated, it was carried principally by company-grade officers, NCO's, clerks, and the like. Weight, 6 pounds. Developed during World War II from Garand principle.

3.   Pistol, Caliber .45 M-1911 A-1: The standard United States side arm, a large semiautomatic pistol, with great stopping power and an effective range of some 25 yards. Developed and issued prior to World War I, it was carried by field-grade officers, signal linemen, gun crews, tankers, and men whose duties or other burdens precluded carrying of rifle or carbine.

4.   Browning Automatic Rifle, or BAR: Firing the same cartridge as the Rifle, M-1, either semi- or full automatic, the BAR could be operated either as a shoulder weapon or from a bipod. With a rate of fire of almost 500 rounds per minute, it was the principal automatic weapon of the rifle companies, one or more being issued to each rifle squad. Weighing 16 pounds, it was developed from Browning's principle during World War I.

5.   U.S. Machine Gun, Caliber .30, M-1919 A-3 (Light Machine Gun, or LMG): An air-cooled, 32-pound fully automatic machine gun, with bipod and shoulder rest; recoil-operated on the Browning principle, capable of sustained fire of 450–500 rounds per minute. Firing the same cartridge as the Rifle, M-1 and BAR, it was the infantry platoon machine gun. Developed in World War I.

6.   U.S. Machine Gun, Caliber .30, M-1917 A-1 (Heavy Machine Gun, or HMG): A heavier version of the above, water-cooled and tripod mounted, and thus capable of both a greater, longer, and more accurate rate of fire. Issued to the Weapons Company of the infantry battalion. There were approximately 500 machine guns of both types in the U.S. infantry division.

7.   U.S. Machine Gun, Caliber .50, Browning: Weighing 82 pounds, this large-caliber machine gun was mounted on trucks, tanks, and other vehicles, and not carried into close infantry combat. Air-cooled, but with a heavy barrel, the .50-caliber machine gun fired approximately 575 rounds per minute, to a range of 2,000 yards. Approximately 350 scattered throughout the infantry division.

8.   Rocket Launcher, 3.5-inch or 2.36-inch (Bazooka); Rocket launchers, developed during World War II, fire a hollow shaped charge capable of penetrating thick armor plate. The 3.5, which replaced the obsolete 2.36 in 1950, weighed 15 pounds and fired an 8.5-pound charge. There were some 600 bazookas in the Korea infantry division. Characterized by a large and distinct backblast, the aluminum tube generally was not effec-

tive beyond 75 yards against medium armor. Widely issued as infantry antitank weapon.

9.   The 57mm, 75mm, and 105mm recoilless rifles: Infantry-carried artillery. They develop high blast from escaping gases on discharge, but no recoil, as with howitzers or cannon. The obsolescent 57mm could be shoulder-fired, while the newer and heavier guns were crew-served, firing from tripods. Effective against infantry and fortifications, such as bunkers, they fire regular shells with a flat trajectory over long ranges. The 105mm was developed during Korea.

10.   Infantry mortars, 60mm, 81mm, 4.2-inch: Mortars are primarily antipersonnel weapons, consisting of simple, sealed-breech tubes and base plates, which throw high explosive shells at a high angle, capable of reaching into valleys, trenches, and into defilade impervious to direct fire. The 60mm mortars were carried into position with the rifle companies; the 81mm's were handled by the weapons companies, and the 4.2-inch fired by a special mortar company within the regiment. The 81mm, with an effective range of 4,000 yards, to 1,800 for the 60mm, weighs more than 100 pounds and is not easily transportable in rough terrain by foot troops. The 4.2-inch, virtually an artillery weapon, is normally vehicle mounted.

11.   The Quad .50: This was a half-tracked vehicle of World War II vintage, mounting four .50 machine guns capable of being fired as a unit. Developed as an antiaircraft weapon, with the advent of fast jet craft it became an antipersonnel weapon capable of hurling an immense amount of fire into hillsides and valleys against advancing infantry, or of throwing long-range harassing small-arms fire against enemy routes by night. Firing as many as 100,000 rounds per day, the Quad .50 could go over hills like a vacuum cleaner, sucking them devoid of life.

12.   The Dual 40: Also developed as an AA weapon, the Dual 40 was a fully tracked vehicle with a tanklike silhouette mounting twin Bofors 40mm antiaircraft automatic cannon. It was also used to support the infantry line, in the same manner as the Quad .50.

The artillery weapons. During Korean operations, the standard U.S. artillery of World War II, the 105mm, 155mm, and 8-inch howitzers and rifles were employed in tremendous quantity. Developments were made in direction, spotting, and radar-sensing. Toward the end of the conflict, Korea was primarily an artillery war, with both sides dug in and cannonading each other rather than employing maneuver.

Armor. At the outset of the fighting, to its tremendous disadvantage, the United States had no tank in the Far East capable of engaging the obsolescent Russian T-34. The light M-24, primarily a reconnaissance vehicle with thin armor plate and light 75mm cannon, was augmented during August and September, 1950, with various U.S. interim model medium tanks, such as the M-26 Pershing, mounting a 90mm gun. Gradually, the old M4A3E8, the World

War II workhorse, the Sherman, fitted with a newer high-velocity 76mm gun, became the principal Korea battle tank. It had a high silhouette, light armor, and an inadequate gun, but it was more maneuverable in the alternately steep and boggy Korean terrain than more modern tanks, such as the heavy-armor, heavy-gun British Centurion III. Failure to mass-produce a good main battle tank was one of the Army's principal weaknesses during the period; the concentration was more on seeking an effective antitank weapon than relying on the more expensive tank itself.

The Communist Nations

Throughout the fighting, the enemy was adept at capturing and employing U.S. weapons and equipment. During the first ninety days, the North Korean People's Army secured enough equipment from ROK and U.S. divisions to outfit several of their own; and the Chinese Communist Forces, on entrance, were in many cases equipped with U.S. arms shipped to the Nationalist Government both during and after World War II, all of which had fallen into Communist hands. The Chinese (as the ROK's) also had a considerable quantity of surrendered Japanese arms and ammunition, from rifles to field guns. The principal source of armament for both North Koreans and Chinese, however, was Soviet Russia. Just as the United States provided 90 percent of all munitions used in the United Nations forces, the Russians designed, mass-produced, and delivered the bulk of all Communist weapons.

As with American arms, the majority of Russian equipment was of World War II vintage.

Russian weaponry, as Russian equipment in general, has one marked characteristic: it is extremely rugged, of the simplest design consistent with efficiency, and very easy to maintain, making it in many cases more suitable for the equipping of peasant armies than the more sophisticated U.S. arms. Despite its simplicity and lack of refinement, it is good.

1. Infantry rifles. The Communist forces were equipped with a miscellany of shoulder weapons, from the Russian 7.62mm carbine, a bolt-action rifle of 1944 vintage, to Japanese 7.7mm Imperial Army rifles, taken by the Soviets from the Kwantung Army in 1945 and turned over to the CCF. The tendency in Communist armies has been to discard the rifle in favor of the submachine gun, less accurate, but able to throw a much higher volume of fire in the hands of unskilled personnel.

2. The Submachine Gun 7.62mm PPSh 41 (Burp Gun): Designed during World War II, the PPSh 41 submachine gun indicated the Soviet belief that highly accurate small arms were wasted in the hands of ground troops, while a large volume of fire was a requisite. Cheap to make, simple to operate, and thoroughly dependable under any battlefield conditions, the Soviet submachine gun was the best of its class during World War II. Fired either full or semiautomatic, it held a magazine of 72 rounds, with a cyclic rate of 100 per minute. Inaccurate except at

close ranges. Toward the end of the war, Chinese infantry carried submachine guns or grenades almost exclusively while on the offensive.

3. The Tokarev 7.62mm Semiautomatic Rifle: This rifle, fitted with flash hider and bipod, served a purpose similar to that of the U.S. BAR.

4. The Degtyarev 14.5mm Antitank Rifle, PTRD-1941: This extremely long, ungainly weapon was designed against armor of the early World War II type. With the advent of thicker plate it became an anti-vehicular rifle, and was used for long-range sniping against personnel. Each NKPA division carried 36 of these, called by Americans the "elephant" or "buffalo" gun.

5. The machine guns: Several varieties of light machine guns were used by the NKPA and CCF, together with the Coryunov heavy machine gun, which was wheel-mounted. Russian machine guns were generally 7.62mm, an excellent military cartridge.

6. The mortars: While as with other arms, a miscellany of calibers and types was found in Communist armies, the standard Russian makes predominated. Because of its ready transportability by hand and its cheapness of manufacture, the mortar was a favorite weapon of both the NKPA and CCF. An NKPA regiment contained six 120mm mortars; each of its three battalions had nine 82mm's; and the smaller 61mm was found at company level. The smaller Soviet mortars had an added advantage of being able to fire U.S. 60mm and 81mm mortar ammunition, of which the Communists captured great stores. The American tubes, unfortunately, could not reciprocate. Other infantry support weapons, such as rocket launchers and recoilless rifles, were not standard enemy issue; they were employed only when captured.

Artillery. The artillery support of NKPA and CCF divisions closely followed that of the World War II Soviet division, though initially the CCF left most of its heavy artillery behind on crossing the Yalu. A division contained twelve 122mm howitzers, twenty-four 76mm field guns, twelve SU-76mm self-propelled guns on the T-34 chassis, and twelve 45mm antitank guns. In addition, each of the division's three regiments had four organic 76mm howitzers. The 122mm rifle was also furnished by the Soviets. With the exception of a few Japanese pieces, Communist artillery was Soviet-made, and during the later stages of the fighting appeared in quantities reminiscent of the Soviet massed artillery used in front of Berlin in 1945. Larger, long-range artillery, such as the 152mm gun, were used sparingly, in contrast with U.S. employment of medium artillery (155mm) in great quantities; the CCF had a marked reluctance to fire on targets they could not observe.

Armor. The Russian T-34/85, the Soviet main battle tank of World War II, which appeared in final form during the winter of 1943–1944, remained the Communist battle tank throughout. The T-34, weighing 35 tons and capable of 34 miles per hour, had excellent traction and was admirably suited to the terrain of Korea, where heavier American tanks such as the Patton found rough going. The T-34, mounting an 85mm gun and two 7.62mm machine guns, was considered by the Soviets an obsolescent tank in 1950. Their heavier, more modern tanks, such as the Josef Stalin III, were never furnished to satellite or auxiliary armies. In the first weeks, 150 T-34's, spearheading the NKPA attack, raised havoc with both ROK and U.S. forces. Later, both a preponderance of American armor and airpower reduced Communist armor to a minor role; it was carefully concealed and hoarded, and rarely employed.

Since both combatants tended to use old and obsolescent armament—such as the T-34/85 and the Sherman M4A3E8, or the 1944 7.62mm rifle and the pre–World War II M-1—no comparison of weaponry is particularly significant or valid in the Korean War. In general, Communist equipment proved adequate, and in its class comparable in performance to American.

Of definite significance, however, is the fact that the Soviets had developed entire new families of small arms and supporting weapons, superior to those of World War II, which they were placing in mass production. The Western nations, including the U.S., while they had such weapons on the drawing boards, did not produce them. In a future limited conflict, the West might find itself outclassed in the field of conventional weaponry.

INDEX